GLOBAL RIVALRIES FROM THE COLD WAR TO IRAQ

GLOBAL RIVALRIES

FROM THE COLD WAR TO IRAQ

Kees van der Pijl

Pluto Press

LONDON • ANN ARBOR, MI

First published 2006 by Pluto Press
345 Archway Road, London N6 5AA
and 839 Greene Street, Ann Arbor, MI 48106

www.plutobooks.com

British Library Cataloguing in Publication Data
A catalogue record for this book is available from the British Library

ISBN 0 7453 2542 4 hardback
ISBN 0 7453 2541 6 paperback

Library of Congress Cataloging in Publication Data applied for

10 9 8 7 6 5 4 3 2

Designed and produced for Pluto Press by
Sage Publications, B-42, Panchsheel Enclave, New Delhi 110 017
Typeset from disk by Star Compugraphics, Delhi
Printed in the European Union by
Antony Rowe Ltd, Chippenham and Eastbourne, England

For Ki

FOR ALL THE REASONS

Contents

List of Tables and Figures

Preface

In early 2003, when the UN Security Council refused to give the United States and Britain the go-ahead for an invasion of Iraq, the Murdoch press blasted those withholding their consent as cowards, pasting weasel heads and necks on photos of French, German and Russian diplomats. In the United States there was a boycott of French wine, and French fries were re-baptised 'freedom fries' to express disgust. The British foreign secretary, Jack Straw, more seriously put the blame for the highly unpopular decision to go to war on ... President Jacques Chirac! It seemed as if rivalries were reverting to the period preceding the First World War, when, to give but one example, scientists in Paris 'discovered' that German urine was more toxic than French.

How, then, does the furious dispute over Iraq square with the idea that history has forever moved beyond rivalry, a thesis most famously developed by Francis Fukuyama in his 'End of History' argument of 1989? Hasn't the world become unified under a single economic system—capitalism—with an 'international community' policing it in the name of democracy and human rights against a handful of remaining 'rogue states'? This was obviously the view of Condoleezza Rice, then US national security adviser (although she had earlier expressed scepticism). After the invasion, Rice qualified the French principle of 'multipolarity' as 'a theory of rivalry, of competing interests and, at its worst, competing values', belonging to a bygone age.[1] A comparable position has been adopted by the Left, or so it seems—witness Hardt and Negri's best-selling *Empire*. Their claim—that world capital has in the process of globalisation effectively absorbed the state system into itself—has become a near-orthodoxy, well beyond the alternative, 'anti'-globalisation movement.[2]

My argument in this study is that the appearance of planetary unification and homogenisation of the global political economy, not unlike the situation a century ago, hides a more profound drift to social crisis and conflagration. Early in the First World War, Lenin criticised Karl Kautsky's expectation that the imperialist states would eventually draw together and jointly exploit the colonial periphery (the stage of 'ultra-imperialism'). Lenin claimed that under capitalist conditions, this could only be a temporary respite from rivalry. 'There is no doubt that the development is going *in the direction* of a single world trust that will swallow up all enterprises and all states without exception,' he wrote in 1915.

> But the development in this direction is proceeding under such stress, with such a tempo, with such contradictions, conflicts, and convulsions—not only

economical, but also political, national, etc.—that before a single world trust will be reached, before the respective national finance capitals will have formed a world union of 'ultra-imperialism', imperialism will inevitably explode.[3]

Many things have changed since these lines were written (not least, of course, the rise and demise of the Soviet state born in the Russian revolution). But the argument against the idea of a stable, collectively managed capitalist world order remains valid. The process of breakneck liberalisation driven by transnational capital creates profound instabilities; the mindless propagation and practice of privatisation and economic competition produces extreme inequality and precariousness; and those worst affected cling to ethnic, national, and religious bonds, which are themselves in the process of dissolution and transformation. Adding to this explosive brew today are the deleterious effects of the exhaustion of society and nature by capitalist exploitation.[4]

The rivalries apparent in the contemporary world are again being exacerbated by the very speed of the unifying drive of capitalist 'globalisation'. But these rivalries do not develop at random. They evolve *according to a specific historical structure which contains, from the start, the 'ultra-imperialist' moment in the form of a relatively unified 'West'*.[5] As I will argue in Chapter 1, this structure first emerged in the struggle between a liberal, English-speaking, Protestant-Christian world created through overseas settlement and trade in the seventeenth century (what I call the *Lockean heartland*); and a series of *contender states* beginning with France. In this struggle, in which the rulers of France and later rivals of the West faced the already established primacy of the heartland, two state/society complexes have crystallised.[6] In the Atlantic heartland, the capitalist class became the ruling class as an already transnational force, maximising its freedom under the liberal state theorised by John Locke. In a society like France, on the other hand, a state class imposed itself on society; from Colbert to Napoleon (or even, some would say, de Gaulle) it demarcated a concentric unit developing under a rationalistic planning doctrine.

The original constellation of an English-speaking West confronted by France develops over time into ever more complex patterns, eventually comprising the entirety of the global political economy—hence, *global* rivalries.[7] Taking off in the century between the English Glorious Revolution in 1688 and the American secession in 1776, social and political development on a world scale came to revolve around a protracted struggle between an expanding Lockean heartland seeking to open up the rest of the world through an aggressive liberalism, and a succession of contender states offering an alternative, shorter, but usually more brutal route forced upon it by the Atlantic West. France challenged the first British empire; Germany, Italy and Japan confronted the second British empire and the United States; the

Soviet Union challenged the wider West; in the 1970s a broad coalition of Third World states even wanted to institute, through the UN, a politically controlled world economy along contender state lines. China would appear to be the primary contender today. In the end, most contender states have been incorporated into the expanding heartland *without entirely overcoming the prior faultlines.* Indeed, with the world economy today apparently more integrated than ever, the West itself seems to be drifting from its post-war Atlantic moorings before our eyes.[8]

So does capital not unify the globe after all? This is where *political* economy comes in. The original 'West' offered capital accumulation the unique constellation of a self-regulating, transnational social space in and from which to expand—an 'internal extraterritoriality' in which it can thrive. But it simultaneously forced the societies on its perimeter into the contender posture, which creates rival economic units, bound to succumb again to Western pre-eminence, usually after a war of dispossession. Rivalries *among* the contenders, meanwhile, have been ruthlessly exploited by the leading heartland states (first Britain, then the United States) by 'active balancing'.[9] Class relations are always imbricated with rivalry—whether we are looking at the original democratic revolution that established the heartland/contender state configuration, the phase of Euro-Atlantic integration necessitated by the challenge of Soviet state socialism, or the comprehensive neoliberal drive accompanying the globalisation of capital today. Indeed resistance to exploitation is often deflected into hatred of others, and discontent may easily become antagonism with the English-speaking West, from which capitalist discipline—'reform'—is most vigorously propagated and pursued.

For the purposes of the present work, I take the transnational-English versus national-French fracture as a *core structure*, with which more complex configurations can be described and understood, not unlike the atom in natural science.[10] Social and ethno-cultural relations, state forms, geopolitical relations, and the economy proper—all are at some point implicated in this core structure. This departs from the state-centric approach of mainstream international relations (IR) theory. But then, as Richard Ashley has argued, international structure should not be seen as 'an external joining of states-as-actors', but traced back to 'a deep, internal relation prior to and constitutive of social actors'.[11] It is this insight which lies at the basis of the critique of the standard IR paradigm and the development of a more comprehensive international or global political economy.[12]

Chapter 1, then, traces the core structure of global rivalries back to the early contests between the expanding English-speaking world and its first rival, France, through the seventeenth and eighteenth centuries. It discusses the Lockean and the 'Hobbesian' forms of the state that crystallised in the period and takes the argument to 1945. I build on this to discuss the origins of European integration (Chapter 2), which I claim was intended as a trans-national constellation extending the original heartland, but which, due to its origins in the contender state experiences of France, Germany, and Italy, reproduced forms of political organisation ultimately incompatible with it. Gaullist France especially epitomises this incompatibility, something which transpired most clearly in the period when the United States was leading the fight against revolution in the Third World (Chapter 3). In the early 1970s, East-West détente, Third World emancipation, and a powerful groundswell of popular democracy entered into a historic convergence, discussed in Chapter 4. In response, ruling class ideologues and policymakers in the West sought to rescind the class compromises of the post-war period, drawing inspiration from the earlier counter-attack against social democracy in Chile. This then developed into a pre-emptive, neoliberal counter-revolution on a global scale. Chapter 5 documents the first phase of this process. In the cir-cumstances of what I call the 1970s interregnum, neoliberal hardliners relied on transnational violence in a range of forms, among other things to clear the field for a sanitised form of democracy that ideally no longer includes the right to vote for a society different from a capitalist one.

The neoliberal counter-revolution included the transformation and par-tial integration of the contender states of the Third World (Chapter 6) and the Soviet bloc (Chapter 7). After the collapse of the USSR, a powerful brake on overt rivalry within the wider West was removed; the inner tensions of Euro-Atlantic unity were certainly exposed in the aftermath of the war over Kosovo, when the EU adopted the Lisbon strategy of neoliberal 'Americanisation'—*against* the US (Chapter 8). This marks the high point of neoliberal transnationalisation in Europe. Clearly this was not much appreciated by the electorates of France and the Netherlands, who in 2005 turned out in great numbers to reject the neoliberal European Constitution, boldly reclaiming the right to vote on the nature of the social order.

The question whether the expanded West holds together will be put to the test now that China has emerged as the next contender (discussed in Chapter 9 against the backdrop of the 'Asian Crisis'). This coincides with the end of the twentieth-century monopoly of the Anglo-American oil giants in the world energy markets. Russian companies have entered the race to supply the world's growing energy needs, both in the New Great Game un-folding in Central Asia and in the Middle East; the Russian state is again strengthening its hold on the process (Chapter 10). The foray of Lukoil, Soyuzneftegas and other companies into Iraq in the period leading up to the war was part of the set of forces that activated Washington and London to invade the country. On the other hand we should not expect France, for example, to be a steadfast opponent of Anglo-American imperialism just because it challenged Britain in the eighteenth century or more recently in

Iraq. Both Chirac and German Chancellor Schröder cynically used the 'peace dividend', won by their stance on Iraq, to intensify neoliberal 'reform' at home. Ultimately, the wars to dispossess the world's remaining state classes are common undertakings of a globalising capitalist class, even if the very process of privatisation will foster competitive interests and rivalry.[13]

In the concluding chapter, I raise the question whether the 'War on Terror' declared by the US in response to the suicide attacks of 11 September 2001, does not represent the demise of the Lockean project altogether. The War on Terror has certainly suspended the human rights strategy by which the West aimed to refract the collectivist aims of successive contender states into individualised, 'private' aspirations.

* * *

What is offered in this book is based on ideas developed over a long period. The theme of a Lockean heartland challenged by successive contender states goes back to an initial sketch in 1987 in *The Marxist Review* (published in Calcutta and edited, at the time, by my respected friend Ajit Roy). It was thenceforth developed in a range of papers and books, but never as the central theme.[14]

When I joined the University of Sussex in January 2000, new influences prompted me to rethink various aspects of the project. The first-hand experience of life in the English-speaking world too played its part here. Intellectually, the Department of International Relations and Politics and the Centre for Global Political Economy at Sussex have been invaluable sources of inspiration, as can be gleaned from the notes and references. In particular, Ronen Palan's conception of a free space for capital, created with the help of states but shielded from democratic politics (elaborated in a range of works, notably *The Offshore World* of 2003), resonates in the analysis of the heartland that I develop in the present study. Others whom I want to thank (with the usual disclaimers) for support, encouragement and constructive criticism at various stages of this project are Jeroen Merk, Johnna Montgomerie, Anastasia Nesvetailova, Henk Overbeek, James Perry, Or Raviv, Chris Sanders, Jan Selby, Robbie Shilliam, Benno Teschke and Duncan Wigan. Colleagues of the Arts Computer Unit at Sussex were always at hand at critical moments. In Paris, François Fourquet, Bernard Guibert, Geneviève Schmeder and Claude Serfati, and, from Australia, Peter McMahon, critically commented on theses developed in this book. In addition, my work with Otto Holman on European integration, at the University of Amsterdam, and our discussions after my move to Britain have in many ways shaped the present study.[15]

In February and March 2005, I had the opportunity to present the main argument of the book, then being finalised, to colleagues and students at the London School of Economics at the invitation of Michael Cox, and at the University of Paris-13 at the invitation of Pascal Petit. In March–April I taught an intensive graduate course at the University of Auvergne at Clermont-Ferrand, organised by Klaus-Gerd Giesen, again largely based on the manuscript. I thank those participating in these events for helping me get a final check on some of the theses I develop here. I also thank Robert Webb and the entire team at Pluto and Ritu Vajpeyi-Mohan, Vidyadhar Gadgil and Ashok Chandran at Sage, for their combined effort in producing this book with great skill and efficiency.

Notes

1. Quoted in the *Financial Times*, 19 December 2003; on Condoleezza Rice, cf. P. Golub in *Le Monde Diplomatique*, July 2005. Cf. Fukuyama (1989, 1992).
2. 'Along with the global market and global circuits of production has emerged a global order, a new logic and structure of rule—in short, a new form of sovereignty. Empire is the political subject that effectively regulates these global exchanges, the sovereign power that governs the world' (Hardt and Negri 2000: xi). Alternatively, this unification has been argued as a transnationalisation or globalisation of Western state power; see Robinson (2004) and Shaw (2000). On the anti- and alternative globalisation movements, cf. Rupert (2000).
3. Lenin, in his introduction to Bukharin's book on imperialism (Bukharin 1972: 14).
4. 'Exhaustion', in addition to the consumption of resources and the pollution/destruction of the biosphere, also refers to the limits up to which social bonds and the neurophysiological make-up of people can be exploited; cf. Funke (1978) and Brennan (2000). For an analysis of the 'no' to the project for a European Constitution in France and the Netherlands in these terms, cf. B. Stiegler in *Le Monde Diplomatique*, June 2005, pp. 22–3.
5. I use 'moment' here in the sense of a weight contributing to a movement, i.e., 'momentum', not as a fraction of time.
6. The term was used by Robert Cox (1986). I will come back to the antecedents of the term 'heartland' in Chapter 1.
7. This is not a linear process, but one that proceeds through ruptures, crises and wars (the same applies, incidentally, to the constitution of the heartland itself—one has only to think of the English and American civil wars, the Wall Street crash, or the world wars). But then, the very idea of a smooth 'spread' of social, economic, or political patterns is ruled out by the structural discontinuities between societies and the inherent volatility of conflict; by the mutual disjunction of experience across different parts of the world; and, ultimately, by the irregularities of the Earth's climate, geography and geology.
8. As argued persuasively by Todd (2004). In the same vein, a privately commissioned report to the US government by Georgetown scholar Simon Serfaty, reported in the *Financial Times*, 3 June 2004, argues that as the US and Britain seem unable to disentangle themselves from their ill-fated adventure in Iraq; they run the risk that 'much of Europe might now view strategic separation [from the US] as a viable response to an unnecessary cultural clash with an Islamic world progressively united by the misuses of American power.' Russia and China might increasingly be viewed as alternative strategic global partners; France and Germany would lead a 'smaller but more cohesive [EU] as a rampart against the allegedly irresponsible uses of American power'; while Russia under Putin could resort to again restoring the Slav units of the former USSR and Kazakhstan into a single bloc.

9. The concept used by Benno Teschke in his work on the emergence of the modern state system (2003). See van der Pijl (1998: 87–8), for a schematic representation and key historical examples of this process of playing off contenders against each other.

10. Thus a study on the history of chemistry concludes that the value of concepts generated by insight into atomic structure 'does not lie in the calculations ... but in their enormous fruitfulness in supplying models.... With these models a much more sophisticated structure theory of organic chemistry is possible. Because of this theory the determination of still unknown structures is facilitated; from the relationships between the theories and the properties, synthesis and what may be described as chemical architecture are advanced immeasurably' (Schneer 1969: 273). I take the notion of a core structure from Ritsert (1973), who identifies the 'commodity' in Marx's *Capital* as such a structure. The core structure does not represent a rationality 'unfolding' into an immanent totality in the Hegelian sense; mutations impose themselves from the outside on the initial configuration as much as they ramify out from it. What organically 'grows', is not the real sequence of events (or the interconnections between events across a widening space), but the evolving picture, which derives its transparency and logical coherence from being connected to the core configuration, in an empirical reference structure to which all events can be meaningfully connected—up to a point: as Ritsert notes, 'the "orthodoxy" of theory derives from the dogmatism of relations' (ibid.: 38).

11. Ashley (1986: 287).

12. For the term, 'Global Political Economy', see Gill and Law (1988) and Palan (2000). My preference for 'global' here resides in the emphasis on processes not confined to relations between states (inter-national), and because 'global' also has the association of comprehensive, suggesting the inclusion of such aspects as the anthropological, the psychological, the geographical, etc., in the analysis. As a critical approach, Global Political Economy challenges the assumption of an ahistorical realm of interstate relations, and seeks to historicise the successive geopolitical orders through which global social development takes place (cf. R.W. Cox 2002: 79). But it should not take the arena of actual geopolitics for granted (cf. Rosenberg 2000: 15).

13. At the time of this writing, France and the US are jointly raising the pressure on Syria, as the French government feels robbed by the Syrians' embezzling of aid to Lebanon, and by the awarding of a gas contract to an Anglo-American consortium after having been initially agreed with Total (*Le Monde*, 13 November 2004; A.G. in *Le Monde Diplomatique*, June 2005, p. 12).

14. See van der Pijl (1987, 1989, 1996a, 1996b, 1998).

15. See Holman and van der Pijl (1996, 2003). On the work of our group in Amsterdam, see Overbeek (2000) and the special issue of the *Journal of International Relations and Development*, 7 (2) (2004), edited by Bastiaan van Apeldoorn.

List of Abbreviations

AAA	Argentinian Anticommunist Alliance
ABB	Asea-Brown-Boveri
ABCA	America, Britain, Canada, Australia
ABM	Anti-Ballistic Missile
ABN–AMRO	Algemene Bank Nederland–Amsterdam Rotterdam Bank
ACC	Allied Clandestine Committee
AEG	*Allgemeine Elektrizitätsgesellschaft*
AFL-CIO	American Federation of Labour—Congress of Industrial Organizations
AIOC	Azerbaijan International Operating Co.
ALADI	*Asociación Latinoamericana de Integracion*
AMF	Asian Monetary Fund
ANC	African National Congress
APEC	Asia Pacific Economic Cooperation
ARAMCO	Arab American Company
ASEAN	Association of South East Asian Nations
ASEM	Asia-Europe Meeting
ASIO	Australian Security Intelligence Organisation
ASIS	Australian Secret Intelligence Service
AWACS	Airborne Warning and Control System
BASF	*Badische Anilin und Soda Fabrik*
BBC	British Broadcasting Corporation
BCCI	Bank of Credit and Commerce International
BCH	*Banco Central Hispanoamericano*
BDI	*Bundesverband der Deutschen Industrie*
BDM	BDM International Corporation (originally Braddock, Dunn and McDonald)
BfV	*Bundesamt für Verfassungsschütz* (Federal Security Service)
BKA	*Bundeskriminalamt* (Federal Bureau of Criminal Investigation)
BND	*Bundesnachrichtendienst* (Federal Intelligence Service)
BNL	*Banca Nazionale del Lavoro*
BOSS	Bureau of State Security
BP	British Petroleum
BR	*Brigate Rosse* (Italy)
CAP	Common Agricultural Policy
CBS	Columbia Broadcasting System

CCF	Congress of Cultural Freedom
CCP	Clandestine Committee for Planning
CDS	*Centro Democrático e Social* (Portugal)
CDU	*Christlich Demokratische Union Deutschlands*
CEA	Atomic Energy Commissariat (France)
CENTO	Central Treaty Organisation
CEO	Chief Executive Officer
CFP	*Compagnie Française des Pétroles*
CHEKA	Extraordinary Commission to Combat Counterrevolution and Sabotage
CIA	Central Intelligence Agency
CIPEC	Council of Copper Exporting Countries
CIS	Commonwealth of Independent States (former USSR)
CMEA	Council of Mutual Economic Assistance
COINTELPRO	Counter Intelligence Program (USA)
COMECON	*see* CMEA
COMINTERN	Communist International
CORFO	*Corporación de Fomento de la Producción* (Chile)
COSATU	Confederation of South African Trade Unions
CPC	Caspian Pipeline Consortium
CPD	Committee on the Present Danger
CPSU	Communist Party of the Soviet Union
CSCE	Conference on Security and Cooperation in Europe
CSFB	Crédit Suisse-First Boston
CVRD	*Companhia Vale do Rio Doce* (Brazil)
DASA	Daimler Aerospace AG
DC	*Democrazia Cristiana* (Italy)
DEA	Drugs Enforcement Agency
DIA	Defense Intelligence Agency
DIHT	*Deutsche Industrie und Handelstag*
DM	Deutschmark
DPG	Defence Planning Guidance
EADS	European Aeronautic, Defence and Space Company
EAEC	Eurasian Economic Community
EBRD	European Bank for Reconstruction and Development
EC	European Communities
ECB	European Central Bank
ECE	Economic Commission for Europe
ECOSOC	(United Nations) Economic and Social Council
ECSC	European Coal and Steel Community
EDC	European Defence Community
EEC	European Economic Community
EFTA	European Free Trade Area
EMU	Economic and Monetary Union

ENI	*Ente Nazionale Idrocarburi* (Italy)
EPC	European Political Community
ERT	European Round Table of Industrialists
ESAF	Enhanced Structural Adjustment Facility
EU	European Union
EURATOM	European Community for Atomic Energy
EURODIF	European Gas Diffusion Consortium
FBI	Federal Bureau of Investigation
FCF	Free Congress Foundation
FDI	Foreign Direct Investment
FDN	National Democratic Front (Nicaragua)
FLN	National Liberation Front (Algeria)
FLNA	National Front for the Liberation of Angola
FMLN	*Frente Farabundo Martí para la Liberación Nacional* (El Salvador)
FRELIMO	Front for the Liberation of Mozambique
FTAA	Free Trade Area of the Americas
G-5, G-7, etc.	Group of 5, 7, etc.
GATT	General Agreement on Tariffs and Trade
GDP	Gross Domestic Product
GDR	German Democratic Republic
GE	General Electric
GHH	*Gutehoffnungshütte*
GI	Government Issue (enlisted US military personnel)
GITIC	Guangdong International Trust & Investment Corp.
GM	General Motors
GNP	Gross National Product
GPU	State Security Organisation (USSR 1922–34)
GUUAM	Georgia, Ukraine, Uzbekistan, Azerbaijan, Moldova
HP	Hewlett–Packard
IAEA	International Atomic Energy Agency
IBM	International Business Machines
ICC	International Chamber of Commerce *or* International Criminal Court
ICFTU	International Congress of Free Trade Unions
ICTY	International Criminal Tribunal for the Former Yugoslavia
IEA	International Energy Agency
ILO	International Labour Organisation
IMF	International Monetary Fund
INF	Intermediate-range Nuclear Forces
IPC	Iraq Petroleum Company
IR	International Relations
IRG	Interregional Group of Deputies of the Supreme Soviet
ISI	Interservices Intelligence (Pakistan)

ITS	International Trade Secretariat
ITT	International Telephone & Telegraph Corporation
KAL	Korean Airlines
KGB	Committee on State Security (USSR)
KKR	Kohlberg, Kravis & Roberts
KLA	Kosovo Liberation Army
KMT	Kuomintang
KWU	*Kraftwerk Union*
KYP	Central Secret Service (Greece)
LAFTA	Latin American Free Trade Association
LDP	Liberal Democratic Party (Japan)
LTCM	Long-Term Capital Management
MAI	Multilateral Agreement on Investment
MBA	Master of Business Administration
MBB	Messerschmitt-Bolkow-Blöhm
MCA	Music Corporation of America, Inc.
MDB	*Movimento Democrático Brasileiro*
MFN	Most Favoured Nation
MI5	Military Intelligence 5: British Security Service
MI6	Military Intelligence 6: British Secret Intelligence Service
MIC	Military-Industrial Complex
MITI	Ministry of International Trade and Industry
MLF	Multi-Lateral Force
MNC	Multinational Corporation
MNR	National Revolutionary Movement (Mozambique)
MP	Member of Parliament
MPLA	Popular Movement for the Liberation of Angola
MPS	Mont Pèlerin Society
MVD	(Agencies controlled by the) Ministry of Internal Affairs (USSR)
NACC	North Atlantic Cooperation Council
NAFTA	North American Free Trade Agreement
NATO	North Atlantic Treaty Organisation
NEP	New Economic Policy
NGO	Non-Governmental Organisation
NHM	*Nederlandsche Handelsmaatschappij*
NIEO	New International Economic Order
NIIO	New International Information Order
NLF	National Liberation Front (Vietnam)
NSA	National Security Agency
NSC	National Security Council
NSDD	National Security Decision Directive
OAS	Organisation of American States
OECD	Organisation for Economic Cooperation and Development

OEEC	Organisation for European Economic Co-ordination
OPEC	Organisation of Petroleum Exporting Countries
OPT	Outward Processing Traffic
OSCE	Organisation for Security and Cooperation in Europe
OSS	Office of Strategic Services
OYAK	Organisation for Mutual Assistance of the Armed Forces (Turkey)
P-2	*Propaganda Due* (Italy)
PASOK	Pan Hellenic Socialist Movement (Greece)
PC	Personal Computer
PCE	*Partido Comunista de España*
PCF	*Parti Communiste Français*
PCI	*Partito Comunista Italiana*
PCP	*Partido Comunista Português*
PD	Presidential Directive
PHARE	Reconstruction Programme for Central and East European Countries
PIDE	*Polícia Internacional a da Defesa do Estado* (Portugal)
PKI	*Partai Kommunis Indonesia*
PLO	Palestine Liberation Organisation
PRB	*Poudres Réunies de Belgique*
PRI	*Partido Revolucionario Institucional* (Mexico)
PT	*Partido dos Trabalhadores* (Brazil)
RAF	*Rote Armee Fraktion* (West Germany)
R&D	Research and Development
RENAMO	*see* MNR
RTS	*Radio Televisija Srbije* (Serbia)
SAC	*Service d'Action Civique* (France)
SALT	Strategic Arms Limita tion Talks
SÄPO	Swedish Secret Service
SCO	Shanghai Cooperation Organisation
SDECE	Foreign Documentation and Counterespionage Service (France)
SDI	Strategic Defense Initiative
SEATO	South East Asia Treaty Organisation
SI	Socialist International
SPD	Sozialdemokratische Partei Deutschlands
SS	*Schützstaffel*
Star 21	Strategic Aerospace Review for the 21st Century
TABD	Transatlantic Business Dialogue
TC	Trilateral Commission
TCO	Tengizchevroil
TNC	Transnational Corporation
TPC	Turkish Petroleum Corporation

TRACECA	Transport Corridor Europe-Caucasus-Central Asia
TUC	Trades Union Congress
UBS	Union Bank of Switzerland
UK	United Kingdom
UKUSA	UK–USA Security Agreement
UN	United Nations
UNCTAD	United Nations Conference on Trade and Development
UNCTC	United Nations Commission on Transnational Corporations
UNDP	United Nations Development Programme
UNESCO	United Nations Education, Science and Culture Organisation
UNICE	Union of Industrial and Employers' Federations of Europe
UNIDO	United Nations Industrial Development Organisation
UNITA	National Union for the Total Independence of Angola
UNMOVIC	United Nations Monitoring, Verification and Inspection Commission
UP	*Unidad Popular* (Chile)
US(A)	United States (of America)
USSR	Union of Soviet Socialist Republics
VEBA	*Vereinigte Elektrizitäts- und Bergwerks AG*
WACL	World Anti-Communist League
WEU	Western European Union
WFL	World Federation of Labour
WFTU	World Federation of Trade Unions
WFS	World Social Forum
WTO	World Trade Organisation

1 Fractures and Faultlines in the Global Political Economy

THE MAKING OF THE 'WEST' AND THE CONTENDER STATE CHALLENGE

> In Third World countries I felt I had dropped into the past, and I had never accepted the notion of timelessness anywhere. Most countries had specific years. In Turkey it was always 1952, in Malaysia 1937; Afghanistan was 1910 and Bolivia 1949. It is twenty years ago in the Soviet Union, ten in Norway, five in France. It is always last year in Australia and next week in Japan. Britain and the United States were the present—but the present contains the future.
>
> Paul Theroux, *The Kingdom by the Sea*, 1984

In order to study foreign relations properly, one has to abandon the Eurocentric mindset; but to understand global rivalries in today's world, we must first investigate the West and its specific history. This is how I will approach the subject matter in this study. I begin by looking at the origins and early development of the relationship between the emerging English-speaking realm and its continental rivals.

The Anglo-French antagonism that will serve as the core structure of our analysis was grafted on late-medieval contests within a ruling class of warriors-landowners on both sides of the Channel.[1] Relations of exploitation and struggles over living space are primordial here; 'national' entities only emerged after centuries of fighting over land occupancy and income. Scandinavian Vikings had raided the British Isles since the ninth century, subduing the Saxons and others wherever they settled. In 1066, England was integrated again into Romanised, feudal Europe by the Duke of Normandy, William the Conqueror (himself a descendant of Viking corsairs). The Norman kings of England retained large tracts of territory in France; the Hundred Years' War in the fourteenth century merely saw the most intense fighting in a protracted struggle over further redistribution. Crucially, however, England became a unified entity right from the conquest. France, with a population six times as large, only came into its own in the mid-fifteenth century, when it made peace with Burgundy, then an ally of the English monarchy. In 1558, England finally surrendered its last holdout, Calais. This absolved the state of having to fight costly land wars and kept taxes on its subjects within negotiable limits.[2]

In the sixteenth and seventeenth centuries, social and political development acquired a new cohesion and direction as a *democratic revolution.* Affecting all of northwest Europe, the democratic revolution evolved through struggles against feudal-aristocratic rule, royal absolutism and the hold of the Roman Catholic church on spiritual and cultural life. Its first, bourgeois, phases—the Reformation and the Enlightenment—entailed the reordering of the form of the state and its relationship with society in ways suiting the needs of the commercialising landlords, merchants and the artisans of the towns. The English and the French revolutions are the defining moments in this process, although even in those epoch-making events the 'bourgeoisie' was never a cohesive class but an amalgam of diverse social forces loosely united by urban residence and commercial activity and outlook. Generally the bourgeoisie in Europe was averse to radical political change because their businesses tended to be part of a system of royal or feudal monopolies and licences.[3] Only when the privilege-granting authority (prince or city) could no longer accommodate an expansion of their field of activity and/ or mental horizon would elements from the bourgeoisie be drawn into the struggles erupting from religious disputes, popular discontent, or fights among different sections of the nobility.

The democratic revolution eventually resulted in parliamentary states with a unified national economy. But this was achieved only after a series of separate revolts and restorations, which moreover tended to be disjointed, spread across different societies as 'moments' of the larger transformation. Political revolutions sent their waves of refugees, ideas, agents and armies across borders into other societies, where they activated social forces that were waiting or lay dormant, thus reconnecting processes of change into a single flow. In this sense the long-term emancipation and formation of the bourgeoisie as a class and the revolutionary convulsions of the Reformation and Enlightenment epochs merged into one comprehensive process.[4] However, the unevenly timed capture of state power in the democratic revolution, and the varying degrees to which the ascendant bourgeoisie was involved in it, also shaped the distribution of geopolitical space. In the wars of religion on the continent and in the British Isles, different patterns of state/society organisation and foreign involvement became apparent for the first time. Hence the bourgeois phase of the democratic revolution can be argued to have created the heartland/contender state structure, which has, after the Glorious Revolution of 1688, over-determined every democratic revolution.[5] Let us look at this in some detail.

The North Atlantic Aspect of the Reformation

The Reformation was the first stage of the democratic revolution in Europe. It had the effect, in the words of Edmund Burke, 'of introducing other interests into all countries than those which arose from their locality and natural circumstances'[6]—a shift of spatial coordinates primarily induced by the growth of commerce and private property, enclosure and displacement. The outcomes of the Reformation entailed major geopolitical consequences: the partition of the German and Spanish empires along confessional lines, and, crucially, the establishment of an English-speaking 'West'.

Protestantism is rooted in the idea of an unmediated covenant with God. Thus, in the context of Christianity, it articulates the rise of individualism, a key aspect of the rise of a commercially minded bourgeoisie. Indeed, till today Protestant Christianity accompanies the spread of capital across the globe, with the militant evangelism of both very much in step with each other.[7] Back in the sixteenth century, the Lutheran reformation triggered the Peasant War and the revolution of the princes in Germany, ripping up the empire; a settlement was reached in 1555 by the Peace of Augsburg. Meanwhile, in England Henry VIII made himself the head of a separate Anglican church through the Act of Supremacy of 1534, dividing the landholdings of the church of Rome among his barons. If we have to define these events by reference to a single principle, it would be *sovereign equality*: the lord of the land is made the supreme authority in deciding on its religion, thus placing religious authority firmly under worldly authorities treating each other as equals. Sovereign equality, an aspect of absolutist state formation, enshrines the preoccupation with dynastic territoriality carried over from the warrior aristocracy. But it is simultaneously over-determined (as was, in Perry Anderson's view, absolutism as such) by the rise of the bourgeoisie. Without ever being the protagonist in the process, the presence of the ascendant bourgeoisie is felt at every step—carving out unified, mutually exclusive jurisdictions which create 'national' economic spaces, and separating a political-administrative and legal sphere from that of religion essentially serves the needs of the bourgeoisie.[8]

Neither Anglicanism nor Lutheranism (nor, for that matter, absolutism) was able to keep up with the pace of social change driven by the spread of private commercialism. In the revolt of the Low Countries against the Spanish Habsburg empire that erupted in the 1560s, the economic aspect found a more suitable ideological vehicle in Calvinism.[9] The Thirty Years' War (1618–48), fought across the princely states and cities of Germany, was triggered by the insurrection in Lutheran Bohemia against the German Habsburgs; it was eventually decided by the interventions of France and Sweden. The Westphalian Treaties of 1648 terminated the wars of religion by replicating the Augsburg principles of sovereign equality for the European continent as a whole. England, in the throes of its own religious civil war, was not a signatory. Its interests were pointing in a different direction, towards a policy of active balancing dictated by commercial interests, and a rupture with dynastic commitments and territoriality.[10]

The special position of England, created in the Reformation phase of the democratic revolution, can only be understood if placed in the perspective of the *conquest of the North Atlantic and settlement in North America*. The concept of an English-speaking *heartland* has its origin here.[11] Columbus may have discovered the Caribbean islands for his Iberian sponsors, but a Venetian—'John Cabot' in English—pursuing the earlier Viking attempt was the first to find land across the North Atlantic. Under a mandate from King Henry VII, and with the promise that he could govern the lands he found as long as he paid the crown 'one-fifth of the capital gain', Cabot landed in Newfoundland in the summer of 1497. He returned to England to organise a fleet of five ships stocked by London and Bristol merchants, but perished on a second voyage. Preying on Spanish treasure fleets sailing home from the Caribbean now became a favourite occupation for English sea captains in the Atlantic, and control of Barbados, Bermuda and other Spanish holdouts would matter much more to the English than North America.[12] Hence there were few vested interests opposed or even involved when in 1578 Queen Elizabeth gave a former courtier, Humphrey Gilbert, letters amounting to a colonial charter (the first of its kind) for settlement in North America. These letters granted him the right to establish a colony anywhere along the coastline stretching from Labrador to Florida, to which the queen claimed title on the grounds of Cabot's landing. Gilbert, we read in Angus Calder's *Revolutionary Empire*, 'was the first Englishman to attempt a New World Utopia'. Conscious of the scarcity of land and the religious divisions at home, he offered feudal holdings in North America for sale to wealthy Catholics, while projecting, under his own rule, colonies for the poor as well.[13]

Catholics did join the Atlantic trek, but the mainstream of seventeenth-century migration to North America was made up of (Calvinist) Puritans fleeing the restorative Anglicanism that accompanied the absolutist ambitions of Charles I. Brushing aside attempts to introduce feudal land ownership, they created overseas replicas of their home communities as sectarian Christian 'New Jerusalems'. 'English birthright'—the right to resist state encroachment that dates back to the Norman conquest—was thus transplanted across the North Atlantic, and would be appealed to at the time of the American secession.[14] Overseas settlements developed as a spatial dimension of the democratic revolution. The process can even be understood as a lateral extension of the eventual civil war on the British Isles; it certainly served, for a time, as a safety valve postponing it (emigration would dry up after the 1650s, only to resume 200 years later). In the meantime, the vast space and resources on the other side of the Atlantic, in combination with the optimistic pioneer mindset of the settlers, created the society that would bring the United States to pre-eminence within the English-speaking world. A subordinate, forced migration of African slaves provided workers for the sugar plantations in the Caribbean and Brazil, and later for the southernmost North American colonies. English merchants operating from London and Bristol, their first royal charter dating from 1572, competed in this lucrative trade with Iberian slave traders and the Dutch.[15] On the other hand, the English merchant-adventurers were late-comers in the Asian trade, which South American gold and silver had made possible for the Portuguese, Spanish and the Dutch. But when the English did arrive in the Indian Ocean, they would exploit the region far more effectively than their competitors.[16]

North America and, at a later stage, Australasia would always occupy a special place in the British empire, not comparable with even the most important colonies such as India. Toynbee argues that the Old Testament allegory of the 'chosen people', dear to English Protestants (they liked to see themselves as the descendants of the 10 northern tribes of Israel dispersed in pre-Biblical times), fed conceptions of racial superiority that legitimised slavery as well as the extermination of the native peoples.[17] The English Revolution established the 'West' as its new frame of reference with all these associations. As Eugen Rosenstock-Huessy writes,

> 'Western World' replaced Western Church and Roman Empire, but it kept the supernatural, religious background and atmosphere which surrounds these two millennial words. Western World was a programme for hegemony, as 'Europe' was for France. The word 'Western' had an appeal. It announced a beginning and a prerogative of Western man.[18]

The establishment of the heartland incorporated the notion of sovereign equality into the divinely ordained union. In the 1640s Massachusetts proclaimed effective independence, but could not develop an economy to sustain it.[19] Of course, there would be a respectable delay before the entities making up the British empire would actually enjoy anything like sovereign equality, and the process always entailed its own frictions and rivalries. But the transnational spread of English-speaking society had by then transplanted a language, a literature, a legal culture privileging property and contract, a political culture centring on the idea of an innate right to resist the state, and a shared belief in the universal validity of these against others. This allowed the heartland to develop as what Bastiaan van Apeldoorn calls a 'transnational space for the exercise and reproduction of capitalist class rule';[20] or, in the words of a historian of the British Commonwealth, as a 'system of interlinked groups, organizations and societies within the greater community *that was able to avoid in a very large measure the growth of rigidities and compartmentalization in its political, economic and social structure*'.[21] This unique constellation was the result of an equally unique transformation of state power that provided the heartland with the specific state–society relationship which alone makes transnational integration possible.

The Hobbesian and Lockean Moments in Bourgeois State Formation

In the course of the English Civil War, the transformation of the state towards a bourgeois form passed through two stages. The first was the state described in Thomas Hobbes' *Leviathan* of 1651. This marks the concentric phase of the English bourgeois revolution, the moment when Cromwell assumed the mantle of Lord Protector and unified the British Isles into a single sovereignty. Hobbes, an admirer of the new natural science, captures the aspect of atomisation in a society subject to the centrifugal force of privatisation and commercialism. In his quest to find the force that binds the floating particles together again, he postulates a social contract that unifies society under a tentacular state (the original frontispiece of the book shows a crowned, sword-wielding ruler whose coat of mail is made up of minute human figures streaming towards him). Although a monarchist himself in the circumstances, Hobbes was not an advocate of the divine right of kings. The Hobbesian state is a new, impersonal entity separate from society, which does not allow any residual authority other than its own.[22] Perhaps because the bourgeoisie was not the overt protagonist of the revolt, Hobbes was not yet able to fully gauge its ability (and that of the commercialising aristocracy, which in England retained its political prerogative) to direct social development without active state involvement. As to the American colonies, to him they were, at best, a safety valve for the surplus poor.[23]

Cromwell's autocratic, 'Hobbesian' state adopted a foreign policy in line with the pre-bourgeois notion of stable alliances. The Protestant Commonwealth in the British Isles actually sought to bring the Dutch fellow Calvinists into an enduring union. It was felt, Pieter Geyl notes, that 'the two Protestant sea powers could form an invincible combination'. A solemn embassy of 246 diplomats and clerks dispatched to The Hague in March 1651, was mandated to negotiate 'the closest possible bond between the two nations ... nothing less than union within a single state'.[24] But the Dutch merchant oligarchy was wary of the revolutionary belligerency that motivated the offer. They could dispense with Protestant militancy and were only too well aware that their newly sovereign republic, which lacked a centralised state power, would be overwhelmed as soon as England recovered from its civil war. The Dutch preferred to continue trading and actually provided the seagoing merchantman capacity that ensured the survival of English-speaking colonies in North America and in the Caribbean.[25]

Yet, in the Protestant union episode we may observe how the Hobbesian state pursues aims which still belong to a calculus of territorial addition, in the tradition of sovereign equality codified on the continent in 1648. It does so on the basis of new principles, both of which also belong to the first phase of the democratic revolution: Protestantism (as a mobilising ideology capable of forging popular national unity) and mercantilism. The state under the Protectorate inaugurated 'centralisation of government … to an extent never felt in Britain before'; the economic counterpart was a policy of 'national aims prevailing over local feelings'. 'England must be heavily armed, and must use its arms to further projects thought to be in the nation's interest.'[26] Upon the empty-handed return of the embassy from The Hague, the Protectorate therefore set out on a collision course with its beloved sister nation. Thus the commercial motive prevailed over Protestant alliance politics; the tactics of active balancing over solemn commitments. The Act of Navigation of the same year 'nationalised' the right of access to English ports, a state imprint on what used to be granted as royal privilege to special interests, domestic and foreign.[27]

Let us keep in mind that the Hobbesian state, in theory and in (its first approximation in) practice, articulates (a) concentric development; (b) a 'revolutionary' ideology mobilising its social base; and (c) a foreign policy backing up the claim of sovereign equality by a powerful military. This will help us understand the later experience of contender states, which remained congealed in the first phase of bourgeois transformation for a more protracted period.

The second experience of state formation, still within the larger frame of the Protestant phase of the democratic revolution, culminates in the Glorious Revolution of 1688. John Locke's *Two Treatises of Government* provides the theoretical argument for this event. It was based on a different set of experiences from Hobbes; the civil war was in its closing stages, and Locke advocated the withdrawal of the state from social life, *after* the Hobbesian state had suspended local autonomies and privilege-based special freedoms. The enclosure movement privatising land ownership had been largely completed, and possessive individualism was now becoming the middle-class norm. Locke theoretically articulated the new conditions in line with the tradition of gentry self-regulation that had been the backbone of the English social order since the Middle Ages. Importantly, he also took the wider 'West' as the starting point for his understanding of how a civil society operates under the rule of law guaranteed by the state. Inspired by self-government in North America, Locke had as a colonial official co-authored the constitution of the state of Carolina well before he wrote the

Treatises.[28] The Lockean state, governed by a constitutional monarch controlled by a parliament, is the true bourgeois political formation; a state
that 'serves' a largely self-regulating, 'civil' society by protecting private
property at home and abroad.[29]

France, too, was present in Locke's thinking, but only as a negative. The
Dutch provinces on the other hand provided a model of constitutional government attractive to the Whig commercial aristocracy. In this respect Locke
was closer to the Dutch oligarchs, and even the Orangist middle classes
who clung to their newly-won sovereignty, than to Cromwell's ideas about
a quasi-imperial union. Indeed the resumption of the civil war began when
Charles II persisted in fighting a costly war against the Dutch in 1672 in
alliance with Louis XIV, whose fleet construction programme and geopolitical
ambitions the British bourgeoisie had identified as the more urgent threat.[30]
The Glorious Revolution sealed the Stuarts' fate when their son-in-law,
Dutch Stadtholder William III, became constitutional monarch and a flow
of funds was set in motion that would give Dutch investors stakes in the
English national debt, the East India Company, and the Bank of England,
which ranged between one-quarter and one-third by the mid-eighteenth
century.[31] Holland thus became an ancillary of the Lockean heartland that
was the crowning achievement of the Protestant phase of the bourgeois
revolution. The new formation—in which, unlike the Protestant union plan,
the separate states retained their formal sovereignty (which the 13 North
American colonies would attain in 1776)—was the final transformation of
the covenant theology of the Puritans into a social contract among men,
both in terms of sovereign equality and in terms of a social contract underlying sovereignty itself.

Distance and different conditions would continue to produce friction,
actual fighting, and, with the subsequent ascent of the US within the heartland, fierce rivalries. All along, the democratic element that runs through
the Lockean project was most pronounced in North America. Attempts to
create a 'Dominion of New England' under King James therefore met with
stiff resistance. But when news of the Glorious Revolution reached Boston
and other settlements in early 1689, bloodless takeovers followed each
other in quick succession. Massachusetts in particular hailed William as a
Calvinist Messiah and the North American colonies drew closer to the mother
country 'than ever before'.[32]

Enlightenment and Structural Rivalry

In the Enlightenment wave of democratic revolution that follows the
Protestant phase, the emerging heartland/contender state structure created
under the lead of Britain becomes apparent. Of course, this history, like
others, 'must begin from the assumption that what may be described

retrospectively as stages in development ... came about because specific actors made particular choices based on the limited information they possessed; and moreover, that they were probably oblivious to the larger and longer-term impact of their decisions.'[33] Yet while thousands of differences between 'England' and 'France' may be cited, one stands out: in the course of the seventeenth century the French monarchy tried, by a 'controlled' version of the transformation of the type that was taking place in the Netherlands and in England (including overseas trade and settlement), to match its competitors, but failed to do so.

The Reformation had a profound impact on the geopolitical perspective of France's rulers. The French monarchy had long been fighting the English and Flemish in the north while trying to battle its way into Italy at the expense of the German emperors. By the mid-sixteenth century, however, the challenge of a Protestant revolution at home threatened to draw France into the wars of religion in Germany, and led to the shift of focus which would eventually involve it in the Thirty Years' War.[34] The monarchy certainly sought to disentangle the country from religious strife by creating a 'nationalised', Gallic Catholicism that placed a government prerogative in the way of papal influence. On that basis, Cardinal Richelieu, the effective ruler from the 1620s, felt able to revoke the freedoms granted to the Huguenots, the French Protestants. But by cracking down on their strongholds in the Atlantic ports such as La Rochelle (which were effectively trade entrepôts controlled by the Dutch), he also eliminated the enterprising, seagoing element in the French bourgeoisie, while simultaneously antagonising the merchant oligarchy of the United Provinces.[35] Richelieu's parallel attempt to create a North American appendage to metropolitan France, a French-speaking 'heartland', failed because the French colonial fleet could not be protected from Scottish privateers operating in the North Atlantic. In the end the Jesuit order had to intervene to save at least Quebec from what should have become 'New France'.[36]

In terms of state formation, the bourgeoisie in France also failed to obtain a form of state suiting the needs of the commercial and urban classes. Instead it was drawn into the *Fronde*—the rebellion of the provinces and the feudal estates against the centralising monarchy—and it shared in the defeat. In 1685, three years before the Glorious Revolution in England, the Huguenots were dealt the final blow when Louis XIV decreed that they were to be expelled from France altogether. Thus the French bourgeoisie was relegated to a subordinate position in the absolutist state. It reappeared partly as a *state class* of patrician notables and partly as a loose collection of middlemen dependent on favours from above.[37] The bourgeois role thus remained confined to merchant capital parasitic on the state, an obstacle rather than a vehicle of development towards capitalism.[38] *But precisely because France happened to be closest to the English experience in time and space, it could not stray away from the lead given by the British. In an embrace* as close as the one between these two countries, there is very little freedom for the weaker party to experiment in terms of ends; although it will be forced, by the same logic, to rely on different means. It must perforce close the gap with the 'first mover' in order to prevent being dispossessed and subjected, and it did so by a revolution from above, using the state as a lever to accelerate social development.

The attempt by Colbert, minister of Louis XIV, to catch up through a mercantilist policy by decree, failed to synchronise the private profit motive and the public interest, as had so successfully been done in the Netherlands and England. The prior reduction of the Protestant-bourgeois element was both a symptom and a further cause of that failure.[39] Challenging Holland by enlisting the support of the Stuarts backfired as well, when France found itself having to fight both of them from 1688 to 1697 and again in the War of the Spanish Succession from 1701 to 1713. Under the Peace of Utrecht that settled this conflict, French power on the continent was effectively placed under English tutelage; the English for the first time became signatories to a European geopolitical order, which they intended to operate by active balancing.[40]

The burden of geopolitical competition was now placed disproportionately on France, but the imperative to modernise was mortgaged by having to consolidate the monarchical-landlord class structure at the same time—a ruling class will not abolish itself for the greater good. Original expropriation under the French kings therefore did not really take place. It was literally original *accumulation*, the amassing of an initial investment fund through intensified exploitation of the peasantry under the old regime.[41] France thus remained stuck with an absolutist state still on the threshold of the Hobbesian transformation. For a century to come—in the wars of the 1688–1714 period, in the Austrian War of Succession (in the 1740s) and the Seven Years' War (1756–63)—it fought the English for control of North America and India and the routes leading there. Throughout these conflicts, the presence of British settlers proved a decisive advantage for the English, just as it had in England's prior rivalries with Holland.[42] Certainly, the American bourgeoisie broke away from Britain soon after the Seven Years' War, but this was entirely in the Lockean spirit—resistance to state encroachment, self-regulation under the law, and bourgeois control of parliamentary institutions, private property and free enterprise. Mercantilist prohibitions on the development of manufactures motivated the English-speaking settlers to rebel against British imperial control. We are reminded here that the establishment of the heartland too involves shocks and conflicts, indeed intense rivalries. Yet, as early as the 1820s, the common heritage prevailed when the two states jointly established their informal empire over Latin America after that continent's emancipation from Iberian overlordship.[43]

The second consequence of the suppression of Protestantism in France concerns the ideological mutation that occurs when bourgeois self-interest is no longer expressed as Calvinism or in other religious terms, but as a straightforward political critique of absolutism. The expulsion of the Huguenots at the end of the seventeenth century left behind a Protestant ideological legacy in Paris with its epicentre in the convent of Port-Royal, which was also a philosophical academy. The achievement of this current of thought, Rosenstock argues, was that 'the French nation could escape the intellectual impasse created by the Reformation and Counter-Reformation.'[44] The seminal figure here is Blaise Pascal, the mathematical prodigy and philosopher, who retired in Port-Royal. Pascal situates the individual human being, alone with his/her religious belief, in 'the eternal silence of infinite spaces' thrown into relief by the discoveries and the new astronomy. The straightforward language in which he attacked the vacuous scholasticism of the Jesuits became the model for Voltaire's satires. The Christian theological heritage was now no longer subjected to rival inter-pretations; it moved from the quest for the grand message hidden in the texts to the question of how that message functions, which elements it is made up of, and what it rules out and cuts off. This is the moment in intel-lectual history, Foucault claims, at which 'the *commentary* makes way for the *critique.*'[45]

In eighteenth-century France, this produced the synthesis between the social forms and ideas spreading from across the Channel, and the rationalist-scientific tradition developed on the continent. The Enlightenment denotes the growth of a transnational liberalism through which the Glorious Revolu-tion resonated in contender state Europe (and in turn influenced outlying areas such as the Americas), while shifting its intellectual framework to bourgeois radicalism.[46] Its vehicle of choice, Freemasonry, advocated the separation of church and state, the advancement of science, and civil liber-ties. Freemasonry played a key role in the spread of these ideas from Britain, but the specific conditions it encountered abroad imparted a radical, anti-clerical and rationalistic twist to them. A term like 'civil society' in Locke's *Treatises*, for instance, was translated as 'republic' in the French edition (printed by Dutch Freemasons), the edition probably used by Rousseau.[47] Here too we are looking at a transnational process of class formation, a process, to quote Edmund Burke again, of 'combining parties among the inhabitants of different countries into one connexion ... and [from which] are likely to arise effects full as important as those which had formerly arisen from the jarring interests of the religious sects.'[48]

Now the political consequences of *this* round of revolution, as Burke also concluded, were potentially much more dangerous and could altogether destroy Lockean liberalism and its tradition of gentlemanly self-regulation. Not only did socialism already emerge in the French revolution; the revolu-tion also modernised the contender state facing the first British empire.

The innovations wrought by Napoleon produced a rationalisation of state power and the concentration of initiative and ingenuity in the state well beyond the Hobbesian prescriptions.[49] The Napoleonic state provides us with the outlines of the general contender state model: concentric development driven from above, using the state as a lever; a 'revolutionary' ideology mobilising the social base; and a foreign policy backing up the claim of sovereign equality with a powerful military. This creates a state which develops in its own right, to a point where its constructive and organising role in society vastly outstrips anything the British or US states can achieve under normal conditions. Therefore we should not understand the heartland/contender structure only as a matter of lead and lag. Once the contender state has developed to its full momentum, the core structure evolves into what Laurent Cohen-Tanugi calls 'the antinomy between administrative regulation, the juridical by-product of the modern state; and what is called, in the Anglo-Saxon countries, the rule of law—with its traditional characteristics and in the conditions under which it arose, that is, the liberal state and the market economy *prior to the era of the welfare state*'.[50]

SYSTEMIC AND TRANSNATIONAL RIVALRIES

Let us now look at the aspect of capitalist development in the evolving core structure. Capital, as a discipline over society and nature, is not an instrument wielded by the heartland in its relations with contenders. Certainly heartland states will back up this discipline with their own coercive capacity, but, as I will argue here, capital is not identical to the West. It is a historical corollary of the heartland/contender structure, but it tends to escape the confines of bounded spaces and imposes itself on global society as an *extraterritorial* discipline.[51]

States demarcate legal spaces on the principle of territoriality, over which they exercise exclusive sovereignty. Capital, on the other hand, was historically formed in the interstices between feudal productive structures such as the manor and the guilds, and as long-distance trade and finance, outside the jurisdiction of the sovereign entities of European society. Once it was blended into a single, comprehensive process with its focus in the English-speaking world, it again began to exercise its discipline on separate societies by taking control of the nodal points linking them, like commercial exchanges, credit, migration, etc. Thus, it can exert competitive pressures on wages and living/working conditions—for example, through free trade and equality of access.[52] Although it will seek to use state power to defend its interests, capital can never allow itself to be locked up within a single political jurisdiction. It must, in the Marxist perspective, develop into a historical force organising the world economy as a whole, if it is to fulfil its 'civilising mission' and prepare a superior form of society. This it cannot do if there is a superior authority in place to begin with. After all, even a Lockean, liberal state may resort again to administering the economy politically and restrict private property and contract, as evidenced by the New Deal in the United States and the wartime emergencies across the English-speaking world. Compared to the territorial organisation of space by states, capital therefore tends towards a 'nomadic' pattern of organisation, moving between different jurisdictions. It operates in an imaginary 'smooth space' that cannot be internalised by states. As Ronen Palan has argued, there is a structural incompatibility between the two ways of organising social space; ruling classes exploit this by organising their state power separately from economic power, which they bracket off from the political process through offshore investments and other forms of extraterritoriality.[53]

The specificity of the Lockean heartland in relation to capital, then, resides in the unique combination of states retaining their formal autonomy, and a wider space organised on a shared principle of the sovereignty of property and contract, and, hence, of capital. This transnational space, while external to each of the taken states separately, is internal to the heartland as a broader configuration.[54] True, quasi-state structures such as the Bretton Woods institutions are operating in the wider transnational space, but they are not set up as channels for synthesising and articulating a collective will, as are states. They constitute a technical and statistical infrastructure preferentially accessed by the strongest heartland states, but not (as in the case of the United Nations and universal international organisation in general) in any parliamentary sense. Ideally they are impermeable to democracy. The heartland is therefore best understood not as some massive central island but as a networked social and geo-economic structure comprising a number of (originally English-speaking) states and a regulatory infrastructure. *Expansion* occurs on two dimensions: one of capital, to global proportions; and the other of the West, which by definition has a more limited reach. In their combined advance across the globe, the two progress in tandem as a way of life, a culture, and a politics, with their means of coercion complementing capitalist discipline.[55]

Against this powerful complex of forces, staking their claim to the planet as a whole, the contender states have to build up a rival apparatus of wealth creation *within* their separate jurisdictions, at best harnessing the resources of satellites. Usually the contender state class is most successful in doing this in the initial phases of the catch-up effort. In the 'economic miracles' following revolution and/or war, a state-led economy can grow extraordinarily fast to the point where it again reaches the trend line determined mainly by population size.[56] But the very success of the catch-up effort then needs a further adjustment of social relations to match the requirements of the more developed economy, a risk few contender state classes have been willing to take for fear of being dethroned. The state class may revolutionise agriculture and break the mould of backward mentalities on the land; it may industrialise, it may even resort to capitalist forms and allow markets to function (as in China today). But it always does so while holding on to political sovereignty. The modern classes it spawns, capitalist or otherwise, will by the logic of the division and socialisation of labour develop more varied interests not necessarily confined to the national economy. At some point they will seek the reduction/restructuring of the directive state, and engage with the rest of the world autonomously on their own terms. The result will be a crisis in which the virtual 'war economy' by which the contender state has attempted to match the heartland's achievements must either enter the test of an actual confrontation or undergo a civilian trans-formation, discarding the structural separation from the West.[57]

In both cases, the chances that a given state class can retain its hold on power are extremely limited. It can propel its society and economy to the very threshold of the level of development reached in the heartland, but there it must leave it. Yet the fact that the centralising authority (monarch or central committee) in these states has been compelled to emulate the Western pattern of development brings into being economic assets, which then become available for expropriation by a transnational capitalist class. Hence rivalry may in a perverse sense serve as a mode of expansion of capital, even if this proceeds through crises and violent conflagrations be-tween the Lockean West and 'the tormented political forms which liberalism then confronted as its military competitors'.[58]

Should we therefore see this as a transcendent 'mechanism', a 'system' which allows the participants no choices? Not if we understand it properly. The apparent 'systemic' aspect resides in the limited number of choices that are possible, given the evolving heartland/contender structure, in com-bination with the tendental globalisation of capitalist discipline. As long as the Atlantic ruling class can ensure that no catch-up strategy will leave key resources or industrial assets in the hands of an unreformed contender state class, or otherwise removed from the regulatory structures under Western control, it might in principle allow a non-Western country to become the 'workshop of the West', just as Britain was once the 'workshop of the world'. But as the example of China acutely demonstrates, a contender state class may want integration on its own terms, or (as in the case of the Third World coalition for a New International Economic Order in the 1970s) it may want exemptions from the prevailing rules of the game. Therefore, the ruling classes and states of the heartland have all along pursued a double strategy: first, trying to dominate, penetrate and integrate peripheral societies; and second, waging *wars of dispossession* against entrenched state classes.[59] The original English-speaking heartland has waged these wars with the help of ad hoc coalitions, usually enlisting the less dangerous con-tenders in a policy of active balancing against the most acute threat: the continental coalition against Napoleon; France and Russia against Germany; and China against the USSR. This results in the phenomena of the *vassal state* enlisted as a heartland ally, but allowed to retain the Hobbesian state/society complex (e.g., Japan and South Korea); and of a *secondary contender* which just avoids challenging the heartland politically (e.g., Brazil or Turkey).[60]

So far, only the European Union (EU) has approximated the heartland in terms of an 'internal extraterritoriality'. The overlap between the original English-speaking West and the EU (as well as the differences in the way they originated) has continued to generate frictions and rivalries, notably in the case of Britain. The UK first remained outside the EU, and then negotiated structural competitive advantages relative to the EU (for which it has in turn mobilised a domestic mass base with the help of populist scares about a supposed European 'super-state').[61] It is true that the EU of today has developed towards a heartland-like structure by relying on forms inherited from the contender state experience. From the Marshall Plan onwards, liberalism was often imposed through state intervention rather than state withdrawal, and, along the way, rivalry with the English-speaking heartland reproduced a set of 'European' attitudes and interests, including in the geopolitical sphere, like the relationship with Eastern Europe and Russia. So while there are powerful unifying forces (which are also cultural: the EU, as Abram de Swaan reminds us, becomes more 'English-speaking' with every enlargement),[62] the structural similarity at the end of the road has been achieved by different, often incompatible, strategies.

I will discuss the relationship between European integration and the Atlantic heartland extensively in the course of this book. Here I just note that there also exists an important *time differential* between the original heartland and the EU in terms of their structural affinity to transnational capital. The greater longevity of the former has made the leading English-speaking states dependent on three areas of specialisation: control of the financial system, control of worldwide energy flows, and military-industrial development.[63] The paradox of the dismissal of 'old Europe' by the US secretary of defence in the run-up to the invasion of Iraq is that the EU in key respects represents a new version of the principles of structural affinity or 'coupling' between the transnational state organisation and capital, which gave the English-speaking heartland its historical advantage as far back as the Glorious Revolution and the American secession.[64] This would apply to a greater willingness to recognise the sovereign concerns of less developed states, a more activist attitude to the crisis of the biosphere, and less reliance on the use of military power in diplomacy. Ultimately, there is no need to assume that European imperialism is any more 'benevolent' than that of the United States; the ruling classes on either side of the Atlantic seek to uphold and advance what I call the global sovereignty of capital. The only benevolence displayed is the renunciation of the use of military force—against each other, that is, not against the rest of the world.[65]

We can now sum up, obviously with all the limitations of a schematic representation, the main characteristics of the developed core structure (Figure 1.1).

Figure 1.1
Three Spheres of Rivalry

Struggles over primacy in the English-speaking heartland	Rivalries with/among integrated former contenders (shaded)	Current frontier of rivalry

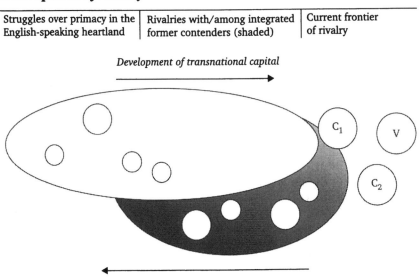

Development of transnational capital

Emancipation of transnational class society from the state

Notes: C_1 = Primary contender; C_2 = Secondary contender(s); V = Vassal state(s)

On this two-dimensional plane, only classical inter-state or *peripheral* rivalries are visible; most obviously on the heartland/contender divide, but also in the relations between states in the other two spheres. With the growth of transnational interests, a *third dimension* of rivalry emerges. On this dimension, we can observe two types of rivalries:

- *Transnational* rivalries, which are inherent in the internal extraterritoriality of the heartland, the wider West, the EU, and so on, in areas where such relations are beginning to develop. Here, states exploit the structural accessibility of integrated societies to state power other than their own, in order to influence the political process there. As we will see, this includes transnational covert action, an aspect of relations among 'allies' that tends to be overlooked. This form of rivalry

is obviously imbricated with transnational class relations, but necessarily involves competing state powers operating transnationally.[66]
- *Systemic* rivalries, complementing transnational rivalries and lending meaning to them. Systemic rivalries are about competing approaches to organising the transnationalised space (heartland, wider West, world). As Harold van Buren Cleveland wrote at the height of Atlantic tensions in the mid-1960s, 'the most important political struggles of [the twentieth] century have not been peripheral conflicts in the nineteenth-century manner. They have been systemic, ideological conflicts among national states as actors in and constituents of wider than national political systems. Their struggles have not been simply about the interests and the power of the separate nations but about the political organization and the ideological tendency of the wider systems.'[67]

The most important systemic shift involving transnational rivalry in the period analysed in this book involved the internal antinomy within the West between state-led development and administrative regulation on the one hand, and, on the other, the Anglo-Saxon heritage of the unadulterated 'rule of law', i.e., property rights and contract, which had been limited by class compromise.

From Democratic Revolution to the Sovereignty of Capital

The experience of English-speaking countries has given rise to the assumption that liberal development proceeds naturally, in step with the inherent rhythm of daily life and the inborn characteristics of the human species. A contender state, on the other hand, proceeds on the assumption of *planned* action, the coercive moulding of the human and natural material, because relative backwardness is its acknowledged starting point. In reality, on both sides of the heartland/contender state divide, society is a product of constant intervention, as ruling classes absorb elements and signals coming from each other and from subordinate social forces, and adapt and anticipate. But in the process of interactive socialisation, the heartland usually has the advantage of experiencing the process of social change first, setting the standard of 'normalcy'.[68] This is further helped by the global centrality of the English language, which, in combination with the Anglo-American dominance in the entertainment business, conveys hegemonic messages smoothly and apparently effortlessly.[69]

The process of establishing and renovating the hegemonic consensus of the West is achieved through an infrastructure of informal networks, from business boardrooms to the more prestigious planning bodies. These bring together, in the private surroundings required to allow the expression of differences, key statesmen, media managers, and other 'organic intellectuals' of the transnational capitalist class.[70] At this level, systemic rivalries are being articulated and, ideally, overcome. In the contemporary world, the Bilderberg Conferences, the Trilateral Commission, the World Economic Forum and a range of comparable bodies are active in this sense. They operate within the heartland, but also on its perimeter, as interfaces with the aspiring bourgeoisie from the contender states. They generate (along with parallel networks of joint directorates, think tanks, inter-governmental and multilateral structures) the hegemonic formulas that underpin the systemic orientation of the wider West, its *comprehensive concepts of control*. A concept of control provides the ideological framework that in a given age provides overall cohesion to the class consciousness of the capitalist class, and at the height of its 'comprehensiveness' sets the limits of the possible/thinkable for society at large. A concept of control can only be operative in a Lockean state/society complex in which rival interests can organise freely before they compete for political office; the process of transnational class formation in that sense steers party competition within the national political systems. As Gramsci recognised, transnational class networks 'propose political solutions of diverse historical origin, and assist their victory in particular countries—functioning as international political parties which operate within each nation with the full concentration of the international forces.'[71]

Lockean liberalism, on which the heartland's rise was premised, today still provides the integral calculus for capitalist class rule. However, the growth of working-class power and the prestige of socialism, which coincided with the contender state challenges posed by Germany and the USSR, forced the heartland ruling classes to seek compromises beyond liberalism. Locke's prescriptions and the gentlemanly liberalism that they codified were ill-equipped to deal with the growing concentration and centralisation of capital, the deepening socialisation of labour within and between corporations, the separation of (stock) ownership from management, and, for that matter, with mass politics. Hence, as Friedrich von Hayek argues in the opening chapter of *The Road to Serfdom*, German ideas about state intervention after 1870 began to reverse the eastward spread of English liberalism that had occurred in the two preceding centuries.[72] In 1947 Hayek himself set about rectifying this with the help of a planning and propaganda network of right-wing economists and philosophers, the Mont Pèlerin Society (MPS). The *neoliberalism* they developed was not meant to be a return to laissez-faire; it self-consciously presents itself as a new doctrine, able to cover all aspects of life by reference to market mechanisms, in order to avoid meeting the needs of modern society by state planning. Rescinding the compromise with labour was at the heart of the neoliberal enterprise, and the need to restrict the power of trade unions was formulated at the first MPS conference.[73]

At the time, these ideas stood no chance against the Keynesian concern with stabilising large-scale industry by sustaining consumption, supported by a broad consensus in which organised labour was a willing partner. State intervention was generally seen as the obvious solution to problems in society and the economy. The contender state legacy thus merged with the shift in the balance of class forces, into what Robert Cox has dubbed the 'welfare nationalist state'—welfare in exchange for loyalty to the nation. The growth of working-class militancy, against the backdrop of the parallel consolidation of the Soviet Union, tilted this compromise further to the left by the mid-century. Through Roosevelt's New Deal and the Marshall Plan, *corporate liberalism* (or 'embedded liberalism') became the hegemonic concept of control in the extended heartland.[74]

Corporate liberalism, I would argue, represents the furthest point of development of the democratic revolution in the West. It takes the ideas of popular sovereignty and universal human rights and seeks to accommodate, *within the capitalist order*, the aspirations for socialism spawned by them. Thus in the context of the rivalry with the state-socialist contender—which we know as the cold war—the welfare state, the 'mixed economy' and a range of related phenomena were pursued in competition with more radical demands emanating from both the domestic working classes and the contender states. In the West itself, this culminated in proposals to socialise profits and give the trade unions a voice in investment decisions; on a global level, it led to proposals to impose codes of conduct under UN control on transnational corporations and to planned interdependence with the Soviet bloc economies. But as we will see in later chapters, by now the Right was mobilising along a broad front. When corporate liberalism unravelled in the crises of the early 1970s, the Hayek programme acquired an unexpected relevance as an alternative concept of control that might guide and inspire a capitalist counter-revolution.

What Hayek proposed was a fundamental disjuncture between market outcomes and the ideological claims of the democratic revolution. This is a crucial mutation, to which I will come back in Chapter 5. It marks off a new epoch, which begins with the coup in Chile in 1973. Indeed, the Allende government had taken the democratic revolution to the point of using parliamentary means to realise a socialist programme, rather than placing itself outside democratic legitimacy by a direct seizure of power. But precisely because its credentials were impeccable in this respect, democracy in Chile was unacceptable to the rulers of the West; Pinochet's terror regime on the other hand was broadly deemed a suitable, if painful, method to introduce the neoliberal alternative. Chile thus became the laboratory of the Mont Pèlerin Society's market fundamentalism. The new constitution imposed on the ravaged country in 1980 was officially designated as the 'Constitution of Liberty', after the title of Hayek's book.[75]

The neoliberal counter-revolution of the 1980s, associated with the names of Margaret Thatcher and Ronald Reagan, has superficially restored the primacy of the West in the global political economy, around a concept of control based on the express rejection of popular aspirations for anything other than individual wealth. Certainly 'human rights' and 'democracy' continue to be selectively promoted—in Ukraine but not in Pakistan, for example. But the global neoliberal offensive is conducted in the name of 'freedom' as defined by Hayek, never as social justice or democratic emancipation. Today, property rights and capitalist discipline overrule all else. As Tony Blair put it in a speech to the New York Stock Exchange in late 1998, the string of financial crises rocking the world at that time did not mean that 'market disciplines have failed, but that in a global economy the absence of such disciplines can have devastating effect. Countries must put in place the right policy framework.'[76] Neoliberal 'good governance' is in that sense premised on a crystallisation of sovereign capital on a global scale. It induces a general condition of *stasis*, captured by post-modern culture and celebrated in statements such as Francis Fukuyama's *The End of History*. Of course the suggestion of universal homogenisation is wildly premature. The ability of different societies to submit to capitalist discipline is limited, and the very pressure to radically adjust to (neo)liberalism paradoxically reactivates the specific heritage of each separate society in new combinations, in a process that Robert Boyer calls 'hybridisation'.[77] As a result, cleavages of a 'civilisational' nature—religious and ethnic divisions—are enhanced in ways undermining the global sovereignty of capital, igniting and/or exacerbating the rivalries we are witnessing today.[78]

Certainly the West continues to exert pressure on other societies to submit to capitalist discipline, and consciously probes for partners in the target states willing to play its game. Condoleezza Rice, on the eve of her appointment as George W. Bush's national security adviser, saw her main foreign policy job as 'finding peace, security, and *opportunities for entrepreneurs in other countries*'. While advocating a policy of confrontation with 'rogue states' like North Korea and Iraq, the policy towards China should in her view be guided by the fact that change in that country is being led by 'people who no longer owe their livelihood to government'.[79] In other words, the West should be looking for the aspiring bourgeois element in those contender societies, where the state drives forward the catch-up development process, but who are not themselves the core state class. This strategy, which seeks to exploit what Gramsci labels *passive revolution*, is itself a legacy from the spread of the democratic revolution, and the Enlightenment is an early example of it. A passive revolution combines a 'revolution from above' without mass participation (Gramsci speaks of 'successive small waves of reform' and 'interventions from above of the enlightened monarchy type') and a creeping, 'molecular' social transformation, in which the progressive class (in this case, the bourgeoisie) finds itself compelled to advance in a more or less surreptitious, 'compromised' fashion.[80]

This aptly sums up the nature of change in a contender state, and integration into the expanding West was long premised on it. But what emerges today in the hour of a contender's demise is no longer a broad-based bourgeoisie, in the sense of an entrepreneurial middle class employing a working class sharing its world-view in key respects. What we are witnessing instead is a 'class effect' of the global sovereignty of capital, in which competing capitalist oligarchies, relying on an auxiliary cadre of professional middle classes, face the nameless billions increasingly concerned with social and/ or physical survival.[81] This 'class effect' occurs universally; 'reform', in the sense of deepening commodification and privatisation, is no longer a one-way process in which only the non-Western societies are on the receiving end. The West itself must bow before the deity of capital, and global society in its entirety acquires the ubiquitous 'Third World' characteristics of extreme inequality and insecurity that are in evidence today.

INDUSTRIAL COMPETITION AND CAPITALIST DISCIPLINE

Let me conclude this chapter by going over the main catch-up episodes that followed the industrial revolution, to the point in time where Chapter 2 begins. The heartland enjoys the initial advantage, forcing the society it confronts into the contender posture. The actions and achievements of the contender state in turn affect developments in the heartland; in the process, capital becomes an autonomous force, imposing its discipline in both directions through geopolitical competition. However, the 'West' is not by any means a fixed entity. There were persistent tensions between Britain and the United States, as well as with Canada, Australia and New Zealand. Yet the spatial coordinates of the heartland were extended step-by-step in spite of friction; first, in 1803 when Napoleon had to sell Louisiana, shortly after it was purchased from the Spanish, to the US government. This freed up the American Midwest for colonisation and large-scale agriculture.[82] The West thus became an economic reality, the terrain of a widening, combined process of agrarian revolution and industrial revolution, opening up vast spaces for renewed settlement and investment in the course of the nineteenth century.[83] It was in this setting that capital in Britain reached the stage of industrialisation. Having defeated Napoleon with the help of a reactionary coalition on the continent, British industry gave the country an almost unassailable position until well into the nineteenth century. Home to only 2 per cent of the world's population, the UK accounted for 40–45 per cent of world industrial production as late as 1860, when it became the financier of US industrialisation.[84]

The need to catch up, in order to prevent peripheralisation and dispossession, was now placed squarely before the ruling classes of all other societies, a thesis extensively covered in the literature.[85] Geopolitical rivalry always serves as a (two-way) enforcement mechanism, on which capital then grafts its own discipline. Thus the French revolution reinforced the conviction among English factory owners—an idea articulated by Ure and Bentham—that the strictest discipline over the workers was an essential requirement for capital's proper functioning.[86] Second, the Continental System, by which Napoleon sought to create an early version of a closed European economy, locked out British products and forced the UK government to adopt measures to compensate for the loss. The steps taken in the area of infrastructure, protection, policing the workers, and development of colonial markets, all testify to the impact which the contender state has on development within the heartland, dispelling the idea that capitalism somehow grows within it, and that the confrontation with the contender state is external to it.[87] Finally, the French annexation of Holland and the disruption of financial networks on the continent in the Napoleonic wars turned London into the key international capital market.[88]

To provide some measure of the catch-up processes in the ensuing period, I rely on the method developed by Giovanni Arrighi, who defines an 'organic core' facing the rest in the world economy. This core consists 'of all the states that over the last half-century or so have occupied the top positions of the global hierarchy of wealth and, in virtue of that position, have set (individually or collectively) the standards of wealth which all their governments have sought to maintain and all other governments have sought to attain.'[89] Arrighi puts the weighted average GNP per capita of the 'organic core' (made up of North America, Western Europe, Australia and New Zealand) for the period 1938–88 at 100, and then looks both at internal distribution in the 'core' and at the catch-up efforts of non-core states as a percentage of the core's GNP per capita. In Table 1.1, I apply a non-weighted version of this method for the earlier heartland/contender rounds, adding the incidences of war and revolution and their consequences for overall distribution. In the table, cotton spindlage capacity in the heartland has been set at 100, in order that the growth of the contender economies relative to the heartland in this first-generation industry can be read from the table.

The American Civil War reminds us that in this period the English-speaking West itself was still subject to shocks accompanying the phased transformation of the 13 settler colonies into the modern United States. In the course of the nineteenth century, the challenge to the heartland subsides: the rival industrial capacity of the three main contenders, which stood at a third of the heartland's in 1834, declined to a quarter by 1867. The crippling effects of revolution and war on the contenders are evident from the table. In France, the bourgeoisie rose twice in an attempt to seize political power (in the 1830 and 1848 revolutions); both efforts were neutralised, but under the subsequent restoration they undermined the

Table 1.1
Heartland-Contender Development, Revolution and War, 1834–1913 (cotton spindlage capacity)

Total for Heartland = 100	1834	1852		1861		1867	1913
Great Britain	87.7	76.6	|	72.9		81.0	64.5
			(Crimean War)		Civil War		
United States	12.2	23.4		27.1	|	19.0	35.5

Contenders in %							
		1848 Revolutions	|			Franco-Prussian War	
France	21.9	| 19.1	|	12.9		16.9	\\ 8.6
					Austro-Prussian War		Paris Commune
Prussia-Germany	5.5*	3.8		5.3		4.8	12.6
Austria-Hungary	7.0	5.9		4.2		3.6	5.6

Source: Calculated from Landes (1969: 215, Table 5).
Note: *1836.

contender state posture by fostering laissez-faire liberalism in the passive revolution.[90] Bismarck on the other hand developed his belligerent foreign policy through a revolution from above as a means of disciplining the German workers, while enlarging the human and material resource base. The establishment of the Second German Empire crowned his achievements, and the violent suppression of the Paris Commune in a way complemented the domestication of the labour movement in Germany itself. But it was not till the twentieth century that all this came together in a really life-threatening challenge to the heartland.[91]

To establish how the discipline of capital emancipates from the coercive force applied by states into an autonomous social force, we must look at the transnationalisation of the relationship between productive and money capital. The centrality of the London capital and exchange markets, established during the Napoleonic wars, for most of the nineteenth century was a function of British pre-eminence in trade and industry. Banks, set up to perform clearing functions and extend credit, at this point still relied on capital that reached the City from the English provinces and ports.[92] The value of British foreign investments in the early 1850s was twice the French stock of foreign investment, so one may conclude that in terms of power exerted through that channel, Britain easily held the advantage. Still it was the *British* capitalist class, relying on its own state, which imposed economic discipline abroad. The same applies to its efforts to open up export markets by unequal treaties, first with Latin America, and then with China, Persia, and the Ottoman Empire.[93] The Cobden-Chevalier free trade treaty imposed on France by the UK in 1860 was also an unequal treaty, and it both triggered and undermined the French attack on Prussia.[94]

At this point the United States began its rise as an industrial economy that would prove decisive in the defence of heartland pre-eminence in the twentieth century. The triumph of the protectionist North in the American Civil War suspended the role of the US as a raw material supplier to the former mother country. But, in addition, it had the effect of creating the extra-territoriality which till today characterises the capital markets of the City of London. As Paul Langley writes, when Britain declined relative to the US and Germany, 'London-centred credit creation became materially less reliant upon capital newly accumulated through British trade and industrial production. Instead, it took place largely on the back of mobile capital in general and capital accumulated through previous rounds of credit creation.'[95] The adoption of the gold standard was very much part of the general drift towards the concentric economic development of the period, but the authority it bestowed on the Bank of England placed this institution in a powerful position to discipline other economies by imposing financial orthodoxy. Yet this was no longer a function of the British or even the wider heartland economies, or politically controlled by them.[96] In other words, capital now operates through its own disciplinary mechanisms, which are relatively autonomous from state power.

Nobody has better captured the process of autonomisation of transnational capital from its UK origins at this juncture than Karl Polanyi in his famous remarks on the role of *haute finance*. Certainly his equation of this role with peace has been challenged, but few will dispute that in terms of capitalist development, high finance acquires its 'offshore' status as a cohesive, disciplinary force at this point. Thus the Rothschilds, Polanyi claims, 'were subject to no *one* government; as a family they embodied the abstract principle of internationalism; their loyalty was to a firm, the credit of which had become the only supranational link between political government and industrial effort in a swiftly growing world economy.' Hence,

> Gold standard and constitutionalism were the instruments which made the voice of the City of London heard in many smaller countries which adopted these symbols of adherence to the new international order. *The Pax Britannica held sway sometimes by the ominous poise of heavy ship's cannon, but more frequently by the timely pull of a thread in the international monetary network.*[97]

This sums up how capitalist discipline is imposed directly, outside, or aside from, the jurisdiction of the separate states—but note Polanyi's use of the term *constitutionalism* as an 'instrument': the Lockean transformation of the relation between state and society is the pre-condition for the transnational functioning of capital.

Among the English-speaking countries a new political format for dealing with disruptive unequal development developed at the same time. Britain was overtaken industrially by the United States between 1880 and 1910, but the Atlantic 'swing mechanism', in which periods of real accumulation absorbing money capital alternated between the US and Britain, kept frictions within limits. From 1870 onwards, Canada, Australia and Argentina also became part of this Atlantic economy, with the City of London serving as the pivot. By 1914, London commanded a stock of foreign investment valued at £20 billion pounds sterling; France's stood at slightly more than £2 billion and Germany's at around £1 billion. Nearly 50 per cent of British investments were in the US and the settler colonies, weakening the British economy but strengthening the heartland.[98]

Politically, the heartland drew closer together in 1911. In that year the UK and the US concluded the Arbitration Treaty outlawing war between them, and the British Commonwealth was effectively created at the 1911 Imperial Conference.[99] Here, then, we see the transnational space, which, as I noted earlier, is external to the separate states, but internal to the heartland as a broader configuration.

The new contender, Germany, did not enjoy any of the advantages of this wider structure. Its rise was predicated on the conquest of the iron ore and coal areas of Lorraine and the unification of the German state in 1871. True, its rise was spectacular, since the new heavy industries through their many forward and backward linkages enabled a much more rapid breakthrough to international prominence than the relatively sedate effects of what Senghaas calls (in the case of France and Austria-Hungary), the 'textile route'.[100] But while the second-generation industries intensified the concentric development of the contender state, they also accelerated the formation of a massive proletariat, which the imperial autocracies in Central and Eastern Europe were ill-equipped to deal with. Preparation for war therefore became the main concern of the emperors of Germany, Austria-Hungary and Russia, at a time when France and England already saw the parliamentary domestication of the labour movement as the paramount challenge. The attempted revolution in Russia in 1905 only heightened the emperors' concerns. With characteristic candour, Emperor Wilhelm II in the next new year's message to his chancellor, Bülow, summed up his programme as (a) 'shoot, decapitate, and break the socialists, if necessary with a bloodbath', and (b) 'after that, war abroad; but not before and not overhasty'.[101]

The nature of the challenge to the heartland in 1914 was therefore a complex one. There was the straightforward rivalry of Germany, but in addition powerful tremors were rising from the depth of the social structures of both the main contender states and the heartland. Social and cultural liberalisation, and artistic and technological innovation were electrifying the air everywhere; the new power of the ascendant working class added a weight that could turn these changes into a qualitative break with the past. The war, then, was simultaneously a civil war against all those who were associated with these developments—a war fought by the ruling classes against their own populations; and a contest against each other over spheres of influence in the Balkans, investments and railway projects.[102]

Its outcome confirms the heartland/contender state divide. On one hand we have the victorious West (with France tentatively integrated into it), championing a resurrected economic liberalism and international organisation to preserve the peace; and on the other the contenders subjected to shock-like adjustments—revolution in Russia; revolution and counter-revolution in Germany, Italy and Japan; the break-up along national lines of Austria-Hungary.[103] As has been observed often enough, the Second World War was therefore a foregone conclusion, the continuation of a war of dispossession of the anti-status quo powers. In Table 1.2, the steel industry is taken as the sector in which to observe the strength of the catch-up effort across the heartland/contender divide around the first half of the twentieth century. Again, note the massive blows that revolution and war dealt to the contenders' development efforts.

The world wars constituted an acute emergency for the ruling class in the heartland. In the contest with the Axis powers, all wartime economies

Table 1.2
Heartland-Contender Development, Revolution and War, 1880–1957 (steel production)

Total for Heartland = 100	1880	1900		1910		1925	1938		1950*	1957*
					First World War		Second World War			
United States	42.8	61.3		72.8		75.5	62.7		78.3	74.5
Great Britain	44.2	29.5		17.8		12.3	23.5		14.4	15.6
[France]	13.0	9.3		9.4		12.2	13.7		7.3	9.9
Contenders in %										
Germany/[FRG]	23.6	38.2		36.0		12.0	51.8		10.5	18.2
			Russo-Japanese War			1917 Revolution				
Russia/USSR	9.9	13.0		9.7	/	3.1	39.6		23.8	34.7
Japan	–	–		0.8**		2.2	14.3***		4.3	9.4

Sources: Calculated from Hexner (1943: 324–5, Appendix VI); Economic Commission for Europe (1959: 22, Tables 16, 17); Japan figure for 1910 (1913) from Moore (1981: 288).

Notes: *Steel plus finished iron.
**1913.
***1939.

were developed to their full potential, an early example of a Keynesian full-employment economy.[104] The 1938 figures for the contenders, adding up to more than 100 per cent (from 17.3 in 1925), remind us of how, in this age of steel, the centre of gravity in global economic development shifted away from the heartland, inflecting the hegemonic concept of the Atlantic ruling classes away from Lockean liberalism as well.[105] But then, the heartland's pre-eminence is also gradually shifting to new grounds, to be expressed as a *qualitative* advantage, a capacity to move ahead to new levels of socialisation of labour. The West restructured its advantage by reorganising the steel industry to supply the automotive complex of 'Fordism' and support a mass consumption society, and not by producing more steel, as the contender economies (including the USSR) continued to do.

Yet again, the discipline of transnational capital in 1944, as organised through the Bretton Woods institutions, was initially almost a function of the new pre-eminence of the United States. But the control over the IMF and World Bank wielded by the West (by the distribution of voting power and the reliance on the US dollar as the international reserve currency) obtained a first, 'private' counterpoint with the creation of an offshore Eurodollar market in the City of London in the late 1950s. The 'Polanyi moment', i.e., the quasi-independent operation of *haute finance* directly imposing the discipline of capital, transpires in the 1970s—first, by the uncoupling of the dollar from gold, greatly expanding the liquidity of the Euromarkets; and second, by the reimposition of neoliberal discipline in 1979, through the rise in interest rates, on the global credit economy that had grown up around them.[106] Finally, transnational companies developed to a size where they too could emancipate themselves from state tutelage into a collective disciplinary force in their own right. The 'multinationals' emerged from the Atlantic war economy that was put in place from 1939. Paul Virilio puts it boldly but accurately when he notes that 'Eisenhower appeared as a kind of inter-state chief of state during the war. With that he initiated what the multinationals would later reorganise.'[107] In Western Europe, this entailed laying the groundwork for a spatial constellation comparable to the heartland, as we will see in Chapter 2.

Notes

1. Teschke (2003: 124). A first sketch for the argument of this chapter can be found in van der Pijl (2001b).
2. Schwartz (1994: 29). Around 1570, England had 3 million inhabitants and France had 19 million (Calder 1981: 22).
3. al-Khafaji (2004: 79–81). I will speak of bourgeois revolution when the private aspirations of the property-owning middle classes determine the orientation of the democratic revolution; and of socialist revolution when forces committed to social and economic democracy prevail.
4. Rosenstock-Huessy (1961: 32); cf. Brucan (1978).

5. Laffey and Dean note that over-determination differs from multi-causality (which, they write, suggests 'a multiplicity of externally related causal factors'), and refers instead to 'a complex process of causality which functions in a contradictory social whole, composed of a multiplicity of distinct, but internally related and mutually constitutive, practices having a tendency—because of their spatio-temporal separation within complex social formations—to drift apart' (Laffey and Dean 2002: 100).
6. Burke (1934: 328).
7. Cf. the essays in Nederveen Pieterse (1992).
8. Anderson (1979: 22–3, 40, 48). On the German revolution of the princes as the triumph of the principle of nation over empire, and its relation to Lutheran democratisation of the church, cf. Rosenstock-Huessy (1961: Chapter 13, 359–452).
9. Calvinism was an urban movement carried from country to country by emigrant traders and workmen (Tawney 1952: 92). Tawney emphasises that Puritanism, not Anglicanism, was the real reformation in England. Cf. Calder (1981: 52) on the connection between Calvinism, literacy, urban centres, trade and overseas expansion.
10. Teschke (2003: 263, cf. 243–4). On the interventions of France and Sweden in the Thirty Years' War, cf. Anderson (1979: 98–9 and 177–8, respectively).
11. The concept of 'heartland' of course borrows from Halford Mackinder's geopolitical nomenclature. Mackinder in 1904 used 'heartland' for the Tsarist Russian Empire, and argued the centrality of the Eurasian land mass in world politics on account of British imperial setbacks and the new strategic importance of railways (cf. Mackinder 1962). The Mackinder heartland thesis was the silent assumption that lay behind the persistent concern of Anglo-American policy 'to prevent the domination of the Eurasian landmass by a hostile power' (Dougherty and Pfaltzgraff 1971: 54). This was expressed, for instance, in what I call the 'Rapallo syndrome' in Chapter 7. The Lockean heartland denotes the evidently superior capacity of the Western bourgeoisie and transnational capital to control not a particular portion of the globe, but the political economy of world society in its entirety, transcending geopolitics to the degree that they are able to subdue internal rivalries, the challenge of successive contenders, and class struggles within their own sphere.
12. Calder (1981: 15–6, 167).
13. Ibid.: 81.
14. Gramsci characterises the English-speaking settlers as 'defeated but not humiliated or laid low in their country of origin'. Hence they were able to bring to America a level of development and civilisation which could continue to evolve with 'an incomparably more rapid rhythm than in Old Europe, where there exists a whole series of checks ... which generate opposition to speedy progress' (Gramsci 1971: 20). Robison and Hadiz, referring to Cumings (1989), note that 'in North America, migrations left the peasantry and aristocracy behind, resulting in the transplantation of Lockean liberalism in a vacuum, without the feudal or revolutionary socialist elements of the European amalgam. By contrast, the Iberian migrations to Latin America were primarily clerical, rural and military' (Robison and Hadiz 2004: 37–8n.). On English birthright, cf. Rosenstock-Huessy (1961: 293).
15. Phillips (2000: 30–31).
16. Schwartz (1994: 38–9); cf. Frank (1998).
17. Toynbee (1935, Vol. 1: 211–2); cf. Rosenstock-Huessy (1961: 266–70).
18. Rosenstock-Huessy (1993: 295).
19. Calder (1981: 235–8).
20. van Apeldoorn (2004: 157–8).
21. Hall (1971: 106, emphasis added); see also Nairn (1973: 75), on the Anglo-American tradition of informal empire (notwithstanding its formalisation in the British case).
22. Hobbes (1968: 223, 227); King (1974: 57–8); Calder (1981: 225).

23. Macpherson in Hobbes (1968: 47–8, 56). On the colonial settlement of the poor, see (ibid.: 387).
24. Geyl (1969: 82, 83).
25. Calder (1981: 178).
26. (Ibid.: 232–3). The Protestant union still fits closely with the pattern of absolutist dynastic union; cf. Teschke (2003: 225–6).
27. On the Navigation Act and its anti-Dutch intentions and consequences, see Padfield (2000: 90). Anderson (1979: 58) prematurely qualifies the Anglo-Dutch wars as 'capitalist'; Teschke (2003: 256ff.), has a sharper eye for the uniqueness of Britain and its policy of 'active balancing' on the continent.
28. Laslett in Locke (1965: 277n., 325n.). In New England, 'there was a degree of self-government ... approached in Stuart England only within those villages ... where there were no gentry in residence' (Calder 1981: 187; cf. Dunbar-Ortiz 2003: 87–8).
29. For Locke, the sanctity of property and contract are so central to his thought that even after a victorious war a conquering state cannot simply confiscate enemy property or abrogate existing contracts (Locke 1965: 443).
30. The manuscript of *Two Treatises of Government* had the mock title, 'On the Gallic Disease', a reference to the strong, directive state which he had come to reject, and of course to venereal disease, associated by the puritan English with France (Laslett in Locke 1965: 75). On the relations with Holland and France, see Padfield (2000: 99–101).
31. Boxer (1965: 110).
32. Several of the ideologues of the Parliamentary party in the English Civil War were returnees from exile from North America; Cromwell himself 'looked to New England rather than Scotland' in matters of theology and church organisation (Calder 1981: 217, cf. 212). On the Glorious Revolution's effects in North America, see ibid.: 384–5, 388.
33. Palan (2003: 80).
34. Rosenstock-Huessy (1993: 153–4).
35. On the Huguenots and French absolutism, see Anderson (1979: 94–6); on Dutch merchants' control of French Atlantic ports, see Padfield (2000: 75).
36. Calder (1981: 178–9). Charles I actually stimulated the migration of entire clans of troublesome Scots to Canada in order to tilt the balance against the French. By the end of the seventeenth century, British settlers outnumbered the French in North America by a ratio of 20:1 (ibid.: 388).
37. Teschke (2003: 178), Moore (1981: 42–3). On the concept of state class, see R.W. Cox (1987: 366–7) and Elsenhans (1991: 78).
38. This is a general point powerfully made in al-Khafaji (2004).
39. Padfield (2000: 98).
40. Bobbitt (2003: 132).
41. Lefebvre (1976, Vol. 2: 35–6). Teschke highlights how the concept of property underlying royal absolutism, and the class structure of rentier landowners, stood in the way of an expropriation comparable to that in England. In addition, wine growing did not have the same dislocating effects as sheep rearing, cf. Moore (1981: 46). Marx used the term 'original accumulation' in quotation marks because what really characterises the preparation for capitalism is the *expropriation* of the direct producers. I profit here from discussions with Robbie Shilliam, and the critique of my own use of original accumulation instead of expropriation by Isam al-Khafaji (2004: 78).
42. Arrighi (1978: 57–8).
43. Nederveen Pieterse (1990: 312).
44. Rosenstock-Huessy (1993: 163).
45. Foucault (1966: 94) discusses the ideas of Port-Royal extensively. The convent of Port-Royal, south of Paris, adhered to Jansenism, a Roman Catholic heresy emphasising individual conscience. Cf. Wahl (1962: 30–5), and the entry for 'Pascal' in *Chambers' Biographical Dictionary*.

46. Gramsci (1977: 12). The Enlightenment would also engender the socialist offshoot of the democratic revolution. Marxist socialism reflects the contender state experience by the recognition that a coercive moment is necessary for the shaping of new social relations—hence it could so easily degenerate into state socialism in later contender episodes (cf. Goldmann 1971). In the English-speaking world, the attitude to the state is negative, and the Left developed only as liberal radicalism with varying doses of charity.
47. Jacob (1991: 111); cf. van der Pijl (1998: 103–6).
48. Burke (1934: 329).
49. Gramsci (1971: 117); Lefebvre (1976, Vol. 2: 29).
50. Cohen-Tanugi (1987: 24, emphasis added). An antinomy is a blocked contradiction which cannot be overcome in a new synthesis.
51. In a crucial passage in the *Grundrisse*, Marx writes that capital 'is not, as the economists believe, the *absolute* form for the development of the forces of production … it is a discipline over them, which becomes superfluous and burdensome at a certain level of their development' (Marx 1973: 415).
52. 'There is no capitalism in itself,' Deleuze and Guattari argue, 'capitalism is *at the crossroads of all kinds of formations*' (1988: 20, emphasis added). Capitalism therefore is neither British nor French; it 'is a global social formation, with the historical evolution of social forces tendentially also becoming global in character' (Overbeek 1990: 3). Capital is understood here as the competitive exploitation of living labour power, which at some point 'escapes' the control of the actual capitalists and develops into a comprehensive discipline over society and nature seemingly beyond the control of even its beneficiaries.
53. Palan (2003: 15, Chapter 7); cf. 'Nomadology', in Deleuze and Guattari (1988: Chapter 12).
54. The idea that capital occupies the structural free space between the sovereignties of states has also been argued by Immanuel Wallerstein (1974), but even apart from its rigid economic determinism, World System Theory is entirely state-centric and does not recognise spatial variations in geopolitical organisation as in the heartland/contender state pattern.
55. This is not because of some mysterious coincidence but because the social class that secured the political conditions for the process of capitalist development—the English Whigs, the Federalists, etc.—also put in place the original Lockean constitutions.
56. Jánossy (1968: 12 and *passim*).
57. Virilio and Lotringer (1997: 12).
58. Rosenberg (1998: 13).
59. In the 1950s, a study group led by Harvard political scientist W.Y. Elliott defined the 'Communist threat' more broadly as any independent economic policies of socialist or nationalist countries proceeding 'in ways that reduce their willingness and ability to complement the industrial economies of the West' (quoted in Chomsky 1985: 6). This also informs the analysis of US expansion by William Appleman Williams (1962).
60. The notion of 'vassal state' is taken from Castells (1998: 277).
61. Houweling (1997).
62. Chapter 8 on the EU in de Swaan (2001) is subtitled, 'The more languages, the more English'.
63. I take this enumeration from Halevi and Varoufakis (2003: 69).
64. On the theory of 'structural coupling' developed by Bob Jessop, cf. Palan (2003: 72–4).
65. In terms of the overall use of force, the 'democratic peace thesis' can be dismissed as propaganda. While military conflict is rare among democracies, overall 'there is little difference in the war involvement of democracies and other regimes' (E. Weede, quoted in Houweling and Siccama [1993: 404]); cf. Halperin (2004).
66. The essays in Keohane and Nye (1973) remain required reading on transnational political relations.
67. Cleveland (1966: xxx–xxxi).

68. On the concept of socialisation, see van der Pijl (1998: 14–24) and van der Pijl (2004). Polanyi's analysis of how the self-regulating market relied on violence and attendant social protection to be able to function at all remains crucial here (Polanyi 1957).
69. de Swaan (2001: 192–3).
70. Cf. Gill (1990). For transnational networks of interlocking directorates, cf. Fennema (1982) and Carroll and Fennema (2002); on planning groups, cf. Carroll and Carson (2003) and Graz (2003); on think tanks, cf. Stone (1996).
71. Gramsci (1971: 182n.). The notion of a concept of control striving for comprehensiveness has been developed by Bode (1979), Overbeek (1990) and Holman (1996), and in my own work from 1984, most recently in 2004. A concept of control combines what Bob Jessop calls an 'accumulation strategy' with a 'hegemonic project' (Jessop 1983).
72. Hayek (1985).
73. Walpen (2004: 56–8, 116); Cockett (1995).
74. R.W. Cox (1987: 164–89). I have defined corporate liberalism in van der Pijl (1984: 22 and *passim*) and in Overbeek and van der Pijl (1993: 11–4). The term 'embedded liberalism' is from Ruggie (1992). Elsewhere (van der Pijl 1984: 22, 76–89; Overbeek and van der Pijl 1993: 9–11) I have distinguished a prior phase of a 'state monopoly tendency' but leave that aside here.
75. Walpen (2004: 176).
76. Quoted in Langley (2002: 132). Global governance along these lines is increasingly accompanied by violence; cf. Duffield (2001).
77. The term is borrowed from Robert Boyer (2001: 43); see also Palan and Abbott (1996).
78. Huntington (1998); Chua (2003).
79. Quoted in *Financial Times*, 25 July 2000 (emphasis added).
80. Gramsci (1971: 114); cf. editors' notes in ibid.: 46. For Gramsci, the French Revolution is the starting point of the process.
81. The term 'class effect' comes from the structuralist Marxism of Louis Althusser, applied to class analysis by Poulantzas (1971). I use the term to denote the reversal of driving forces between 'local' class formation and the formation of capital.
82. Skolnik (1969: xix).
83. Senghaas (1982: 34, 66).
84. Ibid.: 31.
85. See Trotsky (1978) for the theory of combined and uneven development. Cf. also Löwy (1981) and Rosenberg (1998). Further, see Gerschenkron (1962); Senghaas (1982); Berend and Ránki (1982); Schwartz (1994); al-Khafaji (2004).
86. E.P. Thompson (1968: 888); Meeus (1989: 126).
87. Ruigrok and van Tulder (1995: 41), quoting Kennedy (1987: 129–30) and R.W. Cox (1987: 57).
88. Langley (2002: 49).
89. Arrighi (1991: 42). I note in passing that Arrighi departs here from the state-centric hegemonic cycle assumptions of the World System school that he is associated with; cf. Arrighi (1994).
90. Chang (2002: 36–7). Senghaas (1982: 61) notes that in the nineteenth century, economic growth on the European continent under protectionism was always higher than in the free trade period from 1860 to 1875–80.
91. This is corroborated by Houweling and Siccama's findings on the relationship between the occurrence of war and shifts in the relative power position of states (defined as a composite of quantitative indicators). They show that redistributive conflict (war plus being overtaken) in the nineteenth century exclusively affected the contenders. The heartland states were occasionally involved in wars but these were not the consequence of prior shifts in relative power. Thus Britain took part on the side of France in the Crimean War in the 1850s, after which France overtook Russia in the 1860s. Defeat

and decline gave the jolt which triggered the revolution from above in the Tsar's empire. The abolition of serfdom in 1867 marked the first attempt to break the feudal mould of the countryside. Germany overtook France (and Russia) on the eve of the Franco-Prussian war in the Houweling/Siccama table (though not in cotton spindlage capacity, since Germany's rise was expressed notably in heavy industry; cf. Table 1.2 of this book) (Houweling and Siccama 1993: 401, Table V).

92. Germain (1997: 47–51). Of the merchant banks, Barings, originally from Bremen, was set up in 1762 and Rothschild and Schröder's in 1804; cf. van der Pijl (1998: 107).

93. Kenwood and Lougheed (1971: 43, Table 3); Chang (2002: 53–4). Only after the First World War did these countries regain the autonomy to set their own tariffs.

94. Houweling and Siccama (1993: 401, Table V). The recovery in French spindlage capacity was an accidental effect of the US Civil War. On the domestic background of the French attack, see Marx-Engels Werke (1965, Vol. 13: 448).

95. Langley (2002: 51).

96. Helleiner (1999: 140); Langley (2002: 55).

97. Polanyi (1957: 10, 14, emphasis added). The critique of the equation of this order with peace (an early version indeed of the democratic peace thesis) is developed in Sandra Halperin (2004).

98. Kenwood and Lougheed (1971: 45, Table 4, 47); Williamson (1968: 82). Thirty-five per cent of British exports between 1860 and 1910 were destined for European markets, 25 per cent for North America and Australia and New Zealand, and 40 per cent for the remaining periphery. Continental Europe's foreign trade (imports plus exports) was mainly with other European countries (80 per cent between 1830 and 1910) (Senghaas 1982: 91).

99. Hall (1971: 67).

100. Senghaas (1982: 45).

101. Quoted in F. Fischer (1984: 25).

102. Alff (1976: 17); Schmitt and Vedeler (1984: 20).

103. Edward Hallett Carr's *Twenty Years' Crisis* already prefigures the heartland/contender state argument, based on the experience of the inter-war years. Cf. Carr (1964) and the collection of essays on Carr edited by M.E. Cox (2000).

104. Cf. Halperin (1997; 2004); Virilio and Lotringer (1997: 16).

105. The Houweling and Siccama (1993: 401, Table V) power transition data referred to earlier show that in the period 1900–55 the UK was overtaken by several other states, but the USA was not thus overtaken.

106. The appearance of an actual 'Euro' may cause some confusion here; 'Euromarkets'/ Eurodollar/Euro-capital markets, are markets dealing with (mainly) US dollars outside the formal jurisdiction of the American monetary authorities (although not outside their reach, as became clear in 1979). On the Euromarkets, see Burn (1999); on the continuing role of New York, see Langley (2002: 67, 97).

107. Virilio and Lotringer (1997: 31). We may see this connection embodied in the person of Jean Monnet, the 'father' of European integration. In both the world wars, Monnet served in the Allied logistics structures operating from London, and was in between a prominent investment banker in the Atlantic economy (at one point as head of the Bank of America holding company) (for Monnet's network dating from these experiences, cf. my 1984: 225–6).

2 Integration and Rivalry in Europe and the Middle East

COLD WAR ANTECEDENTS OF EUROPEAN INTEGRATION

European integration has its origins in the onset of the cold war—the stand-off with the USSR as the new contender. But as I will argue in this section, there were persistent tensions between the different states involved in the process; Atlantic liberalisation and Franco-German reconciliation required different, often incompatible, solutions.

In the cold war, the hegemonic self-evidence and naturalness of Western life, epitomised by the US, was contrasted with the forced marches and high-pitched ideological mobilisation of the Soviet Union. A month after the launch of the Marshall Plan in June 1947, State Department strategist George Kennan in his famous 'X' article argued that the United States should seek to project abroad the image of a bold, purposeful world power, 'coping successfully with the problems of its internal life' and demonstrating a 'spiritual vitality'. Together this would make Russian communism 'appear sterile and quixotic'.[1] A cohesive American posture, Kennan predicted, would impose 'added strain on the Kremlin's foreign policies' and demoralise its supporters. Indeed, as he summed it up in a second *Foreign Affairs* article,

> If the necessary alternatives are kept before the Russian people, in the form of the existence elsewhere on this planet of a civilization which is decent, hopeful and purposeful, the day must come—soon or late, and whether by gradual process or otherwise—when that terrible system of power ... will be

distinguishable no longer as a living reality, but only as something surviving partly in recorded history and partly in the sediment of constructive, organic change which every great human upheaval, however unhappy its other manifestations, manages to deposit on the shelf of time.[2]

In this view, the process of 'constructive, organic change' has its epicentre in the West, while forcing shock-like adjustments on other societies. But the issue facing the heartland states at the end of the Second World War was that continental Western Europe had a long history of state initiative and direction; a precipitate liberalisation might destabilise the structures of capitalist class rule altogether. Given the depletion of British power in the Second World War, the United States had to assume a leading role in trying to synthesise the element of state intervention and the need to integrate the continent into the wider West. But US society was in no mood to assume new foreign responsibilities. European visitors in the post-war years sent back almost standard accounts of an economic giant reined in by inward-looking provincialism and an obsession with subversion. French academician André Siegfried, writing in Le Figaro in early 1950, saw this in the context of a new sense of vulnerability from foreign aggression. Lindbergh's flight across the Atlantic in 1927 had brought home this new potential; and nuclear weapons, Siegfried felt, were being developed aggressively to overcome this fear. Whoever expressed the slightest doubt, or defended interests other than 'national security', risked being victimised by the FBI's communist witch-hunt and the congressional inquisition of Senator Joseph McCarthy. 'Anti-communism appears to haunt the United States not unlike the spy scares one sees on the outbreak of wars.'[3]

Clearly this was a far cry from the smooth handling of 'the problems of its internal life', which Kennan had argued would allow American pre-eminence in the post-war world. Indeed the only ground on which the Truman administration could justify renewed foreign involvement was by raising the spectre of a communist onslaught on the West. When the British government notified Washington in the spring of 1947 that it was no longer able to prop up the embattled rulers of Greece and Turkey, the Truman Doctrine, with its promise to assist every country fighting communist 'aggression', was the answer. But anti-communism at home and abroad did not inspire much enthusiasm in Europe, where communists held government office in several countries on account of their resistance record and the prestige of the USSR, although the latter was rapidly eroding.[4] Therefore the Marshall Plan, announced three months later, offered a welcome change of angle. The plan was a bold forward projection of the American New Deal and its Fordist mass production economy. Democrats in the US, and Christian and Social Democrats in Europe, could now embrace anti-communism more easily, because the combination with mass consumption and the welfare state offered a progressive alternative. Anti-communism in turn helped in depoliticising workers into consumers, a key ingredient of the Fordist project. Since many viewed the large US corporations of the managerial revolution as the harbingers of a 'mixed economy' beyond capitalism, Social Democracy could make the claim that it was a progressive alternative to communism.[5]

In the circumstances, US cold-war strategists were able to develop democratic socialism as the high road of their involvement in Europe. Paradoxically, in light of the narrow-minded anti-communism at home, the Congress of Cultural Freedom (CCF), set up in 1950 under CIA sponsorship, sought to mobilise European intellectuals as far to the left as possible. As disillusion with Soviet state socialism was easily mobilised and the crude turns of Stalinist party politics alienated the outer fringes of communist influence, the CCF and the (interlocked) European Movement were able to gain ground. These groups and their publications breathed a spirit of noncommittal internationalism, mixed with elements of existentialism and progressive Christianity. But US involvement was not only about the spread of ideas. The mobilisation of European intellectuals had all along been accompanied by the clandestine penetration of Social Democracy and the trade union movement, leading to splits and defections.[6]

With the concept of *totalitarianism*, the shift of allegiance of moderate European leftists obtained a powerful rationalisation, one that is meaningful for our discussion. Totalitarianism conveniently stresses the continuity between fascist and Soviet dictatorship by focussing on the one aspect they share—the tentacular state characteristic of the contender posture—while obscuring the political and economic differences.[7] Yet these differences determine the way in which the contender state will engage in the global political economy and take on the heartland. Thus, in the case of the Axis powers, catch-up industrialisation had certainly been pursued under the auspices of the state, but it was managed in practice by powerful bank-industry combinations ('finance capital') that had set their sights on foreign markets. Wars of aggression were therefore not the result of any quirks of the Führer, the Duce, etc., but a necessary means of redistributing markets and spheres of influence, given that the banks commanded little capital on their own to pave the way by peaceful means for industries under their sway. If the fascist state partly suspended capitalist discipline for its own society, this was to provide a cover for a return to the world market later.[8]

Every contender state, Gramsci explains, 'is connected on the one hand with tendencies supporting protection and economic nationalism, and on the other with the attempt to force a particular state personnel ... to take on the "protection" of the working classes against the excesses of capitalism.'[9] 'National socialism' captured these elements in its own specific way: after destroying the socialist labour movement, it provided a degree of protection through authoritarian corporatism coupled with racist extermination of the 'foreign' in its midst. Its social-imperialist ideology was built on a notion of the 'have-not' state—the 'proletarian nation' arrayed against the 'plutocratic' heartland.[10] But the Leviathan, confiscating its own society and imposing the necessary homogeneity required for civil society, never included the expropriation of the capitalist class. The fascist state represents a final, violent resurrection of the contender state posture in the case of the countries concerned. The anti-communism of the propertied classes merged with Germany's imperialist quest for *Lebensraum* in the east, with Japan's Asian Co-Prosperity Sphere, and with Italy's drive into North Africa.

Soviet state socialism, on the other hand, inherited from the 1917 revolution the aspiration to social equality. However murderous the imposition of state control over society in the civil war and its aftermath, this foundational ideology continued to distinguish it from fascism's utopia of racial purity. It also lacked the expansionist drive triggered by uneven capital accumulation. The USSR relied on the communist movement as a means of influencing events beyond its borders, but the cruel instrumentalism into which this degenerated as early as the 1920s worked to undermine the communist parties abroad, and would, in the end, drag most of them along in the demise of the Soviet state.[11] State socialism was the more complete contender configuration, based on the suspension of private ownership altogether. 'The particular state personnel' entrusted with the protection of the working classes held state power exclusively and were not answerable to a capitalist class as were the Nazis, the Italian fascists, and the Japanese militarists. All this is obfuscated by the totalitarianism theorem, which adopts a comparative politics perspective and entirely ignores the political economy aspect. Instead it poses the relations between democracy and dictatorship in Manichean terms, as a problem of political ethics and morality alone.

The 'American Plan for Europe'

The Marshall Plan was based on blueprints for US involvement in Europe that had already been written during the war.[12] Overcoming the mutual antagonisms that had exposed European states to revolutionary takeovers was mandatory, now that the Left had emerged from the war with newfound power and self-confidence, and the USSR had risen as the new contender. Therefore, as former European commissioner Robert Marjolin writes in his memoirs, 'The essential part of America's plan for Europe was the creation of a European market which, however imperfect, ... exerted a moderating influence on national policies.'[13] This market was premised on the Fordist mass production/consumption economy through which the American ruling bloc hoped to meet working class aspirations, but which it had been hesitant to pursue in the United States alone. However, the diversity of class and national interests entering into the projected unification of Western Europe was such that a liberal format of integration was not a foregone conclusion.

Post-war reconstruction across the European continent had initially been undertaken under the auspices of class coalitions historically associated with the contender state experience, in some cases reinforced by communist parties. Certainly the United States enjoyed enormous prestige in Europe at this point, and several countries undoubtedly took large loans from the US between 1944 and early 1947 to finance reconstruction and cover deficits. But the prospect of increasing dollar indebtedness without a modernisation of industry only reinforced the desire for European self-sufficiency and a diminished US role.[14]

Britain, under a Labour government committed to introducing a welfare state, did not therefore renounce its liberal birthright. In the Bretton Woods discussions with the US, Keynes, the British negotiator, successfully resisted an immediate overhaul of the imperial preference system, and this respite, combined with the victory over the Axis, fed the illusion that Britain was still a world power. In the Foreign Office, it was felt that the UK might recapture a leading role in Europe by working with the USSR to contain a German resurgence, and even constitute a 'Third Force' between East and West.[15] The Treasury, however, had handled the huge US loan which the Labour government had negotiated to stay afloat in 1945. It instead 'was insistent that Britain's best interest lay in a withdrawal from Europe, a concentration on trade with the Sterling Area and a "special relationship" with the United States.'[16] The Marshall Plan vindicated this perspective.[17] The Attlee government, careful to cover its nationalisation and welfare programmes by scrupulously protecting the overseas commitments and interests vital to the British ruling class and the City, therefore insisted that the Organisation for European Economic Co-ordination (OEEC, precursor of today's OECD, and established to ensure trade liberalisation by the Marshall countries) remain an intergovernmental organisation with a council of ministers taking decisions unanimously.[18] Further, the OEEC was used to prevent any integration from developing beyond Churchill's plan for a 'Council of Europe' of governments united against communism.[19] When the Korean War broke out in June 1950, the British government even proposed to wrap up the OEEC entirely and turn its activities over to NATO.[20] This sums up the approach to integration to which the UK has remained committed all along.

To the extent that the Marshall Plan aimed at cracking open the closed reconstruction economies on the continent, removing communists from government, and consolidating a liberal bloc around the English-speaking states, Britain was entirely in step with the United States. Meeting the challenge of the Soviet contender was the one area where the English-speaking states could act in concert all the way. The political shocks that followed the refusal of Eastern European states to accept the Marshall Plan were conveniently interpreted as signs of the dictatorial reality of communism, rather than recognised as the dilemma of state control versus liberalisation (a condition of the Plan) in economies struggling to catch up.

Social Democrats were forced out of the government by the communists in Czechoslovakia in February 1948; Yugoslavia, where the USSR had no comparable means to impose bloc discipline, became the target of a vicious campaign, which further damaged the image of communism abroad.[21] The Labour government used the Prague 'coup' to initiate secret negotiations in April with the transatlantic English-speaking countries, the United States and Canada, not so much out of concern for Eastern Europe but to consolidate the cold war allegiances of Western Europe and put in place an intervention machinery in case of Left defections. NATO, established a year later, served both purposes without yet providing much by way of a military alliance.[22]

The positive aspect of the Marshall Plan—to kick-start the transformation towards Fordism—broke with traditional liberalism. We are looking here at a *qualitative* change, which renders beside the point claims that the plan amounted to only a modest contribution to a basically European effort.[23] Paul Hoffman, the Marshall Plan administrator, rightly called it a contest 'between the American assembly line and the Communist party line'.[24] Hoffman's concern was shared by the French investment banker and wartime Allied logistics manager, Jean Monnet, who was convinced that only a profound transformation of European society along the lines of the American New Deal would provide an alternative to socialism.[25] Corporate liberalism in the context of an Atlantic political economy would allow Fordist mass production of consumer durables to develop in a *transnational* space, which cannot itself become politicised by nationally institutionalised collective bargaining.[26]

However, the envisaged Fordist transformation was looked on with distrust in the western occupation zones of Germany and in Italy. Here the idea of making wage concessions to the working class in order to provide them with purchasing power was still repugnant to large segments of the ruling classes. In addition, until well into the 1950s West Germany retained key aspects of the contender state configuration. The Federal Republic was governed essentially from the chancellor's office; until the restoration of sovereignty in 1955, Adenauer would be his own minister of foreign affairs, and the Christian Democrat party was very much an appendage of the state. The party only gradually 'adapted the political thinking of the older conservatism, which was state-oriented and, in principle, remote from or even hostile to political parties, to the emerging "late-capitalist" class society of a new type.'[27] The modernising managerial cadre on the other hand was ready to develop a class compromise with labour in the context of Fordism. But they lacked political clout until the early 1960s; only then did the 'crony capitalism' and rigid conservatism of Adenauer's inner circle begin to give way to self-regulating civil society and a representation of the broader capitalist class and managerial cadre in parliament and the government in Bonn. Paradoxically, this obtained its political expression in the rise of the SPD.[28]

In Italy, the Democrazia Cristiana (DC) held a comparable position as a state party. But it was less monolithic and could therefore, unlike its West German counterpart at this stage, accommodate the rise of a corporate liberal fraction supported by Fordist industry in its own ranks.[29]

The Breakaway of the 'Six' from the Wider Free Trade Area

In 1949–50, Monnet and his associates in the French state and planning structures developed a strategy to lock West German industrial resurgence into a 'European' framework with real regulatory powers. An organised European economy might then consolidate the temporary advantages that planned modernisation was yielding in France, or at least allow peaceful, negotiated redistribution—as was made possible in the English-speaking heartland on the basis of liberalism and the rule of law. The Federal Republic, in turn, was willing to reciprocate French 'European' initiatives as a way of regaining sovereignty and economic strength.

The Marshall Plan included delivery of continuous wide-strip rolling mills for the steel industry, to mass-produce cheap sheet steel for industries such as packaging, household appliances and automobiles. Two of these mills were being shipped to France, triggering a centralisation of capital in the French steel industry's main regional groupings (the north and Lorraine). One mill was erected in the Ruhr area in Germany. British Steel operated three of these mills, while other countries were given less advanced rolling mills.[30] Before the war, the all-powerful International Steel Cartel had agreed to keep the continuous rolling mill, an American development of the 1920s, away from the continent in order to stabilise the market at a high profit rate for the associated producers.[31] Cartel steel prices thus blocked the development of a mass market for consumer durables and, with it, economic compromise with the working class. Fordism requires the subordination of the 'old' steel industry to the automotive complex, enforcing competitive steel prices. This subordination, in which one sector is geared to a supplier role for another, creates a structure of 'socialised labour' between them, with all the attendant characteristics of socialisation, such as long-term investment planning and sales agreements.[32] But who will act to achieve this subordination and create the structure of socialised labour that is required?

In the United States, the restructuring of relations between the steel industry and the ascendant automobile and appliance industries was achieved largely by market forces. The old steel industry, supplying the railway, construction and heavy equipment sectors, was allowed to be ravaged by the crisis of the 1930s, after which the federal authorities enforced a class compromise on business in the New Deal. The US state certainly intervened when it expanded steel capacity during the war; but in 1945 this was parcelled out to business for free. American automobile companies then secured the partial suspension of market freedom for steel companies by effectively imposing supply agreements on them.[33] In Europe, the steel cartel had postponed a comparable restructuring. The heavy industry bloc in Germany had been a key factor in the rise of Hitler, imposing its accumulation conditions on the Nazi-occupied economies. The war then served as the 'executor' of the crisis. But this did not mean that an alternative was in place in 1945, because the retrograde coal and steel and heavy chemicals bloc had also drawn the viable, 'world market' industries into the abyss.[34]

With two continuous wide-strip mills under construction, the French steel industry faced the prospect of massive overproduction if European markets were not opened one way or another.[35] The dismantling of the Ruhr's heavy industry, which the French were committed to continue, made West Germany the obvious market for French steel. The US and Britain on the other hand were increasingly unwilling to undermine West German production potential in light of the mounting tensions with the Soviet Union. One way out, which became increasingly likely, was a resurrection of the pre-war steel cartel, and, with it, the entire configuration of the Right that had blocked the only possible project to save Europe from socialism: 'the American assembly line'. In 1948, the US government had already launched the idea of extending international control of the Ruhr (part of the Potsdam agreement imposed on Germany at the end of the war) to the industrial areas of Belgium, Luxemburg, and the Lorraine region of France. Adenauer and his cabinet, exasperated by seeing the Ruhr heavy industry combines being taken apart and literally shipped off to France, were willing to sign up to any arrangement that would put an end to this, as their core political constituency was in the Ruhr and Rhineland areas. They also hoped to reopen the issue of the Saar coal-producing region, which had been annexed by France in 1945.[36]

As pressure mounted to find a structural solution, Paris in the end preferred a European control structure to an Allied one. In May 1950, following consultations between Monnet and Hoffman, and some arm-twisting of the French by US Secretary of State Acheson, the plan for a European Coal and Steel Community (ECSC) was made public by Foreign Minister Robert Schuman. American policymakers were puzzled whether this was not just the pre-war steel cartel under a new name, especially when the executive High Authority (of which Monnet would become the president) selected the cartel's Luxemburg offices as its headquarters. Paul Hoffman, himself a former auto executive, had to explain in a closed US senate committee that the project was really about making mass consumption possible by higher wages and competitive steel prices. 'Henry Ford introduced us to that new principle, and, when he did so, he started a revolution that we are still benefiting by,' Hoffman told the senators, expressing his confidence that 'the Schuman Plan may have that result in Europe.'[37]

The ECSC did create a structure of socialised labour in which the coal and steel industries were integrated into the larger steel-using economies of the six participating states, although the automotive component was still in its infancy. After the outbreak of the Korean War, military production actually had to compensate for limited civilian home markets. Even so, the coordination of investment plans and (some) control of prices of the steel industry, *worked to create a level of policymaking through which a transnational class interest could take precedence over the democratic constraints faced by individual governments.*[38] The High Authority here was less important than the parallel European Court of Justice, because the court pointed in the direction of a transnational legal space in the Lockean sense. The discipline of capital could then be enforced by court actions initiated by plaintiffs suffering from market imperfections or infringements of anti-cartel law, rather than by a political institution.[39] Discipline could also be imposed on labour with the help of the free market for (selected) steel products established by the ECSC. In 1953, when it was Monnet's turn to enlighten US senators, he pointed out how, in the event of a steel strike in France, the Schuman Plan would allow raising output in low-wage West Germany with the help of the German trade union representative on the High Authority.[40] Thus the different elements of a transnational structure, in which national politics and class relations are kept from invading a space that is preferentially available to capital, fell into place in Western Europe.

The question why Britain did not join the ECSC can now be answered as well. It is true that the UK had not been invited, and that preparations for the Schuman initiative of 1950 and the preliminary negotiations were conducted without informing the British government to begin with.[41] But the British economy would ultimately have to achieve the same type of transformation towards a Fordist configuration that was on the agenda of the continent, so why did it not join the ECSC? The answer is that, irrespective of the government's colour, the ECSC was far too interventionist. The Labour government had secured the subordination of the steel industry to the integrated Fordist structure by nationalisation, and there was no reason for the then biggest coal and steel producer in Europe to surrender to a control regime worked out by its competitors on the continent. In addition, the British trade union leadership was acutely aware that socialisation in a *transnational* context removes from democratic control the industrial infrastructure created to support private capital. As Henk Overbeek concludes, 'The Labour Party and the trade union movement were mostly opposed to the scheme for fear that their priority of full employment would not stand up to the rationalisations foreseen in the Schuman Plan.'[42] So the historical pivot of the original Lockean heartland remained outside the tentative steps taken in Europe towards a transnational structure aimed at emulating it.

Socialisation of basic industries through nationalisation froze UK basic industry and the entire infrastructure in a pre-war configuration in need of massive new investment. But with the City oriented to international place-ments and arbitrage, this investment would not be forthcoming. As the 'Six' geared towards Fordism, industrial Britain dangled at the tail of this development, unable to keep up. Stuck in a late-imperial posture, with a bloated arms industry producing the entire spectrum of weapons, from air-craft carriers and tanks to bombers and electronics, under American pressure the country continued to devote a large share of its national income to de-fence even after the Korean War.[43] This worked to restrict domestic demand, and diverted scarce investment and engineering resources away from the mass consumption industry complex. It kept the UK dependent on arms exports and foreign military involvement, although occasionally, as in the question of West German rearmament, to which we return in the final sec-tion of this chapter, it allowed British diplomacy to produce a solution straight from the intergovernmental book.[44] Otherwise, to the present day the UK remains uneasily perched in between the original English-speaking heartland and the comparable structures that have evolved from continental integration.

ANGLO-AMERICAN REDISTRIBUTION AND STATE FORMATION IN THE MIDDLE EAST

The ability of the United States to take the lead in Europe interacted with a redistribution of power among the leading heartland states elsewhere. Flexible redistribution is inherent in liberalism, but on the periphery of the process may trigger violence nevertheless. In this section, I look at how the decline of Britain and the rise of the United States worked out in the Middle East, in combination with the process of indigenous state forma-tion there.

The two world wars effectively dispossessed the ruling classes of Germany, Italy and Japan of their colonies, semi-colonies and spheres of influence, and, hence, of overseas resource bases under their control. The victorious United States and Britain, along with Canada and Australia—with France, to which we come back later, as a junior partner—practically monopolised this pillar of Western power, notably the energy sector and, to a lesser extent, non-fuel minerals. The US had achieved pre-eminence in the heartland by an active Open Door strategy, but Britain had meanwhile come to rely on a complex network of colonial and semi-colonial positions, formal and infor-mal empire. In the hour of the UK's most serious predicament, during the struggle with Hitler's Germany, Winston Churchill appealed to President Roosevelt to join forces with Britain and its empire to preserve the 'kind of civilisation for which they stand'. This sentiment was reciprocated by the Roosevelt administration, but not necessarily on the conditions Churchill had in mind. Rather, Washington thought in terms that prioritised the open-ing up of world markets, including the British system of imperial preference, even though the two sides emphasised the unity of 'civilisation'.[45] The negotiations on the Atlantic Charter in December 1941, on the United Nations Declaration of January 1942 and on the Lend-Lease programme of American aid to Britain (agreed in February 1942) record the continuous wrangling between American pressure for access and non-discrimination and the UK government's attempts to hold on to imperial preference and spheres of influence.

The collapse of the Ottoman empire—which once stretched from the Balkans to the Arabian peninsula—at the end of the First World War opened up an important new arena of rivalries over energy resources. Rivalries between the United States and Britain were both triggered and complicated by the simultaneous stirrings of national independence and state formation in the region. Initially, jurisdictions were carved out at will by the imperialist powers. France and the UK had already in 1916 agreed to divide Mesopotamia (today's Iraq), which they had identified as a potentially oil-rich area. It was proposed to enlarge the supply from neighbouring Iran, then the preserve of the British state-owned petroleum company, Anglo-Persian Oil (today's BP). The French claim on the area around Mosul in the north was later downgraded to a right to oil production from that region, as part of a wider deal that gave France the mandate over Syria and Lebanon, and Britain over Mesopotamia and Palestine.

The mandate system was only a thin veneer covering imperialist division of the Ottoman empire, made necessary by US Open Door propaganda and the creation of the League of Nations on the principle of national self-determination. But as the British prime minister, Arthur Balfour, stated in 1918, 'I do not care under what system we keep the oil.'[46] A year before, Balfour had underwritten the Zionist claim to establish a Jewish state in the ancestral homeland of Palestine, partly to command Jewish loyalties in the context of the Russian revolution and partly to place a sympathetic watch over the Suez canal. When British troops occupied the defunct Ottoman empire on the heels of the Arab revolt made famous by the British agent, T.E. Lawrence (of Arabia), the 1919 uprising against the occupation of the Anatolian homeland brought the creation of a modern Turkish state a step closer.

Under General Mustafa Kemal ('Atatürk', chief of the Turks), the process of building a strong state, unifying its social base and driving forward development through a revolution from above would turn the country into a power in its own right, coveted and manipulated in the rivalries that would unfold in the ensuing period.[47] The formation of a state class and the expropriation and persecution of non-Turkish business elements and their ethnic constituencies all testify to the nature of the transition.[48] Turkey claimed a share in the oil exploration of its former empire; it also challenged the border with Iraq. But the Turkish Petroleum Company—a consortium of Royal Dutch Shell, Anglo-Persian, the new French state oil company CFP (today's Total) and a consortium of US oil majors put together by Standard Oil, NJ (today's ExxonMobil), each holding less than a quarter in order to allow the Armenian founder of Turkish Petroleum, Gulbenkian, to have 5 per cent—remained closed to the Turks. Under the so-called Red Line agreement confirmed in 1928, the TPC consortium (later renamed Iraq Petroleum Company) agreed that no oil exploration should be undertaken in the Middle East (including Turkey, but excluding Kuwait and Iran) without consulting the other members of the cartel.[49]

All agreements of this kind, however, are bound to succumb to uneven development. The extension in May 1942 by the United States of Lend-Lease aid not only to Iran but also to Red Line Iraq, on conditions of equal access, demonstrated American willingness to obtain forward positions. By the 1930s, US oil companies had already won concessions in the Arabian peninsula as well. The established British corporations in the region, entitled to a share under the cartel agreement but sceptical about the quantity of oil hidden below the desert sands, had refrained from joining.[50] Churchill towards the end of the war openly challenged American conceptions about free access and he was especially keen to obtain assurances that the US would not further encroach on British Middle East oil leases. This led, in 1944, to the Anglo-American oil agreement, which again aimed at stabilising the existing spheres of influence among companies from the two countries and preventing nationalisations and contracts with outsiders that might impinge on the established UK–US distribution. But US domestic producers, who at that time still accounted for two-thirds of world oil extraction, balked at the idea that the International Petroleum Commission, established by the agreement, would also dictate output levels for them; and their influence in the US Congress was much larger than that of the US oil majors involved in the Middle East. These majors, in turn, were unwilling to accept the existing division of spheres of influence with a retreating empire.[51] US statesmen closely related to the oil companies not only wanted free access to Middle East resources but also sought rights to establish military airfields in Saudi Arabia at the end of the war. Eventually the US consortium operating in Saudi Arabia, ARAMCO, would supply almost half the Western European oil requirements in the Marshall Plan period, most of them subsidised by Washington.[52]

Britain was at this point in full retreat from imperial positions, first of all in India. Here, the westernised indigenous bourgeoisie organised in the Indian National Congress made a compromise possible, as both sides feared the mounting revolutionary tide in the colony. Indeed, as Ajit Roy has written, the transfer of power in August 1947 constituted 'a limited revolution from above to abort a threatening revolution from below'.[53] The violent break-up along sectarian lines, which created a Muslim Pakistan on the western and eastern extremities of the subcontinent, was part of the hand-over of power, since the Congress leadership feared the Hindu–Muslim unity in the mass wave of strikes and mutinies that had erupted the year before. This set India on the path of its own experiment of state-led development as a secondary contender, while Pakistan drifted to vassal status.[54]

Iran was the first arena of overt redistribution among the heartland states. Like Turkey, the country had in the 1920s been transformed by a revolution from above. Under Reza Khan, a military officer who crowned himself Shah, the state assumed its confiscatory posture by establishing a foreign trade monopoly and state investment funds. But it did not succeed in breaking the religious mould of Iranian society. Unlike Turkey, in Iran 'the mosque [remained] the one institution completely independent of the state.'[55] Given the proximity to the Soviet Union and the presence of a strong communist party, the Tudeh, in 1949 the United States decided to defuse growing anti-Western feeling and ensure that Iran would be given a better royalty deal with Anglo-Persian. To this end Washington dispatched a senior diplomat to mediate between Teheran and London.[56] Within a year, the Korean war raised Iran's importance as an energy source, and the movement to rewrite the royalty agreement now assumed political dimensions. Following elections in 1951, Mohammed Mossadeq, the new prime minister appointed by the Shah, nationalised Anglo-Persian's holdings. The US proposed to mediate, but it did not conceal the fact that it expected American companies to take part in oil production in Iran.[57] American and British diplomats and undercover operatives worked closely together in trying to destabilise the Mossadeq government, organising all possible forces to the right of the secular nationalists, including anti-Western Islamic clerics. After the coup that ousted Mossadeq and restored full powers to the Shah in August 1953, Anglo-Persian's share of Iranian oil production was reduced to 40 per cent, the remainder going to its partners of the Red Line cartel.[58]

Under what the Shah called the policy of 'constructive nationalism', Iran resumed the revolution from above as a vassal state under US protection.[59] Turkey had already been reduced to this status in 1947, when it was forced to give up the neutrality it had tried to maintain in the Second World War. In the period between the promulgation of the Truman Doctrine and the country's accession to NATO in 1952, it continued its policy of state-led development. It relied on US funding to do so; but then a vassal pursues state-driven economic development under special licence, not out of love but for tactical reasons. Iran and Turkey together with Pakistan became part of a defensive perimeter against the USSR, a 'northern tier' committed to projecting Western power regionally and suppressing the domestic Left.[60] The shock-like adjustments which characterise development in a state-regulated society continued to dominate political life. The Shah kept himself in power until a volcano of accumulated resentment blew him out in 1979; Turkey and Pakistan witnessed frequent military coups and internal revolts (the Kurds in Turkey and the breakaway of Bangladesh from Pakistan in 1971). State initiative continued to characterise development. In Turkey, the military, which took power in 1960, actually introduced a state planning organisation to reinforce their hold on domestic industry. But repressive statism is never an end in itself. It flows from the weakness of the bourgeois element that compels the ruling class to act through the state to develop the country. In the words of a Turkish legal scholar, 'It is thus out of national necessity and not through any doctrinal fantasy that the Republic has adopted statism as a principle of action.'[61]

Israel, Suez, and the Synchronisation of Anglo-American Middle East Policy

The creation of a Jewish state in Palestine in 1948 provoked a series of events which set the neighbouring Arab states as well on the path of self-assertion by state-led development. This tended to pit them against Britain, the dominant imperialist power in the region. In turn it created opportunities for the United States to gain influence at its closest ally's expense. The UK would resort to a last stand at Suez, but, in sharp contrast to France, eventually resigned itself to the position of a junior partner in the heartland, celebrated as the 'Special Relationship' with the United States.

All development outside the heartland begins with the attempt to unify a given society, beginning from the state downwards; Israel, an exceptional creation in many respects, is not an exception on this score. Jewish settlement in the British mandate of Palestine increased in the interwar years, albeit not as much as immigration to the United States. Thus the foundations for a Jewish state and those of a powerful lobby ensuring unquestionable US support for Israel were being laid simultaneously.[62] The Zionist project relied on capital injections distributed through Jewish immigration networks. Combined with infrastructure spending by the British authorities, this created the assets controlled by an aspirant Jewish state class.[63] As elsewhere, this class spawns a parasitic bourgeoisie handling the projects undertaken by the state; but this bourgeoisie at some point throws off the 'yoke' under which it has matured. As Jonathan Nitzan and Shimshon Bichler write,

> The state acted as a cocoon for [capital] accumulation. The budding corporate conglomerates were initially employed as national 'agents' for various Zionist projects. Eventually, though, their increasing autonomy helped them not only shed off their statist shell, but also change the very nature of the state from which they had evolved.[64]

The socialist ideology, which served to integrate a working class of Sephardic Jews immigrating from the Middle East, provided the unique form of social protection that makes 'shortening the transitions' possible. Conflict with the Arab world, which dated from the Palestinian uprising in

1939 and became endemic in the foundational war of 1948 that drove the Arabs from their towns and land, served to integrate the recent arrivals into a national idea.[65]

The UK by then no longer supported the state it had pledged in the Balfour Declaration. It feared antagonising the Arabs and, hence, British oil and strategic interests. This swung the country away from the Balfour Declaration upon the approach of the Second World War. It also pitted the British, as the occupying power after the war, against a right-wing Zionist terrorist movement. Washington on the other hand was concerned about the socialist element in Zionism, and as late as 1947 worried that Soviet support for Israel might endanger American oil interests.[66] Finally, France, committed to holding North Africa under its control and fearful of Arab nationalism, was early on a strong supporter of the Jewish state. It even negotiated to provide Israel with a nuclear reactor (for which Britain would later supply the heavy water).[67] French policy at the time undermined the US strategy of bringing about an Israeli-Egyptian rapprochement to keep the USSR out of the Middle East. But once Arab nationalism, triggered by the Zionist project, assumed its militant posture, US policy too switched towards supporting Israel.[68]

In Egypt, Syria and Iraq—the 'soft Arab interior' of the Middle East, hemmed in by the 'northern tier' established by Washington, and with Israel pointing right into it—the establishment of strong states was initiated by military coups in the 1950s. The plotters hailed from sections of the provincial bourgeoisie who aspired to share the privileges that flow from state power.[69] The Free Officers' revolt in Egypt and the subsequent coups in Syria and Iraq, in James Gelvin's words 'not only laid the groundwork for a further penetration of society by the governments of those three states, but also redefined the legitimising norm for governments throughout the region .... These regimes permanently strengthened the authority of the state not only by crushing alternative "centres of power" but by augmenting the welfare policies initiated by their predecessors.'[70] The creation of a politically homogenised space under a single, effective state committed to development, the hallmark of the Hobbesian state, was also dictated by the wide differences between city and countryside, religious and secular traditions, ethnic cleavages, and tribal structures.

Gamel Abdul Nasser, who emerged as Egypt's power-holder two years after the 1952 coup, advocated the unification of all Arabs and the destruction of Israel. He abolished existing parties and organisations (including, after some delay, the Muslim Brotherhood), and kept 'the popular masses firmly under control through a panoply of political, trade-union and ideological structures tied to the state apparatus'.[71] To finance Egypt's development needs in the absence of domestic oil sources, Nasser turned to the idea of raising the toll income from the Suez Canal through the 50/50 scheme obtained by the region's oil-producing countries (two-thirds of transit shipping through the canal at that time comprised oil tankers) and harnessing the water power of the river Nile.[72] The UK, the co-owner of the canal company along with France, tried to assuage Nasser by withdrawing its military garrison. But in 1955 the British also insured their interests with a military alliance against Arab nationalism: the Baghdad Pact (with Iraq, then still under the Hashemite monarchy, and the 'northern tier' of Turkey, Iran and Pakistan).

The Suez crisis of 1956 marks the intersection of state formation in Egypt and redistribution among the English-speaking states. Imperial retreat fuelled mounting Franco-British belligerency; this led to the fateful military intervention, while Israel attacked through the Sinai. Washington wavered at first; the State Department even consented to World Bank financing of the Aswan dam on the river Nile.[73] When World Bank funding was withdrawn as a result of domestic lobbying in the US, Nasser seized the Canal. The Anglo-French-Israeli attack coincided with the Hungarian uprising against communist rule, but although the USSR clamped down brutally in Budapest, this could not obliterate its growing appeal in the emerging Third World. One year earlier, 29 Asian and African states including China and India had, at their meeting in Bandung in Indonesia, declared their commitment to decolonisation, non-intervention, equality among nations and neutrality in the cold war.[74] Here was a contender bloc in the making, and Nasser, meeting with Nehru of India and Tito of Yugoslavia, further formalised this in 1956 as the Non-Aligned Movement. So, unless the United States wanted to push the Bandung group into the arms of the post-Stalinist Soviet leadership enjoying new prestige (highlighted by the Sputnik space launch), it had to unequivocally distance itself from old-style colonialism.[75] Indeed as the contours of a broad and potentially powerful contender bloc were beginning to take shape, Eisenhower, bolstered by his landslide re-election the day before, issued an ultimatum to the invading powers and took joint diplomatic action with the Soviet Union to enforce withdrawal from Suez.[76]

The revolution from above in Egypt now took a state-socialist turn with the nationalisation of all foreign holdings in 1957. To discipline the Egyptian bourgeoisie, the nationalisation of the large indigenous monopolies followed in 1963.[77] But as Anouar Abdel-Malek writes in his classic study, one cannot initiate a socialist revolution (the professed goal of the Nasser regime) 'without mobilisation of the popular masses, rural and urban, and the revolutionary intelligentsia; certainly not by relying on a political apparatus committed to a fight against the Left, and by that fact open to all forms of penetration'.[78] Towards the end of his life (he died in 1970), Nasser even attacked his own creation, the Arab Socialist Union, because it had become an obstacle to state control of society. 'Along with a cadre of aides, advisers, and clients, [he] developed a political style of "pre-emption",' writes Joel

Migdal. Thus society was kept in a state of flux and the crystallisation of alternative centres of power was undercut. But in the end, Nasser failed to suppress the forces that would, under his successor Sadat, tilt the Egyptian state away from its original commitments and into a vassal role for the West.[79]

In Britain, the Suez crisis precipitated a change of guard in the Conservative Party. Harold Macmillan took over from Eden, whose ideas about a role between the great powers had lost all relevance. The United States and Britain were now better able to coordinate their responses to the radicalisation process in the Middle East. For Macmillan, repairing the tattered alliance with Washington was a top priority, for which he was well placed.[80] The heartland 'Special Relationship' allowed a division of tasks which smoothed the process of redistribution as Britain continued to retreat and the US pressed forward. Under the Eisenhower Doctrine of January 1957, the US sought to enlist the conservative monarchies of Jordan and Iraq to corner Syria. But the Syrian military rulers responded by joining Egypt in what became the United Arab Republic, a temporary constellation of mainly propagandistic significance. A year later, the king of Iraq was deposed by Nasserist officers.[81] The restored unity of purpose between the US and the UK rested on a joint rejection of Arab nationalism; the remaining differences were tactical. Britain considered an invasion of Iraq too risky; instead it decided to bolster the sheikdom of Kuwait as a secure holdout and oil tap, while confining military action to Iraq's western neighbour, Jordan.[82] London disapproved when US marines landed in Lebanon, but as Irene Gendzier writes, 'the coup in Baghdad ... led to the finalization of the decision to separate Anglo-American interventions in Jordan and Lebanon, while consolidating cooperation farther east.' The overriding aim, Eisenhower cabled to Macmillan, was that 'the Persian Gulf area stays within the Western orbit',[83] and this has remained the strategic objective ever since.

Meanwhile the Baghdad Pact was buried along with the king of Iraq. The shift from British to US pre-eminence in the area was reflected in the formation of CENTO, a US-sponsored defence alliance with Iran, Turkey and Pakistan: the 'northern tier'. Washington also encouraged Israel to move closer to Turkey and Iran, while Ethiopia and Sudan were approached to join a 'peripheral alliance' surrounding the radicalised Arab interior. In addition, Eisenhower proposed 'building up King Saud as a major figure in the Middle Eastern area' as an alternative to Nasser.[84] This followed on an idea of the Shah of Iran, who had suggested to Washington that they could raise the Saudi monarch's prestige by casting him in the role of 'Keeper of the Holy Places.' Thus, in the words of Irene Gendzier, 'the marriage of oil and politics in the oil kingdoms was readily framed in the language of religion, a combination with political potential in the struggle against Nasserism, Ba'thism, and other expressions of populist and radical Arab politics.'[85]

THE RESURRECTION OF THE STRONG STATE IN FRANCE

Unlike Britain, France was not able to resign itself to the outcome of the Suez crisis by restoring the 'Special Relationship', because little in the way of such a relationship had ever existed. In this section, I look at how France instead restored elements of its historic contender position to defend its interests within the wider West, a restoration symbolised by the figure of Charles de Gaulle. His return to power came at the end of a series of military and defence-related setbacks for France; it also represents, paradoxically, a moment in the country's deepening integration into a Lockean constellation taking shape in Europe.

Modern France emerged as a contender state challenging the English-speaking heartland, but it had been integrated into the expanding West early on against German ascendancy, even fighting two world wars on the side of the West. As a result French capital had been able to preserve a significant overseas raw material base. Relying on state support for its mineral companies, the French state class and large sections of its business community were naturally suspicious about the intentions of the English-speaking states whenever they propounded Open Door policies.[86] Never strong enough to challenge the heartland's hold on global mineral reserves, there was always the temptation for France to break ranks and obtain, though diplomacy, preferential access to off-limits mineral resources such as those in the USSR, a strategy which also appealed to the dispossessed former Axis powers.

In 1945, the dilemma for French diplomacy consisted of how it could combine its fear of a resurrection of German political-economic power with the class interest of meeting the Soviet and communist challenges. Monnet, as we saw, devised a transnational framework of industrial integration that facilitated a Fordist transition along Atlantic lines, but defence and colonial issues were left unresolved. Thus France's military security was initially anchored in the Western Union, the alliance with Britain created in 1947 at Dunkirk, and widened in 1948 by the Brussels Treaty. These alliances committed Britain to the defence of France and the Low Countries from attack by Germany, and were complementary to the wartime Grand Alliance with the USSR. But economic integration of the Western occupation zones of Germany, to which the hesitant French had to consent once Marshall aid came on stream, greatly exacerbated East–West friction. In early 1948, the Soviet representatives threatened that an economic partition of Germany as pursued by the US and Britain risked a breakdown of the Four Power control structure, which included arrangements for access to West Berlin. As tensions mounted, the Federal Republic unilaterally introduced a new currency in June, whereupon the USSR banned the use of the new DM in their zone (including West Berlin), while blocking all routes to the city.[87]

Given the consolidation of Soviet power across Eastern Europe, and with secret negotiations among the English-speaking states about a new military bloc in progress, Britain and the US decided to call the Soviet bluff and break the blockade by flying in supplies to West Berlin. The blockade was still in place when the NATO treaty was signed in April 1949. Ernest Bevin, the Labour Foreign Secretary, who had initiated the tripartite talks a year earlier, actually considered the prolongation of the Soviet blockade to be a useful tool in securing the ratification of the NATO treaty by the member states. Even so, Joyce and Gabriel Kolko conclude, the formation of NATO was first of all 'the outcome of Europe's desire to prevent a resurgent Germany from yet again disturbing the peace, to which the United States added its desire to strengthen Western Europe's ability to cope with internal revolt as well as to sustain a psychological mood of anti-Soviet tension'.[88]

De Gaulle, the leader of the Free French in the war, who headed the French government from 1944 to 1946, had been intent on regaining complete control of the overseas territories. It was he who launched the country's armed forces into the re-conquest of Indo-China.[89] With de Gaulle sidelined, the successive governments of the Fourth Republic soon had to turn to the United States to meet the costs of its colonial war. When Mao's revolutionary armies reached the Sino-Vietnamese border, Paris re-baptised the war against the communist-led Viet Minh as a contest between Freedom and Dictatorship. The cash-strapped French already relied on tribal people in north Laos to provide auxiliary troops, encouraging them to grow poppy for income. The outbreak of the Korean War in June 1950 only added to the urgency of bolstering the French position in this contest, and the French mission dispatched to Washington in September 1951 had little difficulty in gaining US support.[90] Well might Ho Chi Minh, the Viet Minh leader, ask for US assistance in making Vietnam an independent state and refer to America's own Declaration of Independence; as a long-standing communist leader he was obviously unacceptable to the West.

Having thus become dependent on US support to hold on to Indo-China, France now faced an American strategy of re-arming West Germany against the Soviet Union. In September 1950, with the North Korean invasion of the south in full progress, US strategists (some of them pre-war investors in Germany) were able to obtain a public statement from Secretary of State Acheson that 10 West German units (the reference being to divisions) were to be formed under NATO command. Amidst public uproar over this statement, Acheson sought to calm the waters by conceding that France was entitled to a voice in this matter. Monnet, confident on account of the recent success with the Schuman Plan, then got René Pleven, another of his wartime collaborators and prime minister of France, to propose a European Defence Community (EDC).

The Pleven Plan of October 1950 comprised a federal structure like the one planned for coal and steel. A European minister of defence would be responsible to a European Assembly voting a common defence budget. The actual European army would consist of 'combat units', each comprising a

German contingent of approximately battalion strength. Defence production, another French area of strength as long as a German arms industry remained outlawed under the Potsdam agreement, was also to be 'Europeanised'. The aim of the plan was to place German rearmament under tight European (meaning French) political control, while continuing to bind West Germany into the Western alliance. With the French army engaged in a colonial war in Vietnam, US presence in Europe was still deemed essential. But its federal European format sat uneasily with the plan's proposal to entrust command to the American commander of NATO forces in Europe.[91] Since German rearmament was in effect made conditional on prior political federation of 'Europe' (otherwise the Assembly voting a common defence budget and the responsible European defence minister would hardly be imaginable), why would a sovereign united Europe want to hand over operational command to an American general?

The US and British responses to the Pleven Plan were dismissive. Adenauer on the other hand cautiously welcomed it as a possible way out of the military occupation of Germany. France was put under serious pressure to raise the size of the envisaged German contingents in the plan. It was only because it feared a break with the US, on whom it depended for arms and supplies in Vietnam (the US covered 70 per cent of the costs of the Indo-China war from 1950 to 1954), that the French government was willing to continue the negotiations at all.[92] The US now began to overtly reciprocate Adenauer's attempt to bargain rearmament for sovereign equality. In August 1951, industrial controls were relaxed and the state of war was suspended unilaterally by the Western occupation powers, a major step towards restoring sovereignty to the Federal Republic. When the Bundestag in February 1952 renewed its support for the EDC negotiations despite overwhelming popular rejection of rearmament, it actually attached a number of conditions, such as a settlement for the Saar coal region then under French control, full NATO membership, the removal of all restrictions on German industry, an end to occupation and a restoration of full sovereignty, and, significantly, release of Nazi war criminals. Hence, in one and a half years, the Pleven initiative had run aground in the face of the US–West German cold war agreement. In February 1952, the *New York Times* was led to caution: 'It was Germany against whom we had to fight for survival in two World Wars ... not France.'[93]

As the Americans continued to push for German rearmament, in 1951 support for European federation also arose among key US representatives on the ground. It was felt that anti-communist resolve in Europe was weakening and that the Western alliance, which guaranteed American presence, might unravel again. If a military bloc were to be formed, integration around the Fordist project was considered crucial. A rearmament along national lines would constitute a 'threat to standards of living, which cannot be depressed materially without endangering public support for the rearmament program'.[94] In his first report as NATO commander, Eisenhower expressed his concern about the growing tide of neutralism in Europe, and in July 1951 he publicly announced support for European unification as a way out of the dilemma. The US Congress in 1952 made its aid policy for Europe conditional on unification, and a Senate report on Western Europe expressed the wish 'to see Europe strong enough eventually to stand on her own feet. To permit integration in the military and economic field to become effective, there must be … some kind of political federation which should of course be shaped by the Europeans themselves.'[95]

In March 1952, the Soviet Union made a final attempt to prevent West German rearmament through NATO. It proposed to reunify Germany as a neutral state with the right to its own armed forces. The *New York Times* qualified the proposal as a gesture meant to seduce those elements in France and Germany opposed to Western defence plans into breaking ranks, and such attitudes no doubt existed, especially in France and in those areas of Germany under its control.[96] In May, however, the foreign ministers of the 'Six' proceeded to sign the Treaty of Paris establishing the EDC, with the command of EDC forces entrusted to NATO. Article 12 of the treaty more specifically indicated that the organisation would have internal security tasks as well.[97] The Commission, as a supranational executive organ, was relegated to a secondary role next to the Council of Ministers, an important shift heralding the later evolution of European integration. Votes in the Council would be weighted according to military contribution, so that France under the new rules could be outvoted by West Germany if the others, or just Italy, decided to side with it.[98]

Amidst general dissatisfaction with the outcome and with ratification still pending, the foreign ministers in September, in line with Article 38 of the EDC treaty, established an ad hoc Assembly chaired by Belgium's Paul-Henri Spaak to write a draft treaty for a European Political Community (EPC). Thus it was hoped that the planned European army could be provided with a federal political canopy. At this point, advocates of economic liberalisation, who felt that events were moving too far in the direction of a closed supranational union, sought to steer the integration project back into an Atlantic format. The Dutch government wanted a customs union made part of the EPC; Belgium and West Germany even advocated a full common market and a coordinated economic policy.[99] But the incoming Eisenhower administration, and Secretary of State Dulles in particular, prioritised the defence aspect. Dulles had been a corporate lawyer for German interests in the United States before the war and an acquaintance of Monnet's from the latter's investment banking days. While he seemingly reinforced the Frenchman's integration concerns, the context in which he operated was different. Balancing the budget was a primary concern, and getting out of Europe a popular theme. EDC fitted into this perspective. 'Out of its ratification,' Dulles told US senators in April 1953, 'will come a substantial

German force which will be the greatest shield that we could get, and ... with that in creation we can gradually cut down our aid.'[100] But neither the condition, attached by Congress to the Mutual Security Assistance act of 1953 (the military aid programme that followed on the Marshall Plan), that the EDC be ratified nor Dulles' 'agonising reappraisal' threat worked to calm French fears of a German resurgence. In August 1954, prime minister Mendès-France put the treaty before parliament without an indication about how to vote, and a procedural motion effectively buried it.

The need to hold the wider West together and integrate West Germany militarily into the Atlantic bloc then prompted the UK government to propose a solution through the Western Union, the 1948 Brussels Treaty organisation. For Britain, the ECSC was not a basis to build upon, and the new Conservative government was as concerned as France over a German resurgence. Anthony Eden, the foreign secretary, hoped to create a German market for British arms exports and thus balance the Federal Republic's growing export advantage; France, through the Western Union, would still have nominal control over West German rearmament. Dulles was critical of this solution because it failed to increase 'European' supranationality to which the Eisenhower administration was committed from the viewpoint of allowing the US to disengage. But Britain now assumed the responsibility of ensuring the broadest possible Atlantic unity.[101] Also, the 'New Look' defence doctrine of 1954, which made the massive retaliation doctrine explicit and implied that any war would be a nuclear one from the start, made the technical issue of the size of West Germany's NATO contribution less urgent.[102] In May 1955, the renamed Western European Union (WEU) came into being. The Federal Republic was granted official and effective sovereignty and incorporated into NATO. The USSR in the circumstances felt compelled, in light of the breach of the Potsdam Agreement on Germany which prohibited the country's rearmament, to formalise its control over Eastern Europe into a military alliance including the German Democratic Republic—the Warsaw Pact.

The EDC saga, usually presented in accounts on European integration as a failure, was in fact a landmark episode in the restoration of the Federal Republic's sovereignty. This in turn is a crucial component of the integration process if it is to avoid ending up as a truly supranational quasi-state controlling its social-economic foundations, which would compromise and politicise the transnational expansion of capital. As Wilhelm Grewe, a key participant in Bonn's rehabilitation diplomacy, observes, the (separate) visits of Dulles and Eden at this juncture 'showed clearly how the political weight of the Federal Republic had increased; until then it had not been part of the political style of the Occupation Powers to have their foreign ministers travel to Bonn for political consultations with the chancellor.' While this greatly enhanced the personal rapport between Adenauer and the overseas visitors, the chancellor felt profoundly bitter about Mendès-France.[103] But then, for France the course of events was a disaster. The military saw the outcome of the Second World War and its post-war strategy thrown into disarray, because, in the meantime, the French Vietnamese army had suffered its dramatic defeat at Dien Bien Phu in May 1954. This would be followed by Suez, the withdrawal from Morocco and Tunisia, and the failure to subdue the uprising in Algeria. It seemed as if the only way France would be able to hold its own in the world would be to first take an active part in the construction of Europe.

The Last Gasp of the French State Sector Strategy — Euratom

Nuclear energy under human control emerged as a heartland monopoly, with the United States, Britain and Canada (as a supplier of uranium) initially in the drivers' seat . The 1943 Quebec Agreement aimed to obtain control over the world's uranium stocks in order to keep them not only from Nazi Germany but also, under a secret Anglo-American agreement of 1944, from the USSR. Since the world's largest known uranium reserves were in the Belgian Congo, it was of momentous importance for Europe's future in this area that Paul-Henri Spaak, as foreign minister of Belgium's government-in-exile in London, had in early 1944 conceded the priority right of the US and the UK to purchase fissile materials from Congo. In a further step to secure their monopoly of atomic weapons, the US in 1946 proposed to place all nuclear technology under UN control, with the threat of armed intervention in case of breaches of the inspection regime. The parallel with today's concerns about weapons of mass destruction is obvious. Not unlike some of the so-called 'rogue states' today, the Soviet Union (and in fact many Western states as well) found the American proposal highly inequitable and instead proposed that the US first give up its own nuclear weapons before international controls were installed.[104] In 1946, a separate ABCA agreement, also signed in Quebec, committed the USA ('America'), Britain, Canada and Australia to a joint military arrangement, which was prior and in many respects, superior to NATO. This agreement provided for the sharing of top-secret military information. The agreement specified certain categories: in addition to the four signatories (category 'A'), there were friendly states (category 'B') with whom information could be shared selectively, and, finally, the enemy (category 'C').[105] This sums up, in a nutshell, the overall geopolitical/economic configuration and the nature of the relations between the English-speaking heartland, the integrated former contenders and the current contenders. But was France in category 'B' or a 'C'?

France had its own domestic uranium supply and was keen to turn this into an asset for its post-war reconstruction. In 1945 General de Gaulle's national unity government set up an Atomic Energy Commissariat (CEA in French) even before nationalising the remainder of the energy sector. On the eve of the Second World War, French researchers Frédéric and Irène

Joliot-Curie had succeeded in obtaining a chain reaction of uranium in heavy water (H_3O) from a partly French-owned factory in Norway. The stock of heavy water had been shipped out just before the German invaders got there, and eventually allowed the US to test and produce the atomic bombs dropped on Japan in August 1945—and prevent the Nazis from making one in time.[106] But France was frozen out of any technology exchange by the Quebec group, and when the US and Britain refused to let it have either reactor technology or enriched uranium, the French went it alone. With natural uranium as fuel, heavy water as coolant, and plutonium as a by-product, the first experimental reactor became critical in late 1948 (in 1952 graphite technology with carbon gas as a coolant was introduced). The CEA initially resisted a weapons programme, but in December 1954, in the wake of the military disaster at Dien Bien Phu, with the EDC off the agenda and German rearmament imminent, a French bomb was discussed at a cabinet-level meeting with the CEA. What resulted was an informal go-ahead.[107]

In the meantime, the United States dramatically altered the overall setting for nuclear energy when it liberalised, under the 'Atoms for Peace' policy of December 1953, existing restrictions on foreign trade in enriched uranium and nuclear technology. American companies such as Westinghouse and GE could now compete abroad for reactor sales. With the cheap energy supply in the US domestic market, exports were mandatory for private capital accumulation in this sector. By 1957, the US had agreed the sale of research reactors with 35 countries.[108] To prevent the proliferation of atomic weapons, the US also proposed an International Atomic Energy Agency (IAEA, established in 1956 under the auspices of the UN), which would control the sales and purchase of fissile materials and take care of safety and inspections. The world market for nuclear equipment and fuel was thus liberalised, and the French found themselves saddled with a costly nuclear programme of their own. It was this situation that prompted them to seek a European solution. In combination with US concerns about keeping the inevitable military dimension under control while capturing the European market, this would eventually converge on the Euratom proposal. Once again, France and the US, for different reasons, were on the same track in 'European' matters. But West Germany had by now sufficiently recovered to effectively thwart being tied down to a European arrangement of French design.[109]

There was concern in various quarters in Europe that its energy needs might make it dependent on Middle Eastern oil or US coal, and nuclear power was discussed from this angle both in the OEEC and in the ECSC. The military implications were of course profound. In France in particular, it was feared that technology and defence interests might once again be prejudiced by Anglo-American schemes.[110] Monnet on the other hand thought that an atomic energy community based on the ECSC might obtain enriched uranium and cheap light-water technology from the US under the Atoms for Peace policy, while letting a European agency control its use and find outlets for high-priced French surplus nuclear fuels. All along, the French attempted to negotiate forms of obtaining or producing enriched uranium, which by then they recognised as the 'fuel of choice'. Since the US objected to letting France obtain this technology via Britain or getting a preferential import arrangement, Monnet made a joint enrichment facility part of the Euratom proposals.[111] However, West Germany by now felt free to make its own demands. It would contemplate a Europeanisation of nuclear energy only in combination with general economic integration—why should the Germans in the end rely on France or a supranational arrangement for a technology they could in due course acquire from the UK, the US or Norway? It was this conclusion which convinced Monnet that going in for a Common Market was the only way to save atomic energy integration.[112]

This, then, was the point at which the French strategy of trying to lock West German resurgence into a 'European' embrace, allowing France to capitalise on its current strengths and control the inevitable redistribution, encountered and was eventually overtaken by German (and Dutch) interest in a Common Market. The two strategies may be understood in terms of, respectively, the creation of a European supranational structure in the contender state tradition, and the shaping of a civil-legal European space in which transnational capital could be liberalised along 'Lockean' lines, with the state subordinated to capital. Paradoxically, it was only after France had gone through its painful adjustment to the Common Market in this second sense (and discarded its colonial heritage) that the new 'Europe' was firmly set on the course towards a transnational liberal constellation, in which the national state retains its prerogatives within the larger structure, subject to common rules.

German preference for the Common Market meanwhile did not mean that the Federal Republic was no longer interested in atomic energy and its possibilities. On the contrary, the bloc of newer industries and their owners and managers, gravitating to the centre of power and displacing the iron and steel interests associated with Adenauer, set their sights on entering the nuclear cycle to regain world market positions lost in the war. Chemical industry and the big electrical engineering firms, the latter often working with US partners and licences, signed up to US enriched uranium, light-water technology. They thus gave up on French (or British) natural uranium technology and, hence, on European integration in this sector. With the restoration of West German sovereignty, they obtained a crucial ally in Franz-Josef Strauss, the right-wing Bavarian, now appointed minister of atomic affairs. Working closely with company representatives, Strauss energetically steered the Euratom negotiations away from the original French proposal to a looser arrangement allowing West German capital to continue developing a world market strategy with its US partners. German capital's willingness to subscribe to costly French technology in a Euratom set-up evaporated completely, especially when a glut in nuclear fuels in 1956 brought prices down.[113] In addition, when Strauss moved to the defence ministry in 1957, West Germany set its sights on becoming a threshold nuclear power with its own plutonium production capacity. As part of this policy, Strauss ensured that the aircraft industry of Bavaria was geared up to provide the planes required to deliver nuclear weapons.[114]

Given American interest in a joint European structure to which the US could sell its light-water technology and thus undermine the French alternative and its military potential, and its concern to have the supranational European supply and purchase monopoly in place, the Americans prevailed on the Germans to opt for a tight arrangement of the ECSC Six, rather than a less stringent arrangement worked out in the OEEC—which the US also opposed in order to prevent British technology from leaking to France. The Federal Republic therefore went along with Euratom not only as part of a compromise that secured the Common Market, but also because the US government threatened to suspend technical and supply agreements if the Germans would not sign.[115] But the rival national and corporate interests at stake, and the shadow cast by defence considerations, made the chances for actual nuclear energy integration minimal.

De Gaulle's Return to Power

The French departure from Vietnam was followed by the Suez crisis. For Britain, the attempt to seize the canal was a matter of oil flows and financial position; a run on the pound started immediately following the start of military action.[116] For France on the other hand, the Suez action was part of its colonial war to retain control over North Africa. (Nasser backed the Algerian National Liberation Front [FLN], providing logistical support and training facilities.)[117]

Algeria was the closest the French came to a large overseas settler colony. When oil was discovered in the Sahara in 1956, two years after fighting with the FLN had erupted, its determination to hold on to it in light of other setbacks could only increase. A local heavy industry linked to indigenous energy sources became the crown jewel of the projected long-term integration with the mother country. But the forces facing the French were part of the wider Arab revolt, and the FLN shared many characteristics of the military revolutionaries in Egypt, Iraq and Syria. As Michael Löwy notes, it mobilised the disorganised Arab middle class displaced by French settlers, while the most energetic Algerian workers lived in France as migrant labour.[118] The failure of the Suez operation—meant to deprive the Algerian FLN of its supply base in Egypt—and the US role in disciplining Paris caused a general demoralisation and swell of anti-American sentiment. But if we are to understand the putsch that would eventually return de Gaulle to power, the much-decried weakness of the French parliamentary system of the Fourth Republic should also be seen for what it was. Although it had been declining in strength ever since liberation, the French Communist Party still had the single largest parliamentary faction, and the constant reshuffle of government coalitions owed as much to this fact as it did to the setbacks in the colonies and in European policy.

In February 1958, Washington sent Robert Murphy, a diplomat with a history in North Africa that would make his very presence suspicious in French eyes, to mediate in a dispute between France and French Algeria's neighbours Morocco and Tunisia. Saharan oil was by now central to French concerns; and when word went out that Murphy had been discussing the possible transfer of the French naval base at Bizerta to NATO, fear of being displaced by the US again led to a 'nightmare of American oil tycoons out-witting the French ... and turning North Africa into an "American sphere"'.[119] Irresponsible actions by the French army in Algeria revealed its growing frustration and contributed to what appeared to develop into a revolutionary situation. In April 1958, French troops seized power in Algiers. Suspicions raised by the Murphy mission played a role, but the formation of the centre-left Pflimlin government raised the spectre of a much graver danger: that of a revolutionary FLN government in Algeria granted independence by a government in Paris that was communist-supported or at least communist-tolerated. In May, a frightened parliamentary majority called in General de Gaulle to counter the threat of a paratrooper attack on Paris and avert civil war. The General had for years been intent on using a dramatic occasion to stage a *coup d'état*; the army, increasingly acting in defiance of the government, provided it.[120] In fact, as Alexander Werth has written, the Right, fearing a conflation of Algerian independence with a surge to the left at home, 'imposed de Gaulle on France by threatening her with civil war.'[121] At the time, the Gaullist network and the colonial die-hards seemed fairly indistinguishable, but that would change. Once in power, de Gaulle had a new constitution adopted, which greatly reinforced the executive branch of government. This was further strengthened by the constitutional changes to the Fifth Republic obtained in 1962.[122] He also succeeded, through skilful manoeuvring, to solve the problem of the decolonisation of Algeria in ways preserving access for French capital in the longer run.

In the changed circumstances of France's integration into the expanded West and into the incipient structures of 'Europe', de Gaulle's putsch allowed the resurrection of the contender state legacy, perhaps best characterised as a 'shielder state' in the nomenclature proposed by Palan and Abbott.[123] This state allowed French capital to raise the rate of exploitation and con-tinue the modernisation and restructuring of industry on which a success-ful integration was premised. But the conditions under which the need for this restructuring had been brought home to French society (both the ruling class and the larger population) left a legacy of rivalry with the United States and its allies. This legacy, as we can see today, would play a crucial role in recasting the European integration process towards a transnational Lockean structure, and yet simultaneously re-position it one further remove from the English-speaking heartland.

Notes

1. Kennan (1951: 120).
2. Ibid.: 141. On Kennan's role in the onset of the first cold war, cf. M.E. Cox (1991) and Yergin (1977).
3. A. Siegfried in *Le Figaro*, 14–15–16 February 1950. Sections of the US military had in the 1920s already mobilised the fear of airborne attack to foster weapons development projects; cf. Jenkins (2002).
4. James Reston qualified McCarthyism as a hangover from pre-war isolationism, which 'minimized the confidence overseas in American justice and American institutions' (*The New York Times*, 18 October 1953)
5. Carew (1987: 204).
6. Scott-Smith (2002). Cf. Christopher Lasch in *The Nation*, 11 September 1967. The CIA-sponsored trade union publication in Europe, the *New Leader*, proposed the decertification of the French CGT as a tool of a foreign power and championed legislation to allow the prosecution for treason of communists by reference to the Nazi-Soviet pact of 1939; cf. *New Leader*, 28 January 1952, pp. 17–8. Cf. also van der Pijl (1984: 150–6) and Godson (1976).
7. Arendt (1966); Friedrich and Brzezinski (1963); cf. Scott-Smith (2002: *passim*). The concept has been resurrected in the ideological preparation of the neoliberal turn in Social Democracy; cf. Giddens (1985: 295–301).
8. I have analysed the rise of Germany as a contender state in van der Pijl (1994); cf. F. Fischer (1984) and Halperin (2004).
9. Gramsci (1971: 262).
10. Gramsci (1978: 289, 450). For the notion of social imperialism, cf. Wehler (1985).
11. Claudin (1975). I have analysed Soviet socialism as a contender state in van der Pjil (1993a); see further Chapter 7 of this book.
12. Eakins (1969); Jones (1955); Gimbel (1976).
13. Marjolin (1989: 212). I base myself in this section on van der Pijl (1978), also titled 'An American Plan for Europe'.
14. Kolko and Kolko (1972: 163); cf. Gardner (1971).
15. Overbeek (1990: 94).
16. Burnham (1990: 177). Britain had lost a quarter of its national wealth in the struggle with Nazi Germany, more than any other belligerent, and its export markets in 1944 were less than one-third of the 1938 level, as manpower and industrial plants had been converted for war purposes. Net income from overseas investment in 1945 was less than half that in 1938 (ibid.: 17).
17. The total amount the US government spent on the Plan was $12.8 billion (85 per cent in the form of grants), the equivalent of 1.2 per cent of American GNP during the four-year plan period. Two-thirds of the Plan credits and deliveries went to Britain (the largest recipient with 25 per cent), France, Italy and West Germany. Ninety per cent of the total were food supplies and industrial deliveries (notably, energy-generating equipment and modern machinery) (Marjolin 1989: 231; Gauthier 1993: 124–5).

18. Another area where British influence worked to consolidate a conservative approach was the restoration of the property rights of private capitalists who had been associated with the Nazis. This extended to the intervention of City economic statesmen on behalf of the Wallenbergs of Sweden, who had during the war assisted German capital in keeping their overseas assets from confiscation. Cf. van der Pijl (1984: 174–5) and Aalders and Wiebes (1995). On the domestic and Atlantic capitalist interests associated with the rise of Hitler to power, cf. Gossweiler (1975) and Stegmann (1976).

19. Robert Marjolin was Secretary General of the OEEC and his memoirs (1989) amply document the British role. The Council of Europe was eventually established by treaty in 1949, with its seat in Strasbourg, and still plays a role today as a forum and judiciary for human rights across Europe. It is an intergovernmental organisation separate from the EU and should not be confused with the European Council, the regular EU summit meetings established in 1974.

20. Marjolin (1989: 239).

21. Kolko and Kolko (1972 : Chapter 14); Claudin (1975: 489–500, 536–48).

22. Wiebes and Zeeman (1983); on the internal security structures, cf. Müller (1991).

23. This is the thesis of Alan Milward (1984). Productivity growth in the OEEC over the period 1948–52 was 27 per cent, with gross investment growing by more than 30 per cent (up to 1951) and output growth was already 25 per cent over the 1938 level by 1950 (Marjolin 1989: 226); but cf. Jánossy (1968) on post-war economic miracles (referred to in Chapter 1 of this book). Although he misses the centrality of Fordism in the post-war transformation of Western Europe, Marjolin rightly notes that expressions like a 'Marshall Plan for the Third World' fail to recognise that it was only in post-war Western Europe, where industrial assets were damaged but not entirely destroyed and where an educated and highly skilled work force was available, that 'an inflow of capital representing only a fraction of what would have been necessary to rebuild it from scratch'—i.e., the real Marshall Plan—could achieve these results (Marjolin 1989: 228–9).

24. Quoted in Carew (1987: 8), and *Senate Foreign Relations Committee 1949–50*: 183–4.

25. On the ideas developed in this respect in wartime London, see Marjolin (1989: 126–7), and of course Monnet's own memoirs (1976).

26. Fordism raises labour productivity to the point where wages can be paid that allow workers to spend a large part of their income to purchase durable consumer goods (first of all, cars). This revolutionary mode of accumulation creates a mass market for industrial goods and redefines the worker as a consumer. Cf. Rupert (1995a). See also van der Pijl (1984: 18–20, 90–4).

27. Leggewie (1989: 299).

28. Simon (1976: 171).

29. Galli (1995: 68, 78).

30. ECE (1953: 18, Table 16); cf. Freyssenet and Imbert (1975).

31. Thus the French 'Comité des Forges' controlled *Le Temps*, the pre-war newspaper of record (after liberation its assets were taken over by a collective of journalists to publish *Le Monde*). The authoritative study on the International Steel Cartel is Hexner (1943); a key study on the history of steel in Western Europe is Jacobs (1988).

32. See for an assessment made at the time, ECE (1953). Cf. also ECE (1959). For a discussion of the concept of socialisation as used here, cf. van der Pijl (2004).

33. Steiner (1964: 41–2); Miller (1971: 152).

34. Goralczyk (1975: 38); cf. Sohn-Rethel (1975) and Gossweiler (1975).

35. ECE (1959: 22, 31); Diebold (1959: 17).

36. Haussmann (1952: 33–41); Marjolin (1989: 272–3). The Saar would eventually be returned to the Federal Republic in 1955.

37. *Senate Foreign Relations Committee 1949–50*: 546–8.

38. Haas (1968: 194). With coal rapidly losing ground to oil, in this industry the ECSC basically worked as a structure facilitating its demise in a more or less equitable way. It also facilitated the task of a government in 'selling' the closure of mines by invoking a higher authority (Milward 2000: 63).
39. Statz (1975: 144). This has become the key to understanding the modus operandi of the EU; cf. Cohen-Tanugi (1987) and Holman (2004).
40. Kolko and Kolko (1972: 468).
41. Young (1999: 51); Diebold (1959: 53–4).
42. Overbeek (1990: 96).
43. 'British rearmament in response to the Korean War would not have approached its awesome magnitude had it not been for U.S. prompting' (Rosecrance 1968: 12).
44. Strauss (1962: 111–3).
45. Roosevelt-Churchill (1975: 122–3); T.A. Wilson (1970: 176–7). For a recent discussion of this civilisational connection of the English-speaking countries, see Jenkins (2002).
46. Quoted in Yergin (1993: 189).
47. Löwy (1981: 185–7).
48. Rustow (1965: 178–9); Rodinson (1977: 124) gives the percentage distribution of ownership of enterprises in the Ottoman empire, with Greeks owning 50 per cent and Armenians 20 per cent in 1913.
49. Yergin (1993: 204–5); Larson et al. (1971: 67–71).
50. Yergin (1993: 281–2 and Chapter 15, *passim*). Of course we know now that the Arabian peninsula holds one-third of the planet's proven oil reserves.
51. Roosevelt-Churchill (1975: 453, 459, 499); G. Kolko (1968: 493); *Senate Foreign Relations Committee, 1947–48:* 49–53, 71–82, 325ff.
52. Gendzier (1997: 22–3).
53. Roy (1986: 31).
54. Bettelheim (1971); Chibber (2003).
55. Halliday (1979: 19).
56. Yergin (1993: 453). George McGhee, the US representative in this matter, was himself an independent oilman.
57. Yergin (1993: 459).
58. Richelson and Ball (1990: 15, 230); Yergin (1993: 467). As recently published CIA documents have confirmed, US agents posing as 'communists' organised a campaign of threats and attacks against the Shia clergy, in order to mobilise the Islamic population against the nationalists and the Left; but then, the social base of the Mossadeq policy was already very narrow (M. Gasiorowski in *Le Monde Diplomatique*, October 2000, p. 11; Halliday 1979: 25–6).
59. Savak, the new secret service of the Shah, was jointly set up by the CIA and Israel's Mossad. In 1958, Trident, a joint organisation of the Mossad, Savak, and Turkey's security service TNSS was set up; Trident was a subsidiary of an arrangement between the CIA and the Mossad for covert intervention in places difficult for the US services to access directly (Richelson and Ball 1990: 173). Mossad had already assisted in the coup that ousted Mossadeq (Gendzier 1997: 151). On Trident, cf. ibid.: 375; for the 'constructive nationalism' quote, cf. ibid.: 289.
60. Koopmans (1978: 142–3). See Gendzier (1997: 28–35, 154) on Turkey's role in the US strategy.
61. Quoted in Rodinson (1977: 128).
62. Badeau (1968: 27) compares the role of the Jewish lobby in the US to the situation at the end of the nineteenth century when 'a large Irish immigrant population devoted to Irish independence constantly injected the "Irish question" into American politics, especially in large Eastern cities.'

63. Nitzan and Bichler (2002: 94); the reference is to the Yugoslav politician, Djilas, who used it to describe the class formed in the state socialist countries (Migdal 1988: 155).

64. Nitzan and Bichler (2002: 96).

65. Ben-Gurion and the original leadership saw war as 'the principal and perhaps only means of increasing welfare and keeping moral tension. Without them, we wouldn't have a fighting nation, and without a fighting regime we are lost' (quoted in Nitzan and Bichler 2002: 102).

66. Migdal (1988: 166); Gendzier (1997: 36). Menachem Begin and Yitzak Shamir were former terror chiefs who became prime ministers in the 1970s.

67. *The Guardian*, 4 August 2005.

68. Gendzier (1997: 155). US aid to Israel amounted to $100 million in 1948 alone, the same amount as spent on Turkish defence under the Truman Doctrine bill a year earlier (Gendzier 1997: 37, cf. 28).

69. al-Khafaji (2004: 187).

70. Quoted in ibid.: 207. The new leading cadres in Egypt, Abdel-Malek (1968: xix) notes, were 'recruited notably from the lower and middle bourgeois strata, but they include some from the old ruling groups'. Indigenous education also meant that the new leaders were further removed from the ideological influence of the West (Badeau 1968: 45).

71. Löwy (1981: 178); Abdel-Malek (1968: xiii).

72. Yergin (1993: 480–1); on the land reforms in Egypt, see Migdal (1988: 184–90, 193–9).

73. In 1954, on the other hand, the US had given Israel the green light to attack Egypt, after it found that Egypt was buying Soviet arms (Gendzier 1997: 209–10).

74. Singham and Hune (1986: 66).

75. For the US, the possibility of an oil embargo by an enraged Arab world ruled out supporting a neo-imperialist adventure (Yergin 1993: 479–98); the Egyptians had to the end expressed their preference for World Bank funding over Soviet offers (Abdel-Malek 1968: 107).

76. Eden (1960: 458); Richelson and Ball (1990: 233).

77. Migdal (1988: 230); in addition, there were clampdowns on the labour movement and the communist party (Löwy 1981: 178–9).

78. Abdel-Malek (1968: xxxiii, emphasis added).

79. Migdal (1988: 205).

80. In addition to other ruling class credentials, as a member of the liberal European pressure group established in wartime London (ELEC), Macmillan's Europeanism was less suspicious to the City than that of his rival, R.A. Butler, who had been associated with the pre-war appeasers in the Foreign Office at the time of Munich. Macmillan also enjoyed a good working relationship with Eisenhower dating from the North African campaign in the Second World War (Young 1999: 95; Overbeek 1990: 99).

81. Gendzier (1997: 11).

82. Ibid.: 301–2.

83. Ibid.: 12–3.

84. Amineh (1999a: 217–8); Yergin (1993: 497); Gendzier (1997: 255, 322).

85. Gendzier (1997: 288).

86. Tanzer (1980: 25 and *passim*).

87. Kolko and Kolko (1972: 488–90). The money reform, replacing the old Reichsmark by the Deutschmark at a rate of 10:1, was the work of Ludwig Erhard, the minister of the economy and a student of the German neoliberal economists, Eucken and Röpke. He joined Hayek's Mont Pèlerin Society at its second meeting (Cockett 1995: 110).

88. Kolko and Kolko (1972: 499). On the internal security dimension, cf. Müller (1991) and Wiebes and Zeeman (1983).

89. Werth (1967: 414).

90. Lacouture (1966: 9). A US military assistance group to assist the French had already been set up in 1950 (Fall 1967: 83). On the Hmong auxiliaries and poppy growth, see McCoy (1991: 112–4, 138–9).
91. Monnet (1976: 406); cf. McGeehan (1971: 64) and Alphand (1977: 224).
92. Grosser (1978: 172–3).
93. *The New York Times*, 18 February 1952, quoted in McGeehan (1971: 187–8, cf. 181).
94. Quoted in *The New York Times*, 23 September 1951.
95. Quoted in Beloff (1963: 96); cf. Eden (1960: 163).
96. *The New York Times*, 12 March 1952; *Die Welt*, published in Hamburg in the British occupation zone, rejected the Soviet proposals, but the *Badische Zeitung* (French zone), recommended careful study. Newspaper articles translated in *La Documentation Française, Bulletin quotidien*, no. 2130, 14 March 1952.
97. Grewe (1979: 149); Kniazhinsky (1984: 91).
98. George and Bache (2001: 69).
99. Goedhart (1978: 115); R.T. Griffiths in Middlemas (1995: 27–8).
100. *Senate Foreign Relations Committee, Executive Sessions 1953*, p. 323.
101. Spaak (1971: 178, 188); Hellema (1979: 125–6).
102. Eden (1960: 151); McGeehan (1971: 232).
103. Grewe (1979: 197).
104. van Splunter (1993: 25, 76–7).
105. The British hoped that under this agreement they would have access to the knowledge needed to build their own bomb, while keeping it out of the hands of the French (Leigh 1989: 4).
106. Aalders and Wiebes (1995: 93–106); cf. Klinkenberg (1971). The United States dropped a uranium bomb and a plutonium bomb, produced by two rival corporate consortia, on Hiroshima and Nagasaki. Germany almost obtained a uranium bomb (uranium is a weapons-grade explosive if enriched by centrifuge technology). All forms of nuclear energy generation involve enriched uranium or plutonium at some point, so strictly speaking there is no nuclear process which is per se 'civilian'.
107. Beumer et al. (1981: 5–7, 26).
108. van Splunter (1993: 193–4).
109. Deubner (1977: 12 and *passim*).
110. Milward (2000: 205); Deubner (1977: 52).
111. Deubner (1977: 51); Beumer et al. (1981: 35).
112. Monnet (1976: 472).
113. Beumer et al. (1981: 35); Deubner (1977: 65, 145).
114. Bufe and Grumbach (1979). I will come back to this when discussing the 1962 *Spiegel* affair in Chapter 3.
115. Deubner (1977: 54–8, 98); Klinkenberg (1971: 139).
116. Actually the United States enforced compliance in the case of Britain by leaning on the IMF to withhold requested emergency financial aid (Yergin 1993: 492).
117. The UK imported almost two-thirds of its oil by way of the Canal, and only a fraction through IPC pipelines; France received half of its imports through the Canal (the US was most dependent on pipelines). 'For Paris ... Suez was Nasser, and Nasser was an ally of the [Algerian] FLN' (Gendzier 1997: 157). For an overview of colonial wars fought at the time, see Halperin (2004: 266, Table 8.2).
118. The Algerian Communist party was a section of the metropolitan PCF dominated by French settlers; it denied that the Algerians wanted separation from France (Löwy 1981: 170–1).
119. Werth (1967: 15); for Murphy's role in North Africa during the Second World War, see van der Pijl (1984: 124–5). The suspicion that the Americans were colluding with the FLN to gain access to Algerian oil was widespread, but de Gaulle in the final negotiations

in 1961–62 succeeded in obtaining assurances about access for its local oil company (later Elf-ERAP, today part of Total) (Beker 1996: 229; Yergin 1993: 526–7).

120. Sulzberger (1972: 32–4).
121. Werth (1967: 20, cf. 21–9).
122. The constitutional changes under the Fifth Republic in 1958 and 1962 are analysed in Duverger (1968).
123. Palan and Abbott (1996); this would be a case of 'hybridisation' as defined by Boyer (2001).

America's Crusade in Asia
and the Euro-Atlantic Rift

THE ILLUSION OF AN ATLANTIC EUROPE

European integration was originally devised as a means of synchronising class compromise with mass consumption, allowing peaceful redistribution transnationally, and solidifying the enlarged West against the Soviet contender and communism. It requires however that an economic space, which is removed from national states, parliaments and social organisations, be created; ideally this space should be self-regulated by market forces, i.e., by capital. This is one half of the European project. Around 1950, the most obvious route to re-integrating a West German economy lacking sovereign status was through a quasi-state structure at the 'European' level that constrained the sovereignty of all. The inevitable redistribution that a German *Wirtschaftswunder* would entail (primarily at the expense of France) could then be handled by monitoring investment and restructuring in the pivotal heavy industry sector, while ensuring free trade in a range of its products.

However, the high authority entrusted with this task, even in the hands of a Monnet with his credentials as a pre-war international investment banker, might become an enduring structure of a contender type, filling the new transnational space with the political legacy of continental Europe—state direction, class politics and protectionism. Hence, as I will argue in this section, the state, paradoxically, had to regain the lost ground to allow the development of European integration along liberal lines. That is the second half of the European project, and de Gaulle would be its exponent in the 1960s. Reviled by liberals, he executed the Lockean programme—not because he was himself a doctrinaire liberal, but because intensified competition required a stronger state to raise the rate of exploitation of labour and return certain international prerogatives to France.

The liberal strand in the European class structure was hesitant to accept the compromise with organised labour. Traditionally averse to developing the domestic economy, it had its strongholds in Britain and on the continent (in the trade-dependent economies of the Benelux countries). The Benelux and Italy had joined the 1950 breakaway of the 'Six' from the wider OEEC area with definite reservations about the element of closure towards the outside world, fearful not least of a Franco-West German entente that would call the shots through bilateral agreements. Their concerns were expressed in the plan for an OEEC free trade area put forward by Dirk Stikker—the liberal foreign minister of the Netherlands and an Atlanticist member of the Dutch corporate elite—one month after the Schuman Plan had been made public, but nothing came of it.[1] It would not be until 1959 that Britain, confronted with the fact that the 'Six' pressed ahead with the Common Market in 1958, organised the European Free Trade Area (EFTA) with the OEEC states not included in the EEC (the 'Seven').

The Korean emergency pushed liberal aspirations into the background, while raising the profile of a West German contribution to the Western political and economic line-up. But as Alan Milward writes, 'European security, in the full sense of the word, did not crucially depend on a German army. It did crucially depend on German prosperity. This was the issue which had to be resolved and which had become more pressing every year since the great revival of the Federal German economy in 1949–50.'[2] With the EDC debate still occupying the high ground, in early 1953 J.W. Beyen, Stikker's successor as foreign minister of the Netherlands, submitted proposals meant to create an economic integration route separate from defence and political issues. The Beyen Plan gained the support of the Belgian government once Paul van Zeeland, a liberal financier by background and committed to the OEEC free trade zone project, was replaced in April 1954 as foreign minister by Spaak, who shared the corporate liberal perspective championed by Beyen. In May 1955 the two men worked out a joint, 'Benelux' memorandum to put the Common Market on the agenda after the security aspect had been taken care of in an Atlantic structure (NATO/WEU) that same month.[3]

Beyen made his career as a bank director holding directorships in Dutch companies, including Philips and Anglo-Dutch Unilever. These firms were at the time highly dependent on continental European markets, and Unilever especially was intimately involved in post-war planning. The company had gone to great lengths to try and retain a presence in Germany under Hitler; when Beyen joined the board in London in 1940, the work he and fellow director Paul Rijkens did for the Dutch government-in-exile included plans for the economic re-integration of Germany after the war.[4] The insertion of agriculture into a Fordist set-up was another area of joint Dutch and Unilever interest. The Netherlands was home to Europe's most advanced agricultural sector, with excellent export prospects. Farm productivity however still lagged behind the USA (the European average was half the US figure); it had to be raised in order to increase the share of workers' incomes available for purchasing consumer durables. In addition, modernisation would release the labour reserve hidden on the land for industry. Therefore, just as the steel industry had been 'socialised' relative to the automotive complex, the countryside was to be turned into a resource base for Fordism, including a new agro-industrial sector. That this had to be achieved on a European scale was because only a transnational structure would allow restructuring by an authority that was not answerable directly to the farming population.[5] Unilever was the kingpin of a strategy to achieve all this. Active in agriculture, fisheries and frozen products for the growing self-service retail sector catering to customers with refrigerators, and producing soap for use in washing machines, the company, like no other in Europe, embodies the agro-industrial aspect of Fordism.[6]

There was a logic to Beyen's role in exploring a new route towards European unity in the 1950s, after the unifying dynamic of the Marshall Plan had receded. But integration was always part of the broader Western line-up. While Beyen was active on the European front, Paul Rijkens and a group of men he had worked with in wartime London took the initiative to open a parallel channel of Atlantic consultation, the Bilderberg conferences.[7] Initially it was difficult to find interlocutors on the other side of the Atlantic. As the *Economist* noted at the time, there no doubt existed a reservoir of internationalism in the United States, but the communist witch-hunt had made Americans 'wary about joining organisations, especially those which smack of the foreign and the strange'.[8] Yet Eisenhower (*after* his election, though) instructed the CIA to cooperate. With Unilever footing the bill, the first Bilderberg meeting in the Netherlands in 1954 brought together a cross-section of the Atlantic ruling class and cadre to discuss European integration and the defence community project in the frank atmosphere which a closed-door session allows.[9] At a second conference (in Garmisch-Partenkirchen in the Bavarian Alps) a year later, the theme of creating a Common Market was at the centre of discussions.[10]

The Atlantic bond representing the wider West and the foundations of the European component thus developed in tandem. Yet 'Europe' was necessarily organised by coordinated state intervention, even though its architects aspired to a transnational state/society complex comparable to the original English-speaking heartland. This explains the alternation of unity and rivalry, and liberalism and state direction, that has characterised Atlantic and European integration ever since. Networks like Bilderberg take their place in this context. They function not as single-minded conspiracies, but as flexible, open structures in which the conflicting lines of development can be identified and synthesised. Ruling class strategists rely on these networks to elaborate a hegemonic strategy aimed at winning over intermediate strata; they can thus establish a bloc of forces committed to a comprehensive, broadly accepted concept of control. This presumes a keen appreciation of the real balance of forces, both in the geopolitical arena and in class terms. Disagreement and discussion are therefore ultimately as vital as a measure of compromise and consensus. There is a real diversity of interests in capitalism, albeit unified under a common discipline; transnational, systemic rivalries were therefore in evidence at various junctures, but always could be overcome. Only in the 1970s, when the West began to re-orient to neoliberalism in response to the challenges of a global democratic drive, would this involve real ruptures and internecine violence. In the 1950s, agreement necessarily revolved around the mixed economy and the 'end of ideology', code words for the corporate liberal concept prescribing Keynesian state intervention, class compromise and the managerial revolution.[11]

The 'Action Committee for the United States of Europe', launched by Monnet in an advertisement in the *New York Times* in June 1955, did not, in contrast to Bilderberg, include active businessmen. Yet class compromise was likewise the necessary point of departure. The growing centrality of West Germany in the European equation also required Monnet to specifically seek to include the German Social Democrats. The US was West Germany's fastest growing export market, and among the 'Six', West Germany was rapidly becoming the most important market for the others. Germany's import requirements, shifting from food and raw materials to engineering products and semi-finished goods in the course of the 1950s, exerted a dynamic, modernising effect on the neighbouring economies.[12] Integrating a West German and Italian membership into transnational planning bodies was crucial to facilitate a European socialisation of labour in the sectors concerned, and to avoid a resurgence of old antagonisms. Recruiting anticommunist Social Democratic and trade union representatives also allowed Monnet to try and reinforce the political centre ground where it might otherwise be too weak; US-sponsored anti-communism in the former Axis powers tended to reinforce older prejudices against Social Democrats. The admission of leading members of the SPD and trade union officials into the Action Committee worked to consolidate their commitment to 'Europe', and, in turn, to influence Schumacher's SPD.[13]

The inner circle thus created then broadens and works to demarcate the limits of political feasibility and 'relevance'. As Alfred Grosser writes, there existed—across the Action Committee, Bilderberg, and comparable groups—a 'Society of Europeans' around Monnet (crucially including key Americans). Whoever was outside the bounds of this 'society', also tended to be marginalised from the mainstream integration process.[14] Once colonialist revanchism in Britain and France had ended in failure, it was this 'Society of Europeans' that pressed forward to establish the EEC.

Compared to the ECSC (and with the important exception of agriculture), the EEC, established along with Euratom, represents the first major step towards liberalising the transnational European space that has since developed into the EU of today. When the foreign ministers of the 'Six' met at Messina on the island of Sicily in June 1955 to discuss the Benelux memorandum, an important step had been taken towards restoring West German sovereignty. Military issues dominated public debate and policy, oddly out of step with the subsiding cold war and the appearance of the non-aligned Third World on the horizon of world politics. Therefore the committee that was set up under Paul-Henri Spaak at Messina to work out the details of a fresh start to the integration process felt free to shift the emphasis away from the integration format of the ECSC and the abortive EDC and EPC projects. Widening ECSC competencies was explicitly ruled out, and the committee had to look into new institutional arrangements adequate to the changed international situation.[15]

The greater degree of liberalism envisaged in the new project also allowed the inclusion of the UK in this round of integration planning. Spaak even showed the Benelux draft to the British government before the other member states had a chance to look at it. But politics in Britain, as in France, was at this point hostage to imperialist illusions. The British position was that most issues under discussion were already taken care of in existing institutions such as the OEEC; furthermore, the Tory government also began to project a global strategy, hoping to achieve a free market for industrial products in Europe while conserving its reliance on cheap food imports from the Commonwealth.[16] It is a reminder of Anthony Eden's position outside the 'Society of Europeans' that he could conjure up the vision of a large free trade zone comprising the Commonwealth and Europe, built around the OEEC and with Britain at the centre; a bloc that 'had almost limitless possibilities and would be an effective counterpart to the Communist bloc *and to the United States.*'[17] This was the worldview that spawned the Suez debacle and to which the US responded in kind.

That the French government of Guy Mollet, formed in January 1956, joined the expedition to recapture the Suez Canal by force seems out of character with the number of Bilderberg and Action Committee men in the cabinet. But then, the French predicament in Algeria poisoned political life and the government was unable to withstand the military and the colonialist frenzy that it whipped up.[18] When the UK withdrew from the Spaak committee work, France faced the Federal Republic alone, and its negotiating position was further undermined. German officials largely wrote the final report, working closely with some of Monnet's associates.[19] Only when French troops had come home from the Suez adventure was Mollet free in

March 1957 to sign the Treaty of Rome establishing Euratom and EEC—both emphatically defined as *new* institutions, separate from the existing coal and steel structures.[20]

The French integration strategy, which built on the contender state model and which had served its purpose in the geopolitical and industrial conditions of the first post-war decade, was thus effectively buried. Indeed the French state and the economic azssets it commanded, would first have to regain a position of strength if US–British liberalisation pressures and West German competition were to be met effectively. This, as I have argued at the end of Chapter 2, was to be the achievement of de Gaulle.

The Gaullist Adjustment to European Liberalisation

Gaullism in France would play a crucial role in moving the European pole in the Atlantic political economy away from the United States. It also, paradoxically, worked to demarcate clearly the sovereignty of the state from the transnational space for capital, which created a structure in Western Europe that moved closer to the original English-speaking heartland. In all respects the Gaullist project represents a great leap forward for French capital, even if the specific circumstances in which the resurrection of elements of the contender experience was pursued limited the shelf-life of the directive state.

First, a devaluation linked to monetary reform and fiscal stringency served to raise the rate of exploitation of the workers. Wage growth in the entire Gaullist period (until 1969) would remain below the post-war average, while productivity went up. In the long run this allowed the transition from an economy centred on old-style family businesses and over-saving to Fordist mass production, concentration of capital, and development of the domestic market.[21] If one takes the long-term view, Marjolin concludes in his memoirs, France may have been the great beneficiary of European trade liberalisation.[22] Of course, the mass of the French population has expressed a different opinion on several occasions, from May 1968 to the referendum on the neoliberal European Constitution in May 2005; but, on balance, French capital and the upper class controlling it would certainly agree.[23]

In the area of his paramount personal interest, geopolitics, de Gaulle had been watching events from his self-imposed exile in Colombey-les-Deux-Eglises. He considered the EEC treaty one further instance of sacrificing French interests to the Western concern of reinforcing Germany. From the over-hasty termination of the First World War, at Versailles, and on to the appeasement of Hitler, Germany had all along received preferential treatment from Britain and the United States. In de Gaulle's judgement, the governments of the Fourth Republic had again signed away vital interests, allowing West Germany to recover at the expense of France in an

Atlantic, cold-war context, under the guise of European 'supra-nationality'.[24] As soon as he had settled in the presidential palace, therefore, de Gaulle reopened the debate on the nature of the European integration process. This was not, as so often maintained, meant as an attack upon it, but intended to recast it towards a liberal, intergovernmental structure in the spirit of Lockean transnationalism—but a *European* one.[25] This implied that its relation to NATO, including the WEU patch-work by which the Federal Republic had been made part of the Atlantic defence structure, had to be restructured as well. In de Gaulle's judgement, the Federal Republic had been the main beneficiary of integration, without ever negotiating a proper political agreement. This left open the possibility that German ambitions might surface again, with geopolitical consequences potentially lethal to France; at the same time, the US role in Europe was also left suspended in mid-air after 1945. Hence the French president decided to create a political axis based on a personal rapprochement with Adenauer. But the Federal Republic would have to accept its post-war frontier, adopt a constructive attitude towards the East, forgo the possession of atomic weapons, and be patient about reunification.[26]

The fact that the political authority under which the European institutions were operating had been left undefined, de Gaulle argued, was being used by the Brussels 'Eurocrats' to claim an unwarranted latitude for themselves. In private discussions with Adenauer, he stressed that there was only one supranational institution in Europe, the ECSC with its High Authority. However, the other two institutions (the EEC and Euratom) behaved as if they too had been awarded such directive powers.[27] In reality they were under the authority of the Council of Ministers; in this respect the Treaty of Rome already marks a step in the liberal, inter-governmental direction as compared to the Schuman plan set-up. To enforce the constitutional reality in the field of foreign policy, the French president first ensured that there would be a meeting of the foreign ministers of the 'Six' every three months.[28] Having obtained Adenauer's consent, he then instructed his government to prepare a detailed programme for political cooperation of the EEC countries. In October 1961, basing itself on the French cabinet plan, an EEC intergovernmental commission chaired by the French representative, Christian Fouchet, laid out proposals to mandate an intergovernmental directorate with working out a coordinated foreign and defence policy. The EEC Commission could then manage the Common Market on a day-to-day basis, because in de Gaulle's view only elected governments enjoying real political authority can decide questions involving the sovereignty of states.[29]

Adenauer supported the Fouchet plan and so did Italy. But the Netherlands and Belgium were opposed. They expected much from British accession to the EEC and from the post-Suez realignment, which had brought Britain back into the US fold. 'The truth of the matter is that these small northern countries feared, above all, a Franco-German hegemony, which at that time would have meant a French hegemony,' Marjolin writes. 'They were being true to their traditional policy of seeking in Britain a counter-balance [and] through Britain, it was America they were counting on.'[30] However, just as the Gaullist position had its allies outside France, the liberal element was not confined to the Low Countries. Liberals in the CDU close to the Atlanticist fraction of the German ruling class and capital, such as Ludwig Erhard and Gerhard Schröder (the foreign minister appointed in 1961), were looking beyond France.[31] They were receptive to the Kennedy administration's clarion call for an Atlantic free trade area, and did not want de Gaulle to stand in the way.

Latching on to the liberal interpretation of integration, the 'Kennedy Round' of trade negotiations aimed to remove the disparities between the highly varied US tariffs (some as high as 50 per cent) and the EEC's common external tariff, and to reduce tariffs overall. Especially significant in the American proposals was the so-called Dominant Supplier Provision, a zero tariff applying to those products in which 80 per cent of world trade was accounted for by the US plus the EEC and Britain (which Kennedy and prime minister Macmillan hoped would soon be admitted into the EEC). The Dominant Supplier Provision aimed at liberalising the most advanced sectors, while preventing a further outflow of US capital trying to jump the external EEC tariff by direct investment to Europe.[32] This was an ambitious attempt to establish a socialisation of labour in the most advanced sectors, the pivot of a single North Atlantic market in the spirit of the original Marshall/OEEC project.[33] It would extend the heartland, as a transnational space for capital, to Western Europe and yet leave the English-speaking states in control, because (as we will see in the final section of this chapter) the United States simultaneously sought to rein in the nuclear ambitions of its NATO allies and re-centralise the strategic balance with the USSR in Washington, with the UK as a junior partner.

The impact of the Kennedy offensive for Atlantic unity, which I have de-scribed at length elsewhere, was momentous but short-lived.[34] It resonated even within the French government. Five ministers resigned in protest in May 1962 over de Gaulle's obstinate rejection of American leadership, and rumours about attempts to sideline the president were rife.[35] Clearly the domestic consensus commanded by the Gaullist project had already nar-rowed considerably when in January 1963 de Gaulle first rejected the British bid for EEC membership, and then concluded a Friendship Treaty with West Germany. The treaty was a mini-Fouchet plan for the two states, with a defence aspect that restored a military capacity outside the NATO command structure—a signal challenge to US leadership. However, the Friendship Treaty was too narrowly focused on France to suit the taste of the Atlanticists in the Federal Republic and their constituency in the ascendant world market interest in German capital. Its ratification in the Bundestag brought this out clearly. A preamble declared the inviolability of West Germany's existing multilateral treaties—NATO and EEC—thus practically emptying the pact with France of content. 'This preamble and the unanimity with which it was adopted, put things right, and the treaty, thus understood, lost its quality as an exclusive political alliance and became an administrative expression of the Franco-German reconciliation which had already been decided twelve years earlier with the Schuman Plan,' Monnet concludes in his memoirs.[36] It certainly spelled the end of Adenauer; Erhard took over as chancellor in the autumn of 1963.

Politically, de Gaulle had lost an important ally, but the structural effect of the resurrection of aspects of the contender state in the context of the EEC remained operative. Monnet too estimated that in the end the reinforcement of the executive in France served to facilitate European integration, because 'in order to delegate sovereignty, authority has to be well established.'[37] The French used their new punch to book a few final successes of the sectoral integration strategy. This first of all concerns the Common Agricultural Policy (CAP). Agriculture, as indicated, should ideally be 'socialised' for Fordist industrialisation, in much the same way as the coal and steel industries had been. The American New Deal had achieved just that, and in Europe the Dutch had already pioneered key aspects of such a strategy before the war.[38] France had the greatest agricultural potential, given its vast land mass, range of climate zones and tradition of quality foodstuffs. Right after the war the French state launched a massive investment programme meant to turn the country into an agricultural exporter, a strategy in which conservative patriotism mixed with economics.[39] The French aim, as earlier in steel, armaments, and atomic energy, was to lock West Germany into a 'European' arrangement that would consolidate the French advantage; but neither was the CDU constituency in West German agriculture averse to a CAP subsidy regime. Hence in January 1962, Sicco Mansholt, the Dutch Labour politician and gentleman farmer turned EEC Commission vice-president, found the necessary manoeuvring space to insert agriculture into the Common Market, with a common fund as a mechanism for operating the policy on the basis of its own income and expenditure.[40]

The CAP illustrates that integration by methods borrowed from the contender tradition, as earlier in coal and steel, is not something that can be applied tactically and removed again later. It works as a structure of socialisation also in the sense of a norm-setting context, engendering a particular outlook among the social forces harnessed by it.[41] This may explain why the CAP, planned as a component of Fordist restructuring, soon lost its modernisation aspect and degenerated into a protectionist system of price supports, which till today absorbs almost half the EU budget, although some of its foundations are being reformed along neoliberal lines. This in itself will not rule out rivalries on the Atlantic fracture—on the contrary.

The CAP gives Europe, notably France, the ability to exert its influence in the shaping of global food policies. Here the existence of an EEC association policy with former colonies must be mentioned. This was a second late instalment of the French sectoral integration strategy. Ideas to embed the French sphere of influence in Africa in a 'European' arrangement circulated from the early 1950s onwards. In the final negotiations on the EEC, West Germany and the Netherlands consented because their corporations had meanwhile become investors in French dependencies and were profiting from the existing infrastructure there. But it was not until France had disentangled itself from the Algerian quagmire before the EEC association policy with its former colonies was finally put in place in Yaoundé in 1963.[42] The association policy consolidated France's sphere of influence in sub-Saharan Africa, where Paris had retained the control of the key levers of power in the monetary and defence sphere that it had lost in Southeast Asia.

ASIAN KILLING FIELDS: INDO-CHINA AND INDONESIA

Franco-American rivalry in the second half of the 1960s cannot be understood without reference to the war in Vietnam, just as the rising tide of Third World economic nationalism, which the EC countries would seek to accommodate in the 1970s, cannot be properly assessed without taking into account the United States' rampage in Southeast Asia. In this section, I draw the broad contours of this process.

US policy in the Pacific differed in fundamental respects from its post-war European strategy. Japan, unlike Germany and Italy, was not identified as part of a strategically endangered area; and yet, the West had much less of a foothold on the Asian mainland. With Japan, there existed no affinities such as the English-speaking bond, or even an emigration connection as with the rest of Europe. US citizens of Japanese origin had been interned during the war, and the Japanese ruling class could not rely on elite groups like the European exiles in London to negotiate with the Americans, or utilise rivalries among occupying powers. In Japan, General MacArthur had sole responsibility. The willingness of the US to allow Western European integration to take off in the 1950s was therefore not matched by initiatives encouraging reconciliation between Japan and its neighbours. Instead of a forward projection of a transnational heartland, Japan, one of the historic contenders to heartland pre-eminence since the Meiji revolution from above in 1868, was encouraged to switch to a vassal role with the West.[43] Under the Yoshida doctrine of mercantilism, restrained remilitarisation and 'subordinate independence', Japan got permission to retain what has been called its '1940 economic structure', a privately owned but state-managed economy geared to winning a total war.[44] Yoshida actually resigned in protest when the Japanese cabinet intensified this policy in 1954 in ways that he thought

were approximating socialism. But Japan's state-monitored economic development continued to enjoy American patronage on account of the willingness of the Japanese ruling class to side with the West in the cold war, and
the structures of the contender state economy were left very much in place.[45]
As in West Germany, the purging of Japanese owners and managers and
the de-concentration of the *zaibatsu* trusts controlled by them was put on
the back burner in 1947–48. In the absence of a transnational structure
like the one created in Western Europe, the stand-alone contender state
would be replicated throughout East Asia, until the collapse of the USSR
removed the necessity to ensure their vassal role in the cold war.

Washington's Japan policy was an early instance of friction with its
European allies, including the UK. US advisors working with MacArthur
geared Japan's economy towards exports by forcing wages and prices down,
whereas London had expected that a democratic policy imposed on Japan
would include the development of a domestic market to reduce competitive
pressures overseas.[46] Japan, then, became the lone US kingpin in the un-
folding geopolitical struggle in Asia. Apart from its own military expenditure
in the country, Washington ensured that the country became the second-
largest recipient (after India) of World Bank loans. Once Mao's forces had
taken Beijing, it was considered opportune to accommodate rather than
resist the organisation of a peaceful version of the wartime 'Asian Co-
Prosperity Sphere' to support the rapidly expanding Japanese economy.[47]
Thus the strategy of replicating state-monitored export economies across
the region was resumed under the 1930s doctrine of the 'Flying Geese'.
In this image, Japan leads a flight of geese, first as the exporter to the
others, then as an investor passing on the role of exporter to others in the
flight, and eventually as the dominant power passing on the investor and
exporter roles further down the flight as more geese join.[48]

The first 'goose' to join the flight was Taiwan after it became the refuge
of the Chinese nationalist leadership driven from the mainland; it was soon
followed by South Korea once the war with the North ended in armistice.
The strategy of these two client states of the US was initially based on an
import-substitution industrialisation strategy, complementing their mineral
and agricultural exports. The UK colonies, Hong Kong and Singapore, served
as regional trade entrepôts.[49] The industrial 'geese' were not receptive to
foreign investment; the money that did flow into the region between 1951
and 1960, was on official account rather than private investment.[50] Politically, the 'geese' were secured by dictatorial regimes. Taiwan was kept under
the fist of the nationalist Chinese exiles. The strength of the democratic
movement in South Korea on the other hand forced the Americans to allow
their initial strongman, Syngman Rhee, to be replaced by General Park
Chung-hee in 1961.[51] By this time, American strategists had concluded
that unless the 'Flying Geese' project were able to rely on Southeast Asia's

mineral and forest riches, Japan and other states might be tempted to seek an accommodation with communist China and other socialist states. Thailand, Vietnam and Indonesia were therefore defined as part of a wider regional constellation in which revolutionary change could not be tolerated.[52]

Inheriting France's War in Vietnam

The French defeat at Dien Bien Phu happened in May 1954, on the first day of the conference on the Korean War in Geneva. The communist Viet Minh, formed in 1941 to fight the Vichy French and the Japanese, had effectively won independence; but the new Soviet leadership, keen to improve the international climate, put heavy pressure on it to accept a temporary partition between north and south Vietnam, as in Korea. In the expectation that the Viet Minh would easily win the elections, to be held within a year, the French began early on to negotiate a diplomatic understanding with Hanoi.[53]

Washington, as we know, had other plans. Rejecting an offer to take over the 40,000-strong mercenary force that the French had relied on, the CIA began to build up the anti-communist, anti-French Ngo Dinh Diem as their man in Saigon. This issue, as well as the question of who would train the army and how, were the chief areas of friction with France. In the background lurked another matter—control over Saigon's heroin business. From the days of their fight against the Viet Minh, French military intelligence had protected an army of Saigon river pirates controlling this trade (the Saigon police chief was its head). If Diem were to have real power in South Vietnam, he had to challenge the gangsters over the issue of their control of Saigon and the rice-growing Mekong delta. Advised by E.G. Lansdale, the CIA architect of the defeat of the communist insurgency in the Philippines, Diem's forces drove out the river pirates in savage battles in April–May 1955. This left Diem as the real ruler of the South, and his infamous brother Nhu in control of Saigon's opium business—thus keeping open a back-channel to France through Nhu's partners in the Corsican mafia. When Emperor Bao Dai, who lived in France, ordered Diem to come to his Rivièra residence to hand in his resignation, Diem instead deposed the emperor, declared a republic, shelved the planned elections, and dismissed his French advisers, including in April 1956, the remaining French troops.[54]

The United States also prevailed on Diem to blockade the communist North. This amounted to a policy of starvation, given that the North depended on substantial rice imports from the South, which was the larger of the two. France was completely sidelined, its remaining interests undercut. As D.F. Fleming notes, 'the US was trying to seal off North Vietnam from the South, to boycott the economy of the North and was threatening to blacklist French business pursuing a contrary policy.'[55]

When John F. Kennedy won the US presidency, one of his key planks was to develop a progressive response to the rising tide of revolt in the Third World. But his space for manoeuvre was constrained by the fear of being seen as weak in the confrontation with communism.[56] In January 1961, the month Kennedy assumed the presidency, the Moscow conference of communist parties endorsed a strategy of wars of national liberation as its common strategy. Much of this, as Gabriel Kolko has argued, was primarily a matter of Sino-Soviet rivalry, but the Kennedy administration took it as a confirmation of their own cold war view of the world.[57] The US decision to enter the Vietnam war was taken as part of a perceived struggle with communism in Asia, notably against China; the aim of aiding the 'Flying Geese' strategy of its vassal Japan, can be seen as over-determining that struggle in the sense that, ultimately, the rationale to fight communism is the defence of private property and capital.[58]

The US had demonstratively turned its back on the Geneva conference when it came to Vietnam, and the election commitment was laid down anyway in an unsigned declaration. The day after the closure of the Geneva conference, the US and a number of heartland allies and local vassals moved to establish a Southeast Asian defence organisation, SEATO, composed of the US, the UK, Australia and New Zealand, and France, Thailand, the Philippines and Pakistan.[59] Along with NATO and CENTO—the northern tier containing the Middle East, soon to be added—this created a global chain of vassal alliances connected to the West. Yet formal membership (as in the case of France) did not guarantee that a country's overseas interests were taken care of; neither should these blocs be seen as fighting machines ready for action. The aspirations of regional elites were directed towards development (partly for personal enrichment, for sure) but not war. Thus in Thailand, a member of SEATO, the military seized power in 1958 and began a crash programme of fostering private enterprise following World Bank recommendations, while outlawing trade union activity. However, the rulers in Bangkok doubted the American commitment to the region; it was not until 1962 that they were willing to sign up as a US ally, knowing that they were exposing themselves to the wrath of their neighbours and communist insurgency.[60]

Vietnam was a rice-growing, largely pre-industrial society with incipient forms of state centralisation, obviously strongest in the communist North. The revolt in the South falls into the category of peasant wars, and it is the American intervention displacing the French—and meant to keep the large communist contenders at bay—which incorporates Vietnam into the evolving structure of rivalry as understood in this study.[61]

The National Liberation Front was formed in the South in 1960. Its formation was a response to the extreme repression of Diem's regime with its military tribunals and summary executions; it came five weeks after a foiled rebellion of his elite parachute regiment had revealed the brittleness of the dictator's power. Kennedy and his entourage were well aware that this was no basis on which to build a reformist strategy in the Third World. On the eve of the new president's inauguration, several South Vietnamese leadership candidates were flown to Washington for policy talks.[62] Diem also alienated Washington by enlisting British advisers with expertise in Malaya to conduct the war on his own terms, as he feared losing control of his army if he relied only on the Americans. In 1962 the US military took direct control of the war, creating a single command structure for the region that covered Thailand and South Vietnam, and embarking on a crash programme of constructing large military bases. As they began to cultivate the South Vietnamese military as potential 'nation-builders', the Americans were acutely aware of the fragility of the capacity of their proxies to hold the line, especially when Buddhist monks joined the protests against the Diem regime.[63]

De Gaulle, who had himself ordered the re-conquest of France's Indo-Chinese colonial empire in the wake of Japan's defeat, records in his memoirs his warning to Kennedy that the Vietnam intervention would turn out to be a disaster for the West. The more the US would fight the Vietnamese in the name of fighting communism, the more the communists would become the champions of national independence.[64] But this warning only raised American suspicions that the French might be plotting to recoup their lost influence. When in 1963, Diem's inner circle suddenly began to seek a rapprochement with opposition forces and the North, the US decided to act. Although French involvement was marginal at best, the US, with 16,000 advisers in the country, feared it was being outmanoeuvred by an unexpected realignment of forces, 'a game ... that Washington thought concealed a plot between Paris, Hanoi, and Nhu'.[65] Having rejected American offers to step down, the dictator and his brother were eventually abducted by South Vietnamese troops and killed—20 days before the assassination of Kennedy himself. These changes cleared the way for installing an officers' regime which the president's advisers had been arguing for and which, as a National Security memorandum put it, would allow the 'benevolent authoritarianism' of the military to 'create national unity and hold power in trust for the less competent civilians.' Since the US controlled aid to the military and handled direct training, the war now became entirely an American affair, and the commitment of ground troops began its steep rise to more than half a million men by 1968.[66]

Congressional support for the war was obtained when an exchange of fire with North Vietnamese torpedo boats was reported in August 1964.[67] With a further, fictional attack added for good measure, the Gulf of Tonkin resolution authorised the president to 'take all necessary steps, including the use of armed force' against 'aggression in South-East Asia'. This opened up what Jan Pluvier calls 'South East Asia's bloodiest period of history ... both on account of the war in Indo-China, which exceeded all prior wars in terms of the scale of violence; and on account of the massacres in a number of other countries, compared to which similar events in the colonial age and under Japanese occupation, pale into mere incidents.'[68] But as the architect of the Tonkin Resolution, Senator William Fulbright, warned two years later in a statement regretting his role, the Vietnam war was costing the United States dear in its relations with its allies. The Atlantic crisis that broke in 1966 with the withdrawal of France's military from NATO (to which we turn in the final section of this chapter), was in Fulbright's view not a matter of any quirks on the part of de Gaulle, who had expressed his fear of being drawn into America's overseas wars; rather, it was 'representative of a widespread loss of European confidence in American policy and judgement'.[69] This could only become stronger when the US persisted in fighting the war even after Indonesia, Southeast Asia's largest prize, had been secured for the West by a murderous coup in 1965–66.

The Indonesian Crisis and the Creation of an Anti-Communist Bloc

The struggle against Asian communism covered a redistribution of regional influence, at the expense of the former European colonial powers and in favour of Japan. As late as 1960, most raw material exports from Asia were still destined for the UK and the EEC; the United States mainly imported sugar from the Philippines and also around a quarter of non-communist Asia's rubber exports. Japan's economic relations with Southeast Asia on the other hand were still very limited. By the 1990s, however, before it faced the double challenge of the resurgence of China and the post-cold war offensive of the West, Japan had risen to undisputed regional primacy, commanding a 'Flying Geese' formation that extended across all of East and Southeast Asia.[70]

Indonesia, like Vietnam, was a predominantly agricultural society, with cash-crop plantations for export controlled by Dutch and British merchant houses. But it is the world's fifth largest country by population, and commands vast forest and raw material resources, also in foreign hands until the Sukarno period.[71] The Dutch never made much effort to come to terms with the nationalist element that began to make its impact in their colonial empire in the 1930s, and Sukarno rose to prominence during the Second World War by utilising the Japanese occupation to reinforce his movement's position for the period after the war. This sealed the unwillingness of the Dutch to work with the nationalists and prevented a compromise with a domestic bourgeoisie as the British achieved in India.[72] Instead, they launched a colonial war to regain control over Indonesia, trying to play on ethnic and religious differences in the colony to reduce the territory to be ceded to the nationalists. However, the US, confident that Sukarno had proved his anti-communist credentials when he cracked down on the communist party in 1948, threatened to suspend Marshall Plan disbursements if the Dutch did not stop their second military campaign. This forced the Netherlands to acknowledge Indonesia's independence a year later.[73]

The main challenge to Sukarno's ambition of developing Indonesia was the problem of land distribution on the island of Java, home to two-thirds of Indonesia's population—all development must begin with mobilising income, people and resources in agriculture. A populist strategy of defending 'Indonesian' interests was hardly sufficient to overcome class conflict in the countryside, though. Class conflict was also compounded by religious divisions and the ethnic diversity of a vast archipelago, which owed its formal unity only to Dutch colonialism. One consequence of the Bandung conference of non-aligned states in 1955 was a treaty with communist China to settle the status of Indonesia's Chinese minority, but from 1959 onwards government measures against commercial activities in the countryside forced tens of thousands of Chinese small traders back to their ancestral homeland and gave rise to tensions with Beijing.[74] In 1957 Sukarno began a tentative process of tightening central authority over the mosaic of ethnic and religious groups by declaring a state of emergency. Inspired by Nasser, he simultaneously moved against Dutch economic interests. This inaugurated a process of confiscation of the social basis by the state in the Hobbesian sense, provoking an insurrection of local Islamic groups and the military on the mineral-rich island of Sumatra, which gained CIA support but failed.[75]

Yet Sukarno's state was far from a fully-fledged Leviathan. His 'five-year plans' were mostly window-dressing to back up his prestige with foreign leaders. What did begin to emerge was a state class of army generals committed to Indonesia's integrity and with an appetite for enriching themselves. The expropriation of Dutch economic assets and the repatriation of hundreds of thousands of Dutch citizens to Europe allowed the military to reinforce their already important positions in the economy (except for the oil industry which remained 90 per cent foreign-owned). Nesting themselves in profitable positions in forestry and other business ventures alongside an ethnic-Chinese capitalist elite, the generals and colonels developed into a proto-bourgeoisie facing the Left (although there were nationalist and communist currents in the army as well).[76] It is here that we should look for the origins of the army's takeover in 1965, and the paradoxical fact that the anti-communist military thereafter remained committed to a strong state driving forward development.

In the intervening years, Sukarno, uneasily perched between the ascendant military state class and the powerful Indonesian Communist party (PKI), attempted to keep the party on board at the elite level even after the suspension of democracy, if only to stave off the Islamic parties, which constituted a threat of a different kind. A timid land reform in 1960 did little to address the tensions brewing in the Javanese countryside, and Sukarno now began to stoke up foreign conflicts to steer clear of domestic strife. In the early 1960s, he raised the stakes in the lingering conflict with the Netherlands over New Guinea, the western half of Papua New Guinea remaining under colonial rule; he also sought a confrontation with Britain over the formation of Malaysia, a combination of the Malayan peninsula with the British-controlled part of the Indonesian island of Borneo (Kalimantan). In the first conflict, the United States was able to defuse a confrontation. The Kennedy administration sacrificed Dutch interests in order not to antagonise Asian feeling, and New Guinea was eventually ceded to Indonesia.[77] The formation of Malaysia, on the other hand, was a more complicated issue; the new state initially aroused enmity on the part of the Philippines but not of Indonesia. Yet Sukarno's ire led him to take his country out of the UN in late 1964 and move closer to the Soviet Union and China, whose leaders by then shared his concern about another pro-Western state in the region.[78] Sukarno therefore allowed the PKI and the unions to mobilise against the United States in mass demonstrations, while accepting military aid from the Soviet Union.

This then led sections of the Indonesian military, who feared that further alienation of the West would threaten their privileges as a state class, to secretly enter into negotiations with the US military and intelligence services. The US had intimated earlier that they were ready to support a coup; in 1963 they had already threatened to cut aid if oil legislation that US companies considered tantamount to expropriation were put into effect.[79] Measures against foreign capital, in combination with a movement for radical land reform on Java, created dangerous tensions. In 1965, with Sukarno suffering from ill-health, a group of left nationalist officers made a coup attempt in order to pre-empt a right wing, US-supported coup. This allowed General Suharto, the commander of the strategic reserve, who had been informed of the initial coup but had kept aloof, to clamp down on it quickly and effectively. Presenting the original coup as an attempt at revolution by the PKI, the new rulers unleashed a popular movement of violent reprisals—Muslims against communists, landowners against landless peasants, ethnic Indonesians against Chinese, and Right against Left. CIA and State Department messages document the close involvement of the United States in what was obviously a campaign prepared well in advance.[80] Anywhere between 500,000 and 1 million people were murdered, a fact celebrated in the American media as 'the West's best news for years in Asia'.[81]

Pogroms against ethnic Chinese had been part of the massacres. With China itself in the throes of the 'Cultural Revolution', there was little chance this time for repatriation. A top echelon of Chinese tycoons, whose business connections were indispensable to the military state class, on the other hand secured positions in Suharto's immediate entourage.[82] Indonesia broke off relations with China; in early 1967, it again became a member of the IMF and the World Bank. As indicated, the new rulers did not simply discard the earlier non-aligned position internationally. Certainly they were more interested in ASEAN, the regional bloc set up in 1967, than in the wider mobilisation that would produce the NIEO movement. But Adam Malik, the foreign minister who was a Sukarno hold-over, was able to resist American pressure to move closer to the West also because Indonesia had large debts to the USSR. When US pressure persisted, Malik actually called on Japan to assume a leading role in the development of Southeast Asia.[83]

Japanese capital took up the invitation with a zeal that would provoke a growing anti-Japanese sentiment and explode in riots against Japanese property in the early 1970s. Yet with ASEAN in place, the original design of the US to provide a cover for extending the 'Flying Geese' programme to Southeast Asia—through the twists and turns of revolution and repression, unity and rivalry—ended up being almost entirely realised.[84] ASEAN was initially set up to defuse tensions among the participating Southeast Asian states and stabilise them politically. Only later did it become a platform for the regional capitalist economy. But Washington was all along concerned about making it look like something civilian, not a military alliance like SEATO.[85]

In Indonesia itself, the Americans had good reason to operate under the cover of a foreign donor conference under Dutch chairmanship. Contrary to what the term 'donor' would suggest, in the decade beginning from 1966 this intergovernmental conference presided over a sevenfold growth in the country's foreign debt and a massive impoverishment of the population. US direct investment rose from $106 million to $1.5 billion over the same period.[86] But these figures are dwarfed by the size of the plunder of the archipelago by its new rulers. As Robison and Hadiz document, the tentative Leviathan established in 1965–66 drew the state, through a revolution from above, 'more deeply into relationships with capitalists, cronies, and "fixers" that revolved around a vast system of benefices and rents'.[87] As the years went by, however, Suharto gradually dissociated himself from the state class of fellow generals, and began, through the medium of presidential foundations (*yayasans*), to accumulate wealth for a smaller circle—his family and a group of associates from the ethnic-Chinese capitalist class. This led to resentment in the army, but it also undermined the possibility that a self-confident middle class would emerge from its 'molecular' advance, as Gramsci assumed would happen in such situations. What crystallises instead, after the supposed removal of the Hobbesian state, is a ruthless oligarchy, confident that it can control society through electoral politics as well.[88] This, as we shall see, set the pattern for other countries in the decades that followed.

The Anomaly of the Continuing War in Vietnam

With communism in Indonesia literally exterminated, China in turmoil, and its European NATO allies increasingly apprehensive, the rationale for the US intervention in Vietnam began to unravel. The joint US/South Vietnamese 'pacification' policies in the countryside, meant to eradicate resistance and win over the landed population, merely served to radicalise the peasantry. The erratic violence of the US military, far from home in a country whose language and culture they and their commanders had no inkling of, made winning any 'hearts and minds' a chimera. The rapaciousness of the indigenous landlord class, who used American power to collect rents from the villages, rendered the political project hopeless. In 1965, generals Nguyen Van Thieu, who was close to the Chinese minority, and Nguyen Cao Ky (a racist air ace who had flown raids into North Vietnam from Laos while transporting opium on other routes) took over power. The two men, fierce rivals, were prevailed upon by President Lyndon Johnson at a meeting in Hawaii in 1966 to begin a constitutional process that would turn South Vietnam into a stable democracy capable of defending itself. A Vietnamese MP, who proposed a law to prevent Ky from running, was assassinated, but in April 1967 the *New York Times*, with a naiveté we have seen repeated recently in Iraq, preferred to report that a surprising 83 per cent of registered voters had 'risked reprisals threatened by the Vietcong' to cast their vote. Glowing press accounts of the democratic virtues of the Vietnamese population could not, however, disguise the fact that the military initiative had gone over to the NLF and North Vietnam.[89]

American strategy now became a defensive one of gaining time to allow the South Vietnamese army to display its supposed nation-building skills. In late 1966, 40 per cent of the by then half a million US troops were being used solely for the defence of bases.[90] The American military responded to the growing stalemate by ever-more furious air attacks on the North. All major cities of North Vietnam had already been hit and the dike and irrigation systems of the Red River delta damaged when the new wave of bombardments began. The war's parameters in tons of ordnance used, the final death toll of around 3 million Vietnamese, and the use of chemical and other banned weapons were all signs of a world power having abandoned all restraint or humanity. This and the visual cruelty of the Vietnam war, televised straight into living rooms the world over on a daily basis, swung world opinion against the US, merging into the left-wing tide to which we return in the next chapter.[91]

Against this background, France, Canada, and UN secretary-general U Thant openly began to advocate mediation. In September 1966 de Gaulle declared that the establishment of US authority in Vietnam had 'revived the war in the form of national resistance,' a war which he warned would prove as fruitless as the one France had waged in Algeria.[92] It was indeed feared in Paris that 'Vietnam' could escalate into a world war (the North Vietnamese on the other hand suspected that the real reason why France was seeking to get the US out of Vietnam was to find a way of returning there themselves).[93] In Britain, Harold Wilson, the Labour prime minister elected in 1964, refused to send troops, hoping that rhetorical solidarity would secure US help to prop up the pound.[94] Washington was in fact willing to do a deal on this basis, as long as Britain maintained its military positions in Southeast Asia to cover the Americans in Vietnam. In early 1967, however, Wilson too, jointly with Poland and the USSR, tried to get a compromise peace on the rails. But the Americans, still convinced they were winning the war, refused to stop the bombardment of the North as a prior condition to negotiations. Wilson, feeling that he could afford to distance himself from the US, decided to withdraw from 'east of Suez' anyway, even though this contributed to the devaluation of the pound later in the year.[95] The Indonesian coup generally lessened the urgency of Western military presence, and ASEAN also served to cover Britain's retreat from Singapore.

In 1968, the Tet offensive of the NLF completely destroyed the illusions about the United States having the upper hand. Although the spectacular uprising decimated the NLF and increased the weight of the regular North Vietnamese army in the struggle, the images of bloodstained and bewildered US diplomats running around the Saigon embassy grounds, guns in hand, sent shock-waves across the world.[96] In March, President Johnson scaled down the bombing of North Vietnam to calm the domestic opposition. However, by that time American society was descending into a deep crisis. The assassination of black leader Martin Luther King in April 1968 (after he had begun speaking out against the war) was followed by rioting all over the US; Lyndon Johnson's surprise withdrawal from politics briefly before this made it clear that the Vietnam adventure had to be ended one way or another.[97] In May, negotiations between US and North Vietnamese delegations began in Paris, although little was achieved. Johnson put pressure on Thieu to make compromises, but as transpired later, presidential candidate Richard Nixon secretly encouraged the South Vietnamese leader not to give in but wait instead for a better deal once he, Nixon, was elected—thus denying the Democrats a successful deal on the eve of the presidential contest.[98]

Once in office, the Nixon administration too found itself unable to end the war. Certainly the national security adviser, Henry Kissinger, was able to increase the rivalry between the USSR and China through a policy of active balancing that brought the president to Beijing in 1972. However, the strategy of 'Vietnamisation'—building an army that would allow the withdrawal of US troops—was fraught with corruption and economic dislocation. The 320,000 US troops in Vietnam in 1970 (down from 540,000 in 1968), developed into the largest growth market for Southeast Asian heroin, with around 10 per cent of the troops addicted or regular users.[99] In the same year, Kissinger widened the war to Cambodia, ousting the country's leader, Sihanouk. Pressure from Indonesia and Japan, who feared that the Chinese were beginning to extend their influence to Cambodia, contributed to the US decision to intervene, and the Indonesian military played a role in the coup in early 1970 that brought a pro-US puppet to power.[100] A further episode in the seemingly endless chain of bloodbaths in Southeast Asia unfolded when Cambodian 'Marxists' began applying ideas about re-ruralisation conceived in exile in Paris. The 'killing fields', which took some 300,000 lives after the Khmer Rouge, their vanguard party, conquered power in 1975, stand as a grim memorial to the destruction of Indo-China. It is also testimony to great-power cynicism, because, as the US moved closer to China against the USSR, this relationship included Western cover for the Khmer Rouge as well.[101]

In a final Asian drama, the US threw its weight behind its vassal Pakistan in the crisis that led to the secession of Bangladesh in 1971. To explore the opening to China, Kissinger had used the good offices of the Pakistani military dictator, Yahya Khan, an ally of Beijing. Khan had initiated a return to civilian rule but responded with brutal violence to the election victory of Sheikh Mujibur Rahman in East Bengal. Anywhere between half a million and 3 million civilians died, while millions of refugees poured into India. India intervened and in a short war in December 1971 presided over the independence of what became Bangladesh. Washington considered the new state too far to the left and in 1975 supported a military coup that entailed the murder of Mujibur, whom Kissinger had earlier compared to Allende. In Pakistan itself, the defeat would usher in a new generation in the military who set their sights on an Islamist renaissance. This determined the course of Pakistani involvement in Afghanistan during the Soviet intervention, and resonates in anti-Western terrorism today.[102]

The defeats of the United States culminated in April 1975, when the world watched the last helicopters carrying South Vietnamese officials lift off from the roof of the US embassy in Saigon, fleeing the North Vietnamese tank columns rolling into the city. In December, President Ford and Secretary of State Kissinger in a meeting with Suharto gave the green light to invade East Timor, an Asian outpost of the Portuguese colonial empire that disintegrated in the 1974 revolution. This added a few more hundreds of thousands to the death lists of America's crusade in Asia. Defending the decision 20 years later, Kissinger referred to the 'context of the period' and the reality of 'dominoes' actually falling all around.[103]

GAULLIST FRANCE AND THE REMAKING OF THE POST-WAR ATLANTIC ORDER

The US predicament in Vietnam could not but expose the fractures and fault-lines within the wider West. It certainly contributed, through several episodes such as the May 1968 revolt, to reactivate the process of European integration. The integration 'relaunch' would culminate in 1973 with the accession of Britain under Edward Heath (along with Ireland and Denmark) to the EEC. Kissinger notes in his memoirs that, uniquely among British political leaders (except perhaps Eden), Heath dealt with the US 'with an unsentimentality totally at variance with the "special relationship"', adding that this may have been caused by the British prime minister's 'dedication of a vision of Europe quite similar to de Gaulle's'.[104] This was not a matter of subjective preference. As noted before, the integration process requires an unequivocal separation of state sovereignty from the transnational space for capital, in order to prevent parliamentary and social democracy from spilling over into the wider arena. In addition, by 1972 the challenge to be met was the strength of the domestic Left, with the USSR having become a conservative force eager to negotiate with the West and consolidate the geopolitical positions won in the Second World War. In both areas, a too-close association with the US had become a positive liability for most Western leaders, and it was a sign of the depth of the West's crisis that this feeling now cut across the original heartland.

De Gaulle is the dominating figure in the movement of 'Europe' away from the Atlantic constraint. In the circumstances created by the American preoccupation with Southeast Asia, the 'Gaullist' perspective also became relevant for other states, thus contributing to the overall rift. The issue of nuclear strategy is important in this respect because here geopolitics is anchored in vital class positions. When it appeared that Nixon and Kissinger were willing to engage in far-reaching agreement with the USSR, the ruling classes of Europe faced the prospect of having to maintain their power, domestically and in the relations with the Soviet bloc, *without* the ultimate 'stick' of US military might, specifically the nuclear deterrent force.[105]

De Gaulle had already defined the French position in this domain in the late 1950s. In 1959 he opened the chess game concerning NATO nuclear strategy by asking the US and UK to remove their nuclear-equipped air force units from French soil. A year later, France tested its first nuclear weapon, the product of the country's nuclear programme discussed in Chapter 2. With this powerful, if largely symbolic, asset in the French arsenal, de Gaulle then proposed to Eisenhower and Macmillan to create a triumvirate in NATO in recognition of their independent nuclear armaments and their different interests in the rest of the world, which required a differentiated projection of power. For France, this concerned the relations with West Germany and with the USSR, as well as its surviving connections to Indo-China and sphere of influence in Africa, then still including Algeria as a colony.[106] But the other EEC states had no nuclear arms, and when the French in the discussions on the Fouchet Plan in 1962 raised the issue of a military option outside NATO, there was an uproar which coincided with a brewing crisis in West Germany.[107]

The Federal Republic, too, was claiming greater freedom of manoeuvre and less Anglo-American tutelage in its foreign policy. The country's leaders considered the growth of integration primarily through the prism of national sovereignty and their own strategic goals, notably reunification. Therefore they had to move carefully, balancing the short-run advantages of backing Gaullist 'recalcitrance' with the long-term association with the English-speaking world in the cold war. Adenauer's defence (and former atomic energy) minister, Franz-Josef Strauss, now sought to make the country a threshold nuclear power, if not more.[108] Foreign Minister Schröder on the other hand represented the Atlantic perspective, which included in 1961 acceptance of Kennedy's plan to rein in the nuclear ambitions of the European allies through a joint NATO nuclear force, the Multi-Lateral Force (MLF).[109] With the MLF plan, inherited from his predecessor, Kennedy intended to provide a cover for the projected engagement of the US in the restive Third World under the 'flexible response' strategy. However, the MLF was bound to exacerbate the divisions in the Federal Republic. Strauss wanted to adapt the Lockheed F-104G Starfighter (assembled in his fief, Bavaria) to make it capable of delivering nuclear bombs to Soviet targets. In early 1962, he was exploring possibilities of buying missiles from Paris and supporting the French nuclear programme financially in exchange for a share in the military results. Although he openly attacked Washington's new strategy, in June he visited the US to buy $120 million worth of Pershing missiles.[110]

The 'Atlanticists' around Schröder and in the other parties kept Strauss under fire on his defence policy, but Adenauer protected him. In October, just before the Cuban missile crisis broke out, an article in one of the channels of Atlanticist opinion, *Der Spiegel* magazine, criticised Strauss on the basis of obvious inside information. This led the defence minister to have a number of journalists arrested. He also initiated proceedings against politicians, including Helmut Schmidt, the future defence minister and eventual chancellor. Since the Cuban missile crisis had erupted in the meantime, Strauss tried to justify his actions in light of the emergency, but he had to step down amidst public uproar.[111] Yet the urgency of an independent nuclear policy in the eyes of sections of the ruling classes in Europe was not diminished; on the contrary.

The Cuban missile crisis had the effect of reminding the world's leaders of the dangers of the nuclear arms race. It certainly terminated the brief period of intense East–West confrontation that had preceded it.[112] A textbook case of the autistic interaction among large bureaucracies that briefly pushed the world to the brink of nuclear annihilation (even closer than assumed in the immediate aftermath), the crisis was solved by Khrushchev's restraint rather than his opponent's; but the American president too drew lessons from the crisis. The nuclear test ban negotiated with the USSR was ratified by the Senate as a sign of a willingness to defuse the cold war. Paradoxically, this created unease in France and other European countries. When Kennedy, meeting with Macmillan in the Bahamas in December 1962, obtained an agreement to place British US-supplied, Polaris-armed nuclear submarines under NATO command, de Gaulle had no choice but to veto the accession of the UK to the EEC, because this amounted to placing the Common Market again under American political tutelage, which he had contested all along.[113]

De Gaulle persisted in trying to get the Germans on board. From his January 1963 'veto' press conference onwards, he sought to tie them to a French nuclear alternative to the MLF. In 1964 he approached Chancellor Erhard with an offer to put France's nuclear arsenal at the disposal of 'Europe'. West Germany would be asked to contribute financially to the French defence budget, but without a command role. Erhard rejected the proposal, not so much out of principle but because the Federal Republic would have no operational control.[114] When Erhard, visiting Washington in June, declared his commitment to the MLF, France warned against a US–West German military alliance outside the arrangements by which the EDC crisis had been solved in 1955 (NATO and WEU). Pompidou, de Gaulle's prime minister, qualified the prospect of such an alliance as a breach of the Franco-German Treaty of 1963. He openly wondered whether the MLF strategy was not, 'in the last analysis ... directed against France'.[115] Indeed, in November 1964 when Erhard concluded a bilateral defence agreement with the United States, French control of West German armament levels, obtained in the WEU arrangement, was effectively removed. A month later, the Americans quietly buried the entire MLF strategy, but this did not mean that the issue of US control over NATO nuclear arsenals was off the table.

The 'Empty Chair' and NATO Crises

The EEC crisis of 1965–66 (the 'Empty Chair') and France's withdrawal from NATO's military organisation in 1966 brought to a head the underlying frictions generated by the attempt to unify the West as an enlarged heartland against the cold war contender, the USSR. The president of the European Commission after 1958, Walter Hallstein, who was to become the architect of the 'Empty Chair' crisis, represented the inveterate anti-communism of

Korean War vintage. As Adenauer's right-hand man in foreign affairs prior to the restoration of sovereignty, Hallstein, under the doctrine named after him, refused diplomatic relations with any country recognising the state-socialist German Democratic Republic in East Germany.

De Gaulle, on the other hand, giving up the strategy of challenging the organisation of Atlantic relations directly, began in 1964 to develop a policy of rapprochement with the Soviet bloc under the slogan 'Europe from the Atlantic to the Urals'. French companies, like their competitors from Italy, Belgium and other countries, had been in breach of the US-imposed trade embargoes with the Soviet bloc all along, but in October 1964 France concluded a five-year commercial treaty with the USSR. This was followed in early 1965 by an agreement on scientific and technical cooperation in the field of nuclear energy. In the same period, a range of commercial and cooperation agreements were concluded with several East European state-socialist countries. These steps were obviously noted with concern in Washington, as they amounted to an attempt to demarcate a space removed from the historic pivot of the West, and moving into highly sensitive areas to boot. To large sections of French business on the other hand, this was one area where, under the Hallstein Doctrine, France had little to fear from its main rival in Europe. De Gaulle certainly wanted to cajole the Federal Republic into breaking with that policy; on the eve of a planned visit to Paris by Erhard in January 1965, he welcomed the Hungarian and Rumanian foreign ministers, concluded an agreement with the Soviet Union on the exchange of radio and TV programmes, and made other diplomatic gestures. All of this was meant to put pressure on West Germany to join the opening-up towards Eastern Europe and, through it, to accept the Gaullist concept of integration. The issue of German reunification, de Gaulle underlined, 'will not be settled by the direct confrontation of ideologies and forces of the two camps today rivalling each other in the world.'[116] But he would first have to wait for the 'Grand Coalition' of the CDU and the SPD to assume government power in Bonn.

In march 1965, Hallstein made a trip to the US to confer with President Johnson and Defence Secretary McNamara. On his return, he reaffirmed in a public statement his position that European integration could not be an alternative to Atlantic cooperation. When he added, on the same occasion, that the Commission was in favour of integration in the foreign policy and defence fields, this could not but set off alarm bells in France. But Hallstein may also have slightly overestimated his own importance here.[117] Events now took a turn which superficially make it appear as if France became isolated in both Europe and NATO. In fact, although harmful to the stature of de Gaulle himself, the crisis would result in the general adoption of the principles which the French president had championed from the moment he took power.

As argued earlier, European integration, as a means of peaceful redistribution of unevenly developing capital operating from separate jurisdictions, ideally establishes a transnational sphere free from parliamentary or social democracy. The Commission therefore had to restrain its political ambitions as well. As David Calleo writes,

> Contrary to widespread theory about the evolution of the [European Communities], their significance, which is very great, rests neither upon those few supranational functions which the Commission performs, nor upon their lingering pretensions to become a European central government. Rather, the Communities have come to play their crucial role as the central locus for continual, organized consultation and bargaining among the national governments and bureaucracies of Europe.[118]

Over time, the transnational socialisation of basic industry, agriculture, and a number of other pooled activities creates a space which generates class and interest formation at the European level, potentially inviting politicisation in turn. The European Parliament, supposedly there to control the Commission, would be the obvious channel for such a political process. But as Otto Holman has argued, there would instead emerge a European 'Trias Politica'—comprising the member states' governments, the Court of Justice, and the Commission—controlled not by the Parliament but by European big business.[119]

When the EEC Commission under Hallstein tabled plans for an accelerated economic union and allotted itself the proceeds of the common external tariff (which would have given it control over the equivalent of some $2.3 billion annually), the plan radically altered the balance within the EEC at the expense of the member states.[120] Coming on the heels of Hallstein's trip to Washington, it also appeared as a coup to return the entire 'European' enterprise back into the Atlantic fold. France therefore withdrew from its obligation to forgo its veto power in the Council of Minis-ters; it recalled its 'European' representatives in July 1965. This effectively brought the EEC to a standstill. De Gaulle, vilified from all sides, rightly claimed that the transfer of sovereignty to the Commission was premature—pending clarification of what he qualified as 'errors or ambiguities in the Treaties relating to the economic union of the Six', the member states could not be expected to alienate vital prerogatives.[121]

The ill-conceived attempt of the EEC Commission to force the pace of supranationalism was not resisted by Gaullist France alone. In the circumstances it went against the interests of all member states. In the mid-1960s their business communities still relied too heavily on the national states to allow a leap into the dark of this magnitude. The ECSC and EEC treaties contained strong anti-cartel provisions, and, like the American anti-trust legislation of the beginning of the century on which they had been modelled, this fostered consolidation of cartel partners into large firms. Such consolidation in 1960s Europe was being actively pursued under national state auspices; and if the EEC provided the framework for it, the Brussels authorities themselves were not (yet) identified as trustworthy guardians of the capitalist interest.[122] On the other hand, French big business was beginning to show dissatisfaction with de Gaulle's 'Grandeur' policies, which had until then worked to unify a broad bourgeois coalition against the working class; but capital had become stronger and the northern European pattern of a selective class compromise with organised labour was beckoning. The president's populist invocation of the threat of 'a [Brussels] technocracy that was for the greater part foreign and that was bound to encroach upon French democracy'[123] meant little to the larger companies and their cadre, and the bourgeoisie felt uneasy with Gaullist politicians defending 'the right of peoples to communism'. De Gaulle's appreciative comment, made on a state visit to the USSR in June 1966, about the role of the Soviet Union in warding off 'the danger of American hegemony' was equally disturbing and ran counter to the ruling class interest of integration into the wider West.[124]

When the 'Empty Chair' crisis was settled in Luxemburg in January 1966, it restored unanimous decision-making for issues in which 'very important interests' were at stake.[125] This confirmed the principle that the state cannot relinquish its sovereign power in a liberal arrangement. Paradoxically, then, it was the French contender state legacy that served to ensure that the integration process remains anchored in the liberal tradition pioneered in the English-speaking heartland; Gaullist 'obstinacy' had run its course and served the further progress of European integration. As one perceptive observer commented at the time, 'the tradition of strong central administration in France may prove to be a greater obstacle to the European unity movement than General de Gaulle himself.'[126] With respect to the Atlantic bond, France announced its intention to withdraw from NATO's military organisation in March 1966, although Gaulle privately assured president Johnson that France would nominally remain in the alliance. The conflict over nuclear policy and the bitter divisions over dealing with Third World decolonisation lay at the root of this decision. De Gaulle used the occasion to expose the existence of secret protocols committing each NATO state's security services to assist in preventing communist parties from coming to power, with special arrangements in place for France and Italy. This involved, according to a US Joint Chiefs of Staff document dating from 1952, 'political, paramilitary, and psychological' actions which were to be kept secret from the host governments. For France at least, this sort of intervention would henceforth be seriously impaired; we return in Chapter 5 to the cases of Greece, Portugal and Italy.[127]

'Nationalism', then, is not a category that tells us much about the supposed obstacles to integration.[128] Rather, Atlantic and European integration from the perspective of transnational capital should ideally not transgress the boundaries of the separate states and establish sovereignties beyond them—other than that of capital. This is why the capitalist interest in Europe could at this juncture live with 'nationalist' politicians within certain limits. First, because they reaffirmed a principle of liberalism vital to business, and, second, because they helped to redraft the geopolitical map away from the Atlantic heartland and demarcate a space in which 'Europe' could profit from the geopolitical and geo-economic advantages of its own making. De Gaulle would retire from politics in the wake of the 1968 explosion, but the legacy he left allowed Willy Brandt, first as foreign minister in the Grand Coalition, and then as chancellor, to pursue an active policy of opening up to the east. In this light it should come as no surprise that Brandt in his memoirs devotes a laudatory 20 pages, titled 'The Great Charles and Little Europe', to de Gaulle.[129] For here was the groundwork of detente and international compromise (notably also on the North–South dimension), and a European policy overtly constructed from a national interest vantage points, for which Brandt would later win acclaim—perhaps also because he did not articulate this strategy, as did de Gaulle, in terms antagonising the United States.[130]

Monetary Battle Lines

The post-war monetary order was based on the overwhelming productive and financial clout of the United States, which in 1945 held 90 per cent of the world's monetary gold reserves. The dollar, established as the international reserve currency, had its price fixed against gold, and private finance was restricted from crossing borders except for financing trade and foreign investment.[131] The British pound sterling remained a secondary international currency in the shadow of the dollar, notably to finance international trade. The offshore Eurodollar and Eurocapital markets in the City of London on the other hand developed independently from national economies, preparing the post-1979 return to an era of financial hypertrophy equivalent to that of the *haute finance*, which Polanyi noted as imposing its discipline 'by a timely pull of a thread in the international monetary network'.[132]

American capital was a crucial factor in getting the Fordist project in Western Europe under way on the foundations laid in the Marshall Plan period. The establishment of the EEC's common external tariff threatened to disadvantage US exports to the Common Market, and US companies were exhorted to hop over the tariff by direct investment rather than waiting for the next round of trade negotiations. At the time, the US balance of trade was still positive, but its balance of payments had slipped into the red, both as a result of investment and overseas military expenditure.[133] Kennedy's far-reaching trade proposals already referred to, as well as his 'Atlantic Partnership' offer—each conceived on the assumption that the UK would join the EEC—signalled the high hopes for drawing the West together into a single political economic structure. De Gaulle's veto simply renewed the urgency of foreign direct investment (right after 1958, US investment mainly flowed to 'other Europe', effectively meaning Britain). The Lockean connection is crucial here: in the words of a prominent business economist, 'The norms that govern relations between business and government in the United Kingdom are similar in many respects to those of the United States ... the national atmosphere [generated by the political processes] in the United Kingdom is close to the norms with which US business feels at home.'[134]

In countries with a contender state tradition, on the other hand, the 'atmosphere' is different. The state here is an active presence in the economy. Corporations enjoy privilege and monopoly on account of their relations with government, and they are embedded in finance capital structures organised around big banks. Nevertheless, direct manufacturing investment by US corporations in Europe grew from $2.1 billion to $6.5 billion in 1964 and $12.2 billion in 1969, although conflicts about the extraterritorial application of US trade laws, referred to earlier, led to friction, notably with France.[135]

With manufacturing being shifted abroad, the US lost ground within the wider heartland as it diverted productive forces to military preparedness and foreign interventions, notably the war in Vietnam.[136] If we take the key sector in the Fordist era—the automobile industry—as an indicator (as presented in Tables 1.1 and 1.2), the redistribution at the expense of the United States clearly transpires both within the extended heartland and with Japan (presented in Table 3.1 as a 'vassal state'). The USSR, on the other hand, victorious but devastated in the Second World War, had to bear the brunt of a sustained arms race with the West and was never able to catch up in this sector, even disregarding the fact that private car ownership only later became part of the Soviet concept of economic development. In the critical post-war transition years (1953–65), Soviet defence expenditure as a percentage of GNP was three times the West European average and 10 times that of Japan.[137]

The real Atlantic rift erupted not directly over the industrial shift, but over the value and role of the dollar. The investments referred to above brought key foreign assets into US companies' ownership, but these were paid for by a currency rapidly losing its value due to the eroding industrial power of the United States. This also threatened the international reserve role of the American currency. The French government, concerned over the foreign invasion, was bent on enforcing gold convertibility of the dollar— a policy associated with the name of Jacques Rueff, a neoliberal economist and a member of Hayek's Mont Pèlerin Society. Rueff had been the architect of the monetary reform after de Gaulle's takeover in 1958; his commitment

Table 3.1
Heartland-Contender Development, Arms Race and War
(passenger car production)

Total for Heartland = 100*	1960		1982
		Arms Race, Vietnam War	
USA	54.4		31.3
[EEC] (including UK)	42.0		61.3
Contenders in %			
Japan ('vassal state')	1.3		43.3
		(Arms Race)	
USSR	1.1		8.3

Source: Calculated from Dicken (1986: 283, Table 9.1).
Note: *The figures add up to 100 with the (small) shares of Canada and Australia, which are not shown in this table.

to squeeze inflation out of the French economy led to the drastic reduction of French workers' incomes in the first decade of the Fifth Republic. The convertibility enforcement, then, set in motion a steady flow of gold across the Atlantic. Various administrative measures meant to restrict dollar convertibility into gold did not prevent a dramatic reduction of US gold holdings. In 1959, the US still held 51.5 per cent of the world monetary gold stock; 10 years later this had decreased to 27 per cent. Gold held by the European states (not counting Britain) doubled in the same period. The amount of dollars (convertible into gold) held was almost twice the size of the remaining US gold holdings, so that in 1969 the US Treasury would not have been able to pay off short-term claims. Under the terms of the Bretton Woods agreement, the United States was insolvent.[138]

Rueff had already proposed a devaluation of the dollar at the time of the 'Empty Chair' crisis. The US would then be able to honour dollar convertibility and pay out gold to foreign holders, but no longer profit from the artificially high exchange rate to buy up overseas assets. A return to the gold cover of the American currency was by now a European interest, but then, as Eric Helleiner has argued, the gold standard (even in the diluted form of a gold-dollar standard) is much more compatible with nationalist economic policy than often assumed. Indeed, Hayek was fearful of the gold standard because a national monetary policy can always come under the influence of democratic politics; hence he favoured a free market of currencies instead.[139] As with other aspects of the Gaullist position, the remaining EEC members did not want to desert or confront the United States on this issue, and de Gaulle's gold policy was abandoned by 1966. The 1967 devaluation of the pound—the first defence line of the dollar—has already been mentioned. After that, the loss of US economic clout (including a decline of the American share in world trade from 25 per cent in 1964 to

10 per cent in 1969 in spite of inflation) 'made the dollar's hegemony an anomaly left over from wartime conditions.'[140]

In 1971, the Nixon administration decided to cut the dollar off from the gold standard. This created, by default, a market regime for the world's currencies through the system of flexible exchange rates, eventually agreed on two years later. Though the outcome would be very much in the spirit of Hayek's ideas, the actual measures were introduced from a rather narrower, quasi-mercantilist mindset that included a 10 per cent tariff mark-up on all imports into the US. 1971, then, was a high point in Atlantic rivalry, as well as straining relations with Japan, because the United States effectively cancelled a foreign debt of $68 billion by no longer honouring its obligation to convert dollars into gold. As Riccardo Parboni argues, 'the United States chose the tempo and form of the crisis, and thus managed to effect a devaluation of the dollar that would not compromise its dominant position as international means of payment.'[141] US money creation, amounting to 10 per cent per year, now began to fuel worldwide inflation for a number of years. Dollars held abroad were accumulating in the London Euromarkets, which in 1979 would eventually be brought under control again by the US Federal Reserve. But in the intervening years they seemed far removed from any systemic discipline, and instead 'passively' provided credit finance for the industrialisation of the Third World and the modernisation of Soviet bloc industry. This became part of the worldwide advance of forces contesting the pre-eminence of the capitalist West, to which we turn in Chapter 4.

Notes

1. Stikker held directorships in the NHM, the colonial pillar of today's ABN–AMRO bank, and in Heineken; in the late 1950s he would be appointed secretary-general of NATO. Cf. Stikker (1966) and van der Pijl (1984).
2. Milward (2000: 119–20).
3. Ibid.: 189–92; Marjolin (1989: 246); cf. Spaak (1971: 235).
4. Its directors, D'Arcy Cooper and Rijkens, were members of the Anglo-German Fellowship, the core body propagating appeasement to Hitler (Overbeek 1990: 69; Rijkens 1965: Chapter 5). Cf. Studiegroep (1942, 1944). It is testimony to the degree of understanding these men had of the problems they were facing that it was Rijkens who recruited David Mitrany, the 'father' of functionalist integration theory, as an adviser to Unilever in 1944. Mitrany was himself involved in British post-war planning and remained with Unilever until 1960 (Mitrany 1975: 31).
5. The 'socialisation of agriculture' thesis was first developed by my student in Amsterdam, Mark Goedhart, in 1978, in the context of our project on European integration. Of course, lobbying in Brussels is often mentioned as a form of influence. But clearly this is a far cry from having a hand in the legislative process. That internationalist politicians consciously sought to bypass domestic constituencies was already evident in the planning of Benelux in wartime London (Spaak 1971: 78–80).

6. C. Wilson (1968: 13–4); cf. Afanasiev and Kolovnyakov (1976: 24, 122). Unilever had one foot in the EEC and one in EFTA, the free trade zone established by the UK in 1959. Therefore it could declare in a 1963 statement, following the rejection of British EEC membership, that Unilever was 'in' whatever happened (quoted in C. Wilson 1968: 11). On Unilever's European profile, which gained it the epithet of the 'seventh member state' in the late 1960s, cf. Sampson (1968: 104–9).

7. The initiators of the Bilderberg project included Joseph Retinger, secretary to the Polish government-in-(western)-exile; Paul Rijkens; the Dutch Prince-Consort, German-born Bernhard; and Paul van Zeeland (Rijkens 1965: 145–6).

8. *The Economist*, 26 February 1955.

9. Rijkens (1965: 141, 143).

10. Eringer (1980: 30). Cf. the lists of participants in the appendix to Eringer's study.

11. This applies to the Congress for Cultural Freedom mentioned in Chapter 2, the European Movement (Retinger, the secretary of Bilderberg, was also secretary general of the EM), and the Carnegie Endowment led by Joseph Johnson, secretary of the American Bilderberg section from 1954 (P. Thompson 1980: 162, 166, 179). I have written at greater length on Bilderberg in van der Pijl (1984: 182–4; 1998: 121–2).

12. Milward (2000: 353); Deubner (1977: 54 and *passim*). As Milward notes, after the Marshall Plan credit lines expired, West Germany replaced the US as the supplier of Europe's equipment and machine tool needs, which countries paid for by exporting to the German market. The concentration of the economies of little Europe on Germany re-presented a shift away from their prior exports to the British market and prefigured the establishment of the Common Market (Milward 2000: 136–55, 167–71).

13. Grosser (1978: 141–2); Monnet (1976: 483).

14. Such outsiders included the German Social Democratic leader, Kurt Schumacher, on the left, or Anthony Eden on the right (Grosser 1978: 139; Deubner 1977: 46–7).

15. Milward (2000: 196); cf. Spaak (1971: 228).

16. The UK did not want trade liberalisation to take shape within Europe first, behind an EEC common tariff, even though this was not itself a breach of GATT, which allowed a preferential tariff policy as an interim measure (Overbeek 1990: 97; Marjolin 1989: 245).

17. Eden (1960: 337, emphasis added).

18. cf. Werth (1967: 18). The point-man of the 'Society of Europeans' in the Mollet government was Christian Pineau; cf. Marjolin (1989: 253–5).

19. Spaak (1971: 231, 245–6); Marjolin (1989: 282–3); Grosser (1978: 197).

20. Deubner (1977: 121–2, 116–7).

21. Delaunay (1984: 235, Table 52); on the restructuring of business, see Djelic (1998).

22. Marjolin (1989: 322–3; cf. 259). On 1 January 1959, France was able 'to make the same tariff cuts and the same advance towards alignment with the common external tariff as her EEC partners.' Actually it was at the insistence of the French government that intra-Community trade restrictions were being dismantled at an accelerated rate. By the end of 1961, quantitative restrictions, on which the French economy had relied for a century, had been practically removed, while intra-Community customs duties saw a reduction by 50 per cent in mid-1962.

23. I note in passing that all capitalist development is characterised by the trend towards concentration and centralisation of capital, so that the expropriation of smaller capitalist is its constant accompaniment. This classical Marxist thesis has received a novel elaboration in the work of Nitzan and Bichler as 'differential accumulation'. Cf. Bichler and Nitzan (2004), and Nitzan and Bichler (2000, 2002).

24. de Gaulle (1970: 178–9, 182).

25. This is an example of Boyer's (2001) concept of 'hybridisation', in which a national economy under the pressure to integrate more closely into the world economy mobilises

its own specific resources to improve the competitive position of the capital operating from its jurisdiction. Milward (2000) recognises the aspect of the persistence of the state in the new European context ('the European Rescue of the Nation-State') but fails, like all mainstream theorists, to account for capital as a structuring force. Hence there are no classes and certainly no class politics in his work. The same applies to the equally indispensable and yet limited work of Ernst Haas (1968).

26. de Gaulle (1970: 186–7).
27. Adenauer (1968: 63).
28. de Gaulle (1970: 196).
29. Ibid.: 206. As de Gaulle explained again in 1962, 'the only Europe that is or could be possible is that of states, leaving aside, of course, that of myths, fiction, and shows' (quoted in Newhouse 1967: 21).
30. Marjolin (1989: 329).
31. Schröder (not to be confused with the later Chancellor of the same name) had been appointed over the opposition of Adenauer's 'Europe clique', who considered him as 'Washington's man' in Bonn (Newhouse 1967: 135). Cf. Monnet (1976: 515–6).
32. J.W. Evans (1967: 5–6).
33. The OEEC was itself revamped in 1961, when the USA and Canada joined the renamed Organisation for Economic Cooperation and Development (OECD), which aimed to coordinate economic policy.
34. See van der Pijl (1984: 195–201).
35. Lerner and Gorden (1969: 69). There were stirrings of a leftist Popular Front against the OAS, the die-hard colonialists who felt betrayed by de Gaulle's negotiations with Algeria, and who were terrorising the country with the bombing campaign; on the other hand, there were reports about an anti-de Gaulle bloc being formed by Atlanticist elements in France, including some of Monnet's associates (Werth 1967: 272, cf. Chapter 9, *passim*). Maurice Duverger highlights the fact that only the 1962 referendum and constitutional reform lent democratic legitimacy to the putsch of 1958 (Duverger 1968: 18–9).
36. Monnet (1976: 551).
37. Ibid.: 504.
38. Goedhart (1978).
39. Milward (2000: 253); Goedhart (1978: 54–5); Afanasiev and Kolovnyakov (1976: 27).
40. In addition to a free internal market (with a common external tariff) for agricultural products, a system of intervention was developed based on high market prices and purchases (or export subsidies) in case of excess production (Goedhart 1978; Newhouse 1967: 56). For the different segments of agriculture and their interests, cf. Maraveyas (1996).
41. Thus in steel, corporations in Europe in the 1960s tended to be less market-oriented than their American counterparts. They were very efficient for sure, but concentrated their innovations in *process* improvement, whereas US steel corporations, dependent on competitive advantage in an environment that is more uncertain (apart from the bilateral oligopoly arrangements with the automobile firms and other large steel consumers), tend to be *product* innovators (Miller 1971: 100–1; cf. *NRC-Handelsblad*, 20 December 1975).
42. Overbeek (1979: 61–4); Swann (1992: 338); cf. Hargreaves (1988: 78–83). The idea of finding suitable 'moderates' among African nationalists, to ensure a smooth transition while retaining rights of access, is a theme that runs right through the negotiations.
43. For the Meiji revolution from above that instituted the directive state in Japan, see Norman (1940) and Sansom (1950: Chapter 13, esp. 339–51).
44. Park (2004: 84); Hartcher (1999: 189). The term '1940 economic structure' comes from Japanese academic Yukio Noguchi.
45. Hummel (2000: 131).

46. Kolko and Kolko (1972: 519). However, the Americans had little concern with the other members of the Allied Council for Japan, and, as the British member of the Council put it, 'treated it with frivolous derision' (quoted in Reischauer 1965: 48).
47. Halliday and McCormack (1973: 14–5); Reischauer (1965: 38).
48. The 'Flying Geese' metaphor was coined in 1937, in the period of Japanese expansion in Asia that would end in the Second World War, by the Japanese economist A. Kaname, on the basis of the experience of the Japanese textile industry. Industrialisation develops through periods of free trade and protectionism, from import to domestic production to export, at which stage inter-state conflicts will become more probable (Bernard and Ravenhill 1995: 172–3).
49. Deyo (1989: 34).
50. Adam (1967: 25).
51. C. Johnson (2002: 25–6).
52. Pluvier (1999: 290–1); G. Kolko (1988: 174).
53. McCoy (1991: 193).
54. Ibid.: 144–56, 160; *Time*, 9 May 1955. Cf. Young and Kent (2004: 246–7).
55. Fleming (1961, Vol. 2: 697); cf. Fall (1967: 89); Lacouture (1966: 10–3, 34).
56. Bassett and Pelz (1989: 227).
57. G. Kolko (1988: 128–9).
58. On the grounds of US intervention in Vietnam, see Kahin (1986) and Werner (1985). As Philip Everts noted in a study of Thailand written during the Vietnam war, the mutual conflicts and territorial claims among South and Southeast Asian states were far more acute than any threat from China, and these conflicts brought more advantages to China than it could ever have achieved through actions of its own (Everts 1968: 18).
59. Fall (1967: 8).
60. Pluvier (1999: 295–6); cf. Everts (1968).
61. Löwy (1981: 134–5); cf. E. Wolf (1973); N.K. Vien in *Le Monde Diplomatique*, April 1973, p. 12. As late as 1975, only 12 per cent of the overall Vietnamese labour force was employed in industry, declining to 10 per cent in 1987 once the end of the war allowed the population to recover (CIA Handbook of Economic Statistics data in *Newsweek*, 17 July 1989). When the Americans were forced out of Vietnam, they left behind an industrial infrastructure in the Saigon area that they had erected at the cost of US$12 billion (W. Burchett in *De Groene Amsterdammer*, 22 October 1975). On Vietnamese economic development after the war, cf. G. Kolko (1997).
62. Lacouture (1966: 26, 35). On Nhu and the drugs trade, see McCoy (1991: 197, 203). On Kennedy's Vietnam policy, cf. Hess (1993: 82–3).
63. G. Kolko (1985: 132–3). On the evolution of the political science of intervention and nation-building in providing rationales for the war in Vietnam, see Gendzier (1995); Chomsky (1969); Packenham (1973).
64. de Gaulle (1970: 269).
65. Lacouture (1966: 83).
66. G. Kolko (1985: 117). Troop levels from Young and Kent (2004: 343, box).
67. The Pentagon had all along organised raids into North Vietnam through Laos and the Gulf of Tonkin (Young and Kent 2004: 334; McCoy 1991: 205).
68. Pluvier (1999: 293–4).
69. Fulbright (1970: 128); the resolution is discussed on pp. 57–9. Johnson was apparently aware that he was presenting Congress with a fake incident when the resolution was passed; cf. Hitchens (2002: x).
70. Adam (1967: 24, Table 2); cf. Bernard and Ravenhill (1995), and Chapter 9 of this book.
71. Having been forced to admit British capital under a treaty of 1834, the largest foreign plantation owners in Indonesia were HVA (Dutch) and Harrisons and Crosfield (UK)

(*Fortune*, July 1948, p. 91). The history of Royal Dutch Shell begins in north Sumatra in the late nineteenth century (Gerretson 1971, Vol. 1: 55).

72. Idenburg (1961: 130–1).
73. Stikker (1966: 137); cf. van der Pijl (1984: 168) for further details and references.
74. Wertheim (1992: 158–9).
75. G. Kolko (1988: 175). On the nature of state formation in Indonesia, cf. Lombard (1981).
76. Pluvier (1999: 306–14); Wertheim (1992: 145–6). Also in 1957, the 'Henry Ford' of Indonesia, W. Soerdyadjaya, an ethnic-Chinese entrepreneur, set up Astra International, which would grow into a $2.5 billion operation in the early 1990s and control 60 per cent of the country's car market, assembling for Toyota, BMW and others (*Newsweek*, 29 March 1993). On the penetration of society by the military state class, see *Le Figaro*, 7 July 1973.
77. de Beus (1977, Part V: 244–403). The New Guinea issue saw the final episode of Paul Rijkens' role as a class strategist, when he formed a group named after him which sought to negotiate with Sukarno directly, in order to safeguard the interests of Unilever and other Dutch companies from the confrontation and the eventual military expedition; cf. Rijkens (1965: 160–81).
78. In 1965 Singapore became a separate political entity dominated by an ethnic Chinese population.
79. Pluvier (1999: 336); G. Kolko (1988: 176).
80. G. Kolko (1988: 180–1); Wertheim (1992: 173–205).
81. *Time*, 15 July 1966. On the continuing repression in Indonesia into the 1990s, cf. the articles in *The Observer*, 28 July 1996 (which also contain information about the role of the UK in the 1965 coup).
82. Wertheim (1992: 167–8); cf. *Neue Zürcher Zeitung*, 20 June 1973.
83. Pluvier (1999: 346).
84. Anti-Japanese riots erupted in 1974 and complicated the Suharto regime's efforts to bring Japanese instead of US capital into its industrialisation projects in the outlying areas such as north Sumatra; cf. *Neue Zürcher Zeitung*, 4 February 1975.
85. There had been an earlier attempt to unite Malaysia, the Philippines and Indonesia in 'Maphilindo', three countries in which the Malay ethnic group is dominant (Adam 1967: 14–8). Singapore and Thailand were the additional members of ASEAN; cf. Bowles and MacLean (1996).
86. G. Kolko (1988: 183–4). On the resistance in Indonesia to US pre-eminence, cf. F. Cayrac in *Le Monde Diplomatique*, November 1972, p. 21.
87. Robison and Hadiz (2004: 30). In the later phase and after the fall of Suharto, the financial press became more forthcoming about the web of business interests centred on the Suharto family, the Salim group of the Chinese-Indonesian tycoon, Liem Sioe Long, and the investment firm of the Islamic convert, but equally Chinese-Indonesian, 'Bob' Hasan. Cf. diagrams and articles in *Financial Times*, 17 October 1995, 13 February 1997 and 16 January 1998.
88. Of the 150 parties registered for the first elections after Suharto's downfall, more than 90 were apparently bankrolled by Suharto family members or associates (Robison and Hadiz 2004: 231).
89. *The New York Times*, 9 April 1967; Young and Kent (2004: 339); McCoy (1991: 215).
90. G. Kolko (1985: 166, 211).
91. On US war crimes in Indo-China, see Hitchens (2002: 19–43); G. Kolko (1985; 1997); I will come back to this in Chapter 11 of this book. One particularly brutal aspect of the US counter-insurgency effort was the Phoenix programme. Started in 1967, it included targeted assassinations, abduction and torture. Such was the brutality of this programme that Australian secret service officers working for the CIA had to swear never to reveal what they had witnessed. The Phoenix programme was scaled down after 1969 because of the excessive abuse of its victims (Richelson and Ball 1990: 232).

92. Quoted in Werth (1967: 412). When visiting Moscow in 1966, Soviet leaders told the French president that China was trying to provoke a war between them and the US by obstructing the delivery of Soviet aid to the Vietnamese through China. Since the USSR had to send supplies by ship to Haiphong, then routinely under US air attack, the accidental sinking of a Soviet supply vessel could trigger such a war (ibid.: 408–9).

93. Ibid.: 406; report of Soviet ambassador Zorin regarding conversations with the North Vietnamese ambassador in Paris in 1969, in *Soviet Foreign Policy During the Cold War: A Documentary Sampler*, available at www.seas.gwu.edu (17 November 1997, p. 16).

94. Ponting (1989: 191–2).

95. Ibid.: 224–5; Dorril and Ramsay (1992: 86). On the Polish-Soviet initiative, see Soviet documents on *Soviet Foreign Policy During the Cold War: A Documentary Sampler*, www.seas.gwu.edu (17 November 1997, p. 13).

96. Caute (1988: 1–8); Servan-Schreiber (1969: 9–28).

97. Hoffmann (1978: 33–7).

98. The back-channel through Chinese-born, right-wing society hostess Anna Chennault was discovered by the outgoing Johnson administration, but both Johnson and Hubert Humphrey, the Democratic presidential candidate, felt that US national interest would be damaged by exposure (Hitchens 2002: 7–16; *The Guardian*, 9 August 2000).

99. McCoy (1991: 223); G. du Jonchay in *Le Monde Diplomatique*, October 1972, pp. 12–5; troop levels from Young and Kent (2004: 343, box).

100. The Asians' fears of Chinese expansion were motivated by a conference of the 'Indo-Chinese Left' held in Guandong, in the absence of a Soviet representative. General Lon Nol, the new strongman, later signed the letter (which the Americans had written for him) requesting US intervention (Daniel 1970: 416–9; Scott 1986: 25; *De Volkskrant*, 13 January 1972).

101. C. Johnson (2002: 12). In 1974, Khieu Sampan, one of the Khmer Rouge leaders, could still could promise a 'veritable peace in Cambodia' (in *Le Monde Diplomatique*, November 1974, pp. 1, 8), a year before taking power. Chinese support for the Khmer Rouge under Pol Pot would crystallise the conflict with Vietnam and the USSR, and entailed the support of the United States for the Khmers. Cf. John Pilger in *De Volkskrant*, 2 May 1998; background in Richard Gott in *The Guardian*, 12 November 1979.

102. Hitchens (2002: 46 and Chapter 4, *passim*); Colodny and Gettlin (1992: 48–9); N.R. Chanda in *Le Monde Diplomatique*, December 1972, pp. 6–7. On Pakistani Islamism, cf. Chapter 10 of this book.

103. On another occasion (still in 1975) he even claimed that 'we are living in a revolutionary situation.' Quotes in Hitchens (2002: 97, 103). In the research for my novel, *The Seizure of Power* (1992, in Dutch), I found that, against the background of separatism in the Moluccan islands and Irian Jaya (former Dutch New Guinea), the Indonesian intelligence services were in 1975–77 actively involved in stirring up unrest among the Moluccan diaspora in the Netherlands in order to destabilise the Social Democratic majority government critical of Indonesia's handling of the Timor crisis.

104. Kissinger (2000: 141).

105. The role of nuclear weapons in 'extended deterrence', as a means to create space for pursuing more specific strategies under the nuclear umbrella, has been argued cogently by Mike Davis (1982).

106. As the French president put it later, 'there is no common policy in the Congo or in Berlin or in the Far East' (quoted in Sulzberger 1972: 839–40; cf. 586). Cf. Kniazhinsky (1984: 216).

107. British intelligence in this period intercepted diplomatic cipher traffic in and out of the French embassy in London, passing on strategic information to the US (P. Wright 1987: 111–2).

108. Bufe and Grumbach (1979).

109. Newhouse (1967: 29).
110. Kirchheimer and Menges (1965: 96–7); Sulzberger (1972: 881).
111. A former FRG defence ministry official was arrested in Spain through the good offices of the Franco dictatorship, thanks to the excellent relations of Strauss among the European Far Right. We return to this in Chapter 5 (Kirchheimer and Menges 1965: 104).
112. Allison (1971); Garthoff (1987).
113. Spaak (1971: 313); Beaufre (1966: 62). The British also saw nuclear weapons as a negotiation tool, but with the US, not with the USSR (cf. Dorril and Ramsay 1992: 55–6).
114. Newhouse (1967: 34–7).
115. Quoted in ibid.: 40. In addition, West Germany refused to accept France's proposals for a higher grain price because it did not want to subsidise French agriculture so generously as to allow de Gaulle to finance the French nuclear deterrent (Kniazhinsky 1984: 299, 219; Newhouse 1967: 30–1).
116. Quoted in Newhouse (1967: 51–2).
117. The fact that the Hallstein proposals were endorsed by the Action Committee for the United States of Europe at its twelfth session in West Berlin only illustrates the Atlantic credentials of Monnet's enterprise and to what extent its animators, like Hallstein himself, belonged to an age that was passing (Newhouse 1967: 86).
118. Calleo (1976: 20).
119. Holman (2004).
120. 'The majority of the Commission,' writes Marjolin (himself a commissioner at the time), 'wanted to introduce a real institutional innovation and alter extensively, radically, the balance of power that had been written into the Treaty of Rome' (Marjolin 1989: 349). Cf. Kniazhinsky (1984: 221). Incidentally the Federal Republic was wary of extending the Commission's power relative to the Council's, because the Brussels bureaucracy was seen as French-oriented and unwieldy (Newhouse 1967: 68; Marjolin 1989: 349).
121. Quoted in Marjolin (1989: 353).
122. This transpired among other things in the wave of state-monitored business consolidation in the EEC countries and Britain in the mid-1960s, in the spirit of meeting the 'American challenge'; cf. van der Pijl (1984: 244–9) and Servan-Schreiber (1969).
123. Quoted in Monnet (1976: 569); cf. Newhouse (1967: 92, 125–6, 147). On the comparison between a north European pattern of selective class compromise and south European confrontation, see Farhi (1976).
124. The politician, René Capitant, quoted in Kniazhinsky (1984: 300); de Gaulle, quoted in Werth (1967: 407).
125. Kniazhinsky (1984: 205); Marjolin (1989: 354).
126. Newhouse (1967: 65).
127. Willan (1991: 27–8). Foreign minister Couve de Murville protested to the US about undercover activities in France as early as 1960; cf. van der Pijl (1984: 226). In 1965 this came to a crisis when the Moroccan left-wing leader Ben Barka was abducted and assassinated in Paris, with fingers pointing to the US (Backman et al. 1987: 180). In France Gladio, the NATO undercover network (which I return to in Chapter 5) is said to have involved the close friend and adviser of François Mitterrand, François de Grossouvre; cf. Müller (1991: 52) and Le Crapouillot, 59 (1981), p. 97.
128. Cf. Farhi (1976).
129. Brandt (1990).
130. Cf. the chapter on Brandt in von Braunmühl (1973: 55–92).
131. Gowan (1999a: 16–7).
132. Polanyi (1957: 14).
133. Cf. van der Pijl (1984: 194) and Marjolin (1989: 341).
134. Vernon (1973: 209).
135. US portfolio investments rose from $1.8 billion in 1957 to $5.4 billion in 1964 and remained at that level for the period we are looking at (Vernon 1973: 71, Tables 3–4).

136. The loss of US competitiveness by the Vietnam war was argued by Seymour Melman in 1970.
137. Maddison (1971: 137).
138. Calculated from Davidson and Weil (1970: 42). As the same authors note, gold stocks had hardly increased in absolute terms in that decade despite new South African mines being opened and the receipt of gold payments for Soviet grain imports.
139. Helleiner (1999: 147–8 and *passim*).
140. G. Kolko (1985: 285).
141. Parboni (1981: 8). The dollar was devalued by approximately 30 per cent of its value (Duménil and Lévy 2004: 33); the 68 billion figure comes from Pollin and Zepeda (1987: 15).

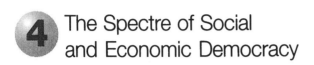

The Spectre of Social and Economic Democracy

MAY 1968 AND THE NEW FREEDOM

In his comments on the 1848 uprising in France, Marx writes that its contribution to the world revolutionary process should not be judged by its own 'tragi-comical accomplishments', but by the 'solid, powerful counter-revolution' it provoked.[1] In this chapter I will argue that the May 1968 movement, the drive for a New International Economic Order (NIEO), and the proposals to establish a control regime for transnational corporations under UN auspices also fit this description. This is not to denigrate what was an authentic, if highly diverse and contradictory, tide of democratic aspirations. But as we can see today, it did serve to mobilise the neoliberal groundswell that restored heartland primacy in the global political economy, sweeping away all before it in the 1980s and 1990s. Indeed the fury of the response indicates that the aforementioned movements were obviously tampering with a vital limit—the democratic revolution that created the 'West' was threatening to push beyond capitalist property relations. This was well captured by two Soviet authors when they observed in 1982 that

> the movement of social protest of the 1960s contributed to ... the ideological thesis according to which true and consistent democracy in social-political life is possible only as the limitation or even negation of capitalism. On the contrary, a number of [neoliberals] in the middle 1970s formulated the opposite thesis: 'true', i.e., 'rationally organized' ... capitalism, is possible only as the restriction of democracy.[2]

International relations played a key role in igniting the democratic radicalism of the 1960s and its ramifications at the global level. The rise of the Third World gave fresh meaning to concepts like socialism and imperialism, a world away from the stale formulae of the cold war.[3] In Western Europe, antiquated academic institutions proved ill-equipped to absorb the exploding student masses. They presented a microcosm of arrogant incompetence, which seemed to apply to the established order at large. How else was one to explain the crimes committed by successive American governments in Vietnam, and the mealy-mouthed support for that policy from the 'allies'? To a new generation, to whom the experiences of the Depression and the Second World War no longer applied and who had high hopes of social mobility, the images flowing in from all corners of the world required radical answers.[4] In the US, the demobilisation of millions of troops, who gained entry into higher education under the GI Act, produced a cosmopolitan student culture in the 1960s; student radicalism on the American campuses blended with black emancipation and opposition to the war in Vietnam, for which black soldiers were being mobilised far out of proportion.[5]

The ground-breaking anti-imperialist student movement actually occurred in Japan. The US–Japanese Security Treaty signed in 1951 gave the US the exclusive right to maintain bases in the country, and more particularly allowed the Americans to intervene militarily in case of a 'civil war'. This effectively restricted the democratic option to re-electing the vassal state party, the LDP. Well before any other youth movement had come into existence, Japanese students were organising mass demonstrations against the renewal of the Security Treaty. In 1960 they forced Japan's then prime minister, N. Kishi (a holdover from the country's wartime leadership), to step down; President Eisenhower had to cancel his visit to the country for security reasons in the same year. The mass struggles against the Security Treaty were a crucial force in shaping *Zengakuren*, the militant left student federation of 1960s fame.[6]

There was a powerful cultural undercurrent to the social changes wrought by the youth movement of the late 1960s and early 1970s, pointing towards increased individualisation and a greater variety of tastes and consumption patterns. The paradox of the May movement is that in spite of the unprecedented rejection of US power, the English-speaking world simultaneously provided the language and symbols that would restore a cultural hegemony that was more profoundly 'American' than anything that went before. The spirit of Jack Kerouac's cult novel, *On the Road*, or the hedonism associated with sexual licentiousness and recreational drug use, emerged from a counter-culture that thought of itself as revolutionary. But capital, too, is a revolutionary force, always looking to incorporate social inventions for profit. Mass consumption was therefore transformed rather than transcended by the youth culture, crystallising between Carnaby Street and San

Francisco Bay. The new pop music, incorporating elements of the blues but sidelining high-brow modern jazz, was a key component of this and fortunes were made in it.[7] When in a parallel development, Steve Jobs placed the personal computer in the layman's hands, he inaugurated a new dimension in mobility just as Henry Ford had done with the Model-T. But consumption patterns were leaving the black austerity of the Detroit automaker far behind. The musical *Hair* popularised erotic entertainment and the number of sex shops in Paris rose from 3 to 45 within the year 1970 alone.[8] As David Caute writes, 'The hippy-rock-drugs culture disturbed the Puritan ethic but it also served as an experimental space station for the new, dynamic capitalism. Thousands of artisan workshops emerged to pioneer products and pleasures which big business would later mop up.'[9]

This was of course far from evident at the time, and thus the challenge to capitalist discipline posed by the radical departures from Fordist regimentation was a real concern. Among the most astute of contemporary analyses was that of Daniel Bell, the red-baiting intellectual of the McCarthy era and author of the 'End of Ideology' thesis. Bell argued that the welfare state tends to disconnect individuals from the material and psychological limitations of their economic position. Just as the Fordist economy increases 'discretionary income' (that part of income used to develop a consumption style of one's own choice beyond the necessities of life), so, Bell claims, 'the expansion of higher education and the extension of a permissive social atmosphere has widened the scope of *discretionary social behaviour*.' On this basis, youngsters of relatively modest background can emancipate from the strictures of class, and begin to think that for them too life is a terrain of unlimited possibilities and participation. 'As the traditional class structure dissolves, more and more individuals want to be identified, not by their occupational base (in the Marxist sense), but by their cultural tastes and life-styles.'[10]

This, in Bell's view, becomes a political problem because the young are drawn towards an 'adversary culture', the struggle of the free creative spirit against the conventions of society that is inherent in modernism. Everybody thus begins to think they are entitled to join the *avant-garde* of society and clamour for radical change on the assumption that society has arrived in a sphere 'beyond necessity', 'at the end of history, in the kingdom of perfect freedom.'[11] What therefore has to be challenged is the context in which a mass-based 'adversary culture' takes shape. The solution that emerges from Bell's analysis is *to restore micro-economic rationality in each individual's life-cycle* and remove the social dimension of Keynesian demand management and redistribution. However, around 1968 such ideas were held only on the margins of the profession of economics, by the followers of Hayek and Friedman. The ascendant force at the time was the Left, a Left breaking away from the encrusted structures of representative socialism.

Forward and Back to Economic Emancipation

The New Left crystallised out of a revival of interest in unorthodox or marginalised varieties of Marxism, from Rosa Luxemburg to Wilhelm Reich, Antonio Gramsci and Herbert Marcuse. Its intellectual origins go back to the crisis in the communist movement following the Soviet clampdown on the Hungarian uprising in 1956, but its mass base dates from the 1960s.[12] The 'Situationist International', a collective of Paris-based artists and academics, deserves pride of place among the contemporary expressions of the New Left, because the very accuracy of its ideas exemplify how a revolutionary worldview can be accommodated by existing society if it is not pursued as a practical project by the revolutionaries. 'Situationist theory,' Caute writes, 'inherited from Dada and Surrealism the vision of a playful society in which individual self-expression would replace the solemn and false masks worn by those trapped in the productive process.'[13] Guy Debord, founder and (with Raoul Vaneigem) the most important and best-known of the Situationists, develops a critique of passive consumption and the mediatisation of society in *The Society of the Spectacle* of 1967. The 'spectacle', 'the sector which concentrates all gazing and all consciousness', has become the central node of rule in contemporary society. Today—the age in which the 'Big Brother' TV show has replaced the image of Orwell's 'Big Brother' dictator controlling his subjects day and night, we can perhaps appreciate the perceptiveness of Debord's observations on how human subjectivity in contemporary society is being objectified and commodified by creating a closed media circuit in which daily life is encapsulated. Alienation, Debord argues, has reached the point where all autonomous existence is being turned inside out and daily life becomes a pathetic replica of the mediatised lives of celebrities from the world of spectator sports and entertainment.[14]

The dynamics of social change have apparently been displaced from the productive process into the process of consumption: from 'being' to 'having'; but the joy of consumption is not even in 'having' real things any more, but in 'being' in the temple of the spectacle, satisfying our desire for symbolic gratification.[15] Yet this transformation is simultaneously an opportunity to shift popular aspirations for a better society to a level *beyond economics* and tackle the very structures of alienation and political class relations. To achieve a socialist society, Debord claims, we must also emancipate ourselves from the economic definition of revolution. Combating alienation is more important than fighting for better wages, because the Fordist system has found ways of buying off political aspirations with economic concessions, and has transformed the conscious producer into a passive consumer addicted to a numbing 'spectacle'. For Daniel Bell, as we saw, the emancipation from the economy is a challenge that must be countered by *reverting* to the economy. For Debord, on the other hand, 'the proletariat cannot itself come to power except by becoming the class of consciousness.'[16]

The May movement would evolve along these conflicting lines. It was sparked off by the student movement, but unexpectedly triggered a social explosion of unprecedented proportions that would resonate across Europe and beyond. On 13 May, Paris saw a million-strong demonstration under the banner 'Students, Teachers, Workers—Solidarity'; 10 days later, some 10 million workers, roughly half the working population of France, was on strike.[17] De Gaulle hurried to consult with French military commanders in Germany, as revolution seemed around the corner. There had been a build-up of working class power over several years; the scarcity of labour emboldened workers to challenge established hierarchies in the workplace and management speed-up practices. But from the May revolt onwards, class struggles were beginning to be experienced by many 'as signs of an incipient social transformation—the beginning of the transition from capitalism to socialism'.[18]

Traditional labour parties and trade unions initially had great difficulty coming to grips with these movements. In 1969 Harold Wilson, the Labour prime minister of the UK, summed up the concerns of established Social Democracy when he observed that 'we face the problem of an assertion of the power of the factory floor, a problem ... which is growing throughout Europe, [and] to which no country has so far found an answer.'[19] The communist parties too were ill-prepared for the May revolt. The French Communist party tended to look upon the students as spoiled brats (*'fils de papa'*) and famously prevented them from fraternising with the workers in order not to forfeit the chance to gain material improvements. But then, Soviet communism and Marxism-Leninism had little appeal left among the young, and Che Guevara and Mao became the heroes of the movement instead.[20] Far-left intellectuals tried to pitch in with their own brand of abstract radicalism: Toni Negri was prominent among the authors of lyrical eulogies of 'proletarian violence' that would guide small groups of students on their way to 'armed struggle' in the 1970s.[21]

Popular Fronts in Europe?

In Greece, far-right military seized power in 1967, but otherwise (neo-) fascism as a mainstream force was confined to Portugal and Spain. Hence, where it was available, Social Democracy was propelled into the foreground to deal with the emergency. In 1969, socialists were in government in 14 countries. As those most experienced in achieving an equilibrium between popular aspirations and the 'realities' of cold war and capitalist structural constraints, the socialists were best-placed to accommodate and contain the groundswell of desire for change; even so it would take time to absorb New Left impulses and adjust to the new mood. Government power was no mean asset here. To graduates filling the ranks of a rapidly expanding new managerial and technical middle class *cadre*, the specific blend of left political tradition and the job opportunities offered in the growing state apparatuses of late corporate liberalism was attractive.[22] In Rudolf Bahro's classical phrase, the cadre in society, and Social Democracy in government, embody 'the compromise of interest between the layer of specialists drifting to "transcending the system" and the part of management oriented to "system reform"'.[23] With the option of mass violence closed in most countries, their hour struck in the aftermath of the May movement.

However, in the process of developing policies that meaningfully dealt with the aspirations of a radicalised following, Social Democratic governments tended to take risks which, seen from the United States, for instance, were potentially jeopardising long-term class and geopolitical interests. West German trade unions successfully propagated co-determination structures across Europe; in several countries, plans for subjecting investment decisions to the scrutiny of such corporatist bodies—and thus potentially politicising them—were being considered, often in combination with the codes of conduct for transnational corporations which we return to in the final section of this chapter. Profit on capital too was made the topic of debate. Ideas about the socialisation of a (usually minute) slice of corporate profits were in the air everywhere, pursued furthest in Sweden; although, as Magnus Ryner has shown, even that country's wage-earners' fund proposals were always meant to take the sting out of more radical working class demands.[24] Still the notion itself amounted to contesting the principles on which the power of capital is based. Eventually, therefore, the socialist role would be restricted to what I will call the 1970s 'interregnum' in the next chapter.

Willy Brandt had been foreign minister in the West German Grand Coalition and was elected chancellor of an SPD majority cabinet in 1969. Early on he came to personify the threat—as perceived in Washington and among conservatives everywhere—that events in Europe were slipping out of control. Brandt's role in shaping a European response to the Soviet 'Peace Offensive' under Brezhnev was inspired by ideas on a 'convergence' of the systems of East and West under common technical imperatives. With his close adviser, Egon Bahr, the chancellor developed a strategy of 'change through rapprochement', in which the West could gain the upper hand if only it dared to act on the assumption that corporate liberal capitalism and state socialism were operating under similar constraints. All along, Brandt's aim was to let the necessities of modern production prevail over their political distortion in Eastern Europe and thus activate the centrifugal forces in those states into direct interaction with the West.[25] But a lot of time was spent on convincing the uninitiated that this did not mean surrender to socialism. Even in the Socialist International, Brandt had to defend the need for dialogue with the GDR, although the organisation adopted his detente strategy as policy in 1972.[26] In a speech to the National Press Club in April 1970 in Washington, Brandt likewise stood his ground, professing to a sense of duty '25 years after the end of the war, to try ... and overcome the deadlock of the European frontiers.'[27] The depth of mistrust is perhaps illustrated by the fact that a year later the chancellor had to reassure a meeting of the German business organisation DIHT that talk of a 'socialist Europe' or the 'Yugoslav model' had nothing to do with his *Ostpolitik*.[28]

Careful to remain the balancing force in the centre, the SPD government countered the political radicalisation of West German society (including the party rank-and-file and student membership) by laws enacting professional interdictions for leftists, the *Berufsverbote*.[29] Brandt's adage of 'risking more democracy', however, began to draw growing criticism, as the mood shifted to the need for a *reduction* of democracy.[30] In 1974, in the wake of a landslide re-election, Brandt was forced to step down—an event that was part of a broader campaign against the reformist Left to which I come back in the next chapter. Undaunted, he continued to work for detente and Third World development as chair of the revamped Socialist International and in other roles. With his fellow party leaders in Austria and Sweden, Kreisky and Palme, he championed greater transparency of the world economy and political oversight. In this perspective, the SI should become a component of the regulatory infrastructure of the Western world, along with the EC, OECD, the Club of Rome (the environmental pressure group), and the UN.[31] This complemented the drive for a New International Economic Order and amounted to a politicisation of the transnational economic space hitherto reserved for capital.

At this juncture, the unease about the progressive encapsulation of capital accumulation by class compromise was articulated in the thesis of the 'ungovernability' of Western democracies. In a seminal report to the newly formed Trilateral Commission, Samuel Huntington identified two key problems underlying this ungovernability: one, the equation of democracy with equality; the other, an epochal shift to welfare expenditure, away from defence and paid for by inflation.[32] As Henry Ford II put it in 1976, co-determination schemes then in the process of being 'Europeanized' were threatening companies' 'freedom of decision ... by restrictive legislation and by the efforts of some elements of organized labour and well-intentioned but uninformed critics to participate in the shaping of business decisions'.[33] Clearly the 'problems' had their focus in Europe, whereas 'solutions' were being debated across the Atlantic.

In this respect an even more acute threat to Western hegemony was the resonance of the workers' and students' movement in the communist parties of Western Europe. The danger here was no longer primarily a matter of a link-up with the Soviet bloc. The intervention in Czechoslovakia in 1968 had effectively terminated direction by Moscow as far as the Western European parties were concerned. Instead they developed towards a normalisation and de-radicalisation that came to be known as 'Eurocommunism', a trend manifest in those southern European countries where communism had a purchase among a modern proletariat and Social Democracy was weak, and also in Japan.

Eurocommunism can be traced back to the experience of the anti-fascist Popular Front strategy of the 1935 Congress of the Communist International. Both had their origin in developments in communist parties outside the USSR, and Moscow adjusted to them belatedly and with difficulty.[34] The Spanish Communist Party (PCE), operating underground, adopted the Eurocommunist programme of commitment to parliamentary government and respect for the geopolitical division of Europe, in preparation for its return to legality after Franco; the party's strength was still an imponderable, and the intention of adjusting party strategy to the change from a Hobbesian to a Lockean state-society complex was important.[35] In response to the 1973 coup in Chile, Italy's PCI, the largest communist party in Western Europe, reaffirmed its commitment to parliamentary procedure and existing geopolitical arrangements. Since Allende's scrupulous observance of constitutionality had not prevented Pinochet's seizure of power, however, the PCI general secretary, Enrico Berlinguer, wanted to go further. Partly reflecting the shift among the PCI's own membership and following (in the absence of a strong Social Democracy) and partly in order to gain the confidence of the broad middle strata in Italian society old and new, Berlinguer proposed dropping the 'metaphysical' qualification of Italian Christian Democracy as the 'Right' and instead developing a 'Historic Compromise' with it.[36] The need to ward off West German interference after the replacement of Willy Brandt by Helmut Schmidt, was a further inducement to the Eurocommunist strategy shift.[37]

In France, Eurocommunism was rather an opportunistic label because the French Communist party neither cared as much for the niceties of political theory as did the Italians nor did it have to present its credentials as the Spanish party did. The PCF, as indicated, tended to adopt positions dictated by straightforward working-class interests in the material sphere first. Even so, in 1974, the three parties met to discuss strategy. The French communists' Common Programme with Mitterrand's revamped Socialist party, with its provisions for the nationalisation of France's large corporations, was equally threatening to Western interests.[38]

The 1974 revolution in Portugal was not itself part of the Eurocommunist trend, as the Portuguese communists stuck to traditional Leninist positions. But along with the disintegration of its African colonial empire, the affirmation of post-war European borders and East–West cooperation at the Helsinki Conference in 1975, and the mounting tide of progressive reform in the Third World, it seemed as if the 1960s workers' and students' movement by several intermediary stages and structures was beginning to push the West on the defensive. The rise and growing legitimacy of the PCI in

Italy was in particular a source of great concern. At the Puerto Rico G-7 summit in 1976, President Ford and the leaders of Britain, West Germany and France between them took the decision not to give any aid to Italy in case the PCI were allowed to enter the government.[39] Also in 1976, a communist party conference was convened in East Berlin at the joint initiative of the Italian and Polish parties to 'clarify mutual positions' (i.e., to discuss fundamental disagreements). When the conference surprisingly produced what seemed to be genuine consensus on the need to combine detente with advancing democracy in the specific circumstances of each state (a nod to Eurocommunism) and to support a New International Economic Order, concern in the West that the Left was gearing up to an offensive posture that was realistic and flexible, could only increase.[40]

Henry Kissinger, speaking to an elite foreign policy audience in Boston in March (in his last year as secretary of state), did not fail to raise the alarm about communists masquerading as democrats. Observing that the ties binding the West were not tactical but 'a union of principle in defence of values and a way of life', i.e., linked to capitalism, he cautioned that whatever their pronouncements on policy, the communist parties were the antithesis of democracy. Were they to gain power,

> They would inevitably give low priority to security and Western defence efforts
> .... They would be tempted to orient their economies to a much greater
> extent towards the East ... steer their countries' policies toward the position
> of the non-aligned.[41]

In Chapter 5, I return to the 'strategy of tension' by which the challenge of the Left was met in the second half of the 1970s. Here we must first investigate the demands of the Third World, with which European governments had been seeking a rapprochement since the OPEC price hike of 1973.

THE MIDDLE EAST AND OPEC AS NEW CONTENDERS

The origins of the Organisation of Petroleum Exporting Countries (OPEC) have to be seen against the background of a surge of national independence struggles in the late 1950s in the Middle East and Latin America. In 1958, a popular insurrection brought down the dictatorship governing Venezuela, the key foreign oil supplier to the United States. The oil minister in the new civilian government, Pérez Alfonso, discontinued the policy of unrestrained sales and instead proposed to Washington to establish a hemispheric oil quota system in which Venezuela's relatively expensive oil would be assured a stable market. But throughout the period of OPEC's formation and early activities, no state of the then Third World could on its own have developed a contender state position challenging the West; they could do so only as a bloc. Indeed, having been rebuffed by the Eisenhower administration over his quota plan, Pérez Alfonso began soliciting allies at an Arab Oil Congress in Cairo in April 1959. The Cuban revolution three months earlier and the ensuing expropriation of US-owned assets on the island state inevitably strengthened the hand of those who wanted to renegotiate economic relations with Washington, just as did the demand by the new rulers in Iraq that the concession to the Iraq Petroleum Company be reviewed. In Cairo, Pérez formed a small committee with representatives of oil exporting states, both radicals and conservatives, to ratchet up the recently agreed 50/50 royalty cut with the oil companies to 60/40.[42] The governments of these states (Venezuela, Saudi Arabia, Kuwait, Iran and Iraq), jointly accounting for 80 per cent of world oil exports, established OPEC in 1960. We should not understand this as a solid bloc, because after Iraq had revoked the IPC concession, its exports stagnated, in contrast to the massive growth of Saudi and Iranian oil production through the decade. What was beginning to change, however, was the effective hold of the United States on world oil prices.[43]

The first attempt to use the 'oil weapon' to bolster the political and economic position of the OPEC countries came in 1967, when Egypt imposed a naval blockade on Israel. US President Lyndon Johnson in response proposed to send in the US Navy under a UN Security Council resolution, stating privately that he wanted 'to see [Harold] Wilson and de Gaulle out there with their ships lined up too'.[44] In June, the Israeli armed forces, ordered to pre-empt an expected Arab strike, defeated their enemies in the Six-Day War. Arab oil ministers promptly called an oil embargo against the US and Britain.[45] The Israeli occupation of the Sinai and the closure of the Suez Canal, in combination with the loss of Nigerian oil due to the civil war in Biafra, led the United States to propose that the OECD take on the (re-)distribution of oil supplies among the Western countries. But disagreement among the NATO allies was such that, in spite of considerable arm-twisting, France, West Germany, and Turkey abstained from the motion that recommended a diversion of oil to the embargoed countries (the US and the UK).[46] Although the Arab boycott was thwarted by the majority decision, clear rifts had once again emerged between the English-speaking countries and the others.

Egypt's challenge to the West had obviously been exhausted and the country slipped into a crisis. In 1968, large-scale student and popular rebellions were violently suppressed by the army and police. 'The real logic of the Nasserite experience,' Löwy concludes, 'was the manipulation of state power by a military stratum of petty-bourgeois origin ... and the last years of Nasserism witnessed epidemic public corruption, as the managers of state enterprises enriched themselves in collaboration with private contractors and businessmen.'[47] We see here a more general phenomenon of the state-monitored catch-up economy, in that private capital can expand in construction, trade, agriculture, services and transport, while the state takes on the bulk of investment. This, as Isam al-Khafaji has shown, feeds—through the constant transfer of resources via state orders and commissions—a parasitic bourgeoisie, to the point where it reaches a size and strength that allows it to demand further liberalisation. This internal process happened in Egypt first, because it was the first Arab state to embark on a state-led development process; the turnabout under Anwar Sadat in 1971, from a contender to a vassal of the West, 'came at a time when the ideology of state interventionism worldwide, as well as the superpower competition and economic nationalism in the Third World were still the basic ingredients of the international system.'[48] However, the economic nationalisms of the aspirant contenders in the Third World were too diverse and disjointed to pose a threat to the West. As Löwy has written, their state classes hesitated to 'cross the Rubicon' and move on to socialism.[49] Thus Algeria, his example of 'Bonapartist normalisation', undertook a land reform in 1971, also expropriating French oil companies operating in the Sahara to kick-start original accumulation. But neither policy was pursued sufficiently vigorously to produce the expected result. The country continued to rely on French and other foreign oil companies through majority Algerian-owned joint ventures.[50]

Confining ourselves here to the Middle East, the 'White Revolution' launched by the Shah of Iran in the late 1960s intensified the confiscatory hold of the state on society, and foreign ownership of economic assets was limited to 25 per cent. The revolution from above included land reforms that came close to collectivisation, driving peasants off the land and into the rapidly expanding cities at a rate of between 300,000 and 330,000 a year from 1966 to 1977. But by the mid-1970s, the imbalances created by precipitate urbanisation and private capital accumulation parasitic on the state-driven development effort led to food dependence.[51] In addition, importing advanced technology for the catch-up effort paradoxically created unemployment among the new urban masses, for whom the Shi'a clergy served as the 'focus of opposition' that would eventually sweep away the Shah and his clique.[52] But then, unlike Algeria, Iran developed as a heartland vassal and this made the Shah's regime particularly vulnerable when the tide of anti-Western sentiment mixed with democratic aspirations. In Turkey too, the state-driven modernisation project alienated large sections of the population, notably the Islamic peasantry of Anatolia. When the urban Left became more prominent in the late 1960s, the bloc hitherto supporting the import substitution policy unravelled. The state class, organised around OYAK, the company run by nationalist generals and the largest concentration of economic power in Turkey, felt seriously threatened, as did the private capitalist class with their pro-Western outlook. In 1971, the army seized power amidst mass disturbances.[53] The disjointed pace of industrial development in the countries mentioned is illustrated in Table 4.1.

Table 4.1
Industrial Growth Rates in Middle East and North African Countries and Major Political Changes, 1960–80

	1960–65		1965–70		1970–81	
			Average Annual Growth in Per Cent			
Algeria	1.5	Military Coup	13.3		11.6	
Egypt	20.0		3.8	Sadat Takeover	9.3	
Turkey	12.7		11.6	Military Coup	6.3	
Iran	9.8		14.6		18.6	Islamic Revolution
Developing Countries' Average	6.7		6.5		6.0	

Source: World Bank data in Amineh (1999a: 356, Table 9.8).

As we can see from Table 4.1 the shock-like adjustments characteristic of the contender state experience, each entailing a radically changed pace of growth (upward or downward), hit each country separately and with highly varying results. It is this volatility which brings home the need for a stabilisation of external economic conditions in a multilateral framework if industrial development is to proceed more evenly, and this exactly was at the heart of the NIEO programme that was triggered by the OPEC price hike.[54]

The OPEC Revolt

The oil shock of 1973 accelerated the retreat of the English-speaking West from imperial positions across the globe, heightening the domestic and international crisis of legitimacy in the face of the advancing democratic revolution. Simultaneously, it activated and politically synchronised the aspirations of the disparate array of contender forces: the Soviet bloc and the emerging Third World coalition.

The retreat of the West was expressed in a series of monetary crises, beginning with the devaluation of the British pound sterling in 1967. This, as we have seen, had initially been postponed as part of negotiations with the United States about British support in the Vietnam war, but the Wilson government announced in 1968 that it would not be able to hold the line, and the withdrawal from military commitments 'east of Suez' began three years after that. US President Nixon in response signed a National Security Memorandum mandating an expanded US presence in those areas affected by the UK retreat, but with the American military bogged down in Vietnam, the best Washington could hope for was that the Shah of Iran and the King of Saudi Arabia would continue to effectively act as US vassals in their respective spheres of influence.[55] However, to bolster the position of two prominent OPEC states at a time when world oil demand was catching up with available supplies—with the centrality of the Middle East accordingly enhanced—was a risky measure. With the market power of the oil exporting countries structurally increased because of the rise in demand, a new crisis could easily destabilise the relations between oil producers and consumers.[56] The decision by the Nixon administration in August 1971 to suspend gold convertibility of the US dollar was such a crisis. As indicated in the previous chapter, the amount of dollars in circulation increased by 10 per cent annually for three consecutive years, and the OPEC countries were immediately affected. They lost around half a billion dollars in income within the first five months after the closing of the gold window.[57] The response was to seek upward revisions of royalty agreements, and, in dialogue with the companies—which also needed higher prices—to arrange a coordinated price hike.

Libya set the pace for these developments. Following the closure of the Suez Canal in the aftermath of the Six-Day War, Libya's oil had become more important, and in 1969 radical officers deposed the ruling monarch. The new regime under Colonel Qaddafi became a guiding force not only in raising oil income but also in establishing a connection between detente, Third World development, and forcing foreign capital to respect host state priorities; the programme, in short, of the subsequent drive for a New International Economic Order. Libya's mineral riches had been developed by a maverick company, Occidental Petroleum of the US, which was also active in East–West trade. Unlike the majors, Occidental could afford to ignore the wider geopolitical aspects of the global energy economy, and it built its position by undertaking joint development programmes with Libya. Qaddafi's revolution from above started from these foundations; in the early seventies, the Colonel launched a second, 'cultural' revolution aimed at solidifying a popular base and championing a blend of nationalism and Islamic-Bedouin culture. He also turned the screws on Occidental, raising the royalty to 55 per cent within a year after taking power.[58]

Oil from Libya was sold mainly to Europe, which relied on this source for around 30 per cent of its oil needs. Qaddafi used this dependence to develop excellent relations across the Mediterranean, shopping for French jets and West German chemical factories, and even taking a major share in Italy's industrial crown jewel, FIAT. With the United States, on the other hand, relations quickly deteriorated when Washington was asked to vacate its important Wheelus air base.[59] Indeed, until very recently relations with Libya have been a source of intense Atlantic rivalries to which I will come back later. In the 1970–73 period, the initial Libyan royalty increase set in motion a series of profit-sharing renewals, first by the Shah of Iran, who also successfully claimed 55 per cent. Venezuela then introduced legislation that authorised claiming 60 per cent. The oil companies now drew together and proposed a comprehensive arrangement with all OPEC countries.[60]

The Western oil companies did have an urgent interest in price rises. They were keen to diversify, both in terms of global oil extraction and in refining, petrochemicals and distribution downstream. But oil company profits had been stagnant from 1966 onwards, and cash flow was insufficient to finance such plans. In May 1973, the Aramco partners, Mobil, Exxon, Texaco, and Socal (today's Chevron), met secretly with the king of Saudi Arabia to discuss the price issue. They kept the Nixon administration informed about what they reported as an Arab intention to raise prices.[61] In the course of 1973, US and European independent oil brokers began a buying spree, reading the signs that the buyers' market in oil was ending and prices were expected to go up.[62] Because continental Europe and Japan were much more dependent on Middle East oil than the United States, while the major companies (the Seven Sisters) were US and British (British-Dutch in the case of Royal Dutch Shell), there was bound to be a strong aspect of rivalry involved in any price change. Basically, the Seven Sisters cartel was being widened to include the OPEC cartel, and out of this emerged the broader cartel of big oil, OPEC and all other oil producers, all riding the waves of the great energy bonanza that would soon become reality.[63]

But the *political* thrust of events does not fit into this picture. The radical countries in OPEC—Iraq, Libya and Algeria—defined themselves as champions of the rising Third World, and the Israeli connection in turn made the US the key enemy (along with its client states, such as South Africa and Portugal). Hence the formation of a contender bloc of oil-exporting states was primarily directed against the US, and it rallied around demands for global equity that places the episode in the context of the democratic revolution—irrespective of the domestic democratic deficit in most states. The picture is further complicated by the fact that the Middle East war of 1973 which triggered the oil crisis was launched by Sadat, the new president of Egypt, who had terminated the country's radical stance. As Daniel Yergin argues, Sadat aimed to restore fluidity to the Middle Eastern situation by striking a military blow at Israel and then proposing a settlement; an impossibility as long as the Sinai was in Israeli hands and Egypt in a humiliating position. Sadat's problem was that Washington had so far not reciprocated his turn towards the West, not even after he expelled 20,000 Soviet advisers in 1972. He therefore turned to Syria's Assad for the planned military strike, and to Saudi Arabia for deploying the oil weapon against the West.[64]

The OPEC ministers were actually meeting in Vienna to discuss prices when Egyptian and Syrian forces launched their surprise attack on Israel. Although briefly thrown into disarray, the Israeli forces soon recovered as US war *matériel* to replace their losses was airlifted in (while the USSR was supplying Syria). When the tide of war turned against the Arabs once again, the OPEC ministers decided to raise the price of oil to $5.11 per barrel and to do so unilaterally, no longer in negotiations with the Western oil companies. In mid-October 1973, the Arab states agreed on an oil embargo against the US and the Netherlands, later extended to Portugal, South Africa and Rhodesia, three states engaged in racist wars and oppression in Africa. Britain significantly was not affected because, uniquely under Conservative prime minister Edward Heath, it had kept its distance from the Kissinger line and favoured a conciliatory policy towards the Third World.

With the Middle East still at war, East–West tensions flared up briefly when Soviet leader Brezhnev proposed that the US and the USSR jointly impose a ceasefire on the ground to prevent the impending rout of Egyptian troops, threatening that the Soviet Union would intervene unilaterally otherwise. With Nixon incapacitated by the Watergate affair, Kissinger and General Haig, the new White House chief of staff imposed on the president, decided to engage in a dangerous poker game by calling a nuclear alert to scare Moscow off. Luckily for the world, the next day fighting stopped and ceasefire negotiations were opened. The oil embargo remained in place, and prices now skyrocketed to around $16 in a few months' time.[65] The claim that the companies are always beneficiaries of a price hike is borne out by the fact that between third quarter-1972 and second quarter-1974, oil majors' profits would rise by about 150 per cent.[66]

Euro-Arab Rapprochement and Rivalry with the US

It is difficult today to appreciate the profound concern at the time that a full-blown Third World revolt was in the making, but this was certainly the mood. It reminds us of the intensity of the perception of a structural threat and goes some way towards explaining the ferocity of the counter-offensive, the first shots of which were fired in Chile later in the year. The OPEC challenge worked to isolate the United States politically, and the mounting tide of Third World demands in its wake only reinforced this isolation. As Fred Bergsten, who resigned from the National Security Council in 1971 in protest over Nixon's unilateralist measures, wrote in the summer of 1973,

> The United States is the least responsive to Third World needs of any industrialized country at this time .... The United States regards developing countries both large and small (e.g., India and Chile, not to mention Indochina) solely as pawns on the chessboard of global power politics. *Rewards go only to the shrinking list of explicit collaborators.*[67]

With the US stake in the Third World growing, Bergsten warned that the opportunities for raw material-producing countries to use their power against the West were increasing as well. Four countries (Chile, Peru, Zambia and Zaire-Congo) supplied more than 80 per cent of exportable copper, and had organised themselves as a cartel (CIPEC); two others accounted for more than 70 per cent of world tin exports; four countries for more than half of the world's natural rubber; and four for half the world's bauxite supply (Jamaica, Guinea, Guyana and Surinam; with Australia added, 90 per cent). The four major coffee producers had also begun to work together; the same was the case for timber, and so on.[68] In fact, both the copper and the bauxite cartels would be undermined by US vassal states breaking ranks and by actual destabilisation by the US (in the case of Chile and Jamaica), but this would transpire only later. In mid-1973 Bergsten still feared that Third World leverage

> could have a double bite on the United States if used discriminatorily against it, *thereby benefiting the competitive positions of Europe and Japan ...* [as] was attempted in oil by some Arab countries in 1967 and has been actively sought at least by Italy and France in the recent past.[69]

Identifying the additional danger of monetary instability as a result of potentially massive cartel rents, Bergsten also did not fail to point out that military action would only make matters worse, as Vietnam had demonstrated. Any action by the US antagonising Third World countries would also benefit America's rivals who 'will usually be waiting in the wings with money and long-term purchase contracts—in the same way that Japanese and European companies wasted no time entering Chile in the wake of its nationalization of U.S. firms.'[70] Given the profound divisions among the Western states and between them and Japan, and the competitive race for binding Third World states to each bloc, Bergsten advocated the establishment of trilateral import cartels for raw materials, beginning with oil.[71]

When the OPEC price hike came, there was profound mistrust of the United States in Europe and Japan. Nixon, who had severely tested Western solidarity with his monetary and trade measures, appeared to be delegating conduct of foreign policy entirely to Kissinger. The latter's conception of the US as a 'global power', with Europe only as a regional partner (a theme expounded in his 'Year of Europe' speech earlier in 1973), had not inspired much confidence across the Atlantic, and the nuclear alert during the October war inspired even less. Also, there was widespread feeling in Europe that the 'Seven Sisters' had given in a bit too eagerly to OPEC price rises. Since some 80 per cent of the increased dollar income was deposited in international banks, primarily Anglo-American banks, it was felt that US and British business were making a lot of money from the higher energy bill paid by the allies.[72]

This undermined any common stance against OPEC. As economics minister (and future prime minister) Nakasone put it in mid-1973, 'It is inevitable that Japan will competitively follow her own independent direction. The era of blindly following has come to an end.' Japan should therefore position itself 'on the side of the oil producing countries'.[73] The United States on the other hand responded with heavy-handed counter-measures. Thus when Libya right after the OPEC oil shock began a drive to nationalise foreign oil companies, Washington, concerned about a domino effect, responded by locking the country out of the international oil market. Of course this US policy won the active support of the Anglo-American majors.[74]

France was the main opponent of Kissinger's proposal to respond to the OPEC challenge with a consumers' cartel, the International Energy Agency (IEA). Certainly de Gaulle's departure in 1969 had improved relations with Washington. US–French collaboration in neutralising the dangerous rivalries that existed between their respective intelligence and undercover security forces, some of which were involved in heroin trading, smoothed conflict in a sensitive area.[75] But in energy matters and in relations with the Middle East, there was no comparable understanding because interests were simply too diverse. The United States at the time relied on Middle East oil for only 8–12 per cent of its requirements (one-fifth of a total import dependency of 39 per cent); Japan for 85 per cent (with a total import dependency of 98 per cent), and Europe for 60 per cent (92 per cent total import dependency).[76] Washington could therefore take political risks in the Middle East which were unthinkable for the others. 'You only rely on the Arabs for about a tenth of your consumption; we are entirely dependent on them', French president Pompidou told the Americans. 'I won't be able to accept ... a situation which requires us to forgo Arab oil, for even a year.'[77]

Kissinger, meeting with foreign minister Michel Jobert in September 1973 in his new capacity as US secretary of state, encountered hesitation and evasion when he proposed to draw closer together. 'You are nationalized in Algeria, and then our companies go in to take your place,' he told Jobert. 'We might be nationalized somewhere else, and we are replaced by others .... The present method of dealing with the question is suicidal.'[78] But the European governments and Japan had lost confidence in the United States— over Vietnam, over the collapse of the monetary system, and over the tendency in Washington to seek unilateralist solutions. While the IEA was being discussed, the US government's energy strategist, Thomas Enders, simultaneously proposed that the United States should aim for energy self-sufficiency by a protectionist high-price, high-domestic consumption policy and thus try to bring world market oil prices down and drain the OPEC dollar surpluses.[79] Another tack considered was to use the one resource with which the US could always strike back: *food*. The American government in response to the OPEC price hike ordered studies into the food vulnerability of particular countries, given that the United States accounted for 35 per cent of world wheat exports and practically monopolised soybean exports, which only a future development of Brazil's soybean production might challenge. The US also dominated the rice trade and supplied the bulk of Japanese corn imports. A 1974 CIA report on 'World Population, Food Production, and Climate' drew together these facts and identified the possibilities for applying pressure on specific countries, friend and foe alike.[80] Direct reprisals against oil producing countries were also being considered.[81]

In light of its misgivings about US policy and partly in response to the general mood of class and international compromise, in December 1973 the EC, recently expanded to include Britain, Denmark and Ireland, called for a *Euro-Arab Dialogue*. The Dialogue was an obvious alternative to a consumers' cartel, although the European states were reticent about this aspect. France, the main force behind the project, actually preferred a UN conference on energy, but this would have left the United States completely isolated, given its earlier commitments and pronouncements. Not unexpectedly, Kissinger considered the Euro-Arab Dialogue an absurd proposal, bound 'to institutionalize the Atlantic differences'.[82] But the Americans also were able to play off different European governments against each other. Thus, in West Germany Kissinger worked with Helmut Schmidt, Willy Brandt's critic within the SPD. Schmidt, Kissinger notes, 'would not participate in the attempt to turn Europe against America,' and at an energy conference in Washington in February 1974 already represented the West German position.[83] Brandt, on the other hand, speaking for the rotating EC presidency, in a conversation with Kissinger defended the right of the European countries to meet with the Arabs, although he too was coy about the institutional format of the actual Dialogue. When the US Secretary of State learned that it had been officially announced at a press conference while he was conferring with the chancellor, he prevailed on Nixon to cancel a planned trip to Europe in protest.[84]

Brandt shared Pompidou's position that the energy issue should be solved through dialogue and compromise. But, as we saw, he was also considered a security risk on other grounds and was forced out of office in April 1974. When there was also a change of guard in Britain (Heath replaced by Wilson) and France (the deceased Pompidou was replaced by Giscard), Atlantic cohesion was reinforced, but the Euro-Arab Dialogue was not suspended. There is no doubt that at this point the idea of trying to establish energy agreements outside the control of the Anglo-American oil majors was gaining ground. It is here that we must look for the material element in Europe's willingness to adopt a moderate, compromising position on the issue of the NIEO. West Germany in particular sought to restore independent access to energy sources by long-term state-to-state credit and delivery arrangements, which were judged a better way of achieving energy security than direct investment. Bonn channelled development aid to its energy suppliers, Iran and Algeria, and increased the state share in VEBA, the national oil company.[85] VEBA was one of the smaller European oil firms (often already state-owned), which in 1976 asked the EC to help them secure the same conditions of access to Arabian oil sources as those already enjoyed by the Seven Sisters. The group, which also included ENI of Italy, and the companies that today form Total (Elf and CFP from France, and Petrofina from Belgium), wanted a cartelisation of the European oil market, which they argued was a 'political' market anyway.[86] ENI of course has a long history of maverick oil exploration challenging the US majors; its head, Enrico Mattei, concluded spectacular deals with Iran and the Soviet Union before his plane was blown up on the eve of a trip to newly independent Algeria in 1962.[87]

Energy was not officially part of the Euro-Arab Dialogue. But it is obvious that the Dialogue created a communication channel that had the potential to link the Arab world preferentially to the EC. This would inevitably include oil deals at some point—an issue that would again be part of the considerations behind the Anglo-American invasion of Iraq in 2003, as we will see in Chapter 10. From the radical Arab side, it was argued that Europe and the Arab world had a joint interest in challenging the dominant position of the US dollar, and that controls should be imposed on the activities of transnational corporations.[88] By late 1976, the Arab countries had in fact replaced the US as the EC's main trading partner. EC imports from the Arab world had by then grown by almost 200 per cent since 1971, while exports (mainly to North Africa, Saudi Arabia and Iraq) grew by more than 300 per cent.[89] The Libyan participation in FIAT has been mentioned already; Iran's participation in Krupp and Eurodif (France's uranium enrichment project) illustrate that this was part of a tendency to more durable alignment. The Libyan deal with FIAT was part of a triangular transaction which also included the Soviet Union, and it highlights the drift of continental European society into networks of interest and power removed from its post-war Atlantic moorings.[90]

THE DRIVE FOR A NEW INTERNATIONAL ECONOMIC ORDER

Let us now look at how the drive for equity and democracy developed into the New International Economic Order campaign, and, more particularly, the codes of conduct for transnational corporations. This went to the heart of the organisation of the global political economy, and if the emancipatory process was always disparate and contradictory, the combined threat to Western power and privilege was never in doubt.

In 1962, the UN General Assembly, enlarged by an influx of newly decolonised states, had already carried a motion proclaiming the sovereignty of peoples over their natural resources. But it was only the OPEC shock that provided the Third World with the clout to begin a process of *renegotiating decolonisation*, with the aim of adding an economic dimension to formal state sovereignty. So if we are looking at what is no doubt a contender state bloc, we have to remind ourselves that, unlike the Soviet bloc, the NIEO coalition sought to reformulate the compromise that was decolonisation rather than to achieve a different economic system altogether. The aim was improvement of the conditions under which the integration into the capitalist world economy was to proceed, not its destruction.[91]

'Democracy' in the case of the NIEO refers therefore to equity in the global political economy between states and state classes holding power in them relative to the West, and not to domestic democracy, which was deficient and often absent.[92] As with all other contender state experiences, the NIEO drive was a response of state classes to the combined threat of being dispossessed by the West and/or dislodged by a revolution from below. Thus the military in Peru, intent on emancipating themselves from foreign control, were simultaneously driven by 'a strong antipathy toward working-class or revolutionary socialist politics'.[93] In India, Indira Gandhi's government actually called a National Emergency to block radical alternatives at home in the wake of the oil price hike and the 1974–75 crisis.[94] The 'unfinished bourgeois revolutions', which stop short of achieving social equality domestically, are therefore condemned to seeking solutions at the international level. This is the only way a measure of redistribution can be achieved if a state class does not engage in redistribution of land or income in its own society.[95]

Without the United Nations framework, the possibility of achieving a minimum of cohesion at the international level would not have existed. The states prominent in the NIEO drive always clung to the UN system and avoided Western-controlled alternatives; as late as 1980 Mexico still refused to become a member of GATT, the liberal counterpart of the UN trade and development body, UNCTAD.[96] The UN framework was the only feasible political meeting ground for progressive state classes with their colleagues from Brazil, Indonesia, the Philippines and other right-wing dictatorships. The Soviet bloc states were involved marginally at best (the exception being Cuba), and so were the East Asian newly industrialising states. Yet the common denominator of their development aspirations, the *initiating role of the state*, allowed state classes of highly varying political orientations to come together in the NIEO coalition, but only through the structure for which state sovereignty is the entry ticket—the UN. From a heartland perspective, on the other hand, this was in itself the problem. As the US ambas-sador to the UN, Daniel Moynihan, put it, the developing countries were engaged in 'a systematic effort to create an international society in which government is the one and only legitimate institution', based on the vision of '*the all encompassing state*, a state which has no provision for the liberties of individuals'.[97] Or, in the words of political scientist Stephen Krasner, the NIEO aimed at a comprehensive, UN-monitored system of 'authoritative allocation'. The South, by taking 'two legacies of the North— the organisation of political units into sovereign states and the structure of existing international organizations—[used] them to disrupt, if not replace market-oriented regimes over a wide range of issues.'[98]

The tone was set by the meeting of the Non-Aligned Movement in Algiers in September 1973, where, among many other alarming statements, detente was claimed to be part of 'the struggle against imperialism'.[99] Algerian president Boumedienne, in his capacity as president of the Non-Aligned Movement, next called for a special session of the UN General Assembly to discuss raw material issues. From these discussions emerged the following set of demands:

- An increase in development aid;
- Renegotiation of outstanding debts;
- The right to expropriate foreign assets and control of transnational corporations;
- Access to technology;
- Access to 'Northern' markets; and
- The establishment of a stabilisation fund to even out raw material price fluctuations.

In the sixth special session of the General Assembly in May 1974 and in the regular session in December, the 'Declaration Concerning the Establishment of a New International Economic Order' and the 'Charter of Economic Rights and Duties of States' were duly adopted as signs that the Third World states were converging on a common platform.[100] The general unwillingness to engage in domestic redistribution was brought out by the fact that the special session in its Action Plan asked the developed countries to finance 'industrial projects, *particularly export-oriented production*, in developing countries'.[101] The neoliberal ideologue, Edwin Feulner, Jr. had a point when he wrote that the NIEO call for 'self-determination' was disingenuous because 'the wealth which the [Less Developed Countries] wish to redistribute does not exist internally, or where it does exist the leadership elite refuses to redistribute it. The leaders of those nations have decided to redistribute someone else's wealth.'[102] But behind that intention was also a real aspiration to develop.

In 1975, a UN meeting in Lima dedicated to industrial development (out of which UNIDO emerged as a specialised agency) agreed upon a target for a Third World share of world industrial production of 25 per cent in 2000, up from 7 per cent at the time. *This was the core challenge the NIEO drive posed to heartland pre-eminence, and the one that the West would never grant under the prevailing political conditions.*[103] Still the industrialisation goal was not itself impossible, if one looks at the rates of growth that were occasionally achieved by states separately, as illustrated in Table 4.1. In addition, there were now ample credit opportunities available, given that a considerable slice of additional OPEC income was being recycled through the London capital market and other Euro-capital markets. This allowed the states classes of the Third World and the Soviet bloc to finance their investment and modernisation plans by borrowing, under their own control and ownership—something they obviously greatly preferred to leaving industrialisation in the hands of transnational corporations, because this is what distinguishes a state class from a comprador bourgeoisie selling off its countries' assets. Credit-financed, state-monitored industrialisation made it possible to restrict the activities of foreign business, even if credit lines were often diverted into the pockets of the ascendant private capitalist element developing within or alongside the state classes.

The OPEC shock and the NIEO drive were accompanied by a profound undercurrent of cultural and political anti-Western development that would survive the reversals suffered by the global reform project. In the Algerian case, the politically motivated Arabisation of education (in a situation where an English- and French-speaking cadre was needed) produced an Arab-speaking, academically trained youth for whom there was no employment in the end. The Arab-Islamic identity that was being propagated from above was not even rooted in popular culture; it was a modernism in its own right that would in due course fuel an opposition to the corrupt state class.[104] Islamism in this sense develops as the counterpart of a half-hearted development-cum-embezzlement effort in a range of countries (Hindu fundamentalism in India might be another example). Of course this would become most prominent in Iran, which in 1979 exploded in revolt against the West. But the ideological drift away from Western values also affected a relatively stable US vassal like Turkey, which in this period upgraded its relations with its Arab neighbours, notably Iraq, and with India, a key trading partner. Attempts by the Shah of Iran to organise a common pro-Western regional bloc and mobilise Turkish support against Iraq were rejected, and the Turkish leadership instead began to seek a rapprochement with Europe.[105] Although this foundered on the crisis over Cyprus (to which I return in the next chapter), Turkey's drift away from the West even included exploratory discussions with the Soviet Union. In 1977, a pipeline linking Kirkuk in northern Iraq to Turkey's Mediterranean coast secured the country's oil needs, in addition to providing transit fees.[106] It would take until 1979, against the background of the incipient neoliberal offensive, before Turkey's flirtation with the NIEO drive was shelved, although in today's moderate Islamic government we may again discern the undercurrents of protest against the corruption of the pro-Western state class that surfaced in the late 1960s and the 1970s.[107]

Israel had by now become a convenient target of general Third World wrath on account of its occupation of Arab lands. The Jewish state shifted to enhanced militarisation in the late 1960s, partly to offset the feared contraction of US involvement and partly in response to the growing strength of a non-racist Israeli Left.[108] Between 1967 and 1973, defence expenditure ran as high as 23 per cent of GDP, attracting big private conglomerates into the armaments sector alongside the state's own holding companies.[109] This contributed to preparing the ground for a further confrontation with the Arab neighbours by broadening the bloc of interests committed to military solutions. The OPEC and NIEO drives meanwhile worked to isolate the country, culminating in the condemnation of Zionism as racism by the UN General Assembly in 1975. Israel as a result moved closer to some of the less savoury Third World regimes, such as South Africa and Central American dictatorships like Guatemala and El Salvador. As we will see in Chapter 6, the Jewish state critically contributed to defeating progressive developments when the US Congress hesitated in the face of ferocious repression and genocide. South Africa's Jewish community was the highest per capita contributor to the Zionist project in the 1970s, in return for which Israel assisted in subverting the embargo against the apartheid regime.[110]

Finally, the NIEO drive, like the OPEC shock, also reactivated the Atlantic faultline. European states for a variety of reasons saw opportunities to profit from the isolation of the United States. Social Democracy was able to largely direct the European response to the NIEO in a spirit of compromise. In February 1975 in Lomé, capital of Togo, the expanded EC agreed to a new format for its association policy with its former colonies. With its provisions for trade preferences, price guarantees and industrial cooperation, the Lomé Convention provided a comprehensive response to the demands of the Third World, when such a deal was strongly resisted at the global level by the United States. (At Giscard's initiative, a comprehensive North–South conference convened in Paris in 1975, only to disband without result two years later.) Indeed American conservatives reproached the EC for giving in to the radical Third World, judging the Lomé Convention 'in some respects a prototype for future attempts ... to build a NIEO', although there were also moderates pleading for compromise.[111]

The most articulate positive response was meanwhile forthcoming from a transnational class of technocratic, managerial cadres, often themselves active in multilateral institutions. This strand was historically connected to Social Democracy and hence also European in orientation.[112] The Dutch economist, Jan Tinbergen, in his capacity as chair of the Council for World Development Policy of the Socialist International, led a group of specialists in 1974 to write a report for the Club of Rome on the issue of the NIEO. The report, subsidised by the Labour-led coalition government of the Netherlands, concluded that 'the relentless operation of market forces' had created economic chaos on a global scale. It proposed a comprehensive New International Order, not just for the economy, but for the political system as well.[113] Here we encounter a transitional programme which is certainly threatening to capital in the short run, but which also departs from the Third World demands by proposing a global programme *beyond national sovereignty*. Sovereignty was considered no longer adequate to deal with a range of problems, such as those involving the deterioration of the biosphere, the exploitation of the deep sea and the exhaustion of resources. The potential for a conflation with the interests of transnational capital in the longer run is obvious, even if the Club of Rome cadre perspective, with its emphasis on environmental issues, was itself suspect.

The Brandt Commission, named after the former chancellor and launched in 1976–77 by World Bank president McNamara, following the same perspective recommended enhancing the 'moment of regulation', albeit as a means to stabilise the capitalist economy by extensive infrastructural supports.[114] Tinbergen too thought that 'planning' should not be taken too literally as 'detailed and comprehensive planning' but rather in the sense of a loose planning framework curbing unstable markets.[115] But in the same period, irrespective of these reservations, the drive to curb the freedom of transnational corporations was gathering strength.

Challenging the Sovereignty of Capital

At the Lima UNIDO meeting, the United States resisted the 25 per cent Third World share for 2000 on the grounds that industrial development cannot be an issue of UN diplomacy, because 'redeployment of industries should be a matter of the evolution of economies rather than a question of international policy or negotiation.'[116] Kurt Waldheim, the UN secretary-general, on the other hand, was of the opinion that the consequences of international productive investment were too momentous to be left to private corporations and hence 'could not, and should not, remain outside the purview of international institutions which had effectively developed means of monitoring, and to some extent regulating, other aspects of economic intercourse.'[117]

Thus the issue of controlling transnational corporations was placed on the UN agenda, and the United States would inevitably be at the receiving end of such a drive. Transnational business at this juncture was an overwhelmingly Anglo-American phenomenon. In 1966 US corporations accounted for 60.8 per cent of accumulated world foreign direct investment, British corporations for 17.8 per cent, French corporations for 4.5 per cent, and Canadian corporations for 3.6 per cent, followed by West German and Japanese firms.[118] The critique of TNCs was always formulated from the vantage point of national sovereignty, in terms of the disproportionate hold on host economies and the extraterritorial jurisdiction of the mother countries (mainly the US and the UK) of the transnational corporations.[119] The presence of the TNC, whether in Chile or in France, was experienced as an extension and lever of Anglo-American power in 'private' guise.[120] Spokesmen for American capital were therefore pessimistic about the control drive. As Milton Friedman famously remarked in 1975, it might well turn out that capitalism 'would prove to be only a brief historical accident.'[121] Or as the CEO of a major US chemical company put it, 'The issue is one of survival. At stake may well be not only the survival of the [transnational corporation, TNC] but the continued existence of the private enterprise market system that has served us so well for so long.'[122]

Certainly the integrated former contenders and vassal states were also home to sizeable private corporations—of the 460 largest industrial corporations in 1970, 260 were American, but 51 were Japanese (with the largest Japanese corporation, Nippon Steel, occupying twentieth position in the overall ranking).[123] But their degree of transnationalisation was much more modest. In the EEC, in the late 1960s there were calls to merge continental European companies into entities that could meet the 'American challenge'—an issue particularly strong in Gaullist France, and mixed with criticism of the US war in Vietnam. The paperback edition of Servan-Schreiber's best-selling Le défi américain, in which the case was made for consolidated European corporations, tellingly opens with a preface on the blow dealt to the US by the Tet offensive in South Vietnam.[124] Various proposals to facilitate Europe-wide company mergers had been under discussion from the mid-sixties, but without much result. The pace of intra-European corporate mergers lagged dramatically behind the continuing takeover wave by US corporations. As EC Commission president F.-X. Ortoli complained in 1975, 'the possibility of controlling our future is slipping away from us, for there continuously appear new centres of economic, financial, and political decisions that are foreign to our member-states and to our Community.'[125]

The idea of a code of conduct for transnational corporations had already been suggested by the International Congress of Free Trade Unions (ICFTU) in 1969. In that year, the ICFTU suggested that the ILO undertake a review of labour relations issues raised by transnational corporations. A year later, it proposed that the UN develop a code of conduct with trade union participation. In 1972, it was decided that the ICFTU would work out a code jointly with TNC unions, the International Trade Secretariats (ITS); this resulted in the 'Multinational Charter' of 1975 asking for binding regulation of transnationals.[126] The trade union cadre also brought its influence to bear on the UN and its specialised agencies. In the ILO, a 'Tripartite Meeting on the Relationship between Multinational Corporations and Social Policy' was held in 1972. The recommendation to undertake further study into the desirability of guidelines for multinationals was adopted by the ILO in early 1973.[127]

In hindsight, the threat posed by projects for regulating transnational corporations' international activities can easily be belittled. The proposals put forward by trade unions and Social Democracy had little bite, especially if we take into account the fact that a degree of regulation is necessary also from the point of view of capital itself. The 1977 British Labour government project for a code regulating investment in South Africa, which followed the promulgation of the relevant principles by the American vicar, Rev. Sullivan, earlier in the year, served as a legitimation for, rather than an obstacle to, investment in the apartheid economy.[128] Yet at the time there was real concern on the part of prominent capitalists. Why this was so becomes clear when we turn to the simultaneous pressure on this issue exerted by the Third World states in the context of the UN.

Proposals here included the provision that each country should as a priority establish a special TNC monitoring agency, which would gather information for national and international use from TNCs, other governmental bodies and trade unions. The national agencies should be given the power, the ability and the duty to obtain information on all relevant activities of TNCs within their boundaries, and should monitor all flows of inward and outward investment.[129] The role of transnational corporations (particularly ITT, but also the US copper corporations) in the destabilisation of the Unidad Popular government in Chile acted as a catalyst for raising the issue of regulation of multinational corporations in the context of the UN.[130] Building on prior discussions in ECOSOC since 1968, UN reports on Chile and the UNCTAD III Conference in Santiago in 1972 turned regulation into a general Third World concern. Some countries, like Brazil and Mexico, had a 30–40 per cent foreign share in manufacturing industry and were in the front line of the drive for regulation.[131] The tone of their demands was bold and threatening, although hardly anti-capitalist. Foreign investment was welcomed, according to the Programme of Action adopted by the UN General Assembly in its sixth special session, 'both public and private, from developed to developing countries in accordance with the needs and requirements ... and determined by the recipient countries'.[132] National sovereignty was accorded preference over corporate interests, in regard to natural resources as well as to 'all economic activities'. In order to exercise effective control and safeguard resources, a state was entitled to any means suitable, 'including the right to nationalization or transfer of ownership to its nationals, this right being an expression of the full permanent sovereignty of the state'.[133]

As indicated, the fear that the host country was inviting the extraterritorial jurisdiction of the corporation's home state along with the transnational corporation was one factor in favouring foreign lending over direct investment.[134] But in that case, corporations operated by the Third World state classes had to obtain advanced means of production in the free market. This led to their quest for gaining control over production technology. The first instance of Third World control of the flow of investment, the Andean Pact's Cartagena Agreement of 1969, covered both aspects by drafting a common system regulating foreign investment and the transfer of technology.[135] UNCTAD III set up an expert committee to investigate the possibility of guidelines for multinational corporations, with special reference to the transfer of technology.[136]

In the second half of 1973, a 'Group of Eminent Persons' appointed by ECOSOC to study the TNC issue started its activities.[137] In 1974, the UN established a Centre on Transnational Corporations, which became a focal point for information on their operations and an irritant to the US.[138] The

OPEC shock and the NIEO drive lent a new edge to the movement and when countries were struck by the crisis of 1974–75, the attitude towards transnational corporations in some cases hardened into outright economic nationalism. In Brazil in 1976, an 'Administrative Council of Economic Defence' began monitoring the activities of the subsidiaries of foreign companies and fined several of them for price-fixing.[139] National sovereignty was the starting point for the Third World states; the envisaged UN regulation was preceded by regional arrangements on which national legislation should be modelled. Thus the Andean Pact adopted its 'Decision 24' to create a common regulatory framework for foreign investment to be followed by the different member states.[140] The Pacific Basin Economic Council too issued its own 'Charter on International Investments'.[141]

On the trade union front, the World Congress of the ICFTU in Mexico subscribed to the Multinational Charter in October 1975.[142] The ILO itself adopted a declaration with the conclusions from the aforementioned tripartite meeting in 1977, but this declaration only contains non-binding recommendations and cannot by any means be considered an infraction of the sovereignty of capital. The trade union/Social Democratic orientation was not to stress the question of formal status too much, but rather to emphasise a pragmatic way of implementation based on transparency. As one TUC official put it, 'Central to any implementation machinery is an effective international system for information disclosure and for consulting on this information.'[143]

The Socialist International interpreted the NIEO movement as a chance for politicising the regulatory structure of international capitalism, which, as I have argued, invades the free space for capital in the Lockean constellation and which business will always seek to resist. In 1977, the SI Study Group on Multinationals was set up. Its report, approved in September 1978, recommended, among other things, to support the position of the Group of 77 and make an eventual UN code of conduct legally enforceable. 'If only voluntary codes can be obtained at the international level,' the report stated, 'they should at least be accompanied by an effective complaints and supervision machinery which allows governments and trade unions to submit individual cases where the code has been infringed.'[144] Within the OECD, this position was reflected in the support for binding regulation on the part of the Dutch and Swedish governments.[145] The SI Report also recommended that

> Each country should as a priority establish a special MNC monitoring agency which would gather information for national and international use from MNCs, other governmental bodies and trade unions. The national agencies should be given the power, the ability and the duty to obtain information on all relevant activities of MNCs within their boundaries and should monitor all flows of inward and outward investment.[146]

This approach, coming from a political tendency enjoying full legitimacy and participating in the governments of several important countries, must have been felt as a particularly threatening one in the boardrooms of US and UK transnational corporations, particularly as it came on top of proposals for the socialisation of profit and workers' co-determination. In 1979, when the committee dealing with the application of the OECD Guidelines (for Multinational Enterprises, adopted in 1976) recommended setting up national liaison offices ('contact points') with approximately the task recommended by the SI Report, the business advisory committee to the OECD warned that these offices 'should not assume the function of a judicial or quasi-judicial forum' since this would 'run counter to the concept of voluntary guidelines.'[147]

In the US and, to a lesser extent, Britain—the 'injured' parties of the control drive—the targeting of the transnational corporation was seen as a consequence of the political incapacity of the Third World states. 'The tendency of local governments to look outward to explain internal troubles,' Walter Wriston of Citicorp wrote, 'has made the world corporation a scapegoat and object of concern.'[148] In fact, US foreign investments began to level off in the latter half of the seventies. In 1977, overseas assets of US corporations reached a high of 20 per cent of US corporate assets (non-financial only) and declined thereafter, although income from abroad continued to rise, especially after 1980.[149] As we will see in Chapter 8, US corporations would continue to occupy key positions in the transnational networks of joint directorates, but the general level of (active) transnationalisation of the US economy would continue to decline, while the transnationalisation of all other economies would increase.[150]

The challenge posed by the NIEO, with the Third World revolution rising behind it, had already become more manageable when actual negotiations about codes of conduct began in 1976–77. These, as can be expected, dragged on for several years. What the representatives of capital continued to fear most was not the idea of a code of conduct in itself but the dynamic it might set in motion. As one manager put it, the business world worried 'whether such an international code might not gradually evolve into a mechanism which would unduly limit and restrict ... the activities which constitute the core responsibilities of business.'[151] Collaboration on the part of the capitalist class and the major capitalist states in the development of codes of conduct was therefore practically confined to guiding the regulatory impulse into channels of desirable synchronisation and international standardisation. Even then, caution prevailed. In 1977 the OECD acknowledged that its own (largely pre-emptive) guidelines, 'though voluntary in origin, may ... in the course of time ... pass into the general corpus of customary international law even for those multinational enterprises which have never accepted them.'[152]

When the intergovernmental working group of the UNCTC began the preparation of a draft code in 1977, the advanced capitalist countries were already in a position to demand that any code would have to be balanced by the establishment of standards for the treatment of TNCs in addition to standards for their conduct.[153] This idea, accepted by ECOSOC in its 'Mexico Declaration' in 1980, signified the reversal of the regulatory drive and the challenge to corporate sovereignty. Ultimately, the only regulation project to emerge from the Third World drive in the UN, the 'Set of Multilaterally Agreed Equitable Principles and Rules for the Control of Restrictive Business Practices' of 1980, has to be understood as an extension of existing anti-trust legislation in the US and the EC. It contributes to the establishment of the operational conditions for capital in the sense of a 'level playing field', i.e., as a way of guaranteeing maximum competition and the interdiction of non-economic arrangements interfering with it.[154] By that time, however, the movement had clearly lost its momentum and was itself becoming the target of a sustained counter-offensive.[155]

Notes

1. Marx-Engels Werke (Vol. 7: 11).
2. Zamoshkin and Melvil (1982: 225, emphasis added); I have adapted the terminology to the understanding of 'neoliberal' used in the present work.
3. On the rediscovery of imperialism theory, cf. Magdoff (1969) and Jalée (1973); the revisionist cold war historians, adopting a historical materalist perspective, include William Appleman Williams (1962) and Joyce and Gabriel Kolko (G. Kolko 1968; Kolko and Kolko 1972), who also played a prominent role as anti-war activists.
4. Garaudy (1971: 32–3). Garaudy came in conflict with the majority in the French Communist Party leadership over their negative attitude to the student movement. The number of students in France—the stage of the actual May 1968 revolt—had tripled since 1960. On the new student profile, see N. Weber (1973: 27–9).
5. The Black Power movement was violently repressed by the COINTELPRO operation mounted by the FBI. The intimidation of black leader Martin Luther King culminated in his assassination in 1968; cf. Richelson and Ball (1990: 294); Scott (1986). Student protest against the war blended with a rejection of the technocratic arrogance with which it was being waged; cf. Chomsky (1969).
6. Harada (1970).
7. Cf. Koopmans (1977), and M. D'Angelo in *Le Monde Diplomatique*, June 1998, p. 25.
8. This aspect of the cultural transition is well captured in the cynical novel by Michel Houellebecq, *Les Particules élémentaires* (Paris, Flammarion, 1998) from which I borrow a few details here.
9. Caute (1988: 49).
10. Bell (1971: 31–2).
11. Ibid.: 44. The term 'adversary culture' comes from Lionel Trilling. Note the reference to the 'end of history', which was later taken up by Fukuyama to celebrate the triumph of the neoliberal counter-movement.
12. Childs (1980: 23).

13. Caute (1988: 200). In the Netherlands, around 1966 the Provo movement shocked established society by silly actions and then ridiculed the heavy-handed response to them by the authorities. Provos were arrested for distributing raisins to passers-by; the sculptor and novelist Jan Wolkers was arrested for carrying a live white chicken in public.
14. Debord (1967: 22, 45–6); where I have consulted the English translation by Black and Red of 1977 at www.marxists.org/reference/archive/debord/society.htm, the reference is to the numbered theses in which Debord presents his argument.
15. Debord (1967: Thesis 17). We see this in the selling of branded products, the consumption of which is motivated by 'experience, life-style, attitude, reputation and image' rather than by the physical item per se (Merk 2004: 134). Cf. also van der Pijl (1998: 13–4), on the spirit of 'mana' by which we may describe the good feeling evoked by branded consumer goods. What opens up here is the world of 'libidinal political economy' identified by Freud in *Civilisation and its Discontents* and elaborated among others by Deleuze and Guattari (1988) and at Sussex by Ronen Palan and Earl Gammon.
16. Debord (1967: Thesis 88). Marcuse's *One-Dimensional Man* of 1964 denounced the same aspect—the comprehensive encapsulation of the working class in the Fordist project—and the need to create a centre of resistance outside it.
17. Singer (1988: 20).
18. Piore and Sabel (1984: 169). 'Car workers in particular had become strong enough to seriously limit management control' (CSE 1980: 8). Extremely tight labour markets gave a strong position to workers notably in West Germany, France and Japan (Mandel 1974: 169); cf. Esping-Andersen (1990).
19. Quoted in Nairn (1973: 7).
20. Goldmann (1971); Caute (1988); cf. Marcuse (1971).
21. For a selection of Negri quotes, cf. Willan (1991: 184); cf. Guattari (1976: 147–8) for the argument that the main-stream working class organisations had become machines of oppression.
22. Fisera (1978: 11, 52–3); cf. Singer (1988: 29). By 'cadre', I mean the class of salaried functionaries entrusted with tasks of planning, social integration, and supervision (see van der Pijl 1998: 136–65). In France and Italy, communist parties had local power and communism was anyway often a training school for a Social Democratic career, as for instance in Spain, when, after Franco, an entire judiciary had to be recruited from proven non-Franquist background.
23. Bahro (1980: 157).
24. Ryner (2002: 138–9 and *passim*).
25. See Elsenhans and Junne (1974: 564).
26. Günsche and Lantermann (1977: 135).
27. Brandt (1971: 115).
28. Ibid.: 259–60; cf. von Braunmühl (1973: 75).
29. U. Mayer (1979: 390).
30. In his memoirs, Brandt notes that he came seriously under fire following the landslide victory in the general election of 1972, with his rival Helmut Schmidt reproaching him that the party was drifting towards a 'Nenni party' position (Brandt 1990: 295). (Nenni was the leader of the left Italian Socialists, ineligible to form a government during the cold war.)
31. Günsche and Lantermann (1977: 143).
32. Huntington in Crozier et al. (1975: 73, 110).
33. Bursk and Bradley (1976: 11).
34. Carrillo (1977: 119–150); Levi (1979: 16); cf. Carr (1982).
35. Childs (1980: 29–30); cf. Muhal-Leon (1980).
36. Berlinguer (1976: 19–25, 32); Roy (1978: 47) speaks of 'the shadow of NATO'. On the splits in the DC, cf. Posner (1977: 815–6).

37. Abse (1985: 8) argues that the PCI was used to deflect labour militancy. Cf. Russo (1979); Boni and Geissler (1977: 1477).
38. Kriegel (1977) considers the 'Euro' label misleading and instead speaks of a 'national communist temptation' to which the parties responded by deradicalisation. Cf. Levi (1979: 18), who stresses the aspect of 'polycentrism'.
39. Hodgson (1979: 293); Axt and Deppe (1979: 82).
40. Conference documents in Conferentie (1976); the Eurocommunist parties and the Yugoslavs and Romanians succeeded in having the principle of consensus accepted in matters of doctrine, giving them effective veto power (Russo 1979: 93).
41. Quoted in Hodgson (1979: 284–5). Out of office, Kissinger continued to campaign actively against Eurocommunism. In mid-1977, he claimed that allowing communists into Western European governments would narrow the Atlantic bond to its bare bones, and reduce NATO to an essentially German–American alliance (*NRC-Handelsblad*, 10 June 1977); in January 1978 Kissinger was the presenter in an NBC documentary in which he argued that Eurocommunism was merely the attempt of East European communism to cross the Berlin Wall into the West; cf. Elliott and Schlesinger (1980: 56).
42. Yergin (1993: 510–8); on the background and politics of the Venezuelan government in that period, see Löwy (1981: 180–2).
43. Yergin (1993: 534–5; Kissinger (2000: 855).
44. Quoted from National Security Council documents in Ponting (1989: 227). Wilson preferred to go in jointly with the US straightaway, ignoring the UN, but his cabinet feared another Suez.
45. Yergin (1993: 555); Ponting (1989: 227–8).
46. Yergin (1993: 556).
47. Löwy (1981: 179).
48. al-Khafaji (2004: 267).
49. Löwy (1981: 165).
50. Apart from the parasitic bourgeoisie that forms on the margin of the state-driven development effort, the need for foreign expertise in Algeria also created a market for commissions among high state officials, which would reach a level equal to its foreign debt (Beker 1996: 230–1; cf. Löwy 1981: 173–4).
51. Amineh (1999a: 310, 332, 347, 349, Table 9.6); Halliday (1979: 122).
52. Halliday (1979: 19); Panah (2002: 286).
53. Koopmans (1978: 198–202, 208–10, cf. 211, Table 12). On the difficulties facing the military in business, cf. H. Boirond in *Le Monde Diplomatique*, June 1972, p. 13. The big private holdings are Koç, Haci Ömer, and Sabanci (H. Boirond in *Le Monde Diplomatique*, June 1972, p. 13; the obituary of Sakip Sabanci in *The Guardian*, 16 April 2004).
54. Krasner (1985: 40).
55. Klare (2001: 59); cf. remarks by Undersecretary of State Joseph Sisco, quoted in ibid.: 60.
56. Yergin (1993: 566–7).
57. Cf. Parboni (1981: 8). For the losses to the producing countries, see *De Volkskrant*, 11 January 1972; *The Guardian*, 31 October 1973.
58. Yergin (1993: 577–80); Barnet (1980: 43); cf. P. Aarts, 'Libië', in Aarts (1983: 108–17).
59. Kissinger (2000: 860–1).
60. Yergin (1993: 580–1).
61. Barnet (1980: 44, 46); A. Marx (1974: 53); Lockwood (1974: 56–8).
62. Yergin (1993: 591). In April, James Akins, the top energy specialist in the US State Department and ambassador to Saudi Arabia, had already warned in an article in *Foreign Affairs* that an 'oil crisis' was around the corner.
63. *Le Monde*, 4 June 1973, identified the oil companies as the objective 'allies' of OPEC on this ground; the same was the case in *Financial Times*, 1 October 1973; cf. Kissinger (2000: 866).

64. Yergin (1993: 606).
65. Ibid.: 611–2.
66. Cf. Bichler and Nitzan (2004: 57, Figure 4.10); cf. Nitzan and Bichler (1995: 462, 467).
67. Bergsten (1973: 104–5, emphasis added).
68. As *Foreign Policy* characterised it in a subsequent issue, paraphrasing Che Guevara's famous revolutionary slogan about Vietnam, 'One, Two, Many OPECs', *Foreign Policy*, 14 (Spring 1974), p. 56.
69. Bergsten (1973: 109, emphasis added; cf. 107–8); for the fate of the Bauxite Association and CIPEC, cf. Barnet (1980: 142–3).
70. Bergsten (1973: 116).
71. Ibid.: 121; cf. MIT oil specialist Morton Adelman in *Fortune*, December 1976, pp. 189–90.
72. G. Corm in *Le Monde Diplomatique*, August 1974, p. 26.
73. Quoted in Yergin (1993: 599).
74. *The Times*, 10 September 1973.
75. The 'French connection' in the heroin supply chain, linking Turkish poppy harvests to the US via Marseille, was imbricated with the activities of the SAC, a 5,000-strong militia established by de Gaulle in response to the events May 1968. The SAC included many Corsican and French gangsters and was being used by French intelligence (the SDECE) as a covert action force. Under Nixon, US drugs enforcement agencies (with French help) were able to crack down on this trail. The Nixon-Pompidou rapprochement of March 1970 and the joint narcotics programme agreed on in February 1971 were, to quote Peter Dale Scott, 'not so much simple police actions as political operations against a common enemy: intransigent Gaullist remnants ... inside and outside of SDECE and SAC' (Scott 1986: 23). The long-standing enmity between the CIA and the French secret services was buried at this point, and there emerged a Far Right connection, which would later play a role under Reagan (McCoy 1991: 67–9).
76. *Le Monde*, 17 October 1973; *The Economist*, 22 November 1975. According to the latter source, oil expert Peter Odell estimated that the North Sea could cover Europe's gas and oil needs by the 1980s.
77. Quoted in Kissinger (2000: 897).
78. Kissinger (2000: 872); cf. Sabri Abdallah (1979: 117).
79. *International Herald Tribune*, 28 November 1974.
80. Barnet (1980: 156).
81. Kissinger (2000: 891–4). By leaking confidential think-tank memoranda on how to act in case of another oil price hike and/or embargo, the United States effectively threatened military intervention; while the 82nd Airborne division and Marine Amphibious forces conducted practice in a desert, Washington hinted that the USSR would reciprocate Western reticence in the Czechoslovak crisis of 1968 in the case of a US intervention in the Middle East (*US News and World Report*, 2 December 1974).
82. Kissinger (2000: 884).
83. Ibid.: 909.
84. Ibid.: 930–1.
85. Krägenau (1975: 77–8); *Frankfurter Allgemeine Zeitung*, 26 November 1973 (oil imports in *Finanz und Wirtschaft*, 15 April 1978; the figures are for 1977).
86. *De Waarheid*, 30 September 1976. In late 1974, the EC Commission openly condemned the cartel practices of the Seven Sisters (*De Volkskrant*, 19 November 1974).
87. Yergin (1993: 503–5, 519, 530); *Financial Times*, 26 October 1995; *De Volkskrant*, 25 November 1997.
88. Sabri Abdallah (1979: 117–9).
89. *Newsweek*, 11 October 1976.
90. Ognev (1984: 447); cf. Galli (1995).
91. Lake (1987: 220).
92. Kannapin (1984: 43); cf. Heuwinkel (1978).

93. Petras (1970: 132).
94. Roy (1986: 43).
95. G. Kolko (1989: 45); Löwy (1981: 165).
96. Even though president Lopez Portillo was more pro-business than his predecessor Echeverría (1970–76), Krasner (1985: 56).
97. Quoted in Feulner (1976: 63, emphasis added).
98. Krasner (1985: 124).
99. *Fourth Conference* (1973: 58).
100. Sabri Abdallah (1979: 117); Dupuy (1989: 33); Overbeek (1982: 147).
101. Declaration Concerning the Establishment of a New International Economic Order (1974: 24, emphasis added).
102. Feulner (1976: 66).
103. The NIEO drive was now strong enough to ensure that at the Lima UNIDO meeting, 82 states voted in favour of the Plan of Action, seven abstained, and only the United States voted against (Feulner 1976: 5; Kannapin 1984: 73).
104. Vieille (1988: 237); Beker (1996: 233).
105. *Neue Zürcher Zeitung*, 9 and 14 September 1973.
106. B. Féron in *Le Monde Diplomatique*, August 1974, p. 5; the pipeline was built by West German contractors (*Newsweek*, 10 and 17 January 1977).
107. Önder (1998).
108. *Frankfurter Allgemeine Zeitung*, 8 September 1973; A. Kapéliouk in *Le Monde Diplomatique*, August 1973, p. 5; and December 1973, p. 5.
109. Nitzan and Bichler (2002: 128–9); IDB (Israel Discount Bankholdings) and Koors are the best-known; for a list of Israel's main conglomerates, see ibid.: 86, Table 3.1. On the generals in politics, see V. Cygielman in *De Groene Amsterdammer*, 15 August 1973 and J. David in *Le Monde Diplomatique*, February 1973, p. 5.
110. *New Statesman*, 11 February 1977, pp. 176–7; *Newsweek*, 20 February 1978. The Israeli ambassador to South Africa qualified the embargo as the 'hypocrisy of the majority of UN members' to which his state could not be a party.
111. Feulner (1976: 5). The moderates included Senator Jacob Javits of New York; cf. Bursk and Bradley (1976: 38).
112. Cox (1979); de Senarclens (1990); Gosovic and Ruggie (1976: 325).
113. Tinbergen (1977: 5, 15).
114. Brandt (1971: 271).
115. Tinbergen interview in *Wirtschaftswoche*, 31 March 1978.
116. Quoted in Feulner (1976: 35). This section builds on van der Pijl (1993b).
117. In Bursk and Bradley (1976: 35).
118. Calculated from Busch (1974: 117, Table 1).
119. US corporations had to invest less and less, relative to the assets they gained hold of as a result. Even if we discard the growth of bank investment (where this is always the case), in 1977 the value of their foreign assets was three times what they had actually invested, whereas in 1950 foreign assets were still covered to a rate of 65.6 per cent by actual investment (UNCTC 1989: 11, Table 1.8).
120. Baade (1980: 13).
121. Quoted in *Fortune*, 4 January 1988.
122. F. Perry Wilson, Chairman and CEO of Union Carbide Co. in Bursk and Bradley (1976).
123. The 46 British corporations constituted the third-largest national set. Busch (1974: 123, Table 5).
124. Servan-Schreiber (1969).
125. Quoted in Kniazhinsky (1984: 161); Holland (1975: 323–9). On the growth of TNC activity, cf. Dicken (1986: 61).
126. de Kemp (1985: 42–3). The chemical workers' ITS of Charles Levinson was opposed to this plan; cf. Etty and Tudyka (1974: 360).

127. de Kemp (1985: 50–2).
128. Ibid.: 102.
129. SI Report on Multinationals (1978: 169).
130. On ITT, cf. Sampson (1974).
131. Dicken (1986: 64).
132. Quoted in UNCTC (1980: 5).
133. Quoted in ibid.: 7.
134. Frieden (1981).
135. UNCTC (1980: 25).
136. de Kemp (1985: 54–5).
137. The political representatives (in contrast to experts) were mainly from the Third World. The employers' organisations were also represented, but trade unions were not. Therefore, the ICFTU and the Christian Democratic WFL boycotted the hearings. Only the AFL-CIO and the Communist WFTU testified (de Kemp 1985: 57; Ruhwedel 1976: 263).
138. In 1992–93, the Centre was dissolved and the monitoring of FDI moved to UNCTAD, which publishes an annual World Investment Report.
139. *Newsweek*, 10 May 1976.
140. UNCTC (1986: 5).
141. Bursk and Bradley (1976: 23).
142. de Kemp (1985: 72).
143. Pursey (1980: 279).
144. SI Report (1978: 169).
145. de Kemp (1985: 87).
146. SI Report (1978: 169).
147. Quoted in de Kemp (1985: 153).
148. Bursk and Bradley (1976: 32).
149. UNCTC (1989: 10, Table 1.7); Duménil and Lévy (2004: 34, Figure 3.2).
150. UNCTC (1989: 23; cf. 22, Table 1.16).
151. Lawrence McQuade (of Procon and W.R. Grace) in Bursk and Bradley (1976: 44).
152. OECD, quoted in Baade (1980: 9).
153. UNCTC (1986: 6).
154. de Kemp (1985: 123).
155. The counter-offensive would set its sights on a code of conduct *for states*, the neoliberal Multilateral Agreement on Investment (MAI). Resistance to the MAI would in turn reactivate the democratic drive to restrict the discipline of capital and transform it from a state-centric approach to a truly global format, which would achieve its first success in Seattle in 2000 (Mabey 1999; Rupert 2000).

5 Transnational Rivalries and the Neoliberal Turn

CONTENDING FORCES IN THE STRATEGY OF TENSION

In response to the democratic tide discussed in the last chapter, a rift emerged between an ascendant fraction of the heartland ruling class intent on discarding the compromise culture of the post-war period altogether and those who remained committed to corporate liberalism. In the remainder of this study, this rift will be shown to have activated all the fractures and fault-lines of the global political economy. Class struggle and international relations would henceforth be accompanied by transnational, systemic rivalries between the English-speaking West (which converted to neoliberalism first) and those governing classes, notably in Europe, hesitant or unable to follow suit.

The Pinochet coup in Chile in 1973 worked as a powerful rallying point for the neoliberal New Right of the Mont Pèlerin Society and its offshoots; it demonstrated that violent shock therapy could reverse the leftward drift and allow the remaking of society entirely on market principles. But Chile seemed at first to be very much an isolated breakthrough. Everywhere else, politics was becoming stuck in an immobilising embrace between capital and labour, between East and West, and between North and South. This immobility then sparked off radicalism on the extremes of the political spectrum, from fringe left groups resorting to terrorist violence to the rather better equipped, assorted rightists. These radicals all became the pawns in a chess game that has gone down in history as the 'strategy of tension', in which they—the self-styled 'red' revolutionaries isolated in most cases from any working class following, and the 'parapolitical' right-wing vigilantes—were manipulated by the covert arm of established state power.

The underworld of the secret services is a vector of the political infrastructure that is either ignored (often, one would assume, out of a sort of academic chastity) or turned into the explanation of everything under the sun. The latter approach comes under the heading of 'conspiracy theory', a branch of populist elite theory. Conspiracy arguments revolve around the theory that the ruling elite is in total control of society. It can therefore even stage events ostensibly harmful to itself, only to dupe 'the people' even more. Thus the East Coast establishment supposedly created the Soviet Union to rip off the decent folks in the mid-west and keep the arms business going; Bush ordered planes to fly into the Twin Towers to be able to go after Saddam Hussein; and so on and so forth. Yet to dismiss covert action altogether as a dimension of politics is equally naïve. True, such action cannot alter the broader course of history or the structural configuration of forces in the global arena. But it can intimidate, and has in certain cases restored movement and fluidity in situations where the social and political order has become deadlocked. Terrorism, I would argue, is *always* a sign of deadlock, but there is more to covert action than terrorism. When stagnation and decay erode the inhibition on violence, which under normal circumstances sustains the preference for peaceful solutions, the covert world is always available to shore up crumbling power structures.[1] The fascism of the 1930s comes to mind here, but in the circumstances after the Second World War it is preferable to speak of *parafascism*. It is by this term that the former Canadian diplomat and expert in this shadowy domain, Peter Dale Scott, denotes the political actions of the covert world in the transnational class struggle. Parafascism differs from the original in that it does not articulate the right-wing, 'revolutionary' posture of certain contender states, but serves as an arm of the heartland states and ruling classes in manipulating local extremisms through provocation and penetration.[2]

The 1970s can then in this respect be understood as *a parafascist replay of the 1930s 'interregnum'*, a blocked situation of which Gramsci famously noted that the old was dying, but the new could not yet be born.[3] In the beginning of the 1970s, there was broad acceptance in the West that 'some modification of the rigidity of the French state ..., of the clientelistic character of Italian Christian democracy and much publicly owned industry in Italy, or the reform of the Spanish constitution' were desirable. But a role for communists in solving these issues was rejected, and there was as yet no basis for neoliberal 'reform'.[4] Hence, in the absence of bourgeois forces capable of making the necessary transitions on their own, the covert world obtained a room for manoeuvre that it would not otherwise have enjoyed. As the report of the Pike Committee of the US House of Representatives, established to investigate the role of the CIA in the late 1960s and early 1970s, concluded, 'US foreign policy lacked a long-term direction and ...

the government ... often resorted to covert action by the CIA as a short-term solution to problems that really required long-term remedies.'[5] These covert actions were not necessarily conspiracies from up high, but often improvised responses by the lower echelons or rogue elements.[6]

The intelligence world is an area in which the 'ethnic' dimension of the original Lockean heartland—the 'special relationship'—has remained intact to a surprising degree.[7] Its post-war structure goes back to the spring of 1941, when American military representatives delivered a model of a Japanese enciphering machine to British specialists at Bletchley Park trying to break the Nazi secret codes. In return, the British supplied advanced cryptographic equipment which they had developed themselves. The US reached agreement in the same year with Canada to use data gained by Canadian signal monitoring. In 1942, UK/US agreement was expanded to include covert action and sabotage operations; Australia and New Zealand were brought into these arrangements in the course of the war, and in 1947 the UKUSA agreement, also known as the UK–USA Security Agreement or 'Secret Treaty', was concluded. It created a structure in which signal intelligence (telephone and other communication intercepts) was shared between the so-called First Party (the US), and the Second Parties (Australia, Britain, Canada and New Zealand). Each partner had specific regional responsibilities. Covert intelligence coordination was even more restricted—to the US, Britain and Australia.[8] But, as we will see later, this did not protect the governing classes of these countries from being disciplined themselves.

In the interregnum emergency, this constellation of forces also activated a set of parapolitical relays among the so-called Third Parties to the UKUSA agreement—the intelligence services of West Germany, Denmark, Norway, Japan and South Korea. In addition, they activated a number of less formal intelligence connections with Taiwan, Israel and South Africa.[9] Also interlocked with the NATO intelligence infrastructure, finally, was the parafascist network that surfaced in Italy in the wake of the collapse of the USSR and became known under its Italian name, *Gladio* ('sword'). Based on official agreements involving the secret services, the Gladio networks (each in fact named differently) were formed from 1951 onwards—first in France and Italy, the countries with the strongest communist parties.[10]

There has never been a situation in which this vast machinery of covert action was even remotely free from fierce internal rivalries. We saw in Chapter 3 how de Gaulle even made public the secret NATO protocols in this area when France withdrew from the military organisation. Inter-service rivalries also abound. However, in light of the hierarchy of control and the one-way flow of information through the UKUSA channels, the capacity of the US secret services to manipulate the incidence of what in the intelligence world is called 'political action' must be seriously considered.[11] I begin with southern Europe.

Intervention and Rivalry in Greece, Cyprus and Portugal

Greece enjoys the doubtful honour of having been the first NATO country to have had a dictatorship imposed on it by this very organisation, supposedly protecting democratic freedoms. But this brutal episode acquires its full meaning only if we see it in the perspective of the state role in the transition to industrial society.

Greek society has long been dominated by a merchant diaspora spread across the port cities of the eastern Mediterranean, the Black Sea coast and the Middle East. The Greek state, ruled by a conservative oligarchy already bailed out once in 1947 by the US, thus has an importance well beyond its actual territory. Since commercial capital and the famous shipping dynasties—connected to the oil trade through providing the early tanker fleets—had no interest in industrialisation, this became a state task; but the spectre of communism haunted the reactionary ruling class and acted as a brake on domestic development.[12] NATO membership in 1952 only added to the immobility of the Greek state. The intelligence service, KYP—used for internal surveillance (along with a branch of Gladio created in 1955)—worked closely with the CIA, which coordinated its intelligence gathering in the Balkans and the wider Middle East from Greece.[13] As industrialisation and foreign investment began to undermine the clientelistic social structures, doubts arose in the Greek oligarchy about whether class conflict could be contained by parliamentary means, and this then triggered the 1967 military coup.[14] However, US support for the colonels' regime, part of an ill-conceived attempt to create a Mediterranean counterpart to the EEC, only facilitated the European governments' efforts to develop links with Greek politicians in exile.[15]

Under pressure from mounting popular dissatisfaction, in July 1974 the Greek junta, encouraged by Washington, supported a military coup on the island state of Cyprus. Its leader, Bishop Makarios, considered too close to the Third World NIEO movement, was deposed. The coup provoked an intervention by Turkish troops to take control of the part of the island inhabited by the Turkish minority, creating a partition that has remained in place to the present day and which continues to complicate EU expansion.[16] However, a rebellion in the Greek army brought down the junta in Athens in the wake of the invasion. After the restoration of civilian rule, Greece withdrew from the military organisation of NATO in August.[17] The new conservative government instead sought succour from the EC—to hold off the Left, rein in the remaining junta supporters in the security apparatus, and reinforce its position vis-à-vis Turkey, towards which Kissinger, the master balancer, had swung US support.[18] The episode left a legacy of anti-American feeling in Greece, which superficially gave a left veneer to the preparation for EC integration. But nationalisation of the country's largest private business conglomerate in 1976 was part of the dispossession of the oligarchy, not a return to the strong state; the return to democracy was fundamentally a liberalisation in the Lockean sense.[19]

The revolution in Portugal in 1974 coincided with the crisis over Cyprus, at the high point of challenges to the West. Portugal controls the strategically important Azores, and has historically functioned as a bridge between Brazil and the Portuguese-speaking African empire and the outposts in Asia, a geopolitical constellation with great economic potential.[20] In the late 1920s, the modern Portuguese state emerged as a right-wing dictatorship under Salazar, imposing itself on society through corporatist structures aimed at controlling the rise of social classes, in classical 'Hobbesian' fashion. By joining the British-sponsored EFTA in 1959, Salazar gave up economic autarchy for a degree of integration; but the need to retain control of the African colonies haemorrhaged the state budget, and capital for industrialisation had to be attracted from abroad. In the 1960s, when industrialisation took off, Portugal became a supplier of textiles and simple electrical goods, whereas it had earlier been a supplier of port wine, sardines and cork. Under the Caetano government, industrialisation was further ratcheted up, with shipyards, steelworks and a petrochemical complex at Sines. Altogether, industrial employment rose from 29 to 35 per cent of the workforce between 1960 and 1980.[21]

A controlled loosening of the state hold on society, attempted under Caetano to adjust to these changes, was defeated in 1972 by a reactionary coalition of landowners, colonial capital and old Salazarists. The state class was in a process of dissolution and NATO support weakened due to the crisis of US power, when the colonial army, bogged down in fighting left-wing rebels in Angola, Mozambique, and Guinea-Bissau, rebelled on 25 April 1974 by placing carnations in the barrels of their weapons. For a brief period, the fall of the dictatorship appeared to evolve into a socialist revolution. The left-wing officers abandoned the idea of EC membership entertained by Caetano; instead, they envisaged Portugal as a bridge between Europe and Africa, or as the initiator of a Mediterranean bloc linked to OPEC and the NIEO (then on the ascendant). Meanwhile land reform, nationalisations (respectful of foreign capital) and a rise in workers' living standards were achieved. But as provisional governments succeeded each other in quick succession, no stable power structure was put in place.[22] On the contrary, the expropriations and the delinking from the world market in the years following the Carnation revolution did mobilise strong counter-revolutionary forces. Parafascist elements of the former secret police (PIDE) and reactionary officers like General Spinola were involved in a series of foiled plots. The small peasants in the north and centre of the country (as well as small businessmen) suffered from ill-conceived economic measures taken by the provisional governments of 1974–75, and became available as a right-wing mass base. Counter-revolution could always raise the spectre of a seizure of power by the neo-Stalinist Communist Party (PCP), a worthy product of the strong state and Portugal's isolation.[23]

In 1976, backed by the newly revamped Socialist International, Mario Soares, a democratic lawyer groomed by Willy Brandt to become the head of a modern Social Democratic party, took office at the head of a socialist minority government on the waves of an SI campaign to 'save' a radio station resisting the left-wing military. Characteristically, Soares was mistrusted by Kissinger, who told him in no uncertain terms that he risked becoming the Kerensky of the Portuguese revolution.[24] Yet Atlantic rivalries remained muted; unlike the Cyprus crisis, there were tensions as well as complementarities between the SI approach and the Kissinger line. These were gradually resolved and fine-tuned by Western loans to the Soares government. By mid-1977, credit was made conditional on IMF supervision of economic policy, effectively neutralising the threat to capitalist class relations.[25] When a crisis erupted over IMF conditionalities in 1978, Soares' choice of the ultra-right CDS as a coalition partner and his willingness to overrule his own party convinced Western observers of his trustworthiness. The Carnation revolution was also thus steered, amidst great difficulty, into a transition from the tentacular state to a Lockean, liberal configuration.[26]

At this point the EC was taking on tasks which the US and NATO, compromised by their support for the Iberian dictators and the Greek colonels, could no longer handle. The role of West Germany, especially through the Socialist International and other channels of SPD influence, should be seen in this perspective. The decision to have the (otherwise powerless) European Parliament directly elected was also an aspect of the new role cast upon the EC. European elections would serve to provide cohesion to the socialist alternative to southern European (Euro-) communism and consolidate the Social Democratic majority at the EC level.[27]

The Strategy of Tension in Italy

The Eurocommunist departure of the PCI in Italy added to the fear in several Western capitals that the 'Mediterranean' tendency in the ruling Christian Democrat party—led by Moro, Fanfani and Andreotti[28]—would reciprocate this strategy for its own ends. This might then conceivably lead to a belated Gaullist turn in Italy, away from NATO and into an embrace with the Arab world and the Soviet bloc. The 'Mediterranean' orientation in the DC represented a tendency in the Italian bourgeoisie and state class that has its roots in progressive Catholicism and nationalism. The strategy of Enrico Mattei (the head of ENI until his death), to strike out-of-area energy deals in the late 1950s, has already been mentioned; the Italian public sector corporations more generally charted a course of developing the domestic market and engaging in dialogue with OPEC and the Soviet bloc.[29] Certainly the state sector was no longer the dynamic, modernising force that it had been up to the mid-1960s. It had become hostage to the DC, which, through nepotism and politically motivated investments in the south of the country, was trying to turn round its sagging political fortunes.[30] In the crisis of 1974–75, the state sector was severely hit, registering record losses, and corruption scandals were the order of the day. Aldo Moro's secretary, S. Freato, thus operated a financial back-channel to procure funds for Moro's role as a politician, and he was accused at one point of taking illegal kick-backs from Italian oil imports under direct deals with the producing countries (Libya, Iran and Saudi Arabia).[31]

The rival DC faction, the 'American party in Italy',[32] enjoyed the confidence of the Atlantic security infrastructure and the heirs of the fascist past in the Italian state. Secret service chief de Lorenzo, the founder of Gladio in Italy, attempted a coup as early as 1964; when the plan was foiled, the Gladio training camp on the island of Sardinia had already been designated to house the PCI and Socialist party leaderships.[33] The Atlanticists in the Italian state and politics were boosted when, following France's withdrawal from NATO's military organisation, the Mediterranean naval command was moved to Naples. When the strategically important island state of Malta in 1971 joined the non-aligned movement and closed its ports to Western warships, Italy's importance to the West could only increase.[34]

In response to the radicalisation of society after 1968–69, all the main tendencies in the DC developed more or less secretive activities to retain power in the changed circumstances, but the Atlantic faction obviously had the best connections.[35] Licio Gelli, the Grand Master of the *Propaganda Due* (P-2) Masonic lodge, had by that time become the informal head of Italy's parallel power structure, available in an emergency. Gelli had contacts at the highest level in Washington as well as with the Vatican. In 1969 Kissinger and General Alexander Haig, his NSC deputy and a Roman Catholic with important political connections in Italy, authorised Gelli to begin recruiting some 400 Italian top military and intelligence figures into P-2 to give it an operational capacity to deal with the Left's advance.[36] But the unsavoury background and the links of many of these personalities to neo-fascism in Italy and abroad (Spain, Argentina, Greece, etc.), combined with the risks of staging a coup in a country with a powerful communist party and bordering on Tito's Yugoslavia (coup plans were exposed in 1964, 1970 and 1974), led to fierce disputes between the CIA and the State Department. Kissinger, at that time still the National Security Adviser, apparently found himself mediating between the two on several occasions. In 1973, Italian neo-fascists with links to P-2 conducted a series of high-profile terror attacks, for which explosives had been obtained from US bases in West Germany.[37] However, after Nixon's abdication from the presidency, CIA funding of ultra-right groups abroad dried up; as was later revealed by Andreotti, interior minister at the time, the Right then turned to the mafia for funding.[38]

When Aldo Moro, then foreign minister, visited Washington in 1974, he was subjected to a grilling by Kissinger over his supposedly pro-Arab leanings and his refusal to allow US planes to use Italian bases to supply Israel in the 1967 Six-Day War. In addition, he was told off on the subject of his conciliatory attitude to the growing influence of the PCI. Kissinger warned Moro that criticism of the CIA role in Chile should not lead to a situation in which Italy went communist while the US stood by. During an evening meeting, an unnamed US intelligence official told Moro in confidence that he was in danger; as Philip Willan relates, Moro 'was advised that groups *on the fringes of the official secret services* might be brought into operations if he did not abandon his policy of negotiating with the communists.' Moro was seriously taken aback and confessed to an aide that he contemplated leaving politics altogether.[39]

As we have seen, the 'Historic Compromise' had been elaborated by the PCI in response to the Pinochet coup in Chile. But the premise that a left-wing government must seek the middle ground, because it will not be able to confront the entire middle class in an imperialist context, alienated the PCI from the formations further to the left.[40] The Left critique centred on the thesis that factory automation had been only sparsely introduced in Italy, and that the manual working class therefore wielded a power which it would lose in the near future. It should therefore press for more radical solutions as long as it enjoyed this advantage, especially since US imperialism was paralysed by Vietnam—but this too was only temporary.[41] There was a broad array of groups to the left of the PCI subscribing to this argument, such as the *Il Manifesto* group, which had a sizeable following and its own newspaper. But smaller formations on the extreme left, such as the Red Brigades and Workers' Autonomy, adhering to an 'abstract', Brechtian revolutionism, wanted to provoke violent insurrection.[42]

In June 1976, the PCI polled 34.4 per cent of the votes in parliamentary elections, coming within five percentage points of the DC. I have already noted in Chapter 4 how—at the Puerto Rico summit a week later—the US, UK, West Germany and France agreed to isolate Italy in case of participation in the government by the communists. This 'private' agreement was taken without consulting Canada, Japan or Italy (represented at the G-7 by Moro). However, Helmut Schmidt leaked the decision to the press to make the threat more effective, and the DC took care to keep the communists on the shortest possible leash. The PCI had won the right to be consulted on major policy issues, but under pressure from the senior NATO states, foreign policy was excepted from this 'programmatic convergence'.[43] Meanwhile Carter had succeeded Ford in the US, ostensibly inaugurating a change away from Kissinger-style covert action. Yet in late 1977, when pressed on the issue, Carter's National Security Adviser, Zbigniew Brzezinski, argued that a promise not to intervene was 'an offensive requirement'.[44] In the trial of the plotters of the 1974 neo-fascist coup attempt, the head of Italian intelligence had already told the judge that 'from now on there will be less and less talk of neo-fascist terrorism and more and more of red terrorism.'[45] Was this a sign that the covert world had switched to using *left* extremism? In 1976, a supplement to a US Army field manual dating from 1970 was made public in the Turkish press (and subsequently in other countries). This recommended penetration of 'insurgent' groups by US agents in case an allied government proved 'passive and indecisive' in the face of 'communist subversion'. In 1981 the entire document was found hidden in the luggage of the daughter of Licio Gelli, just after the membership list of the P-2 lodge had been made public.[46]

Whether these exposures were themselves part of attempts to influence events, or accidents revealing that the strategy of tension by provocation was still operational, cannot be stated decisively here. We do know that when the Andreotti cabinet was on its last legs in January 1978, US ambassador Richard Gardner was recalled to Washington, and the State Department issued an unequivocal statement that the US would not accept government participation by communists in Europe. But the uproar with which this was greeted across the European political spectrum, and the fact that the 'American Party in Italy' was in disarray over the Lockheed disclosures in the US, only strengthened the hand of the Mediterranean faction in the DC to pursue its negotiations with the PCI. In July, the communists declared their support for a new Andreotti government without entering it.[47] On his way to the parliamentary confirmation of the Andreotti cabinet, Moro, then president of the DC, was kidnapped by the Red Brigades and held hostage in one of the great dramas of post-war political history.

Moro's captivity became a painful episode of obviously conscious incompetence. There is no point going over all the tragicomic details of the 'search' under the auspices of a special crisis committee in the interior ministry, which included, as was later revealed, many P-2 lodge members vehemently opposed to Moro's policies. The minister of the interior, Cossiga, even invited Gelli to attend some of the meetings.[48] For three weeks, a US State Department official joined the deliberations in camera, returning to Washington briefly before Moro was killed.[49] There are serious indications that the abduction and assassination were not the work of the Red Brigades (BR) on their own.[50] They at least had assistance from the mafia, acting in cahoots with the US and Italian security services, although there is also evidence of other mafia groups involved in trying to *find* Moro on behalf of contacts in the DC.[51] The loose threads in the evidence seem to warrant the following scenario. The DC president was abducted by the BR with the assistance of groups close to the security services (or in them) and/or the mafia;[52] held captive by the BR and 'tried' by them;[53] and finally released to another group (possibly the mafia, possibly Mossad) to be killed and disposed of. His body was found in the back of a car parked symbolically in an alley in between the headquarters of the DC and the PCI, the two parties of the

Historic Compromise.[54] The decision to have Moro killed was indeed eminently political. The always intractable Gelli, in a TV interview in 1989, claimed that Moro had almost been released but that those in the government who did not want to see Moro free had prevented it.[55] Bettino Craxi, the socialist moderniser, alone among the mainstream party leaders, advocated negotiations with the kidnappers. He also took care, though, to hint at the similarities between the BR and the PCI as violent revolutionaries, thus catering to the mood of those who wanted to move beyond class struggle altogether into the world of individual achievement and pleasure associated with neoliberalism.[56]

Leonardo Sciascia's reading of Moro's letters from captivity highlights the shift out of the corporate liberal class compromise and towards a more authoritarian state, separate from society and capable of executing a neoliberal programme. In a letter in which Moro refers to Senator Gui—one of those exposed as having accepted Lockheed bribes—and his colleague Taviani, the DC leader asks whether their calls for a hard line to demonstrate the power of the state might have been suggested from abroad. Such a stand, Moro suggests, is not appropriate for Italy, where compromise and flexibility are needed; although it may be suitable for the US, Israel and West Germany, 'which have quite different grounds to reject a moment of reflection and humanity.'[57] Taviani, he writes, had been party to a campaign against him, Moro, on account of supposed communist support. But given Taviani's past functions as minister of defence and minister of the interior, and his protracted role in dealing with the security apparatus and his intimate contacts with the US, doesn't '[Taviani's] harsh posture concerning me, perhaps reveal an American and German hand?' Is it possible, Moro asks again in a subsequent letter to the DC leadership, that 'all of you, unanimously, wish my death on account of a purported state interest which somebody whispers maliciously into your ears?'[58]

This then was the crowning achievement of the strategy of tension, a strategy developed to discipline Europe at a critical juncture for the West. Terrorism in its offensive mode, Gianfranco Sanguinetti writes, is the strategy of the desperate and the zealots; in its defensive mode, it is always and only states themselves which resort to terrorism, either because they have landed in a real social crisis or because they fear one. The aim of creating a terror scare is to convince the population that, whatever may separate it from the state and the government of the day, they at least have *one* enemy in common: terrorism. That is why 'terror' must always be depicted as *absolute evil*, and never approached realistically; only thus can the struggle against it be proclaimed as a general interest, the general good.[59] Of course one cannot avoid thinking of the US 'war on terror' when reading these lines today.

Nothing happened to PCI leader Berlinguer, but the Historic Compromise was buried with Moro.[60] After the elections of 1979, a right-wing DC government was formed under Cossiga. The communists effectively became the accomplices of the strong state and the neoliberal austerity policies, to which Berlinguer committed himself out of a quasi-Protestant 'anti-capitalism'. By now the Italian employers had come to the conclusion that, given the zealous 'anti-terrorist' position of the PCI, they were worth much more in the opposition than in the government. In 1980 FIAT was able to restore discipline in its factories; two years later Confindustria, the employers' organisation, felt strong enough to call an end to the automatic inflation correction in their wage policies. One more year, and Craxi would emerge at the head of the government, ending the era of DC rule altogether.[61]

DISCIPLINING THE HEARTLAND IN THE INTERREGNUM

Just as Italy had shown the rest of bourgeois Europe how to deal with the working class after the Russian revolution, it led the way in devising strategies to deal with the rise of the Left after May 1968. The most eager pupil, in the 1930s as well as the 1970s, was Germany.[62] That country's pivotal position for the wider West had been enhanced by the weakening of US leadership. The Atlantic crisis tended to politicise 'Europe' and differentiate conditions in the EC member states; as a result there emerged, as Hans-Jürgen Axt and Frank Deppe have argued, a hierarchy of power at the European level. The challenge of the Left required a chain of command, which inevitably led to the most 'secure' European state, West Germany under Schmidt. Bonn now assumed a range of 'responsibilities' with respect to the European 'weak links'. These responsibilities notably included, in addition to the challenge of Italian communism and the revolutionary crisis in Portugal, attempts to influence the French Socialist Party, signed up for a coalition with the PCF, and guiding the transition out of Francoism in Spain.[63] But was the Federal Republic itself secure enough? Let me first briefly go into this issue, before turning to events in the English-speaking states.

As we saw in the last chapter, Helmut Schmidt rose in the SPD as a rival to Willy Brandt, who had by 1974 become a positive security risk for the West. In a sense, Brandt embodied a 'Historic Compromise' all by himself—a leftist by US standards, and a legitimate holder of government office in a major European country. When Brandt, after his landslide re-election, launched into broadening class and international compromise to deal with the consequence of the oil price hike, he was deposed. Significantly it was on his return from a trip to Algeria and Egypt in April 1974 that he was informed of the arrest of Günther Guillaume, his right-hand man, as a GDR spy, and forced to resign. Helmut Schmidt was ready to take the place of a man whom he felt was gambling with West Germany's Atlantic commitments; the FDP minister of the interior, Genscher, who had been informed of Guillaume's spying eleven months earlier but kept it under wraps, was actually in favour of switching to the CDU altogether.[64]

Why then did the Federal Republic, supposedly the guardian of order in Western Europe, succumb the way it did to the terrorism of the Baader-Meinhof group? Was there an interest on the other side to reinforce the state, or even a transnational interest in keeping the Schmidt government under pressure? The head of the federal criminal bureau (BKA) later claimed that if there had been the necessary political will, the entire terrorism phenomenon could have been eradicated early on.[65] The emergency legislation (*Notstandsgesetze*) and professional interdictions, through which the Brandt government and its predecessor (the Grand Coalition of CDU and SPD) had sought to shore up state security, gave extensive powers to the state; but the security apparatus and the judiciary had not been properly denazified and were a world away from the SPD. So were politicians like Franz-Josef Strauss, a prominent figure in the transnational Right to whom we return below.

Andreas Baader, Ulrike Meinhof and friends, calling themselves the 'Red Army Fraction' (RAF), pulled off a number of bank robberies as part of their 'urban guerrilla' campaign, modelled on the Uruguayan *Tupamaros*. In 1972 they were arrested, but the RAF continued under a 'second generation'. A law suspending constitutional rights was promulgated to deal with the terrorist challenge in early 1975, and, in a spiral of repression and radicalisation, the actions of the RAF became more violent as well. In the autumn of 1977, they assassinated the West German employers' chief and former Nazi, H.-M. Schleyer. Simultaneously, a Palestinian commando group hijacked an airliner, demanding the release of Baader and others from prison. After German special forces had raided the Mogadishu airport in Somalia to free the passengers, the SPD minister of justice in the Schmidt government, H.-J. Vogel, claimed that 'our people have had in these weeks a new and stronger feeling about the relation of a single individual toward the state ... the people, especially younger people ... *learned that the state, in order to uphold its functions and protect life, may also demand services and sacrifices.*'[66]

Indeed terrorism, whatever its origins, always works to mobilise and galvanise the power of the state and the established order, while paralysing the forces of democracy. At first, this strategy had its centre of gravity domestically, in the various Western countries affected; after 1980, the strategy of tension, by then a cohesive doctrine, was extrapolated to the international sphere, as terrorism and adventurism began to be deployed internationally by the West against the Soviet bloc and progressive governments across the globe. But the neoliberal offensive, by which the West restored its pre-eminence over the contender forces in the 1980s, was also premised on changes in the English-speaking countries.

Watergate

Richard Nixon was not a moderate like Moro or Brandt; on the contrary. Yet, paradoxically, he too was involved in what risked becoming a sort of Historic Compromise, through his spectacular opening-up to China and the Soviet Union. In fact, the crude tactics of the Nixon White House in dealing with the opposition to the war in Vietnam, once it spread to the establishment media and think tanks and the Democratic Party, were crucial in assembling the coalition that would apparently vindicate the basic values of American public life. In true US heroic mode, the exposé was made possible through the courage and perseverance of two young journalists, Bob Woodward and Carl Bernstein. The fact they worked for one of the most prestigious establishment newspapers is usually left in the background, and it is not generally known that Woodward was a former Navy liaison officer who knew Alexander Haig personally from his period in the military. Let me briefly recapitulate what seems a more probable chain of events, beginning with two key figures in Nixon's entourage, Kissinger and Haig.

Henry Kissinger had risen as an advisor to Nelson Rockefeller, heir of the Standard Oil dynasty and kingmaker in the Republican party. Kissinger always retained a keen eye for the interests of the US oil majors, as we saw in the Euro-Arab Dialogue episode. Where Kissinger's and Nixon's views on foreign policy happened to come together was on the issue of nineteenth-century style 'secret diplomacy'—Kissinger because he had studied the restoration of a European state system after the Napoleonic wars, and fancied applying a classical balance of power *Realpolitik*; and Nixon because he distrusted the large federal bureaucracies in Washington, notably the State Department (along with the press, the 'liberals' and so on). To pursue an innovative foreign policy based not on ideology but on US interests, the two men were led to upgrade an institution inherited from earlier presidencies, the National Security Council (NSC), to support a foreign policy conducted directly by the White House. As we saw, Nixon had already operated a secret back-channel to influence the ongoing negotiations with Thieu in the presidential campaign of 1968. Once in office, he intended to use secret diplomacy to engineer his own way out of the Vietnam quagmire. However, as Len Colodny and Robert Gettlin document, the Joint Chiefs of Staff in the Pentagon were highly suspicious of what Nixon and Kissinger were up to in Vietnam. They launched a spying operation through a junior officer, who had by late 1971 already passed on to his military superiors thousands of messages copied from Kissinger's secret diplomatic correspondence.[67]

General Alexander Haig was Kissinger's deputy at the NSC, and it was he who planted the Pentagon spy on him. Haig had been a field commander in Vietnam, and was in an ongoing battle with Kissinger to get Nixon's ear. But he also had to cover his back as a (very fast rising) officer by simultaneously supplying the Joint Chiefs of Staff at the Pentagon with information on the much despised 'Dr.' Kissinger.[68] In June 1971, Kissinger made a tour of Southeast Asia from which he secretly took a short break to fly to Beijing and confer on the possibility of a Nixon visit. This trip had been made possible by the mediation of Pakistan's dictator, Yahya Khan, who thus earned Nixon's support to clamp down on the revolt in Bangladesh, referred to in Chapter 3. When details of US backing to Khan appeared in the press, the White House, not trusting either the CIA or the FBI, decided to form an intelligence unit of its own to probe the leaks which were undermining the White House/NSC foreign policy. Thus the 'Plumbers'—a group of operatives with a common background in the Bay of Pigs CIA operation against Fidel Castro in 1961—were created. The Joint Chiefs by now knew of Kissinger's feelers towards mainland China and the secret talks with the Vietnamese, but Nixon in turn found out about the Joint Chiefs' spying operation. He feared however that challenging the military might jeopardise his re-election, as it would reveal the back-channel he and Kissinger were using to prepare their Triangular Diplomacy, a policy of actively balancing the USSR and China to extract the US from Vietnam.[69]

The Watergate saga begins when White House counsel John Dean directed the 'Plumbers' into the Watergate building to find compromising material on any Democrats using the services of a Washington call-girl ring. The police caught them red-handed, and on one of the burglars found an address book with the name of a former CIA man still on the White House staff list. In June 1972, an article by Bob Woodward appeared in the *Washington Post* reporting this. Woodward was then a junior reporter, having left a job as a lieutenant in the US Navy, most recently as a 'briefer' of the NSC on behalf of the Joint Chiefs. Shuttling between the Pentagon and the White House, a briefer provides the NSC with military information, and Woodward in this role developed a close acquaintance with his contact at the Nixon NSC, General Haig, who in turn would become the master of ceremonies in the unmaking of the president.[70]

Nixon was unaware of the break-in when Dean reported the Plumbers' arrest to him, but true to character he immediately advised him to begin playing off the FBI and the CIA against each other in order to undermine any investigation.[71] A series of articles in the *Washington Post* on the existence of a secret fund used for the re-election of the president, in breach of newly enacted election laws, only confirmed his sense that the media were after him anyway. Certainly he was re-elected by a landslide in November 1972. But a month after the inauguration, the Senate formed a committee to investigate Watergate. Nixon now stepped in to deal with it directly, but

Dean's earlier handling of the issue fatally implicated the White House, and the president was soon forced to dismiss his chief of staff Bob Haldeman, his aide Ehrlichmann, and, finally, Dean, to protect himself.[72]

The detente policy with the USSR and the spectacular visit to China had won Nixon an election, but also gained him bitter enemies at the Pentagon. In 1971, his unilateral monetary and trade policy had already alienated a different bloc of forces, the East Coast establishment committed to Atlantic unity and global liberalism. It says something about the confusion that accompanied the unravelling of the corporate liberal concept of control that some in this latter bloc were considering a change of policy along the lines of European social democracy. The advocates of imperialist militarism in the Pentagon and the military-industrial complex, on the other hand, wanted to win the wars in Southeast Asia and up the ante in the arms race with the Soviet Union. All of them considered Nixon's policies a disaster. As Kissinger puts it, 'conservatives who hated Communists and liberals who hated Nixon came together in a rare convergence, like an eclipse of the sun.'[73]

Haig now emerges as the executor of Nixon's demise, in the crucial role of White House chief of staff after Haldeman's dismissal. Although grateful to Nixon for promoting him to four-star general, Haig shared the concern of the Joint Chiefs that the blood sacrificed in Vietnam was being negotiated away by his rival Kissinger. He continued to ensure military access into the Kissinger back-channel, while simultaneously working with friends in the Democratic establishment. Supplying confidential information to Woodward as well as to the Senate Committee, Haig was able to completely demolish Nixon's position by revealing, without the president's knowledge, the existence of a secret taping system. He then encouraged Nixon to resist the public prosecutor's attempts to get hold of the tapes; and thus led the president straight to his downfall.[74]

With Gerald Ford as caretaker president, the first signs of a new hegemonic bloc in the American capitalist class, committed to a return to multilateralism, were soon apparent. Kissinger stayed on, but he had to accept that the grounds were shifting. The basis for a new policy was being laid by a prestigious planning body, the Trilateral Commission (TC) organised by David Rockefeller and his adviser, Zbigniew Brzezinski.[75] Jimmy Carter, seeking the advice of this body to develop a coherent foreign policy, criticised the key disjuncture in the Kissinger diplomacy, which was 'too paranoid and too interventionist with regard to left-wing movements on the geopolitical periphery, and too friendly with Leonid Brezhnev and the historical bastion of communist power'.[76] The Carter administration, inaugurated in 1977 and stacked with TC members, attempted to bring coherence into policy, and recapture the initiative with a 'human rights' policy. This represents a momentous choice, as it no longer drew the line as between the Right and the Left, but as between the Lockean heartland and the Hobbesian state.

Disciplinary Covert Action in Britain and Australia

Harold Wilson, the British Labour leader who served as prime minister from 1964 to 1970 and again from 1974 to 1976, eventually resigned of his own accord. But the attempts to destabilise him have been well researched and powerfully illustrate how in the 1970s interregnum, the fear of the Left on the part of the City, the secret services and sections of the press provoked unprecedented adventurism in British politics. Not that Wilson was ever a socialist, let alone a communist. As Stephen Dorril and Robin Ramsay write, he was rather 'the young expert, the man with the slide rule' annoyed with the aristocratic amateurs who ran the City. 'Private enterprise,' Wilson claimed, 'requires to be guided, instructed, even bullied by the state if the national economy is to prosper.'[77] Clearly this was not the view held by the propertied classes, and to them Wilson represented the cadre mind-set which can easily drift out of control.

Prominent among those who entertained the illusions of a British 'Third Way' between East and West, and annoyed by US urgings to rearm and restrictions on trade with the USSR, the young Wilson, in his various government positions after the war, was involved in large-scale commercial projects with the Soviet Union, involving the export of jet engines and the import of timber and grain. Wilson's trips to Moscow and the business acquaintances made by him found their way into the dossiers of the secret services and would eventually resurface in the early 1970s.[78] When he rose to Labour leader following the sudden death of Hugh Gaitskell in 1963, and was elected to lead the government the next year, Wilson became the target of intelligence surveillance. In some of the wilder allegations, he was even suspected to have been involved in a supposed KGB assassination of Gaitskell, the Labour cold warrior.[79]

The City was concerned because Wilson's hostility to its role in the economy was well known. To support the pound (as part of a deal on maintaining UK positions east of Suez, already referred to in earlier chapters), Wilson and his chancellor of the exchequer, James Callaghan, even relied on a financial agreement with Wall Street and the monetary authorities in the US, thus avoiding reliance on the Bank of England.[80] Another set of enemies was mobilised when the more doubtful cousins of the white English-speaking family, Southern Rhodesia and South Africa, unleashed their secret services on Wilson following Rhodesia's unilateral declaration of independence in 1965. A British intervention to bring the colony to heel was ruled out on the basis of misleading information about the military situation, but agents of the African minority regimes now actively began plotting a coup which involved members of the royal family.[81]

Concerned about Soviet penetration, in the summer of 1965 the CIA undertook a secret review of the British counter-intelligence service, MI5.

This spying operation in the UK, in overt breach of US–UK intelligence co-operation agreements, was revealed by (a sympathetic) Peter Wright in *Spycatcher*. Since the US government acted on several occasions on the basis of apparent knowledge of classified British cabinet documents, Wilson knew at the time that something was going on.[82] Certainly the 'Special Relationship' was at a low ebb, not least because of disagreement over Vietnam and the related devaluation and east of Suez issues. But when the CIA's counter-intelligence chief, J.J. Angleton, used a visit to Britain in 1965 to confer with MI5, not only over the Burgess spy ring but also over Wilson, it was obvious that the Americans were becoming a party to something that went beyond disagreement.[83]

By now, Callaghan had emerged as a right-wing rival to Wilson's leadership.[84] But the British Right, concerned about the growing power of the Left, was already looking beyond Labour. In 1968, newspaper magnate Cecil King of the Mirror group began a campaign to overthrow Wilson and replace the Labour government with a national unity cabinet backed by the army.[85] A full-fledged campaign of defamation against Wilson came on stream, but then Labour unexpectedly lost the 1970 election. Since the coffers of the Labour Party were practically empty, Wilson turned to some of his East–West business friends to fund his private office. Against the background of massive industrial strife under the Conservative government of Edward Heath, this swung the anti-Wilson machine into high gear for its final run.[86]

When Wilson returned to office in 1974, the campaign against him merged into the broader offensive by the heartland secret services and the ascendant New Right. An actual parafascist force, composed of a few hundred former Special Operations officers and assorted mercenaries, ready to engineer a coup against the Labour government, reinvented itself a few times before passing under the 'command' of retired general Walter Walker, a former senior NATO commander. Walker liaised with a group in the Conservative party around intelligence operative Airey Neave, the key backer of the New Right alternative to Heath, Margaret Thatcher.[87] But the right wing of the Labour government was also adjusting to the counter-offensive against the Left. On the issue of whether the Wilson government should deliver on arms deals with Chile inherited from the Tories now that Pinochet was in power, Callaghan argued that withholding arms from that brutal dictator would be a victory for communism.[88] Late in 1974, Wilson called another election, which Labour won, but again by a small margin. His hope of enlarging his majority significantly was thwarted—as was the hope of his detractors to get rid of him by a Tory victory.[89]

In 1975, plans for a coup entered a more serious stage. They were based on NATO contingency plans for a war in Europe, and required the cordoning-off of various key transport nodes, such as Northern Ireland, the port of Liverpool and Heathrow airport. There were various signs that military exercises to 'secure' these nodes were afoot; the Cunard Line was even approached by military men, asking whether they could provide a ship to be used as a floating detention centre to lock up ... the Labour cabinet![90] But the takeover plans did not have active CIA support, a precondition for success. Certainly Wilson had become embroiled with the US intelligence community on several counts, not least over his reticence to continue paying for expensive satellite signal intelligence under the UKUSA agreement. There were several US monitoring stations in the UK, and the Wilson government was not privy to what spy satellites picked up from Soviet and Chinese high-frequency communication and telephone traffic. Only after Wilson stepped down did George Bush (Sr.), the head of the CIA, negotiate a sharing agreement with Callaghan.[91] Only belatedly did Wilson take steps to stem the attacks; because, according to Dorril and Ramsay, he knew that he would soon leave office and could take some risks. He sent a letter to US Democratic leader Hubert Humphrey with questions about the role of the CIA in Britain and in Angola, bypassing MI6 and MI5, whose heads he confronted directly with evidence on the campaign against him. Bush flew to Britain to deny involvement (though conceding a CIA role in Angola). Challenged by Wilson, the director of MI6 accused his counterpart at MI5, who then apparently apologised to Wilson for what he called a private vendetta by an 'unreliable' section of MI5.[92]

Drawing a line under the corporate liberal orientation in economic policy, the Callaghan government outlined a neoliberal monetarist programme submitted to the IMF in 1976, although, as Henk Overbeek writes, 'it would take a new Tory government to broaden the scope of the new liberalism and transform it into a explicitly political strategy.'[93] I will come back to this in the final section of this chapter. Let me conclude this section by briefly investigating how Australia too was brought into line at this juncture.

Like Wilson, Australian Labour party leader Gough Whitlam is best understood as a representative of the cadre class, which in the 1960s became the dominant social force in Social Democracy. He was elected in late 1972 on a programme of belated Keynesian reforms and nationalistic resource politics, which effectively aligned mineral-rich Australia with the NIEO project. The attempt by one of his ministers to establish direct links with key member states of OPEC, the decision to withdraw Australian troops from Vietnam, and the decision to extend diplomatic recognition to mainland China then provoked the intelligence infrastructure of the heartland into action.[94] Australia is a Second Party in the structure of heartland intelligence, but this bond never extended to the left-of-centre political forces. Upon taking office, Whitlam found out that the Australian secret service, ASIS, was employing agents in Chile to destabilise the Allende government as part of the CIA strategy that culminated in the Pinochet coup. Ordering the ASIS to stop with this activity, he also instructed its sister organisation ASIO to end the security probes into his staff.[95] In August 1974, the Labour government, concluding that its instructions were being sabotaged, set up an official commission to investigate the intelligence community. A year before, a government inquiry took files from the offices of the ASIO on the grounds that it was withholding material from the government; the heads of both ASIS and ASIO were dismissed in due course.[96] This raised the question of who actually holds power, and the answer would come soon. The CIA had all along intervened with and infiltrated Australian parties and trade unions, but its attitude hardened after it had installed an important listening post at Pine Gap in central Australia to monitor communications surrounding Soviet missile tests. The head of CIA counter-intelligence at the time expressed concern that US data collection was being put into jeopardy by 'a party that has extensive historical contacts in Eastern Europe'.[97] When the Australian government made public the fact that Pine Gap was a CIA operation and threatened not to renew its lease, US agents responded by making damaging information about Whitlam available to the Australian intelligence services.[98]

Throughout Whitlam's tenure as prime minister, Rupert Murdoch—the press tycoon then on the threshold of the transnational expansion that would turn him into a key supporter of Thatcher and the media kingmaker of Tony Blair and George Bush Jr.—kept him and his ministers under fire. Revelations concerning Whitlam's private life and supposed financial deals with Iraq and Pakistan were given extensive coverage, and the minister responsible for applying the Keynesian policy, as well as his colleague for minerals and energy who had been soliciting OPEC funding, were forced out of office as a result of Murdoch press campaigns.[99] In November 1975, Whitlam himself was dismissed, on a pretext, by Governor-General (acting head of state) Sir John Kerr, himself a former liaison officer with US intelligence and a member of CIA front organisations in the 1950s and 1960s. The US had by then threatened to sever intelligence links with Australia, a member of the heartland inner circle. British intelligence too was part of the operation against the Labour government, intercepting secret communications with the Australian foreign affairs ministry.[100] Meanwhile the removal of a prime minister judged too far to the left was not just a gesture to satisfy the Right. It paved the way for a sharp turn in policy towards neoliberal monetarism under the conservative government of Malcolm Fraser, which would remain in office until 1983. As in the UK, the sharp anti-inflationary, anti-union neoliberal turn, which would deal a major blow to the country's manufacturing sector and workers, could build on preparatory work by the treasury secretary in the prior Labour government, who had already tuned in to the new line.[101]

The instrumentality of 'unleashing' the intelligence services on a left government may be obvious, although it is only in hindsight that we can see that it also served to bridge the interregnum between corporate liberalism and neoliberalism. In other countries too, key figureheads of the compromising tendency in the political class were removed at this juncture. This often happened under dramatic circumstances. In France, Robert Boulin, expected to succeed Raymond Barre as prime minister, died in a scandal fomented by the Gaullist right wing; in the Netherlands, the 1977 elections were held amidst a terror emergency, burying the Labour-led government of Joop den Uyl in spite of a massive election victory for his party. A year later, the Christian Democratic parliamentary leader, Willem Aantjes, was removed by rekindling his wartime behaviour as a youth of 18, after he had declared that the introduction of the neutron bomb by NATO would raise the issue of Dutch membership of the alliance.[102]

NEOLIBERAL CIVIL SOCIETY AGAINST THE STATE

Let me now turn to the structural changes that were made possible by the personnel changes and the terror scares. What is it about neoliberalism that allows it to become the hegemonic formula, once the strategy of tension and actual violence has restored fluidity to social development and politics? This is what will concern us in this section.

A concept of control such as neoliberalism is not a ready package which can be 'applied'. It is, as Gramsci writes of Hegel's 'Spirit', 'not a point of departure but a point of arrival, it is the ensemble of superstructures moving towards concrete and objectively universal unification and it is not a unitary presupposition.'[103] Certainly Hayek and the Mont Pèlerin Society had elaborated the key neoliberal principles long in advance; but neoliberalism as a concept of control crystallised only once the period that I call the interregnum had seen the demise of the most exposed representatives of the corporate liberal counterpoint. Other options were floated too, and were seriously considered before being discarded again. What is realised in the end, however, is never an abstract blueprint; everything that happens on the road to neoliberalism, all the unforeseen complications and grim details, contribute to and are implied in the new relations. This is what in the end determines the ethical and political status of neoliberalism.

The restructuring of democracy as 'civil society' *against the state* is the pivotal transformation in the neoliberal counter-revolution. Fukuyama's 'End of History' thesis claims that liberal capitalism and parliamentary democracy have progressed in tandem for more than a century, and have triumphed together over the 'totalitarianism' of the major contender states. In fact, though, *democracy had its wings clipped before capital could re-impose its discipline under the neoliberal concept*—the shock therapy was first applied, literally, to Chile.[104]

As I have argued in Chapter 1, the democratic revolution is at the root of modernity. It is a process of progressive emancipation—first of the bourgeoisie, but always with the implication that the remainder of society will follow. Its early development includes, as a spatial aspect, the crystallisation of the heartland/contender state structure of modern international relations, through which class formation and democratisation are thenceforth refracted. In the 1960s and early 1970s, democratic emancipation moved into a critical zone, contesting the exploitation both between social classes in the same society and between societies as such. Eventually, through the class struggles in which the response to these challenges took shape, capital would establish its sovereignty on a world scale.[105] Since this is only possible under a universal Lockean state/society complex, there evolved a parallel campaign to delegitimise its 'Hobbesian' counterpart, the tentacular state. Once more we are not looking at a preconceived strategy, but at a process of continual adjustment and repositioning. This is brought out by the successive attempts to develop a response to the rise of the Left and the contender formations.

The threat of a worldwide deepening of democracy elicited the formation or reactivation of a series of think tanks and planning groups advocating a militant response to the challenge of the Left. In Europe, there was the Pinay Circle, a breakaway from the Bilderberg conferences, and extensively enmeshed with the covert world; in East Asia, the Moon network, the World Anti-Communist League, and so on. In the US, the same period produced the Smith Richardson and Olin foundations, the more comprehensive and ambitious Heritage Foundation (interlocked with the Mont Pèlerin Society through its director and MPS treasurer, Edwin Feulner Jr.), and the revamped Committee on the Present Danger, a neo-conservative group of cold warriors.[106] These networks would eventually determine the profile and programme of the Reagan administration to a considerable extent. Their recommendations were invariably uncompromising and aimed straight at the perceived threat. Thus the Heritage Foundation early on attacked the moderates in the US who were willing to even consider the demands of the NIEO coalition.[107] In the circumstances of the 1970s, however, it would have been very dangerous to mount a counter-offensive against the radical Third World (or, for that matter, against the Soviet bloc) without first establishing a degree of unity of purpose between the ruling classes of the wider West. The Trilateral Commission branched off from the Bilderberg conferences around 1973 for this very reason. Abandoning the NATO framework with its cold war hierarchy and military-industrial involvement (as exposed by the Lockheed bribery scandal and its ramifications in Europe and Japan), the TC more consciously projected a civilian profile and a sophisticated, Gramscian 'intellectual' posture contrasting with the secrecy of Bilderberg.[108]

To avoid rivalries of the type that Bergsten, in his call to arms against OPEC, had warned would result from unilateral responses, the TC offered a prestigious channel of communication, while commissioning reports that offered in-depth analyses of the problems at hand. The fact that it soon (in 1975) came up with the key report on the 'Crisis of Democracy', referred to briefly in Chapter 4, testifies to the centrality of the issue. Daniel Bell had already indicated that the development of Fordism creates a situation where a general emancipation becomes possible, and that the very dynamic of modernism privileges the 'adversary culture'. In other words, a continuing democratisation opens the way to socialism. Bell's solution was to find ways of bringing back the proportionality between individual economic resources and political aspirations. The 'Crisis of Democracy' report pursues the same line of argument. Its authors, Michel Crozier, Samuel Huntington and Joji Watanuki, argue that relative affluence has created a problematic 'syndrome of values'. They express concern about the 'stratum of value-oriented intellectuals' critical of existing authority (what they call 'adversary intellectuals'); although they note, importantly, the parallel growth of a stratum of 'technocratic and policy-oriented intellectuals' (our managerial cadre). They conclude, 'In recent years, the operations of the democratic process do indeed appear to have generated a breakdown of traditional means of social control, a de-legitimation of political and other forms of authority, and *an overload of demands on government*, exceeding its capacity to respond.'[109]

The authors also highlight the difference between the English-speaking West, where industrialisation and democratisation have developed in tandem, and Germany, Italy, Japan and other countries (our contender states), where democratisation has historically lagged behind industrial-isation. This creates specific imbalances which expose the political order in these countries to critiques of 'bourgeois democracy' from various angles.[110] In other words, the dangers to the established order are most acute outside the Lockean heartland.[111] The solutions, one may infer, must therefore come from the West; and they were in fact being applied at this very point in time by the covert world: the Atlantic intelligence infrastructure and its parafascist auxiliaries. But the longer term requires a more enduring restructuring, which the authors of the *Crisis of Democracy* report still fail to elaborate. Thus Huntington in his chapter notes that democracy has come to be identified with equality, as referred to earlier, but he does not develop a solution.[112] It is the same with the authors' concern with inflation, which they see as a symptom of ungovernability (worldwide dollar inflation serves to buy off the contender blocs with cheap credit, national inflation makes nominal wage increases easy). In the Trilateral Commission's discussion of the report and in its recommendations, added at the end of the published report, the way forward is sought within the conditions prevailing at the time: thus, non-inflationary growth must be achieved through state *planning*, while 'advocatory journalism' must be reined in to 'restore the balance between the government and the media'. In other words, the *state* is called on to restore its own authority and rectify economic malfunctions. But this leaves the contender state aspect of the challenge to the West in place, including the overarching role of the United Nations.[113]

The Market for/against Democracy

The Trilateral approach aimed at a deradicalisation of Third World demands by creating a negotiated framework in which challenges would be handled flexibly, avoiding conflict and bringing the West's greater resources and resourcefulness to bear in the long run.[114] The underlying orientation was never one of real compromise; we are looking at a comprehensive bid for hegemony that seeks to encompass, as another TC report put it, 'a global system where the communist philosophy withers and has no new converts'.[115] But given that the contender state posture was not itself challenged, a further deepening of the Western response was needed, and here the neoliberal programme developed by Hayek and his co-religionists in the Mont Pèlerin Society takes its place.

In *The Road to Serfdom* (1944) (the writing of which he coordinated with Karl Popper's *The Open Society and Its Enemies* [1945], as part of a project meant to discredit the economic and philosophical arguments for collectivism), Hayek already develops the thesis that state intervention in the economy inevitably leads to dictatorship. More specifically, he identifies the modern cadre as the historical subject of this dictatorial drift, because of its illusory claim to be able to run society on the basis of planning. But the amount of information necessary for accomplishing this task is impossible to obtain; only the market mechanism, Hayek argues, can be trusted to effectively regulate the modern economy.[116] This does not imply a return to laissez-faire. Neoliberalism is a true utopia, built around a resurrected early-modern type of humanity that can take the place of the mass-produced Fordist subjects marching in step to collectivist servitude. This new human type, entering into cooperative relations among 'vitally satisfied men', knows only 'competitively determined freedom', not a freedom obtained through collective emancipation.[117]

The ascent of neoliberalism (as we now know it) to hegemony was never a foregone conclusion. Attempts by the Mont Pèlerin Society to build an alliance with American neo-conservatives, for instance, initially failed because political, 'value-oriented' right-wing thinkers hesitated to accept Hayek's proposals to replace the *just society* of the original democratic revolution by the *free society* governed solely by the market. Thus the neo-conservative, Irving Kristol, in 1970 wrote that there is

> no better way of indicating the distance that capitalism has travelled from its original ideological origins than by contrasting the most intelligent defender of capitalism today [Friedrich von Hayek] with his predecessors ... [However], despite Professor Hayek's ingenious analysis, men cannot accept the historical accidents of the marketplace ... as the basis for an enduring and legitimate entitlement to power, privilege, and property.[118]

Hayek's approach is, however, congruent with the original Lockean programme because it *fundamentally contests the guiding role of the state in social and economic development*—irrespective of whether that state enjoys democratic legitimacy. The state, with its instruments of redistribution, planning and crisis management, must step back before the abstract individual. The neoliberal interpretation of this individuality hinges on the notion of *choice*. Extended to all spheres of life by neoliberal thinkers like Kenneth Arrow and Anthony Downs, rational choice and, more specifically, 'Public Choice' theory identifies state regulation and redistributive policies as the cause of economic malfunctioning. The need, first identified by Bell, to restore micro-economic logic to each individual's existence, can now be addressed in a way that accommodates the very aspirations that ran through the May 1968 movement: autonomy, creativity, self-realisation. The 'free rider problem'—Bell's 'discretionary social behaviour' by people who have not actually paid for things they enjoy—can be solved if the structure of social solidarity on which the welfare state is based is removed.[119]

Although neoliberalism is a political and social programme of truly totalitarian dimensions, its rise was predicated on the restoration of the 'market' as the regulatory mechanism in society. Hence economics as a discipline is a crucial vector in its advance. Indeed the 'neo-classical' economics approach, in combination with Popper's neo-positivism, both of which were able to establish themselves as academic orthodoxy in the 1960s, paved the way for neoliberal hegemony. Neo-classical theory provides an integral micro-economic doctrine set against the state role in the economy. While behaviourism advanced in the actual social sciences, 'academic economics as taught in most American universities was subtly transformed into a fighting ideology of the "West".'[120] The Swedish central bank began awarding Nobel Prizes for economics in 1969, and the prizes for Hayek and Friedman (in 1974 and 1976, respectively) mark the crisis of the Keynesian orthodoxy both in the real economy and academically, raising the prestige of its opposite number.[121] As Enrico Augelli and Craig Murphy have argued,

> The apparent triumph of neoliberalism in the 1980s may, in fact, have something to do with the ready availability of a vast middle cadre, made up of academically trained neo-classical economists, at the very moment that a powerful leadership element formed in reaction to the economic crisis of the 1970s.[122]

As economics, neoliberalism enshrines capital as the sovereign force in organising society. The sole agencies that it explicitly recognises are the property-owning individual, who is 'free' to engage in a competitive quest for improvement; and the market, which is the regulator of this quest. Capital, as the mobile wealth that has already accumulated and has entrenched itself politically, is obscured as a social force by resurrecting an imagined universe of individuals, some of whom happen to own Microsoft, and others only their own labour power, or not even that. Neoliberalism thus naturalises capitalist relations by taking the economic definition of man as the starting point for an integral social science, while leaving 'outcomes' entirely contingent. The structural problem of modernism identified by Bell—the 'adversary culture'—is likewise solved by individualisation and a restoration of micro-economic rationality. These combine to discipline the individual's choices and tailor them to his/her actual budget. If not, the citizen is taking risks that can become unmanageable. The process of neoliberal restructuring ('reform') thus turns the 'free' individual into a force contributing to the dynamic instability of a rapidly developing capitalism, because, given 'risk', 'choice' has far-reaching consequences that may decide one's life experience in its entirety.[123]

Finally, the counterpart of the emasculated state, whose sovereignty recedes before the sovereignty of capital, is an emasculated society. The new concept of 'civil society', which has taken the place of the older uses of the term, is conceptualised primarily as the *opposite* of the coercive state, thus adding to the delegitimation of the contender tradition, and, by implication, of all development not controlled by transnational capital.[124] It also implies a changed concept of democracy as a competitive game within set limits. Just as economic competitors are not supposed to challenge the nature of the market economy itself (which is why the state has to be separate from the economy and refrain from taking on any activity which private subjects can handle), the participants in the democratic competition must accept the given, 'level playing field'; that is, the existing social-political order. *Political competition cannot therefore include those who want to change the existing order.* No freedom for the enemies of freedom. As Fukuyama writes, 'in most advanced democracies the big issues concerning the governance of the community have been settled'; this of course includes the 'choice' of economy. Hence inequality cannot become an election issue.[125] This is the implication of bracketing the economy off from the sphere of political choice, or, to use Stephen Gill's phrase, *constitutionalising* it into a foundational aspect of society. 'Responsible' political elites must therefore agree not to contest the principles of social organisation; the emotional energies of the electorate should be reserved for issues of identity and morality.[126]

Of course, interest in elections under these conditions can only decline. Why vote if the principles on which society is run are placed out of reach for the voter? Paradoxically, the only real excitement marshalled by this sanitised form of democracy occurs when 'people power' is used to remove a contender state class from office. But once the pop concerts and round-the-clock mass rallies televised around the world have helped to install the neoliberal alternative (as has happened in a number of former state socialist societies), the meaninglessness of choosing among candidates holding different babies but all committed to privatisation soon imposes itself again.

Indeed it tells us something vital about neoliberal, sanitised democracy—'polyarchy'[127]—that those like Brandt or Moro (leave alone a socialist like Allende), who were willing to include in the democratic process those committed to changing society, *had to be eliminated before the 'competition' could be opened*. The historical, inherently revolutionary process of general emancipation on which democracy was based since the Reformation and the Enlightenment (punctuated by actual revolutionary crises, and with *equality* the inherent longer-term objective) is then ideally terminated. We are lifted into an a-historical universe, because history has achieved its purpose. Instead of modernism with its promises of a future beyond necessity, we enter the hall of mirrors that is *post*-modernism, a Nietzschean world in which the only future is one's own, in *this* life; the only aspiration meaningfully entertained is that of individual improvement.[128] For the after-life, there is religion; but only for the after-life.[129]

In this light, however, the 'No' to the European Constitution in 2005 may come to mark a historical turnabout, certainly because there were earlier signs of profound dissatisfaction with the neoliberal trend. Likewise, the political shifts occurring in Latin America are suggesting a more than incidental change of course. Indeed the persistence of the state and its capacity to reconnect with emancipatory democracy is the great fear of today's New Right. James Buchanan titled a 1990 talk in Sydney, 'Socialism is Dead But Leviathan Lives On'. Feulner in his fiftieth anniversary MPS speech in 1999 again identified the state as being inherently connected to socialism; he speaks of the need, significantly, for a 'constitutional revolution'. Clearly, the neoliberal conscience remains haunted by the suspicion that the re-making of democracy along rational choice lines may not have done the job after all. New threats keep popping up to complicate the reduction of politics to individual choice. As Feulner warned in his 1999 speech, 'New causes, like environmentalism, health care reform, and others, threaten to expand Leviathan's power even further.'[130]

Neither does neoliberalism enjoy a monopoly *internationally*, thus producing new frictions. Certainly it would seem as if a planned economy is no longer a possibility *within the confines of a single state*. Yet the state as such has weathered the storm, and in both China and Iran (and in Russia), it is driving forward development in ways that should not be confused with 'capitalism' just because they take place with private proprietors riding high. In fact, the capitalism espoused by the Chinese, or even by some EU leaders, is suspect by the standards of neoliberalism. In this perspective, competition cannot be one policy among others, because this would imply that there exists a social force which can choose competition or decide otherwise; in other words, a sovereignty superior to that of capital. The neoliberal doomsday machine, once switched on, must remain beyond human control.[131]

Margaret Thatcher and the Limits of Covert Action

How the contenders challenging the West in the 1970s were dealt with, and how this entailed new rivalries, will concern us in the remainder of this study. Here I confine myself to a few brief points on how the covert aspect of the neoliberal restructuring receded again before the broader geopolitical and economic configuration of forces, taking the example of Margaret Thatcher.

Mrs. Thatcher was the exponent of an ascendant transnational neoliberal class bloc that obtained a focus in the UK as an instance of Gramsci's 'international political parties, which operate within each nation with the full concentration of the international forces'.[132] Her involvement with the more shadowy aspects of the neoliberal counter-offensive was profound, and would remain so. But it is important to see that the interregnum was really that: an exceptional state that was temporary, before the more enduring, 'regular' forces associated with capitalist rule resumed their directive role under a new hegemonic concept of control that was truly *comprehensive*, no longer dependent on violent interventions.

In the course of the 1970s, the transnational capitalist class mobilised against the Left and the global reform drive. The International Chamber of Commerce in Paris (ICC) was a particularly vocal component of the incipient counter-offensive.[133] Two key executors of the neoliberal policies applied to Britain make their appearance in this connection at the twenty-fifth ICC Conference in Madrid in 1975: US businessman Ian McGregor (who as head of British Coal in the 1985 miners' strike would lead the attack on the miners' union) and Rupert Murdoch (instrumental in defeating the printers' unions of Fleet Street as owner of part of the British press). At the ICC conference, a Committee on Social Responsibilities chaired by McGregor recommended mounting an offensive against the critics of capitalism, boldly proclaiming that 'making profits' was the true sign of social responsibility on the part of business. Murdoch, involved at that very moment in the destabilisation of the Whitlam government in Australia, was the rapporteur on the issue. The robustness of the report's conclusions can only be appreciated if one realises that the general drift at this point was still in the direction of controlling transnational corporations and socialising profits. The ICC secretary-general, Swedish bank director C.-H. Winqwist, emphasised at the conference that the Committee's recommendation to use the free press more self-confidently as a means to educate the public in the basics of capitalism (notably on the 'true role of profit') had to be acted on urgently. Otherwise, 'the attitude of government and society toward the business community, already highly critical in many nations, could become downright hostile, and that might mean the end of the free economic system as we know it today.'[134]

Another powerful push for neoliberal policies was the 1979 turn to monetarism by the US Federal Reserve under Paul Volcker, to which I return in the next chapter. This decision, inspired by the theories of Friedman and the Mont Pèlerin Society and its US offshoots, threw the credit-financed catch-up plans of the Third World and the Soviet bloc into disarray by raising real interest rates. But the blow extended to all states run on the principle of Keynesian deficit financing. If we also take into account the decision (also in 1979) to deploy new nuclear missiles in the European NATO countries, it will be clear that the Thatcher phenomenon is part of a broad trend of reasserting both the geopolitical pre-eminence of the heartland and the global discipline of capital.

As the ideological exponent of this development, Margaret Thatcher's political talents were deployed in weaving a coherent narrative around it, combining the heartland's innate superiority, the futility of the idea of socialism—or *any* historical alternative even in the distant future ('There Is No Alternative', *TINA*)—and, of course, throwing a bone to the Tory countryside. First, the state as a focus of loyalty is replaced by the notion of an *ethnic connection between democracy and the rule of law and being English*, which as we saw harks back to the origins of the West. Indeed Thatcher emphasised that democracy, an innate trait of the white English-speaking peoples, had taken root only belatedly and incompletely even in continental Western Europe. As she put it on a later occasion, the 'special relationship' with the United States denotes

> A common heritage as well as the language .... The basic things [we share] are the enlarging of freedom backed up by a rule of law, backed up by economic liberty .... This has been longer in our psyche, I think, than in anyone else's .... When you are dealing with Europe, it is nothing like the same length of time: [Democracy in] Germany [is only] in the post-war period; France [has had] one form of government, one government, after another.[135]

The individualist, neoliberal philosophy is then grafted on the heartland connection. There has to be a social contract 'between the individual and *the nation*', open to 'the free citizen, unmediated by any group as far as is possible'. Indeed, in another of her famous statements, she claimed that 'there is no such thing as society.'[136] Given the ethno-political definition of English-speaking democracy, foreigners cannot enter this social contract except as individuals. Thatcher's political mentor, Enoch Powell, had already campaigned against immigration, but his overt racism made him unattractive as a mainstream candidate. Thatcher on the other hand felt free in her election campaign to warn that Britain risked being 'swamped by people with a different culture'.[137] Once in Downing Street, she took care to cultivate an even narrower nationalism and make it as homely as possible. Leading a TV team through her new living quarters, she stressed that the furniture and the paintings were all British and if not, would soon be replaced by home-made items.[138]

The Chilean connection was a major source of inspiration. It remained an important link, including in the 'arms for Iraq' episode that would eventually end her career as prime minister. Early on, Mrs. Thatcher organised a meeting of experts from her government and the Chilean junta to compare notes on economic policy. When Hayek criticised her later for not sufficiently following the Chilean example, she had to explain to him, ironically, that the 'possibilities' in Britain, given its consensus culture and parliamentary institutions, were more limited than in Chile under Pinochet. Her trade minister and protégé, Cecil Parkinson, in an exchange with Chilean critics in 1980, likewise defended moderation as a drawback that had to be accepted.[139] Of course, the civil war methods employed by the Thatcher government in dealing with the trade unions, and the destruction of British mining and manufacturing and the corollary legacy of social destitution and drugs use, as well as the war crimes committed in the 1982 conflict with Argentina over the Falklands, bring the Thatcher years closer to the Chilean experience than formal political distinctions would suggest.

It soon became apparent that the covert element in the Thatcher 'revolution' also had to observe certain limits which it may not have been aware of. The neoliberal economic programme was enacted with lighting speed,[140] and Britain in due course took up its role in the offensive redeployment of the West. But it would seem that the Atlantic security apparatus resisted a makeover of the regular intelligence structures by zealots. When Thatcher's liaison to the parafascist Right, Airey Neave MP, announced in early 1979 that, if elected, the Tory government would reorganise the British secret services, he and the UK ambassador to The Hague, Christopher Sykes (proposed as the new head of MI6), were both assassinated. Neave's plans had been intended, as a sympathetic observer qualified them, 'to clean out the crooks and amalgamate MI5 and MI6.' But the former Colditz escapee obviously underrated the capacity of these powerful bureaucracies—embedded, as we saw, in one of the key transnational structures of the English-speaking heartland—to hold their own against adventurers.[141]

Abroad, the attempt of the transnational Right to support the bid of Franz-Josef Strauss to the chancellorship in Bonn, a covert campaign of which Thatcher assumed patronage, likewise ran into opposition from the established security forces. Of course, this campaign failed to get their man into the chancellery in Bonn. Helmut Schmidt was removed by other means; after his re-election, his government was brought down when Count Lambsdorff, the leader of the pivotal liberal coalition partner (the FDP) and a prominent member of the Atlantic ruling class himself (a member of the TC, etc.), crossed the floor in late 1982 to join forces with the Christian Democrat opposition. Helmut Kohl, who would not have beaten Schmidt in an election, was thus crowned chancellor of the Federal Republic. Anyway Strauss, the pugnacious right-winger, lacked a real basis beyond his fief, Bavaria; his candidacy had been a fairly hopeless exercise. Yet the episode provides a unique glimpse into this type of covert operation, because it was being monitored by the West German security service, the *Bundesamt für Verfassungsschütz* (BfV). The BfV report ended up in the hands of the Bavarian's old nemesis, *Der Spiegel* magazine, probably as a result of inter-service rivalries, which were rife at the time.[142]

The campaign entitled 'Victory for Strauss' was launched in September 1979 by Brian Crozier of the Institute for the Study of Conflict, a New Right organisation. Crozier's network and the Strauss campaign were inter-locked with the Pinay Circle, the aforementioned breakaway group from Bilderberg, named after the French conservative politician and former prime minister, and one of the key nodes in the neoliberal Atlantic New Right.[143] According to the BfV report, Thatcher received the Strauss campaign group in her residence, Chequers, shortly after her own election. But even with the head of MI6, Arthur Franks, on board, the Crozier group stood little chance.[144] The BfV report is important for another reason: it reveals how the conspirators planned the use of 'terrorism' to raise the profile of the candidate as a strongman needed to bring order, and also discloses the presence of senior NATO intelligence officers promising 'political action' as well as the role of editors of the quality press promising propagandistic support and 'revelations'.[145] Its aim was not achieved, but the intelligence on the 'Victory for Strauss' campaign shows that the tactics used in the inter-regnum from which neoliberalism emerged triumphant had by the late 1970s become routine for a range of groups and institutions that we would not normally associate with the extreme Right. Yet at the same time, we can only conclude that these very tactics were again being abandoned be-cause the systemic transition was now well on track in the West.

Notes

1. In the words of Robert Cox, the covert world offers the contradictory face of 'a revolu-tionary potential of popular resistance and a parasitic symbiosis with established power that enables covert elements both to prey upon society and to do some of the dirty work required to sustain established authority' (R.W. Cox 2002: 120).
2. Scott (1986: 15); cf. Scott and Marshall (1991: 1–7).
3. With the result of a range of 'morbid phenomena'—first of all, fascism (Gramsci 1975, Vol. 1: 311).
4. Hodgson (1979: 278).
5. As summarised by Willan (1991: 114). The Pike Report was actually more critical of the government's use of the CIA than of the organisation itself. The House voted not to release it but the text was published in full in *The Village Voice*, 16 February 1976.

6. My reading of the murky histories of terror/counter-terrorism is that the original perpetrators tend to be 'authentic', acting upon their own convictions; but that the forces supposedly protecting their targets from them sometimes prefer to lower their guard, out of equally authentic disgust with policies or because they are allowed (or, in exceptional cases, ordered) to do so. As the state tends to reinforce its surveillance capacities in response to terrorism, it is usually able to restore, along with 'normalcy', the directive power of the ruling class as well. But all along there is of course the 'constant' of blundering, incompetence, Murphy's law (what can go wrong, will go wrong), coincidence, etc.

7. The CIA has been characterised as 'a *Bruderbund* of Anglophile sophisticates who found powerful justification for their actions in the traditions of the Enlightenment and the principles enshrined in the Declaration of Independence' (E. Thomas, quoted in Scott-Smith 2002: 79). There is also a network of Roman Catholics of Irish origin in the CIA, interlocked with Catholic parapolitical networks at home and abroad. The OSS head, William Donovan, and later CIA prominents such as Colby, Casey, McCone and others are representatives of this Irish Catholic strand (van Wesel 1992: 258–62).

8. Richelson and Ball (1990: 151); Leigh (1989: 6–7, 31, cf. 34–5). Ireland is not itself part of the infrastructure of heartland intelligence, although it is the oldest settler colony; Canada is obviously considered a weak link.

9. Richelson and Ball (1990: 170).

10. The European headquarters were initial in France, and the network was called the Clandestine Committee for Planning (CCP). In 1964, as rivalry with Gaullist France was intensifying, the headquarters of the renamed Allied Clandestine Committee (ACC) were shifted to a location in Belgium. In addition to NATO countries, Spain, Austria, Switzerland and Sweden had their own stay-behind networks (in the event of a Soviet occupation) linked to Gladio in various ways (Müller 1991: 17, 52, 57–60; cf. F. Vitrani in *Le Monde Diplomatique*, December 1990, p. 3)

11. cf. Club Turati (1975: 39); cf. S. Wright (1998). The incidence of terror scares in NATO countries was highest when left/left-of-centre forces were gaining ground. Thus, from 1969 to the early 1970s, when reformist Social Democrats were on the ascendant in West Germany and the Netherlands, these countries were targeted by heightened terrorist activity. In southern Europe, on the other hand, terrorists seemed particularly motivated in the latter part of the decade, the period of the United Left programme in France and the Historic Compromise in Italy. 1976 was the peak year of terrorist incidents in both France and Italy (Mickolus 1980).

12. Holman (1987–88: 17). For the role of the Communists in the resistance to the Nazi occupation, see G. Kolko (1968: 172–93).

13. Müller (1991: 54–5); the information in Agee and Wolf (1987: 154–5) (originally published 1978) about 'a nucleus of a citizen army against a left-wing coup' run by a Greek-American CIA officer obviously refers to this, then still unknown, Gladio network.

14. Vergopoulos (1987–88: 110). The coup of April 1967, 'Operation Prometheus', was executed by a group from the KYP led by Georgios Papadopoulos, a former Nazi collaborator and subsequent head of the military junta, on the basis of a NATO emergency procedure drawn up in 1950 to deal with a communist attack. The coup was aided by Exxon and its Greek-American partner, Tom Pappas; Nazi exile groups like the Paladingruppe also supported the KYP in the coup. The CIA actually used the past Nazi connections of Papadopoulos to ensure his recruitment as an agent (Scott 1986: 16; Müller 1991: 55; Kowaljow and Malyschew 1986: 22–3, 33). The Esso Pappas group was a conglomerate also involved in heavy industry, e.g., Hellenic Steel; cf. *Newsweek*, 12 July 1976.

15. Holman (1987–88: 28). On the NATO/Junta connection, see R.S. Someritis in *Le Monde Diplomatique*, August 1972, pp. 1, 3.

16. The United States had advance knowledge of the impending coup and the intention of the plotters to kill Makarios (Hitchens 2002: 80–2; *Le Monde*, 15 August 1974).
17. Reiding (1975: 164–5); Holman (1987–88: 29 and *passim*). France became an arms supplier (in addition to the US) to Greece soon after the fall of the junta; cf. *Neue Zürcher Zeitung*, 21 August 1974.
18. *The Guardian*, 31 July 1974. The conservatives had polled one-third of the votes in the last elections (1964) before the coup; now, on the basis of the countryside vote, they emerged as the largest formation. This effectively frustrated the attempt to bring the the perpetrators of torture during military rule to justice; cf. *Journal de Genève*, 15 August 1975.
19. On the nationalisation project of the Commercial Bank of Greece and other components of the Andreadis group, cf. *Newsweek*, 6 September 1976. The fact that the conservatives from the start appropriated the issue of Greek EC membership isolated the left pro-European forces as long as PASOK stuck to its anti-NATO/anti-EC position. PASOK dropped the left posture soon enough, but it was not till the early 1980s that pro-EC elements within the party could gain the upper hand over the 'American' faction (*NRC-Handelsblad*, 23 November 1984; *Neue Zürcher Zeitung*, 1 June 1979; *Financial Times*, 24 June 1976).
20. Portuguese-speaking countries are among the world's main suppliers of several key resources, e.g., iron ore (Brazil, Angola) and diamonds (Angola).
21. Rother (1987–88: 91); Holman (1987–88: 25).
22. *Le Monde*, 9 August 1975; W. Burchett in *De Groene Amsterdammer*, 2 December 1975, pp. 1, 12; K. van Meter and A. Echegut in *Le Monde Diplomatique*, May 1978, p. 3.
23. Rother (1987–88: 92); Spinola, a member of the Pinay Circle, sought support for a coup from the Bavarian fiefholder Franz Josef Strauss and Deutsche Bank chief H. Abs, but although he obtained substantial funds on a European tour, his ambitions were foiled. But then Spinola was not the choice of the potential opposition forces (Roth and Ender 1984: 90). On the PCP, cf. Smith (1979), who sees the party as a product of the most isolated society of Western Europe.
24. Rejecting this comparison with the Russian liberal leader who briefly held power before the Bolshevik revolution pushed him aside, Soares apparently retorted, 'But I don't intend to become a Kerensky', upon which Kissinger snapped, 'Neither did Kerensky.' Quoted in A. Echegut in *Le Monde Diplomatique*, September 1984, p. 13.
25. Rother (1987–88: 95–6).
26. A. Echegut in *Le Monde Diplomatique*, September 1984, p. 13. This also had to do with the US need to develop a counter-revolutionary strategy in Portuguese Africa, which it could not do without Portuguese support (cf. Mittelman 1977: 62). In 1986 Portugal joined the EC along with Spain.
27. Axt and Deppe (1979: 91, 165).
28. Andreotti is one of the most complex political figures of post-war Italy. He was a member of the 'Mediterranean' faction in the DC and close to the Sicilian Mafia. He was also the real head of P-2 and the superior of Gelli, according to the widow of the director of the Banco Ambrosiano, who was found dead hanging from a bridge in London in 1982 after a financial scandal involving the Vatican (*De Volkskrant*, 4 February 1989)
29. M. Pirani in *Le Monde Diplomatique*, December 1971, p. 3.
30. *Financial Times*, 4 March 1977.
31. Willan (1991: 259, 268); *Newsweek*, 8 December 1986.
32. Club Turati (1975: 41).
33. In 1991 it was revealed that between the 1964 coup project and the next attempt in 1970, the Gladio network had worked with Italian neo-fascists in the contested Austrian province of South Tirol in preparing the bloody train bomb attack on the Italicus express in 1970 (*Humo*, 25 April 1990; *Frankfurter Allgemeine Zeitung*, 3 August 1991).

34. Willan (1991: 16). If Italy and Spain were also to close their harbours to US ships, the Sixth Fleet would have had to conduct its operations in the Mediterranean from Norfolk, Virginia (Hodgson 1979: 302).
35. Sciascia (1978: 14).
36. *Humo*, 25 April 1990; *The Observer*, 18 November 1990; *De Volkskrant*, 24 November 1990.
37. Testimony of the head of Italian counter-intelligence from 1971–75, *The Guardian*, 26 March 2001.
38. Within the CIA, revelations about narcotics deals had already led to the dismissal of James J. Angleton by the rising star and original architect of Gladio, William Colby (Scott 1986: 4).
39. Willan (1991: 220, emphasis added), based on a selection of Italian newspaper sources, interviews, and transcripts from the Moro court case. Moro collapsed during his US stay due to the strains (his wife later testified that he had actually been threatened), and cut short the visit with four days; cf. ibid.: 275.
40. In light of the preventive terror unleashed by the Right against this strategy, one observer concluded that a Chilean situation was already developing even before the PCI had entered the government; cf. F. Scianna in *Le Monde Diplomatique*, April 1978, p. 3.
41. Cf. Scholten (1975: 53, 166); Sanguinetti (1982: 67).
42. I use 'Brechtian' in reference to Brecht's 1930 play 'The Measure' (*Die Massnahme*) on the decision by a small group of communists to apply the death penalty on one of their number, with his consent, in order to enforce party discipline.
43. Hodgson (1979: 293–4, 280–1).
44. Quoted in ibid.: 298.
45. Quoted in *De Volkskrant*, 3 December 1990.
46. Willan (1991: 209). Excerpts of the US Army Field Manual (FM 30–31) found in Gelli's daughter's possession were published in Italy by the magazine *Panorama* in July 1981.
47. Hodgson (1979: 298–9).
48. Willan (1991: 225); *De Standaard*, 13 January 1989.
49. The eccentric journalist and confidant of the Italian secret state, Mino Pecorelli, himself a member of P-2 enjoying access to the security apparatus, was proven on several occasions to have information that could only have come from the highest government sources. Pecorelli was killed in the long string of assassinations that surrounds Moro's death. Among his papers were found draft articles with interviews of Andreotti and others who accused the US of having orchestrated the kidnap (Willan 1991: 245).
50. Sanguinetti (1982: 72). This book gives many examples, as does Willan's (1991), of signs that the BR, which supposedly abducted Moro, was being remote-controlled by the security services. Never, he notes, did the BR captors address the working classes, and no secrets really painful for the DC, which Moro carried around with him, ever reached the public, although he threatened to reveal them on several occasions in his letters.
51. Willan (1991: 260–6). Sciascia, a Sicilian himself, who did not have the knowledge of later trials and revelations, writes that the there is a hint of the Mafia code of practice in the BR actions (1978: 134).
52. Moro's bodyguards held their fire apparently because they recognised somebody from the security services among those holding up Moro's cavalcade; one Mafia gangster in 1993 confessed that he had been part of the BR kidnap gang, but that in turn implicates the police because the same man was at the time an informer of a regional commander of the *carabinieri* (*NRC-Handelsblad*, 15 October 1993). (I use the term 'Mafia' without specifying the different 'Mafias', i.e., Cosa Nostra, N'Drangheta, etc.)
53. In one 'confession', Moro speaks implicitly about American involvement in the strategy of tension, which he claimed was meant to bring back Italy to 'normality' after the disruption of 1968 (Willan 1991: 276–7). Willan notes that statements on Andreotti's

links with the CIA, and on Gladio, were omitted from the BR typescript, an indication that sensitive information was consciously deleted (Willan 1991: 291; Sciascia 1978: 33).

54. Willan (1991: 307, 320).

55. Quoted in ibid.: 325. The further history of Gelli, his arrest and the amazing story of how he walked out of a Swiss high-security prison while awaiting extradition fall outside the scope of this study. David Yallop's (1984) book on the supposed assassination of Pope John Paul I in the same period contains important information on the parallel state in Italy without being necessarily convincing on the actual assassination; cf. Bernstein and Politi (1997: 174).

56. Abse (1985: 31–2).

57. Quoted in Sciascia (1978: 71–2).

58. Quoted in ibid.: 72–3, 89. In a later revelation, the BR 'commander' of the Moro operation, Moretti, implied that it was the fear that Moro had already revealed vital government secrets which prevented the government from accepting Moro's release, which Moretti claimed the BR were ready to agree to (cf. Robert Katz in *International Herald Tribune*, 4 April 1994). Helmut Schmidt sent a telegram to the Italian government after the death of Moro, in which he proposed a closer Italian-German collaboration in combating terrorism, 'also to set an example for Europe and the entire world' (quoted in *De Waarheid*, 17 March 1978).

59. Sanguinetti (1982: 53, 54–5).

60. When P. Mattarella, the leader of the DC in Sicily, was assassinated in 1980 on the eve of the inauguration of the first regional government under the Historic Compromise, it was clear that this solution was not going to be tolerated under any circumstances (Sanguinetti 1982: 13, 16). The Mattarella assassination also led Andreotti to distance himself from the mafia again, and he introduced anti-mafia measures which he later claimed as proof of his lifelong anti-mafia stance (*Financial Times*, 23–24 September 1995).

61. Abse (1985: 33–7). Looking over Craxi's shoulder already was his key backer, the construction and media tycoon and P-2 member Silvio Berlusconi, later prime minister himself (Craxi fled later to Tunisia, on the run from Italian justice). On Craxi's rise, see P. Allum in *Le Monde Diplomatique*, March 1984, p. 3.

62. Sanguinetti (1982: 73).

63. Axt and Deppe (1979: 54). The key study on the transition in Spain, from Hobbesian modernisation under Franco to integration into the heartland, is Otto Holman's *Integrating Southern Europe* (1996).

64. M. Wolf (1997: 201–2). Federal counter-espionage, which obtained the information on Brandt from British code-breakers at GCHQ, passed the information to Genscher in May 1973 (Dorril 1991; Leigh 1989: 231). Cf. Brandt's own account (Brandt 1990: 303–6, 326, 333).

65. Cf. Roth and Ender (1984: 63–4). The head of the Federal intelligence service, BND, was in favour of the *Ostpolitik*; given that the counter-espionage agency worked with the British in collecting material on Brandt, the possibility of UK and other foreign involvement cannot be ruled out. Cf. the concluding section of this chapter.

66. Quoted in *Newsweek*, 21 November 1977 (emphasis added). In the same episode, the imprisoned founding members of the RAF group died in their Stuttgart jail, amidst allegations of assassination and even rape. On the RAF phenomenon, cf. Wisnewski et al. (1993) and M. Wolf (1997).

67. Colodny and Gettlin (1992: 11–3).

68. Ibid.: 42–3. In four years Haig rose from colonel in Vietnam to four-star general, a career bound to make him enemies in the Pentagon.

69. Ibid.: 48–9; cf. S. Alsop in *Newsweek*, 9 July 1973.

70. Colodny and Gettlin (1992: 190); on Woodward's naval career, see ibid.: 70–1, 83–5.

71. Ibid.: 175–77, 201–2; *The Presidential Transcripts* (1974: 103).

72. Colodny and Gettlin (1992: 245–6, 267).

73. Kissinger (2000: 983); cf. Mankoff (1974: 108).

74. Haig arranged that his old friend and deputy director of the CIA, General Vernon Walters, was hired as a translator (!) at the secret talks between Kissinger and Le Duc Tho (Walters spoke French); he brought in his old pal and CIA agent, Herbert Butterfield, to the White House; and he worked with the Democratic opponents of Nixon through Joseph Califano, a deputy defence secretary under Kennedy and Johnson, who was part of a circle that included Katherine Graham, the owner of the *Washington Post* (Colodny and Gettlin 1992: 302–5, 339, 358). He was not himself 'Deep Throat', the source of Woodward and Bernstein's reports; that, as revealed in May 2005, was a disaffected deputy director of the FBI.

75. See Gill (1990) for the definitive study on this commission and its place in the change from Nixon-style unilateralism to a global projection of power under Carter and Reagan.

76. Hodgson (1979: 292–3).

77. Dorril and Ramsay (1992: 167); Wilson quote in ibid.

78. Leigh (1989: 39–49); Dorril and Ramsay (1992: 5).

79. In 1965, the US began operating a listening station in Virginia which monitored British diplomatic transmissions (Leigh 1989: 227); cf. Dorril and Ramsay (1992: 14, 25, 78); (P. Wright 1987: 273, 363–5).

80. Dorril and Ramsay (1992: 81).

81. When discovered, the plotters got away lightly, testimony of the sympathy in the British ruling class for the settler friends in southern Africa. Within the Conservative party, the Rhodesian issue mobilised a powerful far Right current, which broke ranks with the party line for the first time (Leigh 1989: 106; Dorril and Ramsay 1992: 88–9, 96–8).

82. P. Wright (1987: 274–6); Leigh (1989: 96, 102–3); Dorril and Ramsay (1992: 109).

83. Dorril and Ramsay (1992: 115).

84. When Callaghan moved from the Treasury to the Home Office, he became privy to files collected on his colleagues and he enjoyed the confidence of those forces who were after Wilson (Leigh 1989: 149); Callaghan was the only Labour leader trusted by the secret services (Dorril and Ramsay 1992: 242).

85. Leigh (1989: 157); P. Wright (1987: 369); detailed discussion in Dorril and Ramsay (1992: 173–82).

86. Leigh (1989: 192). Heath incidentally did not fare much better than Wilson. A bachelor and conciliatory by nature, he was equally mistrusted by the far Right as a supposed security risk. The services fed information about the Red Menace to him continuously, but were disappointed by his composure (P. Wright 1987: 359–60). In February 1974, faced with a miners' strike coming on the back of the oil crisis, Heath called an ill-advised election, after which Wilson returned to power.

87. Leigh (1989: 219–21); Dorril and Ramsay (1992: 230–1, 266–7); further fascinating detail on coup planning is given in Chapter XLIII (pp. 282–90) of their book. For a candid insider's view, see James (1996: 48–9). James Reston reported on the Walker militias as part of the option to combat inflation under a state of emergency; see *International Herald Tribune*, 31 August/1 September 1974.

88. Quoted in Dorril and Ramsay (1992: 252–3).

89. Ibid.: 271. It is not without interest that at this point, union leaders were still able to assure Labour that printers would not allow smear stories to appear; something which would no longer be possible after Rupert Murdoch took the fight to the printers' unions.

90. Leigh (1989: 223–4); cf. P. Wright (1987: 371–2).

91. Leigh (1989: 226).

92. Quoted in Leigh (1989: 250). On the letter to Humphrey, see Dorril and Ramsay (1992: 302–3); on Wilson's motives, see ibid.: 308.
93. Overbeek (1986: 22). The breaking point within the Conservative Party was Heath's commitment to class compromise; cf. Overbeek (1990: 161).
94. Kaptein (1993: 85–6).
95. Whitlam also found out that the ASIS was also assisting the Americans in Vietnam. His steps to extricate Australia from the war caused great consternation in US intelligence circles. The new Australian government was qualified 'as North Vietnamese, as North Vietnamese collaborators'. At this point Angleton even considered breaking off intelligence cooperation with Australia altogether (quoted in Richelson and Ball 1990: 260; cf. Leigh 1989: 232).
96. Leigh (1989: 232).
97. Quoted in Richelson and Ball (1985: 266).
98. While the mildly left policies of the Whitlam government provoked the intelligence infrastructure into action, there was also an element of rivalry involved between two American secret services, the National Security Agency (NSA) and the CIA. The CIA was operating a signal intelligence facility in Australia, which in 1975 became subject to public debate; the organisation wanted to prevent the uproar drawing the attention of the NSA, which was apparently very resentful of the fact that the CIA was moving into an area that had been its preserve for so long (Richelson and Ball 1990: 267, 251); cf. *De Volkskrant*, 26 January 1988).
99. The press campaign was also revenge for a refused bauxite mining license; cf. Tuccille (1989: 40–1) and Kaptein (1993: 87–8).
100. Richelson and Ball (1990: 267); Leigh (1989: 233).
101. Kaptein (1993: 88–9).
102. *NRC-Handelsblad*, 5 November 1979; on Aantjes, *Haagse Post*, 29 October 1988.
103. Gramsci (1971: 446).
104. Fukuyama (1992). A more accurate assessment of the nature of the democratic triumph of the West can be found in Robinson (1996) and Görg and Hirsch (1998), which differentiate between *forms* of democracy. See also the Zamoshkin and Melvil (1982) quote in Chapter 4 (n. 2).
105. The states of the NIEO coalition and the UN, and every contender state before that, have asserted their sovereignty over capital; only in the abortive project of a Multilateral Agreement on Investment (MAI), referred to at the end of Chapter 4, can we observe a complete reversal. Short of this, the multilateral infrastructure of the Bretton Woods institutions, the WTO and the international capital markets today approximates a global sovereignty of capital.
106. Ferguson and Rogers (1986: 86–8); Scheer (1982). Cf. van der Pijl (1998: 98–135) for a historical analysis of the transnational class networks, from Freemasonry to the World Economic Forum and the Business Council on Sustainable Development.
107. Feulner (1976).
108. According to a participant in the twenty-third Bilderberg Meeting at Megève (France) in 1974, Bilderberg 'had seemed to lose its sense of direction' (quoted in Eringer 1980: 31); a year later, the Church Committee hearings in the US Senate exposed Bilderberg's chairman, Holland's Prince Bernhard, and other Bilderberg luminaries such as Franz Josef Strauss, as having been part of a bribery network for the sales of US airplanes in Europe, using the World Wildlife Fund (set up by the Prince in 1961) as a cover (Sampson 1978: 271f). The idea of a 'Gramscian' intellectual role of the TC has been developed by Gill (1990).
109. Crozier et al. (1975: 8, 9, emphasis added).

110. Ibid.: 5–6.
111. Ibid.: 30–1, 37, and 149, respectively on Europe and Japan. Watanuki considers Japan to be relatively shielded from these issues because of the existing reservoir of traditional values.
112. Huntington condemns John Rawls' *Theory of Justice* for propagating this identity between democracy and equality (in Crozier et al. 1975: 62); cf. Zamoshkin and Melvil (1982: 225) and our Chapter 11.
113. Cf. also the discussion of the Crisis of Democracy report in Robinson (1996: 68–9).
114. Christopher Makins, then deputy director of the Trilateral Commission, called the TC report 'Towards a Renovated International System' an example of the gradualist or reformist approach to the NIEO (quoted in Sklar 1980: 25).
115. Quoted in Gill (1990: 202). The initial funding for the TC came from David Rockefeller, George Franklin and David Packard; from the Ford Foundation, the Lilly endowment, the Rockefeller Brothers Fund, the Kettering Foundation (GM partner) and the Thyssen Foundation; and from corporations GM, Sears, Roebuck, Caterpillar, Deere, Exxon, Texas Instruments, Coca Cola, Time, CBS and the Wells Fargo Bank (Sklar 1980: 86). The aim was to create a forum in which the transnational bourgeoisie could develop hegemonic concepts of control applicable to the required international multilateral order.
116. Cockett (1995: 81–2); Hayek (1985); Pasche and Peters (1997).
117. W. Röpke, quoted in Walpen (2004: 58).
118. Kristol (1971: 17, 20). Cf. Walpen (2004: 172), on the Montreux MPS meeting of 1972, where Kristol was told off by Milton Friedman on account of his position. I will come back to the term 'neo-conservative' in Chapter 7.
119. Walpen (2004: 53–4); cf. the beginning of Chapter 4 of this book.
120. C. Johnson (2002: 184; cf. 188).
121. Further Nobel prizes would follow for G. Stigler, J. Buchanan, M. Allais, R. Coase, G. Becker and Vernon Smith (in 2002), although at some point we are of course looking at the MPS awarding these prizes to its own members (cf. the list in Walpen 2004: 212).
122. Augelli and Murphy (1997: 33). They add that 'it is possible that the size of this middle element may be disproportionately large compared to the "mass" element of the transnational neoliberal "party", and that a broader public reaction to the arrogance, impudence and short-sightedness of economics ... may turn out to be one of the weaknesses of transnational neoliberalism.'
123. As Alex Demirovic has written, the permanent anticipation of a potentially wrong choice and the possibility of missing a chance overstrains the individual to the point where he/she is thrown back onto him/herself, thus undermining the capacity to imagine/engage in collective action capable of changing the conditions (quoted in Walpen 2004: 243).
124. Cf. Biekart (1999), and Colás (2002) on the ambivalences of the displacement of the history/state/class nexus by the new, post-historical, civil society/social movements approach.
125. Fukuyama (1992: 317). Cf. his discussion of Nietzsche's 'last man'.
126. This constitutional process is usually informal, but occasionally explicit, as in the rules governing the European Bank for Reconstruction and Development, or the EU's proposed European Constitution today (Gill 1995 and 2003; cf. Todd 2004: 35–6; Görg and Hirsch 1998).
127. Robert Dahl's term applied by William Robinson (1996).
128. Emancipation as a general concern is shifted to overcoming those limits on full individuality and choice that potentially result from differences in gender/sexuality,

'race' and disability; cf. Fukuyama's (1992: 294) enthusiastic endorsement of this approach. Workplace protection infringes neoliberal logic; but once in a wheelchair, one is rolled back into the universe of equal rights. But let's not forget that even these compensatory emancipatory terrains are under fire from the far Right; cf. Berlet (1995).

129. The MPS explicitly attacked liberation theology; cf. Walpen (2004: 203).

130. Ibid.: 269, 251–2, quotes on 254.

131. Thus one prominent neoliberal thinker cites the statement by former EU commissioner Karel van Miert—that competition is not an aim in itself but a means to an end—as an example of the mistaken assumption that there can be a legitimate authority retaining a prerogative to limit competition (W. Möschel in *Neue Zürcher Zeitung*, 26–27 March 2005).

132. Gramsci (1971: 182 n.), as cited in Chapter 1 (n. 71).

133. Paul (2001: 105–8).

134. Bursk and Bradley (1976: 30–1). On Murdoch's right-wing views and militant support of Israel, cf. the very complimentary book by Tuccille (1989); cf. Special Report in *Newsweek*, 12 February 1996.

135. *Newsweek*, 8 October 1990.

136. 'No such thing as society' quote in Walpen (2004: 234); Barker (1982: 44).

137. Quoted in Barker (1982: 15). This was not a personal quirk; in the run-up to Thatcher's election, the Select Committee on Race Relations recommended an immigration quota for South Asians. The London *Times* approvingly recommended also elaborating a nationality law and identity cards, cf. *Times*, 22 March 1978 (the Select Committee report was dismissed as retrograde babble by the *Financial Times* on the same day).

138. Garton Ash (1983: 11).

139. Walpen (2004: 81, 232); Parkinson statements in *El Mercurio*, 30 October/5 November 1980.

140. *Le Monde*, 27 July 1979, opined that election promises (on tax reductions, reduction of the state role in the economy, and limitations on trade unions' rights) had seldom been so promptly honoured.

141. James (1996: 47). The planned head of MI5 (later EC Commissioner), C. Tugendhat, narrowly escaped an attempt at his life. Neave's killing was done by an unknown breakaway group from the IRA (he was shadow Northern Ireland secretary), but the type of fuse used in the bomb was only available to the CIA at the time (ibid.). On Neave's connections, see Leigh (1989: 220, 224).

142. Richelson and Ball (1990: 22). The monitoring in question (on which the leaked reports were based) was done by Bavarian intelligence agent H. Langemann.

143. Among the participants of the Pinay Circle meeting in Washington in December 1979 were Paul Volcker, chairman of the Federal Reserve; Ed Feulner of the Heritage Foundation and the Mont Pèlerin Society; European Commissioners K.-H. Narjes (also a TC member) and F.M. Pandolfi, a former Italian finance minister and member of the P-2 Masonic lodge; and William Colby, former CIA director and organiser of the Gladio undercover network in Europe (Roth and Ender 1984: 86; cf. Teacher 1993). Cf. James (1996: 10–1) on the many links to Thatcher. Cf. *The Observer*, 6 April 2003, on the membership of Norman Lamont, Thatcher's Chancellor of the Exchequer. This article claims that the Pinay circle had already been founded in the 1950s by Pinay and Adenauer.

144. As was the head of the French intelligence service SDECE, A. de Marenches. His status is perhaps illustrated by the fact that he was given an audience with the president-elect, Ronald Reagan, in late 1980, to present his view of the world (B. Woodward 1987: 24–5). De Marenches was a maverick operator, with a US wife, and not always in line with French policy; cf. Backman et al. (1987).

145. Friendly journalists were to be relied on by the Crozier campaign to defend the 'free society' against communist subversion; demonstrations should be organised; *personalities who posed an obstacle to the campaign goal should be discredited.* More specifically, the hand of the KGB behind terrorism should be emphasised. The editor of the *Neue Zürcher Zeitung* promised a series of articles highlighting that Schmidt was endangering the unity of NATO, etc. (excerpts of the BfV report [Langemann memorandum] to the minister of internal affairs of the state of Bavaria, 8 November 1979, in Roth and Ender 1984: 47, 59–60, 86–8; Teacher 1993).

6 From Pinochet to the Reagan Doctrine

LATIN AMERICA'S CONTENDER STATE EXPERIENCE AND ATLANTIC RIVALRY

In this chapter, we turn to the 'southern axis' of the neoliberal offensive. To place it in perspective, I begin by looking at the historical development of the contender positions of Brazil, Mexico and others, as well as Chile—the experimental station to which the principles of social organisation developed by Hayek and Friedman were first applied.

Soon after winning independence in the early nineteenth century, Latin America landed into the sphere of influence of the English-speaking heart-land. Certainly France had on various occasions tried to take the place of the dispossessed Iberian powers first; most spectacularly when Napoleon imposed a treaty on Spain to cede Louisiana, the mid-western swathe of the North American continent. But as noted in Chapter 1, the US purchase of Louisiana opened a new era of expansion for the heartland instead. The Monroe Doctrine of 1823 (with Britain a silent partner) ruled out any renewed colonisation of the American continents, while securing privileged access to its mineral riches and plantations in agreement with the merchant classes and latifundia owners.[1]

The particular state/society configurations that emerged from Spanish and Portuguese colonial rule were easily integrated into the informal, Anglo-American 'imperialism of trade', but remained ill-prepared to resist it and develop. The Iberian legacy of counter-reformation and military parasitism barred the way to a modern bourgeois state. As Gramsci noted in the 1930s,

> in these regions of the American continent there still exists a situation of the *Kulturkampf* and of the Dreyfus trial, that is to say a situation in which the secular and bourgeois element has not yet reached the stage of being able to subordinate clerical and militaristic influence and interests to the secular politics of the modern state.[2]

As in Europe, the imposition of a Leviathan subordinating sectoral and regional interests was a precondition for homogenising the social substratum into a national civil society. But the colonial heritage and the orientation towards commodity exports did not engender the sort of class compromises which industrial development requires.[3] Only when the world wars and economic crises weakened the heartland hold on the subcontinent would a series of 'semi-revolutions from above' reorient the state classes to greater autonomy and industrial development. This also reactivated rivalries on the Atlantic axis; the peculiarity of Latin American development is that the mutation to a contender state mode in the largest countries, which necessarily pitted them against the United States, interacted with the rise of new contenders in Europe, Germany first of all.

In Mexico's revolution from above under Cárdenas (1934–40), Brazil's under Vargas (1937–45), and Argentina's under Perón (1944–55), to name only the most important, 'state power emerges as the principal structure and real dynamo of bourgeois power.'[4] They were 'semi-'revolutions because import-substitution industrialisation never reached the stage where the old agrarian-commercial oligarchies were dispossessed to inaugurate a complementary revolution on the land. Certainly the political basis of the state was broadened through class compromises with organised labour, but populism implied that workers were kept in a passive role.[5] Hence the 'nationalism' of Latin American leaders was always ready to turn against the working classes again, as part of a return to export promotion and realignment with the landed interests. As Otto Holman has argued, in the Iberian mother countries, dictatorships held on to power long enough for the Hobbesian constellations to mature and mutate into Lockean ones on the basis of stable class compromises. Latin American politics on the other hand remained volatile, slipping back easily while potentially subject to revolutionary transformations.[6]

Brazil is the epitome of the Latin American contender state experience (which has typically been that of a 'secondary' contender, avoiding a direct confrontation); it remains a pivot of global rivalries today. Brazil evolved as a slave economy supplying sugar, gold and, finally, coffee to Europe. Unlike the Spanish colonies, it did not achieve its independence through an anti-colonial liberation struggle; the Portuguese regent proclaimed himself emperor in 1822. The Brazilian state then developed by gradually expanding the imperial bureaucracy to the point where it can be characterised, in the words of Bolívar Lamounier, as 'a Hobbesian construction, not in the vulgar sense of violent or tyrannical domination, but just the opposite way, meaning that certain legal fictions had to be established lest naked force becomes imperative.'[7] The Brazilian semi-revolution from above occurred when the centre of gravity in the country's class structure and regional balance shifted away from the mining, coffee-growing and commercial–financial interests concentrated in the Minas Gerais and São Paulo regions to the state of Rio Grande do Sul with its manufacturing and family-farmer profile. In 1937 Getúlio Vargas, the southern leader, established a semi-fascist political order, the *Estado Novo*, while presiding over a massive expansion of industrial production, estimated at between 50 and 60 per cent over the period of his rule.[8]

The inroads made by the ascendant contenders, Nazi Germany and Japan, through barter deals and trade agreements with Brazil, Peru and others, threatened to broaden the challenge to the heartland at this juncture; this was certainly the case when a large number of countries in Latin America suspended interest payments on their debt partially or fully to weather the crisis and use funds for development. To handle the smaller rebels, US-trained National Guard commanders could be entrusted to ensure 'good citizenship', a policy first tested in Cuba in 1933. But the larger countries were governed by state classes capable of mobilising an industrial proletariat. To deal with them, Washington had to switch to a policy of diplomatic persuasion, the 'Good Neighbour Policy'. President Roosevelt even went to Buenos Aires in 1936 to plead for inter-American solidarity against foreign military attack, but also against commercial and cultural penetration.[9] Nazi Germany became an important export market for Brazilian coffee and cotton and a source of industrial imports. It even replaced Brazilian trade with the United States to a significant extent. In addition, the air links from Brazil (and Colombia) with Axis capitals in Europe caused friction, and Pan American Airways' grip on hemispheric air traffic was only tenuously maintained.[10]

In the case of Mexico, acute rivalries between the West and the ascendant contenders across the Atlantic and Pacific likewise created the space for the country's drive to gain control over its social and economic base. When in 1938 the always restive southern neighbour nationalised the US-controlled oil industry, German and Japanese buyers were available to offset a threatening American boycott of Mexican oil. As Lloyd Gardner concludes, the eventual settlement of the dispute 'owed a good bit to Axis competition.'[11] The Mexican state too conforms broadly to the Leviathan that we expect to lead the development effort by confiscating its social base. The state class ruled through the PRI, 'the government disguised as a party'.

Import-substitution industrialisation under Cárdenas was meant to compensate for the loss of raw material exports in the world depression. But whereas the PRI successfully mobilised peasants, workers and other groups and thus prevented them from organising independently, the emergent bourgeois element tended to evade this form of incorporation. The parasitic growth of a bourgeoisie feeding on the state-led economy, which, as we saw, is a feature of the contender state experience, was an aspect of Mexico's 'revolutionary' political structure early on. 'Many members of the powerful new industrial class that had emerged by the mid-1940s never even became members of the party, let alone subsumed within sectoral confederations.' Instead, Migdal writes, the new entrepreneurs organised themselves in a Chamber of Manufacturing Industries, which negotiated with the state to obtain special privileges.[12]

Towards the end of the Second World War, with the defeat of Germany and Japan imminent, Latin America also got a taste of the redistribution within the heartland when the United States put pressure on Britain, the main foreign customer of Argentina, to embargo strategic materials in response to Perón's takeover of power in 1944.[13] This was part of a broader offensive by which the United States sought to recoup the influence in Latin America lost in the 1930s. It involved renegotiating outstanding debts, which brought reduced interest rates, extended redemption terms and debt write-offs of up to 80 per cent.[14] For Mexico and Bolivia, this was made conditional on rescinding the expropriation of US oil companies, to which Bolivia yielded but Mexico's state class did not. In Brazil, Vargas was ousted by the military in 1945. A year after the war, Washington proposed to Perón that Argentina, in order to normalise relations, liquidate German investments in the country and move away from Britain (which was already selling off its own assets). It was feared that Argentina might build an anti-Yankee bloc with Chile and its vital copper deposits. However, when the Argentinean strongman unexpectedly declared himself a Western vassal in the cold war, he was able to gain sufficient manoeuvring space to remain in power until 1955, when it was his turn to be deposed by his generals.[15]

Hence the formal sovereignty of the Latin American states, in combination with popular sentiment against the United States, placed a limit on the restoration of Western hegemony, even when the US in 1948 organised the Organisation of American States (OAS) as a cold-war, free-enterprise version of the Monroe Doctrine. US State Department planner George Kennan set the tone when he recommended that in an emergency, Washington's clients south of the border should be allowed to apply 'harsh governmental measures of repression'.[16] Given the predatory grip of US investment on the Latin American economies, conflict was bound to flare up. Between 1946 and 1951, US companies invested $1.6 billion in the region but carried back $3.1 billion.[17]

From the Cuban Revolution to Pinochet

The small states of Central America and the Caribbean, where National Guard commanders held power on Washington's account, were obviously the most vulnerable because the development option was never explored. In January 1959, Havana fell to a ragtag guerrilla army enjoying massive popular support. The Cuban revolt gained worldwide resonance because it was an authentic popular movement impossible to reduce to 'the hand of Moscow' or even communism. This was a Third World revolt in the spirit of Bandung, and it was also judged as such in Europe. When prohibited by Washington to sell arms to Fidel Castro's government, British prime minister Macmillan presciently warned Eisenhower that US policy would force Cuba into the arms of the USSR.[18] But as US sugar companies were being confiscated along with Havana's mafia-controlled leisure industry, John F. Kennedy made much of the Cuban issue in the presidential campaign, accusing his opponent Richard Nixon of having 'presided over the communization of Cuba'.[19]

Unwilling to stop a CIA 'Contra' operation planned earlier, Kennedy had to swallow the debacle of the Bay of Pigs landing in April 1961. He and his cabinet now feared that the USSR, which had meanwhile assumed strategic responsibility for Cuba, would see Washington's failure to back the invasion militarily as a sign of weakness.[20] In fact, Khrushchev was shifting resources away from the military, and he too was concerned that the other party would think he was backing down. The Soviet decision to deploy missiles in Cuba then prompted Kennedy to impose a naval blockade on the island state, the closest the world has been to a nuclear holocaust. As mentioned in Chapter 3, Kennedy was sobered by the experience. But his promise not to invade Cuba, as part of the compromise with Moscow, mobilised the Cuban exiles in Miami against him.[21] Cuba henceforth developed as a state-socialist outpost, paradoxically combining a continued agrarian export structure centring on sugar with a policy of supporting global reform and revolution.

A month before the Bay of Pigs invasion attempt, Kennedy announced the Alliance for Progress, a grand plan to defuse further revolutionary change in Latin America. Agreed at the Inter-American summit in Punta del Este in August 1961, the US promised $1 billion assistance annually in what began as a reformist attempt to 'persuade the developing countries to base their revolutions on Locke rather than Marx.'[22] But countries that risk being overwhelmed by the West must first establish a state power that unifies society and mobilises its available human and natural resources; Hobbes, not Locke, is the reference point here. Cuba's representative at Punta del Este, Che Guevara, rejected the American proposals, but there was also fierce criticism from those who signed up. As we saw, Venezuela had at this juncture just taken the initiative that would lead to OPEC, and the Chilean and Uruguayan representatives spoke out forcefully for a system of preferences that would make room for their commodity exports.[23] The contours of the later NIEO movement were becoming visible, and Brazil may again serve as the illustration that this rested on structural constraints, not on a prior political programme.

As the largest economy with the greatest potential but also with a potentially explosive mix of extreme class and simmering ethnic divisions, Brazil was at the centre of the changes which the United States sought to channel towards liberalism. But in 1963 the Johnson administration cut back on the civilian component of the Alliance for Progress, prioritising police aid and counter-insurgency training for Latin American officers (at the School of the Americas in the Panama Canal zone). Brazil was then in turmoil, with mass strikes backing the government's refusal to reduce the state role in the economy on the recommendation of the World Bank. The disintegration of the elite-based Brazilian party system as a result of intensifying class struggles in the early 1960s raised the spectre of another Cuba, this time in the largest economy of the subcontinent.[24] Like the *Estado Novo* in the 1930s, the military coup of 1964 was motivated by the 'necessity of making the revolution from above before someone else succeeded in starting one from below'.[25] The contender state posture was not abandoned; under the doctrine of 'national security', the confiscatory state merely imposed tight discipline on the working class, terrorising the Left. Otherwise, as Klaus Esser writes, the military's Action Programme of 1965 'was not essentially different from ... [the prior government's minister of the economy] Furtado's *Plano Trienal*', except for the reliance on foreign capital.[26]

Peru is another case of development through the imposition of a strong state, but a conflict with Washington over the status of the local subsidiary of Standard Oil, N.J. (today's Exxon), forced it into a more contentious, left-wing position in the face of greater US leverage. The purchase of fighter jets—refused by the US—from Gaullist France provoked a punitive suspension of American aid. This triggered the decision by the Peruvian army to take power in 1968.[27] Hence there was already a more defiant aspect to Peru's revolution from above, which was also populist in that it sought to improve the situation of the peasantry 'without permitting its effective mobilization'.[28] In line with the global drift to the left, a land reform enacted in 1969 expropriated sugar plantations both from national landowners and US companies. Nationalisation of copper mining on the other hand stopped short of harming American owners, because the Peruvian military hoped to negotiate an expansion of mining activities and an increase in copper exports.[29] However, the Nixon administration was not going to give free rein to Latin American attempts to reduce the role of transnational capital. In Bolivia, steps towards nationalisation of foreign property taken by the Torres government were cut short by a US-sponsored coup in 1971 that brought Colonel Hugo Banzer to power.[30]

In neighbouring Chile, Salvador Allende's election victory by a relative majority in 1970 represents a further drift to the left. The contender state experience here had been historically dominated by the attempt to wrest the country's mineral riches from foreign control. Chile conquered the Peruvian and Bolivian nitrate areas in a war in the early 1880s. Nitrate sold to European agriculture as fertiliser was controlled by British capital; President Balmaceda's attempt later in the decade to restrict the foreign grip ended in failure.[31] In the twentieth century, copper became the prime export commodity, a sector 90 per cent owned by US capital.[32] A Popular Front government in the 1930s set up a public institution to stimulate industrialisation, CORFO, without succeeding in upgrading industry from its secondary role next to mineral exports. In response to communist gains in local elections, in 1946 the ruling Popular Front president even moved to the US camp in the cold war, and it took until the late 1950s before the left bloc was able to recover from the experience. This then led to the Unidad Popular (UP) government, elected in 1970 on a programme of socialist transition by consent. In his inaugural address, President Allende made a reference to Engels' thesis that in a constitutional state, a parliamentary majority may peacefully guide society to socialism; he also promised that control of the state sector industries would be placed in the hands of the workers.[33]

As we have seen, the contender posture of a state in the international arena is relatively independent of its political orientation. In Chile, the nationalisation of foreign companies in 1971 was even agreed upon unanimously, in spite of bitter right-wing opposition to the UP government otherwise.[34] Chile now assumed a leading role in the mobilisation of the Third World that would culminate in the NIEO programme. The UN Development Programme convened in Santiago in 1971; UNCTAD was formed a year later. Allende actively engaged with the Andean Pact established in 1969, itself an early example of the later NIEO drive with its rules on foreign investment.[35] Chile's contender posture at this juncture in many ways confirmed the fears in the West that a broad revolt in the Third World was in progress. In 1972, CIPEC, the organisation of copper exporting countries modelled after OPEC, met in Santiago and adopted resolutions condemning the machinations of US copper companies against Chile. In his speech to the UNCTAD conference in the same year, Allende argued for the need to develop an answer, through the UN, to the impending satellite communications revolution, which otherwise would place control over global information flows in the hands of US capital.[36]

The new government was keen to try and diversify Chile's economic relations and reinforce its economic ties with the EEC and Japan. But the Western ruling classes were hardly in the mood to support a socialist experiment. In a speech unwittingly highlighting the later turn of events, Allende noted concern among NATO countries that Italy might choose to follow the 'Chilean road'.[37] In fact Nixon and Kissinger moved to destroy the UP government even before Allende had been installed officially. Intelligence documents headed 'Immediate Santiago', which are in the public domain today, spell out how the US aimed to 'overthrow Allende by a coup', preferably before his confirmation as president, but planned to 'continue vigorously beyond this date ... utilizing every appropriate resource.' Actions should be 'implemented clandestinely and securely so that the USG[overnment] and American hand be well hidden.'[38]

In a first, critical move, the commander of the army, René Schneider, was assassinated in October 1970 by a gang of parafascist military, operating under instructions from Washington.[39] This removed an important obstacle, because Schneider was committed to upholding the Chilean constitution and keeping out of politics. Allende was confirmed nevertheless, but a panoply of destabilisation measures was then put in place, including the suspension of food credits (as will be remembered, starvation was part of the US response to Third World demands). The credit refusal deprived Chile of its annual imports of 200,000 tons of wheat, greatly exacerbating the plight of the new government, in spite of a small increase of domestic food production in 1970–71. An attempted renegotiation of the Chilean debt, the highest in the world (after Israel) in 1971, also ran aground on American obstruction.[40]

The Pinochet coup took place in September 1973, half a year after the elections of March. The increase in the UP vote from 36.2 to 43.4 per cent in this poll made the chance that Allende would be turned out of office in the statutory elections of 1976 less likely.[41] The coup was welcomed by the propertied classes and the right-wing parties, including the Christian Democrats. Unlike Cuba, where nearby Florida provides a refuge for around one-eighth of the island's population, the Chilean bourgeoisie had to engage in the fight against redistribution and expropriation directly. But perhaps the fury it displayed, and the support for killing and torture afterwards, was also fed by a deeper indignation about the invasion of the prior elite political system by mass politics.[42]

Chile's isolation under the terror regime of the junta allowed a drastic reversal of economic policy, unmitigated by international institutions or even inhibitions among the military. A year after the coup, with thousands murdered and trade union activity suspended, the wage share in the national product was reduced by almost half, while the state's budget deficit was brought down from 24.7 per cent in 1973 to 2.6 per cent in 1975. Building on these first steps, a group of advisers around Milton Friedman, working with the junta's own economic experts, then elaborated the shock therapy that should guide the terror-stricken country into the promised land of neoliberalism once and for all. As Friedman emphasised in a letter to Pinochet, the restructuring was not meant as a shift in economic policy only, but intended to remake society entirely.[43] This happened, it should be remembered, when the NIEO drive was still in full progress. Indeed, as Pinochet would declare with characteristic bravura, on the renewal of his tenure as president in 1981,

> Seven years ago we found ourselves alone in the world with our staunch anticommunist stand against Soviet imperialism and with our resolute advocacy of a system of social market economy, against a socialising statism then prevailing across the Western world .... Seven years ago we were almost alone. Today we are part of a global categorical tendency. And I tell you, gentlemen: whoever may have changed his views, not Chile![44]

At the heart of the neoliberal transformation is the dismantling of the contender state posture. The liberalisation of the economy, in Chile as elsewhere, hinged on the financial sector, set free from the tight controls under which it had operated before. In combination with a liberalisation of transnational financial flows, a small oligarchy of family dynasties among the emergent transnational capitalist class was able to reap the fruits of the privatisation of state assets and dispossession of the state class.[45] In early 1977, the junta issued a new foreign investment code, which restored 'national treatment' for investors (i.e., all rights enjoyed by nationals) and a better tax regime. The new openness to transnational capital was one of the reasons for the country's withdrawal from the Andean Pact and its NIEO-style investment code.[46] Under these conditions, domestic industry declined from the peak of 29.5 per cent of GNP in 1974 to 20.7 per cent in 1980, recasting the development model away from domestic industrialisation—which was seen as the bedrock of a national bourgeoisie, of an organised working class, and, ultimately, of communism.[47]

The Brazilian 'Miracle' and its Overseas Supports

The murderous assault on the Chilean attempt at socialist democracy resonated across Latin America. In Argentina, Pinochet's coup was interpreted as a reinforcement of Brazil's influence on the continent. The government of the ailing Perón, who had returned earlier in 1973, intended to use its domestic uranium deposits in cooperation with India to develop a nuclear industry.[48] When Perón's widow, Isabel, took over in 1975, death squad terrorism by the vigilantes of the parafascist AAA aimed to break the Left, as a precondition for emulating Brazil's economic success.[49] The military coup in March 1976 seems the logical conclusion of this development. Recently declassified documents reveal how Kissinger, then in his final year as secretary of state, urged the Argentinean junta to speed up the restoration of 'stability' before human rights concerns on the part of the US Congress would interfere.[50] Estimates of the death toll in Argentina run into the tens of thousands. These include victims of the transnational intelligence and death squad network, Operation Condor, a Chilean initiative for which Argentina became a favourite hunting ground. In 1976 the Uruguayan secret service was allowed to assassinate the former president of its parliament and a minister in Buenos Aires, while their Bolivian colleagues executed former president Torres, also in Argentina.[51] Otherwise, the repression hardly reached a positive stage. The collapse of the dictatorship after the ill-conceived Malvinas/Falklands war with Britain in 1982—launched when the country was almost bankrupt—only accelerated capital flight.[52]

The military junta ruling Brazil on the other hand continued to preside over a process of substantive development. Here, Gabriel Kolko writes, 'The state-based elite appears in relatively "honest" forms .... It is strictly technocratic and defends the autonomous interests of its empire—amounting to 32 per cent of all assets of the top 300 corporations in 1974 (especially iron and steel and oil)—against foreign interests if necessary.'[53] Their sober assessment of the country's needs certainly explains why Brazil was the first foreign state to recognise the revolutionary government in Lisbon in 1974. Conscious of the $3 billion annual energy import bill, the Brazilian generals extended offers of technology and capital to Portugal and its breakaway African colonies in exchange for oil.[54] The crisis of the mid-1970s forced the country to enhance its self-sufficiency: Petrobras began a programme to develop alcohol-mixed car fuel to avoid oil imports, and Brazil built the world's largest hydroelectric dam at Itaipu in this period.[55] But under the surface of what may have appeared as a drift into the NIEO coalition (of which Mexico had meanwhile become the most vocal supporter in Latin America), there emerged, under the pressure of economic difficulties, the first signs of liberalisation as well. The tentacular state was openly criticised in the São Paulo financial press, and Ernesto Geisel (the general who headed Petrobas, and was then appointed president of the country), attempted to introduce a measured 'democratisation' from above through a closely monitored two-party system.[56]

The imbrication of Brazil's contender state posture with Atlantic rivalries reached a critical threshold when the generals began negotiating a nuclear programme with West Germany. Brazilian industrialisation had shifted the export package away from coffee to a sizeable manufacturing component and a stronger connection with Europe. By 1974, European imports from Brazil were twice US imports, while capital flows from European countries equalled those from the US.[57] European investment was already gaining ground in consumer durables when the nuclear deal with the Federal Republic of Germany added a new dimension.[58] West Germany had put its ultra-centrifuge uranium enrichment programme, which the US feared could become a cheap route to an atomic bomb, into a joint enterprise with Britain and the Netherlands in 1968.[59] In 1972 France responded by setting up a rival enrichment programme based on uranium diffusion with south European countries, including Franco's Spain. In 1975 this project, Eurodif, obtained a billion-dollar loan from the Shah of Iran, which signalled that country's own nuclear ambitions. Not only did this raise the spectre of oversupply of enriched uranium in the longer run, but of proliferation as well. In 1968, the year of the Non-Proliferation Treaty, some 200 tons of enriched uranium (which has to be reported in grams) were unaccounted for, probably as a result of secret shipments to Israel.[60]

In 1974, in response to India's nuclear test, the US convened a group of countries including the USSR to discuss a ban on exporting enrichment plants. The move to include Moscow highlights to what extent frictions with West Germany at this point overrode cold war concerns (it had been Soviet policy all along to supply only nuclear fuels and no enrichment technology to foreign users, and to require that spent fuel rods be sent back). But given temporary demand for enriched uranium as well as the potential geopolitical gains, neither the Federal Republic nor France were willing to give up equipment exports in this domain.[61] The German–Brazilian deal concluded in June 1975 dramatised the differences. Comprising uranium exploration in the Amazon, the transfer of enrichment technology, and eight 1,200-megawatt nuclear power stations (to be supplied by the combination of AEG and Siemens, KWU), it was qualified at the time as a replay of the US-German rivalries of the 1930s.[62]

The Brazilian dictatorship, like other unsavoury partners (such as apartheid South Africa and the Shah's Iran) of the European nuclear producers France and West Germany, thus seemed on the way to become a self-supporting nuclear power. Brazil was already working with Aérospatiale of France and MBB of West-Germany (both part of today's EADS) to develop licensed production of long distance missiles.[63] The US and Canada responded to the Brazilian deal by putting uranium deliveries to Germany on hold, while the IAEA, backed by the US and the USSR, launched a deep probe of the country' nuclear programme. The Germans had tried to hide their activities behind Euratom, but the EC nuclear watchdog, E. Jacchia, was on their trail and favoured closer monitoring of what Bonn was up to.[64] In 1976, after Gaullist prime minister Chirac had been replaced by Raymond Barre, a member of the Trilateral Commission, France switched to the US side. The Schmidt government on the other hand was not willing to yield to US pressure, and only promised to reconsider future nuclear exports to Brazil.[65]

Brazil's neighbours were equally concerned. Those states that could afford it, such as Venezuela, expressly sided with Carter's human rights policy as a way of reinforcing their position in the hemispheric diplomatic equation.[66] With a new generation of fast breeder reactors—developed separately by West Germany and France—on the horizon, in 1977 the Carter administration took the initiative to reverse the drift to a plutonium economy and further restrain enriched uranium trade and technology diffusion. In 1978, a new control regime under the IAEA was put in place, although West

Germany and Japan persisted in their objections. It was only as a result of popular resistance to a 'plutonium economy', and the collapse of large-scale electricity investment after privatisation, that the nuclear energy option (almost) disappeared as a scenario for the future; leaving only nuclear proliferation as an acute concern.[67]

OLIGARCHIC PRIVATISATION IN THE DEBT TRAP

The Third World industrialisation drive, like Soviet bloc modernisation, was financed in large part by OPEC oil income recycled through the London Euromarkets. In this section, I will analyse how the United States slammed the brakes on this process towards the close of the 1970s by a sharp deflationary turn, gaining leverage over the contender states by bankrupting them.

The ample credit available in the inflationary 1970s allowed the NIEO as well as the Soviet bloc state classes to evade the external control mechanisms built into official aid and foreign direct investment (FDI). Easily contracted loans gave the state classes direct control over investment decisions and hence, ample opportunities for corruption too, with a heavy top-slice taken by predatory private operators in most Third World countries.[68] Whereas foreign direct investment accounted for 30 per cent of external capital flows into Latin America in the 1960s, and bank loans and bonds for 10 per cent (the remainder was mostly official development aid); in the 1970s, banks and bondholders accounted for 57 per cent and FDI for 20 per cent.[69] The uncoupling of the dollar from gold worked as an accelerator. The flow of funds in the form of international bank lending rose from $132 billion in 1973 to $435 billion in 1977 and $665 billion in 1979, about half of which flowed to the Third World. With real interest rates negative in several years because of high inflation, the circuit of money capital to the Third World allowed a select group of contender states such as Brazil to join oil-producing states like Iran in expanding their infrastructure and industrial assets.[70]

Western banks operating from the City of London were thus effectively financing the NIEO coalition and the Soviet bloc, the contender coalition against the heartland that was in the process of coalescing around joint demands at the UN. Senator Frank Church, whose high-profile investigations of the Lockheed bribery and other scandals briefly turned him into a potential presidential candidate, therefore opened an inquiry into the size of OPEC deposits in US banks. A 1977 report for his committee warned that 'enormous financial surpluses are concentrated in the hands of a very few countries which cannot spend them for goods and services', and that these were potentially hostile countries—as they had shown by using the oil weapon against the West.[71] The banks, however, refused to cooperate with the Church committee and effectively torpedoed its investigation. They rightly claimed that the emerging global financial system hinged on the

Eurodollar markets, not on their Arab clients. Indeed the depositors were in fact highly vulnerable. This would be proven true when, under new extraterritoriality provisions in the Export Administration Act of 1979, the US authorities froze the assets of Khomeini's Iran both in the US and in US banks abroad. European banks had not been consulted but were fearful of an Iranian loan default and had to follow suit. The head of Deutsche Bank complained that the Euromarkets could not function if disrupted by political unilateralism, but the United States would go much further than this in meeting the challenge of Third World nationalism.[72]

Concern over the inflationary financing of state-led development, as well as the inflationary sustenance of the corporate liberal class compromise with organised labour, was articulated by neoliberals like Milton Friedman. In Chile he advised Pinochet, and in the US he was a leading voice in the so-called Shadow Open Market Committee advocating a neoliberal, monetarist turn.[73] Their hour struck when Paul Volcker was made head of the Federal Reserve in August 1979, in what William Greider calls 'the most important appointment of Jimmy Carter's presidency'.[74] At his confirmation hearing in August, Volcker identified declining business profitability (from 6.6 per cent in the 1960s to 3.8 per cent in the 1970s) as a sign that inflation was undermining the operation of the economy. The cause of inflation was traced widely to the capacity of the Third World states to obtain better terms of trade with the West, most spectacularly of course in the case of oil.[75] From the annual conference of the IMF, held that year in Belgrade, Volcker took home the view that inflationary growth on a world scale was creating 'dangerous instabilities', and on 6 October, a day after his return, he followed the monetarist advice to regulate interest rates by reducing the money supply rather than setting them directly. In the words of an economist at the Federal Reserve, he 'slammed on the brakes and threw the economy into the windshield.'[76]

Yet the 1979 intervention was not as straightforward as celebratory accounts in later years would have us believe. Monetarism, André Drainville has argued, is not a direct application of a prior principle to the money world, but 'a specific and contradictory mediation of neoliberal restructuring', just as neoliberalism itself is 'a cluster of negotiated settlements, a collection of hesitant, partial and contradictory arrangements'.[77] Thus, contrary to neoliberal economic wisdom, the tightening of the money supply did not diminish borrowing or speculation; at the prodding of the White House, the Federal Reserve even had to resort to imposing actual credit controls. It was this that threw the US economy into a sharp recession, sending down Carter's ratings early in the election year. The Fed then embarked on a series of interest rates hikes, forgetting about monetary targets altogether. Ronald Reagan in the end defeated Carter on the promise to restore the military primacy of the United States in the world and provide a vigorous response to the Soviet and Third World challenges, a promise dramatised by the hostage crisis in Tehran. But the series of further interest rate hikes in the interval between the election and the inauguration would turn out to be 'more effective in destroying the enemies of U.S. foreign policy around the globe than any military operation the United States could ever imagine.'[78]

Internationally, the net result was a turnaround in the long slide of the value of the dollar. As Volcker himself wrote at the time, 'a great world power does not want its policies, international security or political objectives to be impeded by external economic constraints.'[79] But was it really an *American* interest that was being asserted? Here I would argue, with Stephen Gill, that the apparently unilateral resort to US control over the dollar really served to impose the discipline of capital on the world economy.[80] Volcker's initial targets were actually the American creditors of the contender coalition, the banks which he had helped to defend against the Church committee's enquiries as a director of the Federal Reserve Bank of New York. In his new capacity, he 'wanted to shock the banks and the financial markets, even put a little fear in their hearts,' as Greider puts it. The 8 per cent reserve requirement, added to rein in bank lending to doubtful borrowers, obviously did not go down well with the big bankers who had made extensive loans to the NIEO states and the Soviet bloc. The head of Citibank even criticised Volcker for a 'lack of trust in free markets'.[81] This is true to the extent that neoliberalism relies on initial state intervention to create the conditions for its operation as a self-regulating system; once in place, everything, including interest rates, should then be decided by market forces.

In the 1979 monetarist turn, we may also discern how a transnational interest imposes itself nationally as a concentrated force—not an entirely abstract claim, given Volcker's membership of Bilderberg, the Trilateral Commission, former directorship of the Chase Manhattan bank, etc. High dollar interest rates increased the cost of capital globally, but this could only be done from the United States. As Randall Germain emphasises, a comparable move in Europe or Japan would not have had remotely the same effect.[82] In that sense the sovereignty of the United States in the broader heartland is a necessary component of the modus operandi of capital. Committed to remedying what he later called 'twenty years of government policies promoting inflation',[83] Volcker used the central role of the dollar and the relative strength of the US economy at the time to act as executor for a transnational class interest. 'It was an important turning point, almost ignored at the time, for both the U.S. economy and the world's,' writes Greider.

> The value of the hundreds of billions held internationally in dollar-denominated financial assets began to appreciate. The trend, once started, would continue

with gathering force for the next five years—profoundly altering the patterns of world trade and wealth in the 1980s.[84]

From one year to the next, state classes who had borrowed from Western creditors (states, banks, multilateral institutions)—sometimes at negative real interest rates, believing that inflation would eat away the principal in due course—found themselves stranded with massive debts in hard dollars at high real interest rates. With the Reagan administration in place, the determination to manage the global debt economy as a means of destroying the contender challenge from both the Soviet bloc and the Third World could only increase. The incoming treasury secretary, Merrill Lynch banker Donald Regan, urged the IMF in September 1981 to observe a stricter conditionality on loan recipients and to require them to apply neoliberal austerity policies. As to the World Bank, he announced that the US had 'stringent limitations on what we can do and can't do for the [Third World]'.[85] All this worked to dismantle the state-led development effort and free the private element from the constraints imposed on it across the globe.[86]

Rivalry and Privatisation in the Latin American Debt Crisis

The debt crisis broke in August 1982 when the government of Mexico announced that it could not pay the interest on its debt of $90 billion (of a total Latin American debt of $360 billion). As banks stopped lending to debtors struggling to meet their obligations, the crisis inaugurated a new round of original expropriation and rolled back the Third World economic achievements of the past 10 years. In Table 6.1, we can gauge the blow to some of the key member regions of the original NIEO coalition relative to the heartland, from the GNP figures as presented by Arrighi (in the USSR, GNP only collapsed after 1989, cf. our next chapter).

State classes everywhere were thrown into disarray by the debt crisis. The Mexican government nationalised the banks to stem capital flight, raising the number of state enterprises to 760 in 1982 (from 84 ten years earlier).[87] The drop in real wages by 28 per cent (between 1981 and 1984), on the other hand, improved conditions for private capital accumulation. The same is true in Brazil, where wages fell by 43 per cent between 1981 and 1984 and inflation remained at 141 per cent per year, compared to much higher rates of inflation in Mexico and Argentina.[88] Capital flight from Brazil reached an estimated $12 billion in 1989, but never matched the scale on which it occurred in other debtor countries.[89] The relative size of the country and its huge natural resources allowed the state class to compensate for the drying-up of foreign credit by channelling pressures for land and wealth to Amazonia. The assassination of the rubber tapper, Chico Mendes, in late 1988 and the death of a land reform minister are

Table 6.1
**Heartland-Contender Development in the Debt Crisis
(weighted GNP per capita)**

Average for Heartland = 100	1970		1980		1988	
		Volcker Shift				
North America	127.4	|	98.6		109.7	
Western Europe	73.5		103.0		91.4	
NIEO Contenders in %				Debt ⟶ Crisis		
Latin America	15.5		19.8		10.6	
Middle East and North Africa	8.1	Iran Rev.	11.1	Iraq–Iran	7.1	
Yugoslavia	18.0		22.5	War	14.1	Civil War

Source: Compiled from Arrighi (1991).

reminders of the ferocity of the drive to increase the exploitation of the vast Amazon region and the resistance of its indigenous peoples and progressive politicians. Deforestation in the area doubled between 1981 and 1989, but foreign concern about the environmental consequences was dismissed as an attempt to sabotage the development of a potential industrial rival.[90] The Brazilian state paid interest totalling $123 billion between 1971 and 1989 (on a debt that stood at $112 billion in 1989), forcing it to secure its energy needs by barter deals with countries like the USSR and Iraq. By then the military state class had abdicated and the bourgeoisie had moved in. Indebtedness was only alleviated thanks to the decline of interest rates in the 1990s and the securitisation of almost half its outstanding obligations.[91]

The haemorrhage caused by the debt crisis was given a political twist reminiscent of the NIEO days, with Fidel Castro's calls for a moratorium on interest payments in 1984–85. To pre-empt a potential surge of anti-Western resentment, the most important Latin American debtors formed the Cartagena group to work out a common position; Bolivia's suspension of payments and the decision of Peru's new president, Alan García, to limit interest payments to 10 per cent of export earnings indicated the direction in which they intended to go.[92] Hence, in October 1985 US Treasury Secretary James Baker proposed a plan to the 15 most indebted states (including the big Latin debtors but also Yugoslavia) that combined new loans ($20 billion from private banks, $9 billion from the World Bank) with an acceleration of liberalisation. Thus the debtors were asked to restructure their economies along free-market lines, effectively dismantling the contender state posture and the protection against capitalist discipline that it entails, in return for an amount less than a quarter of their combined interest obligations for the 1986–88 period.[93]

The Cartagena initiative and the unwillingness to accept the Baker Plan gained support from West Germany at this juncture, with calls for an alleviation of the debt crisis. The dramatic contraction of markets, notably in Brazil, was of course also detrimental to US exporters and investors. However, the industrial interest was more pronounced in continental Europe, and so was the effect of the debt crisis (as can be seen in Table 6.1). Because of the finance capital structures inherited from catch-up industrialisation, European banks tend to adopt the perspective of the real economy rather than engage in global speculative investment on their own. German banks certainly participated in the 1970s credit spree, but they had a share of only 6.7 per cent outstanding in the international credit market in 1985, against a Japanese share of 24.5 per cent and the US banks' 18 per cent. In Latin America, the West German share was even slightly lower: 6 per cent of the outstanding debt of the eight most indebted countries, as against the US banks' 35 per cent. Deutsche Bank, the biggest German bank and the centre of a powerful financial group (including some of West Germany's largest industrial companies such as Siemens, Daimler-Benz, and others) had doubtful debts too, but these were well covered, whereas some American banks were dangerously exposed.[94] Deutsche's maverick head, Alfred Herrhausen, spoke for a broader interest in European capital when he openly criticised US banks' credit strategies and Washington's responsibility for the debt crisis.[95] Directors from Deutsche Bank and its group were actively developing a broader consensus around a debt pardon at this juncture through symposia and private discussions. But in 1987, when Herrhausen defended his proposals in a press conference at the IMF/World Bank meeting in Washington, he met with intense hostility and actual threats. As we will see in the next chapter, the end that he would meet in 1989 would seem to be primarily connected to his involvement in support for Gorbachev's reform of the USSR rather than to the differences over handling the debt crisis. But there is no doubt as to the fury that his proposals for a pardon elicited, particularly against the background of long-standing frictions over German involvement in Latin America.[96]

Meanwhile the debt crisis worked as an accelerator in bourgeois class formation in the countries affected. Both the privatising element in the state classes of the contender states and the parasitic bourgeoisie that grows under its patronage will ultimately want to join the ranks of the transnational capitalist class, leaving state-led development behind, just as the Whigs in seventeenth-century England abandoned the Hobbesian state when it no longer served their interests. The debt crisis precipitates this process. Failing to meet the obligations on *sovereign* debt effectively means the bankrupting of the state, and 'structural adjustment'—the policy through which the restoration of capitalist discipline and heartland pre-eminence is then achieved (through IMF prescriptions, initiatives like the Baker Plan, etc.)—entails the asset-stripping of the bankrupted state through privatisation. Hence, the unification of society under the state—which is a precondition of development given the fact that the commanding heights of the world economy are already occupied by the heartland—is reversed before it has fulfilled its role entirely. This speeds up the inherent tendency of state capitalism 'to divert resources to private hands', which, as Isam al-Khafaji writes, 'paves the road for economic liberalisation irrespective of the intentions of its political leaders.'[97] Foreign capital also took part in the transition, joining in the asset-stripping of the indebted contender states by debt-equity swaps which permitted the return of transnational corporations at bargain basement prices 10 years after the NIEO had threatened to lock them out.

Whether liberalisation, along the lines of a Lockean emancipation of the ruling class from state tutelage, is really *premature* depends on the level of development reached. In the military dictatorships committed to neoliberalism, privatisation was a disciplinary operation meant to derail the supposed drift to socialism. In Chile, of 507 public companies in 1973, only 70 remained in 1977; in Argentina, the military junta sold the state interest in 370 nationalised companies within two years.[98] Chile rebounded to some extent from the shocks that followed the Pinochet coup; but Argentina's tragic fate, as a society terrorised by parafascist and state violence and looted by its capitalist class and foreign operators alike, seems at the time of this writing to have reached a point where the chances of a resumption of economic development without profound social change appear remote.[99]

Generally speaking, when privatisation transfers the ownership of assets to sections of the state class *before* the 'turn' to liberalisation and democracy is actually made, oligarchies—under the protection of the Leviathan state which they still control—may appropriate huge chunks of property along with a continued hold on state power, even if this is no longer their private fief. The Suharto dynasty's role in Indonesia, analysed by Robison and Hadiz (2004) and referred to in Chapter 3, is a case in point.[100] Mexico is another, of course in different circumstances. In late 1986, its government bilaterally agreed with its creditors to embark on a privatisation and liberalisation project. The principal beneficiaries included the family of president Carlos Salinas de Gortari, who had built a power base in the new ministry of programming and budget (set up in 1976 to steer economic policy away from national development priorities to transnational ones),[101] and Carlos Slim Helu, a member of a tight-knit Lebanese community in Latin America that includes former presidents of Brazil and Ecuador. The Salinas and Slim families were among the 13 families who became multimillionaires through the privatisation of Mexico's telephone company, Telmex.[102] The position of Slim in the top bracket that has emerged from neoliberal oli-garchic privatisation is given in Table 6.2.

Oligarchic privatisation developed amidst further growth of the region's debt, which rose to over half a trillion ($534 billion) in 1994, with a debt-to-export ratio of 280 per cent.[103] The oligarchs have risen along with new

Table 6.2
Wealthiest Individuals in Latin America, 2003, in US$ Billion

Name	Sector	Fortune	Country
Carlos Slim Helu	Telecom	7.4	Mexico
Lorenzo Mendoza	Beverages	4.3	Venezuela
Gustavo Cisneros	Media	4	Venezuela
Joseph & Moïse Safra	Banking	3.6	Brazil
Jéronimo Arango	Commerce	3.4	Mexico
Aloyso de Andrade Faria	Banking	2.7	Brazil
Lorenzo Zambrano	Cement	2	Mexico
Eugenio Garza Laguera	Beverages	1.8	Mexico
Alberto Bailleres	Mining	1.7	Mexico
Andronico Luksic	Mining	1.6	Chile
Gregorio Perez Companc	Oil	1.6	Argentina
Roberto Hernandez	Banking	1.6	Mexico
Alfredo Harp Helu	Banking	1.5	Mexico
Eliodoro Matte	Paper	1.4	Chile
Anacleto Angelini	Paper/Fuels	1.4	Chile

Source: Compiled from *Forbes* data, as in *Le Monde*, 10 November 2003 (some names include family).

transnational capitalist networks created around successive rounds of debt restructuring, and European capital and political influence have increased in the process, once again challenging the United States. Thus Spanish banks have capitalised on historic links with the region and have meanwhile surpassed US banks in terms of loans.[104] As Holman has documented, Spanish banks were crucial players in the post-Franco transition in the late 1970s. They were especially closely involved with the government of Socialist prime minister Felipe González in Spain, whose rise (like that of Mario Soares in Portugal) occurred under the auspices of Willy Brandt and the Socialist International. Of the banks in González's entourage, which were facilitating the inflow of German capital and handling its subsidies to his party, Banco Central Hispanoamericano (BCH), formed in 1991, led the foray into Latin America. In the process, it built on the liberal tradition of the Banco Central with the Latin American connections of the Hispanoamericano parent.[105] With the Luksic family (cf. Table 6.2), Chileans of Croatian origin (and active again in their country of origin as well), BCH has created a network across Latin America that includes some of the largest banks in Chile, Argentina, Paraguay, Uruguay and Peru.[106]

Regional Implications of the Return to Civilian Rule

By the mid-1980s, the new capitalist oligarchies in Latin America were ready to take over power from the military state classes presiding over bankrupt states. Enriched by asset-stripping the contender state, the oligarchs could afford to support their own front men in a civilian game of politics.[107] The West was restructuring its involvement accordingly. As William Robinson explains, from 1979 into the 1980s, the United States began to promote 'polyarchy'—sanitised democracy—confident that the issue of the economic organisation of society had been effectively depoliticised. The debt crisis also contributed by literally discrediting the idea of a national economy.[108]

Formal democracy in Latin America has historically been possible whenever the fraction of the bourgeoisie committed to internal development was able to rely on popular classes willing to accept capitalist property relations.[109] There have also been formal pacts, as in Colombia and Venezuela in the 1950s, committing two parties to peaceful alternation of government power on the basis of electoral competition. The silent presupposition, however, has always been that no attempt at popular mobilisation around the issue of socio-economic reform would be made, because that would upset the mechanism.[110] This certainly applied in the 1980s, because the military dictatorships had destroyed the Left and intimidated the population. The people were longing for a peaceful life without killings and torture, and neoliberal politicians would occasionally warn trade unions that the military were still around, lest they forget.[111]

The return to civilian rule was thus based on the careful observation of the needs of the oligarchies on the one hand and concern for broad-based economic development to neutralise resistance on the other. The NIEO had been a way to maintain this balance, but it had been defeated. In the changed circumstances, regional integration serves the same purpose. Given the unwillingness of the governing classes to 'alter the existing distributive structure in favour of the large majority of the populations of their nations, thereby creating the much greater internal market essential to making autonomous industrialization more efficient and viable', Kolko writes, Latin American common market projects offered 'a way around the small size of internal markets'.[112] ALADI, signed by eleven countries in 1980 (and replacing the LAFTA of 1960), failed, however, to overcome mutual rivalries. The military regimes of Brazil and Argentina in particular were unable to handle pressures for democratisation and integration simultaneously. Brazil rejected the monetarism of its neighbours all along; it kept a proposal by Buenos Aires for bilateral integration in abeyance until the Argentinean junta had gambled away its remaining credit in the Malvinas/Falklands adventure.[113] The civilian president, Raúl Alfonsín, then proposed sectoral integration to Brazil in 1985, and a treaty was concluded in 1988. But not unexpectedly, every further step tended to mobilise sectoral interests against the process and it was discarded.[114] In 1989–90, a new round of negotiations, bringing in Uruguay—and after the downfall of its dictator, Stroessner, Paraguay—then led to the agreement to establish Mercosur as a general common market by 1994 (in 1996, Chile and Bolivia concluded association agreements).

The Clinton administration meanwhile helped to consolidate neoliberal governance in Mexico through NAFTA, the free trade initiative that also includes Canada. NAFTA turns Mexico into an offshore location for US capital and a reservoir of surplus labour, on the lines of the 1960s Border Industrialization Programme.[115] In the US perspective, NAFTA has the political purpose of 'ratifying, supporting and extending the market-oriented reforms enacted by the Salinas regime'.[116] Mercosur, on the other hand, reactivated past rivalries. Washington and the World Bank reacted especially critically to the comprehensive treaty with the EU in 1995, declaring it to be in breach of WTO rules. The United States even made an attempt to rekindle a long-past area of friction between the Mercosur partners by speaking out on the La Plata river issue, offering Argentina a special status as a military ally outside NATO.[117]

For the Brazilian ruling class, this could only signal that there was a premium on diversification of its economic and political links. For Brazil, Mercosur is therefore a political vehicle for larger ambitions rather than a goal in itself. Brazil holds too many assets enabling it to be a world player to allow itself to be chained by a regional integration body; unlike defeated Germany, it has never been in the position where it has been forced to engage in complex agreements with victors and neighbours to restore a sovereignty lost in war. Mercosur will therefore mainly be a negotiating tool for both Brazil and Argentina to protect their interests in an eventual Free Trade Area of the Americas (FTAA).[118] On the other hand there also exists, in Brazil and elsewhere, a growing resistance to neoliberal globalisation that has to be accommodated. This resistance has produced its own transnational webs, such as the World Social Forum convening in Porto Alegre, a focus of opposition to the neoliberal capitalist class organised in the Davos World Economic Forum; and projects for Latin American integration reminiscent of an earlier age of collective economic nationalism.[119]

Hence Brazil has all along looked beyond the Western Hemisphere, consolidating its autonomy relative to the United States by developing a wide range of economic links. Brazilian capital, as we saw, already began questioning the strong state in the 1970s; over the first debt crisis decade, the state sector gradually declined from one-third of the sales total of the largest 500 companies in 1981 to less than a quarter in 1993.[120] Under the Collor government, state heavy industry began to be sold off; under Itamar Franco, this was continued and the aircraft firm, Embraer, was sold off along with a string of steel companies. The creation of Mercosur coincided with the election of F.H. Cardoso, an economist with Left credentials, to the Brazilian presidency. The confidence that he would not stand in the way of private exploitation of the enlarged economic opportunities was rewarded when Companhia Vale do Rio Doce (CVRD, the world's largest iron ore company) was put on the block too. By now, the process of oligarchic enrichment was in full swing, but with a strong foreign investment component.[121] Family dynasties *not* able to jump on the privatisation train lost out, and more and more Brazilian family firms were selling out to corporate buyers, domestic and foreign. All the big names of world business are active in the country, attracted to the Mercosur market and eager to be part of the further expansion of Brazil's international connections.[122]

However, the staggering social inequality of Brazil, the highest among the 40 countries on which the World Bank collects data,[123] inevitably makes the oligarchs' rule fragile. The election of former workers' leader Lula da Silva to the presidency was more a sign of the depth of the social and economic crisis than a solution, but it has revived the contender aspect of Brazilian development under new circumstances. Lula won after a decade of polarised blockage between the workers' party PT and the non-PT bloc, a deadlock that the PT sought to break by developing a hegemonic strategy beyond its own constituency. In 1993, Lula had already begun talking to the business world, promising to stay the neoliberal course except for privatising more carefully and prioritising productive capital over speculative finance.[124] Once in office, Lula's solution to the failure to inaugurate real social change at home has been to link the country's agrarian and mineral resources to the export-led industrial growth of China. In addition he has explored possibilities for a 'G-5' with India, South Africa, China and Russia, in an obvious attempt to bring together the strongest (potential) contender states.[125] In 2004 Brazil concluded extensive agreements with China, under which CVRD ore is supplied to China's steel factories (Brazil is world number one in iron ore and China in steel production), and Brazilian soya (grown on cleared Amazon rainforest areas, and already exported to the EU, excluding US, genetically modified soya) is exchanged for the launch of Brazilian satellites by China, while Brazilian and Chinese oil companies will be collaborating in South Asia, Iran and Latin America.[126]

Why would Brazil under a PT government be pushing for a 'G-5', replicating the format of the G-8 rather than the G-77 of the NIEO days? This can be understood in light of the demise of the United Nations as a framework for collective emancipation. The US already began to distance itself from the UN under Kissinger,[127] but the neoliberal Heritage Foundation, the key think tank behind Reagan, made this its central plank. UNCTAD, UNIDO, the UN Centre on Transnational Corporations, and other instances of expanding the UN role to monitor the world economy, all came under fire when Reagan took over.[128] UNESCO's project for a New International Information Order (NIIO), threatening the hold of Western capital on global media, became the prime target of the attack. Obviously, the NIIO brought out the major underlying weakness of the NIEO coalition—its highly uneven, often dismal domestic record on democracy and freedom of information. This allowed the Reagan and Thatcher governments to target UNESCO, initially by attacking the Senegalese UNESCO head, M'Bow (appointed in 1974), over his Byzantine manners.[129] The closure of the Centre on Transnational Corporations and the reorganisation of the UN Secretariat along business lines effectively turned the UN from a potential framework for control of the world economy into a link in the global infrastructure of sovereign capital, as advocated notably by the International Chamber of Commerce.[130] Although this is an inevitably incomplete process, for states like Brazil the UN no longer offers the possibility to develop a challenge to Western hegemony or capitalist sovereignty.[131]

ATTACKING THE WEAK LINKS OF THE 'THIRD WORLD': AFRICA AND CENTRAL AMERICA

Let me conclude this chapter by looking at the counter-revolution against left-wing regimes in the weaker states of the Third World, black Africa and Central America. First, Africa.

The collapse of the Portuguese empire in 1974 boosted progressive forces across the African continent, but the societies of Sub-Saharan Africa in most cases did not have even the beginnings of an effective state power to launch a development effort in the contender state mould.[132] Given the already existing distribution of wealth and power in the global political economy, aspirant rulers in Africa require extraordinary moral fibre to resist cheap routes to personal riches. But it is precisely here that the West and its parafascist allies have been at hand to remove those who displayed just those precious traits—from Patrice Lumumba of Congo, killed under the auspices of the Belgian state working closely with the United States; and the Mozambican independence leader, Eduardo Mondlane, assassinated in 1969; to Chris Hani, the champion of the young blacks in Soweto, whose killers in 1993 were found to be linked to a transnational far-right organisation operating from the US under the painfully accurate name 'Western Goals'.[133] When the Portuguese revolution of 1974 threatened to bring to power left-wing insurgents in Angola, Mozambique and Guinea-Bissau (and in the Indonesian archipelago of East Timor), and the Ethiopian emperor, Haile Selassie, was deposed in the same year by a left revolution, a more structural response was in order. But as we saw, this was the era in which long-term solutions were in short supply. In the circumstances, defending Western interests temporarily became a responsibility of the apartheid regime of South Africa.[134]

South Africa is the economic powerhouse of the African continent, a state-led economy and vassal of the West. Conquered by Britain in the Boer War against Dutch settlers, the country's gold, chrome, manganese, coal and diamond resources were redistributed to British and English-immigrant capital. In the 1920s, the state embarked on an industrial development strategy, in part to protect the Dutch-Afrikaner proletariat from competition from black labour. Iscor (a state iron and steel company), Escom (electricity supply) and other ventures became the core of a state sector that was to expand greatly in the 1960s and 1970s. In the 1960s, the South African state class set up a state-owned arms industry, Armscor; so that when French arms supplies were cut under the UN sanctions of 1977 in the context of the NIEO drive, the apartheid regime had its own military-industrial infrastructure in place. In 1970, the public sector's share in fixed capital stock surpassed that of the private sector.[135]

The apartheid system served as a means of regulating the labour market and maintaining high rates of exploitation by organising the black labour supply in separate reservations ('Bantustans') and townships. In the mid-1960s, resistance organised by the African National Congress seemed beaten and a decade of growth set in, encouraging the state class to seek more foreign investment. By way of diversifying from British influence, the regime attracted US and Japanese capital, while Germany at one point became so prominent that a 'Bonn-Pretoria Axis' emerged that would become particularly important for the Federal Republic's nuclear ambitions.[136] After the Second World War, German and Japanese companies had to develop ways of compensating for their country's dispossession of overseas raw material resources. In South Africa, Japanese firms became investors in the sprawling mineral empire of the Anglo-American Corporation controlled by the Oppenheimer family and in Consolidated Gold Fields. German capital on the other hand was closer to the state sector. In 1976, West Germany was South Africa's second-largest supplier and third-ranking investor, after Britain and the US.[137] West German involvement in Africa at the time had the distinct quality of evading allied controls in the defence field. This applies not only to nuclear connections with South Africa (including uranium mining in the former German colony of Namibia, then under South African control), but also the 25-year lease of an entire province in Zaire by the missile development company Otrag, for use as a test range.[138]

South African economic growth in the years leading up to the world shocks of the early 1970s, fuelled both by credit-financed state and foreign investment, made controlling black labour increasingly difficult. The country also failed, again in part because of its reliance on primitive exploitation, to develop its exports in the more technologically advanced industrial sectors. Therefore the collapse of Portuguese colonialism offered a much-needed chance for the apartheid regime to gain new credentials as an ally in the fight against communism.[139] Washington certainly welcomed this ambition. Kissinger felt all along that closer bonds with the white-ruled regimes were strategically mandatory, given Western reliance on uranium from Namibia, chrome from Rhodesia, and gold and a range of strategic services rendered by South Africa. The US should therefore 'edge discreetly away from any general support for African nationalism.'[140]

Mineral-rich Angola was the key prize among the Portuguese colonial assets. Kissinger, writes the former CIA station chief in Angola, John Stockwell, 'was determined the Soviets should not be permitted to make a move in any remote part of the world without being confronted militarily by the United States.'[141] The Portuguese revolutionary government intended to hand power to the MPLA, but there existed a rival insurgent movement, the FNLA, operating from neighbouring Zaire, today's Congo. Zaire's corrupt president, Mobutu, had been installed by the United States after the assassination of Lumumba, but he had recently turned to China for arms. Only in July 1974 did the CIA join in to support the FNLA; a month later, Moscow threw its weight behind the MPLA as the legitimate liberation movement. A second rival movement to the MPLA, the tribal based UNITA under Jonas Savimbi, was also supported by the CIA.[142] In Mozambique, the Renamo (or MNR) 'Contra' forces, ranged against the left-wing FRELIMO government installed in mid-1975, had been set up by Rhodesian intelligence; South Africa took care of its communications and supplies in order to keep Mozambique in a permanent state of collapse.[143] In 1975, however, under the Clark Amendment the US Congress forbade all covert CIA involvement in Angola, and, by implication, elsewhere. On a visit to Zaire in August, French president Giscard promised to suspend all strategic arms to South Africa.[144]

The MPLA officially declared Angola's independence in November 1975, but so did the FLNA. A South African military column was driving the MPLA forces and their recently arrived Cuban advisers ahead of them in their push to Luanda, while UNITA and South African troops moved along the railway towards the capital from the east. When Nigeria began to extend financial support for the MPLA, it turned out that Washington did not have the means to follow up Kissinger's initial orders to 'seek every means to escalate the Angolan conflict.' In January 1976, the South Africans, confronted with an airlifted Cuban force of division strength with tanks and fighter aircraft, and following the refusal of the Ford administration to acknowledge their military intervention openly, withdrew from the country. French involvement (via Zaire) was terminated the same month.[145]

South Africa was not the only state-led economy in the region. White-ruled Rhodesia, traditionally a tobacco and raw material exporter, also switched to state-monitored economic development after 1965, to deal with the embargo imposed after unilateral independence. By the mid-1970s Rhodesia was the second-largest industrial economy of Africa.[146] After failed assassination attempts on the lives of the leaders of the Patriotic Front, Mugabe and Nkomo, the position of the minority regime and its black puppets deteriorated; we have to remind ourselves that this was still the period of growing Third World power. Even Kissinger, after a tour of the region in early 1976, warned that a compromise solution had to be developed. This was echoed by UK Labour minister Anthony Crosland, who told NATO colleagues that if 'issues were settled on the battlefield, it would seriously lessen the chances of bringing about a moderate regime in Rhodesia.'[147]

This was also the line pursued by the Carter administration. Certainly the new cold war was by now beginning to reach Africa in the form of a campaign against Cuban and Soviet support for the MPLA and other left movements in the region. But this did not itself improve the chances for the Rhodesian regime to survive. National Security Adviser Brzezinski even added South Africa itself to the list of countries where change had to be promoted if an 'apocalyptic alternative' were to be avoided.[148] The social explosion among the million or so inhabitants of Soweto in mid-1976, on the heels of the humiliating withdrawal from Angola, brought home the fragility of the apartheid regime; the furious repression that followed the uprising killed many hundreds—most famously the black leader, Steve Biko—and drove thousands more across the borders to join the military arm of the ANC.[149]

The incoming neoliberal governments in the English-speaking heartland soon found out that the left tide in Africa would have to be turned by different means. The Reagan administration launched a new type of counter-guerrilla warfare, which for the US at least was a 'low intensity' form of conflict. Margaret Thatcher, whose rise had occurred in a climate in which the covert arms of the southern African minority regimes had played a role of their own, was willing to reward the Rhodesian minority regime in spite of Commonwealth protests. But here too, the covert fringe had to cede pride of place to mainstream capitalist interests. Lord Carrington, her foreign secretary—a Bilderberg and TC member with past directorships in Rio Tinto Zinc, Barclays Bank and other blue-chip firms with important interests in the region—arranged a deal with the Patriotic Front that granted continued land rights for the big white landowners in the new state of Zimbabwe.[150]

Low Intensity Conflict and Terror under the Reagan Doctrine

The shift to a new counter-revolutionary strategy in the aftermath of the Vietnam war was adorned with the phrase 'low intensity warfare', because it was obvious that the American public was in no mood to be drawn into another major foreign military adventure on that scale. Ideas about new, cheaper forms of counter-insurgency were circulating well before the Pentagon commissioned BDM Corp in Arlington to write an eight-volume, 3,500-page report (finalised in 1981) meant to underpin the low intensity warfare strategy. In a speech in late 1984, Reagan's defence secretary Weinberger summed up the conditions under which military power could be applied. Vital national interests should be at stake; certainty of victory assured; clear goals set; support of the American public in place; and there should be a constant review of ends and means in light of changing circumstances. Only in extreme cases should US troops be sent in for 'mopping up' operations. The Grenada invasion in 1983 would be the first example of the strategy.[151] Elements of the strategy had already been applied, though, when the province of Shaba in Zaire rose up against Mobutu in 1978. It was left to Moroccan military and French and Belgian paratroops to safeguard the foreign mining interests; Saudi Arabia covered expenses. Planes of the Otrag missile company active in Shaba took care of transport and repatriation along with US transport planes, although Carter would have preferred it to be a European affair altogether. But NATO commander Alexander Haig successfully pressed for greater American involvement.[152]

Haig became Reagan's first secretary of state and, in spite of his short tenure, played a crucial role in developing a new policy. Soon after his confirmation he proposed to exchange the use of the term 'national liberation' with the term 'terrorism' to denote rebel activity in the periphery (he also denied that the term 'Third World' had any meaning). Thus Moscow, on account of its support for national liberation movements, could be identified with terrorism, which Haig in a State Department 'Current Policy' document qualified as the greatest threat to world peace.[153] With William Casey, the new CIA director, he developed plans to actively target unfriendly regimes and 'terrorist' groups. Libya was among the first objectives. In late 1981, US citizens were ordered out of the country although oil continued to be imported; CIA reports about Libyan intentions to assassinate Reagan later proved to be hoaxes.[154] A Senate subcommittee on Security and Terrorism began work in 1982 to investigate the backing of 'terrorist movements' in southern Africa by foreign states. In the same year Casey travelled to South Africa to study how a cordon of counter-insurgency movements against left-wing regimes could be created to protect the apartheid regime.[155] Renamo/MNR in Mozambique and UNITA and FNLA in Angola were included in a Heritage Foundation report in November 1984 that recommended support for Contras in nine countries. Ultra-right drugstore tycoon Lewis Lehrman, involved in a range of private Contra-support networks as well as a board member of Heritage, went to Angola in June 1985 to meet Jonas Savimbi, the leader of UNITA, and brought him to Washington. Congress however still balked at the idea of sponsoring global terrorism and it fell to the Heritage Foundation, Western Goals, the World Anti-Communist League, and various Protestant fundamentalist 'churches' to pick up the tab.[156] In March 1986, Reagan sought to provide new legitimacy to these activities in a message to Congress entitled 'Freedom, Regional Security and Global Peace', which became known as the Reagan Doctrine.[157]

In Africa as elsewhere, counter-revolutionary terror entailed generating human misery, which creates a population exhausted by killing and maiming, and welcoming the 'return' of sanitised democracy of the neoliberal variety. In addition, apartheid was abolished in South Africa once the threat of communism subsided. Privatisation saw the ANC cadre joining in the asset-stripping of the state and becoming millionaires in their own right.[158] But across the continent, a new generation of leaders has emerged in the wake of the defeat of the Left. There is a new element of rivalry at work in Africa that has replaced the divided loyalties of the cold war—a rivalry that works notably against the Francophone rulers who used to rely on patronage from Paris as well as the handful of survivors of the late 1970s national liberation episodes, such as Mugabe of Zimbabwe. The new rift was an aspect of the Tutsi genocide in Rwanda and the subsequent withdrawal of Hutu perpetrators into Zaire, which in turn contributed to the collapse of the Mobutu dictatorship in 1997. The ascendant forces that have emerged from these conflicts tend to be English-speaking leaders such as the new rulers of Uganda, Rwanda, Ethiopia (and independent Eritrea) and Angola. At the time of the takeover in Zaire (again renamed Congo), their combined effort was triumphant. These leaders have been characterised as having left behind their youthful leftism for an economic pragmatism amenable to transnational capital, which may be Western newspaper hype and wishful thinking. But their advance has certainly curtailed French influence in Africa.[159]

Socialists in America's Backyard

In the late 1970s Central America became part of the world-wide collapse of the imperial positions built up by the West in the cold war, and the terrain of a particularly grim counter-revolutionary offensive in the ensuing decade. As George Black has emphasised, the political collapse preceded the economic crisis that provided the mass base for the Left. But to the forces associated with the rise of Reagan in the United States, in particular the 'California Suite' associated with the president's earlier career as governor and including his successive national security advisers, Central America was directly adjacent to their home turf. Seventy per cent of US oil imports reach the country through the Caribbean, and for Sunbelt capitalists in the tourist business, coffee and fruit trade, as well as for the military and some high-tech military suppliers, this is literally their own backyard that cannot be allowed to fall to 'communists'.[160] The Carter administration had shown itself weak in this area too; Carter's conscientious commitment to 'protecting the individual from the arbitrary power of the state' came when revolution was clearly moving beyond a Lockean format.[161] Haig, on the other hand, wanted to inflict a quick defeat of the Left. Like Casey, he was a fervent Roman Catholic, deeply concerned about the supposed suffering of the church in El Salvador, Nicaragua and Cuba.[162]

The Sandinista revolution in Nicaragua in 1979 brought a wide alliance of democratic forces, including business, to power. Its dominant tendency was supported by European Social Democracy, keen to avoid a radicalisation of the revolution. When the United States in early 1980 froze a major loan agreed earlier with the Sandinistas, the Soviet Union sent an expert team to assist in economic development and infrastructure. European concern mounted as a Cuba-like rift with the US seemed to be developing; the call by the Socialist International to support the Sandinista government was responded to by the Social Democratic governments of West Germany, Sweden, Spain and France, but primarily out of a concern to moderate the revolution.[163] In fact the Sandinistas allowed the private sector to retain property rights over three-quarters of the means of production, channelling 80 per cent of state aid to it; but the representative of the business world in the junta was not convinced of their ultimate intentions and joined forces with the breakaway Sandinista group of E. Pastora, operating on the border with Costa Rica. The CIA meanwhile recruited elements from Somoza's National Guard into a Contra force operating from the Honduran border in the north.[164] The Contra operation was exposed by *Newsweek* in 1982, and Congress adopted the Boland amendment denying funds earmarked for toppling the Sandinistas to the government. This shifted operations underground, and in late 1983 a small CIA contingent and Colonel Oliver North of the National Security Council began organising a covert war.[165]

European differences with the Reagan administration were more pronounced in relations with El Salvador, where a powerful left guerrilla force mobilised the landless poor who had lost what little they had in the crisis of the 1970s.[166] The military seized power in October 1979 to deal with the insurgency, inviting the United States to assist in what would become a bloody testing ground for the Low Intensity Warfare strategy that claimed some 60,000 dead. The Salvadoran army was increased from 9,000 men in 1980 to 39,000 in 1985, with a further 10,000 security forces assisting the regular army. Armed by Israel and with US Huey helicopters used in Vietnam, the military applied a displacement strategy reminiscent of America's earlier war, consciously creating refugee populations, which were then politically neutralised.[167] European humanitarian aid to Salvadoran refugees in Honduras spilled over into overt disagreement with Washington when France under Mitterrand in a joint statement with Mexico effectively recognised the left guerrillas of the FMLN in 1981, while the European Parliament condemned the Salvadoran elections as a farce.[168] The elections were intended to isolate the FMLN, who were in no position to accept the invitation to come forward and compete openly for votes; the death squads of Major d'Aubuisson, an alumnus of the School of the Americas, had already killed the entire political wing of the FMLN before the election. The assassination of the moderate archbishop of San Salvador, Romero, while dedicating mass in the city's cathedral, was a signal that nobody was safe.[169]

A third major instance of the Low Intensity Warfare strategy concerned Guatemala. This country had a long history of left-wing rebellion against its oligarchy, and of US intervention to boot. When a guerrilla war resumed in the 1970s, however, the Ford administration imposed an arms embargo in light of the appalling human rights abuses; this forced the Guatemalan oligarchy and army to look elsewhere. Israel, isolated by the anti-Zionist campaign in the UN, offered to step into the breach, supplying arms and advisers for a strategic hamlet plan meant to control the indigenous population. It was also involved in the coup d'état that brought Ríos Montt to power in early 1982.[170] Montt, a Protestant fundamentalist, had links with the religious Right in the US, but otherwise owed his success with the insurgency to a homegrown strategy relying less on the US. Closing off the border with Mexico, in 1982 the army succeeded in subduing the rebellion by a strategy of total warfare against the indigenous population that bordered on genocide. This provoked a new coup ousting Montt a year later, after which the military switched to a strategy of elections and targeted killings to retain power.[171]

In 1983 the United States invaded the small island state of Grenada in the wake of infighting in the ruling left party. In combination with a political shift in Europe (highlighted by the ouster of Helmut Schmidt's SPD), this changed the European perspective on Central America. Certainly Mrs. Thatcher warned Reagan that the invasion of Grenada (a Commonwealth member) would generate anti-Americanism, endangering the deployment of NATO cruise missiles; she condemned 'intervention ... in the internal affairs of a small independent nation, however unattractive its regime'.[172] Otherwise, European politicians did not dare to resist the US, or were just fearful of war. The EC became the largest aid donor to Central America in the years that followed, but political support now went to bourgeois forces, with socialists like Felipe González admonishing the Sandinistas to do more about pluralism.[173] Meanwhile Pope John Paul II began to mobilise conservative clergy in Central America, promoting men like Obando y Bravo, the reactionary bishop of Managua, to cardinal, while sanctioning the Jesuit poet in the Sandinista government, Ernesto Cardenal. The pope equated US intervention with supposed Soviet intervention and remained silent on initiatives, taken with European support, to bring peace to the region.[174]

In late 1983 the CIA raided Nicaragua's ports with speedboats, destroying most of the country's oil stocks. US oil companies were prevailed upon to conduct repair work only if paid in advance; Exxon let Managua know that it would no longer supply tankers. But when steps were taken to mine Nicaragua's harbours, an uproar in Congress, fearful that a Soviet tanker might be blown up, again curtailed US involvement in April 1984.[175] Funds for the opposition and covert operations in Nicaragua were banned. This was again subverted by the North network of private organisations in the US and an array of foreign allies of the Reagan administration, including Saudi Arabia, Taiwan, South Korea, the Likud government of Israel, and others. Retired general John Singlaub, head of the World Anti-Communist League, was a key figure in these networks and also their liaison with the Pentagon. In 1984, the White House arranged that Saudi Arabia would begin paying $1 million a month to the Contras, through an account in the Cayman Islands in Colonel North's name.[176]

A final source of financing the Nicaraguan Contras was the drugs trade. 'The epidemic of cocaine and heroin that has afflicted American cities during the past two decades,' Chalmers Johnson writes, 'was probably fuelled in part by Central and South American military officers or corrupt politicians whom the CIA or the Pentagon once trained or supported and then installed in key government positions.' The Nicaraguan Contras were allowed 'to sell cocaine in American cities in order to buy arms and supplies.'[177] The Medellín cocaine cartel had already been part of the effort before the Congressional ban and provided the planes to transport arms, which on return brought their own merchandise back into the US.[178]

The case of Grenada, the Korean Boeing incident to which I return in the next chapter, and the attack on US Marines in Beirut, all contributed to a change in the political mood in the US. In June 1985, the House voted an aid package of $27 million for the Nicaraguan Contras. In July, the Clark Amendment, which had stood in the way of support for the anti-communist rebels in Angola, was revoked. This cleared the way for the proclamation of the Reagan doctrine already referred to. By now, however, the White House had become entangled in a new channel of covert support for the Contras, a network of arms smugglers supplying Iran in the war with Iraq, in exchange for promises to release American hostages in Lebanon; I return to this in Chapter 10.[179] In the end, exhausted by revolution and the 'low intensity' counter-revolution that killed hundreds of thousands, the countries of Central America, too, turned to sanitised democracy. Elections in 1989 (El Salvador, Honduras) and 1990 (Nicaragua and Costa Rica) returned conservative coalitions into office, burying the threat of the Left.[180]

Notes

1. Nederveen Pieterse (1990: 312); Gallagher and Robinson (1967: 241).
2. Gramsci (1971: 22).
3. Therborn (1979: 101). Extreme differences between rich and poor persist and the state therefore operates under the circumstances of a 'permanent state of emergency' (Sonntag 1973: 174).
4. F. Fernandes (speaking on Brazil) quoted in P. Evans (1979: 42).
5. Ibid.: 39; the term 'semi-revolution' comes from Löwy (1981). As to relations on the land, only in Bolivia, Peru and Mexico was the latifundia system abolished; else-where, it was in fact reinforced, so that large land ownership today accounts for 65 per cent of Latin American farm acreage. In Brazil, some 0.01 per cent of the population owns the greater part of the land (Chua 2003: 65).

6. Holman (1993: 226–7); G. Kolko (1989: 45–6); Löwy (1981: 164).
7. Lamounier (1989: 116).
8. Frank (1971: 206, cf. 203–4).
9. Gardner (1971: 60); on Cuba, see ibid.: 53–7. On the interest moratorium, see Pollin and Zepeda (1987: 14), quoting D. Felix.
10. Frank (1971: 207–8); P. Evans (1979: 68).
11. Gardner (1971: 123).
12. Migdal (1988: 218, 234); Morton (2003: 645). MacEwan (1991: 20), quoting Cypher (1990: 50), notes that the bourgeoisie all along aimed to restore 'free trade', lending a temporary quality to state-led development.
13. Gardner (1971: 202).
14. D. Felix, quoted in Pollin and Zepeda (1987: 14).
15. Kolko and Kolko (1972: 78–9, 415–7). Berle (1962: 20). Argentina was one of the countries that contributed to schemes during the war to sustain the supply of key war materials such as Swedish ball-bearings to Germany; cf. Aalders and Wiebes (1995: 107–18).
16. Quoted in G. Kolko (1988: 40).
17. Berle (1962: 45).
18. G. Kolko (1988: 141–2).
19. Quoted in Paterson (1989: 198).
20. Ibid.: 203–5.
21. At a post-Cold War conference held in Havana in early 1992, it was revealed that on the day Kennedy was assassinated, 22 November 1963, Castro received a French journalist carrying a message from the president with the proposal to normalise relations (Kennedy also had instructed his UN ambassador to undertake exploratory conversations with the Cubans in New York). Cf. A.M. Schlesinger Jr.'s report on the 1992 conference, reprinted in *De Volkskrant*, 21 March 1992. The assassination of Kennedy has been the topic of a range of conspiracy theories and a film by Oliver Stone that is tilted towards the most extreme of these theories. The most convincing explanation holds that Kennedy initially allowed, but in October called off a planned exile landing on Cuba from Haiti. The Cuban exile/Mafia network then used Lee Harvey Oswald, a low-level intelligence asset first employed by US Naval Intelligence as a 'defector' to the USSR and whose latest role had been that of a fake pro-Castro demonstrator for COINTELPRO, to shoot the president. Whether more than one assassin was involved is secondary here (Oswald was a certified sharpshooter though). Apparently the plan was to have Oswald killed immediately afterwards and thus provoke—by branding him a Castro sympathiser—a US military strike against Cuba. This failed because Oswald was arrested alive. He was then shot by a Mafia-related nightclub owner, Jack Ruby, after having been interrogated by the Dallas police (in turn, Ruby later died in his cell). No record of the interrogation ever emerged, and we are left with Oswald's own emphatic statement for the camera that he was 'just the patsy'. Vice-president Johnson took prompt steps to avoid being drawn into a war against Cuba, but there were so many dark personal and political secrets that would have been unearthed by a thorough public investigation of the Kennedy assassination (from Marilyn Monroe's affair with the president to Mafia support for his election), that in the end the Warren Commission Report on the killing looked more like a cover-up. The suspicion of a centralised high-level plot to which this gave rise is contradicted by the relatively clumsy set-up, which rather suggests a Cuban exile/Mafia operation with, possibly, local US intelligence and law-enforcement agents providing cover (Dorril 1992).
22. Kennedy adviser A.M. Schlesinger Jr., quoted in Packenham (1973: 63, cf. 87); cf. Biekart (1999: 149).
23. Quoted in Gerassi (1965: 253).
24. Lamounier (1989: 125); Füchtner (1972: 234); Fernandes (1996: 104).
25. P. Evans (1979: 93).

26. Esser (1979: 57).
27. G. Kolko (1988: 214–5).
28. Petras (1970: 131). 'Peru and Brazil ... with minimum internal security problems were capable of more state-oriented autonomous initiatives, at least during 1965–75, than Thailand or Indonesia' (G. Kolko 1989: 48).
29. Petras (1970: 140, 145).
30. *Time*, 6 September 1971.
31. Frank (1971: 104–11). Bolivia tried in vain to regain access to the sea in the Chaco War with Paraguay; cf. Gerassi (1965: 113).
32. Frank (1971: 125, 130).
33. Allende (1973: 20, 65); Gerassi (1965: 114–8).
34. von Brunn (1973); *Newsweek*, 14 May 1971.
35. Allende (1973: 68–9). Mutual trade in the Andean Pact tripled in three years (ibid.: 141).
36. Ibid.: 142–4, 210. The Chilean president urged the 27th session of the UN General Assembly to adopt Echeverría's Charter of economic rights and duties of states (ibid.: 211–4).
37. Ibid.: 33–4.
38. Declassified documents dated 16 October 1970, at www.seas.gwu.edu/NSAEBB (26 November 1998). On the Western intelligence infrastructure in Latin America, see Richelson and Ball (1990: 118, 234–5).
39. Details in Hitchens (2002: 55–71).
40. Barnet (1980: 157); Allende (1973: 148); *De Volkskrant*, 5 February 1972. All that was achieved at the conference with 16 creditor states in Paris was an extension of the re-demption period to eight years (*De Volkskrant*, 21 April 1972).
41. Arroyo (1974: 18).
42. Migdal (1988: 271). The 1970 election had been the first under general suffrage (Therborn 1979: 90).
43. Quoted in Walpen (2004: 176); economic figures from Catalán Aravena (1984: 45). The wage share in GNP was 52.16 per cent in 1972, and 28.49 per cent in 1974 (ibid.).
44. Quoted in Müller-Plantenberg (1981: 24).
45. The Chilean economy under the liberalised financial regime passed under the control of five main groups: Cruzat-Larraín, BHC (Vial), Matte, Angelini, and Edwards (one of the oldest financial dynasties of the country) (Catalán Aravena 1984: 50); in addition, there was the fast-rising star of the Luksic empire built in the period (*Financial Times*, 12 September 1996; cf. also Table 6.2 in this chapter).
46. *Newsweek*, 4 April 1977. On the principle of national treatment, cf. Braithwaite and Drahos (2000: *passim*).
47. Fernández Jilberto (1985: 185).
48. *The Observer*, 27 October 1974; Pringle and Spigelman (1983: 378–9); cf. P. Labreveux in *Le Monde Diplomatique*, June 1972, p. 17.
49. Merkx (1976: 44). López Rega, the Rasputin behind Isabel Perón and organiser of the AAA death squads, was in close touch with Licio Gelli of the Italian P-2 Masonic lodge discussed in the previous chapter (*Newsweek*, 21 July 1986).
50. According to the verbatim transcript of a meeting with the Argentinian emissary on 7 October 1976, Kissinger said, 'What is not understood in the United States is that you have a civil war .... We want a stable situation .... If you can finish before Congress gets back, the better' (extensive quotes in *The Guardian*, 6 December 2003). In 1976, right-wing military coups also took place in Ecuador, Peru and Uruguay.
51. Condor included Argentina, Paraguay, Uruguay and Brazil, with Bolivia, Colombia and Peru participating in data collection and exchange. It operated as far as Washington, D.C., where a Condor strike killed Allende's foreign minister, Letelier, and his US friend Ronnie Moffitt, in September 1976 (Hitchens 2002: 68; *De Volkskrant*, 7 April 1993).

52. Teubal (1996: 203). Thatcher too was in dire straits, with her popularity at its lowest and 10 per cent unemployment, and urgently needed a victory (Fontaine 1995: 109).
53. G. Kolko (1989: 47); cf. P. Evans (1979).
54. *Frankfurter Allgemeine Zeitung*, 14 May 1974. This also may explain their newfound support for the Palestinian cause (*Financial Times*, 30 December 1974).
55. *Newsweek*, 10 January and 23 May 1977.
56. The 1974 party system was meant to constitutionalise a structural majority for the government party (ARENA) but backfired when the opposition MDB won a majority (Holman and Fernández Jilberto 1989: 11). On the nature of the bourgeois opposition to the state, cf. Therborn (1979: 107–9); *Frankfurter Allgemeine Zeitung*, 20 June 1973; *Neue Zürcher Zeitung*, 16 February 1977.
57. In 1960–62, coffee represented 53 per cent of Brazil's exports, other primary products (iron ore, wood, etc.) 44 per cent, and manufacturing 2 per cent. In 1972, this changed to 25–46–29, respectively (P. Evans, 1979: 67, Table 2.2; *Financial Times*, 30 December 1974).
58. GM and Ford produced cars in Brazil since the 1920s and Volkswagen since the late 1950s, but the VW brand overtook its rivals before itself being overtaken by latecomer Fiat. The truck market was also dominated by European companies. By 1996 Fiat had become the biggest car maker in Brazil; European car makers produced 832,000 cars in the country, against 590,000 by GM and Ford. In Argentina the balance was 599,000 by Fiat against Ford's 49,000 (Fernandes 1996: 111; *Financial Times*, 19 April 1996).
59. Klinkenberg (1971).
60. E. Jacchia in *International Herald Tribune*, 16 September 1977.
61. Pringle and Spigelman (1983: 344–5, 380); *International Herald Tribune*, 4 October 1974; D. Fishlock in *Financial Times*, 19 April 1979.
62. Gall (1976: 21–5). In 1970 KWU had cancelled the Siemens licensing agreement with Westinghouse of the US.
63. *De Groene Amsterdammer*, 6 April 1977. On Brazil's developing links with Japan, including iron ore for steel-making swaps and a range of other projects including bauxite, cellulose factories and agricultural projects, cf. *Newsweek*, 4 October 1976 and 13 February 1978.
64. Klinkenberg (1971: 149); Deubner (1977: x–xi); E. Jacchia in *International Herald Tribune*, 16 September 1977.
65. Deubner (1977: vii, xvi–xvii); Pringle and Spigelman (1983: 380–1). In 1976 Barre and President Giscard cancelled agreements with Pakistan, while South Korea and Taiwan, under intense US pressure, cancelled their agreements with France (ibid.).
66. *Frankfurter Allgemeine Zeitung*, 25 May 1977.
67. On the Carter nuclear policy, see Pringle and Spigelman (1983: 382–5); on the fast breeder programme, see Giesen (1989). A year later the nuclear option received a major blow with the near-meltdown of the Three-Mile Island reactor in the US, and it would be almost buried along with the Chernobyl disaster six years later. Meanwhile the Brazilian–German deal unravelled in the early 1980s under the weight of the debt crisis, although nuclear arms proliferation remains an urgent issue until today. In 1984, only one nuclear power plant had been built, supplying 1 per cent of Brazil's energy needs; one more was planned (I. Sachs in *Le Monde Diplomatique*, November 1984, pp. 10–1; *Newsweek*, 12 May 1986).
68. 'Much of the debts that Latin American and other nations have accumulated since 1955 may be explained by the middle- and upper class' addiction of a life style requiring vast amounts of foreign consumer goods, and here too the national bourgeoisie has failed because of its own contradictions' (G. Kolko 1989: 45).
69. Frieden (1981: 408, 411, 428); Lipietz (1982: 38); Castells (1998: 251).
70. Lipietz (1984: 75); cf. B. Cohen (1986: 21, 23, Tables 2.1 and 2.2) for aggregate lending figures. Cf. *Newsweek*, 26 May 1980.
71. Quoted in Sampson (1982: 140).

72. Picciotto (1983: 31–2); quote of the chairman of Deutsche Bank in Sampson (1982: 275).
73. Lindberg (1983: 198–9).
74. Greider (1989: 46).
75. Ibid.: 75, 101.
76. Quoted in *Newsweek*, 16 June 1987.
77. Drainville (1994: 118, 120).
78. Halevi and Varoufakis (2003: 63); Greider (1989: 182–5, 218–9).
79. Quoted in Parboni (1981: 164).
80. Comparing Reagan's policies with Nixon's unilateral monetary policies, Gill (1990: 107) writes that 'though perhaps not consciously intended, Reagan's policies none the less reinforced the tendency towards transnational hegemony.' This also holds for the Volcker intervention in the run-up to Reagan's election. Peter Gowan (1999a) on the other hand emphasises the continuities between Nixon and Reagan in this respect.
81. Sampson (1982: 138); Greider (1989: 106–9); Citibank quote in *Newsweek*, 16 June 1987.
82. Germain (1997: 158–9).
83. Quoted in *Newsweek*, 16 June 1987.
84. Greider (1989: 207).
85. Quoted in Brownstein and Easton (1983: 18). The head of the Federal Reserve who succeeded Volcker, J.P. Morgan banker Alan Greenspan, was also a militant neoliberal and member of the Mont Pèlerin Society. Greenspan was inspired by the novels of Russian-born émigré Ayn Rand that celebrate radical individualism into a philosophy, and contributed a paper against consumer protection and income tax to a book edited by her (*Newsweek*, 16 June 1987).
86. 'Circa 1980 the US abandoned the doctrine of development for all in favour of the doctrine that poor countries concentrate their efforts on economizing as much as they could …, enhancing their capabilities to service debt and to preserve their creditworthiness' (Arrighi 1991: 51).
87. Data from a speech by US ambassador and banker, J. William Middendorf, II (1986: 5). The Echeverría government had been in a conflict with the private business world for some time, but the bank measures did not stem the capital flight (MacEwan 1991: 22–3).
88. Pollin and Zepeda (1987: 4). Inflation (annual averages) in the period 1981–84 ranged from Brazil's 141 per cent to 362 per cent for Argentina and 667 per cent for Mexico (ibid: 5).
89. As a percentage of external debt, capital flight from Brazil in 1985 was 14.3 per cent, against Argentina's 98 per cent, Mexico's 87.6 per cent, and Venezuela's 100+ per cent (cf. van der Pijl 1995: 115, Table 5.4). At the end of 1988, the amount of capital illegally held abroad was 20 per cent of outstanding debt, minuscule compared to countries like Venezuela (170 per cent) and Mexico (80 per cent) (*De Volkskrant*, 9 June 1989).
90. Kolk (1996: 68, Table 2.2). Cf. S. Hecht in *Le Monde Diplomatique*, July 1989, pp. 18–9; *Newsweek*, 9 January 1989. 'Unless there is serious discussion of debt relief for Brazil, we can sit back and watch the Amazon burn,' one environmental campaigner put it in 1989, but the army prevented Brazilian president José Sarney from attending a conference on the issue in March that year (*Newsweek*, 30 January 1989; *De Volkskrant*, 4 March 1989). Cf. Kolk (1996: Chapter 3, esp. 109–14).
91. Fernandes (1996: 107, 110); cf. Pollin and Zepeda (1987: 10). In 1985, deals were made with the Soviet Union and Iraq to swap oil supplies to Petrobras for, respectively, the construction of oil platforms and Volkswagen cars assembled in Brazil (*NRC-Handelsblad*, 5 March 1985).
92. MacEwan (1986: 2).
93. Pollin and Zepeda (1987: 8).

94. Deutsche Bank had its doubtful debts covered for around 50 per cent by extra reserves, against a rate of 20–30 per cent for American banks (with some bad exceptions like Bank of America and Manufacturers Hanover). Even Citicorp, the biggest US bank, with $14.9 billion Third World debt on its books by the mid-1980s (against total reserves of 4.9 billion), failed to secure re-insurance of its non-performing loans (P. Norel in *Le Monde Diplomatique*, March 1985, p. 9; *Newsweek*, 1 June 1987). Because US banks were also financing Japanese banks, their exposure to Third World defaults was higher than the figure of 18 per cent of the total would suggest; cf. *NRC-Handelsblad*, 31 January 1986 (based on the BIS Quarterly Report).
95. Wisnewski et al. (1993: 158–61).
96. Ibid.: 154, 162. In late 1988, the mood among American banks was shifting, although the worst exposed (mentioned in note 94) and Citicorp stuck to their objections (*De Volkskrant*, 9 September 1988).
97. al-Khafaji (2004: 241). As MacEwan (1986: 8) writes, the reason why the Latin American debtors ultimately did not default was because 'orthodox programs being followed ... do in fact serve the interest of the ruling groups.'
98. *Newsweek*, 26 September 1977; Fernández Jilberto (1985: 199).
99. The buying up of vast tracts of land in Argentina has all the appearances of a closing auction. The Elsztain brothers are the largest landowners today, while George Soros, the philanthropist and self-styled critic of neoliberalism, became the second largest landowner in the country, immediately followed by Luciano Benetton, the Italian textile tycoon. In light of future world food scarcity, these are far-sighted investments indeed (Chua 2003: 65–7; *De Volkskrant*, 5 October 1996). In 1996, the Argentinean armed forces were still the largest landowners.
100. Arrighi (1991: 57–61) also highlights the oligarchic aspect of wealth creation in this context but in a more abstract, general sense.
101. Morton (2003: 638).
102. Chua (2003: 60–2); *Newsweek*, 6 November 1989.
103. Data in *Financial Times*, 21 December 1994.
104. *Financial Times*, 12 March 1999.
105. Holman (1996: 176–7, 187, 196).
106. *Financial Times*, 6 December 1995. On Luksic, which has a 65 per cent share (worth more than 2 billion) in the Antofagasta copper conglomerate alone, see *The Times*, 6 November 2004.
107. The issue of representation versus bourgeois self-rule is addressed in Therborn's (1979) seminal work.
108. 'Where ability or opportunity to construct a national economy are lacking, the state is automatically unable to generate any social consensus around itself, i.e., to make itself a nation state' (Vieille 1998: 223, cf. 221). Cf. Robinson (1996: 89–91), and our discussion of Crozier et al. (1975) in Chapter 5 of this book.
109. Therborn (1979: 109).
110. Roberts (1985: 20).
111. Cf. MacEwan (1986: 12) (the example is from Argentina). The eclipse of the state has also unexpectedly politicised ethnicity along political-economic class lines, notably in countries with Amerindian majorities such as Bolivia, Peru, Guatemala and Ecuador. Cf. Chua (2003: 50) on Felipe Quispe, the indigenous leader of Aymara Indian extraction, and his anti-white movement in Bolivia.
112. G. Kolko (1989: 45); Kaltenthaler and Mora (2002: 84).
113. Kaltenthaler and Mora (2002: 74); MacEwan (1986: 3); *Newsweek*, 25 August 1980.
114. *El País*, 17 November 1986; *NRC-Handelsblad*, 11 December 1986.
115. Between 1974 and 1981, the number of workers employed in special Export Processing Zones doubled to 130,000 in 630 plants (Dicken 1986: 175).
116. Rupert (1995b: 666).

117. R. Seitenfus in *Le Monde Diplomatique*, February 1998, p. 8; Kaltenthaler and Mora (2002: 76). The relative weight of Mercosur at the time was on account of its combined population of 204 million and GDP of $1 trillion, one-eighth of the $8 trillion GDP of NAFTA (population 385.5 million). The Andean Pact had 101.9 million people, with a combined GDP of $240 billion (*Financial Times*, 22 March 1996).

118. Patomäki and Teivainen (2002: 48).

119. On Porto Alegre and the WSF, and on the alternative Latin American Community plan, see Patomäki and Teivainen (2002: 58–9, 53).

120. *Financial Times*, 17 May 1995.

121. The Vicunha group, a textile concern owned by an immigrant family of Jewish-Syrian extraction, first picked up a stake in CSN Steel in 1993, and then used this as a platform to go for control of CVRD through a consortium. In the process, it established itself as a new core of capitalist power by outmanoeuvring the Votorantim group, the hitherto dominant business dynasty (*Financial Times*, 14 December 1994 and 29 June 1998). The controlling family in Vicunha are the Steinbruchs; and in Votorantim, the de Moraes.

122. *De Volkskrant*, 9 June 1995; *Newsweek*, 14 October 1996.

123. Fernandes (1996: 112–4); *Frankfurter Allgemeine Zeitung*, 22 October 1982.

124. Tosi Rodrigues (2000: 256–7).

125. As Lula has put it, 'We want to build a political force capable of convincing rich nations … that they can ease their protectionist policies and give access to the so-called developing world' (*The Guardian*, 28 May 2004).

126. Details in *The Guardian*, 28 May 2004.

127. In 1976 Kissinger ordered a cut in aid to those countries voting against the US in the UN, and the response in the United States to the adoption of the anti-Zionism resolution by the General Assembly proved that there was popular support to begin disengaging from the UN altogether (Feulner 1976: 45).

128. In 1986 President Reagan appointed Roger A. Brooks (a Heritage Foundation luminary who had been the author of several Foundation studies critical of the UN) as director in charge of international organisation at the State Department under Assistant Secretary Alan Keyes, another prominent Heritage Foundation associate. Charged with overseeing the Kassebaum Amendment reducing the US contribution to the UN, they ran into opposition from Japan, which preferred to have a group of 18 experts investigate modes of voting and financing (G.A. Astre in *Le Monde Diplomatique*, May 1986, p. 9).

129. In 1983 Shultz wrote to M'Bow that the US was withdrawing from UNESCO (Fontaine 1995: 256). But his successor, F. Mayor, a militant Spanish catholic, refused to disavow his former chief (cf. interview with Mayor in *Newsweek*, 18 January 1988).

130. Paul (2001) sees the 'Global Compact'—a network of blue-chip corporations aiming to use the UN as a vehicle to spread 'best practice' defined by them—as the defining moment of this reversal of the NIEO drive. Cf. also www.globalcompact.org.

131. Brazil is incidentally one of the states not paying its contributions to the UN; of the larger countries in the Western Hemisphere, only Canada, Cuba and Bolivia have paid their dues. The UN today is financed mainly by Germany and Japan, followed by Russia and China, the remaining EU countries, India, and most of Africa (*Le Monde* supplement, 19 March 2005, pp. 22–3).

132. They have been classed as 'weak states' (Migdal 1988), or even 'quasi-states' (Jackson 1990).

133. Scott (1986: 21–2); *De Volkskrant*, 15 October 1993.

134. The Ethiopian revolution compelled the US to abandon its major intelligence facility in that country, shifting to the British-controlled atoll of Diego Garcia, depopulated for the purpose (Richelson and Ball 1990: 206).

135. In addition, SASOL (oil-from-coal synthesis) and various industrial development ventures, aiming to develop sectors such as chemicals and new technologies, were part

of the state-driven development effort. Singh (1984: 91); Sampson (1987: 133–4); Seidman and Makgetla (1980: 59, Table 4.2B, 67).
136. Sampson (1987: 115–6).
137. Seidman and Makgetla (1980: 37, 81, Tables 4–7, 83). Banks lending to state corporations included Deutsche Bank, Commerzbank, and Bayerische Vereinsbank (Singh 1984: 92). When the debt crisis broke, South Africa's debt to European banks was twice the size of debt to US banks (*Newsweek*, 27 January 1986).
138. *Le Monde*, 5 July 1978.
139. Clarke (1978: 68–70); Stockwell (1978: 185–6); Blishchenko and Zhdanov (1984: 8).
140. Hargreaves (1988: 211). South Africa's Bureau of State Security (BOSS) all along maintained close links with British and US secret services, exchanging information on Communist Party members, anti-apartheid activists, and the political orientation of migrants (Richelson and Ball 1990: 173).
141. Stockwell (1978: 43); background in G. Wright (1997).
142. Stockwell (1978: 67, cf. 44). The Chinese would withdraw when fighting broke out, perhaps to avoid confronting Cuban troops; in Zaire their place was taken by French advisers.
143. *The Observer*, 9 October 1988; cf. Davidson (1980).
144. The reference was to 'continental and air' arms (cf. *Chronologie Internationale* 1979: 111).
145. Stockwell (1978: 217, 232).
146. H. Mayer (1979: 1119).
147. Quoted in Inquilab (1984: 20).
148. Quoted in ibid.: 24.
149. The proximate cause of the Soweto uprising was the fact that the apartheid regime had decreed that black Africans should learn Afrikaans rather than English at school, with the indigenous language as second language (Sampson 1987: 144–8).
150. Hargreaves (1988: 226); cf. M. Holman in *Financial Times*, 14 April 2000.
151. Hippler (1986: 38–40, 45–6); E.R. Alterman in *Le Monde Diplomatique*, May 1986, pp. 1, 6–7; cf. van Creveld (1991).
152. G. Wright (1997); *Le Monde*, 5 July 1978.
153. Quoted in Hippler (1986: 43). In January 1981, Haig based his views on proofs he had seen of Claire Sterling's *The Terror Network*, supposedly exposing a world-wide terror operation managed by the KGB, but dismissed by the intelligence services as fiction. Cf. Roth and Ender (1984: 14–15, 37–8); B. Woodward (1987: 66, 88–9, 92).
154. B. Woodward (1987: 134).
155. Inquilab (1984: 26–8).
156. Marishane (1992); M.A. Lee and K. Coogan in *Le Monde Diplomatique*, October 1986, p. 6; *The Observer*, 10 October 1988. These networks also emerged in the aftermath of the assassination of Indian prime minister Indira Gandhi in 1984 by her Sikh bodyguards. The defence of the suspects was paid for by the representative of the World Anti-Communist League in India, Rama Swarup. Swarup was arrested for espionage in 1986; at his trial the prosecution accused the intelligence services of the United States, West Germany, Israel and Taiwan of spying on India's nuclear programme (Nair and Opperskalski 1988: 77–9; *Lobster*, 17, 1988, p. 8).
157. M. Klare in *Le Monde Diplomatique*, March 1986, pp. 1, 3. Meanwhile the 'terrorism' theme, which had receded into the background due to the new cold war in Europe, came back to centre-stage in the formulation of US strategy. An International Security Council, supported by CAUSA, a far-right network financed by the Korean, S.M. Moon, produced a stream of publications labelling a range of progressive movements as terrorist (cf. International Security Council 1986). A more respectable channel producing a

parallel stream of publications in the same spirit was Ray S. Cline and Yonah Alexander's *Terrorism* book series (cf. Cline and Alexander 1986), and the journal *Political Communication and Persuasion*, edited by Alexander.

158. The best-known example is former COSATU trade union leader C. Ramaphosa (*Financial Times*, 25 March 1997). For the end of apartheid, see Sampson (1987).
159. *Financial Times*, 26 May 1997.
160. Black (1982: 29); cf. Davis (1986: 181–230). For the background of the Reagan cabinet, see Brownstein and Easton (1983).
161. Quoted in Biekart (1999: 153). Carter also authorised CIA support for the opposition to the Sandinistas (B. Woodward 1987: 80).
162. Black (1982: 29); Morris (1999: 455). Both Haig and Casey were members of the elite Knights of Malta, a crusading order of some 10,000 members worldwide. Haig proposed to impose a blockade of Cuba, but Reagan's advisers were afraid of a war (B. Woodward 1987: 83).
163. Biekart (1999: 176). France supplied a handful of military equipment including three helicopters which was taken very badly in Washington (Fontaine 1995: 104).
164. Black (1982: 33). Coordination of Contra activity and of its political cupola, the FDN, was placed in the hands of the US ambassador in Honduras, John Negroponte (Hippler 1986: 140–3).
165. B. Woodward (1987: 203).
166. Jung (1980).
167. Hippler (1986: 118–9, 121). In the period 1972–80 El Salvador imported 80 per cent of its arms from Israel (J. Lemieux in *Le Monde Diplomatique*, October 1984, pp. 16–7). On Israel's role as an 'exporter of West Bank expertise' to the Third World, cf. Nederveen Pieterse (1985).
168. Biekart (1999: 176).
169. The death of Romero, as well as the killings of President Aguilera in Ecuador, General Torrijos of Panama and Peruvian military leader Hoys Rubio have all been linked to the activities of Operation Condor. Cf. Blishchenko and Zhdanov (1984: 68–70, 106–7); Scott (1986: 1); Hippler (1986: 111).
170. Hippler (1986: 123–4); J. Lemieux in *Le Monde Diplomatique*, October 1984, pp. 16–7.
171. Hippler (1986: 129).
172. Quoted in Morris (1999: 503). On the legality of the Grenada invasion and other instances of US gunboat policy in the period, see Holman (1986) and Weston (1987).
173. Biekart (1999: 176–7).
174. Bernstein and Politi (1997: 403–10); C. Antoine in *Le Monde Diplomatique*, May 1987, pp. 14–5; *Newsweek*, 6 August 1990.
175. B. Woodward (1987: 202–3, 231); Hippler (1986: 146); cf. S.E. Crane in *Le Monde Diplomatique*, June 1983, pp. 16–7. A Soviet tanker was actually damaged off the Nicaraguan coast in March 1984 by a mine and suffered casualties (Garthoff 1994: 149).
176. Morris (1999: 497); B. Woodward (1987: 256–7); Hippler (1986: 146–7). Singlaub had been in charge of Operation Phoenix in Vietnam (P. Abramovici and J. Decornoy in *Le Monde Diplomatique*, September 1987, pp. 1, 10–1).
177. C. Johnson (2002: 9).
178. Scott and Marshall (1991: x) give an estimate of $10 million in aid; Chapter 5 of their book focuses on the interconnections between the drugs trade and the WACL network. Cf. *Newsweek*, 23 May 1988.
179. M.A. Lee and K. Coogan in *Le Monde Diplomatique*, October 1986, p. 6; C. Julien in *Le Monde Diplomatique*, January 1987, p. 5.
180. *Newsweek*, 7 May 1990.

7 The Rapallo Syndrome and the Demise of the Soviet Union

THE USSR AS A CONTENDER STATE

The Soviet Union has posed the most serious challenge to the pre-eminence of the West in modern history. It not only mobilised a large population and a vast territory rich in resources; in addition, the state class pushed the contender state posture to its logical limit, as a state socialism with a planned economy. Let me therefore briefly retrace the emergence of the Soviet state from the Russian revolution.

The need for Russia to modernise was brought home to the Tsarist autocracy by the defeat in the Crimean War in the mid-nineteenth century. The emancipation of the serfs in 1861 and the abolition of the administrative power of the landlords set in motion the combined process of a proletarianisation of the workforce and an autonomisation of the state; both these, however, remained seriously incomplete.[1] The Bolshevik revolution, not unlike the French, resulted from the strains imposed on a contender state by its pursuit of a catch-up policy and a corollary military strategy. When the First World War drove millions of Russians into Pomerania and Galicia to fight the modern war machine of the German Second Empire and its allies, the ruling aristocracy around the Tsar lost control and society collapsed in revolution. Amidst the slide into anarchy created by what has been characterised as a 'movement of Christian indignation against the state', the Bolsheviks, along with their working class following in the pockets of modern industry, were able to take the lead by skilfully handling two key issues—an immediate end to the miseries of the war, and land reform.[2]

Lenin, prevailing over intense opposition within his own party, succeeded in defining the seizure of power as a socialist revolution; he then accepted a humiliating peace and ordered the expropriation of the large landowners— all this on the assumption that the impending *world* revolution would legitimate these preliminary steps.[3]

Soviet power survived the onslaught of foreign intervention and defeated the Contras supported by the West. But revolutionary breakthroughs abroad did not materialise, and internationalism—the subordination of inter-state and ethnic questions to the international solidarity among the workers— had to be adjusted to a more realistic understanding of the foreign relations of the Soviet state. In March 1919, Lenin conceded that as things stood the revolution would at best progress as a shock-like process reverberating through the existing state system. As he noted at the Eighth Congress of the Russian Communist party,

> We are living not merely in a state, but in a system of states, and it is inconceivable for the Soviet Republic to exist alongside of the imperialist states for any length of time .... There will have to be a series of frightful collisions between the Soviet Republic and the bourgeois states. If the ruling class, the proletariat, wants to hold power, it must, therefore, prove its ability to do so by its military organisation.[4]

This created a tension between the geopolitical interests of revolutionary Russia as a state and the 'world party' created in 1919 after the Bolshevik model, the Communist International ('Comintern'). Internationalism went through several reformulations at successive Comintern congresses, until it came to denote the solidarity of the world's workers with the embattled USSR.[5] But a socialism confined to Russia would remain subject to the existing configuration of forces in the global political economy, with the heartland occupying the commanding heights. The Western powers, Lenin concluded in his last piece of writing, 'failed to overthrow the new system created by the revolution, but they did prevent it from at once taking the step forward that would have justified the forecasts of the socialists, that would have enabled the latter to develop all the potentialities which, taken together, would have produced socialism.' In combination with the capacity of the ruling classes of the West to buy off their workers, this displaced the future epicentres of revolution further into the imperialist periphery, to China and India.[6]

The Soviet state would in the meantime have to try and play on the rivalries between the imperialist states. A first opportunity offered itself after imperial Germany's defeat in the First World War when Walter Rathenau, a visionary liberal associated with the high-tech industry of the period, proposed to form a Western consortium to develop Russian resources as a means of paying the war indemnities imposed by the Versailles treaty. By gaining access to Russia's oil, ores and grain, Germany might compensate for the loss of European and overseas raw material bases, while finding a market for its heavy industries. The heartland powers and France were not forthcoming in their support for this enterprise, and nationalist politicians instead drafted a straightforward commercial treaty with Soviet Russia (Rathenau considered this a step too far, as did the Social Democrats). The treaty was concluded on the margins of the 1922 Genoa reparations conference, in the small town of Rapallo.[7] The collusion between the two states, both ostracised by the West, was not confined to Russian manganese shipments for German steel production. It also allowed the German army to conduct manoeuvres on Soviet territory in breach of the Versailles treaty. The United States then intervened with a rehabilitation programme, the Dawes Plan of 1924, which tied Germany in with the West again. 'Rapallo' would, however, henceforth remain a code word in Western diplomacy denoting the undesirability of rapprochement between Germany and the Soviet Union. Till today, the 'Rapallo syndrome' plays a role in how the geopolitical evolution of Europe towards the east is perceived from the perspective of the English-speaking world.

Towards a Second Revolution—From above

The formation of a Soviet contender state resisting subordination to the West began with the monopolisation of political representation by the Bolsheviks, backed up by the CheKa secret police and the Red Army. This resulted in what Hélène Carrère d'Encausse calls 'the confiscation of power'.[8] The vanguard principle of the Bolshevik party in many ways prefigured the tentacular state that thinks and acts for society; when Lenin speaks of the 'proletariat as a ruling class', we are really looking at a cadre speaking *for* the proletariat. Thus the party became a vehicle of the state class ruling and governing revolutionary Russia. In 1920, departments of the Central Committee and of the regional party committees were formed to draw up and keep lists of (and appoint) state functionaries. Two years later, when Stalin became General Secretary of the Party, these departments were appointing more than 10,000 functionaries a year, a number that went up further in the years that followed. This was the system of the *nomenklatura*, a registered state class of functionaries eligible for public office. At party elections, recommendations from above were henceforth to be followed, and the party's repression of factions in 1921 anyway made campaigning for office impossible.

In this way the party merged into the confiscatory state. Membership became a pre-condition to gain access to the *nomenklatura*; as a result, the political conjuncture of communism in the USSR was uncoupled from that in the wider world. Whereas communist parties abroad shrivelled, the Communist Party of the Soviet Union (CPSU) enjoyed a spectacular growth, doubling to three-quarters of a million party members in one year

(1923–24) in spite of the reduction in the numbers of the industrial proletariat.[9] 'The party itself,' McAuley observes, 'was changing from being a
party of industrial workers to one of administrators—both because those
who were industrial workers by profession had now moved into government
or party posts and because white-collar personnel were joining the party in
an attempt to preserve or obtain a job.'[10]

After Lenin's death, Stalin could become the personification of the new
Soviet state because he had collected key posts in the domestic power apparatus. People's Commissar for the Nationalities, General Secretary of the
party, and head of the Workers' and Peasants' Inspection, a body set up to
keep an eye on the so-called bourgeois specialists and technicians—all these
were jobs of little interest to the internationalist leadership. They were
looking for signs of the world revolution on which they felt the fate of
Bolshevik power depended, and were active in the Comintern. Stalin's rise,
then, was a corollary of the *switch from the world-revolutionary perspective
to the contender state posture*, and with him emerged a generation of cadres
who had little interest in the niceties of Marxist theory or world revolution.
Instead they were crude and curious, and inventive and quick-witted in
their own way—in brief, real pioneers.[11] Using this cadre basis, Stalin was
able to play off the other leaders against each other, getting rid first of
Trotsky, the key exponent of the world revolution that did not happen. In
show trials in Moscow in the late 1930s, Stalin and his henchmen then
entirely decapitated the internationalist Bolshevik party.[12]

The turn to state-driven industrialisation was the second aspect of the
contender posture. It was launched when Lenin's New Economic Policy
(NEP), meant to give the population a break from the convulsions of war
and revolution and to rekindle economic life, ran aground in the late 1920s.
The fast-growing middle class of enterprising farmers and commercial
middlemen ('NEP men') soon came to face the new cadres emerging in the
socialist urban centres.[13] The non-Russian nationalities—who had been
given a degree of freedom both culturally and administratively, in order to
provide the much-needed cadres capable of governing the Soviet republics—
added a centrifugal aspect to the loosening of revolutionary discipline.[14]
The new government thus came to face two clear-cut internal challenges—
decentralised market relations and national autonomy—which stood in
the way of the necessary mobilisation of investment funds and an army of
labour for industry, 'socialist original accumulation'. But such a mobilisation
was necessary to meet the *external* challenge. When exchange relations
between the ailing urban-industrial sector and the flourishing countryside
became so imbalanced that the peasants refused to supply the cities with
grain, Stalin decided to break out of the impasse in January 1928 by sending
a shock-troop of 30,000 party activists to forcibly requisition grain for the
starving cities. At the same time, the CheKa was wrought into the GPU, an

instrument of violence and state terror, enabling the revolution from above to remove all obstacles in the way of 'constructing socialism in one country'.[15]

Within the leadership, Nikolai Bukharin, who had most actively supported the NEP, now raised his voice to protest the excesses against the peasants. 'It was he who used, in the Central Committee, the strong and provocative term "Leviathan state".'[16] Bukharin's views were based on an analysis of the Nazi state, suggesting that certain characteristics of the 'totalitarianism' in Hitler's Germany were also crystallising in the USSR. In Bukharin's view, the total surrender to state power endangered the humanistic core of the socialist ideal; a theme that would re-emerge under Nikita Khrushchev and again under Gorbachev. In the circumstances of his time though, it sealed Bukharin's fate.[17]

Thus a Jacobin-like revolutionary power, aiming to overthrow the existing structures of the global political economy by world revolution, was transformed into a state class holding the reins of a contender state and facing those very structures from a qualitatively different position. Amidst dramatic instances of mass mobilisation and collective psychosis, the Soviet state deepened its hold on society through shock-like extensions of its power, driving forward the economy through five-year plans, collectivising agriculture, and, in a breathtaking synthesis of terror and economic policy, moving millions of labourers about as virtual prisoners of the state.[18] As a state on the threshold of urban-industrial modernity—facing the Lockean heartland occupying the commanding heights of the global political economy—the USSR first had to establish a comprehensive hold on society. This alone allowed it to defend itself while attempting to catch up with its opponents. In the words of Moshe Lewin,

> The state engaged in a hectic, hasty, and compulsive shaping of the social structure, forcing its groups and classes into a mould where the administrative-and-coercive machinery retained its superiority and autonomy. Instead of 'serving' its basis, the state, using the powerful means at its disposal (central planning, modern communications and controlling mechanisms, monopoly of information, freedom to use coercion at will), was able to press the social body into service under its own diktat.[19]

Of course, a catalogue of unique circumstances—from the birthmark of socialism to the vast surface, immense resources and rich cultural heritages of the societies brought together into the USSR—should make one hesitate to lump the Soviet experience into a single category with Napoleonic France, Wilhelmine/Nazi Germany, imperial Japan and others. But in terms of the uneven development in the global political economy and international relations, it is there that Soviet state socialism belongs—in the succession of contender states; resisting, challenging and finally succumbing to the liberal universe of which the heartland forms the centre.

The first two five-year plans demonstrated what the imposition of centralised state power can achieve if it is not mortgaged to a bourgeoisie feeding on the process, or inhibited by compassion. The figures in Table 1.2 of this book tell their own story, if not that of the dramatic human sacrifices, the triumphs and the terror. The collectivisation of agriculture on the other hand, despite the tremendous cost in lives through violence and famine, did not improve output. The Stalinist campaign reached its greatest fury when economic growth, driven by breakneck industrialisation, hit a ceiling in the late 1930s (from 17 per cent per year in the period 1926–36, back to 10 per cent thereafter). In the prevailing climate, this was officially explained as the result of sabotage. Adjustments to the existing plan and delays in the new five-year plan accompanied the show trials in which Bolshevik leaders 'confessed' their activities as 'wreckers'.[20] While foreign trade virtually collapsed in the 1930s, Soviet industrialisation developed a state-monitored emulation of the more advanced mass production economy being developed in the US. The Soviet leadership paid American engineering firms huge fees to draw the blue-prints for their five-year plans, 'focused ... upon single, clear cut objectives to build new, gigantic, mass-production units to manufacture large quantities of simplified standard models based on proven Western designs without design changes over a long period .... Simplification, standardisation, and duplication became the operational aspects of Soviet industrial strategy.'[21]

Given that the Axis powers represented the most acute challenge to the heartland, the USSR could develop as a secondary contender, even though it was not till the actual Nazi attack in the summer of 1941 that the Soviet Union was accepted as an ally of the West. Stalin all along sought to garner goodwill with the rulers of the West by demanding restraint from the Popular Front governments in France and Spain. Rebuffed in his attempt to set up a collective security bloc against Hitler, he then concluded the 1939 Non-Aggression Pact to gain time. These policies sacrificed the international communist movement, which had enjoyed a brief revitalisation after the 1935 Comintern congress, to the immediate survival of the Soviet state.[22] In the war, the USSR bore the brunt of the struggle against Germany and its satellites, dwarfing the military effort in Europe on the part of the English-speaking states. This was an element in the policy of active balancing on the part of the heartland. The Nazi defeat brought the Red Army as far west as Berlin, allowing the Soviet Union to project a sphere of influence in Eastern Europe; in China, a peasant-based communist movement succeeded in overthrowing the US-supported Kuomintang in 1949. This made the USSR the new contender. It now entered the second stage of its catch-up effort—reinforced by an array of friendly states on its periphery but with the full force of the West openly ranged against it for a contest to the end.

Integration and Rivalry among Socialist States

When the Marshall Plan and the anti-communist crusade dashed Stalin's illusions about an enduring accommodation with the West, the Soviet leadership switched to creating what the dictator qualified as a 'second world market'.[23] In 1949, Poland, the German Democratic Republic, Hungary, Czechoslovakia, Bulgaria and Rumania joined the USSR in the Council for Mutual Economic Assistance (called 'Comecon' in the West). This started the process of extended reproduction of Soviet-style 'Socialism in One Country', initially with minimal division of labour between the partners, and triggering political landslides in the countries involved. The internationalism of the 1935 Comintern congress had inspired the communists in the left coalition governments that took power in Central and Eastern Europe under the protection of the Soviet armies. They had survived the Spanish Civil War and the resistance, but now they had become a liability. Just as the Moscow trials of the late 1930s eliminated the internationalists within the USSR, judicial theatre from the same director between 1949 and 1952 served to kick the East European communist parties into line—first in Hungary and Bulgaria, and then in Czechoslovakia. In Rumania, the attempt to try its leader, Gheorghiu-Dej, was narrowly averted.[24] In a mirror image of what was happening in the West, social democrats were thrown out of governments; Tito was excommunicated. Artur London, a veteran from the Spanish civil war and state secretary in Prague, was one of those tried, but he survived. In his memoirs, he relates how he 'confessed' that his 'Trotskyism' and 'Titoism' had made him averse to the 'patriotic construction of socialism' in his own country. Also, he had continued to trade with the West after 1947, and so on and so forth.[25] In a perverse way, these were accurate accusations; the Popular Front governments in Central and Eastern Europe were not keen to completely forgo diverse foreign connections and economic relations, and this was then held against them as proof of treason.[26]

After Stalin's death in 1953, the gradual relaxation of political control—culminating in Nikita Khrushchev's secret address to the 20th Party Congress in 1956 in which he denounced Stalin's excesses—allowed fresh departures in foreign policy. The logic of the arms race forced the Soviet Union to subordinate its economic policy to the requirements of meeting the Western standard and its successive military-technological innovations; this inflected its catch-up strategy towards defence, perennially lagging behind except when it briefly took the lead in (civilian) space exploration.[27] But as Khrushchev put it, 'international relations, spread beyond the bounds of relations between the countries inhabited chiefly by peoples of the white race, are now beginning to acquire the character of genuinely world-wide relations.'[28] The overtures to India and Egypt, prominent advocates of non-alignment, and the policy of reconciliation towards Yugoslavia greatly raised the Soviet profile in the world, but they also tended to undermine the regimentation of the Central and East European state classes. Mao Zedong on the other hand considered Khrushchev a weakling straying from the Marxist–Leninist line. The Hungarian uprising of 1956, suppressed by Soviet military intervention, and comparable stirrings in Poland solved by political means, revealed the dangers of changing course. National democracy had roots that contradicted Stalinism in these countries; besides, there were the victims of socialist expropriation who were ready to roll back the communist project altogether. The clampdown in Budapest marked the limit to diversity within the Soviet bloc, but did not remove the causes for friction, which reside in the uneven development among the member states of the socialist bloc, and among contender states in general.

All contender state classes attempting to lead their societies to the level of development attained by the heartland face a crisis once they have gone through the breakneck phase of agrarian and industrial revolution and need to move into the next stage of development. The state class, which has isolated itself from society to direct the revolution from above, must now establish a new relationship with the subjects that it has hitherto been moving around, as on a drawing board, by coercion if not actual state terror. Ideologically, the socialist states also have to adjust the doctrine under which they have legitimated the phase of 'socialist original accumulation'. As Herbert Marcuse notes, 'with technological and industrial progress, ... the [magical utilisation of Marxist theory] comes into conflict with more fundamental objectives [and] ... has to give way to more universalist, "normal", and internationalist conceptions.'[29] However, allowing the population a degree of active participation, without letting through a private class associated with the West, requires delicate manoeuvring. The ability to lead the masses through conviction is usually lost in the earlier phase, while the relaxation of absolute control allows the different factions of which the state class itself is inevitably made up to reassert their own interests as priorities of the state. In the USSR, after 1956 such tensions included conflict between workers resisting workplace discipline versus managers' interest in raising productivity; the humanistic intelligentsia's quest for cultural freedom; and the technocratic cadre's need for information. These challenged, in complex and sometimes contradictory ways, the power and information monopoly established by the state class in the despotic phase.[30] Some form of overtly articulated class conflict had to be institutionalised, while retaining the social ownership of the means of production.[31]

Obviously, whatever is achieved here, it is not done by goose-stepping from one phase to the next in unison. To quote one Soviet author, 'while the law of primary socialist accumulation stops to operate in some [countries], it is only beginning to operate in others.'[32] And then how should this institutionalisation proceed: by deepening democracy (say, through council-like forms); by indirect, parliamentary democracy; or by allowing markets to regulate social relations again? Khrushchev tried several options to move beyond original accumulation and extensive industrialisation, but all had detrimental short-run effects on the Soviet economy and in the end spilled over into international rivalries with other socialist states. Thus the decision to liberalise the movement of people within the Soviet Union led to hundreds of thousands of workers migrating back to European Russia from West Siberia and Kazakhstan, creating local shortages of labour. This led to the 1960 decision to demobilise some 1.2 million men from the army, part of the measures by which Khrushchev hoped to 'carry out his far-reaching plan for catching up with and overtaking the United States.'[33]

It is precisely here that the pressure from the West intervenes, if not necessarily directly. But whatever happens in a contender state is *always* overdetermined by the existence of the heartland. In this case, the increase of US defence expenditure and Kennedy's decision to develop counter-insurgency programmes to deal with national liberation movements in the Third World did not allow the demobilisation of so many Soviet ground troops without some form of compensation. This led to the upgrading of the Warsaw Pact (which had until then largely been a dormant organisation) as a source of manpower, and to the decision to deploy missiles in Cuba, which led to the crisis referred to earlier.[34] It also prompted the Soviet leadership to propose a division of labour within Comecon, interrupting the extended reproduction of 'Socialism in One Country' in each state separately. Paradoxically, this led to protests from the countries still in the early stages of development. In 1962 Gheorghiu-Dej of Rumania refused to cooperate with Khrushchev's project for supra-national planning because this 'would have transformed Rumania into a reservoir of oil, a granary, and a supplier of raw materials.'[35]

On the other hand, countries like the GDR and Czechoslovakia, which had been part of Germany's and Austria-Hungary's late industrialisation strategies, were all for deepening the division of labour. In Czechoslovakia, a movement to modernise planning to conform to the needs of advanced technological possibilities emerged in the same period. Given the diverse set of forces drawn into the economy, who were for different reasons less amenable to coercive central planning from Prague (technocratic cadre, women, Slovaks, the young), this would always prove difficult, but the Czechoslovak solution of allowing market relations back into the economy also provoked resistance from workers' collectives and the state-run trade unions, who feared a negative redistribution of income.[36] Driven by a powerful groundswell of democratic demands, the party under Alexander Dubcek chose the market route, and in 1968 even proposed to dismantle the collective ownership of the means of production. This route, as we will see, would later turn out to be the way to privatise state socialism for the benefit of an aspiring bourgeoisie. But the outcome of the actual 'Prague Spring' will never be known, because the Soviet leadership under Leonid Brezhnev, who had ousted Khrushchev in 1964, took the fateful decision to intervene militarily and 'normalise' Czechoslovakia with the help of the Warsaw Pact. Only Rumania refused to participate in the clampdown.

At the other extreme, China and Albania (like Rumania) were still in the process of establishing the foundations of the contender state by a process of 'socialist original accumulation', duly accompanied by indoctrination campaigns assigning 'magical' qualities to a nationalised quasi-Marxism. While Khrushchev was presiding over de-Stalinisation, Mao Zedong in 1958 began a campaign of state-led original accumulation different from the Soviet model established in the 1930s. 'The Great Leap Forward' in China was accompanied by furious attacks on revisionism (nominally, on Tito, but behind him, Khrushchev) and on imperialism. US nuclear power was famously dismissed as a 'paper tiger'. The Soviet Union, seeking a rapprochement with the West, warned the Chinese about US military power; privately, Khrushchev mocked the Chinese experiments with people's communes, the alternative to the collective and state farms of the USSR. In 1959, when it transpired that Moscow was secretly negotiating with Washington to suspend its support for a Chinese nuclear capability, and the USSR declared itself neutral in the border conflict between India and China, a rupture ensued in which Moscow ended all technical assistance.[37] The conflict would lead to border clashes on the Ussuri river. It entered a new phase when China, in an attempt by Mao's entourage to resist the ascendancy of a technocratic tendency in the Communist party, unleashed a radical anti-'bourgeois' campaign, the Great Cultural Revolution in 1966. Once again, the 'magical' use of ideology was in evidence, with successes in oil exploration, for instance, attributed to the correct application of Mao's thought.

ATLANTIC RIVALRIES IN THE NEW COLD WAR

Let me now turn to the era of detente and the rifts between the Western powers that accompanied it. Detente was the main diplomatic aim of the USSR in the Brezhnev period; by gaining recognition of the post-war borders in Europe, Moscow hoped to free the development of economic links from the mortgage of geopolitical issues, such as West German claims to areas incorporated into Poland or Czechoslovakia after 1945. The Soviet 'Peace Offensive' of 1969, coming on the heels of the crackdown on the Prague Spring, was certainly met with distrust in the West. Only when Moscow accepted that the US and Canada would participate in a conference to settle the borders issue, did the Permanent Council of NATO agree in October 1972 to engage in a Conference on Security and Cooperation in Europe, out of which would emerge the Organisation dealing with these issues, the OSCE. In August 1975, at Helsinki, UN Secretary-General Waldheim reminded the participants that the 35 governments signing up to the Final Act accounted for 80 per cent of the world's military expenditure. The idea that at least some of this could now be converted to development in the civilian sphere was certainly at the heart of the Soviet effort to realise the Helsinki agreements.[38]

The economic provisions of the Helsinki Final Act emphasise the need 'to create durable links and thus reinforce long-term global economic cooperation.'[39] The Soviet Union was looking primarily to Europe or even the US to work towards this; its own support for the NIEO project tended to be tactical and political, even though the prestige of the USSR at the UN definitely increased in the early 1970s.[40] With the quadrupling of the price of oil in 1973, however, Soviet energy resources too rose in value, and Brezhnev's vision of 'importing efficiency' by multi-billion dollar deals now became a distinct possibility. Premier Kosygin's caution not to rush into dependence on the West and squander irreplaceable raw material sources was overridden, as were actual challenges to the leadership of the ailing Brezhnev in the run-up to the 25th party congress of 1976. B. Shelepin, who had led the party conservatives who ousted Khrushchev, was himself removed; Yuri Andropov, the head of the KGB, made a bid for the leadership on a platform of detente and democracy. He would have to wait until Brezhnev's death in 1982. After Andropov's short tenure the pendulum swung back again to the party conservatives.[41]

This fateful postponement of the first attempt at renovating state socialism since Khrushchev resulted from the particular tenacity of an ever-smaller circle of septuagenarians holding power in Moscow. The Brezhnev generation in the leadership had begun their careers early, to fill the gaps created when the great purges of the 1930s swept away some three-quarters of the senior Bolshevik cadre (D. Ustinov, Brezhnev's minister of defence, for instance, was put in charge of Soviet defence industry in 1941 at the age of 32). This was the pioneer generation of the revolution from above, born before 1910. The next generation of cadre, born roughly between 1910 and 1925, came too late to benefit from the purges, but 'just in time to be decimated by World War II'.[42] The advanced age of the surviving earlier generation (at the end of the 1970s, the average age on the Politburo was almost 70) made the elite of the Soviet state class even more remote from the changes taking place in Soviet society than they would otherwise have been. Andropov however, through his eyes and ears in the KGB, had a better understanding of the urgent need to achieve a qualitative acceleration in the country's development. Absenteeism and alcoholism among the working population were keeping productivity down, and discrepancies between qualification levels and actual occupation added to the demoralisation among technical specialists.[43] Andropov, like the young Mikhail Gorbachev after him, was the exponent of a centrist and pro-detente managerial cadre, often recruited from the newly urbanising non-Russian republics, who were gaining ground in the *nomenklatura* and were keen to exchange ideological tenets for the principles of Western-style modern management.[44]

As with all contender states, the advances achieved by the Soviet bloc in the 1970s were seriously reversed in the ensuing decade as a result of the debt crisis and the new cold war. Thus passenger car production, a key indicator in the Fordist phase of catch-up industrialisation (cf. Table 3.1 of this book), still rose considerably from 1971 to 1980, notably in Poland and the USSR, bringing these countries to levels of production per capita approximating those of Czechoslovakia (100 per 10,000 in 1971), the GDR and Yugoslavia. But the drying-up of credit, combined with the limited export opportunities for cars rolling off depreciated production lines discarded by European manufacturers, were further signs of what we now know was the beginning of the end, once the West launched its final cold war onslaught.[45]

Euro-Soviet Rapprochement

The roles of French and Italian capital in the Soviet bloc were highlighted by their joint ventures and licensing agreements in the car industry— Renault's Dacia in Rumania, FIAT's Lada in the USSR and the Polonez in Poland. West German interest, on the other hand, was concentrated in the heavy equipment and chemical industries. Even more than the others, Germany also sought to tap into the raw material riches of the USSR. This revived the pattern of the Rapallo Treaty, even if the outlawed military interests of the Federal Republic (missiles and nuclear weapons) would this time be accommodated by the ostracised states of the 1970s: South Africa, Zaire and Brazil.

Ostpolitik began in earnest in 1966 when West Germany experienced its first post-war recession. Between 1966 and 1973, West German exports to the CMEA countries doubled, while exports to the Third World stagnated.[46] As we saw earlier, the 'Grand Coalition' of Christian and Social Democrats, with Brandt as foreign minister, presided over this shift. It drew support from big German capital, notably the Deutsche Bank orbit. Deutsche Bank, launched by Georg von Siemens in 1870, was the largest of the new banks set up to drive forward the industrialisation underpinning Germany's contender posture after the unification of 1871. Apart from the Siemens electrical engineering concern, the Deutsche Bank financial group included major steel producers such as Hoesch and Mannesmann; chemical concerns such as Bayer and BASF; and the car maker, Daimler-Benz, today incorporating Chrysler of the US. On the other hand, the bloc of forces associated with the prior liberal interlude under Ludwig Erhard drew its support from the light industries. Although the fluidity of capitalist market relations and the need to keep business going at all times must be kept in mind here, this latter bloc has historically been centred on Dresdner Bank, which had close ties with the light export industries (its holdings and preferential interlocks with big industry are with Krupp and Thyssen in steel; AEG in electrical engineering; and Hoechst in chemicals).[47]

The foray into the Soviet bloc was led by the Deutsche Bank group. When the Grand Coalition took over, the retiring Hermann Abs even created a duumvirate at the head of Deutsche Bank—a 'Grand Coalition' of one 'socialist' and one Christian Democrat—to ensure that the fine-tuning of foreign economic policy would not be hindered by difficulties in getting through to key decision-makers in the government.[48] Light industry on the other hand was hard-hit by the lifting of import barriers for East European producers in 1966; textile and clothing lost hundreds of thousands of jobs, primarily to the Third World, but also to a growing import share from the East in the period 1969–76. Small business and light industry were wary of *Ostpolitik* and, as a right-wing bloc in Christian Democracy, unhappy with the Grand Coalition.[49]

In addition to his conception of transcending the East–West divide (referred to in Chapter 4 of this book), Brandt saw the development of economic relations with the Soviet bloc in the perspective of developing an independent European growth pole in the Atlantic economy. Technological development in the US was achieved primarily in its defence sector, with which West Germany could not compete; but if the UK were to join the EEC (of which Brandt was one of the most outspoken advocates), a European group in NATO could be formed, which would then competitively utilise the civilian-economic advantages from East–West trade. In August 1970 Brandt signed a treaty in Moscow with Soviet prime minister Kosygin. A few months later, the heads of Mannesmann, Salzgitter (state-owned steel company), GHH (steel), Siemens and the three big chemical companies also travelled to the USSR, while B. Beitz of Krupp had separately accompanied a German minister visiting Moscow earlier.[50] These were the companies that were most closely, although never exclusively, involved in East–West trade. Christian Deubner gives the export shares of West German industry to Comecon for 1981 as 13 per cent for machine tools and rolling mill equipment, 10 per cent for steel tubes, and 9 per cent each for bulk chemicals and iron products.[51] However, there was a qualitative aspect to these percentages, in that they are not subject to extreme market or currency fluctuations; they locked German industrial capacity into the Soviet planned economy. Indeed East–West economic cooperation at this juncture 'switched from individual contracts stipulating the supply of individual types of goods to large-scale, long-term agreements providing for the import of integrated industrial plant, technological processes, and complete plant.'[52] In the crisis-ridden 1970s, such a shift had potentially enormous consequences for the nature of economic development in Europe, with commensurate geopolitical ramifications, and this certainly was how things were understood by Western strategists.

Integration culminated in 1980 with the contract for a gas pipeline from Urengoi in north Siberia to Bavaria, signed by a consortium headed by

Deutsche Bank (for Mannesmann, with assistance from AEG and Salzgitter).[53] This contract for $6 billion worth of gas supplies annually for 25 years— and hence, an equivalent market for exports to the East—set all the alarm bells ringing in Washington, because, as one Soviet commentator put it, 'if the deal succeeds, all the US ... efforts to restrict the granting of credits to the USSR will be brought to nought.' At this point of time, US electronic listening posts in West Germany were monitoring thousands of German phone calls a day in an attempt to gather information about the pipeline project.[54] Spokespersons for the industries involved now argued that it was in Germany's interest to help raise the productivity and efficiency of the Soviet economy, if only to ensure the envisaged Soviet export surplus by which debt service was to be covered.[55] Certainly the United States had its own stakes in the evolving trade with the Soviet Union, from Pepsi-Cola's entry under Nixon to large-scale contracts with IBM and Bendix under Carter. Thomas Watson, of the IBM founding family, was Carter's ambassador in Moscow.[56] But the Reagan administration, building on the freezing of rela- tions in Carter's final year in office under the influence of the arms-industrial bloc (to which I return later), was eager to launch what Assistant Secretary of Defence Richard Perle called a 'well-designed program of economic sanc- tions [that] can both damage the development of the Soviet economy and slow the growth of their defence industrial base.'[57]

This approach gained the upper hand when Poland, hardest hit of all East European states by the debt crisis, declared a state of emergency in late 1981. It was thus that the Polish leadership hoped to avoid the stand-off with the workers of the Solidarnosc trade union movement in the shipyards of Gdansk from deteriorating into political collapse and Soviet intervention. Washington promptly imposed a boycott on both Poland *and* the Soviet Union in December 1981, forcing the USSR to produce the necessary equip- ment and lay the entire pipeline itself.[58] This drew a sharp response from Helmut Schmidt, who had already clashed with Reagan in the summer over the pipeline contract, but who now detected a calculated attempt to sabotage German and European economic interests—the Polish state of emergency in his view was a decision by the Poles, meant to stave off Soviet interference. Defence Secretary Weinberger and UN Ambassador Jeanne Kirkpatrick even wanted to declare Poland in default, and Haig now had to rush in to warn that the European banking system might collapse as a result.[59]

In June 1982 the Versailles G-7 meeting reached agreement on a higher interest rate on credits to the Soviet bloc (12.4 per cent instead of the earl- ier 8.8 per cent), as a compromise.[60] But on his return to Washington, Reagan ruled that the embargo decisions imposed the previous December would also apply to US subsidiaries and licence-holders abroad, thus effectively making the agreement void again. Although European companies were ordered by their governments to go ahead and ignore the US decision, it made dealing with the USSR less attractive in the long run. Haig had meanwhile been replaced; Schmidt, in trouble at home over the NATO missile decision, flew to Washington to express his dismay to the new secretary of state, George Schultz, but to no avail.[61] A year later the US obtained agreement from Western European leaders to cap imports of Soviet natural gas at 30 per cent of energy needs, a further step in the economic war against the USSR. A parallel campaign to let key technical knowledge fall into the hands of Soviet intelligence—but with intentional design flaws that would actually ensure failure—led to serious disruptions in the pipeline project.[62]

Concerned over the Reagan hard line, France's Mitterrand and the new German chancellor, Helmut Kohl, decided to stage a show of European unity. A celebration of the Franco-German friendship treaty, concluded 19 years earlier between de Gaulle and Adenauer, was organised to signal profound dissatisfaction with the state of Atlantic relations. This was heightened when Secretary Shultz in January 1984 declared in a speech in Stockholm that *the partition of Europe after the war had never been recognised by the United States*; thus effectively abrogating US adherence to the Helsinki Final Act. According to Shultz, human rights were the centrepiece of US foreign policy.[63] The implication of this was to delegitimate the confiscatory state of the USSR, with which West Germany and others were seeking a durable rapprochement on which to graft a European strategy. Well might Federal President Weiszäcker in 1983 declare that 'basket two'—economic cooperation—was the most important element in the Helsinki package, or, with Austrian Social Democrat leader Kreisky, defend East–West trade at the April 1984 Trilateral Commission meeting in Rome.[64] In the English-speaking world, from Carter onwards, 'basket three'—human rights and free movement—had been declared central. This placed the Soviet Union at the other extreme of the heartland/contender axis, out of bounds for the wider West.

The economic floor beneath this ideological choreography was laid after the 1982 recession in the United States. The massive deficit spending for defence, by which the Reagan administration climbed out of the pit, triggered a restructuring of economic policy in Europe as the expanding US economy now began sucking in exports from Europe. In the first eight months of 1984, export growth to the rest of the world remained almost stagnant, but West German exports *to the US* rose by 35.9 per cent, French exports by 39.4 per cent, and Italy's by 46 per cent.[65] In France, this was accompanied in 1983 by the abandoning of the initial Keynesian policy and the import restrictions meant to keep Japanese capital from profiting from demand management.[66]

There were also signs of a tentative transformation in West Germany, perhaps not to straight neoliberalism, but towards a synthesis which absorbed elements of the neoliberal emphasis on market regulation and post-materialist ideology and yet left the industrial strengths and class compromise intact. As Richard van der Wurff has argued, this policy aimed at accelerating technological progress in new fields such as ecologically sustainable development, while retaining existing wage and taxation levels. The harbingers of this hybrid concept of control were Oskar Lafontaine in the opposition SPD and Lothar Späth in the CDU.[67] Jacques Delors, who, as minister of economy and finance, was the architect of the 1983 neoliberal turn in France, moved closer to the Lafontaine/Späth concept when he was appointed president of the European Commission in 1985.[68] This reorientation, to which I will return in Chapter 8, also made German and other advanced European companies more dependent on markets in the most developed economies (North America and East Asia) and on developing their own high-tech sector, including an aerospace component. Daimler-Benz was the main force in this process, by its takeovers of AEG and the German aerospace sector; while Deutsche and Dresdner Bank made key acquisitions in the City of London and on Wall Street.[69] East–West economic cooperation on the other hand dried up at a critical juncture in the development of the Soviet modernisation attempt. The German Industry Confederation in its annual report for 1984 acknowledged that because of uncertainties created by the American embargos, the economic *Ostpolitik* was rapidly losing steam. A new opening to the East, Christian Deubner wrote at the time, would henceforth be a matter of weaker industries dependent on protection, a policy possibly pursued jointly with their counterparts in France and Italy, and in British industry.[70]

Military Build-Up and Economic Warfare

Parallel to the *economic* rivalries within the Western bloc, the United States also pursued a policy of outright confrontation that tended to undermine East–West interdependence in the longer run. This policy was driven by a bloc of forces that was, obviously, organised around the 'military-industrial complex' (MIC). But we should understand this bloc as a political formation in its own right, shaped by the specific geopolitical development of the original English-speaking heartland and the wider West.

The 'MIC' in a narrow sense, i.e., the actual military machinery of the United States and its supply lines in the American economy, lost clout because of Vietnam.[71] This allowed the forces clamouring for national liberation and international equality to become stronger everywhere, something felt most acutely in the more precarious outposts of Western influence in the world. *Israel* occupies a special place here, because only the projection of overwhelming power by the US can guarantee its survival as an ethnic colony amidst a hostile Arab world. As dependence on Middle Eastern oil increased, however, the prospect that the West might give in to OPEC and, more generally, to the Third World revolt raised fears that Israel's existence might become part of North–South bargaining, especially after the anti-Zionism resolution in the UN General Assembly made the political status and constitution of Israel an issue in the NIEO campaign. Maintaining a coalition between the military-imperialist constituency, which runs from the Pentagon and military industry to the media and academia, and the energy sector (always suspected of being ready to compromise with the oil-producing countries) therefore became mandatory in order to protect Israel. The growth of the Middle East arms market thanks to oil income provided the basis for such a convergence of interests. As Nitzan and Bichler have demonstrated, by the late 1960s this resulted in a political business cycle affecting the large US arms producers and 'big oil' in tandem.[72]

The connection with the right-wing Zionists was made when the 'Senator from Boeing', Henry Jackson, teamed up with a group, including investment banker and veteran cold-war diplomat Paul Nitze, to campaign for the deployment of an Anti-Ballistic Missile (ABM) system and restoration of nuclear superiority over the USSR. Richard Perle acted as a liaison between Jackson and the ABM group; in 1969 he followed Nitze to the Pentagon as a special assistant.[73] Senator Jackson, Kissinger notes in his memoirs, 'proceeded to implement his [convictions] by erecting a series of legislative hurdles that gradually paralyzed our East-West policy.'[74] The Jackson–Vanik amendment to the 1973 trade legislation tied commercial equality for the USSR to acquiescence in Jewish emigration to Israel, mortgaging detente on the Zionist project. A year later Jackson wanted a tripling of emigration to 100,000 per year and US monitoring of exit visa policy, as Israel wanted more urban immigrants with better skills. Meanwhile the Jackson team led the opposition to ongoing arms control negotiations, undermining the US position on SALT II, the draft treaty covering multiple-warhead ballistic missiles. When they won over Defence Secretary James Schlesinger and the Pentagon in mid-1974, Kissinger felt that detente was a lost cause.[75] Thus the militarist bloc obtained a hold on US policy, which, as we will see in Chapter 10, was still able to influence the decision to invade Iraq almost 30 years later. But the first aim was to raise tension with the USSR.

The alliance of militarists and right-wing Zionists was consolidated in the second half of the 1970s, when a key segment of the New York Jewish intelligentsia, including Norman Podhoretz, editor of *Commentary*, abandoned its traditional left liberal position for a hard-line conservatism.[76] In 1976 the neoconservatives, as they became known, prevailed on CIA Director George Bush Sr., to appoint one of their number—the red-baiting Harvard historian, Richard Pipes—to head a 'Team B' to upgrade current CIA estimates of Soviet military strength. 'Team B,' Robert Scheer writes, 'was successful in getting the U.S. government to profoundly alter its estimates of Soviet strength and intentions.'[77] In this episode Bush followed the lead of the hardliners who laid siege to his own organisation, the CIA; the liaison officer dealing with Team B, John Paisley, fought bitter battles with it, because Soviet defence growth was actually falling and procurement of weapons was even down to zero growth in the period 1976–81.[78] Yet the

'Window of Vulnerability' scare created by Team B, which referred to the supposed gaps in US defence against nuclear attack, worked miracles. It would ultimately contribute to the eventual rebirth of the ABM project as the 'Strategic Defence Initiative' under President Reagan.

Carter's election in 1976 of course pointed in the wrong direction for the cold warriors. Carter, writes Alan Wolfe, was the first Democrat president after the war who, thanks to the preparatory work of Nixon and Kissinger, 'did not *need* the cold war.' But 'defence plants, hawkish labour unions, support for Israel, and macroeconomic stimulation' had worked to rear a powerful cold war lobby in the Democratic Party too, and Carter sought to gain time for his human rights strategy by making concessions to the hard-liners.[79] The neoconservatives had meanwhile organised themselves in the Committee on the Present Danger (CPD), with a separate 'European–American Workshop' chaired by veteran nuclear strategist Albert Wohlstetter (one of Nitze's original ABM group), to win over European politicians to a confrontationist stategy.[80] When Carter drafted Trilateralists like Cyrus Vance and Michael Blumenthal into his cabinet, their places on the board of the Council on Foreign Relations, the elite planning network for international strategy (with its influential journal *Foreign Affairs*), were taken by Nitze, Pipes, the Rostow brothers Walt and Eugene, and other neoconservative CPD prominents.[81]

From Europe, the president was encouraged to raise the temperature of the cold war a little by Helmut Schmidt. It will be remembered that at this point the issue of communists entering governments in Italy and France was still not resolved, and Schmidt, while firm on the economic side, was concerned about the long-term political effects of *Ostpolitik*. In 1978, annoyed by Carter's decision to suspend production of the neutron bomb under the influence of mass protest, Schmidt proposed to upgrade NATO's intermediate range missile capacity in Europe. This would bring Europe's NATO allies back to a more central position in the ongoing arms reduction negotiations between the US and the USSR, while drawing a clearer line between the West and communism.[82] In January 1979, Carter, Schmidt, Giscard and Callaghan, meeting on the island of Guadeloupe, agreed in principle on stationing land-based Cruise and Pershing II missiles in Europe; the US government next decided to budget $2.7 billion for the new MX intercontinental missile. The 'discovery' of a Soviet brigade in Cuba signalled that there were powerful forces at work that sought to generate new crises and scares. The Iranian revolution in February and the seizure of the US embassy in Tehran then prompted Carter to announce a rise in defence spending of 4.5 per cent per year (once again so as to throw a bone at the opponents of the ratification of SALT II, planned for December); and in June the Rapid Deployment Force, the intervention unit for the Persian Gulf under the Carter Doctrine, was declared operational. With Presidential Directive 59,

Carter even committed himself, unknown to the public, to a nuclear war-fighting strategy for the United States.[83]

It was the Soviet intervention in Afghanistan in December 1979 that opened the floodgates of a new cold war. Ratification of SALT II was postponed and in January 1980 an economic embargo was imposed on the USSR in computers and grain. Moderates like Secretary of State Vance had by then left the Carter administration. Giscard d'Estaing and Thatcher's foreign secretary, Lord Carrington, judged the Afghan situation differently and made their reservations public. Helmut Schmidt had for different reasons given up on Carter earlier, and was reported to have flown to California in mid-1979 to confer with Republican foreign policy veterans Kissinger, Haig, George Shultz and David Packard.[84] From the perspective of Europe's rulers, the threat of the Left had receded sufficiently to revert to realistic relations with the USSR, but this was not the intention in the United States.

The Reagan administration included all the big names of the Committee on the Present Danger. Its two terms in office were a bonanza for the American arms industry, compensating for the fact that it had to leave most of the business created by the Iran–Iraq war to its European rivals.[85] Terminating the challenge posed by the USSR was the overriding concern in Washington; and, as we can see today, the final stage of the Soviet contender experience begins when Reagan took office. It was actually the president's personal conviction that now was the chance to spend the Soviet Union into bankruptcy. As he put it in an interview in the fall of 1981, 'they're going to be faced with [the fact] that we could go forward with an arms race and they can't keep up.' Certainly the White House disowned a statement by Pipes earlier in the year that the 'Soviet leaders would have to choose between peacefully changing their Communist system in the direction followed by the West or going to war,' but this was nevertheless the mood in the administration.[86] Pipes also predicted, accurately, as it turned out, that intensified US pressure would force a new NEP on the USSR, neutralising the contender effort.[87] This policy took shape in several steps. In March 1982, Reagan signed a National Security Decision Directive (NSDD 32) directing the relevant offices to work towards a 'neutralisation' of Soviet control over Eastern Europe; in November, he signed NSDD 66, authorising the use of economic sabotage against the USSR itself; and in January 1983, with NSDD 75, the president made regime change in the USSR official policy.[88]

The administration's *public* statements were meanwhile meant to neutralise the growing anti-nuclear movement at home and abroad, and to avoid appearing too belligerent. Yet Brezhnev's proposal for a moratorium on intermediate range missile deployment was not taken up because the Cruise/Pershing II deployment gave NATO a qualitative advantage, targeting Soviet command centres on its own soil; the much-debated SS-20s of the USSR, on the other hand, could not get beyond Iceland. Reagan would only allow negotiations on land-based intercontinental ballistic missiles, which were anyway in the process of being made obsolete by submarine-launched missiles, in which the US had a clear superiority.[89] In June 1982 the president flew to Europe for discussions with Pope John Paul II (with whom he agreed on covert support for the Solidarnosc movement in Poland) and for the G-7 meeting at Versailles, already referred to earlier. This was a more difficult engagement in light of the pipeline disagreements with the European allies. But Reagan felt that they had to be convinced that 'this is our chance to bring the Soviets into the real world and for them to take a stand with us.'[90] We have already seen how he reneged on the interest rate compromise upon his return to Washington, committed as he was to raising the stakes.

In March 1983 Reagan gave a biblical twist to the contest with the USSR when he called the Soviet Union 'the focus of evil in the modern world'.[91] In October, at the 10th anniversary of the Heritage Foundation, the president characterised his crusade as a democratic revolution that was in the process of writing 'the last sad page of the bizarre chapter in human history known as communism'.[92] The 'Evil Empire' speech was addressed to a meeting of the National Association of Evangelists in Florida, and with the religious metaphor Reagan tapped into a deep root of the sense of identity of the English-speaking West. In combination with the Heritage speech, it highlights the conviction that the struggle was entering an epochal final stage, a sentiment shared by many millions in American society.[93] Jerry Falwell, the evangelist architect of the 'Moral Majority' for Reagan, had in the run-up to the election swung round to support for Israel, defending its right to subdue the entire Middle East. Falwell, who until then had the reputation of an anti-Semite, now praised the aggressive policies of the Likud government of Menachem Begin.[94] 'Evil', with its domicile in Moscow, was identified by the Protestant fundamentalist current in the United States; while branding those resisting the West as 'terrorists' was the contribution of the Israeli Right, whose approach to the Palestinian population displaced in the successive wars of colonisation was premised on equating all its political claims with the terrorism perpetrated by its extremist fringes. The combination was baptised at a conference in Jerusalem dedicated to the topic of Soviet support for international terrorism in July 1979. It was attended by Senator Jackson, George Bush (then still a Republican hopeful himself) and 'specialists' such as Jonah Alexander and Ray Cline.[95]

In 1983, the effort to spend the USSR into bankruptcy received a major boost with the launch of the Strategic Defense Initiative (SDI). SDI, or 'Star Wars', took up the old ABM project. It was geared to technological innovation, so that US industry could also compete with rivals closer to home. A project proposed by a group of defence firms based on existing technology was discarded in favour of a rival project from the entourage of nuclear scientist Edward Teller based on new technologies.[96] In addition, SDI aimed at enlisting the allies' research efforts, which in turn forced the states signing up (the UK, Israel, West Germany and Japan) to submit to US export controls. The unilateral colonisation by the Americans of the signatories' research results effectively derailed rival European efforts in the new technologies domain even before they were launched (as was confirmed by the anaemic condition of the civilian European research programme, Eureka, launched by Mitterrand in 1985).[97]

The aggressive US military posture, relying on Cruise and Pershing missiles and high-tech weaponry to destroy Soviet command structures in the early hours of a war, led to growing tensions with the European NATO allies, already at loggerheads with the US over the pipeline issue. At the Williamsburg, Virginia, G-7 meeting in May 1983, Reagan encountered serious disagreement on the merits of the missile deployment from Mitterrand and Canada's Pierre Trudeau; supported only by Mrs. Thatcher, he had to go all-out in defending the hard line with the USSR.[98] Chancellor Kohl had to be leaned on by General Bernard Rogers, NATO commander in Europe, before a visit to Moscow in the summer of 1983, and later in the year Rogers got into an overt conflict with his own German deputy, General Kiessling, over the forward strategy. In a contrived scandal, materials for which were passed on by the CIA to German military intelligence, Kiessling was disgraced and dismissed by West German Secretary of Defence and future NATO Secretary-General Manfred Wörner.[99] In November 1983 the Bonn parliament voted in favour of NATO missile deployment, ignoring mass protest; the first missiles were flown in the next day by US Air Force planes in an obvious act of intimidation, both of the opposition and of the USSR. The Soviet delegation duly left the Geneva INF negotiations in protest.

Tension with the Soviet Union had been raised two months earlier by the Korean Airlines incident. The KAL 007 jetliner was shot down when it penetrated Soviet air space, in what appears to have been a tragic error in a series of incidents involving incursions by US spy planes.[100] Then, in October, the US invaded Grenada. This heightened fears in Moscow that Washington was abandoning all accepted rules of international behaviour.[101] True, Reagan contemplated a conciliatory response to a letter from Andropov, in which the latter proposed to normalise relations. But the president was instead prevailed on by his entourage to tell the Soviet leader off, and Reagan's eventual letter 'ended any chance of a rapprochement with Andropov.'[102] This was taken rather lightly in the White House:

> Reagan's cheerful opinion was that 'the Russians' had finally accepted the fact that they could no longer afford to keep pace with his arms build-up. If not, he was prepared to spend twice as much, if necessary, to force them to come to terms.[103]

Andropov died in February 1984; his successor, Konstantin Chernenko, returned to the negotiating table but died in March 1985. Only then could Mikhail Gorbachev finally take over from the exhausted Brezhnev generation, launching his Perestroika ('restructuring'). We turn to this in the concluding section of this chapter.

RIVAL RESPONSES TO GORBACHEV'S NEW LOOK

Gorbachev's intention, made clear soon after taking power, was to gear the contender role of the Soviet Union to civilian economic development—the new NEP predicted by Pipes. The command structures of the confiscatory state make such radical shifts possible; and the affinity with continental European politics in this respect was reinforced by the common rejection of American belligerence.[104] Perestroika was, in the words of the new general secretary himself, a 'revolution from above', in which 'profound and essentially revolutionary changes [are] implemented on the initiative of the authorities ... necessitated by objective changes in the situation and in social moods.'[105] The Soviet leadership was demoralised by the Reagan policy; Star Wars in particular brought home the gap with the West, which had earlier led to the abandoning of independent military research and a shift to spying and reverse engineering instead.[106]

In his first major policy statement, the political report of the CPSU Central Committee to the 27th party congress in February 1986, Gorbachev ventured beyond routine denunciations of imperialist aggression and decay. His argument that environmental degradation and the depletion of resources were jeopardising 'the very foundations of the existence of civilisation'— and the references to the blind play of 'market forces' and the need to address the issues at the global level—position him outside the traditional contender state posture with its emphasis on national sovereignty. His analysis rather situates him in the strand of thought that we encountered earlier in the Tinbergen report to the Club of Rome and in the Brandt Commission. There was an urgent need, according to Gorbachev, 'for effective international procedures and mechanisms, which would make for the rational use of the world's resources as an asset belonging to all humanity.'[107]

It therefore comes as no surprise that support for the Gorbachev programme was strongest among the intelligentsia, especially the managerial cadre—the same was true in the West. Soviet authors in his entourage paid lip-service to the supposed militancy of the proletariat, but simultaneously noted its essentially defensive position and gradual marginalisation. The cadre on the other hand, in the words of Gherman Diligensky, 'show a greater interest towards global humanistic problems and the humanisation of our way of living' and, if it embraces democracy, it may develop into a 'centre of gravity for other groups inclined towards social and political protest'.[108]

Not that the mood among the cadre was optimistic; as Alexander Bovin, one of the most articulate of Gorbachev's advisers, wrote in *Izvestia* in 1987,

> We must also recognise clearly that the relation of forces on a world scale may change in favour of capitalism, in case Perestroika does not succeed or is essentially limited and restrained ..., in case not socialism but capitalism 'masters' the new wave of the scientific-technical revolution. That is the meaning of Perestroika—seen through the prism of the fate of socialism.[109]

In this respect, the neoliberal counter-revolution, which was turning the new productive forces of the period directly into military threats to the USSR, seriously constrained the freedom of manoeuvre of the new Soviet leadership. In a world in which the heartland enjoys structural advantages resulting from historical precedence, a contender state cannot shift course without facing up to pressure from the West seeking to derail it. As I indicated earlier, the greater openness that accompanies the attempt to move to a higher stage of political articulation allows the diversity of interests and perspectives to become apparent.

In the circumstances, the alternative to Gorbachev's version of Perestroika (with its social democratic accent) emerged in the form of the Yeltsin option of a transition to capitalism. 'What kept Yeltsin and his followers in opposition to Gorbachev,' writes David Kotz, 'was their disagreement with [his] commitment to reform and democratize socialism, rather than replace it with capitalism.'[110] This provided the angle from which the neoliberal forces in the West sought to unhinge the rapprochement between Gorbachev and Western Europe.

Western Strategy against a New Rapallo

The Reagan administration was committed to maintaining the pressure on the USSR and not allowing the restructuring to civilian competition to proceed on conditions set by the Soviet state class. Indeed, whoever is in office, the US *can* ultimately only prevail by bringing its huge military assets into play as a competitive advantage.[111] So when Gorbachev announced a unilateral moratorium in April 1985 on the deployment of intermediate range missiles in Europe and, 10 days later, on nuclear weapons testing, Washington duly rejected both proposals.[112] When the leaders nevertheless agreed to meet in Geneva in November, Reagan was warned by his advisers that, whatever Gorbachev might say, 'intelligence showed' that the new Soviet leader was preparing for war. Reagan was thus groomed to stick to his guns just to thwart a supposed Soviet design. 'Any new move on our part, such as SDI, forces them to revamp, and change their plan at great cost.'[113] Preparing Reagan's meeting with Gorbachev, Donald Regan, the president's chief of staff, analysed the US position entirely in terms of the economic implications of SDI.

> The Soviets [Regan wrote in his memoirs] could not spend more on arms without running the risk of bankrupting the state .... I urged the President to stay strong in dealing with Gorbachev .... Faced with the choice between bankruptcy and a fall from power that would deliver the U.S.S.R. back into the hands of the faction that had all but ruined her economically, [Gorbachev] would have no choice .... The key was SDI. To match it, Gorbachev would have to mortgage the whole future of communism.[114]

A month after the summit, Gorbachev offered to allow US inspection of Soviet nuclear test sites to verify a moratorium; again Washington was not interested. Instead Undersecretary of Defence Fred Iklé chose to use a visit to Munich to exhort the West European allies to abandon the 'principle of stability between East and West' and bring the West's 'technological and economic superiority' to bear on the Soviet bloc.[115] In the meantime the US had prevailed on Saudi Arabia—in exchange for military guarantees—to increase oil production to bring down the price. Between late 1985 and 1987, crude oil prices collapsed from $28 to $17.5 per barrel, reducing Soviet hard currency earnings proportionally.[116] Even the explosion of a nuclear reactor at Chernobyl in April 1986, a disaster which should perhaps have occasioned a more humane look at things, was used by Washington to mount an ideological campaign and declare the USSR outside civilisation. The Murdoch press reported 15,000 dead and reports broadcast by US radio stations beaming into Eastern Europe caused local panic.[117]

The Reagan policy had all along been based on the idea that a comprehensive 'Americanization of Europe' was necessary to fill up the vacuum created by the 'reduction of Soviet cultural presence in Eastern Europe'. It was essential *to prevent a 'Europeanization of East Europe'.*[118] So when Perestroika was responded to benevolently by European politics and public opinion—not least out of exasperation with Reagan's belligerency—concern in Washington could only increase. Certainly the boorish Helmut Kohl made several gaffes, comparing Gorbachev to Nazi propaganda minister Goebbels and then accompanying Reagan to an SS war cemetery. But the West German interest in reunification, fear of war, and economic appetite soon got the upper hand again. Otto Wolff von Amerongen, the most prominent East–West trader in the country, at a June 1986 meeting of the Vienna club of Western business leaders and their Soviet bloc counterparts, repeated familiar arguments about raising the technological level of Soviet industry because 'it is in the interest of the West that the USSR increases its exports ... [and] oil, gas and raw materials are a too fragile and too vulnerable basis.'[119]

Many European business leaders saw American embargo policies as little more than protectionism for US capital. To be eligible for SDI contracts, for instance, the Kohl government had to accept Pentagon monitoring of West German corporations' deals with the Soviet bloc, giving the US authorities insight into minute technical details.[120] Nevertheless political relations between West Germany and the Soviet Union improved in the course of 1986, when Foreign Minister Genscher visited Moscow. At the World Economic Forum in Davos in 1987, he challenged the US and Britain to exploit the opportunities for disarmament and economic cooperation which Gorbachev was creating. But at the Venice G-7 in June, despite heated debate on how to deal with Gorbachev, no agreement was reached.[121] A prestigious West German business delegation led by Mannesman and Deutsche Bank director F.W. Christians (the architect of the gas pipeline deal) attended a meeting on a nuclear-free world in 1987 in Moscow. A year later Christians even made a proposal to turn the Kaliningrad area, the Russian enclave between Lithuania and Poland formerly part of German East Prussia, into a special economic zone where ethnic Germans from the USSR could be resettled.[122] Kohl went to Moscow in 1988, and in October Italian prime minister de Mita visited Gorbachev at the head of a powerful business delegation that included Agnelli of FIAT (to negotiate the production of the Panda model in the USSR). Other Italian companies signed deals for a petrochemical complex planned to be the largest in the world, while banks extended a $1 billion credit to finance the increased production of consumer goods.[123] Obviously, the new policies adopted by Gorbachev worked to remove cold war obstacles to deepening economic integration with the Soviet Union, opening a new arena of expansion for European capital, in direct competition with opportunities in the Atlantic economy.

In the absence of a true consensus, violence once again began to creep in on the edges of the geopolitical spectrum. Sweden, like Austria and Spain, was always seen as a security risk in the development of East–West ties because of its formal neutrality. But Prime Minister Palme's role in the campaign for a nuclear-free world as the head of the commission named after him, his commitment to the UN to convert Sweden's defence industries and his embrace of Gorbachev's disarmament proposals constituted a positive threat. At home, Palme faced a bloc of companies of the Wallenberg group such as Ericsson, Saab-Scania and Asea, eager to comply with Pentagon requirements in order not to miss out on the latest technology and lose markets in the US or, in the case of actual arms production, in other NATO countries.[124] To neutralise this opposition, Palme had sought the support of Volvo chairman Pehr Gyllenhammar, the initiator of the European Round Table of Industrialists and a TC member, in his 1982 election campaign. He thus hoped to win support for a renovated corporate liberalism in the spirit of Lafontaine and Späth's ideas in West Germany and Delors' in Brussels.[125]

In January 1986, when Gorbachev enlisted Palme's support for a denuclearisation in the year 2000 and the unilateral test ban referred to earlier, opposition to the Swedish prime minister's orientation, in both the geopolitical and the social economic spheres, had been building up for years. The day after his public endorsement of the Gorbachev proposal, Palme was assassinated when visiting a cinema with his wife. As so often in these cases, the perpetrator may have had a number of backgrounds and motives. Palme had also been the UN mediator in the Iraq–Iran war, and yet in his government capacity signed weapons exports contracts to the war zone. At a NATO Conference in 1984, Georgetown strategist William Taylor had identified the neutral status of Sweden as a threat in itself; a 'Swedenisation' of Europe would upset the military balance between the Soviet Union and the United States.[126] What we do know is that the Swedish security apparatus, which is closely integrated with the NATO intelligence infrastructure, failed to protect him and went out of its way not to capture the assassin.[127]

The willingness of the Reagan administration to seek violent solutions in breaking the links between 'Moscow' and Europe was displayed in all openness in the attack on Libya. Till today Libya combines the role of an energy supplier to Europe with ties to national liberation movements— 'terrorists' by US standards. Reagan broke off diplomatic relations early in his first term, freezing Libyan assets in the US. In August 1981 he allowed US jets to provoke a fight with Soviet-made Libyan jets in the Gulf of Sidra. This led to widespread criticism both at home and abroad.[128] In 1982 a ban of Libyan oil imports was decreed, but European importers and a number of US corporations, notably Occidental Petroleum, ignored the boycott. Greece, a NATO member state, even proceeded to sign a naval agreement with Libya. This was seen as a direct strategic threat, and in 1984 Secretary Shultz therefore proposed to switch to 'active defence'.[129] In March, Reagan sent a naval squadron of 45 ships including three aircraft carriers and nuclear submarines to the Libyan coast, with express instructions to strike back hard if Libyan aircraft were to respond. This led to the sinking of several Libyan patrol boats and around 70 dead.[130] CIA director Casey however felt that there had been no real reason for the attack. Ten days later, a bomb in a Berlin disco killed a US serviceman; this was declared to be a Libyan terror attack, and in a night operation on 14 April, F-111 bombers operating from Britain hit several cities in Libya, aiming specifically at Qaddafi's personal residence and killing his adopted daughter. France had refused passage to the US planes, forcing them to make a long detour that hampered the operation. The attack was coordinated to be broadcast on prime-time TV in the US, and Reagan himself appeared to explain that the Berlin disco attack was irrefutably the work of Qaddafi and that the US had acted in self-defence.[131]

The air raid created an uproar abroad; Moscow cancelled a meeting planned for May between foreign secretaries Shevardnadze and Shultz. But the bombing was also a warning to European supporters of a neutralist stance in the spirit of the NIEO and Euro-Arab Dialogue episodes.[132] In the summer, Casey and Shultz decided to press the issue and raise tension, more particularly using the conflict in Chad (in which Libya was involved), to force the hand of the French. Vernon Walters, Reagan's UN ambassador and CIA veteran, was dispatched to London, Paris and Rome to convince the European governments; a disinformation campaign simultaneously aimed to instil fear among Libya's neighbours. Walters however had little success on his European tour. Even Mrs. Thatcher could not make herself available and London let it be known there would be no landing facilities for F-111s this time. In France, the US counted on the military to join the US in the fight against Libya, but Mitterrand proved a harder nut to crack. An exasperated Walters warned that the CIA had knowledge of spectacular terrorist attacks to come; these struck Paris that same month.[133] In Italy the message was better understood. In 1986, the Agnelli family, the majority owners of FIAT, consented to the repurchase of the Libyan holding in the company for fear of US reprisals. Because the Agnellis lacked the means to buy out Qaddafi themselves, the deal was done by Deutsche Bank, making it the second largest shareholder of FIAT.[134] On the other hand, when Andreotti resisted the isolation of Libya and questioned the breach of the ABM treaty by Star Wars, the general in the ministry of defence in charge of the ABM dossier was assassinated by the Red Brigades in March 1987.[135]

Atlantic rivalry over relations with the USSR reached unprecedented heights in 1989. Certainly the election of Bush Sr. in November the year before marked a shift of gear to a more cautious attitude. In January, Henry Kissinger flew to Moscow on a mission for the President-elect, to prepare the ground for direct negotiations over the future of Eastern Europe with Gorbachev. But there was a growing feeling in Washington that the situation in the Soviet Union would now develop its own momentum, in the direction of further if not final disintegration of the Soviet bloc and possibly the USSR itself.[136] In February, the communist rulers of Hungary initiated the transition away from a state-controlled economy and one-party rule. The negotiations between the rulers of Poland and Solidarnosc, begun a few days before, heralded a similar political transformation.[137] In light of these events, a report for Bush written in March (and turned into a National Security Directive later in the year) recommended that the US should adopt a 'policy that actively promotes the integration of the Soviet Union into the international system'.[138]

If the strategy, then, was to terminate the contender posture of the USSR once and for all, West Germany should obviously not be permitted to pursue its own interests in ways undermining sustained Western pressure. However, Gorbachev's visits to London, Paris and Bonn in the first half of 1989, under the theme of 'Our Common European Home', testified to his continued popularity. Nothing suggested that the Soviet Union was about to give up its international position. German reunification and a relaxation of Soviet control of Eastern Europe were still on the cards; both were important negotiation chips for Moscow in exchange for aid, even though the proposals for a gradual reform of the planned economy were by then beginning to unravel, notably after the suspension of the state monopoly on foreign trade at the end of 1988. But this could only enhance West German interest in deals, not least concerning the future of the GDR, whose leaders were so obviously out of step with the Gorbachev line. In the United States, on the other hand, Bonn's activism on this front triggered a barrage of apprehensive comment in the media, targeting a policy which, by assisting Gorbachev's reform of Soviet socialism, was prolonging its lease on life.[139]

In April and May 1989, this theme was taken up in meetings of the main transnational elite planning networks. At a Trilateral Commission meeting in Paris in April, a report by Giscard d'Estaing, Henry Kissinger and former Japanese prime minister Nakasone recommended recapturing the initiative from Gorbachev by developing a strategy of long-term, conditional reconciliation, a mixture of 'cooperation and confrontation'. The authors sought to strike a balance between the different positions within the wider West by proposing to give the USSR observer status (not membership, which was rejected by the US) in GATT and IMF, to enable it to get acquainted with the rules of the game. They also proposed joint ventures in light industry (the German interest was in heavy industry) and the creation of a monitoring institution for aid to the former Soviet bloc.[140]

Comparable arguments were made at the 37th Bilderberg meeting a month later in La Toja, Spain. German economic statesmen were conspicuously absent from this gathering, although the topic was the future of Eastern Europe. The attitude towards the Germans was also less benevolent. Bonn's policy towards Gorbachev was criticised by Timothy Garton Ash, foreign editor of the conservative British magazine *The Spectator* and a sceptical observer of *Ostpolitik*.[141] Selected to address a prestigious gathering of European royalty and a cross-section of the Atlantic ruling class, Garton Ash advocated a forward strategy that would make Soviet concessions irreversible, with an active role to be played by the US and Canada in order to ensure that the process be guided by 'Western values'. Warning that there were 'profound differences of approach between the *Ostpolitik* of the Federal Republic of Germany, on the one hand, and the East European policy(ies) of the United States of America on the other', Garton Ash emphasised that what should be avoided was a 'Europeanisation of *Ostpolitik*', which was being talked about in Bonn. Instead he advocated the pursuit of a 'Westernisation of *Ostpolitik*' in order to keep German ambitions in check, because 'Europeanisation can also mean de-Americanisation.'[142] We are reminded of the American concern about a possible 'Europeanisation of Eastern Europe' as quoted earlier; but then, with the cold war subsiding, arguments against a new Rapallo were increasingly argued from the perspective that the United States might be left out of European affairs altogether—an aspect that would return in the arguments for NATO expansion and involvement in Yugoslavia, to which we turn in the next chapter.[143]

A comprehensive Ten Points programme for German and European economic unity was announced by Chancellor Kohl, 19 days after the GDR leadership opened the Berlin Wall on 9 November. The high-speed rail network—through which the newly founded European Round Table of Industrialists had in its first report of 1984 envisaged revitalising the European economy—was given a Paris–Berlin–Moscow extension in the new proposals.[144] From the perspective of the wider West, the need to rein in German rapprochement with Gorbachev now became extremely urgent. The entire post-war settlement in Europe was beginning to unravel and Germany seemed to be reclaiming the dominant position at the heart of the continent that it had lost in 1945—this time in agreement with the Soviet Union, and apparently unconcerned about the incompatibility with a social system inimical to the West. But, as members of the Bush administration had indicated on various occasions in the course of 1989, salvaging the USSR from the crisis of state socialism was out of the question. As Lawrence Eagleburger declared in September, it was not the task of US policy to ensure the success of Perestroika.[145]

How then are we to account for the fact that two days after the presentation of the Ten Points programme, a car bomb killed Alfred Herrhausen, Kohl's closest economic adviser, co-author of the Ten Points and head of Deutsche Bank, the historic bulwark of the independent fraction of German capital? Was it really the case that the extreme-left RAF, the presumed perpetrators, felt particularly angered by somebody who was willing to build bridges with the tottering Soviet Union, and who was on record for demanding greater transparency *in the West* to match Gorbachev's glasnost?[146] Or was he simply the next in line in the tragic procession of Aldo Moro, Olof Palme and others, who stood in the way of the advancing West? We need not doubt the profound concern in Washington and London (and also to some extent in Paris) that West Germany was breaking ranks in dealing with Gorbachev, and might emerge significantly enlarged from it—a position echoed in elite planning groups. True, no death warrants are issued at such gatherings. As the journalist, Will Hutton, put it after participating in the Bilderberg meeting of 1997, 'No policy is made here, it is all talk, some of it banal and platitudinous. *But the consensus established is the backdrop against which policy is made worldwide.*'[147] Now what if—via one of the several senior NATO and defence-related figures present, for instance, at the 1989 Bilderberg meeting—the consensus that the Germans should be restrained had percolated down the security apparatus to the point where some maverick element decided to activate, through provocation or otherwise, a violent fringe group in the belief that a greater evil might thus be averted?

There was certainly no shortage of high-level concern. Within a week of the opening of the Berlin Wall, George Kennan, the architect of containment, spoke out against allowing the two Germanys to unite. The interests of Europe, Kennan argued, should prevail over those of a nation that had plunged the world into two world wars in the twentieth century.[148] This was part of a tidal wave of columns and op-ed pieces openly hostile to a unified Germany, especially in light of the rapprochement with Moscow. As one of these comments put it, the 'German locomotive [is] heading for the East and possibly pulling Western Europe behind it,' and it should be brought a halt sooner rather than later.[149] Mitterrand paid a last-minute state visit to the GDR in December, a vain gesture unable to stem the tide of the country's re-incorporation into the Federal Republic. In March 1990, a meeting of 'experts on Germany' (including Garton Ash) was held at Mrs. Thatcher's Chequers residence (the notes of which were subsequently published in *The Spectator*). Indeed, as TC intellectual Graham Allison, Russian liberal politician Grigory Yavlinski and shock-therapy advocate Jeffrey Sachs conclude in their analysis of Western policy at this stage, there were 'sharp differences' between the 'continentals' led by West Germany and the English-speaking 'islanders' about whether to actively try and shape the future of the USSR jointly with Gorbachev or to just let it slide.[150]

The resulting frictions did not stop the process of German reunification. In May 1990 the GDR ceded, by the treaty introducing the 'market economy' for the new entity, its economic and financial sovereignty to Bonn and the Bundesbank; the five new states officially became part of the Federal Republic in October. Lafontaine, who fought the accompanying election on a ticket of keeping reunification in abeyance, was removed from the race for the chancellorship by an attempt on his life. With the field to himself, Kohl then won over a sceptical electorate by promising 'flourishing landscapes in the East'.[151] However, his appeals to the United States to jointly provide economic assistance to the USSR were consistently rejected 'until economic reforms were "in place".'[152] Secretary of State Baker had told Gorbachev in February that a reunified Germany would have to remain in NATO; the OSCE, which gives the USSR equal rights and in which US influence is much more restricted (also relative to its European allies), would not do.[153] Continuing arms control negotiations had by now assumed the nature of a straightforward capitulation by Moscow. As Raymond Garthoff writes, 'the US administration was unrelenting in pressing its advantage [and] little heed was given to the broader consequences of imposing one-sided compromises on Gorbachev and Shevardnadze.'[154] It was only the need to obtain Soviet consent to a military response to Iraq's invasion of Kuwait in August 1990 that gave Gorbachev a short respite before the final collapse.

Cutting Russia Down to Size

The demise of the USSR was the result of a collapse of confidence within the state class, part of which joined the shift to privatising the economy that was set in motion by forces emerging from the shadow world of criminal gangs and regional bosses. Soviet indebtedness increased from $28.9 billion in 1985 to $54 billion in 1989, and when Moscow adopted G-7 and IMF recommendations for a withdrawal of the state from the economy, it placed the USSR under the discipline of the regulatory infrastructure of Western capital.[155] The indigenous capitalist element surfaced when the suspension of the state monopoly on foreign trade of December 1988 (mentioned earlier in this chapter) opened the floodgates for anybody who could lay hands on low-priced oil and metals stocks and sell them abroad. Privatisation in the USSR was bound to be oligarchic, because there existed no middle class, as there did, for instance, in Hungary and Poland.[156] The careers of the eventual post-Soviet oligarchs—most of them young outsiders able to grab their chance more quickly than the established state class (I will return to them in Chapter 10)—were only made possible, however, because 'a decisive part of the old ruling group tore itself loose from its prior allegiance and turned on the system through which it had ruled.'[157] In other words, the state class abandoned the state-socialist form of the contender effort, switching to a free-for-all in the race for private enrichment.

The dramatic collapse of Soviet society into an ocean of misery and degradation has been extensively documented, even though the process may have bottomed out today. But it is beyond doubt that an extremely unequal society has been created in the process.[158] This should not make us forget that there was a genuine democratic surge, which included the aspect of re-establishing equal relations between the republics making up the USSR. But the Interregional Group of Deputies of the Supreme Soviet (IRG)—established in the summer of 1989, and which included dissident nuclear physicist Andrei Sakharov, Boris Yeltsin and various religious leaders—swung more emphatically towards a neoliberal economic programme after Sakharov's death. This was the point at which, as part of US democracy promotion, the Heritage Foundation and the Free Congress Foundation (FCF) established contact with the IRG to provide it with training and office equipment. A delegation of the IRG, including Yeltsin's chief of staff G. Burbulis, visited Washington under the auspices of the FCF in October 1990, meeting with Vice-President Quayle, several cabinet members and Heritage Foundation luminaries. They carried a letter from Boris Yeltsin, meanwhile elected to the leadership of the Russian Republic (then still part of the USSR), who stressed that he would 'seek to create an economic system based upon universal market mechanisms and the sacred right of every person to property. The entrepreneur will become the chief actor in our economy.'[159]

Once the groups that sought a straight capitalist transition had aligned themselves with centrifugal tendencies emerging at the same time, the centre was put on the defensive. After the breakaway of the Baltic republics and stirrings and actual fighting in the Caucasus (Georgia, Armenia, Azerbaijan), the Russian, Ukrainian and Belarusian Supreme Soviets declared in October 1990 the priority of their laws over those of the USSR, thus undermining the position of Gorbachev at the centre.[160] Gorbachev's attempt to hold the remaining USSR together after the Baltic states had seceded still gained massive support in a referendum in March 1991, with 76 per cent in favour of keeping the downsized Soviet Union intact.[161] But this was not allowed to hold up the process of disintegration, of which Boris Yeltsin had become the undisputed driving force.

The Bush administration now came under pressure from various quarters to forget about Gorbachev and shift support to Yeltsin and other republican leaders. Whereas in the view of one commentator, 'some Western leaders' still banked on the architect of Perestroika, Yeltsin would bring down the Soviet superpower forever and create 'a smaller, looser, more diverse association of free-market economies'.[162] In the spring, Washington turned to Yeltsin as a possible alternative, instructing the CIA and NSA—which had moved into the Soviet Union in force under the new freedoms and had discovered a plot against Gorbachev—to provide Yeltsin with personal and communications security.[163] In June, Bush officially received Yeltsin at the White House. On receiving the available intelligence, the Russian leader could assure his host that he was ready to deal with it—unlike Gorbachev, who had ignored warnings, including one by Bush himself.[164]

When the Yanayev coup came in August 1991, the plotters kept Gorbachev confined in his dacha on the Black Sea. Bush ordered US intelligence intercepts to be given to Yeltsin in Moscow; a US embassy communications specialist was at Yeltsin's side to help him establish contact with military commanders.[165] The coup, a half-hearted and amateurish affair, 'destroyed the very foundation for central authority that the conspirators had so desperately sought to preserve and reinforce.'[166] Yeltsin on the other hand moved quickly and decisively. First, by banning the Communist party, Yeltsin fulfilled the boldest dreams of his supporters at home and abroad. He then moved to place the Soviet institutions under his own authority; in December, after the Ukrainian leadership had declared its unwillingness to join the new Union, Yeltsin moved to bury the Soviet Union altogether and to replace it with the Commonwealth of Independent States (CIS). Gorbachev was forced to resign as president of the USSR, and transferred the control of nuclear weapons to Yeltsin as president of Russia. The image of the lowering of the red hammer and sickle flag on the Kremlin flashed around the world, a dramatic sign of the final demise of the most powerful contender the West had faced so far.

Notes

1. Berend and Ránki (1982: 40–1); Nove (1978: 12–4). On the phased and incomplete movement of peasants from the land into the factories, see von Laue (1967: 74–5). This chapter combines material from van der Pijl (1993a, 1994 and 1997).
2. Lewin (1985: 269); Hough (1990: 48).
3. Claudin (1975: 46–102); Löwy (1981: 56). See also the foreword to Lenin's *Imperialism*, (Lenin, *Collected Works*, Vol. 22: 97–94).
4. Lenin, *Collected Works* (Vol. 29: 153); cf. Bukharin and Preobrazhensky (1969: 257–8).
5. By 1924 this had reached the stage where the idea that the revolution had begun in a periphery was abandoned, and Moscow was redefined as the command centre of the world revolution (Claudin 1975: 113).
6. Lenin, *Collected Works* (Vol. 33: 498).
7. L. Fischer (1960: 236–50); cf. van der Pijl (1984: 69–71).
8. Carrère d'Encausse (1980).
9. Voslensky (1984: 48–50).
10. McAuley (1977: 72); cf. Hirszowicz (1980: 95, Table 3.2), on the class composition of the CPSU in 1917, 1930, 1956 and 1977.
11. Deutscher (1966: 335–6).
12. Medvedev (1976); cf. Rosenstock-Huessy (1961: 483–90).
13. Laird and Laird (1970: 37); Nove (1978: 85–113).
14. Carrère d'Encausse (1979: 25).
15. Elleinstein (1973, Vol. 2: 111). The rise of pathological killers like Beria through the secret police apparatus reminds us that at some point a state confiscating society also develops its own logic and criteria of efficiency, but then, the emergence of a Khrushchev or Gorbachev at the head of the USSR symbolises the capacity to restore the political orientation. On Beria, cf. Stalin's daughter, Svetlana Alliluyeva (1967: 136–8).
16. Lewin (1985: 19–20).
17. Bukharin characterises the danger of the New Leviathan as 'the idea of violence, of coercion as a permanent method of exercising power over society', which, for all its achievements, risks creating 'a dehumanized populace' (quoted in S. Cohen 1974: 362).
18. Harrison (1978: 83) speaks of the Gulag (camp) sector as an economic force in its own right.
19. Lewin (1985: 265).
20. Jánossy (1968: 63–8). Nove (1978: 194–5) sees this ceiling as already having been reached in 1933. Typically, Bukharin (as a former champion of the NEP) 'confessed' that he had been active organising 'Kulak' (well-off farmer) revolts in the north Caucasus and western Siberia as early as 1932 (from the Dutch translation of the Soviet court proceedings, Struik 1938: 126).
21. A.C. Sutton, quoted in Spohn (1975: 246). Sutton's study is well documented, but is part of a conspiracy theory that claims that the USSR is a creation of the East Coast establishment in the US.
22. Carr (1982); Claudin (1975: 24) emphasises that during the war Stalin even went further and disbanded the Comintern entirely without any consultation, to please the allies.
23. Stalin (1972: 31).
24. Burchett (1980: 147).
25. London (1970: 159, 272–6).
26. For an overview of the recent literature on the trials, see L. Richard in *Le Monde Diplomatique*, October 1995, p. 16. As Löwy (1981: 71) notes, the doctrine of 'Socialism in One Country' not only had tactical value in the struggle with the internationalist revolutionaries in the party, but 'owed its inception also to its immediate affinity with the spontaneous nationalistic ideology of the emerging bureaucratic strata.'

27. Holloway (1984: 152–7).
28. Quoted in Kubálkova and Cruickshank (1980: 160).
29. Marcuse (1971: 131, changed to present tense); Konrád and Szelényi (1981) see the alternation between party ideologues and technocratic managers as a general principle underlying state-socialist development.
30. Rakovsky (1978: 44–5, 85–8).
31. Senghaas (1982: 299–300); this was the classical argument of Brus (1975).
32. Senin (1973: 61); Senghaas (1982: 297–8).
33. Tiedtke and Tiedtke (1978: 143).
34. I follow the explanation of the Tiedtkes' (1978) paper on the upgrading of the Warsaw Pact.
35. Marcou (1979: 116).
36. Kosta (1978: 122). Kosta was one of the co-authors of the report *Civilisation at the Crossroads* (1966) (named the Richta Report after its editor), which formulated reform proposals in the name of the 'scientific-technical revolution'; cf. Senghaas (1982: 297).
37. Burchett (1980: 206–7).
38. J. Denis in Helsinki (1975: 22).
39. Helsinki (1975: 60). The Final Act was made up of three main areas, or 'baskets':
    I.   Security in Europe,
    II. Economic, Scientific, Technical and Environmental Cooperation, and
    III. Cooperation in the Humanitarian Domain (a short declaration on Security and Cooperation in the Mediterranean is to be found between II and III).
40. Hough (1986: 99). Brezhnev's statements on the Third World tended to focus on national liberation rather than global reform; cf. *Parteitag XXIV* (1971: 32–3, 35). The enhanced weight of the USSR was certainly reflected in the United Nations when Waldheim invited the Soviet Union for the first time to take part in negotiations on the establishment of a UN peace-keeping force in the wake of the 1973 Arab–Israeli war; throughout this period, the number of Soviet nationals working in the UN Secretariat increased substantially (cf. Shevchenko 1985).
41. Shevchenko (1985: 284); B. Feron in *Le Monde Diplomatique*, May 1975, p. 7; *International Herald Tribune*, 23 September 1976. Oil prices from van der Linde (1991: 102, Table 3.3).
42. Adomeit (1979: 38); the quote is from *Newsweek*, 27 February 1984.
43. Andreff (1983: 280–4); CIA estimates put the Soviet GNP for 1975 at approximately 60 per cent of the US level (Kotz 1997: 37).
44. J. Kolko (1974: 166); *International Herald Tribune*, 9 June 1977. On the growing presence of non-Russian nationalities on the Politburo and Central Committee, see *Time*, 19 April 1971.
45. Elsenhans and Junne (1974: 566); *NRC-Handelsblad*, 16 November 1984. Poland was confronted with a debt of $20 billion (in hard dollars) in 1980, the same as more developed Yugoslavia (Fontaine 1995: 57). On the 'second' cold war, see Halliday (1986).
46. Braunmühl (1973: 87, 87n.).
47. See Fennema (1982: 127, Fig. 6.1, 146, Fig. 6.9); Ziegler et al. (1985: 99, Table 5.1); and Pfeiffer (1993: 239–40, Tables II/IV, 243–5, Tables II/IV).
48. The banking advisers of West German chancellors have been meaningful pointers as to their shared geo-economic orientation. Adenauer was advised by Abs of Deutsche Bank and Erhard by Dresdner's P. Binder. For the Grand Coalition of SPD and CDU, the dual leadership was composed of K. Klasen, an SPD member, and F.H. Ulrich of the CDU. Helmut Schmidt was advised by J. Ponto (of Dresdner, assassinated by the RAF) and Helmut Kohl by Herrhausen (Czichon 1969: 201, 213; cf. Wisnewski et al. 1993).
49. Deubner (1984: 525, 527n.).
50. Braunmühl (1973: 88, 91–2).
51. Figures for 1981 from Deubner (1984: 527n.).

52. Ognev (1984: 447).
53. Sörgel (1985: 1236); *NRC-Handelsblad*, 17 November 1980.
54. Ognev (1985: 35); Richelson and Ball (1990: 262).
55. E.g., an AEG director, quoted in *Frankfurter Allgemeine Zeitung*, 2 May 1978.
56. Levinson (1978: 171, 170).
57. Quoted in Brownstein and Easton (1983: 459).
58. Aganbegjan (1989: 300); Garthoff (1994: 549).
59. *NRC-Handelsblad*, 4 August 1982. In Chapter 6, we saw that bankers of the Deutsche group led by Herrhausen would pay back a few years later by proposing to forgive Latin American debts. The Soviet leadership even felt obliged to reassure Polish leader Jaruzelski that they were not considering intervention under any conditions (Bernstein and Politi 1997: 370; Garthoff 1994: 547n.).
60. Fontaine (1995: 112).
61. In June 1982 Haig had to concede to Soviet foreign minister Gromyko that the sanctions had been imposed without his involvement; he was dismissed by Reagan a week later (Garthoff 1994: 49).
62. Schweizer (1994: 140, 188).
63. Secretary of State George P. Shultz, 'Building Confidence and Security in Europe'. US Department of State press release, 17 January 1984; cf. Garthoff (1994: 561).
64. G.-A. Astre in *Le Monde Diplomatique*, June 1984, p. 16; Garton Ash (1993: 264); Mitterrand and Kohl saw Jaruzelski of Poland as a moderate like Kadár in Hungary (Fontaine 1995: 298–9).
65. *NRC-Handelsblad*, 24 October 1984; the British figure was 15.6 per cent.
66. A. Lipietz in *Le Monde Diplomatique*, March 1984, pp. 1, 6–7
67. van der Wurff (1993); Späth (1985).
68. Deppe (1992: 64–6) argues that Delors sought to salvage corporate liberalism in Europe; Serge Halimi in *Le Monde Diplomatique*, June 2005, pp. 20–1, claims that he instead embraced neoliberalism wholesale. Cf. Ross (1995).
69. Deutsche Bank purchased a share in Morgan Grenfell in London, later taking it over entirely; Dresdner Bank acquired ABD Securities in the US. On Deutsche's strategy, see Mattera (1992: 202). Daimler absorbed AEG in 1982, airplane engine maker MTU and plane manufacturer Dornier in 1985, and MBB in 1990 (L. Carroué in *Le Monde Diplomatique*, November 1990, p. 5). Through its consolidated aerospace subsidiary DASA, Daimler became a partner in EADS, the maker of Airbus. On the rivalry between US and the EU in aerospace production, see Y. Béranger and L. Carroué in *Le Monde Diplomatique*, September 1997, p. 24.
70. BDI (1984: 173–4); Deubner (1984: 532–5).
71. In fiscal 1969, 37 per cent of the US defence budget went into the conduct of the war, to the detriment of weapons development and the modernisation of both the nuclear deterrent and intervention forces. Nixon's Defence Secretary, Melvin Laird, was for this reason strongly committed to a withdrawal from Vietnam (G. Kolko 1985: 313–5, 347–8).
72. Nitzan and Bichler (2002: Chapter 5); N. Birnbaum in *Le Monde Diplomatique*, September 1984, pp. 2–3; Todd (2004: 170). It should be noted here that Zionism originally emerged as a response to anti-Semitism whipped up by imperialist rivalries in Europe, and that it had a powerful left wing which only began its long decline once the state of Israel had been founded.
73. Brownstein and Easton (1983: 500).
74. Kissinger (2000: 985).
75. Ibid.: 1028, cf. 994–5; Colodny and Gettlin (1992: 422).
76. Cf. Landau (1983).
77. Scheer (1982: 54); cf. Wolfe (1979: 25–32).

78. CIA statement in 1983, quoted in Garthoff (1994: 41). Paisley's opponent was the former head of the DIA, General Daniel Graham. The DIA too later conceded that Soviet investment in new weapons in the period 1976–81 did not grow at all (Ferguson and Rogers 1986: 95). Paisley, who challenged the Team B assessments, was found dead in his sailing boat in September 1978, and his memory was clumsily smeared as a supposed Soviet infiltrator; cf. Corson et al. (1989: 93); cf. Richelson and Ball (1990: 257).

79. Wolfe (1979: 40–1).

80. Adler and Haas (1992: 387). A list of the CPD membership in the Reagan government is in Scheer (1982: 145–6).

81. Silk and Silk (1981: 220); on the CFR, see Shoup and Minter (1977).

82. Fontaine (1995: 120, 125); *NRC-Handelsblad*, 25 and 30 August 1986. In a 1983 interview Brzezinski argued that the deployment of INF missiles in Europe was necessary first of all to prevent Western Europe from turning to the East to overcome its current economic malaise (quoted in G.-A. Astre in *Le Monde Diplomatique*, June 1984, p. 16).

83. Scheer (1982: 11).

84. G. Kolko (2002: 46–8). Former CIA director Robert Gates later revealed that the US began to fund Afghan *mujahedeen* guerrillas in mid-1979 (cf. Johnson 2002: xiii). Documents seized in the occupied US embassy in Teheran provide evidence of active US collusion with the Afghan rebels more than six months before the Soviet invasion (Galster 2001: 12, 18–9); cf. *NRC-Handelsblad*, 24 July 1979.

85. Brownstein and Easton (1983: 533) mention 32 members of the CPD; Garthoff (1994: 14) mentions 50. On the oil and arms profits of the Reagan period, cf. Nitzan and Bichler (1995: 467, 462).

86. Quotes from Garthoff (1994: 11, 12), who also mentions a general on the staff of the National Security Adviser being transferred after making unauthorised statements about a 'drift toward war' (ibid: 12n.). On the war-fighting plans, cf. Scheer (1982: 7–9).

87. Pipes, quoted in *Neue Zürcher Zeitung*, 10 November 1982; on the mood in Moscow, see Doder (1986: 44).

88. Schweizer (1994: xiv); Gervasi (1990).

89. Fontaine (1995: 126, map); R.J. Barnet in *Le Monde Diplomatique*, April 1982, pp. 18–9.

90. Quoted in Morris (1999: 460). The CIA had prepared the covert intervention in Poland with Mossad, and also worked through the National Endowment for Democracy and the AFL-CIO (Garthoff 1994: 31). On the role of Mossad, see Schweizer (1994: 34–5). Olof Palme of Sweden was prevailed upon to allow secret shipments for Poland to transit through Swedish ports (Bernstein and Politi 1997: 425).

91. Quoted in Morris (1999: 473); Garthoff (1994: 98).

92. *NRC-Handelsblad*, 19 October 1985.

93. Hal Lindsey's *The Late Great Planet Earth*, with its thesis that Christ's second coming would take the form of a right-wing purge, was the best-selling non-fiction book in the US for an entire decade, with tens of millions of copies sold; cf. Gifford (1988: 22).

94. Landau (1983: 55). On the broader connection between Protestant fundamentalism and Zionism, cf. Nederveen Pieterse (1992: 191–234). In the Protestant fundamentalist imagery, the English-speaking West is the dispersed northern half of biblical Israel and modern Israel is the remaining southern tribe of Judah (Armstrong 1985: 142).

95. Garthoff (1994: 23), who does not mention Bush. Cline was a close friend of Bush from their CIA days, and supported Bush's bid for the Republican candidacy in the 1980 campaign (Callahan 1990: 5). A follow-up conference in Washington in April 1980 also featured Henry Kissinger, Pipes, and a host of key neoconservatives. See Chapter 6, note 157 of this book on Alexander and Cline.

96. There were also reservations brewing on the part of large electronics companies (IBM, HP, etc.) that the indiscriminate confrontation with the Soviet Union (by de-mothballing antiquated battleships, etc.) was not in line with the needs of the advanced sectors in

the US, which were seen to be losing ground to European and Japanese companies. David Packard was appointed to go over defence expenditure with an eye to the role it could play for developing the productive forces to the advantage of US industry, a role military expenditure has traditionally played in a country averse to state intervention. Between 1980 and 1983, Pentagon funding of research and development rose from 62 per cent to 75 per cent of all federal US R&D outlays, and Star Wars took this process further (Junne 1985: 33; Pianta 1987).

97. Junne and van der Pijl (1986: 183–6); Fontaine (1995: 266).

98. Morris (1999: 486).

99. Schweizer (1994: 195–6); Hesse (1984: 11–2); *De Waarheid*, 16 July 1988.

100. Garthoff (1994: 121); Richelson and Ball (1990: 183). On the official US policy of constant probing of Soviet airspace, see Schweizer (1994: 8); on claims about a US spying operation behind the KAL flight's mysterious change of course into Soviet airspace, cf. *International Herald Tribune*, 16 September 1983 and 4 September 1985; *Newsweek*, 2 July 1984; and the book reviews, of studies by R.W. Johnson and Seymour Hersh, by C. Wiebes in *Vrij Nederland*, 19 July and 18 October 1986; cf. Wiebes (1988).

101. On the reaction of Moscow to the Grenada invasion, see Garthoff (1994: 129).

102. Morris (1999: 488). Garthoff (1994: 139) writes that Reagan was actually shocked to learn that the Soviet leadership thought he sought war, but this is perhaps testimony to the extent to which policy was actually developed by his entourage rather than by the president himself.

103. Morris (1999: 498).

104. Risse-Kappen (1994) situates the West German state–society relation in between the Lockean pattern of the United States and the top-down USSR.

105. Gorbachev (1987: 55). Gorbachev had made a special study not only of the NEP experience but also of the Stolypin reforms in Tsarist Russia on the eve of the First World War (another revolution from above) before he took office (Fontaine 1995: 238).

106. See Garthoff (1994: 189) on Chernenko's final attempt to match US defence outlays; and Castells (1998: 30–1) on the military technology gap as the trigger for Perestroika. The loss of confidence is well grasped by Doder (1986).

107. Gorbachev (1986: 22); on the Gorbachev episode more broadly, see Hough (1990).

108. Diligensky (1988: 207–8).

109. *Izvestia*, 11 July 1987. The 'scientific-technical revolution' was the Soviet term for the new technologies developed in the 1970s and 1980s (micro-electronics and new materials—van Tulder and Junne's [1988] 'core technologies').

110. Kotz (1997: 60).

111. This is the thesis of Claude Serfati (2004).

112. Garthoff (1994: 213–4).

113. Quoted in Morris (1999: 544).

114. Regan (1988: 296–7, 298–9).

115. Garthoff (1994: 250); *NRC-Handelsblad*, 3 March 1986.

116. I have corrected the oil price figure in Schweizer (1994: 243)—$30 to $12 per barrel in one year—by reference to van der Linde (1991: 102, Table 3.3); cf. Yergin (1993: 764).

117. Garthoff (1994: 276).

118. Cf. Zimmerman (1981: 100, emphasis added in the quoted part).

119. *NRC-Handelsblad*, 24 June 1986. Other Western participants were Umberto Agnelli of FIAT and Donald Kendall of Pepsi-Cola.

120. Marie Lavigne in *Le Monde Diplomatique*, January 1985, p. 9. The extraterritorial application of US export restrictions harmed research in key NATO allies. France was refused a Cray supercomputer; the Max Planck institute in West Germany could only get one on the condition of enhanced security checks on staff; and research on very high speed integrated circuits was being duplicated in France and Britain because of

American restrictions. ICL of the UK complained in a memorandum about 'growing technological imperialism by the United States' (*Newsweek*, 11 November 1985).

121. Morris (1999: 528, 532); Garthoff (1994: 584); *Newsweek*, 22 June 1987.
122. Garton Ash (1993: 107, 405); Christians had been baptised in Königsberg/Kaliningrad in 1944 (E. Calabuig in *Le Monde Diplomatique*, August 1991, pp. 16–7; *Der Spiegel*, 9/1987).
123. *De Volkskrant*, 18 October 1988.
124. L. Backlund in *Le Monde Diplomatique*, June 1986, p. 13; M. Nyberg, personal communication, 8 January 1988; *NRC-Handelsblad*, 10 August 1984. Perle was sent to European capitals to pressure them to comply with US export restrictions (Schweizer 1994: 49). The overgrown Swedish arms industry is forbidden by law to export arms, but the government can authorise exceptions. In 1983, arms were exported to 41 countries: 45 per cent to the Third World and 36 per cent to NATO countries (Thorsson 1984: 19–21).
125. Aalders (1987: 32); cf. van der Wurff (1993). Bastiaan van Apeldoorn has dubbed this version of corporate liberalism 'embedded neoliberalism'; cf. Chapter 8 of this book.
126. Quoted in L. Backlund in *Le Monde Diplomatique*, June 1986, p. 13.
127. Aalders (1987). Palme too may have been targeted in one of the ramifications of the arms for Iran operation; in early 1987, the director of Sweden's arms export office, C.-F. Algernon, who was the key figure in an investigation of alleged arms smuggling by the Bofors company to the Middle East, was pushed in front of an underground train in Stockholm (*International Management*, April 1987, p. 7). As to the security apparatus, the strong CIA contingent in Sweden operated freely under the protection of the SÄPO intelligence service (Guillou and Wallis 1987: 215, 231). When Hans Holmer, the police commissioner leading the investigation (and a former SÄPO officer) finally began making inquiries, his wife was seriously attacked and threatened (*NRC-Handelsblad*, 10 April, 1986). Palme's nemesis in Swedish politics, Carl Bildt, became leader of the Conservative party in the aftermath of the killing, and then premier on a Thatcherite programme in 1991. This was so out of touch with the country's tradition that it led to a humiliating exit within a few years (Ryner 2002: 154).
128. Morris (1999: 448–9, 451); *NRC-Handelsblad*, 8 January 1986.
129. In May, the State Department intelligence division produced a report listing the options, which included covert action and even regime change (B. Woodward 1987: 263).
130. Ibid.: 315, 319–21. Egypt had been approached to attack Libya but declined; Libyan attempts to get mediation going through Arab and European third parties were rejected by the US. Cf. *NRC-Handelsblad*, 3 April 1986. March 1986 was already a good month for aggressive naval deployment, as two large US warships provocatively entered Soviet territorial waters to within six miles of the Crimean peninsula, gathering intelligence while ignoring signals to withdraw (Garthoff 1994: 269).
131. B. Woodward (1987: 321–3). The suspects of the Berlin disco attack were released without prosecution; GDR spy chief Wolf criticises his own state security for not intervening although they knew that Libyan diplomats had arrived in East Berlin with explosives, and mentions that a Libyan whom the PLO had identified as a US intelligence asset was freely passing through Checkpoint Charlie into West Berlin in a period of heightened international tension (Wolf 1997: 338–9; cf. *De Volkskrant*, 22 December 1988).
132. Morris (1999: 586). Vieille (1988: 224) notes that this attack marks the moment at which the 'system of states on which, in principle, the international order has so far been based ... has become obsolete and no longer bolsters the world capitalist order ... and that the United States has to find other ways of maintaining this system'; cf. *The Wall Street Journal*, 13 January 1986, for the groups favouring an Italian 'crossing of the Alps'. *NRC-Handelsblad*, 16 April 1986.

133. I. Ramonet in *Le Monde Diplomatique*, October 1986, p. 6; B. Woodward (1987: 341–2). There was also talk of Qaddafi's supposed cross-dressing habit, with Reagan at one point proposing to lure the Libyan leader into his wife Nancy's wardrobe. On the Walters trip, see *NRC-Handelsblad*, 2 September 1986. The spokesman of the State Department, B. Kalb, resigned in protest over Reagan's Libya policy (A. Gresh in *Le Monde Diplomatique*, May 1987, p. 21).

134. When Libya bought its 41 per cent share, it had to pay a high price because the bankers making the deal said that this was Libya's entry ticket to Europe; when it sold again, it got a low price because the bankers told the Libyans that its holdings abroad might be seized on political grounds, so they had better act quickly. But Deutsche Bank also saw its role as confirming German independence from America (Galli 1995: 136–8); cf. F. Clairmonte in *Le Monde Diplomatique*, April 1990, p. 15; *NRC-Handelsblad*, 23 April 1986.

135. C. Moffa in *Le Monde Diplomatique*, May 1987, p. 11.

136. Beschloss and Talbott (1993: 25–6); cf. interview with Secretary of State James Baker, quoted in Garthoff (1994: 377).

137. Bernstein and Politi (1997: 522–3).

138. Quoted in Garthoff (1994: 377).

139. Cf. overview in Greiner 1990.

140. This would become the European Bank for Reconstruction and Development (EBRD), another source of controversy, as we will see in Chapter 8 (*Le Monde*, 12 April 1989).

141. In his 1993 book *In Europe's Name*, he gives a scathing account of *Ostpolitik*, mocking the language of peace used by its proponents (Garton Ash 1993).

142. Garton Ash (1989: 5).

143. Cf. Todd (2004).

144. *Blätter für deutsche und internationale Politik*, January 1990, pp. 119–21.

145. Quoted in Garthoff (1994: 382–3).

146. Herrhausen's armoured Mercedes was blown up in the open street, killing the banker but not his driver, a high-tech assassination supposedly the work of the extreme-left *Rote Armee Fraktion* (Landgraeber et al. 1992; Wisnewski et al. 1993; *Het Parool*, 10 April 1993). In the next year and a half, Oskar Lafontaine's candidacy for the chancellorship fell through after an attempt on his life that knocked him off the political stage for several years and, as we will see in the next chapter, made him vulnerable to subsequent attacks when he had recovered; the head of the privatisation trust for East Germany, Rohwedder, was assassinated (cf. also Chapter 8); and CDU moderniser Lothar Späth was removed by a scandal.

147. W. Hutton in *The Observer*, 1 February 1998, emphasis added.

148. George Kennan in *International Herald Tribune*, 14/15 November 1989.

149. Quoted in Greiner (1990).

150. Allison and Yavlinski (1991: x); Garthoff (1994: 433).

151. C. Mohr in *Le Monde Diplomatique*, June 1991, p. 15.

152. D. Batistella in *Le Monde Diplomatique*, June 1990, p. 9; Garthoff (1994: 415).

153. Garthoff (1994: 413).

154. Ibid.: 423n. This position may be linked to the *Discriminate Deterrence* report written by a group composed of Kissinger, Iklé, Brzezinski, Wohlstetter and General Goodpaster. It warned that arms reduction negotiations could acquire a momentum of their own from which it would be difficult to disentangle again (*De Volkskrant*, 3 February 1988). On the other hand Bush declined to actually support the disintegration of the USSR along national lines, in spite of calls for sanctions to enforce Lithuanian independence. Kohl and Mitterrand were even encouraged by Washington to write to the Lithuanian nationalists to suspend the unilateral declaration of independence of March 1990 (ibid.: 425n.)

155. Kotz (1997: 75, Table 5.1). 'The ultimate explanation for the surprisingly sudden and peaceful demise of the Soviet system was that it was abandoned by most of its own elite, whose material and ideological ties to any form of socialism had grown weaker and weaker' (ibid.: 6). Cf. J.-M. Chauvier in *Le Monde Diplomatique*, June 2005, pp. 18–9.
156. Gowan (1999a: 260–6); Brucan (1998: 63, Table 4); Garthoff (1994: 422).
157. Kotz (1997: 153, cf. 94). On the Jewish background of most of the oligarchs and the resulting rise of anti-semitism in Russia as a political force, see Chua (2003: 138–42). Castell's question: 'How could such a veteran, shrewd party ... lose political control', is the obvious wrong question in this perspective—it did not lose political control; there were two different strands seeking to transform themselves and their society (Castells 1998: 7).
158. S. Cohen (1998). For details on mortality rates and other instances of the collapse of Soviet society, see Todd (2004: 210).
159. Quoted in Bellant and Wolf (1990: 31), see also for an overview of FCF training programmes in other East European countries; background of democracy promotion in Robinson (1996)
160. Garthoff (1994: 439); Chiesa (1993: 27).
161. Garthoff (1994: 455–6).
162. F. Coleman in *Newsweek*, 24 June 1991; Garthoff (1994: 464).
163. Hersh (1994: 84–5). Deputy National Security Adviser (until briefly before, Deputy Director of the CIA) Robert Gates was in charge of top-secret contingency planning from the fall of 1989 to early 1991 to study the options in case of a coup against Gorbachev. From 1987, Moscow had become concerned about the inflow of people associated with US intelligence; in January 1989, the KGB and MVD were instructed to prevent Soviet citizens from using foreign undercover contacts for their own ends (Garthoff 1994: 317, 388n., 396n.). From the spring of 1991, the CIA began to provide the president with daily top secret reports on the internal situation in the Soviet Union (ibid.: 448n.)
164. Ibid.: 487; Bellant and Wolf (1990). In July, in a meeting with Yeltsin and Nazerbayev of Kazakhstan, Gorbachev indicated that after the signing of the Union treaty he would dismiss the party conservatives whom he had recently taken on board; but this session was bugged by the KGB, thus alerting the plotters (Garthoff 1994: 473n.; Bellant and Wolf 1990; Hersh 1994: 84–6).
165. Hersh (1994: 85–6). On the role of the 'civil society' networks supported by the Soros foundation in rallying support for Yeltsin, see Pavlovski (1992: 17).
166. Garthoff (1994: 478).

8 America over Europe in the Balkans Crisis

SOCIAL FORCES IN THE CLINTON GLOBALISATION OFFENSIVE

Under Reagan and Thatcher, the United States and Britain led the way in restoring the discipline of capital and the liberal birthright of the heartland. But since neoliberalism develops as a *transnational* strategy, evacuating the confines of state-contained corporate liberalism, it cannot for long be confined to one segment of the global political economy.

Western Europe was the obvious next station for the neoliberal counter-revolution. European capital had on its own already assumed a more activist posture after the collapse of the USSR and the opening of Eastern Europe. Washington was unwilling, however, to allow a return to capitalism in the former Soviet bloc solely under European auspices, or to permit the transition to consolidate corporate liberal capitalism across the wider space now available. The 1990s therefore witnessed a massive forward drive of Anglo-American capital, covered in Europe by NATO. This time, though, US involvement did not hinge on productive investment as in the 1960s. Instead it revolved around investment banking and management consultancy, which make their money from privatisation and flexibilisation. The scions of European capital, organised in the European Round Table of Industrialists (ERT), in the circumstances developed the ambition to meet the American challenge on its own ground. Exploiting the absence of democracy at the level of the

EU, they were able to win over the European governments and the Commission for a comprehensive neoliberal strategy. Whereas the 1960s 'American challenge' was about developing transnational corporations, matching the Anglo-American advantage was now seen in terms of neoliberal 'reform'—privatisation and asset-stripping, predatory enrichment, and intensified exploitation of the population.

In this section, let me briefly review the different forms of economic restructuring that accompany neoliberalism and then look at the gap created between Britain and the US on the one hand and continental Europe on the other. I begin with the large corporation in the United States. It sounds paradoxical that the corporation, which we tend to equate with capital, can itself be placed under a new discipline. Yet this is what happens in the neoliberal context. 'Big capital' in the corporate liberal era had done well in terms of real output: as a share of GNP, the turnover of the Fortune 500 companies in the US reached the 60 per cent level in 1980. They had been losing ground, however, in terms of their relative profit rates.[1] As the large corporations in the post-war period developed into 'fortresses of collective bargaining power', active stakeholders were able to defend their income claims in the inflationary 1970s; the inactive holders of property and profit titles on the other hand were very much crowded out as the real economy stagnated.

To reverse this situation, a new breed of capitalists, fund managers and 'raiders' began a counter-attack in the 1980s. Claiming to represent the interests of the inactive owners of capital, these operators—leading what became known as the 'revolt of the rentier', or 'revolt of the capital market'—targeted the cumulative structures of compromise and social protection that had developed in the large corporation in the Fordist era.[2] Why pay high wages in the US if there are millions of Mexicans willing to work for one-tenth of that wage or less? In the view of Ross Perot, the maverick computer services tycoon who bought himself a board seat on General Motors, there were 'tens of thousands, maybe hundreds of thousands of people at GM who are quite insulated from the harsh realities of the competitive marketplace'; something which he felt could be remedied by breaking up the unity of the corporation as a social structure.[3] This became the high road to squeezing more income out of the real economy. Corporations were transformed into money-making machines for owners and shareholders, and began to be traded wholesale. 'Junk bond' capitalists started purchasing corporations though new techniques such as leveraged buy-outs. They then asset-stripped them, made parts of the workforce redundant, and sold off the surviving parts again at a profit. Michael Milken became the iconic figure among a cohort of swash-buckling operators such as Carl Icahn, I. Boesky, and T. Boone Pickens, before he landed in jail for having ruined a number of savings banks and pension funds.[4] Soon, specialised firms such as Kohlberg, Kravis & Roberts (KKR), took over from the first generation of privateers. In the late 1980s, KKR, with 50 employees, had 19 companies in its portfolio, and more combined assets than the fifth-largest US corporation at the time, General Electric.[5]

At this stage, the effects of global market liberalisation and corporate downsizing began to fuel a stock market boom. Total stock market assets in the US reached $16.6 trillion in 1999, almost twice the size of US GDP ($9.3 trillion; in 1990 it had still been the other way round, with stocks worth $3.1 trillion and GDP $5.8 trillion).[6] The overall direction of the neoliberal 'reform' drive was by now back in the hands of the historic operators of global capital markets, the investment banking communities of Wall Street and the City of London—albeit with some new names added (and most merchant banks of the City sold to foreign owners). Investment banks such as Goldman Sachs, J.P. Morgan, and others became spearheads of the globalisation drive, organising mergers and acquisitions and tracking down new sources of wealth for their clients all over the world.[7] These firms impose, in the sense of Polanyi's *haute finance* (referred to in Chapter 1), the discipline of capital, irrespective of 'nationality'. When the British economy was in free fall in the late 1990s, investment banks operating from the City of London accounted for the handling of 40–50 per cent of mergers and acquisitions, and 30 per cent of the worldwide currency trade.[8] Assisting them in the process was a new cadre active in accountancy houses like Arthur Andersen, Price Waterhouse Cooper, etc., and other 'coordination services' companies—law, insurance, management consultancy, and debt-rating firms.[9]

The public sector too became the target of this bloc of forces. The asset-stripping of state property through privatisation enlarges the field of operation for capital, while bringing huge fees to the investment banks, who act as advisers and arrange the stock market flotation of public property. Under the doctrine of 'New Public Management', utilities like energy, public transport, and the mail and telecom infrastructure; the medical sector, pensions, health and other social insurance; as well as policing, prisons and even military operations abroad, have all been put at arm's length from government and turned into sources of private profit. The English-speaking countries including, notably, New Zealand and Australia have led the way here.[10]

Today we are in a position to assess the outcome of this 'reverse Great Transformation'. In the United States, the wealthiest 1 per cent in the first wave of neoliberal transformation (1977–89) saw their income share increase from 8.7 to 13 per cent of all incomes, with half of the increase (of a total of $200 billion in 1989 dollars) accounted for by interest, dividends and capital gains.[11] From 1980 to 1994, the year the Clinton offensive was unleashed, the richest 5 per cent in the US saw their income share increase by 59 per cent; the richest 20 per cent by 33 per cent; all others by less than that; and so on down to the poorest 20 per cent, who gained nothing.[12] In Britain, from 1983 to 1986, the high tide of Thatcherism, the number of millionaires increased from 7,000 to 20,000, and so on and so forth.[13] The revolution of the rich against the poor has continued ever since, in the process assuming a global sweep. Over the decade 1985–95, the wealthiest fraction of the American capitalist class (defined as those owning more than half a million dollars in liquid financial assets) grew by 6 per cent annually to a total wealth of $16.7 trillion. The same category in Asia increased at a rate of 9 per cent per year; Europe even overtook North America by a small margin. In 1999, the total wealth of those owning a million or more in Europe was $25.5 trillion. According to the World Wealth Report, there were 2.5 and 2.2 million millionaires in North America and Europe, respectively, in that year; 1.7 million in Asia; and 200,000 each in South America, the Middle East and the 'Eastern bloc'. There were 276 *billionaires* in North America, 115 in Europe, 77 in Asia, 32 in South America and 14 in the Middle East.[14]

In Table 8.1, the fortunes of the top bracket of billionaires in the US and Western Europe in 2003 are compared with their fortunes in 2000 (if they were already listed in the top bracket at that time), to illustrate that the upper layer of the wealthiest have continued to improve their position— never mind the stock market crash.[15] Although this is 'raw' wealth, not yet transformed into enduring class power (e.g., by setting up charitable foundations and sponsoring universities, think-tanks and planning groups, as the Rockefellers have done, for instance),[16] the fact that these fortunes are continuing to be made at this pace is an indication of how neoliberalism works out socially.

It must be noted that income disparities under neoliberalism are not a zero-sum game within separate countries. Neoliberalism develops in a tendentially global context and it is at this level that the super-incomes are generated. Thus US corporate profits from foreign direct investment rose steadily towards almost 50 per cent of domestic profits in 2002; in 1980, following the 1979 interest rate hike, other income from the rest of the world (mainly from portfolio investments and interest income) rose to near 100 per cent of domestic profits and remained there. This contributed, we may assume, to the rise of the share of the top 20 per cent in the world income distribution from three-quarters of total income in 1980 to 83.4 per cent in 1990, while the remaining four quintiles all lost in terms of income share.[17] At the bottom end, the number of people living on less than $1 per day increased to from 1.18 billion in 1987 to 1.19 billion in 1998, although in China almost 100 million climbed out of that category in the same period.[18] There is no doubt, however, that the populations in the heartland too have paid dearly for the enrichment of their ruling classes and for the readiness of their politicians, academics, journalists and even trade union

Table 8.1
Wealthiest Americans and Western Europeans, 2003, in US$ Billion (compared to 2000)

United States			Western Europe		
B. Gates	Microsoft	46 (37.5)			
W. Buffett	Berkshire Hathaway	36 (17.3)			
P. Allen	Microsoft	22 (17)	K. & T. Albrecht	Aldi (Germany)	25.6 (13.3)
A.L. Walton	Wal-Mart	20.5 (45.3)*			
H. Walton	Wal-Mart	20.5			
J.C. Walton	Wal-Mart	20.5			
J.T. Walton	Wal-Mart	20.5			
L.J. Ellison	Oracle	18 (29)	L. Bettencourt	L'Oréal (France)	14.5 (10.1)
M. Dell	Dell	13 (7.8)	I. Kamprad	Ikea (Sweden)	13
S. Ballmer	Microsoft	12.2 (10.5)			
A. & B. Cox	Cox newspapers	11 (13.3)*	B. Rausing (family)	Tetrapak (Sweden)	12.9
A. Cox Chambers	Cox newspapers	11			
J.W. Kluge	Metromedia	10.5 (8.6)			
F.F. Mars Jr.	Mars	10.4 (14)*	A. Ortega	Inditex (Spain)	10.3
F. Mars	Mars	10.4	S. Berlusconi	Fininvest (Italy)	10 (8.5)
J.F. Mars	Mars	10.4	H. Rausing	Tetrapak (Sweden)	7.7
A. Johnson	Magellan Fund	9.8 (7.4)	G. Cavendish		
S.M. Redstone	Viacom	9.7 (6.6)	Grosvenor	*Real estate* (Britain)	7.5
C.W. Ergen	EchoStar (media)	8.9	B. Arnault	LVMH (France)	6.7 (8.4)
D.E. Newhouse	*Newspapers*	7.7 (6.6)	S. Persson	H&M (Sweden)	6.7 (5.1)

Source: Compiled from data at Forbes' website (www.forbes.com/2003/02/26/billion aireland.html). Data for the year 2003 has been taken to allow comparison with rankings in other chapters (figures for 2000 are given in brackets; no figures for 2000 are given in cases which were not already listed in 2000). 2003 data for Berlusconi added from *FT Magazine*, 13 November 2004.

Note: *Fortune meanwhile divided through inheritance.

leaders to embrace the neoliberal gospel as the truth. For workers, management techniques and ideologies such as quality circles and benchmarking were developed to intensify work, while accumulation strategies directed at leisure and recovery time have extended the discipline of capital deep into daily life.[19]

The Clinton administration played a crucial role in the process of closing off the escape hatch into social security for those succumbing to these pressures or losing the jobs they were trained for. In 1996 the duty to accept work became the central principle of the social security system, although the mayors of several large American cities warned that it only needed a recession to turn this into a nightmare scenario. This is indeed what happened. Child poverty rose again from 16 per cent in 2000 to 17.6 per cent in 2003, after an initial decline. The same has happened with adults, but then the definition of poverty in the United States underestimates the amount of people below the poverty line by half. By the European definition (poverty is defined as less than 60 per cent of the median income) the 2000 figure for total poverty would be 23.8 per cent (against the official 11.3 per cent). In addition to the 35 million living below the poverty line today, 6.8 million workers who are employed for more than 26 weeks per year constitute the additional category of the 'working poor'.[20] In Britain, the Thatcher shock therapy raised the number of people living below the poverty line from 6 million in 1979 to 11.7 million in 1986. The Blair government sought to deal with the heritage of Conservative rule by a package inspired by the Clinton policy, albeit not as harshly applied. The result is that between 2000 and 2002, the percentage of people living below the poverty line has improved slightly from 21 to 17; one-third of them are single parents, though, blighting the lives of a large swathe of contemporary youth.[21] This then is the broad profile of the alternative to European corporate liberalism that was 'on offer' in the aftermath of the Soviet collapse, and the rich on the European continent were of course willing to try it out.

Europe's 'Rhineland' Legacy in the Balance

Clinton's election coincided with the spring tide of neoliberal globalisation. His initial sponsors were firms headquartered in the state of Arkansas where he was governor; foremost were the retailers, Wal-Mart, of which company his wife Hilary was a director.[22] The New York financial community then invited the candidate, for what the *New York Times* later called a 'job interview', on Wall Street in June 1991. On that occasion, Robert Rubin, Roger Altman and other prominent investment bankers explained to him the need for free trade and capital movements, premised on a reduction of US federal debt and a balanced budget. For all we know, Clinton may already have been well-groomed in these ideas as a member of the Trilateral Commission.[23] Rubin (who had been in the Goldman Sachs investment bank since 1966) became Clinton's treasury secretary; Richard Holbrooke (Lehman Bros., Crédit Suisse-First Boston) was a key player in the Yugoslav drama as assistant secretary of state;[24] while J.P. Morgan's Alan Greenspan remained at the helm of the Federal Reserve. These men became the main advocates of the administration's neoliberal activism abroad. The telecom and computer industries and other industries with an interest in a more active state role in education also supported the Clinton campaign. But this aspect of his mandate soon became mired in controversy and had to be abandoned.[25]

The end of the cold war exposed the rift that had been opening up between the neoliberalism of the English-speaking heartland and the corporate liberalism persisting on the European continent. In his 1991 study, *Capitalism against Capitalism*, French state planner and insurance director Michel Albert famously labelled these patterns 'neo-American' and 'Rhineland' respectively. Now that the common enemy had been defeated, Albert argued, the competitive struggles between these two forms of capitalism was descending into 'an underground war, violent and merciless, but also surreptitious and even hypocritical, like every tribal war within the same creed.'[26] Was he using this only as a metaphor, or do we have to think here, perhaps, of the assassinations of Palme and Herrhausen as well? There was certainly concern at this point that the intelligence apparatuses of the Western states were being employed against each other. The chairman of the Intelligence Committee of the US Senate, David Boren, declared in a press talk in 1990 that 'as the arms race is winding down, the spy race is heating up.' Espionage activity 'against private commercial targets in the United States' was on the increase, 'carried out not by foreign companies, but by foreign governments'.[27] This was confirmed by French intelligence director Pierre Marion, who set up a special branch 'to gather secret technologies and marketing plans of private companies'—both of US companies and others.[28]

Albert, however, clearly refers to *systemic* rivalries. The eclipse of the Rhineland capitalisms of Europe (and their equivalents in Japan and South Korea), which he saw on the horizon, reminds us that capital does not impose its discipline once and for all, but works in a constant process of adjustment and restructuring. If there is a resistance to neoliberalism in Europe (or Japan), this is not because of some innate cultural quality or fixed 'civilisation', but because their contender state structures have engendered different practices and mentalities, less amenable to a full-fledged commodification of social relations. Yet the individualism on which neoliberalism is grafted also made itself felt outside the English-speaking West. The new subjectivity that accompanies it more willingly embraces the ideas of choice and risk propagated by neoliberalism. But because the social landscape remains relatively inhospitable to the radical privatisation and individualisation prescribed by the neoliberal concept, this will tend to develop as a hybrid form which appreciates a greater degree of 'contingency' but retains the elementary notion that the economy is meant to serve and improve society as a collective entity, not the other way around.[29] If we look at the situation on the eve of the Clinton offensive, the structural factors in which this attitude was anchored were as follow:

First, the 'finance capital' pattern of bank-networked industrial groups. This is typical of corporate liberal capitalism, and a legacy of the contender experience; it was a hallmark of capitalism in Germany (e.g., the Deutsche and Dresdner groups discussed in Chapter 7), France and Italy.[30] At the time of this writing, the sweep of neoliberalism is triggering a land-slide in these countries; but finance capital structures were still basically in place at the beginning of the 1990s. In the English-speaking heartland of neo-liberalism, on the other hand, finance capital did not develop as strongly to begin with, either because of the historically separated circuits of money and productive capital in Britain, or because liberalisation and deregulation undermined them where they did exist, as in the US. Indeed American commercial banks joined the hunt for short-term profits in privatisation and takeover activities, as they lost their role in finance capital structures in the 1980s.[31]

Second, in terms of industrial structure, German (like Japanese) capital was still strong in sectors belonging to the original corporate liberal configuration grafted on Fordism (automobiles, engineering and chemicals). In the 1980s, US (and UK) capital on the other hand began to shift to new activities in the information and bio/genetics (biotechnology and pharmaceutical applications) industries, and accelerated its internationalisation. The commodification and privatisation of plant-genetic sequences allowed US and British agro-industrial corporations to extend the discipline of capital over the entire food chain.[32] More generally, US transnational corporations are the key players in the socialisation of labour on a world scale. In 1990, the value of US imports from peripheral economies (the former Third World) compared to domestic value added stood at 1:8; in 2002 this tripled to 1:3.[33] The diminishing relative size of the industrial base (the US manufacturing share of GDP fell from 20 per cent in 1987 to 14.1 per cent in 2001) is therefore not a problem as long as the global productive economy remains centred on the US. New information technologies, to organise vast supply and sub-contracting networks, have made it possible to leave behind the format of the bureaucratic and omnivorous corporate empire building.[34] By the mid-1990s, world trade shares in the Fordist sectors were 21 per cent for Germany and 12 per cent for the US; but in the new industries they were 14 per cent for Germany and 28 per cent for the US. In the distribution of profit between the US, Europe and Japan in the period 1989–94, the same trend can be noticed. In automobiles, for instance, only 23.6 per cent of all profits accrued to US firms against European capital's 46.6 per cent, and Japan's 31 per cent. But the US profit share was almost two-thirds of the total in electronic components and instruments and in data processing and reproduction, the remainder being shared between Europe and Japan.[35]

Third (and finally), there is the aspect of trade union organisation. On the European continent, trade union organisation ultimately weathered the storms of the new cold war and the collapse of state socialism. Raiders like

Perot and Icahn in the US and Murdoch in Britain, on the other hand, were able to inflict historic defeats on labour, robbing it of the structures which alone can prevent the atomisation of the working class.[36]

The UK position within the European Communities was always problematic, given its liberal antecedents as the pivot of the original heartland. On the other hand, the concentric contender tradition had made continental Europeans wary of the neoliberal concept. As Bastiaan van Apeldoorn has argued, in the 1980s national industrial champions on the continent perceived the forces of globalisation more as a threat than as an opportunity. The Single European Act of 1986 sought to restore European competitiveness by an active industrial policy rather than by straight liberalisation, a strategy articulated by the European Round Table, established three years earlier and referred to already.[37] British corporations were not very receptive to this assertive European posture, with its echoes of the contender role. The largest among the British corporations commanded enough capital to compete at the global level directly, whereas the typical large continental company was a big employer but often not in a position to choose where and when it wanted to compete worldwide. But capital on the continent is itself also fractured relative to the neoliberal, globalising model. In Table 8.2, the biggest European corporations have been listed by assets and by employees, resulting in three categories: 'Global' (straight world market competitors), 'Euro-Contender' (internationally assertive from a secure European base), and defensive 'Fortress Europe'.

Table 8.2
Three Orientations in European Capital (1992) and ERT Founding Members

Global Capital	Euro-Contender Capital		Fortress Europe
First 8 (Assets)	Second 7 (Assets)	First 8 (Employment)	Second 7 (Employment)
Royal Dutch Shell*	Daimler-Benz		ABB Asea*
British Telecom	Siemens*		Alcatel Alstom
Glaxo	Hanson	FIAT*	Gén. des Eaux
BP	Deutsche B.	Unilever*	Hoechst
Allianz	Elf Aquitaine	Philips*	Bayer
British Gas	Guinness	Volkswagen	Peugeot
Nestlé*	BAT Industries		

Source: Adapted from Holman and van der Pijl (1996: 68, Table 3.4) for top 15 European firms by assets and by employment; van Apeldoorn (2002: 86, Table 3.1) for original membership of European Round Table, 1983.

In case of double rankings, firms are placed according to highest ranking position in one category.

*ERT founding members.

The lack of overlap between the assets and employment rankings of course highlights structural differences between financial and oil companies on the one hand and labour-intensive productive capital on the other. But within industry, there was also a rift opening up between soaring stock market quotations of innovative science-based companies like Glaxo (or branded foods conglomerates like Nestlé), and the Fordist mass production industries with their vast capital outlays liable to depreciation. Against this background, British firms clearly dominate the 'Global' fraction.[38] German firms, on the other hand, were concentrated in the central column ('Euro-Contender'), with some also in 'Fortress Europe' along with its stronger French component. This broadly fits the different degrees to which neoliberalism had taken hold across the different EC countries around 1990. Obviously, Thatcher's Britain was at the forefront; at the other extreme, France, Italy and Belgium were entrenched in corporate liberalism. The Euro-Contender position was dominated by German capital. It built on the strongest industries oriented to new technologies like just-in-time production to cater to a more demanding, 'individualised' consumer; but it also sought to retain the groundwork of class compromise. In Chapter 7, I mentioned how Lafontaine in the SPD and Späth in the CDU, Palme in Sweden (in a dialogue with ERT initiator Gyllenhammar) and Delors at the head of the European Commission were all exploring a new synthesis, or 'hybrid', between the Atlantic neoliberalism then ascendant and aspects of corporate liberalism.

One aspect of the Euro-Contender and Fortress Europe positions concerned the idea of a common European defence. Meant in part to create a control structure for Germany and rein in any new ambitions, this also brought to the surface older interests of trying to wrest Europe free from American tutelage—also with an eye to technological development spun off from weapons research. In mid-1991, France even reactivated the idea of an independent European military force as an alternative to NATO. However, the plan for a Franco-German 'Eurocorps' met with 'immediate and unambiguous opposition' from the US.[39] A common foreign and defence policy was part of the agreement reached at the Maastricht summit of the renamed EU in December 1991 (this was worked out in some detail in the treaty of Amsterdam in 1997), but the main thrust was towards neoliberalism. The Economic and Monetary Union, with its provisions for combating inflation and controlling deficits, promised to impose a permanent structural adjustment on member states, prejudicing the interests of economies organised around industrial capital and employment (cf. the central and right-hand columns in Table 8.2). Paradoxically, Britain remained outside the EMU. It stuck to its rejection of a harmonisation of taxes on capital, while obtaining an exemption on working hours and trade union rights. This enabled it to make the most of its EU membership and yet maintain world market positions without having to bother about European social legislation.[40] Germany, on the other hand, appeared willing to give up its powerful deutschmark in exchange for the European free market. The establishment of a European Central Bank, setting interest rates and managing (under the tight budget and inflation conditions of the EMU stability pact) a new common currency (the Euro) can even be read as a concession to France and the other member states. By Europeanising a key aspect of economic policy, they obtained a degree of control over the strong currency countries (Germany and the Netherlands). But since the ECB would be 'independent', i.e., free from political and, hence, parliamentary control, its mandate, the stability pact, laid down the neoliberal line 'constitutionally'.[41]

The Maastricht treaty represents a major step towards organising the EU along the lines of the Lockean heartland: a free space for capital, with separate state jurisdictions keeping political sovereignty and democracy away from the larger structure. Indeed only a thin line now separated the new concept from full-fledged neoliberalism, Anglo-Saxon style. This has alternatively been called 'compensatory neoliberalism' or 'embedded neoliberalism', to denote the remaining elements of class compromise and social protection—but these are left for the member states to maintain, *after* the deflationary conditions of the EMU have been met.[42] The real difference, I would argue, was that this neoliberal project was not the result of a prior collapse of the corporate liberal configuration and a Thatcher-like transformation, but a flight forward in the hope that the 'market' would help overcome the imbalances between states and classes. However, the narrow margin by which French voters ratified the treaty was a sign of the limits of consent in this respect (Denmark was even asked to vote again to correct an initial rejection). Given the absence of a popular mandate for the EMU and its socially destructive guidelines, author and Green politician Alain Lipietz ominously warned that it might explode in civil war within a few decades.[43]

RIVAL RESPONSES TO THE CRISIS IN YUGOSLAVIA

In the short run, the momentous changes that occurred at the heart of the European continent reverberated most explosively on its periphery. In this section, I will argue that in the break-up of Yugoslavia the main moments of the neoliberal counter-revolution come together in a vicious spiral: the interest rate hike of 1979, the collapse of the non-aligned and Soviet blocs, and the dismantling of the contender state and its structures of social protection.

Initially, the makeover of state socialism to capitalism was left to the EU,[44] although in late 1991 NATO put in place the North Atlantic Cooperation Council (NACC), a tentative crisis management and rapid intervention structure including the former Warsaw Pact countries. The Bush I administration resisted giving the Helsinki organisation, the OSCE, a larger role, but equally dismissed the aspirations of Hungary, Czechoslovakia and Poland to join NATO.[45] West Germany, for obvious geopolitical and economic reasons, was best placed to capitalise on the opportunities arising from the transformation of the Soviet bloc. German ambitions with respect to Central Europe and the Balkans had a longer tradition in the *Mitteleuropa* policy. Given the role of this policy in unleashing two world wars, its revival in the 1980s was bound to create concerns among its neighbours east and west. The EU set up an aid programme for Poland and Hungary (PHARE), later extended to other countries, but reunified Germany accounted for the lion's share in the actual flow of funds into the Central and East European economies, with Austria in second place.[46] The newly opened economic area offered opportunities for European capital to try and match US patterns of internationalisation in countries like Mexico by runaway investment and subcontracting activities. This included 'outward processing traffic' (OPT, the exports of semi-finished products for finishing, and re-imports of finished products) to Central Europe, in addition to imports of raw materials and semi-finished goods from countries like Bulgaria. OPT accounted for 26 per cent of Hungarian and Czech exports to the EU in 1997; in textile and clothing, the percentages are even higher. Germany was the pivot of both types of trade.[47]

The three Central European states (Czechoslovakia, Poland and Hungary) early on established a collaboration named after Visegrad castle near Budapest. Their association with the EU in December 1991 signalled the aspiration to 'return to Europe'—underpinned by a 55–65 per cent trade dependence on the EU, again with Germany as the key partner, but with Italy and Austria in important positions as well.[48] The uneven integration into an expanding *Mitteleuropa* increased centrifugal pressures within countries with important regional disparities. Czechoslovakia's break-up still was mitigated, however, by the immediate vicinity of Germany and, importantly, elite agreement. Slovakia was the weaker partner with less foreign trade and only a fraction of inward investment (with just 13 per cent of the FDI of Bohemia-Moravia, the Czech half). In mid-1992 its unemployment level was three times that of Bohemia-Moravia (12 per cent against 4.3 per cent). But Vaclav Klaus, the Czech prime minister (and a member of the neoliberal Mont Pèlerin Society), and the populist Slovak leader Meciar agreed on a split in 1993. While there would not have been a popular mandate for the split, neither was it actively resisted.[49]

Concern over the neoliberal orientation of the Maastricht treaty (notably among Social Democrats in the large industrial countries such as France and Germany) also became an issue in the transition process of Eastern Europe. There was widespread criticism in Europe of the shock-therapy applied to Poland, and in light of the collapsing economies and obvious signs of criminal enrichment, little enthusiasm existed for a wholesale application of neoliberal privatisation to the wider European space. These reservations were an echo of the earlier disagreements on how to deal with Gorbachev, and in a few cases they led to the same tragic outcomes. Detlev Rohwedder, a SPD politician and steel manager turned head of the privatisation institution for East Germany, Treuhand, caused controversy by refusing to allow Anglo-American investment banks to play a role in the sale of socialist state property. In April 1991 he was assassinated by a sharpshooter, supposedly from the Rote Armee Fraktion. His successor at Treuhand duly let the Atlantic investment banks enter the process, apparently with no objections on the part of the 'extreme Left.'[50] By comparison, Mitterrand intimate Jacques Attali, the head of the European Bank for Reconstruction and Development (EBRD)—set up for the purpose of privatising the Soviet bloc economies— came off lightly thanks to his taste for expensive office furnishings and executive travel. Attali too wanted to prevent a premature exposure of the former Soviet bloc countries to untrammelled neoliberalism, and he expressly sought to keep funds from ending up in mafia hands.[51] But for neoliberals, 'bandit capitalism' is a necessary phase in the transition. In 1993 the US suspended its contributions to the EBRD until Attali was removed from his post later that year, following a sustained smear campaign in the *Financial Times* and other publications. Under IMF veteran Jacques de Larosière, the EBRD promptly switched to financing the private sector.[52] By now the United States was moving towards active involvement in the geopolitical reordering of the European continent as well, and Yugoslavia became its prime target.

The Bankruptcy of the Federation and the Role of Germany

Yugoslavia was constructed in 1945 on the principle that a strong federal state had to be based on a weak Serbia, which had dominated the pre-war monarchy. The new communist leadership, emerging from the liberation struggle against the Nazi occupiers, therefore agreed to make Serbia's territory smaller (21 per cent of the area) than the actual area inhabited by Serbs (36 per cent of the population). This was achieved in part by granting the Serbian provinces of Vojvodina in the north and Kosovo in the south far-reaching autonomy on account of, respectively, the Hungarian and Albanian population shares. This autonomy was reinforced in 1974. These concessions were in the spirit of socialist nationality policy, which anyway aimed at overcoming these distinctions.[53] But the divide had deep roots. Slovenia and Croatia had been part of the Austro-Hungarian empire, used the Latin alphabet, and were Roman Catholic. Resentful about Serbian dominance in the inter-war years, Croatian fascists welcomed the Nazis in the Second World War, killing hundreds of thousands of Serbs in extermination camps.[54] In the early 1970s, Croat nationalism surfaced again, encouraged by extremist exiles in the United States and West Germany. Future tensions were heralded by a students' movement demand for a greater share of Yugoslavia's foreign currency income to Croatia.[55] There also existed a modernisation differential between the westernmost states, with their manufacturing and tourist sectors oriented to Europe, and Bosnia, Serbia and the rest of the southeast, where the bulk of state-owned heavy industry and mining was concentrated but which were otherwise mainly agricultural. Slovenia's product per head was twice the Yugoslav average, Croatia's 123 per cent; and that of Serbia proper was 93 per cent.[56] All these faultlines were activated when, after a decade of simmering tensions, upon the death of Tito in 1980 a sovereign debt of $20 billion was revealed—a year after Volcker had shut the inflation valve.[57]

Initially the West was unanimous about keeping Yugoslavia's federal unity intact. Priority was given to the country's capacity to service its debt.[58] But the structural adjustment strategy, with its implications of trimming the central state budget and shifting the burden of adjustment onto the working class, tended to raise tensions among different sections of the population while reducing the capacity of Belgrade to balance them by budget-related policies. There now emerged groups in the Yugoslav Communist party who allied themselves to foreign capital, sometimes through the good offices of Western politicians. As loyalties were thrown back to more elementary group levels, ethnic prejudice offered itself as a political tool for rival elites. Yet, in 1989 Prime Minister Markovic, on the advice of the IMF, tried to combat rampant inflation by a policy of re-centralisation. However, since the neoliberal shock therapy he applied hit the heavy industries hardest, mass strikes erupted in Bosnia, Serbia and Macedonia, contributing to a renewed centrifugal drift.[59]

The two republics which initiated the disintegration process were Slovenia and Serbia. Slovenia was seeking independent integration into Western Europe; in the second half of the 1980s, it already conducted one-fifth of its foreign trade with West Germany. Culturally, it was the most westernised republic.[60] After some hesitation, a Croatian leadership around the nationalist, retired general Franjo Tudjman joined the Slovenians in trying to aim for independence of their respective states. The Roman Catholic church, Austria, and, in Germany, the media as well as the state and church of Bavaria, actively supported the aspirations for secession among the Slovene and Croat elites. Indeed, in 1991 the EU had to warn Austria that its membership application would be put on hold if it continued to agitate for the disintegration of Yugoslavia.[61] At this point the US still officially turned down Croatian requests for arms, not least because it was feared that the Yugoslav army might appeal to the Soviet military for help in a real emergency. But the Croats had little difficulty obtaining arms clandestinely from Hungary.[62]

In Serbia, a new leadership mobilised the workers behind nationalism, now that socialism had been ideologically exhausted. Statements by Tudjman condoning the Croat fascist past rekindled old fears, notably among the Serbs living in Croatia and Bosnia. In the mid-1980s the Serbian Academy of Sciences published a memorandum advocating the restoration of Serbian sovereignty over the entire Serbian population and a retraction of the autonomy granted to Vojvodina and Kosovo. This was the programme of Slobodan Milosevic when he purged the Communist party to make the shift to nationalism possible. Of course there were important questions of where boundaries were to be drawn, at the expense of whom, and how the urban areas with their mixed populations were to be dealt with.[63] Privatisation too posed a particular problem in Yugoslavia. Because workers formally owned the country's assets, the liberal leaders in Slovenia and Croatia were paradoxically in favour of nationalisation to bring them under republican elite control. In Serbia, on the other hand, international isolation as a result of its nationalist policy tended to reinforce the strong state in the contender mould. The state class held control of key economic levers: the prime minister of Serbia was also head of Progres (importer of Russian gas from Prime Minister Chernomyrdin's Gazprom); the chairman of the Serbian parliament was also head of Jugopetrol, and so on.[64] Criminal enrichment was also an important aspect of the restructuring. By manipulating recurrent hyperinflation and bank fraud, an elite within the Serbian state class transferred an estimated 26 billion deutschmarks of the population's hard currency savings into their pockets. A network of firms registered in Cyprus, many linked to Milosevic and his family, served to arrange payments for strategic items imported along the Danube.[65]

After the Yanayev coup attempt in August 1991, fears of Soviet intervention in Yugoslavia receded, and Germany now became more assertive. Foreign minister Genscher threatened Belgrade with recognition of Slovenia and Croatia (which had declared their independence in June) if the federal army (which was recruited disproportionately from Serbia) continued to defend the country's unity. Within a week the EU too effectively abandoned its commitment to federal integrity when it established a commission to study peaceful dissolution. But as British foreign minister Hurd readily conceded, the dismemberment of Yugoslavia would not come about peacefully.[66] When fighting broke out between Croatian militias and the federal army, France sought to use its influence in the UN to contain the conflict (and German influence and rashness); Serbia turned to the US for the same reasons. In Belgrade, the appointment of former US Secretary of State Vance to the post of UN emissary to Yugoslavia was welcomed as a sign that the long-standing relations between the UN and non-aligned Yugoslavia were still meaningful, and even as proof of American commitment to federal unity.[67]

There is no doubt that the causes of the dissolution of Yugoslavia were first of all structural. Indebtedness, a loss of confidence, and interest in privatisation among sections of the state class were even more manifest than in the break-up of the USSR. But Germany fatally precipitated events when it unilaterally recognised Slovenia's and Croatia's secession in

December 1991, without requiring guarantees concerning the rights of the Serbs and other minorities in Croatia. This brazen gesture vindicated all the fears rekindled by German reunification, and it complicated ongoing negotiations in Maastricht.[68] The Americans had meanwhile been shoring up anti-Serb forces to the south, establishing a bridgehead among Albanians with the perspective of making friends among the Islamic peoples in the region. At the same time, Germany seemed to be moving in through the northwest, along with Austria and, in a covert role as arms supplier, Hungary, all with the Vatican's blessing. This, Susan Woodward writes, '[gave] the appearance to military planners and politicians in the region that the United States had chosen to divide spheres of influence north and south in eastern Europe with Germany.'[69]

However, the Bonn government soon switched to a more cautious line, resisting further anti-Serb furore in the press and pressures from the Roman Catholic hierarchy. An independent Muslim Bosnia, with its explosive mix of nationalities (including a 30 per cent Serbian population), was understood to be a very risky undertaking. With Bosnia in mind, insiders such as Milovan Djilas had already predicted a bloodbath when Croatia was allowed to secede.[70] But rivalry ignited by Germany's earlier step now led Washington to step in and claim a greater role. The Bush administration, concerned that the German initiative would marginalise the United States in the area altogether, pushed through the recognition of Bosnia at the Brussels NATO summit in April 1992. Encouraged by Washington, the Muslim government of Alija Izetbegovic had called a general mobilisation against the Serbs the day before, and full-scale civil war was the result.[71] Izetbegovic obtained weapons from Iran via Croatia and mafia middlemen. Arms supplies were also secured from Turkey and Saudi Arabia.[72]

When Clinton took over in 1993, Holbrooke was entrusted with channelling weapons to the Bosnian Muslims from regional suppliers, again including Iran. The Serbs in Bosnia obviously enjoyed support from Serbia, although there were important tactical differences between extreme nationalists, monarchists and Milosevic in this respect. Weapons for the Bosnian Serbs were also obtained through the Russian mafia and Israel, which used deliveries to buy safe passage for the Jewish community out of beleaguered Sarajevo. At this point the United States was still not ready to openly attack the Serbs and risk a rupture in NATO. In February 1994, Tudjman was prevailed upon to break off secret negotiations with Milosevic about partitioning Bosnia. In the same month, the first of three bloody mortar attacks on public places in Sarajevo began to fuel calls for foreign intervention—although, as it later turned out, the Bosnian Islamists had in all three cases staged these attacks themselves to arouse public indignation.[73]

At this juncture, Clinton decided to intervene militarily in the Yugoslav crisis. This was not anchored, as in earlier instances of liberal offensives undertaken by Democratic presidents from Wilson to Kennedy, in a mobilisation of domestic social energies and real economic expansion.[74] US economic prosperity under Clinton was premised on low-wage job growth, created by expanding the money supply and bank lending to the private sector, in combination with excessive consumption made possible by the growth of stock market values.[75] The intervention was geopolitically motivated, and catered to interests traditionally allied with the Republicans. The strategic rationale for intervention was provided by a Holbrooke paper in *Foreign Affairs*, in which he argued that 'the West must expand to central Europe as fast as possible in fact as well as in spirit, and the United States is ready to lead the way.' NATO, Holbrooke insisted, would have to be the 'central security pillar' of the new European architecture.[76]

The US president had been exploring possibilities in the same direction by making statements about increased defence spending and US support for post-Soviet Georgia, a bridgehead towards the energy-rich Caspian. This soon led to an amelioration of his chances for re-election, which had looked bleak throughout 1994 (the congressional elections in November left both houses under Republican control), as the arms and oil industries began to take a more favourable look at the administration.[77] US defence strategy at this point was based on conducting two 'theatre wars': one challenging Russia on its own periphery (for example, in the Balkans or along the Black Sea coast), and the other directed against China by challenging it in North Korea, Taiwan or Tibet.[78] For the Balkans, this strategy entailed bolstering Croatia financially and militarily (a US–Croatian military agreement was concluded in 1994), on the assumption that the area eventually would be dominated by two powers, one linked to the West (Croatia) and the other linked to a Slavic bloc with its centre in Moscow.[79]

The NATO Offensive and the Kosovo War

The NATO offensive in the Balkans also drew inspiration from the draft *Defence Planning Guidance* (DPG) for the Fiscal Years 1994–99. The DPG was written in the final year of the Bush I administration, and articulated the neoconservative line that runs from the 1970s Committee on the Present Danger to the subsequent 'Project for a New American Century'. Concerned with new rivalries after the collapse of the USSR, it recommended ensuring that no rival superpower would emerge in Western Europe, Asia or on the territory of the former Soviet Union.[80] 'Potential competitors ... need not aspire to a greater role or pursue a more aggressive posture to protect their legitimate interests,' and the United States 'must sufficiently account for the interests of the advanced industrial nations to discourage them from challenging our leadership or seeking to overturn the established political and economic order.' Therefore, the United States 'must seek to prevent the emergence of European-only security arrangements which would undermine NATO.' Military presence and US overseas bases should bolster the defence of former Warsaw Pact states against Russia as well as Middle East states dependent on the US, such as Saudi Arabia and the other states on the peninsula. In the DPG, even the fight against nuclear proliferation was placed in the perspective of containing its closest rivals—preventing states like North Korea, Iraq, and some of the successor states to the Soviet Union and in Europe, from acquiring nuclear weapons (and other weapons of mass destruction) would dissuade US allies such as Germany or Japan, and others, from themselves developing a nuclear capacity. What is most important, the DPG claims, is 'the sense that the world order is ultimately backed by the U.S.' Given this responsibility, the US would indeed have to contemplate pre-emptive wars against states with nuclear, chemical or biological weapons.[81]

In line with these recommendations, the January 1994 North Atlantic council in Brussels took the decision to expand NATO to Poland, Hungary and the Czech Republic, with further potential members being placed in the waiting room of a 'Partnership for Peace'. This was based on the idea that the Soviet collapse had opened a 'window of opportunity' that should not be left unused.[82] As the US Ambassador to NATO, Robert E. Hunter, put it, 'if history is kind and we are successful, we can see an extension eastward of the European Civil Space. But if history is unkind, NATO will have lost no time and no effort in providing for more robust allies to play a full role in the security of the continent.'[83] The US aerospace industry was at this point extremely receptive to the assumption of 'new responsibilities' by Washington. It was going through a series of mega-mergers (Lockheed and Martin; Boeing-Rockwell-McDonnell Douglas; Raytheon and Hughes), which brought it in close touch with Wall Street bankers assisting in the process. Both groups were looking to Europe for new markets. The 'US Committee to Expand NATO' was chaired by the director of strategic planning of Lockheed Martin Corporation.[84]

In July 1995, not long after Holbrooke's article in *Foreign Affairs* had outlined the larger framework, NATO airpower was unleashed against the Bosnian Serbs.[85] The Dayton agreement between the main parties in the Yugoslav conflict, concluded in November under US auspices, served to demonstrate the usefulness of Western resolve as much as it improved Clinton's chances for re-election, although observers on the ground questioned whether NATO's intervention had been so important after all.[86] Bosnia became a ghost state with a ruined economy, with Swedish neoliberal politician Carl Bildt in charge—and with 16 per cent of the all-Yugoslav debt to service.[87]

Meanwhile, getting NATO into a shape where it would be amenable to the American strategy required serious adjustments. Following the death of the ailing Wörner, the Belgian Socialist politician Willy Claes became

NATO secretary-general in late 1994. Claes took a leaf from veteran US strategist Samuel Huntington's 1993 thesis of a 'Clash of Civilisations' by identifying an Islamic challenge to Western interests, but this went straight against the evolution of US strategy. In October 1995, he had to step down in a bribery scandal.[88] The US State Department then arranged job interviews with potential replacements, in which some more light was thrown on the considerations that were important here (this was, it should be remembered, during the phase when NATO intervention had led to the Dayton agreement). The initial candidate to succeed Claes, the industrialist and former prime minister of the Netherlands, Ruud Lubbers, was interviewed in the US embassy in The Hague in October 1995 by NATO ambassador Hunter and others. Lubbers was found insufficiently militant—a view confirmed when he faced Secretary of State Warren Christopher in Washington a week later.[89] At this point, conservative-ruled France and Britain were still unwilling to follow the offensive turn taken by the Clinton administration. They refused, among other things, to subscribe to the US policy of encouraging Ukraine to edge closer to the West.[90] While the US was overtly cultivating Russia's newly-independent southern neighbours with an eye to their mineral wealth, the main European states had plans for the oil and gas of Russia proper. Lubbers was the architect of a plan named after him, the Energy Charter or Lubbers Plan, which laid down an intergovernmental framework for integrating the former Soviet Union's energy resources into the world economy. True, the Bush administration had co-signed this charter in late 1991, but Clinton's first secretary of the treasury, Lloyd Bentsen, who was close to the big US oil and gas interests, rejected it.[91] Entrusting NATO to the architect of an energy plan that stood in the tradition of securing industrial Europe's energy needs by intergovernmental means made as little sense, in light of the US' forward push towards Central Asia, as Claes' defining of Islam as the enemy. The eventual choice of Javier Solana, a one-time anti-NATO Spanish socialist now willing to subscribe to the offensive position, on the other hand had the advantage of pacifying the French and their insistence on a more pronounced Mediterranean component in NATO.[92] Eventually, this would facilitate France's rejoining NATO's military organisation 30 years after having left it, even though Chirac's condition of a NATO southern command for his country was rejected.[93]

Following Clinton's re-election in 1996, Secretary of State Christopher was replaced by UN Ambassador Madeleine Albright. Christopher was judged too cautious to function in an offensive setting and had been openly critical of Germany's role in Yugoslavia. Samuel Berger, a Washington lawyer with Lech Walesa's Polish government among his clients, was appointed to head the National Security Council.[94] Albright's worldview hinged on the Munich trauma that had sealed the fate of her native Czechoslovakia in 1938. This perspective admirably suited the ascendant US design. It provided a moral component to a completely one-sided interpretation of the Yugoslav collapse, in which Milosevic was cast as a latter-day Hitler and 'genocide' became a term loosely applied to vigilante atrocities. These atrocities were themselves a result of the social crisis and the sense of insecurity it generated, notably towards people considered backward (but with a higher reproduction rate). As Emanuel Todd has argued, even the ethnic cleansing among Croats and Serbs cannot be understood without taking the catalytic effect of a pre-modern Muslim sub-population into account.[95]

For the United States, on the other hand, the Muslim states of Bosnia and Albania were stepping stones in its forward push towards the Caucasus and Central Asia. Albania had exploded in the meantime; when the Berisha dictatorship was brought down in 1996, the state itself dissolved and some 750,000 small arms ended up in private hands in spite of an Italian intervention. The Kosovo Liberation Army led by former Maoists was now in a position to back up radical demands for Albanian autonomy in neighbouring Kosovo and Macedonia. This was to critically shape the further evolution of US policy, especially once the alternatives for energy flows from the Caspian region and the need to shut out Russia came to include a pipeline linking the Black Sea to the Albanian coast, a project to which the US and the EU committed themselves in 1994.[96]

Between 1996 and 1998, Social Democrats won the elections in the main EU states, but the leftward turn would easily be deflected into foreign adventure on the part of the US. In France, a revolt against neoliberal economic policy brought the country to a standstill in the winter of 1995–96, toppling the Juppé government after President Chirac had called a bluff election. Jospin's superficial internationalism certainly did not pose an obstacle to the Clinton drive, and Tony Blair endorsed it. Blair was elected in Britain in 1997 on a 'New Labour' project that built on the Special Relationship with the United States and support for Israel. The ease with which the Labour party had been retooled from a workers' movement into a vehicle of the 'radical centre' committed to neoliberalism reveals the depth of the defeats inflicted on the British working class under Thatcher; globalising business certainly was quick to pick up the scent of further 'reform'. Murdoch's News Corp., Glaxo and Shell all swung to support for the New Labour project, while the new prime minister and several of his colleagues were so close to BP that the company would soon earn the nickname 'Blair Petroleum'. Right after the election, Blair moved to enlist Sir David (later Lord) Simon, former head of BP (a major investor, with its US partner Amoco, in Caspian oil) and a prominent member of the ERT, to propagate British neoliberal 'competitiveness' in the EU.[97]

Social Democratic politics evolved into a real challenge to Atlantic unity only when the 1998 election in Germany replaced Chancellor Kohl by Gerhard Schröder at the head of an SPD/Greens government, with Oskar Lafontaine leading a reinforced Ministry of Finance. It now appeared that the projected renovation of corporate liberalism, which Lafontaine, Späth,

Palme and Delors had begun exploring in the latter half of the 1980s (each from a different direction, though), was after all beginning to find its way from the drawing board into practical politics. The new concept, compensatory or embedded neoliberalism, combines (as mentioned earlier) neoliberal austerity and individualisation with industrial modernisation (notably in the ecological domain), while leaving class compromise basically intact. The SPD subscribed unreservedly to the Delors vision of a Europe united under this concept, even if Schröder's own commitment to the EU was not necessarily that intense.[98]

The composition of the Schröder government, comprising several exponents of the May 1968 student movement and a former lawyer of the Baader-Meinhof terror gang, was sufficient ground to verify its acceptance of Western and 'market' discipline. But Lafontaine's plan to stabilise the exchange rates among the US, the EU and Japan was the real and immediate threat. In Asia, Washington accepted currency pegs to the dollar because there did not exist an integrated bloc capable of challenging America's monetary primacy. In Europe, however, post-war integration was on course to introducing a new common currency meant to facilitate capitalist integration across the industrial economies of the EU. Under the Lafontaine proposal, the Eurozone would then be insured against external currency risks as well. The former radicals in the government were therefore of less concern than the centre-left figure of Lafontaine, who embarked on cutbacks for sure but who also spoke (jointly with his French counterpart and personal friend, Strauss-Kahn) of reining in footloose international finance. In Italy, the post-communist government of Massimo d'Alema likewise favoured an industrial employment strategy and regulation of international financial flows.[99]

Washington's forward push into Central and Eastern Europe and the Balkans therefore provided the obvious mechanism to discipline the new continental leaders. In 1998 itself, the Americans pressured chancellor-elect Schröder to agree to a NATO campaign against rump-Yugoslavia without a UN mandate; d'Alema volunteered to expound on his NATO loyalty in an American newspaper on the eve of an audience at the White House. The acquittal of a US air force pilot responsible for severe loss of life by recklessly diving under a ski-lift cable was a further sign of Italian goodwill towards NATO.[100] These leaders were so concerned to 'protect their flank', one would assume, that they also ultimately sacrificed the main plank in their programmes for its sake. Lafontaine on the other hand resisted the NATO strategy in Yugoslavia all along. As to France, its long climb back into the NATO military structures culminated (in December 1995, at the height of the mass strike movement), in the formal announcement of the country's return to the Atlantic military organisation. This meant that French troops in former Yugoslavia, dispatched under UN auspices, became part of not just NATO, but also of its first out-of-area operation.[101] Even *if* the

Jospin government would have wanted to pursue a different line, this was the situation created by President Chirac under his constitutional prerogative.

However, all NATO allies were against bypassing the UN Security Council in case of military action. The Blair government, to Washington's annoyance, even sounded out the Russian UN ambassador on the subject of a joint Security Council resolution in June 1998. To launch the alliance into a real war, therefore, required adroit manoeuvring and intense US pressure, which Secretary of State Madeleine Albright took upon herself. As State Department spokesman James P. Rubin noted afterwards, 'Albright was so central to NATO's decision to confront the Milosevic regime over Kosovo that it was often called "Madeleine's war".'[102] With NATO's 50th anniversary only a few months away, in January 1999 the Clinton administration used the uproar over a mass grave found at Raçak to press ahead and overcome European hesitations.[103] The Raçak incident allowed Albright to push a plan that would threaten Yugoslavia with NATO attack directly if the Kosovo Albanians were not granted autonomy. With the promise of US ground troops, European allies were becoming more amenable to the idea of wresting a political solution from the Yugoslavs, especially when Albright telephoned them from Moscow in January claiming to have obtained Russian consent. Britain and France were given ceremonial roles in the talks at Rambouillet near Paris to uphold the idea of 'Europe' solving its own problems. There, Yugoslavs and Kosovo Albanians were in fact able to agree 'on nearly every aspect of the political agreement', according to Rubin.[104] Even the presence of an international military force was accepted by the Yugoslav side. But the military annexe to the agreement, which was placed before the negotiators at the eleventh hour, bypassing the Russian delegation, prescribed complete control of Kosovo by NATO.[105] It also gave the alliance a free rein within rump-Yugoslavia proper, including access to broadcasting facilities, tax freedom, etc.[106] This was an obvious dispossession strategy which the Serbian state class could not be expected to agree to.

From all the evidence, it appears that war was premeditated, and its humanitarian consequences subordinated to larger geostrategic designs. Both the CIA and the Pentagon predicted reprisals against the Albanian population in the case of NATO attack, since it was obvious that such an attack would be interpreted as air cover for the KLA.[107] NATO war games even assumed a near-60 per cent displacement of the civilian population in case of war in the not-so-fictitious state of 'Akrona'.[108] But then a quick triumph would allow Washington to write the script for NATO's anniversary celebrations, including a new alliance strategy, while fostering neoliberal globalisation in areas still largely beyond its control. Indeed as Thomas Friedman wrote in the *New York Times* four days after the beginning of the attack, 'For globalism to work, America can't be afraid to act like the almighty superpower that it is .... The hidden hand of the market will never work without a hidden fist—McDonald's cannot flourish without McDonnell-Douglas, the designer of the F-15.'[109]

With a NATO attack obviously on the agenda, reticence in Europe about the consequences of flagrant violations of the UN Charter, of the Helsinki agreements (a 2,000-strong OSCE detachment actually had been allowed into Kosovo in late 1998 to monitor the situation there) and of international law in general was not easily overcome. At Rambouillet, according to State Department spokesman Rubin, Italian foreign minister Dini shared Western discussion documents with the Yugoslav delegation, while resisting a NATO role in enforcing a peace agreement. The French even refused to admit NATO commander Wesley Clark on to the conference grounds.[110] The Dutch government's evaluation of the war claims that 'some southern European member-states', despite strong UK and Dutch pressure, did not consent to further measures against rump-Yugoslavia. The result was that 'the EU could reach agreement on the extension [of the oil embargo] and on further sanctions against Yugoslavia only after the start of the air campaign.'[111] In other words, war was the only way to forge a consensus.

France was soon back in its role as a NATO dissident, protesting US control of the war. Chirac had led the country back into the Atlantic fold and was a supporter of the intervention as such; yet at one point he threatened not to attend the NATO anniversary celebrations in Washington if France's preference for restraint continued to be ignored.[112] All bombing targets were set by US intelligence—even the Chinese embassy later turned out to have been consciously targeted after NATO discovered that it was being used for Yugoslav military communication.[113] Sensitive targets were then discussed for approval over the phone by the politicians, from Madeleine Albright downwards, in which the less amenable partners were pressured with the consensus already achieved by the others.[114] But in addition to actions under NATO command guided by the US, B-2 planes also flew their own missions over Belgrade and northern Serbia straight from bases in the US, as did other American planes from aircraft carriers.[115]

The war had the predicted result of a massive displacement of Kosovo Albanians, who were driven from their homes by Serbian police and the army for tactical military reasons or simply out of revenge. NATO bears full responsibility here, as this outcome had been predicted in detail. After consulting Holbrooke, William Walker—head of the OSCE observer mission in Kosovo and a former American ambassador to El Salvador at the time of some of Central America's most gruesome experiences with US-sponsored terror—withdrew the OSCE contingent on the eve of the attack, thereby removing the last vestige of protection for the population.[116] Several times, Albanian refugee columns were hit by high-flying NATO planes, giving rise to the suspicion that it was not only Serbian thugs who drove them into neighbouring Macedonia and Albania proper. When European resistance to the campaign began to mount due to repeated targeting of civilian objects and the use of cluster bombs by NATO, the US government passed classified satellite images and signal intelligence to the chief prosecutor of the Yugoslavia Tribunal, Louise Arbour. Arbour, a personal friend of Madeleine Albright, then indicted Milosevic and a few fellow leaders for war crimes. This had the effect of suspending all diplomatic dealings with the Yugoslav state, leaving only military options.[117]

The conclusion of the war was nevertheless only reached via mediation by the Finnish president Ahtisaari, Gazprom head Chernomyrdin, and a Swedish investment banker.[118] Compared to the original demands at Rambouillet, the agreement they negotiated was a considerably better deal for Yugoslavia. Serbia's infrastructure was however severely damaged, leading to a drop in production estimated by the IMF at 45 per cent. This came on top of dangerous pollution by the use of depleted uranium and the bombing of chemical plants and oil refineries.[119] For the Balkans, very little was achieved that would warrant the vast human suffering and material destruction. Ninety per cent of Europe's heroin today passes through 'liberated' Kosovo, and Pristina airport is a key transit for smuggled children for prostitution and slavery.[120] But the war was undoubtedly a success from the perspective of the Anglo-American forward strategy. The formal inclusion of Poland, Hungary and the Czech Republic in NATO was complemented by military cooperation with other countries in the area: the initial air corridors for the attack led through Croatia and Hungary into northern Serbia, and through Albania and Macedonia into Kosovo. In the final hours of the conflict, Hungary closed off its airspace to prevent Russian transport planes from supplying a small column that had captured Pristina airport by surprise in an effort to enforce the compromise deal.

AMERICANISATION OF THE EUROPEAN UNION AGAINST THE UNITED STATES?

The Kosovo war was launched to push forward the Anglo-American sphere of influence on the European continent as far as possible, given that Russia was still powerless to prevent this.[121] Its success 'would decisively consolidate US leadership in Europe,' Peter Gowan writes, and by ignoring the UN Security Council, Russia was robbed of a say on what was happening right on its doorstep. The war sealed 'the unity of the [NATO] alliance against a background where the launch of the Euro could pull it apart.'[122] In this section, let me review the war's negative impact on European interests and the simultaneous, perhaps paradoxical, EU turn to neoliberalism.

First, the US forward push has facilitated the access to Caspian and Central Asian energy resources for American and Anglo-Dutch capital by redrafting the geostrategic situation. For continental Europe, on the other hand, independent access to these resources has been restricted. Bombing the bridges over the Danube at Novi Sad in northern Serbia interrupted a river supply route by which around 100 million tonnes of goods a year were transported as late as 1987, blocking wheat and ores and minerals to Austria and Germany.[123] There are important geopolitical—in addition to economic—issues involved here. With the opening of the Rhine–Main–Danube canal in the early 1990s, an inland shipping link has been established linking the Black Sea littoral states (including Russia) with Rotterdam and the North Sea.[124] The political-economic aspect of bombing the bridges surfaced when France and Germany supported reserving EU funds for clearing the river of debris after the end of hostilities, but the UK held up a decision on political grounds. At the time of this writing, the bridges still are blocking the Danube.[125] In fact, after Dayton and the lifting of sanctions against rump-Yugoslavia, hopes had flared up among the littoral states along the Danube that they again stood a chance to profit from 'the growing importance of the Black Sea region as a transit route for Russian gas and central Asian oil'.[126] But precisely because of the oil and gas pipelines run by Gazprom of Russia, Topenergy of Bulgaria, and other regional players, the old fear of Russian penetration revived, whether or not in combination with trepidation over a Russia–EU link outside the control of Anglo-American oil majors.[127] While there is no point in assuming that the bombing was motivated by a single strand in this complex set of rival interests, there is no doubt that the outcome was detrimental to Austrian–German aspirations to link up to the Black Sea and beyond by developing the Danube route. The same holds true for other instances of military actions with intended or unintended economic consequences, such as the bombing of the Zastava autombile complex, which was half-owned by FIAT-Iveco and was under negotiation to be sold further to either FIAT or Peugeot. Zastava in its heyday produced 220,000 cars a year, and would have reinforced the European automobile industry with another low-wage production location comparable to Volkswagen's acquisition of Skoda.[128]

Second, the Kosovo war also concerned the province's mineral resources. Presented in the media almost exclusively as a contested area in terms of nationalities, with sacred places, etc., the real economic importance of Kosovo resides in its underground wealth, which has earned it the title of 'Serbia's Kuwait'. Indeed the ownership of the Trepca complex was one aspect of Serbia's decision to restrict Kosovo's autonomous status. Trepca was, and in fact still is, 100 per cent Yugoslav property, with an estimated value of 4.5 billion euros. It exported zinc, lead and other minerals to a range of European countries, including Russia, and also boasted some 17 billion tonnes of coal reserves.[129] The Rambouillet agreement actually proposed introducing a free market in Kosovo, which would have entailed putting up the Trepca complex for sale to the highest bidder, as part of a comprehensive privatisation of Yugoslav assets in the province, dispossessing the state class. However, the compromise agreement which ended the bombing stipulates that Kosovo remains part of Yugoslavia and makes no mention of property rights. As a result, a complex struggle has erupted, dividing all parties including the Albanians.[130]

The geopolitical balance in Europe was profoundly altered as a result of the NATO forward drive, which has meanwhile been taken further with the wars in Afghanistan and Iraq. The United States has effectively become the doorman regulating European dealings with Russia. Albania, Bulgaria, Macedonia and Rumania, along with NATO members Greece and Turkey, today form part of a group, under US auspices, committed to closer military cooperation and operating a joint force in Bulgaria for peacekeeping and relief operations.[131] As Peter Gowan wrote, even before the Kosovo war,

> For American policy planners, Poland is only one part of the necessary geopolitical wedge between Germany and Russia. In many ways, Ukraine is an even more important prize. A combined Polish-Ukrainian corridor under US leadership would decisively split 'Europe' from Russia, exclude Russia also from the Balkans, go a long way towards securing the Black Sea for the USA, link up with America's Turkish bastion, and provide a very important base for the 'Great Game' for the energy and mineral resources of the Caspian and the Asian Republics of the former USSR.[132]

At NATO's 50th anniversary celebrations in Washington, in the midst of the war, Georgia, Ukraine, Uzbekistan, Azerbaijan and Moldova established GUUAM—adding Uzbekistan to the year-old link already established by the other four. The US, Britain and Turkey are the sponsors of GUUAM, which consolidates the cordon sanitaire referred to by Gowan, while providing a security cover for the countries through which oil transport from the Caspian (but outside Russian or Iranian control) should pass if the US, Britain and Turkey have their way.[133] During the Kosovo war, the military value of GUUAM was made clear on the first day of the NATO attack itself, when Azerbaijan intercepted Russian jet fighters destined for Yugoslavia.[134] Ukraine too closed its airspace to Russian reinforcements for the Pristina detachment in June 2000. Russia on the other hand has been forced on to the defensive. Realising that it can no longer match even a country like Turkey (which has become pivotal in the new geostrategic situation) with conventional weaponry, Moscow has changed its military strategy to include a first-use option of nuclear weapons.[135]

The War as a Catalyst for Neoliberalism

The Kosovo war worked to constrain the manoeuvring space of those in Europe, who, like Lafontaine, envisaged a cautious strategy of European integration, constructed around an innovative industrial policy with some protective structures still in place—to wit, the compensatory or embedded neoliberal concept discussed earlier.[136] But the violent push into the Balkans undermined an enlargement strategy based on economic and social compromises and real transition time. Lafontaine resigned from the German government 12 days before NATO attacked and also vacated his post as chairman of the Social Democratic Party. His attempt at regulating footloose international finance, as he conceded afterwards, was defeated by neoliberal investment bankers and their followers in politics and the press. He also makes clear how the smear campaign against him brought back anxieties dating from the 1989 attempt at his life that knocked him out of the election campaign. Four days after his resignation as minister of finance and SPD chairman, the *Financial Times* ominously announced that 'the battle for European capitalism has begun in earnest', meaning the struggle between the 'Anglo-American model' based on the 'rules of risk and return' against a 'stakeholder capitalism which aims to balance the interests of employees, shareholders, suppliers and the wider community'.[137] This came on top of a statement by Assistant Treasury Secretary Edwin Truman, who according to the same newspaper 'used the strongest language heard from the US administration' on the supposed drift of the Eurozone towards becoming an industrial export bloc rather than a freely accessible part of the open world economy as desired by global capital.[138] This was one of the final salvoes fired at Lafontaine.

In France, the drift was clearly towards breaking up the group structures of finance capital. In 1996, for the first time in French economic history a foreign investment bank headed the league for merger and acquisitions activity, as Goldman Sachs beat French rivals.[139] In Germany, social and legal obstacles to such a transformation remained in force, requiring the US administration and the neoliberal press to keep up the pressure. Attempts at state intervention to hold back the trend were incidental, and anyway often without success.[140] But Chancellor Schröder's weak position in the immediate aftermath of Lafontaine's resignation carried real risks in this respect. Therefore it must have come as a relief that on 8 June, with peace talks over Kosovo in progress, a joint Schröder–Blair statement (on the occasion of the European elections) marked the German government's overt turn to neoliberalism, at least in rhetoric. The 'Third Way' is meant to enlarge neoliberal precepts with a communitarian programme, bringing back a recognition of the need to hold society together. Thus in the Schröder–Blair statement there is support for the market economy, but not for the market society.[141] The neoliberal turn received a generic push, though, when Schröder had a tax package adopted that removed fiscal obstacles to the break-up of the big finance capital groups, in a move which the *Financial Times* wrote had been 'eagerly awaited by the big names of German industry and US investment banks hungry for deals'.[142]

This was not a matter of European capital being caught unawares. In 1993, in the wake of the collapse of the USSR, the ERT advocated the creation of group specifically dedicated to competitiveness, and made a proposal in that spirit to the president of the EU commission, Delors. In three reports, the advisory group of the CEOs of Unilever, ABB, Nokia and BP recommended the modernisation of education in order to improve the European position in the emerging global information economy; the liberalisation of the public sector; and the flexibilisation of labour, which the groups said should not only be employed in ways favouring corporate competitiveness but should also be continuously trained and re-trained to adapt to changing needs.[143] While the Bosnian war was raging, liberal interests on both sides of the Atlantic were brought on board of the Clinton globalisation offensive through the Uruguay Round Agreement of 1994 and its programme for the worldwide opening of hitherto closed economies.[144]

The work of the Advisory Group on competitiveness was translated at the Luxemburg Summit of late 1997 into an employment strategy that committed the EU countries to fostering 'employability' of workers by (re-)training programmes, creating more favourable circumstances for small start-up companies, labour flexibilisation, and the mobilisation of women for paid work, e.g., by opening night shift jobs to women. To ensure compliance, a principle of annual reporting by governments was agreed, so that progress in each of these areas could be monitored.[145] The reconstituted Advisory Group meanwhile produced four more reports. The first one argued that social protection should be oriented to mobility of labour; the second recommended the creation of more competitive European capital markets including the stock exchange, and the concomitant growth of a European pension market. The third report again emphasised labour market flexibilisation, and the final report of 1999 brought the different recommendations together in an action plan that focused efforts in these areas on *catching up with the United States*. The report noted that the US economy had flourished in the 1990s due to its dynamism and openness, and had thus contributed to economic activity in the rest of the world.

The neoliberal restructuring of capital in Europe also affected the network of interlocking directorates among large corporations. Over the first post-Maastricht decade, European capital developed into a pattern reflecting the opening-up of nationally confined finance capital structures on the continent—and their transformation into a rival transnational network separate from the Atlantic one. This can be explained as follows. The 'financial bourgeoisie in power', which, as André Granou argues, takes the place of the state at the heart of the economy as liberalisation proceeds, no longer looks only to its own state for direction and protection. Instead it establishes strategic links horizontally, with other corporations in the wider European space (the first signs of this already produced dissent among the French capitalist class under de Gaulle).[146] These links are usually established by multiple directors, mostly non-executive directors, or 'network specialists' as Meindert Fennema calls them. They concentrate on collecting such positions rather than actually managing corporations, which they leave to the managerial cadre below them. Their multiple (outside) directorships are combined with strategic planning and semi-political functions (advisers to governments, etc.), membership of private planning groups such as Bilderberg, and so on and so forth. The networks of joint directorates thus serve as the ground floor of these channels of information, communication and strategic consensus formation, on which the effectiveness of a concept of control is premised.[147]

In Figure 8.1, based on the 100 'global players' of the business world in 1992 compiled by Mattera, I have drawn the transnational combinations by taking all companies interconnected by two or more directors, as *clusters*. Additionally, I have added firms linked by two or more joint directorates—'satellites'—to these clusters. The level of multiplicity ≥2 is intended to highlight the stronger and, we may assume, strategically more meaningful connections.[148] Their actual strategic orientations (at the juncture of the early 1990s, that is) may in turn be hypothetically inferred by combining their position in the network with the position in the Global/Euro-Contender/Fortress Europe categories in Table 8.2.

Figure 8.1
Clustered Joint Directorates, 100 Transnational Corporations, 1992

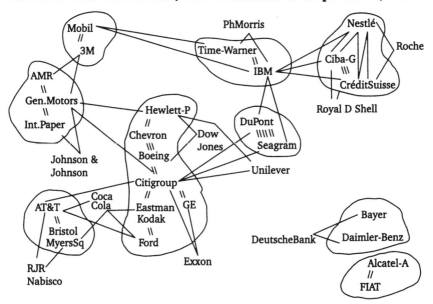

Source: Compiled from Mattera (1992). Clusters of corporations linked by two or more directors, and corporations linked by two or more directors to clusters.

From Figure 8.1 it transpires that the big Anglo-Dutch firms were at this juncture connected into a wider Atlantic network of joint directorates that also contained a Swiss pole (with CS Holding, the parent of Crédit Suisse and the CSFB investment bank, at the centre). The other continental European firms were, however, not connected into this network. At this point they stand apart from it at the multiplicity levels indicated—and within the limits, obviously, of the relatively restricted sample of 100 corporations (Japanese companies in the Mattera list are not connected into the global network at this level). We are looking here at a key aspect of the heartland/contender structure of the global political economy. As Fennema found in his study on international networks of banks and industry for the years 1970 and 1976, the structure of transnational interlocks was made up primarily by interlocks among American, British, Canadian and Dutch firms. West German capital also had many links with Dutch firms, but *hardly any interlocks existed between German, French and Italian corporations*.[149] In the 1970s, therefore, Dutch transnational corporations performed a bridge function between what he calls 'the Anglo-Saxon network', with the West German network as the main bloc of *national* capital in Europe.[150]

By 2000, it would seem that clusters of ≥2 interlocks—and satellites connected by 2 or more directors to clusters—had become (at this density level) disjointed into a continental European and a US network, with the Swiss network now linked to France and Germany instead of interlocked with the Atlantic network. British and Scandinavian companies were distributed over the network as a whole, notably underscoring the new bridge position of capital headquartered in the UK.[151]

Structurally speaking, in market control terms we can no longer speak of a Euro-contender tradition in European capital at this point, and even less of a Fortress Europe bloc *consisting of large companies* (cf. Table 8.2). Between 1987 and 2000, as Bastiaan van Apeldoorn has documented, European corporations inserted themselves into the globalisation trend driven by US and British capital. Sales outside Europe for the top 19 corporations went up from 34 per cent in 1987 to 46.2 per cent in 2000; on the other hand, sales outside the home country but within the EU (which would suggest a specifically European profile) hardly increased. The contender posture with its implications for protection was expressly abandoned, and the rivalry with the US was entirely argued in terms of competition.[152] This did not imply the suspension of the difference between being 'American' and 'European' at the level of the actual capitalist class—on the contrary, in fact. Thus, as the former secretary-general of the ERT remembers, whenever the 'argument was heard that the head of a large U.S. multinational's European operations was running a business as big as many ERT members and making a major contribution to the European economy ..., the answer always came that such a man ... was only a divisional head, *not a bearer of global business responsibility*.'[153] The fact that states and blocs of states like

Figure 8.2
Clustered Joint Directorates, 150 Transnational Corporations, 2000

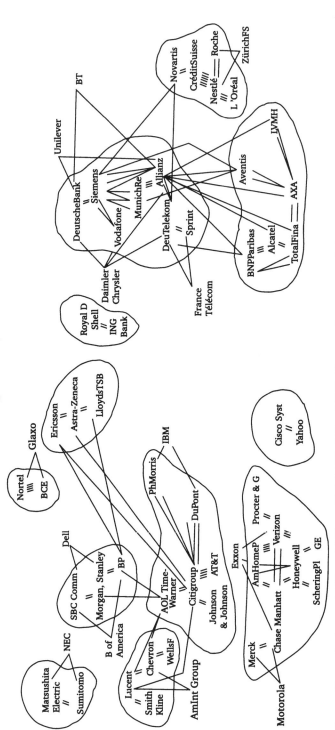

Source: Companies by assets (*Financial Times*, Global 500, 4 May 2000). Clusters of corporations linked by two or more directors and corporations linked by two or more directors to clusters. Data collected with Otto Holman and Stijn Verbeek.

the EU continue to be the main nodal points in negotiating the broader research and development orientations, arenas of class compromise, and partners for the really epochal business deals in the arms and infrastructure field, makes 'citizenship' a persistent requirement and/or advantage. Hence the 'commercialisation of sovereignty' as Palan calls it, is bound to produce rivalries even on a 'level playing field'.[154]

A New Era of Atlantic Rivalry

Immediately after the Kosovo adventure, the heads of government of the EU countries—the European Council—met in Lisbon to discuss a comprehensive strategy that built on the steps recommended by the ERT Advisory Group on Competitiveness in the previous years. But the Lisbon agreement of 2000 also breathed a new spirit of defiance. On the one hand it sought to accelerate the introduction of neoliberal privatisation and flexibilisation; on the other, there was an unmistakeable thrust towards rivalry with the US, expressed in the agreement *to turn the more competitive economy which would result against the United States, and overtake it by 2010.*[155] This sounds more like Khrushchev's boast that Soviet socialism would bury capitalism than a commitment to global capitalism. Again the idea that the capitalist class is in the process of constituting itself at the global level as a homogeneous force, irrespective of nationality or 'regionality', with rivalry suspended, is contradicted by events on the ground.[156] The Transatlantic Business Dialogue (TABD), set up in 1995 in the spirit of the globalisation drive then ascendant, saw its 'success rate' diminish in subsequent years; the annual CEO summit scheduled for 2001 was even cancelled. Issues like the resistance to genetically modified agricultural products and other issues made contentious by protest movements in Europe are seen as souring the climate.[157]

The Lisbon agreement prescribes that the labour participation rate be raised from the current 61 per cent of the active population to 70 per cent in 2010. At the European summit of Barcelona in 2002, it was furthermore decided to raise the effective retirement age by five years.[158] In its preparatory document for the Lisbon meeting, the European Commission also recommended that when employment opportunities would increase, jobs should be filled quickly on favourable market conditions and in ways to ensure non-inflationary growth (i.e., without wage rises). Flexible working hours, more opportunities for part-time work and a review of legislation that protects employment too stringently and imposes excessive redundancy compensation are thus in order.[159] The leaders at Lisbon also wanted an enhanced 'utilisation of Europe's full e-potential', and the creation of a climate in which e-commerce and the Internet can flourish. These aims would allow 'the EU to catch up with its competitors', by forming European companies able to challenge the dominance of such US firms as Microsoft, Intel, Dell and others.[160]

The third pillar of the Lisbon project is the completion of the internal market. This aspect was to be pursued by the removal of remaining obstacles to a single market, through liberalisation of such sectors as gas, electricity, postal services and transport. Simultaneously, integration of capital markets (33 stock markets in the EU as against two in the US, 11 cross-border payment systems as against one), and liberalisation/privatisation of such sectors as pension provision would facilitate access to and increase of the money capital base available for accumulation by European capital.[161]

However, the Lisbon agenda, building on a decade of preparation by the ERT, still had to be made palatable to the populations of Europe. *The EU was always more neoliberal than national governments could afford.* In 2002, UNICE, the EU employers' organisation, complained that concrete measures should be taken to prevent the Lisbon agenda from being derailed; yet in more and more countries, notably in Italy, France and Belgium, powerful protest movements against liberalisation emerged in the first decade of the new millennium. Chancellor Schröder took the unusual step of resigning from the post of chairman of the German SPD (which he had taken from Lafontaine), in order not to lose any more time in trying to convince his party of the necessity of cutbacks, liberalisation and privatisation.[162] From all these signs, one can only conclude that unlike the working classes of the US and UK, the European trade unions have not been defeated and continue to resist the imposition of disciplinary neoliberalism, as was confirmed in the momentous rejection of the European Constitution in France and the Netherlands.

The EU, then, would represent an imperialism as ruthless as the Anglo-American original if only it could overcome its internal rivalries and unify its executive arm. It should certainly not be mistaken as the harbinger of a capitalism with a human face, or anything of that kind. But as I agued in Chapter 1, it *is* the more contemporary attempt at synchronising the geopolitical and economic dimensions of capitalist class rule.[163] The EU countries are clearly ahead of the US in obtaining a hold on such levers of globalising capitalist discipline as reside in global standards, ecologically and socially sustainable capital accumulation, etc.[164] They would be able, for instance, to take the lead in the urgent innovation of desalination technology to secure fresh water supplies in the Mediterranean countries and roll back desertification. Yet the EU is also intent on developing a military capability and command structure, except that military power to project 'full-spectrum dominance' is clearly not in its sights (or means). But then, '9/11' was not averted by the awesome defence and intelligence assets defending the West; and in Iraq, the United States, in the words of a French defence intellectual, 'cannot exercise battle-space dominance a few hundred yards beyond [its command] bunker in central Baghdad.'[165]

The nuances that still exist between the imperial posture of the English-speaking heartland, and the EU in dealing with the outside world are illustrated by an article written by Robert Cooper, an assistant to Javier Solana, the NATO secretary-general-turned-EU security and foreign policy representative.[166] Empire would seem the obvious choice, Cooper writes, except that it no longer works. *'A century of emancipation, of national liberation movements and self-determination cannot be reversed.'* The alternative, tried out by the EU, is to widen the sphere of integration and require candidate members to conform to neoliberal practice in Europe.

> The EU can in some respects be likened to an empire; it is a structure that sets standards of internal governance but in return offers its members a share in the decision-making, a place in the commonwealth. Across central Europe, countries have rewritten constitutions and changed laws to conform to European standards. This is a kind of regime change, but it is chosen, legitimate. *This represents the spread of civilisation and good governance in lasting form.*[167]

The fact that 'Lisbon' came on the heels of the Kosovo war should also remind us of the more classical forms of geopolitical rivalry activated by the US forward pressure. First, the existing structures of European military cooperation, in the perspective of the Common Foreign and Security Policy, were strengthened after Kosovo. In the aborted European Constitution, the member states were committed to improving their military capabilities. True, Solana developed a strategic doctrine that allows Washington to counteract attempts to move towards the creation of an operational European command structure.[168] Yet the industrial assets and structures necessary for mounting an independent EU military role are nevertheless being reinforced. The Lisbon strategy advocates an intensification of space exploration, to which it attributes a strategic importance. Again the idea is to build an aerospace industry and capacity that can beat the United States (in 2003, Airbus, the airplane subsidiary of the European aerospace consortium EADS, for the first time in its history built more civilian passenger planes than Boeing of the US). In addition, the heads of the six most important aerospace companies, in discussions with the EU commissioners entrusted with foreign and defence policy, have launched the Strategic Aerospace Review for the twenty-first century: Star 21.[169] In their report, the aerospace business leaders argue that space exploration is vital for maintaining Europe's *political independence*. Space exploration is connected to general information gathering, innovation and research, geophysical knowledge and development aid, as well as military operations. In addition to Airbus, the development of a European satellite navigation system (Galileo) rivalling the US Global Positioning Satellite system is considered a key asset in this respect. However, the simultaneous requirement that the EU raise defence expenditure to increase the aerospace market runs up against the deflationary effect of the United States role in the world economy and the fact it functions as a Keynesian state on a global scale, prioritising demand in its own sphere and depressing it abroad.[170]

European social development thus remains mortgaged by the EU commitment to an ill-fitting neoliberalism, heartland style. This produces anomalies which express themselves in incomprehension coupled with exaggeration, malfunctions, disagreement and new struggles. The specific characteristics of the continent are not just relics of the past, doomed to be swept away by 'reform'. As Robert Boyer writes, while new financial practices may spread quickly, work and employment practices change only slowly, dependent as they are on workers' competences and apprenticeship, which requires time. And while Europe (or Japan and South Korea) may be ill-equipped to join the financialisation of the world economy on favourable terms, it may well be that in the longer run the heritage of state enterprise and monitoring, class compromise and/or corporate paternalism may provide a better environment for the inevitable return to prominence of new forms of production.[171] Therefore the basic problem with the EU's Lisbon strategy is that it takes a destructive approach to Europe's existing strengths and places all its hopes on a strategy of competing with the US by adopting the American model wholesale.[172]

Notes

1. For the period 1968–78 (Wildenberg 1990: 44, Figure 3). This was, hence, a period of negative 'differential accumulation' in terms of Bichler and Nitzan's analysis of the process which links the profitability of the Fortune 500 relative to total corporate profits (Bichler and Nitzan 2004: 48, Figure 4.3; cf. profit rate graphs for the US and Europe in Duménil and Lévy 2004: 35, Figure 3.3). This chapter builds on van der Pijl (2001a).
2. J. Morris (1982); Wildenberg (1990).
3. Quoted in *Newsweek*, 17 June 1985; 'fortresses' quote from T. Baudoin and M. Collin in *Le Monde Diplomatique*, February 1986, pp. 14–5.
4. I. Warde in *Le Monde Diplomatique*, August 1993, p. 21; cf. Kornbluth (1992).
5. Wildenberg (1990: 89). KKR burnt its fingers when it paid $26 billion for RJR Nabisco in 1992. Between 1986 and 1992 its main rival, Forstmann Little, assembled a comparable portfolio that included Pullman, Gulfstream, General Instrument and a host of other large corporations (*Business Week*, 10 February 1992; *Financial Times*, 13 September 1994).
6. Houben (2004: 48, cf. Table 4). See B. Cohen (1999) on the acceptance of the dollar abroad relative to other currencies. The markets for financial derivatives continued to grow in the 1990s. Between 1992 and 1997, futures and options on interest rates, currency and stock market indexes in combination tripled to a level of $12.2 trillion out-standing; interest rate swaps and options and currency swaps in combination grew from $5.3 trillion to $28.7 trillion in the same period (Duménil and Lévy 2001: 143.
7. A rare glimpse into the machinery of enrichment operated by this set of people was offered in the rise and fall of Boo.com, an internet sportswear retailer launched in 1999, which collapsed in 2000. Boo.com was part of the short-lived myth that everything bought and sold would soon move out of the shops and that even clothing would be bought online. J.P. Morgan, the blue-chip US investment bank, took a stake in Boo and brought

in selected clients to share in the expected bonanza. Lebanon's Hariri family (cf. Table 10.1 of this book) and the Bin Mahfouth banking family of Saudi Arabia (cf. Table 10.1 of this book), Bernard Arnault (Table 8.1 of this book), the Benetton family and the Goldman Sachs investment bank were among those who jointly footed the $135 million bill for the aborted venture. The parasitic nature of the wealth of these 'investors' is underlined by the fact that the main reason given for Boo's failure was the fact that none of them took an active management interest in the operation (*Financial Times*, 19 May 2000).

8. R. Farnetti in *Le Monde Diplomatique*, February 1997, pp. 16–7.
9. Cutler et al. (1999: 10–1).
10. Lane (2000). On the privatisation of the state monopoly of violence, cf. Ortiz (2004); on the prison business in the US and Britain, cf. L. Wacquant in *Le Monde Diplomatique*, April, 1999, pp. 1, 24–5.
11. Houben (2004: 49); *Business Week*, 8 June 1992.
12. Todd (2004: 110, Table 5).
13. B. Cassen in *Le Monde Diplomatique*, June 1987, pp. 1, 19; cf. Duménil and Lévy (2004) for a general picture of the neoliberal revolution in historical perspective.
14. Merrill Lynch, Gemini Consulting and World Wealth Report data in *Financial Times*, 7 July 2000.
15. It is to be noted that compared to the industrial sources of wealth of the richest Asians (Table 9.1 in this book), the richest Americans and Europeans (in Table 8.1) owe their wealth to retail and everyday household items, along with media and, in the US list, the powerful IT companies such as Microsoft, which enjoy monopolies that allow them to impose rents on global customer bases that amount to taxes.
16. Lundberg (1969); Collier and Horowitz (1976).
17. Duménil and Lévy (2004: 33–4, cf. Figure 3.2); Korzeniewicz and Moran (1997), as in Robinson (2004: 152, Table 4.1, 12). The data for the remaining quintiles for 1980–90 is: second quintile, down from 18 to 11.3; third quintile down from 3.5 to 2.1; fourth quintile down from 2.2 to 1.8; and fifth quintile down from 1.7 to 1.4.
18. World Bank data in *Financial Times*, 24 January 2001.
19. On benchmarking, see Sklair (2001: 113–48). According to one company-sponsored report, women in the reproductive age bracket are finding it more and more difficult to actually reproduce (Kreitzman 1999: 18).
20. Houben (2004: 49); A. Daguerre in *Le Monde Diplomatique*, June 2005, p. 4.
21. B. Cassen in *Le Monde Diplomatique*, June 1987, pp. 1, 19; A. Daguerre in *Le Monde Diplomatique*, June 2005, pp. 4–5.
22. Hilary Clinton was a Wal-Mart board member from 1985 to 1992 (*Newsweek*, 24 January 1994). In 2000, R. Walton was the richest man in the world (cf. Table 8.1 in this chapter).
23. *International Herald Tribune*, 16 February 1999; Trilateral Commission membership, 1994 (www.trilateralcommission.com, 16 January 1995).
24. Holbrooke's appointment as UN ambassador in June 1999 was held up a few weeks in the US Senate because of suspected improprieties in his parallel roles as a State Department adviser and a CSFB investment banker (*Financial Times*, 18 June and 1 July 1999).
25. Ferguson (1995: 291, 297–301). Hilary Clinton's abortive campaign for a new medicare system is a case in point.
26. Albert (1992: 26). 'Communism's collapse has weakened the bonds [with Europe and Japan],' columnist Robert Samuelson wrote in *Newsweek*, 24 December 1990. 'In an era of global economic competition, we are less sure of our foreign interests. Are Europe and Japan our allies or our rivals? And our allies wonder whether they really need us anymore.'
27. Boren (1990: 5).
28. *Newsweek*, 23 September 1991; cf. Schweizer (1993) and Hager (1996).
29. Walpen (2004: 242–3). The notion of 'hybrid' used here is from Boyer (2001).
30. Pfeiffer (1993); Morin (1974); Morin data in *The Economist*, 1 July 1995; Galli (1995).

31. Albert (1992: 65–8); van Apeldoorn (2002: 24–5). A key study of the US economy in terms of financial groups in the 'European' sense is Menshikov (1973).
32. Pistorius and van Wijk (1999: 24). Here I should refer to the authors who define capitalist crisis in terms of the exhaustion of the social and natural substratum of capitalism, e.g., Funke (1978: 227–8) and Brennan (2000).
33. Houben (2004: 47). As van Tulder and Junne write in this connection, 'The very concept of what a multinational corporation is may have to change. The development of [new technologies] makes it possible that one single headquarters in one country can direct and control far-flung activities in many countries around the globe without owning any of the productive units any longer—eventually even without possessing any formal assets abroad' (van Tulder and Junne 1988: xii).
34. Lipp (1997: 58); Houben (2004: 46, Table 2).
35. See van der Pijl (1998: 60, Table 2.4).
36. T. Ferguson and J. Rogers in *Le Monde Diplomatique*, November 1981, p. 11.
37. van Apeldoorn (2002: 68–9, 128–9); cf. Holman (1992).
38. Typically, Glaxo and BP were among the top ten foreign donors to US political parties under Clinton, both incidentally subsidising the Republican opposition; three other UK firms, Seagram's and Northern Telecom from Canada, and Murdoch's News Corp., underline the English-speaking connection here. But no other European firms figure in the list. In 1995–96 Glaxo gave $232,000 to the Republicans and BP gave $161,000 (and $50,000 to the Democrats) (*Financial Times*, 26–27 October 1996). The corporations supporting the Republicans at this point were also the backers of Blair's New Labour project.
39. S. Woodward (1995: 174).
40. Houweling (1997); B. Cassen in *Le Monde Diplomatique*, December 1991, pp. 4–5.
41. On the constitutionalisation of neoliberalism in the EMU, see Gill (1998).
42. Ryner (1998) and van Apeldoorn (2002) respectively.
43. A. Lipietz quoted in B. Cassen in *Le Monde Diplomatique*, August 1992, p. 30.
44. I will henceforth speak of EU, even though some of the policies towards Eastern Europe were still formally made by the EC.
45. Garthoff (1994: 427, 497); *Newsweek*, 18 November 1991; P.M. de la Gorce in *Le Monde Diplomatique*, March 1993, pp. 4–5.
46. Holman 1998: 15; *De Volkskrant*, 4 January 1992. By 2001, Germany was still the main investor ($18.5 billion, of which some $15 billion was divided between the Czech Republic, Poland and Hungary); Britain was second, but not in these three countries (of $15.1 billion, $12 billion was in 'other Eastern Europe'); and the US was third, with investments more equally spread, but with Poland first (OECD and Survey of Current Business data in Houben 2004: 54, Table 6).
47. Pellegrin (2000: 284); *Financial Times*, 18 April and 24 May 1995.
48. J.-Y. Potel in *Le Monde Diplomatique*, October 1992, p. 4; *Financial Times*, 18 April 1995; cf. Garthoff (1994: 465).
49. J.-Y. Potel in *Le Monde Diplomatique*, October 1992, p. 4. The incorporation of the Czech economy into the German sphere of influence was highlighted by the purchase and retooling of Skoda by Volkswagen and also, less glamorously, by German sex tourism. German capital accounted for more than 36 per cent of overall foreign direct investment into the Czech Republic by late 1994, with American investment in second place at 21 per cent (*Financial Times*, 2 June 1995).
50. Rohwedder's successor was Birgit Breuel, a prominent neoliberal politician with important connections in the world of investment banking (Wisnewski et al. 1993: 236–8, 260–2). Cf. C. Mohr in *Le Monde Diplomatique*, June 1991, p. 15 on Rohwedder's policy, which Mohr still assumed was being continued by Breuel.
51. The EBRD was characterised as 'one-third EC, one third World Bank, and one-third Banque Lazard or J.P. Morgan' by *Le Monde*, 24 April 1991; cf. Attali interview in *Business Week*, 26 April 1993; Garthoff (1994: 415).

52. 'Bandit' quote from Thatcher's minister of finance Geoffrey Howe, in Gowan (1999a: 230); *Financial Times*, 7 March 1996. Former French foreign minister Roland Dumas ascribed the bringing down of the EBRD head as the work of 'the Anglo-Saxon establishment' (*Financial Times*, 26–27 June 1993).
53. Figures for 1991 in Samary (1995: 19).
54. Kloss (1969: 182–3).
55. F. Feron in *Le Monde Diplomatique*, March 1973, p. 2; *Time*, 27 December 1971; *De Volkskrant*, 24 November 1971.
56. C. Samary in *Le Monde Diplomatique*, July 1991, p. 5. Serbia proper had a level of export orientation equal to Croatia in the early 1990s, but not its autonomous provinces; for Slovenia it was around 25 per cent (ibid.). The modernisation differential is also brought out by the fact that in the mid-1950s Slovenia, Croatia and Serbia reached a reproduction rate of 2.5 children per woman, the developed European level, while Bosnia, Macedonia and Kosovo only reached this important threshold in 1975, 1984 and 1998, respectively (Todd 2004: 64–5).
57. Samary (1995: 11).
58. S. Woodward (1995: 153–5).
59. Gowan (1999b: 85, 88); cf. C. Samary in *Le Monde Diplomatique*, July 1991, pp. 4–5. In the Bush administration, both L. Eagleburger and B. Scowcroft had private business interests in Yugoslavia (S. Woodward 1995: 155).
60. C. Samary in *Le Monde Diplomatique*, December 1992, p. 12.
61. Gowan (1999b: 87); S. Woodward (1995: 101–5); *De Volkskrant*, 18 June 1993.
62. Wiebes (2002: 164); *Financial Times*, 2/3 September 1995.
63. C. Samary in *Le Monde Diplomatique*, November 1991, p. 19.
64. Samary (1995: 75); C. Samary in *Le Monde Diplomatique*, July 1991, pp. 4–5.
65. Wiebes (2002: 215); *NRC-Handelsblad*, 9 March 1996.
66. Quoted in *Newsweek*, 15 July 1991.
67. S. Woodward (1995: 180).
68. The Major government of the UK consented to Germany's move, in exchange for obtaining opt-outs from the Social Charter and EMU, crucial to the Thatcher strategy to be in *and* out of the EC/EU (Gowan 1999b: 92; cf. Houweling 1997).
69. S. Woodward (1995: 159–60); Cafruny (2003: 102); cf. Gervasi (1996).
70. Interviews in *Newsweek*, 22 April 1991; *De Volkskrant*, 11 July 1991.
71. S. Woodward (1995: 196); Gowan (1999b: 94); Carrington interview in Marijnissen and Glastra van Loon (2000: 105). The Muslim population of Bosnia was 43 per cent of the total.
72. Wiebes (2002: 166–7, 185, 189, 205–6). Even the Argentinian president of Lebanese origin, Menem, clandestinely supplied arms.
73. Ibid.: 69–70, 169, 174, 215.
74. Cf. van der Pijl (1984).
75. Duménil and Lévy (2004); *Financial Times*, 22 November 1995 and 19 February 1999.
76. Holbrooke (1995: 42).
77. Ferguson (1996: 63). The strategic backgrounds are analysed in Achcar (1998).
78. Achcar (1998: 104).
79. A. Cowell in *The New York Times*, syndicated in *De Volkskrant*, 2 August 1995.
80. All quotes from the *The New York Times*, 8 March 1992.
81. See the discussion on the DPG in Golub (2004: 23–4).
82. Achcar (1998: 112).
83. Quoted in *Business Week*, 23 January 1995.
84. *Context Newsletter*, 37, January–February 2000, p. 4; *De Volkskrant*, 5 July 1997.
85. Gowan (1999b: 96).
86. N. Both in *De Volkskrant*, 6 September 1995; cf. interview with the British commander of the UN mission, Sir Michael Rose, in Marijnissen and Glastra van Loon (2000: 109).

87. Chossudovsky (1996: 32, 35n.).
88. *Financial Times*, 6 November 1995.
89. *De Volkskrant*, 11 November 1995.
90. *Financial Times*, 28 November 1994.
91. *NRC-Handelsblad*, 7 January 1994. On Bentsen, see *Newsweek*, 21 December 1992.
92. *Financial Times*, 2/3 December 1995.
93. T. Friedman in *De Volkskrant*, 5 December 1996.
94. *International Herald Tribune*, 23 December 1992; *Newsweek*, 10 February 1997.
95. Todd (2004: 66). The conflation of modern and pre-modern structures can give a particularly vicious twist to civil strife, as shown in the case of Lebanon by Michael Johnson (2001).
96. Gowan (1999b: 100); *The Guardian*, 15 February 2001.
97. Ramsay (2002: 64–86); Macintyre (2000); *Financial Times*, 8 August 1994; 3–4 May 1997; 24 March 1998 and 15/16 May 1999.
98. C. Semmler in *Le Monde Diplomatique*, September 1998, pp. 4–5; cf. van der Wurff (1993).
99. R. Kurz and E. Lohoff in *Le Monde Diplomatique*, March 1999, p. 15; R. Rossanda in *Le Monde Diplomatique*, December 1998, p. 6.
100. According to a reconstruction in *Die Zeit* (reported in *De Volkskrant*, May 15 1999), Schröder, the newly elected (but not yet sworn in) chancellor and his foreign secretary Joschka Fischer were on their way to confer with outgoing chancellor Kohl, when a call from Washington asked them whether they would agree to an attack on Yugoslavia without a UN mandate, in an obvious test of the new government. They got a quarter of an hour to reply. Fischer's only complaint, apparently, was that he was sorry that this had to happen just when they were in the government. See also Lafontaine (1999: 242–5); M. D'Alema in *International Herald Tribune*, 22 January 1999.
101. P.M. de la Gorce in *Le Monde Diplomatique*, January 1996, p. 7.
102. J. Rubin in *Financial Times*, 30 September/1 October 2000; M. Klare in *Le Monde Diplomatique*, May 1999, pp. 8–9. The KLA leadership conceded afterwards that it had played the card of provoking NATO intervention, but this of course only worked with an eager partner on the other side (BBC TV, 12 March 2000; Gowan 1999b: 101).
103. cf. Marijnissen and Glastra van Loon (2000: 172).
104. J. Rubin in *Financial Times*, 7/8 October 2000.
105. Marijnissen and Glastra van Loon (2000: 126–7); Ali (1999: 65).
106. Kosovo Agreement (1999).
107. E. Rouleau in *Le Monde Diplomatique*, December 1999, p. 7.
108. *Financial Times*, 21 April 1999.
109. Quoted in Talbot (1999: 33).
110. J. Rubin in *Financial Times*, 30 September/1 October, 2000. On Italian rivalry with the US and Germany in the Balkans, see Circolo PRC (2002: 25).
111. www.parlement.nl, 22 March 2000; emphasis added.
112. *Washington Post*, 20 September 1999.
113. *Financial Times*, 5/6 June 1999; *De Volkskrant*, 18 October 1999.
114. According to the *Washington Post* (20 September 1999), Joschka Fischer was particularly cavalier in this regard, and at one point during a telephone conversation with Madeleine Albright, on estimated casualties of a planned air raid, caused confusion on the other end when he shouted out of anger over a last-minute goal scored by Manchester United against Bayern München, a match which he was watching on TV while discussing bombing targets and expected casualty figures in Yugoslavia.
115. *Het Parool*, 8 April and 7 June 2000; French Foreign Minister Védrine on BBC TV, 12 March 2000.
116. Walker denied this but Holbrooke confirmed it afterwards (BBC TV, 12 March 2000). On the instrumentalisation of the OSCE verification mission by the US, cf. Cafruny (2003: 106).

117. De Wijk interview in Marijnissen and Glastra van Loon (2000: 101); *De Volkskrant*, 29 May 1999; *Financial Times*, 8 June 2000.
118. *Financial Times*, 14 June 1999.
119. *Financial Times*, 14 December 1999.
120. *Le Monde*, 17 May 2003.
121. Ali (1999: 66). The European Commission proposed a 5 per cent increase in EU spending, partly on account of Balkan reconstruction (*Financial Times*, 11 May 2000).
122. Gowan (1999b: 102).
123. Marijnissen and Glastra van Loon (2000: 95).
124. In the 1970s, Soviet and German lawyers were already wrangling about the potential implications of the projected canal, with the Germans fearing Soviet activity on Europe's waterways and a consolidation of Soviet control over the Danube states (*Frankfurter Allgemeine Zeitung*, 30 June 1977).
125. *Financial Times*, 8 December 1999.
126. *Financial Times*, 26 April 1996.
127. Indeed 'the danger in this is that Russia ... could re-establish a stronghold in the Balkans. This could limit Bulgarian independence and cause nervousness among several NATO countries, not least Turkey.' Turkey might be more disposed to developing the alternative to the Danube link to Central Europe, i.e., the Adriatic, and the overland route through Croatia. Actually the conquest of the Krajina region in 1995 restored the oil pipeline that runs from the Croatian coast to Hungary, which the Croatians and the Hungarian oil company, MOL, want to develop to control the Central European energy markets at the expense of the Russians (*Financial Times*, 7 December 1995).
128. *Financial Times*, 10/11 April 1999.
129. E. Rouleau in *Le Monde Diplomatique*, December 1999, p. 7; *De Volkskrant*, 13 July 1998.
130. *Financial Times*, 12 October 1999 and 11 July 2000. The failure to really impose NATO's will and, hence, a neoliberal recipe on Kosovo has left the province and its people in the balance. As to Serbia itself, the dispossession of the state class was achieved in 2003 when its government—which has become mired in perpetual crisis after it handed over Milosevic to the Yugoslavia tribunal in The Hague to release blocked aid money— announced the privatisation of cigarette plants to Philip Morris and BAT; and Beopetrol, the second largest oil retailer, to Lukoil of Russia.
131. *Financial Times*, 9 October 2000.
132. Gowan (1999a: 301).
133. *Financial Times*, 6 May 1999; Reuters dispatch on www.russiatoday.com, 4 May 1999; cf. Amineh 1999b.
134. *De Volkskrant*, 24 March 1999.
135. Cf. J. Kobaladze in Marijnissen and Glastra van Loon (2000: 140). In 1997, I. Rybkin, secretary of the Russian security council, declared that in case of a conventional attack on Russia, the country should be ready to respond with nuclear missiles (quoted in *Financial Times*, 12 February 1997).
136. Ali (1999: 66); Blackburn (1999: 123); cf. Lafontaine (1999).
137. *Financial Times*, 16 April 1999.
138. *Financial Times*, 7 April 1999.
139. *Financial Times*, 7 January 1997.
140. Thus in the takeover of Mannesmann by Vodafone, Goldman Sachs used the knowledge, which it had obtained when advising Mannesmann in taking over the mobile phone company, Orange, against its former client, but a lawsuit against Goldman Sachs failed (*Financial Times*, 1 January 2000; *International Herald Tribune*, 5/6 February 2000).
141. Walpen (2004: 237).
142. *Financial Times*, 15/16 July 2000. In the ranking of European merger and acquisition advisory activity for 1999, Goldman Sachs headed the list, followed by Morgan Stanley, Merrill Lynch and J.P. Morgan (*Financial Times*, 8 March 2000).

143. Houben (2004: 29–31).
144. Gowan (1999b: 96).
145. Houben (2004: 33–5).
146. Granou (1977).
147. Fennema (1982: 208–9); cf. Carroll and Fennema (2002) and Gill (1994).
148. Mattera (1992). On methodological issues, cf. Fennema (1982: 96–7).
149. Fennema (1982: 112).
150. Hence, in 1970 the most central nodes in the transnational network (but owing their centrality to different regional vectors) were US banks and corporations, Dutch and Anglo-Dutch transnational corporations and Deutsche Bank. In 1976, Swiss Bank Corporation (today merged into UBS) entered this core; in 1992 (again amidst mainly US and Anglo-Dutch banks and corporations), CS Holding is among the most densely interlocked (cf. van der Pijl 1998: 61, Table 2.6)
151. Cf. analysis in Holman and van der Pijl (2003); for a list of interlocks of ERT members in 1999, cf. van Apeldoorn (2002: 108–9, Table 3.4).
152. van Apeldoorn (2002: 140, 174).
153. Richardson (2000: 6, emphasis added); cf. Holman and van der Pijl (2003: 80–1).
154. Palan (2003); see also Cerny (1994) and Graz (2003).
155. Houben (2004); van Apeldoorn (2002: 158–89).
156. The reference of course is to Hardt and Negri (2000), Robinson (2004) and comparable approaches prevalent in the anti-globalisation movement.
157. *Corporate Europe Observatory*, 3 October 2001.
158. Houben (2004: 14–5).
159. Quoted in ibid.: 20.
160. Quoted in ibid.: 16, cf. 19.
161. The European Commission looks forward to a growth of pension funds assets from 2 to 3 trillion euros, to which could be added a further 3–5 trillion by 2005 if European pension funds were to achieve the level of assets proportional to those of Dutch pension funds. This would compare to US pension assets, already available for private investment, of $6.9 trillion in 1999 (Houben 2004: 53–4, cf. 48, Table 4).
162. Ibid.: 36–7.
163. The quest for a 'European' alternative to empire is not a matter of benevolence. The revolt in the periphery as much as the anti-capitalist, alternative globalisation movement are forcing the hand of European states in much the same way as in the 1970s, when they were compelled to lend verbal and tactical support to the NIEO proposals. At the Fourth World Social Forum in Bombay in January 2004, a junior minister of the right-wing government in Paris declared that France, with one in four workers employed in export-related activities, aspired to 'a globalisation that is humane and regulated' (*Le Monde*, 17 January 2004).
164. On rivalries in involved in setting global standards, see Graz (2002).
165. François Heisbourg in *International Herald Tribune*, 27 December 2003.
166. Robert Cooper in *The Guardian*, 23 October 2003.
167. Ibid. (emphasis added).
168. Lerouge (2004: 81).
169. EADS, BAe Systems, Rolls-Royce, Thales (formerly Thompson), Snecma, Finmeccanica (Houben 2004: 40).
170. Todd (2004: 106). On Galileo, see ibid.: 239.
171. Boyer (2001: 35, 42); Todd (2004: 248, 250); see also Albert (1992) and Hampden-Turner and Trompenaars (1995).
172. On property rights, see May (2000, 2004) and Braithwaite and Drahos (2000), who emphasise that the West, the US first of all, is largely in control of the rules of global regulation.

9 The Rise of China as the New Contender

CHINA'S REINTEGRATION INTO THE CAPITALIST WORLD ECONOMY

The rise of China as the new contender state and its current 'economic miracle' are at the centre of international attention today; in different ways this is also inevitably activating the faultlines running through the global political economy. Currently boasting the largest proletariat in the world working at the lowest wages, capital accumulation in China profits from ruthless privatisation, transferring state assets by the block into the sphere of private enrichment. Wages are as low as 10 cents per hour, with no independent trade unions allowed. By flooding world markets with goods at an exchange rate estimated at 20 per cent of purchasing power parity, China's ascent has thrown the post-war configuration of Asia into disarray, while exerting downward pressure on wages worldwide.[1] Paradoxically, however, the country's breakneck economic development has also enlarged the manoeuvring space for a range of raw-material supplying states in the South (from Brazil to Angola) in their relations with the West. In this section, I will place the rise of China as the new contender in historical perspective.

China's participation in the Asian commercial economy has a long history. It first peaked in the early fifteenth century when the famous Treasure Fleet under Admiral Zheng He, a Muslim eunuch, sailed in a series of expeditions as far as Arabia and the east coast of Africa. However, the Ming emperors, concerned with maintaining control and defending the inner Asian land frontier against nomad tribes, put an end to China's seaborne exploits.[2]

In the late seventeenth century, the Manchu rulers, who ousted the Mings and remained in power until 1912, entirely closed off the empire to foreigners. An exclusive license for foreign trade was granted to the Hong merchants in Canton, far from Beijing and the tea-growing areas. The British East India Company then devised its strategy of breaking into the empire by smuggling opium in the late eigtheenth century. When the Chinese imperial authorities, concerned over both the loss of silver and the physical and moral degradation among the afflicted population, tried to resist the opium smugglers, Britain declared war to secure access for the drug in 1839. A second Opium War followed in 1857, with France joining in the fight in order not to be excluded from expansion in Asia. This war saw the first stirrings of popular resistance to the miseries inflicted on China by the West. Predators now descended on China from other sides as well. Japan, the first Asian contender following its modernisation in the Meiji Revolution of 1878, humiliated the empire in 1894–95 in a brief war over Korea. The war led to the secession of Korea and the annexation of Taiwan and parts of Manchuria by Japan.[3]

Rivalries among the imperialists intensified as various powers grabbed their own strategic ports and coastal areas in China, anticipating its possible implosion; first came Germany, then Russia, which took hold of Port Arthur. In 1898, anti-Western modernizers at the imperial court staged a palace revolution, but the Manchu empress still prevailed. The court in turn tried to stir up a nationwide movement to expel all foreigners, the 'Boxer' rebellion. After this episode of fruitless resistance, China was again humiliated and turned into what amounted to a collective possession of all the imperialist states. Britain, the hitherto prominent imperialist power in China, at this point enlisted the support of the United States for a policy of collectively guaranteed equal access, the 'Open Door' policy formulated by US strategists.[4] This was a major landmark in the reaffirmation of the English-speaking heartland connection, against contenders encroaching on British tutelage over the Chinese empire.

Rivalries over Northeast Asia also entailed the war between Russia and Japan in 1904–05, which had a profound effect in China. For the first time in modern history, an Asian power defeated a European state, and this served as a signal to Chinese intellectuals that their country too would have to awake from its lethargy. A nationalist revolt against the Manchu emperors led by Sun Yat-sen in 1911–12 did not however produce a stable government. Regional warlords contested his and each other's authority; in 1923, two years before his death, Sun even sought the support of the USSR, aware of the continuing machinations of the Western powers in cahoots with Japan.[5] By now, the Chinese Communist party had begun to get organised in China's port cities. It was fatally encouraged by the Soviet Union to enter into an alliance with the nationalist Kuomintang (KMT), even though the KMT moved to the right under Sun's successor, General Chiang

Kai-shek, allying with the powerful landlord class and pro-Western financial circles. In a series of confrontations in China's main urban centres, the communists were massacred by their allies in the late 1920s, after which Chiang established his government in the new capital, Nanjing.[6]

Still, the elements for a revolution from above that would have turned China into a contender state (at a juncture when comparable states such as Turkey or Brazil were choosing that path) were lacking. Not only was the KMT leadership entirely tributary to the innermost circle of the Chinese financial aristocracy (the Soong and Kong families), but the Chinese bourgeoisie, interested in developing domestic markets and industry and achieving greater autonomy vis-à-vis Japan and the West, also feared the workers and poor peasants more than their own landlord class and its allies. The big proprietors had a disproportionate hold on arable land, 60 per cent of which was held by 10 per cent of the population. Wealthy city-dwellers often continued to receive rents from land they owned in the countryside.[7] In the 1930s, when Japan began to press forward into China, Chiang Kai-shek resisted that advance only within the limits set by the US and Britain. After 1940 the war against the Japanese was given second place to the struggle against the communists. In 1935 Mao Zedong, a long-standing advocate of a peasant-based revolution in China, won the leadership of the party and directed it towards a guerrilla war against the Japanese invaders. The communists had little difficulty wresting the banner of national independence from the Kuomintang, and were able to put their programme of social equity and collectivism into practice in remote provinces, from where they staged their guerrilla war. Between 1937 and 1945, communist party membership increased from 30,000 to 1.2 million.[8] In 1949, the communist armies took Beijing and restored it in its dignity as the historic capital.

The revolution was primarily anti-imperialist and anti-'feudal', that is, directed against the domestic class of large landowners. In 1947 an agrarian reform that confiscated large holdings without indemnity was promulgated in the liberated zones; in the aftermath of the revolutionary takeover, the large industrial monopolies directly associated with the KMT were confiscated, but smaller capitalists were allowed to continue in business. This was the 'national' bourgeoisie meant to work with the communists in building up the Chinese economy. Within the party leadership, Zhou Enlai was the organiser of a strand of opinion supporting the revolution on grounds of national pride, the 'second front'. This tendency would come under repeated attack but finally triumphed in the late 1970s.[9] Nationalisation of industry meanwhile remained limited to around two-thirds of assets. Löwy concludes from this that the revolution in China moved from its '1917' straight to the New Economic Policy, which in Russia had only been introduced to compensate for the ravages of the intervention and civil war.[10] From 1952 to 1976, the year of Mao's death, industrial output grew by

11.2 per cent annually. At various turns, the party under Mao tried to accelerate the development effort by mass mobilisation campaigns, which were characterised by the 'magical' utilisation of Mao's brand of Marxism and were also part of struggles within the leadership. In the Great Leap Forward (1958–61) and the Cultural Revolution (1966–76), significant gains were made but at tremendous cost. Both episodes were instances of the revolution from above; the Cultural Revolution was especially disastrous. 'Rather than in empowering working people ... [it] wore them out with constant campaigns orchestrated from above.' But with unions practically suspended, industrial production stuck to a 10 per cent level of growth.[11] The countryside, on the other hand, fared less well. Accumulation in industry had been realised by creating adverse terms of trade for farm products, and the farming population suffered from the authoritarianism of the commune system. Only by vastly increasing the agricultural workforce could output be doubled over the 1952–76 period. Certainly there was a much better food situation than in comparable Third World countries such as India.[12] But by the close of the Mao era there were mounting imbalances in the economy, which required democratisation and real involvement of the population, or a change in orientation.

Internationally, the Chinese revolution only briefly conducted a radical policy. In the early 1950s it had already shifted to a course which made it one of the founding members of the Non-Aligned Movement by mid-decade. In 1958, parallel to the Great Leap, there was a return to a militant foreign policy that, as we saw, led to tensions with the USSR, which was then on the path of normalisation with the West. Washington imposed an embargo on China and encouraged the KMT survivors, who had sought refuge in Taiwan, to harass and provoke the mainland. Since the US State Department had been purged of its China specialists in the McCarthy backlash over the 'loss' of China and a far-right China lobby held successive governments hostage, it took the Americans a decade longer than others to recognise the fact that the communists in 'Peiping' (the name for Peking/Beijing when Nanjing was the capital) were available for active balancing against the USSR.

Shifting Gear to Nationalism and Capitalism

Even in the Cultural Revolution, when Maoism became a synonym for extreme radicalism, Chinese communism never lost the political culture of peasant nationalism. The Cultural Revolution, a mass campaign of Mao's inner circle in alliance with the army, against the party (over which he had lost control after the disasters of the Great Leap), eventually allowed the party to break completely with communism and shift to a nationalist posture.[13] After the death of Mao, two years of struggles in the leadership ensued. In 1978 Deng Xiaoping was able to stage a comeback and it was he who announced the shift to 'market socialism'. 'China began, in short, to experiment with the second strategy for breaking out of its backwardness', that of straight imitation of the Western model.[14] This was pursued through a resumption of the revolution from above, keeping the Hobbesian state in place. To the people emerging from the ravages and madness of the Cultural Revolution, the promises of material abundance and free initiative were certainly welcome. But there was little otherwise to compensate for the moral degradations and excesses of Maoism's final years, certainly no restoration of autonomy and democracy. As Martin Hart-Landsberg and Paul Burkett write, 'It was the party's decision to marketize the Chinese economy. There were no mass movements seeking to solve China's many economic and social problems by strengthening market forces.'[15]

The reforms began in 1979 as an experiment in selected urban areas. They were accompanied by massive swings in emphasis, from an initial campaign to prioritise the goal of increased steel production, to a swing back to agriculture and light industry first, and so on. Through these shock-like accelerations, a labour market emerged. Managers were encouraged to hire workers on contract instead of permanently; a policy extended to the state sector in 1983. Simultaneously, the private sector was allowed to branch out, its workforce growing from a quarter million at the outset of the reform phase to 3.4 million in 1984.[16] In 1979 Deng, using a term reminiscent of the most painful of humiliations suffered by imperial China, announced his 'Open Door' policy inaugurating four special economic zones in the southern provinces of Guangdong and Fujian. The catch-up logic of the contender state was brought out in his use of the term 'schools' for the expected foreign investments: schools for labour discipline, technology, etc. However, the appreciative opinion held by many that the Chinese communists have been able to avoid the fate of the Soviet Union in the transition tends to overlook the fact that the main difference resides in the complete absence of democracy. In 1982 the right to strike was removed from the constitution, to facilitate the recruitment and exploitation of labour for the industrialisation drive in the coastal zones.[17] The Chinese state class controls the process of economic privatisation in such a way that all transfers of power proceed without mass involvement; whether this will turn out to lead to oligarchic privatisation also by creating political parties from above remains to be seen.

In hindsight, Chinese state socialism has served to prepare the country for a role as one more Asian export economy oriented towards Western markets, especially the US. The shift in gear to an 'Open Door' policy Chinese-style marks the moment when China entered this situation as a competitor. At this point, it changed from being a rival (with the USSR) in guiding the world socialist revolution to a rival of Japan, hitherto the favourite Asian vassal of the US in the confrontation with the two state socialist world powers. All signs, then, were of a 'return to great power politics and rivalry'.[18] More fundamentally, China was emerging as a straightforward contender, willing to confront the West if need be. Unlike Europe, Asia has never been allowed by the US to develop as an integral bloc capable of absorbing redistributive pressures peacefully, and this makes the rise of China such a potentially destabilising event. As Benedict Anderson has argued, the economic growth miracles on the East Asian rim were predicated on three geopolitical and geo-economic conditions. First, the hot wars fought in Korea and Indo-China and the 1965–66 massacres in Indonesia triggered a vast flow of US funds to the region, e.g., by footing South Korea's defence bill or maintaining military bases in the Philippines. This was continued in the final phase of the cold war, when China sided with the anti-Soviet alliance; at the time this did not yet prejudice US support for the others. Second, the Asian 'miracles' profited from Japan's rapid economic rise from the 1960s, which benefited countries such as Thailand through foreign investment. The third condition, however, was the Chinese revolution. As long as Maoist China was developing as an autarchic collectivist economy, its role in the wider Asian economy was negligible. But once it allowed private capital back in, its expansion was bound to disrupt the overall Asian picture entirely.[19] 'In the nineties,' Anderson concludes, 'China was finally in a position to out-compete South-East Asia in manufacturing exports, a situation which seems certain to continue indefinitely.'

> Seen retrospectively, the South-East Asian miracle was thus in part the product of an extraordinary forty-year sequestration from the global market of the greatest power in Asia. The Western attitude towards this process was contradictory and vacillated accordingly.[20]

Certainly the Bush I administration had to join the condemnation of the Tiananmen clampdown on student protesters and impose sanctions; it also did not forget to bolster Japan's military readiness, as we will see later. But the 1991 ban on satellite parts and high-speed computers was lifted in early 1992, and while there were trade frictions, these too remained subdued. Neither did the globalisation drive under Clinton initially affect China. Beijing's decision to peg the Chinese currency to the dollar in 1994 was seen as a move to tie its fate more emphatically to the United States economy at a moment when Washington was gearing up for an attack on Japanese state capitalism (to which I return later). In the mid-1990s there were signs of growing readiness in the West to reciprocate. At the Toronto Bilderberg Conference in May–June 1996, the usual roster of royalty, economic statesmen and blue-chip corporate executives heard former US assistant secretary of defence, C.W. Freeman Jr., deliver a paper entitled 'Let China Awake and Join the World'.[21] Freeman identified China's rise as the linchpin of the displacement of the Atlantic Community by an Asia-Pacific community, and focused on the concomitant need to guide the country into the multilateral regulatory infrastructure of the heartland. China's strategy would be to defuse conflict with its East Asian neighbours and with Russia, while building up a military capacity to reintegrate Taiwan into its jurisdiction—in conflict with the United States, if necessary. In Freeman's view, there was no question that China was succumbing to the centrifugal effects of its crash course towards capitalist modernisation. China 'is well along in its efforts to create the central institutions necessary to manage an increasingly dynamic and integrated national economy', with a growing nationalism among the population to back it up politically. Comparing the Chinese challenge to that of the previous contender state, the USSR, the Freeman paper further notes that

> Beijing China is not an implacable foe of the West or the world order the West has created .... The challenge to the world posed by the rise of China is different. In some ways, it may prove more daunting .... The 21st century will see China resume its traditional pride of place among the world's societies. The question before Europeans and North Americans is not how to prevent what cannot be prevented. It is how to ensure that the rise of China in the new millennium buttresses rather than erodes the international system we have constructed with such difficulty in this century. To that end, we must urgently consider how to speed up China's integration into existing institutions on acceptable terms.[22]

Again I would argue that the contrast with the USSR is mistaken: the anti-Western posture of prior contenders was always a product of the contender experience itself. Its failures and frustrations in one stage guide it towards a more militant, radical confrontation in the next. We may look at France under Richelieu and then Napoleon or at Germany under Bismarck and then under Hitler. In that light, the Russia under Witte and Stolypin, which transforms itself into the USSR after the First World War, is less of a unique experience. And while each contender brings its own special assets and conditions into play and poses its challenge at a given point in world history under circumstances that will always be different, the Chinese challenge to the West *and the response to it* may still be in a benign stage which need not last. The tactical alliance with Beijing was reversed early on by the Bush II administration, and its confrontation strategy appears to have survived the 11 September emergency.

The Transnational Chinese Capitalist Class in the Contender Effort

The formation of a Chinese capitalist class, interlocked with a wider Asian network of ethnic Chinese power holders in the economy and in politics, has become a crucial force in the turn of the mainland to a contender role. Influencing its broad orientation and the speed of privatisation in various ways, the overseas Chinese have become strategic partners of the state class.

As Chalmers Johnson writes, 'China has one major asset not available to most developing nations: the overseas Chinese. This reservoir of talent, capital, and experience is open to a China that stresses nationalism rather than communism.'[23]

The Chinese capitalist class in the Southeast Asian region has roots that go back many centuries. In modern times its role was shaped by relations with Western colonisers and imperialists, for whom Chinese wholesale traders served as middlemen. This has created powerful minorities controlling entire economies. Eighty-one per cent of quoted capital in Thailand is owned by ethnic Chinese, who form 10 per cent of the population; the respective relative percentages in Indonesia are 73:3.5; in Malaysia 61:29; and in the Philippines 50–60:1.8. Along with the Chinese societies of Hong Kong, Taiwan, Macau and Singapore (77 per cent Chinese), these communities have jumped at the opportunities offered by the opening of the mainland Chinese economy to capital. Often, there are particular regional links involved as well, which may structure reintegration: thus Guangdong Chinese went to Malaysia and rural Thailand and rural Indonesia, while Fujian Chinese went to Jakarta, Manila, Singapore, Bangkok and the cities of Indochina. Often, overseas Chinese retain kinship links with communities on the mainland.[24] As David Kowalewski writes, 'Chinese elites, with their transnational connections, are the cutting edge for the outflow of national capital .... Asian [TNCs] are based primarily in Chinese-dominant countries—Hong Kong, Singapore, and Taiwan.'[25] Certainly family-based, owner-managed companies and groups of companies will face all the problems that come with this type of firm, such as limits of expert management, succession crises and problems associated with expansion. But, notes James Mittelman, as Chinese MBAs from the US and other countries return to China, they will bolster the competitive edge of the transnational Chinese capitalist class, raising the level of the challenge to the West.

> While clan and especially linguistic ties continue to reinforce business interests among ethnic Chinese, traditional family linkages are increasingly integrated with professional management practices. Generational divergence within the Chinese networks has challenged the customary, intuitive style of the ageing patriarchs. Modern English-speaking, MBA-toting managers, many of them financial technocrats, reflect the tenets of liberal-economic globalization transmitted by business and law schools not in their ancestral villages but in western countries where they now invest, trade, and borrow.[26]

One problem that complicates the evolution of China as a contender state in this respect is that the actual 'MBA legion' (if they return to China at all) is modest in size. This may inflect the Chinese state configuration towards the pattern persisting in Taiwan; I return to this in the final section of this chapter. But there is no denying that a transnational Chinese business class exists and is organising itself as such. They have formed a common platform in the World Chinese Entrepreneurs Convention (which meets annually)—a Chinese equivalent of the likes of Bilderberg and the Trilateral Commission. In the first year of 'reform' itself, in its August 1979 meeting at Vancouver (the first one outside Asia), prominent figures from the communist Chinese state class joined the overseas Chinese business elite to discuss matters of common concern.[27]

The privatisation of the mainland state class has since developed as a movement of party cadres, who use their party cards to set themselves up as capitalists using 'borrowed' state assets. Investigations by Chinese state institutions and foreign researchers found that in the hands of military, provincial and local bureaucrats, state assets have tended to miraculously melt away, whereas the 'private' sector has continued to grow. By 1995 private capital accounted for 40.4 per cent of non-agricultural employment, 45.1 per cent of retail sales and 47.7 per cent of exports. Under favourable tax rates and declining central state tax income, the state sector (heavy industry conglomerates, banks) is effectively being bled white by this class, applauded from the West as 'reformers' and 'entrepreneurs', but effectively embezzling public property in all kinds of ways. Hong Kong is the key pivot of this process; Li Ka-shing, the Hong Kong magnate (number one in Table 9.1), illustrates how high-level mainland interests were woven into existing relations with the West. Li took over the sprawling conglomerate, Hutchison Whampoa, from its British owners in 1979, while sharing influence with the British Keswick family in Jardine Matheson holdings, the historic British trading firm in Hong Kong. He developed valuable ties with the Deng family as well as with the Thatchers in the UK.[28] But investment into China from the former British crown colony often represents capital from mainland enterprises seeking to evade taxes and other restrictions by 'investing' in Hong Kong and then 'investing' back again, a laundering process called 'round-tripping'.[29] The size of the property passing from state to private hands in these and other ways is such that the key handlers can attract major Western firms as partners. Thus Huang Yantian, president of Guangdong province's GITIC investment corporation, forged links with McDonalds, PPG Industries and Pabst Brewing from the US. In October 1994 Morgan Stanley of the US set up a joint international investment bank with the People's Construction Bank of China (with smaller participations from Singapore and Hong Kong investment companies), etc.[30]

The decision to transform the large public corporations into joint stock companies with state majority ownership has further facilitated the transfer of public property into private hands and given the aspiring bourgeois element grounds to challenge the state's remaining prerogatives. Foreign capital is made part of the transition because of the requirement of a local partner if investments are made in China; this locks transnational corporations into an embrace with the state sector and its privatising offshoots, which are hotbeds of favouritism, corruption and incompetence.[31] It is perhaps a

Table 9.1
Wealthiest Individuals in China, Taiwan, Hong Kong and Other Emerging Asia, 2003, in US$ Billion

China			Taiwan (T) & Hong Kong			Other Emerging Asia		
Name	Sector	Fortune	Name	Sector	Fortune	Name	Sector	Fortune
Ding Lei	Internet	1.1	Li Ka-shing	Various	7.8	Azim Premji	Logistics	5.9 (India)
Rong Zhijian	Various	0.9	W, Th., & R. Kwok	Real estate	6.6	Robert Kuok	Agriculture	3.4 (Malaysia)
Xu Rongmao	Real estate	0.8	Lee Shau Kee	Real estate	3.7	Lee Khun-hee	Electronics	2.8 (South Korea)
			Tsai Wan Lin	Insurance	3.7 (T)	M. & A. Ambani	Various	2.8 (India)
			M. Kadoorie	Various	3.3	Khoo Teck Puat	Banking	2.6 (Singapore)
			Nina Wang	Real estate	2.8	K.M. Birla	Raw material	2.4 (India)
			Patrick Wang	Industry	2.6	L. Mittal	Steel	2.2 (India)
			Y.C. Wang	Plastics	1.9 (T)	Shin Kyuk-ho	Candy	2.2 (South Korea)
			Tsai Wan Tsai	Insurance	1.8 (T)	P.S. Mistry	Various	2 (India)
			Chen Yu-tung	Real estate	1.7	Lim Goh Tong	Games	1.9 (Malaysia)
						Lucio Tan	Tobacco	1.9 (Philippines)
						Ng Teng Fong	Real estate	1.7 (Singapore)
						Kwek Leng Beng	Hotels	1.7 (Singapore)
						Lee Seng Wee	Banks	1.6 (Singapore)
						A. Krishnan	Telecom	1.6 (Malaysia)

Source: Compiled from *Forbes* data, as in *Le Monde*, 10 November 2003 (some names include family).
Note: (T) = Taiwan

sign of things to come that senior Chinese executives have already spoken out for a further reduction of the state role and want the communist party to withdraw from the scandal-ridden, bankrupt banking sector.[32] Table 9.1 shows the still relatively modest status of China's wealthiest, compared to Taiwan and (meanwhile re-incorporated) Hong Kong, and 'Other Emerging Asia' (note the Chinese family names in that column). The Asian Crisis has removed some names from this list, such as Liem Sioe Liong of Indonesia.[33] The development of India, which has so far followed the path of a secondary contender, deserves a longer discussion for which there is no space here; let me just note that liberalisation after 1991 has broadly followed the global trend, with the attendant phenomena of oligarchic enrichment clearly in evidence.[34]

The position of the overseas Chinese in Asia as a mercantile, 'market dominant' ethnic minority all through their history has made them vulnerable to popular discontent, not least when an indigenous bourgeoisie finds the high grounds of the economy already occupied. Mainland China today wields the political clout (in this respect more than it did as a communist state) to offer protection to Chinese minorities abroad. But, in addition, the capitalist transformation has made available a 1 billion-strong population for economic exploitation as labour or customers. This conflation of political and economic motives is what unifies the overseas Chinese capitalist class with the privatising state class into a single social force. We are looking here at a major aspect of what makes the Chinese contender role specific, an aspect that may leave only Japan as a regional target for China's 'nationalism'. I return to this in the last section of this chapter.

Finally, the growth of the ethnic-Chinese capitalist class was always facilitated by the close links between business and politics in the respective countries, which all developed under directive states, as vassals of the West in the cold war. There is nothing specifically Chinese about this; South Korea too has a notable reputation in this respect. Political payments, whether as campaign contributions or plain bribes, are a familiar phenomenon in the countries involved, and there was no reason why one could not, as part of transnationalisation, also shift this flow of funds to politicians in countries other than one's own. The process certainly crossed a crucial threshold when US politicians began to be paid by Asian sponsors, a phenomenon which really took off under Reagan and Bush I. The Chinese entered this game when Clinton began reaching out to them. Various operators of Chinese background reciprocated to the point where their access to the Clinton White House broke into scandal. But then, as former undersecretary of commerce Jeffrey Garten notes, the push into emerging markets like China, India and Brazil 'attracted a lot of foreigners who wanted to play in the new game .... Our firms needed partners, local suppliers, help setting themselves up.' It was from these quarters that shady sponsors of the Clinton re-election campaign emerged, such as former Commerce Department official John Huang and an entire ring of Asian contacts of the Democratic Party, as exposed in a scandal in 1996.[35]

THE ASIAN CRISIS AND THE DISRUPTION OF THE JAPAN-CENTRED ORDER

The Asian crisis of 1997–98 marks the moment in which the rise of the new Chinese economy overturned the cold-war order in Asia. As I will argue in this section, it was this crisis that allowed Western capital to breach the barriers imposed by state-monitored economies of the Japanese type. Of course this does not mean the West therefore 'engineered' the crisis. The twists and turns by which contender states manoeuvre to engage in the catch-up effort send shock-waves through the global political economy which create situations that are unpredictable as such. In each case, the test is not whether a positive theory predicts/explains in detail what happens on the ground, but whether a core structure, like the heartland/contender one developed in this study, can still be developed to meaningfully account for the evolving complex of forces—while at the same time acknowledging the new and the unexpected. Western investors were able to exploit the new openings in the Asian economies because they sensed that the tectonic shifts produced by the rise of China were working in their favour. But just as seismologists who know the location and drift of the faultlines in the earth's crust are not therefore the engineers of earthquakes, investors are hardly in control of the epochal shifts by which capital, from its historical epicentres, continues to advance across the globe.[36]

Japan is the linchpin of the Western position in Asia, the Pacific vassal in the contest with the Soviet bloc and, until the 1970s, China. I have already noted that there has been no integration process in East Asia comparable to that in Europe to guide the uneven development of capital into peaceful channels; it was left to the Japanese state and capitalist classes to organise the wider region themselves. Like all contender states pursuing a capitalist strategy, catch-up industrialisation in post-Second World War Japan operated through finance capital structures (the *keiretsu*, the resurrected form of the pre-war *zaibatsu*), which had the domestic market very much to themselves, thanks to an extensive system of quotas, tariffs and import requirements. The state ensured that industrial activity was spread across the economy but otherwise allowed the leading firms to become the organisers of integral product chains in which every aspect is controlled from the centre. This system, named 'Toyotism' after the car-maker, was transnationalised in the 1970s; the state role, centralised in the Ministry of International Trade and Industry (MITI), strategically identified the tasks for the separate 'flying geese'. Thus Malaysia was targeted for word processors and fax machines, Indonesia for textiles and plastics, and so on. The corporations then organised the actual distribution of productive activity.[37] Japanese capital in this way built up a regional socialisation of labour on a cost base that gave it a competitive edge over the United States. By the 1980s, it had also achieved a technological edge, which US capital sought to tap into to secure its own development through joint ventures and consortia. Kenichi Ohmae at the time called this negotiated market structure (in which Europe was the third partner) 'Triad Power'.[38]

However, the United States was never going to accept such a triangular structure in the longer run. The competitive aspect of its attitude towards Japan was already evident in the 1970s, and the legislative weapons forged to combat OPEC and the NIEO were also deployed against Japanese textiles, consumer electronics and steel exports to the United States. Under the Carter administration, Japan agreed to an 'orderly market agreement' of voluntary export restrictions in 1977. Under Reagan, commercial antagonism became more pronounced. The US pressured Tokyo into opening the Japanese market for computers, auto parts, agricultural products, satellites and beef, not least to protect Reagan's re-election chances in 1984. In fact, as Ohmae noted at the height of the furore over the US trade deficit, the real balance with Japan was almost even, if sales by the 300 largest US multinationals in Japan were set against those of Japanese companies in the US plus Japanese exports. But that of course does not necessarily hold true for each separate congressional district in the US.[39]

Japan still was a loyal ally against the USSR, and Tokyo joined Reagan's new cold war every step on the way.[40] Economic friction never became overt political rivalry. However, the 'Keynesian' expansion by which Reagan sought to achieve recovery, rearmament, and re-election in one go, drove up the dollar and, as we saw, generated a massive surge in imports into the US. Further protectionist measures were taken but a more enduring solution was obviously necessary. In September 1985, Secretary of the Treasury James Baker concluded the Plaza Accord with the other members of the Group of Five (G-5) to arrange a managed equilibrium between their currencies. In three months, the dollar declined in value by 18 per cent against the yen.[41] Washington also obtained agreement that the 'Triad' partners would stimulate their domestic economies to keep the currencies at the equilibrium level. The Japanese government did this by bringing down interest rates—in one year, it lowered interest rates three times. It was this decision, taken in response to US pressure, which drove up the yen and inaugurated a wave of hyper-liquidity that became known as the 'bubble economy', and which lasted until 1991.[42] At the start of the 1980s, the book value of all real estate in Japan taken together was equal to the value of US real estate; at the end of the decade, its value was four times the US equivalent. In 1987, Japanese stocks accounted for 42 per cent of all listed assets in the world, although the Japanese economy represented only 15 per cent of the world economy in real terms—output, employment, etc.[43]

The United States turned into a net debtor country in 1985. Foreign sponsors of the American political economy were needed, and Japanese banks, deregulated by suspension of interest rate ceilings and barriers between deposit banking and security firms, were the first among foreign buyers of US treasury bonds. Japan would continue to meet American deficits in this way, but it of course also gained a weapon to defend itself against US pressure.[44] Meanwhile Japanese capital was pouring into the United States at a rate between $25 billion and $50 billion a year, with landmark takeovers such as that of Columbia Pictures by Sony and of MCA by Matsushita, leading a wave of tariff-hopping investment to maintain market positions in the US. The Japanese ministry of finance reported in May 1987 that of total Japanese FDI, 35 per cent, or $37.4 billion, had been invested in North America (against $21.7 billion in Asia and $20.4 billion in Latin America).[45]

At this point, feeling was widespread that the United States might be forced to cede pride of place to Japan in Asia. Thus Lawrence Krause of the Brookings Institution argued in 1988 that the US should accept the 'shift to Japanese hegemony'. A growing number of Americans were actually working for Japanese paymasters and a study in 1986 showed that from 1980 to 1985, of the 76 former US government officials who went to work for foreign interests, 20 signed up with a Japanese employer.[46] The fact that two-thirds of the more than 400,000 foreign students in the US in 1992 were from Asia further reinforced the idea of a global shift.[47] Paul Kennedy's *The Rise and Fall of the Great Powers*, with its theory of imperial overstretch causing the decline of every great power—i.e., at this point, the US— captured the spirit of the time.[48] The shift from the Atlantic to the Pacific Ocean as the new centre of the world inevitably conjured up a deeper sense of decline of the West, although Treasury Secretary James Baker dismissed the idea that the US would not be the leading power in the emerging Pacific Century as 'ludicrous'.[49] Indeed the notion of the 'Pacific', according to Manuel Castells, reflects 'the psychological and political shock suffered by North America and Europe when confronted with the developmental experiences of Japan first, of the so-called Asian "tigers" next, of the "new industrializing periphery" (for example, Thailand) later, and finally, of China, with India looming on the horizon.' Yet,

> In itself, the phenomenon should not be threatening to the West, since it actually represents the access of billions of people to a higher standard of living, and therefore, the creation of new, very large markets, on which Western companies could also thrive. This is why a growing number of economists and politicians insist on the dismantlement of Asian protectionism as the sine qua non condition for this new Asian prosperity to be shared with a parallel expansion of trade and investment in the world at large.[50]

This became the guiding doctrine in the decade to come. In the late 1980s, the United States was in the grips of a veritable paranoia as far as

Japan's economic rise was concerned, and forces seeking to raise the stakes in economic competition had a ready audience.[51] In the meantime a massive financial crisis was brewing in Japan, which would make the idea of overtaking the United States a pipe dream. The high yen led to an increase in imports, producing windfall profits for Japanese trading companies to the tune of $350 billion between 1985 and 1988, which flowed to the banks; but Japan's large corporations were equally cash-rich, leaving the banks with unused liquidity which then began to pour into real estate. Three-quarters of all lending for real estate purchases between 1985 and 1989 ($623 billion in all) was provided by banks.[52] All along, interest rates were kept low and only in May 1989 did the Bank of Japan raise the interest rate (in several steps) from 2.5 per cent to 5.25 per cent in March 1990. The Tokyo stock market was at that point in free fall, and although the Gulf War worked as a stabilising factor, the total loss in land and stock values as a result of the interest rate hikes amounted to $8 trillion.[53]

Clinton won the election just when the crisis in Japan exploded, and the new president, committed to a neoliberal globalisation strategy, now felt that he could raise the stakes and force a removal of protectionist structures. The cold war had certainly ended, but not the underlying rivalries, past and present, along the heartland/contender state divide. The Department of Commerce under the incoming secretary, Ron Brown, advocated a vigorous 'commercial diplomacy'; his deputy characterised relations with former allies as 'economic war'. As former undersecretary Garten sums it up, 'The culture was electric: we set up an economic "war room" and built a "trading floor" that tracked the world's largest commercial projects.'[54] There was even a 'Team B' (a reference to the group that created the Soviet threat panic in the Carter days), formed by protectionist and anti-Japanese Democrats. It was led by Senator Dick Gephardt, and included company representatives and also Dutch journalist Karel van Wolferen. Van Wolferen was one of the 'Gang of Four' who produced works stressing the supposed anomaly of Japanese state-led development.[55] Finally, in 1994 Clinton himself (at the juncture in which he presided over the offensive turn that would take NATO deeper into Eastern Europe and the Balkans) openly went on the attack against Japan. Specifically targeted were the MITI and the Ministry of Finance. These 'permanent government agencies,' Clinton claimed, had created an economy with 'low unemployment and high savings rates, big exports and no imports—and they want to keep it that way.' Of course he did not emphasise that this had been US policy for Japan in the first place. Instead the president now urged the country's state class to stop impeding the emergence of 'a fully modern state with fair and open trade'.[56]

The end of a particular phase of a contender challenge is usually accompanied by a collapse of the specific political structure that guided it. When Japan was discarded as a vassal state with the end of the cold war, the

Liberal Democratic Party (LDP), another 'state disguised as a party' by which the state class had effectively run a one-party political system, went down with it. Until that time (1993), politics in Japan had evolved as factional struggles under the LDP umbrella; now it 'simply collapsed of its own corruption and redundancy.'[57] A straight neoliberal turn, however, is incompatible with the contender legacy of Japanese society and its economy. The Hosokawa government, which favoured an increased role of 'markets', was out of office within three months. It was at this point that the Clinton offensive switched to high gear. But when Washington stepped up pressure in early 1994 on Tokyo to liberalise imports now that a falling dollar gave the US a competitive edge, the Japanese Ministry of Finance threatened in an oblique way that it might begin to divest itself of US treasury bonds. This unprecedented gesture of defiance showed that the Japanese ruling class was not going to capitulate.[58]

Scattering the Flying Geese

The emergence of China in the global political economy as the new 'world factory' is the deeper cause of what became known as the 'Asian Crisis' of 1997–98. This is not a simple mechanism. The neoliberal globalisation drive entailing hedge fund exploitation of 'emerging markets'; the targeting of Japan by the Clinton administration; the Japanese position within the Asian economies and its history of rivalry with China; as well as the position of the overseas Chinese in the 'flying geese' economies organised by Japan and geared to exports to the US, must all be entered into the equation to understand how the rise of China as the new contender and the financial crisis that spread across East Asia as far as Indonesia are interconnected. But an important bottom line is the tacit deal struck between the United States and China to operate a transnational machinery that links American over-consumption to Chinese over-exploitation, a deal that includes the undervaluation of the Chinese currency, pegged to the dollar. This has the perverse effect of a downward trend in overall world consumption and production, because at the consuming end only the United States can sustain demand by using its structural advantages as the organiser of the world economy and provider of its reserve currency; while at the producing end, the worldwide downward pressure on wages and working conditions due to cheap Chinese exports (low wage costs plus an undervalued currency) depresses demand and production everywhere else.[59] This accounts for the overproduction/underconsumption aspect of the Asian crisis that was exposed by the currency collapses which resulted from short-term financial flows.

The absence of institutionalised regional integration in East Asia and the specific ethnic heterogeneity of the ruling classes within the separate states lend a particular fragility to the regional economic structure that crumbled in the crisis. The 'flying geese' arrangement was never a process of integral replication of the Japanese state-led economic development pattern—unlike the extended reproduction of state socialism, for instance, the different Asian societies and their conception of authority and the state role are incomparably more divergent.[60] Yet in all cases we are looking at state classes controlling their economies to varying degrees through their political power.[61] The Kuomintang in Taiwan controls a vast financial and commercial empire; Mahathir Mohamad's ruling party in Malaysia has links to a large network of businesses; the Suharto children were on the boards of many companies; and the People's Liberation Army of China ran a host of large corporations. However, 'as Asia's middle class becomes larger and more affluent, it will increasingly demand respect from its masters, more say in policy and more transparency in government's relations with business.'[62] Rising behind the middle class, of course, are the masses of the populations in these countries, which also demand a fairer share.

The state classes in each separate Asian country were therefore man-oeuvring within a narrow space set by domestic and international constraints which differed in each case. Rather than relying solely on US military protection and, economically, on the 'Toyotist' supply architecture centred on Japan, they tried to avoid dependence and instead developed patterns of industrialisation 'linked both backward to Japanese innovation and forward to American markets'.[63] Their attitude to Japan remains mortgaged by the wartime experience, the unwillingness to allow a yen bloc to develop, and by the fact that the economies of the countries joining the flying geese later (such as Thailand, the Philippines and Indonesia) are dominated economically by a Chinese minority. Hence the 'national' element in state capitalism is compromised and, to the degree that a Chinese element can direct the orientation of the state, it will always look with one eye to mainland China.[64]

After the Plaza Accord, Japanese corporations used the strong yen to invest abroad, primarily, as we saw, in the US. After 1987, South Korea and Taiwan joined in; their investments flowed to the ASEAN countries and, still at some distance, China. Korea and Taiwan until that time accounted for the largest share of Japanese manufacturing FDI in Asia, but now they themselves became major investors as well.[65] As Mitchell Bernard and John Ravenhill write, 'the integration of Malaysia, Thailand, and parts of coastal China with northeast Asian production has been one of the most marked changes in the spatial organization of the East Asian political economy since the Plaza Agreement.' Competition shifted from a pattern of rival national economies to transnational processes in which local production is made part of wider networks controlled by rival centres.[66] As part of this inner-Asian rivalry, and to retain a degree of independence, the Southeast Asian economies pegged their currencies to the low dollar, thus gaining an advantage in export markets over Japan, South Korea and Taiwan. Trade between these three and the US continued to grow, but at a slower rate because their currencies appreciated considerably. This again motivated their exporters to switch production to Southeast Asia, where wages, e.g., in textiles, were one-third of the Northeast Asian levels (which in turn were one-third of the US) in 1990.[67]

The Southeast Asian economies were thus growing at record rates, with their exchange rates securely tied to the currency of their most important foreign market. However, unlike Northeast Asia, their export-oriented industrialisation was not based on prior import-substitution experience but 'grafted on economies whose small manufacturing sectors are notable for their histories of rent seeking and inefficiency'.[68] This was a corrupt environment, which was now targeted by short-term speculative funds from abroad seeking quick profits. In the enrichment frenzy that caught fire in the Clinton years, hedge funds were scouring 'emerging markets', profiting from the pressures applied to Asian governments, Russia and others to liberalise, privatise, set up stock markets, make currencies convertible and remove capital controls. The most notorious hedge fund, Long-Term Capital Management (LTCM), was established in 1994 and run by a former senior official of the Federal Reserve Board along with two Nobel Prize winning economists; it went bankrupt in 1998. Although LTCM had its capital base in an offshore location for tax reasons, former colleagues at the Federal Reserve bailed out the operation at the cost of $3.6 billion of taxpayers' money—'as good an example of pure "crony capitalism",' comments Chalmers Johnson, 'as any ever attributed to the high-growth economies of East Asia.'[69]

Capital inflows into the Southeast Asian countries were encouraged by the liberalisation of bank lending in the early 1980s (first in Malaysia, last in Thailand), stable (i.e., dollar-pegged) currencies and high interest rates. In late 1996 Japan decided to liberalise its financial markets too; a 'Big Bang' that brought a wave of Western investment bankers to Tokyo and led those who had offices there already to upgrade their operations.[70] All the hype about the Pacific Century seemed after all to be confirmed, in spite of the recent crisis of the Tokyo stock market. Indonesia was estimated to be the world's largest importer of private capital in 1996 and Malaysia was fourth. However, money was no longer being invested in the export industries (which were stagnating) but being diverted into the property sector, in a repeat operation of the Japanese bubble a decade earlier. Real estate loans accounted for an estimated 25–40 per cent of bank lending in Thailand, Malaysia and the Philippines in 1998, in large part funded by short-term credit.[71]

In the summer of 1997, Western fund managers became distrustful of the levels of debt of some of the companies they had invested in, and began to withdraw capital. The result was the mass flight out of the fragile Southeast Asian economies and South Korea that has gone down in history as the Asian Crisis. Thailand led the way with a net private capital outflow of

10.9 per cent of GDP in 1997, compared to an almost equal inflow the year before; followed by the Philippines, which saw net private capital flows come to a standstill in 1997 compared to a 9.8 per cent (of GDP) inflow the year before.[72] Short-term capital debt (debts which have to be paid back within two years) rose to unsustainable levels in South Korea ($74.3 billion compared to $29.1 billion longer-term and unallocated), Thailand ($50.2:$19.2 billion) and Indonesia ($38.2:$21.5 billion). As the Asian states resorted to draconic devaluations (South Korea 48.1 per cent against the dollar between July 1997 and February 1998; Thailand 43.2 per cent; and Indonesia 73.5 per cent) and stock market values collapsed, there was no way in which these debts could be redeemed.[73] In financial terms, the crash of 1997–98 was triggered by 'the swelling debt-to-equity ratios of the [Newly Industrialising Countries], which by 1997 far exceeded the ratios of corporate debt to gross domestic product in the developed countries.'[74] The spread across creditors, mostly non-bank private lenders (investment funds, etc.), for 1998 is given in Table 9.2.[75] Japanese investors were exposed to the greatest extent, but the category 'other' (e.g., in the case of South Korea) highlights the broad international basis of the Gold Rush.

Table 9.2
Private Sector Debt Exposure in Asia to Main Creditor Countries, 1998, US$ Billion

	Japan	US	France	Germany	UK	Other	Total Private	(Grand Total*)
S. Korea	23.7	10.0	10.1	10.8	6.1	42.8	103.4	(125)
Thailand	37.7	4.0	5.1	7.6	2.8	12.2	69.4	(94.5)
Indonesia	23.2	4.6	4.8	5.6	4.3	16.3	58.7	(114.5)
Malaysia	10.5	2.4	2.9	5.7	2.0	5.3	28.8	(47.7)

Source: *Financial Times*, 2 May 1997 and 30 January 1998.
Note: *Total private/public debt in 1996.

Yet financial flows are only a surface phenomenon, the most volatile element of a larger set of forces. The underlying movement of production away from the Japanese-centred Asian economies to China and the over-production crisis due to the deflationary effect of China's low-wage export strategy must be considered the more fundamental causes of the Asian crisis. In 1992 US trade with China already surpassed Japan's (in 1985, on the other hand, US–China trade was still less than half that of China with Japan). This established the China-US axis, although Chinese exports to Japan were still equal to those to the US through the 1990s. But South Korea and Taiwan had also become dependent on the North American market, which was twice the size of their exports to Japan in 1993. Chinese manufacturing production grew between 1980 and 1992 at an average annual rate of about 11 per cent, only slightly behind South Korea.[76] When Vietnam, Myanmar, Laos and Cambodia joined ASEAN in the early 1990s, a range of further low-wage export locations came on stream. Who would absorb all the output of these economies?

China solved this problem for itself when it effectively devalued the (non-convertible) yuan by unifying several managed exchange rates at the low swap market rate of 8.7 to the dollar in January 1994, after an earlier devaluation in 1990. The 1994 (dollar-pegged) exchange rate undercut its Southeast Asian rival manufacturers in export markets. But they received a further blow two years later when the Clinton administration, fearful that Japan might indeed begin to divest itself of US bonds and withdraw capital (as they had threatened), negotiated a 'reverse Plaza Accord'. This time it was the yen that was brought down, throwing the Asian exporters—both North and Southeast—into a crisis, as Japanese exports now became much cheaper and dollar-pegged Asian currencies drifted upwards with the US dollar. Export growth in South Korea, Thailand, Indonesia, Malaysia and the Philippines fell from 30 per cent a year in early 1995 to zero by mid-1996.[77] Thus the rise of China exploded 'the Japan-led regional-national production order, financed by export-oriented foreign direct investment in the "tigers",' concludes Anastasia Nesvetailova, because it 'was no longer balanced by the financial sphere determined by an American-dominated dollar-bloc regime linked to a "yen-appreciating bubble".'[78]

But why was South Korea, alone among the Northeast Asian economies, implicated in the crisis the way it was? The answer is that Korea witnessed a powerful workers' movement fighting for democracy and better wages and working conditions. Real wages in manufacturing in the East Asia/Pacific region almost tripled between 1970 and 1996, and South Korea was among the countries where the gains made by the workers were greatest—a moment of reckoning for one of the most repressive vassal regimes sustained by the United States in the cold war.[79] In addition, there was the growth of a domestic middle class. South Korea also bore the brunt of the overproduction aspect of the crisis. As the editors of *Monthly Review* noted at the time, prices of computer memory chips (South Korea's main export item) collapsed entirely, while markets for cars, petrochemicals, shipbuilding and steel were glutted. Hence the markets on which service on short-term obligations was to be earned were subject to severe competition, which eventually led to the crisis becoming manifest.[80] Here too, a directive state, in this case developing as a vassal of the West, reaches the end of its trajectory. The South Korean state class in the later part of the 1980s relaxed state authoritarianism to deal with the popular movement which previous dictatorships had failed to contain; the revolt of the city of Kwangju in 1980 and the massacre among its inhabitants was the last stand of the South Korean state and its American supervisors. However, as the state class mutates into a political class, it also fractures, becoming dependent on elections. The need to form coalitions with diverse social forces then turns its closeness to business from a positive direction towards being bribed and captured, including by foreign operators.[81]

THE ASIA-PACIFIC GEOPOLITICAL TRIANGLE—THE US, JAPAN AND CHINA

All the alliances and commitments built up by the United States in Asia since the Second World War have been essentially tactical and short-term. In the absence of an integration process, like the one pursued in Western Europe under Washington's protection, there was no common East Asian position to block the playing-off of separate states against each other. Hence the West can continue to conduct a policy of active balancing; and, as I will outline in this concluding section, the US occupies a position of pre-eminence here.

For Washington, the end of the cold war with the USSR heralded the beginning of economic warfare against the former Asian vassals, whose exemption from neoliberal market discipline had expired. The handling of the Asian crisis bears out this thrust, although, as indicated, the actual crisis was the result of erratic movements of speculative finance across a plane destabilised by shifts in the distribution of productive activity. The Asian crisis was followed by renewed capital inflows, no longer speculative money of course, but direct investment to cherry-pick key productive assets at bargain-basement prices. Between January 1998 and February 1999, South Korea saw an influx of FDI of $21.6 billion, divided over 91 deals; Thailand 75 deals worth $10.2 billion; and the Philippines $3.7 billion over 22 deals.[82] Yet the expected bonanza did not materialise further due to underlying overproduction problems, the indebtedness of companies and uncertainties about long-term chances for Asian economies other than China. US financial institutions in particular were keen on entering the closed Japanese bank and insurance sector, but Japan on the whole remains inhospitable to foreign investment (2 per cent of GDP in 2005, compared to 22 per cent for the US).[83]

China continues to be the production location of choice. Unlike the Northeast Asian contenders such as Japan and South Korea, who closed off their economies to foreign investment during their growth spurt, China has opened its doors (with the aforementioned restriction of a mandatory local partner). This relative openness has allowed transnational capital to play a major role in the reorganisation of the Asian economy around China, but has in turn made the country completely dependent on foreign markets and capital to sustain its pace of development.[84] Of the $50 billion-plus annual inflow of foreign direct investment into Asian economies in the years following the crisis, half was destined for China. When China overtook the United States as the top destination of FDI in 2002, $53 billion flowed into the mainland economy alone. In 1990 the ASEAN countries, South Korea and Taiwan still attracted four times the direct investment flowing into China; in 2002 this had been completely reversed.[85] Table 9.3 gives the trend and the sources.

Table 9.3
Foreign Direct Investment in China, 1979–2002 (US$ billion)

	1979–93 Annual Average	1992–97 Annual Average	2002
Hong Kong	9.4	20.7	20.9
United States	4.9	2.9	7.3
Taiwan	1.2	3.3	5.7
Japan	0.6	3.2	4.5
Singapore	0.3	1.9	2.6

Sources: (1979–93) Chinese Ministry of Foreign Trade and Economic Co-operation, in *Financial Times*, 31 August 1994; (1992–97) calculated from Zhou and Lall (2005: 61, Table 4) (realised investment); (2002) *China Monthly Statistics* ('Amount Contracted') in Kim (2004: 175, Table 3).

Two-thirds of FDI inflows into China are in manufacturing, with an upward trend of high-value added sectors such as semiconductors. I have already mentioned that a large slice of the investment into and from Hong Kong is 'round-tripping' by operators from the mainland and tax haven routing; according to one estimate, the Hong Kong figure in Table 9.3 should be discounted by 40 per cent to skim off this moving-around of funds from actual FDI.[86] Along with the overseas Chinese and Taiwan, Hong Kong investment and US contract production (not through investment) typically seeks to engage in low-wage manufacturing for export; Japanese capital goes to intermediate goods production for export to Japan; whereas US and European investment is typically in firms that are expected to cater to the Chinese market. Estimates of the share of foreign firms in China's exports range from one-quarter to half.[87] China is thus now part of the regional 'flying geese' formation—not as the organiser, as Japanese capital was earlier, but as a big goose somewhere in the middle, struggling to move up in the flight. The growing trade deficit with Singapore, South Korea and Taiwan between 1994 and 2004, and the parallel growth of the export surplus with the United States supports the thesis of a growing socialisation of labour in the region with elements of complementarity, notably in electronics, which as a sector best lends itself to parcelling out different production stages.[88]

However, signalling the ambitions of a true contender, the Chinese state class is not content with being the recipient of investment. China aims to become a major foreign investor itself, with a vice-premier announcing that Chinese firms must 'go global'. This strategy, which according to the leadership will benefit not only 'China's development but also the prosperity of the whole world', has already resulted in more than $2 billion government-authorised foreign investment outflow in 2003.[89] The acquisition of IBM's PC arm and a French perfume retail chain by Chinese companies are spectacular instances of their aspirations, if not perhaps sufficient evidence to see a longer trend. But there is no doubt that the Chinese are becoming an active force in the global political economy in their hunt for resources across the continents—energy from Saudi Arabia, Kazakhstan, Sudan and Angola; Cuban nickel, Brazilian iron ore and soybeans, etc. This inevitably restricts, to name but one aspect, US options in dealing with challenges in Latin America, and thus becomes part of global rivalries generated along the heartland/contender fracture.

Now, as we have seen, every contender at some point faces the problem of having to adjust its political system to the class structure that emerges along with the modernisation emulating the heartland. The antagonism with the West can develop into a dynamic of its own in the process; Chinese nationalism can thus precipitate, but not solve, the transition problems that occur when a society finds itself in the 'wrong' type of state/society configuration, unable to merge into the expanding liberal universe. China is already experiencing specific difficulties in restructuring its society to an Asian capitalist format. Thus the aim of the Chinese state class is to create powerful business groups of the finance capital type, like the *zaibatsu/keiretsu* of Japan and the family-owned *chaebols* of Korea. But apart from the class of tycoons composed of overseas Chinese and privatising party leaders, an educated middle class is lacking, due to the shortfall in higher education. In combination with the limited size of the foreign-trained 'MBA' element referred to earlier, this may force the Chinese state class to forego its finance capital strategy and instead seek to follow Taiwan, where the state and the ruling party own or control some 50 per cent of corporate assets, accounting for around 30 per cent of the island's GNP.[90] But that would only further consolidate the contender state configuration and complicate any further transition.

In the Asian crisis, China—itself insulated from currency speculation by capital controls and non-convertibility of its currency—was a tactical ally of the West. Japan on the other hand posed an acute threat to heartland hegemony when it proposed in September 1997 to create an Asian Monetary Fund (AMF) to deal with the crisis. It offered to put up half the initial $100 billion of the fund's capital. The US promptly rejected the proposal, calling it a way of prolonging Asian 'crony capitalism' and an invitation to fiscal imprudence in the stricken countries, given that the Japanese proposals departed from neoliberal orthodoxy.[91] What Washington feared most, however, was the prospect of Japan assuming a larger political role in the Pacific region; earlier proposals that Asian 'super-exporters' shift their energies to 'unification projects in their own region' had also been dismissed for this reason.[92] Robert Rubin's deputy at the Treasury, former World Bank economist Lawrence Summers, was sent on a mission to ensure that the IMF was put in charge of dealing with the crisis. Officially this was intended to maintain overall policy cohesion; but it in fact served as a guarantee that the crisis would be solved on conditions set in Washington. As the *Financial Times* commented at the time,

> In the last three months, as the Asian crisis has broadened and deepened, Mr Summers has been everywhere—putting pressure on the Japanese to reflate their economy, cajoling the Koreans to implement tougher financial reforms, nudging the US Congress not to pull the plug on IMF funding .... More important, Mr Summers has been successful in ensuring that *the entire international rescue operation has been run along US lines*. There was a dangerous moment before the Korean collapse, when momentum was building in Asia behind a Japanese-led plan for a special regional bailout fund .... Mr Summers managed to kill off the proposal and leave the IMF at the forefront of the bailouts— the critical element of the US approach.[93]

In the counter-attack on the NIEO following the debt crisis, strict IMF conditionality had been one of the main mechanisms by which the contender state grip on its society, and the structures of state ownership, finance capital and social protection that were in the way of competitive liberalisation had been removed. From 1969—when only half the number of states requiring IMF assistance were subjected to the full adjustment package—the percentage rose to 90 in 1984 (involving 66 countries), so that IMF Director de Larosière could claim that 'adjustment measures really have become universal.'[94] Not that the actual record was that impressive: in the decade since 1987, when the IMF put in place the Enhanced Structural Adjustment Facility (ESAF) to gear countries to export-led industrialisation and improved debt service, the 36 countries that sought IMF assistance, according to the IMF's own report, did worse than those 43 eligible countries that did not.[95] Hence the 'universal recipe'—a neoliberal austerity policy and the sale of debt-ridden local companies—was far from convincing by the time of the Asian crisis. Also, companies operating in the context of the finance capital structures of state-monitored economies with high savings rates are *always* 'debt-ridden' by the standards of Anglo-American stockmarket capitalism.[96] No wonder that the question arose as to whether 'allies' (to be distinguished from highly indebted Third World countries such as Pakistan, Argentina or the vanquished USSR) should be subjected to the full impact of IMF conditionality.

Thus presidential economic adviser Martin Feldstein, in an article in *Foreign Affairs*, wondered whether it was fair to demand a fundamental overhaul of the South Korean economy to qualify for a $57 billion IMF loan package. This in effect only served to bail out Korea's foreign creditors, whereas a bridging facility to meet short-debt debts might be better for Korea. If a strong economy like South Korea must be placed under IMF discipline, why not the EU? There the same conditions prevail—'labour market rules that cause 12 per cent unemployment, corporate ownership structures that give banks and governments controlling interests in industrial companies, state subsidies to inefficient and loss-making industries, and trade barriers that restrict Japanese auto imports to a trickle and block foreign purchases of industrial companies'.[97] In addition, the ruthless imposition of the neoliberal capitalist model threatened to undermine the structures of vassalage better kept in reserve in the evolving geopolitical configuration. Asian 'moderates' were, according to Henry Kissinger, already complaining that 'Asia is confronting an American campaign to stifle Asian competition.'[98] Yet the prevailing opinion was that the crisis offered an opportunity to rectify the 1945 failure to remake Asia in the image of the West—'a second chance to create democratic, laissez-faire societies across the Pacific Rim'.[99]

The Failure of East Asian Bloc Formation

The smaller Asian economies were hit hardest by the successive shocks that constitute the Asian crisis—the withdrawal of short-term capital, and the IMF assault on the structures of state-monitored capitalist development—but the larger ones held their own. Japan outright refused to follow the IMF recommendations; China had not suffered and was equally unwilling to deregulate; Taiwan too dragged its feet on liberalisation. But around them, Asian economies were severely affected, their state classes dethroned by varying forms of (usually oligarchic) democratisation—most spectacularly in Indonesia, which because of continuing political instability also failed to recover economically.[100]

To the Japanese ruling class, the shock of having been targeted at all created the space to seek a new relationship with the United States—ideally, by inviting it into a Pacific partnership that would limit Washington's ability to play off different states against each other. This option had been raised first in the mid-1980s, when the Takeshita government installed a commission to study the future of trade in the Asia-Pacific region. Redefining the Pacific relationship was also a response to calls for a confrontation with the United States—such as the book *The Japan That Can say 'No'* by the nationalist politician, Shintaro Ishihara (a cabinet minister in the period 1986–88), co-authored with Sony president Akio Morita (who lent Ishihara his support to further an agenda of his own). Ishihara and Morita denounced America's strategy of confiscating, on national security grounds, technologies developed by its allies in the context of SDI, and called on the government not to allow Japanese ingenuity to be sequestered by Washington in this way.[101] In 1989, the government commission under Yoshihiro Sakamoto recommended that Japan should abandon its exclusive concentration on the US market, and create a loosely institutionalised forum to strengthen regional economic integration without antagonising the United States. Conscious of Western sensibilities, the Sakamoto commission even advised that not Japan but Australia should propose these steps; Australian Prime Minister Bob Hawke had raised the idea of an Asia Pacific Economic Cooperation (APEC) on a visit to South Korea earlier in the year. In late 1989, APEC was indeed founded in Canberra, with the USA and Canada, Australia and New Zealand, Japan and South Korea, and the ASEAN countries as members. China, Taiwan and Hong Kong were admitted in 1991; a secretariat in Singapore was set up the year after.[102]

So the English-speaking states were still in a directive role even when, finally, an Asia-Pacific bloc was constituted (just as the US and Britain had been in the case of ASEAN). 'In east or northeast Asia, the United States viewed its military capabilities as sufficient to neutralize the surrounding threat, and thus preferred to maintain its interests in the region through bilateral arrangements,' writes Hun Joo Park. 'The failure to establish multilateral cooperative institutions in Northeast Asia in the post-World War II era stems partly from the American hegemony and its preference for a divide-and-rule strategy [and a] hub-and-spokes pattern of bilateral alliances.'[103] At this point, Japan was still the partner of choice. The Bush I administration sold it the technology of the F-16 jet fighter so that the country could produce its own version, the FSX.[104] This was part of grooming Japan for balancing against China, and it certainly raised the stakes in the Asian arms race that was beginning to pick up, to the point where the Southeast Asian arms market overtook the Middle East as the third-largest weapons sales area after the United States and Europe in the mid-1990s.[105]

Asian state classes were aware of their weakness relative to the US and the multilateral regulatory infrastructure under its control. Neither did they necessarily consider APEC the best solution to defend their interests. Pressures from the United States to liberalise economies and introduce parliamentary systems along with stock markets were resented along a broad front for reasons good and bad. In 1990, Prime Minister Mahathir of Malaysia launched the idea for a free trade zone including Japan and South Korea, but *excluding* the US, Australia and New Zealand. In 1993, finding insufficient support for a proposal which was so obviously directed against the English-speaking heartland, he proceeded with another project—a 'Caucus' within APEC. On several occasions, however, President Bush Sr. and his secretary of state, Baker, warned that this Caucus would 'constitute a trade barrier'—thus hinting at sanctions. In the circumstances, Japan and South Korea saw no advantage in risking the wrath of Washington.[106] Yet there was no denying that 'peace was breaking out in East Asia' after the collapse of the USSR, and this was bound to diminish US influence. China recognised South Korea in 1991, and the government of the Philippines asked the US Navy to vacate the Subic Bay naval base.[107]

There was no way, however, that the United States was going to leave Asia to the Asians. The position developed in the draft Defence Planning Guidance for 1994–99 again provides important clues here. On the subject of Asia, it warns against 'the potentially destabilizing effects that enhanced roles on the part of our allies, particularly Japan but also possibly Korea, might produce.' Nuclear proliferation in the region had been sparked off by South Korea's intentions and was interrupted only when its architect, President Park, was assassinated with US connivance; in the meantime, though, North Korea had set up a rival programme. A potential succession crisis in China was another threat which could not be left to Japan to handle on its own.[108] Washington therefore moved to become more active in the evolving process of regional cooperation. Fred Bergsten—who, as we saw, warned against the proliferation of OPEC-like blocs—was put in charge of an APEC eminent persons group to study the direction the organisation should take. Upon taking office, President Clinton then invited the APEC leaders to an informal summit in Seattle in 1993 where they agreed to work towards an Asia Pacific Community.[109]

Thus the Clinton administration effectively hijacked he APEC process and made it part of the globalisation drive. In late 1994, at the APEC summit in Bogor, Indonesia, participants committed themselves to liberalisation trajectories for the twenty-first century, while in 1995, at Osaka, agreement was reached to unilaterally open the Asian economies to foreign capital. Chile was admitted as a member and the creation of an Asia-Pacific free trade zone was agreed for 2020.[110] This was the juncture, as noted earlier, when the Japanese ministry of finance threatened to divest itself of its US treasury bond holdings, even though Clinton backtracked from his initial Japan-bashing (and also upgraded US creditworthiness by bringing the budget into the black, among other means by cutting social security). In fact there was a divestiture already in progress—in 1989 Japanese investment trusts still invested 60 per cent in US securities and 18 per cent in Asia, whereas in 1994 this was reversed to 13 and 75 per cent respectively.[111] Japan now actively resisted US demands for liberalisation and even became more confident in challenging Washington. In one gesture, Tokyo criticised the priority accorded to Eastern Europe by the IMF and the World Bank, claiming that more finance was needed for East Asian projects. In 1993, the World Bank report, *The East Asian Miracle* (paid for by Japan's ministry of finance), highlighted the positive role of the state in economic development, in a sign of Japan's willingness to stand up for what had been the true basis of its development success.[112] Obviously a rift, which reflected long-nurtured resentment, was opening up between the United States and Japan. Japan's contender trajectory, which had gained a new lease on life during the cold war, was losing its licence, but it was obviously not being abandoned.

Towards China, on the other hand, the Clinton administration showed more leniency. In spite of the Tiananmen repression, it renewed commercial partner status (MFN) for China in May 1994.[113] Yet the centrifugal tendency also affected China and its regional allies, and the country's role as the new contender transpires in the fact that Beijing, jointly with the ASEAN countries, became the driving force behind the idea of an Asian bloc independent from the 'Americanized Pacific-Asian economic regional order'.[114] In 1995, a meeting of the ASEAN states, along with China, Japan, and South Korea ('ASEAN+3'), took place to prepare a common position. These meetings were institutionalised from 1997. Although the preparation for ASEAN+3 coincided with projected negotiations with the EU in the first Asia-Europe Meeting (ASEM), in this part of the world Europe is far weaker than the United States. As Richard Higgott notes, 'the prospect of Asia and Europe balancing against the US, via [ASEM] remains—occasional rhetorical flourishes notwithstanding—a remote prospect.'[115] In no way will the integration of Europe spill over to integration in Asia, or otherwise strengthen the hand of an Asian bloc—which itself remains elusive. China on the other hand, as we will see, does look to the EU to counterbalance US pressures.

The Asian Crisis had the obvious effect of souring relations between the United States and the East Asian states. The APEC summit at Kuala Lumpur in November 1998 virtually collapsed amidst serious disagreements over the causes and handling of the crisis, and 'resistance of Asian policy makers to a strengthened APEC after the financial crisis was caused not only by the lack of tangible benefits but also by a fear of American dominance within the organisation.'[116] But given the preponderant military and economic assets Washington continues to wield, and the blows incurred by the weaker APEC members, the anaemic state of regional integration in the Asia-Pacific area only strengthens the hand of the United States—except that it must now return to active balancing.

Balancing Japanese against Chinese Nationalism

A bloc of its own might have shielded Japan from economic turbulence in the same way that Germany profits from the EU, but no such bloc exists. Japan together with China and South Korea accounted for 22 per cent of world GDP in 2000, which puts the region roughly in the same class as the EU or NAFTA; but intra-regional trade was only 20 per cent of total trade of the three countries, against the EU, 60 per cent and NAFTA's 47 per cent.[117] On their own, Japanese preferences on how to organise the world economy carry little weight. As John Braithwaite and Peter Drahos write, 'The most ironic feature of Japan's consistent comparative impotence across [global business regulation] regimes is that it is a quintessentially unitary realist state actor.'[118] The Pacific Business Forum, set up in 1994 by the president of Itochu Corporation of Japan as a private planning network for the APEC region, champions increasing investment and area-wide product standardisation; but attempts to stabilise markets are inimical to the neoliberal mindset prevailing in the West. At the February 1998 WEF meeting in Davos, a proposal by the president of Sony, N. Idei, to develop greater telecom/ electronics standardisation, was rejected by Columbia professor E. Noam, who argued, typically, that the competitive quest for new technologies should not be slowed down by a process of standardisation negotiations bound to become 'cumbersome and politicised'.[119]

In response to the Asian Crisis, Japan suspended liberalisation of its economy in order to prevent further fall-out. Indeed the country 'has been intensifying, albeit as quietly as it possibly can, its search for more independent policy lines from America and a more pro-active role in promoting intraregional cooperation befitting the post-cold war era.'[120] But the Japanese position does not allow it much freedom; its exports are still highly dependent on the US market. Nevertheless, the Asian Crisis was a turning point. Nationalism was given a lift by popular indignation on how the crisis was handled by the United States. In 1998 Ishihara wrote a sequel to *The Japan That Can Say 'No'*, in which he called for a halt to further Japanese purchases of US bonds. This had such a public resonance that it secured his election as mayor of Tokyo in the following year.[121]

The Chinese response to the Asian crisis, on the other hand, was to intensify its export offensive, improve conditions for incoming foreign investment and apply for membership of the WTO (to which it was admitted in December 2001).[122] In 2000 Prime Minister Zhu Rongji proposed creating a free trade zone with the ASEAN countries (eventually agreed in 2002). But now Japan, fearing marginalisation from the process of regional economic integration, began courting ASEAN countries in turn and agreed a free trade area with Singapore 'in order to counter the ASEAN-China [free trade area]'. Washington too concluded a free trade agreement with Singapore, reflecting its concern to control the rise of China.[123] Finally, South Korea began exploring free trade agreements with both Japan and Singapore— and comprehensively with ASEAN—in 2003-04.[124] The visit of the South Korean president to Japan in 1998 was a breakthrough in the relations between countries whose citizens until recently considered the other 'the most disliked nation'. The 2002 football World Cup held jointly in South Korea and Japan was of equal importance in the thaw.[125]

However, the ability of Japan to build a regional bloc to counter Chinese ambitions towards its southern neighbours (where the overseas Chinese hold economic power) continues to be hampered by its past. The lack of integration and the survival of an imperialist nationalism condition each other here. Because of the failure to engage in regional integration and the unwillingness of the US to allow such integration to proceed, there was also no need for Japan to admit war guilt. With the emperor allowed to stay on, Japan and the Asian victims of Japan's continental war and brutal colonial rule did not have a chance to resolve the problems of fear and mistrust, which deeply underlie and perpetually mar the international relations in the region.'[126] There was no Japanese Willy Brandt to go to Nanking (the place of the worst wartime massacre of civilians), kneel down, and apologise. On the contrary, Prime Minister Koizumi's ceremonial visits to the Yasukuni shrine, where Japan's war dead, including the leadership hanged for war guilt, lie buried, continue to insult its former victims, notably China.[127]

This obviously is not a personal quirk on the part of the Japanese prime minister, but a political gesture catering to a new mood. Nationalism is on the rise again, now that economic crisis and the loss of the lifetime employment guarantee have exposed the Japanese population to insecurity to a degree not seen since the Second World War. Ishihara, the mayor of Tokyo and the man who wants Japan to say 'no', enjoys a growing popularity with his calls for the Japanese government to speak up. But the 'no' isn't aimed primarily at the United States any longer; it is directed *against China*. This does not resonate so much with the older generation, which remains faithful to the pacifism that settled with the dust of the atomic attacks on Hiroshima and Nagasaki. But among the young, this counts for less. A poll amongst 20–30 year-olds held in 2004 by Japan's leading newspaper, *Asahi Shimbun*, revealed a 63 per cent majority in favour of revising the constitution to legalise a regular army.[128] Of course Japan was part of the Western defence set-up all along. With 240,000 men under arms and a defence budget of $40 billion, it is today second only to the US. North Korea's nuclear policy was one reason why it embarked on a policy of military normalisation as early as 1996, effectively abandoning the pacifist principles of the constitution.[129] But in the new context that has emerged in the aftermath of the Asian Crisis, Japan's policy, as Chalmers Johnson has noted, is 'to do everything in its power to adjust to the re-emergence of China on the world stage.'[130] The United States in the circumstances has clearly adopted a policy of active balancing on the side of Japan; the Clinton economic warfare strategy was soon abandoned again. In 1999, Washington decided to embark on a missile defence system essentially directed against China and North Korea, devoting $10.6 billion to it over a five-year period—with Japan as a partner. By joining forces with Tokyo, however, the United States risks being drawn into disputes between China and a number of Southeast Asian states (notably Vietnam) about energy resources in the South China Sea.[131]

China meanwhile, like all contender states before it, has profited from the tactical balancing pursued by the heartland before emerging as the primary contender itself. After Nixon's trip to Beijing had normalised relations, the United States developed a strategic relationship with China under Deng Xiaoping against the USSR. To compensate for the loss of important US monitoring stations in Iran, mainland China was prevailed upon in 1979 to provide the US intelligence community with listening stations to spy on the Soviet Union.[132] Under Bush II, the first signs of an emerging confrontation with China were temporarily eclipsed by the Global War on Terror.

The United States, in the words of one of its ambassadors, has 'never accepted a deterrent relationship based on mutually assured destruction with China' in the way that it accepted the balance of terror with the USSR; the Bush administration certainly would not allow China to develop militarily to the point where the US would have to accommodate to such a balance in the way it did in the cold war with the Soviet Union in the 1970s.[133]

In the first intelligence memo Bush Jr. received as president-elect, three strategic threats were identified: first, al-Qaeda terrorism; second, the proliferation of weapons of mass destruction; and third, the rise of China as a military power—but third only because it still 'was 5 to 15 or more years away.' Soon after, Paul Wolfowitz, in an echo of the statements on the USSR made by Richard Pipes in Reagan's days, stated that 'over the long run the Chinese political system is going to have to change.'[134] Beijing was not intimidated; a few weeks after the inauguration of the Bush Jr., Chinese aircraft forced a US spy plane to land on the island of Hainan. The Americans had to engage in humiliating negotiations to get the plane and its crew back, but only after the Chinese had thoroughly inspected it. The 11 September attacks deflected attention, but they did not stop the Quadrennial Defence Review of the US defence department shortly afterwards from defining Northeast Asia and the East Asian littoral as 'critical areas' for American interests—areas which cannot be allowed to fall under 'hostile domination'. Given that Asia is 'emerging as a region susceptible to large-scale military competition' in which rising and declining powers produce dangerous instabilities, the document sees one state, obviously China (though not named), as the ascendant 'military competitor with a formidable resource base'.[135]

At the time of this writing, the Bush administration is reverting to its original anti-China line, pursuing an idea of Secretary of State Rice to build a vassal bloc with Japan, Taiwan and India as partners in 'containment', while encouraging an aspirant liberal capitalist class in China itself—whom Rice had earlier identified as 'people who no longer owe their livelihood to government' (cf. Chapter 1 of this book)—to gain political ground.[136] Washington's joint statement with Tokyo in early 2005 that the two governments consider the peaceful solution of the Taiwan problem a 'common strategic objective'—which amounts to guaranteeing its current status—could not but infuriate the Beijing government. Taiwan avoided a further deterioration of relations with the mainland only because a parliamentary majority has prevented the Taiwanese government from spending on a record $18.3 billion US arms deal, and by a visit of the pro-Beijing opposition leader to the Chinese capital. The Chinese meanwhile are seeking to cultivate a strategic alliance with the EU, subsidise the Galileo project, and order weapons, although the US has threatened to suspend Atlantic military cooperation if Europe were to supply arms to China.[137]

The Chinese state class too has cultivated nationalism as a new ideological basis for its hegemony. This allows it to display strength and determination to the outside world without having to fear internal dissent in the short run. But as I indicated earlier, mobilising emotional energies, generated by the painful dislocations of privatisation and breakneck industrialisation, in favour of nationalism carries great risks. Nationalism in China has worked well to deflect Tiananmen-style demands for democratisation, but has meanwhile reached an intensity that may propel the Chinese state class to take actions that it would not necessarily have chosen itself.[138] Nationalist fury may turn against the West (as when reports on the casualties of the bombing of the Chinese embassy in Belgrade by NATO came in); but there are more profound forces directing it against Japan. Here, an entire complex of resentments is at work, which does not just go back to the experiences of the Japanese invasion in the 1930s and the Second World War. There is also the fact of Japan's successful contender experience and its prompt response to Western pressures in the nineteenth century; something which the Chinese failed to achieve. This deeper resentment mixes with regional imperialist rivalry resulting from its capitalist format, and with the memories of the Second World War. The fact that Japanese schoolbooks hardly pay attention to the crimes committed during the invasion of China continues to elicit fury across Asia with every new edition in which this painful omission is repeated. The standard Chinese schoolbook on the other hand includes *nine* chapters on this issue, in which the Japanese are identified as 'demons' (*guizi*), who have surpassed the prior crimes committed against the Chinese by the 'Western demons' (*yang guizi*).[139] Obviously we are looking at a highly explosive dynamic of mutual vilification; kept going, paradoxically, by the simultaneous, shared experience of the dislocations that come with contemporary capitalist development.

At the time of this writing, the Chinese economy is expected to overtake the US as the world's largest economy by 2041.[140] But then, *most contender states in history were on a course of overtaking the heartland, had their economies not at some point run aground in political crisis entailing geopolitical confrontation.* The roots of future crisis are not hard to detect. First, China has committed itself to precisely the same export-led growth model that ran into trouble in the Asian crisis, and faces staggering over production in several areas. Investment coordination at the state level was thrown out along with central planning, with massive over-capacity in several sectors the inevitable result. In car production for instance, around half of capacity is idle.[141] Second, China has become dependent on ever-growing resource imports and food to keep its economy going at the current rate. China's energy and petrochemical corporations have emerged as powerful competitors, notably in the chase for the remaining fossil fuel deposits in Central Asia, Africa and the Middle East—as we will see in Chapter 10. China is responsible for 17.5 per cent of world growth and its economic development strategy can only heighten competitive pressures and rivalries throughout the region, to be solved by increased exploitation of society and nature.[142] Indeed the government in Beijing in a recent report expresses concern about the 'ceaseless widening of the gap in income distribution and the aggravated division of the rich and the poor'; while an official of China's Environmental Administration warns that in light of the ravages on society and nature wrought by breakneck industrialisation, 'China's populace, resources, [and] environment have already reached the limits of [their] capacity to cope.'[143]

Uniquely among contender states at this stage of their development, however, China holds a major stake in the American economy in the form of dollars and US bonds—a consequence of its $100 million-plus trade surplus (in 2003) with the United States. As a French expert commented in a newspaper article, 'If China were to cease to accumulate dollars, the result would be an uncontrolled free-fall of the U.S. currency, inducing a systemic shock for the global economy.'[144] However, as the author of the quoted article also notes, the comparison with Japan's comparable trade surplus with, and financial stake in, the US in the 1980s would be mistaken. Not only did Japan's economy contract considerably in the next decade, but

> There was little risk that Tokyo was going to transform its economic muscle into strategic power directed against the United States, which ensures Japan's security in a dangerous and unstable East Asia. China, on the other hand, has its own strategic agenda to press .... The United States will thus have to chart an increasingly difficult course between the risks of appeasement and the dangers of confrontation.

Ultimately, like all contender states before it, and if does not turn towards socialist democratisation, China may come to face the hazardous internal transition from a directive state guiding the development of society to a Lockean configuration. This would involve the dispossession of sections of the state class, transnationalisation, and exposure to the working classes in its own society clamouring for improvement of their lot. It must be expected that this transition will destabilise the wide-ranging geopolitical and economic webs which China's rise has created in the last few decades.

Notes

1. I. Warde in *Le Monde Diplomatique*, March 2005, pp. 1, 6/7.
2. Levathes (1994); cf. Frank (1998).
3. Meskill (1973: 194–201); Frank (1998: 160, 274). The war against China served to consolidate the traditional martial aspect of Japanese society in the context of the contender state (Sansom 1950: 495–7).

4. Dallek (1984: 55).
5. Pelissier (1965, Vol. 2: 186, 214); Meskill (1973: 245–56). Britain and France had secretly promised Japan the German sphere of influence in China at the end of the First World War (Han Suyin 1994: 40).
6. Han Suyin (1994: 80–94). The drama became the decor for André Malraux' famous 1933 novel *The Human Condition*.
7. Pelissier (1965, Vol. 2: 321); Löwy (1981: 90, 115). On the Soong financial dynasty, cf. Seagrave (1996).
8. Löwy (1981: 116).
9. Han Suyin (1994: 213).
10. Löwy (1981: 124); cf. Chapter 7 of this book.
11. Hart-Landsberg and Burkett (2004: 28, 30). The 'Great Leap Forward' is estimated to have led to death by starvation of some 30 million people (cf. C. Johnson 2002: 151).
12. Hart-Landsberg and Burkett (2004: 29).
13. Van Ness (1970: 10, 50); O'Leary (1980: 47).
14. C. Johnson (2002: 151).
15. Hart-Landsberg and Burkett (2004: 30–1).
16. Ibid.: 32–3; *Le Monde*, 16 March 1979.
17. Internal migrants mobilised into the 'miracle' areas have begun forming what one Chinese observer calls 'Chinatowns in Beijing', inhabited by people speaking different dialects, with their own food markets. One such 'Chinatown', Zhejiang in Beijing, had 400,000 inhabitants in 1994, and dominated Beijing's garment industry (*Newsweek*, 7 March 1994; cf. Hart-Landsberg and Burkett 2004: 33, 37).
18. Park (2004: 79).
19. B. Anderson in *London Review of Books*, 20 (8), April 1998; cf. B. Nussbaum in *Business Week*, 1 December 1997.
20. B. Anderson in *London Review of Books*, 20 (8), April 1998. See chronology in *Financial Times*, 6 February 1995.
21. It was published in part in the *Straits Times*, a Southeast Asian journal, on 30 June.
22. www.tlio.demon.co.uk/reports.htm#Kinder (2 April 1998).
23. C. Johnson (2002: 152).
24. Kowalewski (1997: 29); Chua (2003: 23-48); *Financial Times*, 17 October 1995, 16 August 1995, 26 April 1995.
25. Kowalewski (1997: 87).
26. Mittelman (1997: 99); cf. Samuel Brittan in *Financial Times*, 2 February 1995.
27. *Financial Times*, 25 August 1997.
28. *Financial Times*, 25 October 1994, 21 February 1995, 6 August 1997.
29. Zhou and Lall (2005: 45).
30. Hart-Landsberg and Burkett (2004: 44–7); *Business Week*, 9 May 1994; *Financial Times*, 25 October 1994.
31. E. Le Boucher in *Le Monde*, 16 June 2005.
32. Hochraich (2003: 59 and *passim*); *Financial Times*, 29 April 2005.
33. Liem Sioe Liong of Indonesia (where he is known as Sudomo Salim and is close to the Suharto family) was possibly the richest of them all; through his Hong Kong holding, First Pacific, he has US and Australian interests in the food and catering industry and a majority in the Dutch Hagemeyer trading company. However his position has declined, along with the fortunes of his political master (*Financial Times*, 25 October 1994, 21 February 1995, 6 August 1997).
34. On the Indian names in Table 9.1, cf. Roy (1994) and van der Pijl (1998: 131). Liberalisation of the economy after 1991 led to a massive surge in foreign direct investment to $6 billion

in 2003; privatisation saw peak years in 1992, 1995 and 1999 (*Financial Times*, 3 June 2004). Neoliberalism has also led to a resurgence of the caste system. Employment of the 'untouchable' *dalits*, the 250 million-strong underclass, has been reduced by more than 10 per cent since 1991. Forty-three per cent of *dalits* live under the poverty line against 23 per cent of the Indian population as a whole (*Le Monde*, 17 January 2004).

35. *Newsweek*, 31 March 1997. It also exposed links to operators active in the Caspian oil business, cf. *The Washington Post*, 19 March 1997. On the bribery aspect, cf. Kowalewski (1997: 93).

36. Chicago merchant banker and former US Senator Adlai Stevenson Jr. described Asian investment opportunities in early 1998 as 'once-in-a-lifetime'. According to CSFB investment bank, investments of the post-1998 class 'would have been unheard of prior to the crisis, when most Asian companies saw little need or desire to cede control to secure capital' (quoted from the *Financial Times*, 26 March 1998).

37. van den Berg (1995: 389); Ruigrok and van Tulder (1995: 39–62); T. Bouwman in *Le Monde Diplomatique*, November 1984, pp. 12–3.

38. Ohmae (1985).

39. US subsidiaries had sales of $43.9 billion in Japan in 1984, against local sales by Japanese firms in the US of $12.8 billion. The famous $31.2 billion trade deficit of 1984 was almost equal to the difference between these two figures (*Newsweek*, 13 April 1987); a comparable calculation was made by a US trader based in Japan, Bill Totten, in 1994 (*NRC-Handelsblad*, 8 June 1994).

40. P. Chamsol in *Le Monde Diplomatique*, April 1984, pp. 1, 26–7.

41. Hummel (2000: 137–44); cf. *International Herald Tribune*, 1 February 1984; *Newsweek*, 13 April 1987.

42. Hartcher (1999: 64).

43. Ibid.: 69–70.

44. From 1986 to 1990, net savings in Japan were 19.2 per cent of GNP, 16.4 per cent going into home investment, and 2.8 per cent going abroad. The US on the other hand saved 2.6 per cent of GNP and invested 5.1 per cent, so that the shortfall of 2.5 per cent (calculated over US GNP) had to be imported (Hartcher 1999: 233); the net 'penetration deficit' of the US vis-à-vis Japan in 1984 was $100 million (Hummel 2000: 121n.). Cf. *Newsweek*, 12 May 1986; *Financial Times*, 24 November 1987.

45. Tolchin and Tolchin (1989: 8–9, 185); *Time*, 18 June 1988.

46. The most prominent was Lionel Olmer, former undersecretary of commerce in the first Reagan administration and thereafter hired by Nippon Telegraph & Telephone (*Newsweek*, 22 December 1986). Among 'America's 25 Top Asia Hands', in early 1988 *Newsweek* counted investment bankers and private financiers Richard J. Flamson III of Security Pacific Corp.; Eugene Atkinson of Goldman Sachs; Richard Holbrooke; William E. Simon, former secretary of the treasury and trustee of the Heritage Foundation; the ambassador to China, Winston Lord; Maurice Greenberg, president of American International Group; Gerald L. Curtis, director of the East Asia Institute of Columbia University and a consultant to the Japanese edition of *Newsweek*; M. Oksenberg, head of the East-West Center in Hawaii and former adviser on China to the Carter NSC; and Henry Wendt III, head of SmithKline Beecham (*Newsweek*, 22 February 1988).

47. *Newsweek*, 15 March 1993.

48. Kennedy (1987). On the impact of the Kennedy thesis, cf. M.E. Cox (2001: 322–3).

49. Other US policymakers privately added that Japan could only assume a leadership role if it would shed its 'predatory, introvert policies' and 'mercantilism' (*Newsweek*, 22 February 1988; cf. Kennedy 1987).

50. Castells (1998: 215).

51. Hummel (2000: 148).
52. Hartcher (1999: 77).
53. Ibid.: 96–8; *Newsweek*, 24 December 1990.
54. *Newsweek*, 31 March 1997; see also Trilateral Commission membership 1994 (www. trilateralcommission.com, 16 January 1995). The expression 'economic war' was used by J.A. Rollwagen, deputy secretary of commerce and a former director of the supercomputer manufacturer, Cray.
55. *Business Week*, 15 February 1993. The other three were Chalmers Johnson, James Fallows and Clyde Prestowitz; cf. discussion in Hummel (2000: 172–85), who adds journalist Theodore H. White to this group.
56. Quoted in Hartcher (1999: 1). Of course, having an economy with 'low unemployment and high savings, big exports and no imports' is a deeply offensive state of affairs.
57. C. Johnson (2002: 197).
58. Hartcher (1999: 226). The dumping of US Treasury paper works to induce recession in the US by forcing US interest rates up, as was demonstrated in 1987 when Japanese life insurance companies sold large amounts of US bonds, and the interest rate on 30-year bonds went up from 7.5 per cent to 9 per cent in order to keep the product attractive to investors, but with damaging consequences for the rest of the US economy (ibid.: 227). Hosokawa's affection for 'markets' had not prevented him too from strenuously contradicting US preferences (Hummel 2000: 151–2).
59. C. Johnson (2002: 206); Todd (2004: 106).
60. Bernard and Ravenhill (1995: 199).
61. Wade (1990); Deyo (1989).
62. *Financial Times*, 29 December 1995, commenting on developments in South Korea.
63. Bernard and Ravenhill (1995: 172, 177).
64. G. Kolko (1989: 47).
65. Hummel (2000: 146); international production levels in *Financial Times*, 12 November 1996; Japanese FDI in *Financial Times*, 11 June and 5 December 1996; and *Newsweek*, 30 August 1993.
66. Bernard and Ravenhill (1995: 183, 184).
67. Ibid.: 180, 180n.; Castells (1998: 208, Table 4.1); Kwon (2004: 129, Figure 1).
68. Ibid.: 196. In 1992 Thailand reached the GNP/c level of Taiwan in 1978, but had only half the secondary school enrolment (cf. Wade and Veneroso 1998: 9n.).
69. C. Johnson (2002: 216).
70. Hartcher (1999: 253).
71. Nesvetailova (2002: 253–5).
72. *Financial Times*, 8 January 1998.
73. *Financial Times*, 30 January and 20 February 1998; C. Johnson (2002: 213, 218).
74. Nesvetailova (2002: 253).
75. Banks were also seriously exposed though: Bayerische Landesbank at twice its capital base; the French banks, Société Générale and Credit Lyonnais, at around three-quarters of its capital base; and US banks Chase and Morgan at half of capital base (*Financial Times*, 20 February 1998).
76. Castells (1998: 208, Table 4.1); *Financial Times*, 17 October 1994 and 17 April 1997. China's GNP growth over the entire reform period (1978–2004) averages 6.1 per cent annually; Japan's from 1950 to 1973, was 8.2 per cent; and South Korea's from 1962 to 1990 was 7.6 per cent. Hence Chinese growth was not that exceptional, although the scale of the changes certainly is (E. Le Boucher in *Le Monde*, 16 June 2005).
77. C. Johnson (2002: 212).
78. Nesvetailova (2002: 253).
79. Castells (1998: 252); *Financial Times*, 2 April 1996.

80. Notes from the Editors, *Monthly Review*, 49 (10), March 1998. On yuan devaluation, see *Financial Times*, 10 November 1997. Manufacturing growth in *Financial Times*, 4 November 1994; wages growth in *De Volkskrant*, 7 December 1996. From the 1978 turnabout, Chinese annual average per capital income rose almost 7 times in the mid-1990s; even if purchasing power is taken into account, its per capita income was still only one-fifteenth of Japan's and one-twelfth of the US (C. Johnson 2002: 153).
81. Haggard and Mo (2000: 215–6); Wade and Veneroso (1998: 9). On the Kwangju massacre and US involvement, see C. Johnson (2002: 113–22).
82. Wealthy individuals also joined the fray: the inevitable George Soros, dubbed a 'parasite' by Malaysian premier Mahathir, led a consortium that bought up a Thai steel mill; Saudi Prince al-Waleed (cf. Table 10.1 of this book) bought stakes in the car industries of Korea and Malaysia. Paradoxically, US corporations were careful not to appear too eager to buy up assets in the stricken countries, for 'to the extent the IMF is identified with the US, protests against the Fund's policies tend to take an anti-US flavour' (*Financial Times*, 26 March 1998; cf. 30 April 1999; 28 April 2000).
83. *Financial Times*, 30 May 2005. The low FDI stock in Japan is the result of continuing disinvestment in spite of new inflows. The British percentage is 37. Yet in 2000, foreign capital held major stakes in the prized Japanese car industry: Renault had a 36 per cent stake in Nissan, Ford 33 per cent in Mazda, and GM 20 per cent in Fuji Heavy industries (makers of Subaru) (*Financial Times*, 23 March 2000).
84. E. Le Boucher in *Le Monde*, 16 June 2005.
85. Kim (2004: 158, 161); Zhou and Lall (2005: 42).
86. Zhou and Lall (2005: 45).
87. Hart-Landsberg and Burkett (2004: 48); E. Le Boucher in *Le Monde*, 16 June 2005; Zhou and Lall (2005: 47).
88. E. Le Boucher in *Le Monde*, 16 June 2005; Zhou and Lall (2005: 47, 52).
89. Editors' foreword in Hart-Landsberg and Burkett (2004: 5).
90. C. Johnson (2002: 157, 161); Castells (1998: 254–8); Hochraich (2003).
91. Park (2004: 83); C. Johnson (2002: 219); *Financial Times*, 1 July 1999.
92. R. Dornbusch column in *Business Week*, 1 March 1993; cf. *Business Week*, 8 February 1993.
93. *Financial Times*, 15 January 1998 (emphasis added). Summers' economic orthodoxy had made news before this, when he explained that Africa is 'underpolluted' and therefore has a comparative advantage as a dumping ground.
94. Quoted in Chahoud (1987: 46).
95. ESAF countries: zero growth (up from minus 1.1 per cent) in terms of GNP/c, with indebtedness as a percentage of GNP up from 82 to 154; non-ESAF group: GNP/c growth rates of 0.3 in 1980–85 and 1 per cent in 1990–95, with indebtedness up from 56 to 76 per cent (G. Kolko in *Le Monde Diplomatique*, May 1998, p. 7).
96. Wade and Veneroso (1998: 15).
97. Feldstein (1998: 26); cf. the reply by IMF deputy managing director Stanley Fischer in *Los Angeles Times*, 20 March 1998. His boss, Michel Camdessus, had in a 1994 interview still pointed to the high qualities of East Asian countries in terms of institutions conducive to high economic growth (*Newsweek*, 15 August 1994).
98. Quoted in Wade and Veneroso (1998: 21); for other critics, cf. *Financial Times*, 31 December 1997/1 January 1998 [George Soros]; 12 December and 19 December 1997 [Jeffrey Sachs and others].
99. B. Nussbaum in *Business Week*, 1 December 1997.
100. C. Johnson (2002: 220). On Indonesia, see Robison and Hadiz (2004); cf. Zhou and Lall (2005: 62). In the Philippines, the democratisation a decade earlier was certainly a dispossession of the state class around President Marcos but not of the oligarchy (cf. F. Houtard in *Le Monde Diplomatique*, May 1987, p. 26).
101. C. Johnson (2002: 194). On Ishihara, see Hummel (2000: 201–2).

102. Hummel (2000: 154–5).
103. Park (2004: 85, 84), quoting Lowell Dittmer
104. C. Johnson (2002: 195).
105. *Financial Times*, 28 February 1996.
106. Kwon (2004: 103n.); C. Johnson (2002: 216).
107. C. Johnson (2002: 197).
108. DPG quoted in *The New York Times*, 8 March 1992. On the background of the assassination of Park, see C. Johnson (2002: 112–3).
109. Hummel (2000: 156).
110. C. Johnson (2002: 217); Hummel (2000: 156); *Financial Times*, 10 November 1994.
111. Hartcher (1999: 229).
112. Ibid.: 228.
113. The technical term is 'Most Favoured Nation', which suggests privileged status, whereas it actually refers to equal status with other trade partners.
114. Kwon (2004: 103).
115. Park (2004: 82–3); Higgott (2004: 170).
116. Higgott (2004: 162).
117. Park (2004: 81).
118. Braithwaite and Drahos (2000: 478).
119. *Financial Times*, 2 and 3 February 1998. On the Pacific Business Forum, see *Financial Times*, 4 September 1995.
120. Park (2004: 81–2); C. Johnson (2002: 217).
121. C. Johnson (2002: 194).
122. Hart-Landsberg and Burkett (2004: 49).
123. Kwon (2004: 99); Higgott (2004: 164).
124. Kwon (2004: 99).
125. Park (2004: 86, 90).
126. Ibid.: 85.
127. W. van Kemenade in *IIAS Newsletter*, July 2005, p. 5.
128. C. Leblanc in *Le Monde Diplomatique*, October 2004, pp. 16–7.
129. Park (2004: 79, 87, 87n.).
130. The reason why Japan nevertheless seeks to eliminate US military presence (while maintaining a military alliance), is because 'the real fear is that increased American belligerence toward China might invite Chinese retaliation against the bases in Japan' (C. Johnson 2002: 61).
131. Klare (2001: 109–37); C. Johnson (2002: 168). If the project for a thermonuclear fusion reactor has meanwhile brought all parties together again (because of the costs), in the period preceding the decision to build the experimental reactor in France, a US–Japanese bloc was locked in bitter rivalry with Russia and China (*De Volkskrant*, 2 July 2005).
132. Richelson and Ball (1990: 172, 188).
133. Ambassador David Smith quoted by Dan Plesch in *The Guardian*, 13 September 2002.
134. B. Woodward (2004: 12); Wolfowitz quoted in G. Kolko (2002: 120).
135. A. Murray in *The Guardian*, 30 January 2001.
136. Rice quoted in *Financial Times*, 25 July 2000 (cf. Chapter 1, note 79 of this book).
137. W. van Kemenade in *IIAS Newsletter*, July 2005, p. 5.
138. C. Johnson (2002: 156).
139. C. Leblanc in *Le Monde Diplomatique*, October 2004, p. 16.
140. Goldman Sachs study quoted in *International Herald Tribune*, 24–25 January 2004.
141. E. Le Boucher in *Le Monde*, 16 June 2005.
142. Hart-Landsberg and Burkett (2004: 81). The figure for China's growth contribution for 2002 is from Morgan Stanley analyst Stephen Roach.
143. Editors' Foreword in Hart-Landsberg and Burkettt (2004: 5–6). Among the problems, a

report of the Council on Foreign Relations lists forest resource depletion, desertification and flooding; 75 per cent of river water flowing through urban areas is unsuitable for drinking or fishing, while 60 million Chinese have difficulty getting access to water. Of the 10 most polluted cities in the world today, seven are in China (quoted in ibid.).

144. F. Heisbourg, director of the Strategic Research Foundation in Paris, in *International Herald Tribune*, 27 December 2003. It was noted in February 2004 that between January 2002 and October 2003 Asian countries accumulated US $611 billion—Japan 219 billion, China 184 billion and Taiwan 73 billion. This accumulation of dollar holdings funded the US deficit, while exports to the West, notably the US, continued. The US therefore profits from the Asian countries' willingness to keep US bond prices and the dollar up, while themselves keeping their exchange rate down to continue exporting at rates that produce growth at home (Martin Wolf in *Financial Times*, 11 February 2004).

10 Energy Conflicts in the Post-Soviet Era

FROM 'IRAN–CONTRA' TO THE FIRST GULF WAR

China's rise as the new contender has increased worldwide demand for energy, against the background of sharpening rivalries over limited resources. Certainly these should not be envisaged as a fixed stock of things, as in the famous 'Limits to Growth' report of 1972. But there is no doubt that sources of energy and fresh water, and related claims to waterways and territorial waters, have all become potential sources of conflict.[1] In this chapter, I place America's 'War on Terror' in this perspective. The Iran–Iraq war and the two Gulf Wars, I would argue, are best understood in the context of a protracted dismantling of contender positions in the Middle East by the West, including the Soviet Union's in Afghanistan. In the process, Washington relied on Islamists in Saudi Arabia and Pakistan—a decision for which the world is paying the price today. The warning of the last communist Afghan ruler, A. Najibullah, that 'if fundamentalism comes to Afghanistan, [it] will be turned into a centre for terrorism,' was not heeded.[2]

I begin by tracing the rivalry between Iran and Iraq in the period leading to the Islamist revolution. Iraq's development in the 1970s was initially a sideshow to the last phase of the Shah's rule in neighbouring Iran. The 1973 oil price hike fuelled industrialisation ambitions among many contender state classes, (sub-) imperial ambitions among others, and corruption everywhere; Iran combined all of these. The country not only embarked on a crash industrialisation programme, but also became the prime customer of the US aerospace industry, for which the OPEC price hike created an alternative market after the Vietnam boom collapsed in the early 1970s. Of the total US arms sales in 1974, half ($3.9 billion) went to Iran.[3] The Shah used his new power to seize islands in the Hormuz straits, encouraged by Washington, and to stir revolt among the Kurds in Iraq. The Baath regime in Baghdad could only get him to stop this support by giving up its claim to the Shatt-al-Arab, the estuary of the Euphrates and Tigris rivers, and accepting a boundary in the middle. Today of course we chuckle when reading that three years later (in 1978) Iraq made a further gesture to its powerful neighbour by expelling Ayatollah Khomeini, the Shia cleric and opposition leader, who had lived in Iraqi exile for 14 years. But then, who would have predicted at the time that in 1979 the same Khomeini would fly in from Paris as the new ruler in the Iranian revolution![4]

In the same year, Saddam Hussein pushed aside the last remaining Baath leader above himself and took full control. He cracked down on the Iraqi Left, including the Communist party, and allowed the bourgeoisie greater leeway. The class of private contractors in construction and building materials, which had developed in the wave of public investment after the oil price hike of 1973, thus began encroaching on the economic monopoly held by the Baath state class, although the dictatorship remained firmly entrenched. In 1983, in the early stages of the war with Iran, privatisation laws were enacted that made larger corporations possible, including in agribusiness. The formation of a bourgeoisie was further affected by the deportation, on the outbreak of the war, of a quarter of a million Shias, including the Iranian element in the business world of Iraq. Hence, as Isam al-Khafaji notes, there occurred a shift in the composition of the Iraqi bourgeoisie, 'to the advantage of those descending from regions north and northwest of Baghdad, who secured a dominant position in the social hierarchy by the 1980s.'[5] In the wake of the Anglo-American invasion of 2003, the dispossession of the state class would be followed by a return of political entrepreneurs with a Shia background such as Ahmed Chalabi and his orbit, as we will see in the last section of this chapter.

Saddam Hussein's decision to claim the mantle of regional primacy in the face of Iran's collapse into Islamist revolution stemmed from his personal ambition to become a new Nasser defending Arab aspirations. Apart from the more obvious objectives of the war, it also aimed to provide a new focus for a population affected by social change.[6] The Iraqi invasion, launched in September 1980, started a struggle that would last eight years. It killed around a million people, maiming and wounding many more. With an estimated $400 billion spent by both sides on conducting the war, and around $100 billion of property destroyed, it became the most expensive conflict since Vietnam. Total arms sales to the Middle East jumped from $29 billion in 1974–78 to $65.3 billion for 1979–83 and $89 billion for 1984–88, when the fighting finally ended.[7] With much of the accumulated oil wealth of two major OPEC states spent on arms and destroyed in the struggle, the war inevitably became an aspect of the restoration of the primacy of the heartland over the OPEC/NIEO bloc ranged against it a decade earlier. State-led development in both countries was seriously reversed, as always when contenders are encouraged fight it out among themselves. The oil facilities of both were seriously hit; the 1986–87 price drop that 'wiped out the increases of the second oil shock of 1979–81' obviously hit Iraq and Iran as well, further adding to the loss of income.[8]

Iraq's heavy weaponry had been supplied by the USSR and France, but the Iranian revolution broadened its supply base. A European cartel of munitions makers took orders from both sides; during the Iran–Iraq war Britain recouped its position as the world's second-largest arms exporter. The chilling story of Gerald James, whose fireworks company was recruited into the supply operation because established UK munitions makers could not meet the demand to keep the carnage going, offers a catalogue of the deals, takeovers, secret service supervision and dirty tricks that this entailed. Mrs. Thatcher personally supervised large-scale UK weapons deals with Oman, Jordan (the most important conduit for Iraqi purchases), and the record Al Yamama contract with Saudi Arabia, a £60 billion programme in three instalments involving minesweepers, Tornado fighters and helicopters (many of which were also shipped on to Iraq). To pay his way, Saddam had to borrow against the collateral of future oil revenues; Western creditors naïvely believed that this was the way to gain leverage over him.[9]

As has been pointed out repeatedly in the discussions on the 2003 invasion, the West was the main provider of the advanced weaponry with which Saddam Hussein hoped to build his future power. The Thatcher government allowed Iraq to purchase computerised machine-tool facilities in the UK to produce parts for its nuclear programme and other sophisticated weapons systems. Britain also facilitated the exports of components for the 'supergun' designed by the Canadian weapons wizard, Gerald Bull. With the Chilean arms dealer and Pinochet intimate, Carlos Cardoen, British companies set up a nuclear-capable missile production facility near Baghdad.[10] Apartheid South Africa was another pivot for bringing US and British weapons technology to Iraq. Armscor, the state-owned weapons firm, worked with Cardoen in supplying cluster bombs and other outlawed ammunition to Iraq, including super-gun components and missile technology.[11]

US support for Iraq was officially blocked. In 1982, however, Washington became concerned over Iranian successes on the battlefield and secretly began providing CIA satellite information to Baghdad. In December 1983, in spite of reports on Iraq's use of nerve gas to stem the Iranian advance, the Reagan administration signed a confidential directive to do 'whatever was necessary and legal' to prevent the country from losing the war.[12] US chemical companies meanwhile sold pesticides which could be used for chemical warfare, while others supplied—under Department of Commerce licences—biological agents including anthrax.[13] Finance for Saddam was made available through an obscure branch of the Italian BNL bank in Atlanta, but also by blue-chip banks like Morgan-Guaranty Trust of New York.[14] The main supplier of a chemical warfare capacity appears to have been West Germany. MBB, the German aerospace company later absorbed into DASA (today's EADS) also assisted in developing missile capacity. In addition, German companies helped out with Iraq's nuclear programme, which used weapons-grade materials obtained from Latin American sources.[15]

The Islamic revolution in Iran was the last nail in Carter's coffin in the 1980 presidential election. The seizure of the US embassy in Tehran occurred when the president yielded to pressure from the Shah's US financiers and friends to admit the deposed ruler to the US to undergo medical treatment, and froze Iranian deposits in Western banks.[16] However, William Casey, the head of Reagan's election campaign and later CIA director, then entered into secret negotiations with the Iranians to delay release of the hostages in the embassy until after Reagan had been elected. He promised that the US would resume weapons supplies thereafter.[17] This created the undercover channel for much-needed spare parts for the Iranian forces that would develop into the Iran–Contra network. But the Reagan administration could not lift the arms ban when it settled the overseas assets freeze with Iran and only allowed a partial lifting of the US economic embargo in January 1981. As a result, the increment of arms supplies that can be attributed to the Iran–Iraq war largely went to America's competitors, and it left Washington handicapped in dealing with Tehran, and generally in a weak position with regard to the war even when it was harming vital Western energy interests.[18] In the later stages of the conflict, oil tankers in the Persian Gulf came under attack from both sides, and in early 1987 Gorbachev made an offer to Kuwait to lease Soviet tankers to protect them from the Iranians. This prompted the United States to trump Moscow by moving into the Gulf itself with warships protecting shipping lanes. Effectively, the United States joined the Iraqi side as a result, and there was a real danger of a US–Iranian conflict.[19]

Israel's role in the Iran–Contra scandal, which had broken by that time, is important because it reveals the link with the Lebanese civil war. For the Jewish state, Iraq was always the more immediate enemy, and in a daring air raid in 1981 the Israelis destroyed the country's one nuclear reactor before it could be started up. An Iraqi victory, Ariel Sharon later claimed, would have posed a 'much bigger danger than whatever would result from the Islamic revolution'.[20] Yet in 1982, Israel under Sharon's command invaded southern Lebanon in support of the Christian Phalangists—a proxy war with Syria (Iraq's Arab rival) and Iran. It also used the occasion to strike at Palestinian refugee camps in Lebanon, driving Yasser Arafat from the country in August, and allowing Phalangist militias to massacre hundreds of civilians. The US–French multinational force that was deployed in Beirut to try and contain further excesses now came under attack from Hezbollah, the Shia party formed with aid from Iran. Striking twice in

1983, they killed several hundred US soldiers (and 58 French) in October. To avoid further losses, the Pentagon withdrew the remaining troops.[21]

With the US officially disengaging, Hezbollah took or still continued to hold a number of American hostages (including the CIA station chief, kidnapped in early 1985). In the circumstances Washington decided to bribe them free by using the covert supply route to Iran via Israel.[22] In January 1986, Reagan signed the finding authorising the deal (over the opposition of the State and Defence departments); National Security Adviser McFarlane, Oliver North and a team of CIA agents went to Iran to hammer out the details.[23] At the NSC, North handled the transfer of spare parts and anti-tank missiles, working along with Israeli, Iranian and other arms traders. The huge profits made on the covert arms deliveries to Iran were then used to fund the Contras in Nicaragua in spite of the congressional ban, in what William Casey called 'the ultimate covert operation'.[24] But, as Paul Vieille has written, 'the war in Lebanon cannot be fully understood in terms of rivalry between world powers and regional powers, or between religious groups and sects; its is also a blend of drugs and arms trafficking and organised crime, enveloping both sects and governments.'[25] Poppy and hashish growing are concentrated in the then Syrian-occupied Bekaa valley in Lebanon, and drugs traded for weapons made the country the pivot of illicit transactions for the wider region, with all the famous traffickers involved in intractable webs of swindle and intrigue.[26]

When Reagan authorised the Iranian arms-for-hostages plan, US narcotics agents of the Drugs Enforcement Agency (DEA) had become deeply involved in the Lebanese drugs underworld, along with the CIA, again with the aim of obtaining the release of hostages. Agents of the Defence Intelligence Agency (DIA), dispatched to Lebanon to find hostages, ran into the CIA-DEA arms-for-drugs operation that was part of the Iran–Contra network. Inter-service rivalry along with genuine exasperation led to a decision to return and report to Washington. However, Iranians and Syrians close to the Assad family in power in Syria had infiltrated the drugs route to the US run by the CIA-DEA. Concerned about exposure, they arranged to have the plane carrying the DIA team back to the US blown up. This happened over Lockerbie in Scotland, in December 1988.[27] The disaster was conveniently pinned on Libya, keeping the CIA's contacts in Syria and Iran away from public view.[28]

The next chapter of the West's relations with Iraq begins when Iran accepted a ceasefire in July 1988. The Bush I administration was aware that Saddam was using funds obtained in the United States to finance arms purchases; France continued to supply Iraq with advanced weapons, including Mirage 2000s to be assembled in the country. Saddam Hussein in turn invested part of his estimated $10 billion fortune in French companies. In the late summer of 1989, however, the FBI raided the BNL offices in Atlanta, as Israeli concern about Saddam's military capability was beginning to resonate in the United States. In September, the CIA reported to the US National Security Council that Iraq was building a sophisticated, full-spectrum arms production infrastructure with technology obtained in the UK. Yet we are not looking at a straightforward US–UK rift: in the same month, as revealed by a subsequent congressional investigation, Iraqi scientists attended an advanced thermonuclear detonation seminar in Portland, Oregon.[29]

The White House and the State Department continued to put pressure on the Department of Agriculture and the Treasury to extend credits to Iraq because Saddam was still considered a potential ally.[30] As late as January 1990, the US felt close enough to the Iraqi leader to urge him to launch a campaign in OPEC to raise the oil price, although this was also motivated by the desire to let him have the means to demobilise his armies and thus ensure stability in the region.[31] In Britain, on the other hand, a radical turn-about in the Iraq policy was made and the Thatcher government began removing all traces of its earlier involvement in the arming of Saddam. A spate of assassinations of key players in the British supply effort included the killing of Gerald Bull, the designer of the super-gun, in March 1990.[32]

Thus we get to the first Gulf War. Saddam Hussein, bankrupted by the war with Iran, began complaining to Kuwait over that country's all-out oil production strategy and the exploitation of deposits on the Iraq–Kuwait border by Kuwait. Even at this point, the US was so keen to maintain its connections with Iraq that the Bush I administration sent ambivalent signals about whether it would tolerate a military solution to Saddam's conflict with Kuwait. As US warships were patrolling the Persian Gulf in late July 1990, US ambassador April Glaspie, summoned to meet Saddam Hussein, made the notorious remark that she was under 'direct instruction from the president so seek better relations with Iraq', specifying that the US had 'no opinion on the Arab–Arab conflicts like your border disagreement with Kuwait'. This has been raised as evidence of an attempt to trick the Iraqi dictator into an adventure.[33] It may also have been an expression of the real hesitation regarding whether or not to build up Saddam Hussein as a regional power and US ally, now that Iran was a lost cause. Glaspie's were not the only signals in that direction. Five months earlier, when General Schwarzkopf outlined the danger Iraq posed to its neighbours in the US Senate, Assistant Secretary of State J. Kelly told Saddam in Baghdad that the US considered him a 'force of moderation'. A US senate delegation in March confirmed that line. Yet the preparation for a showdown with Saddam would seem to have been the stronger element all along, also given the neoconservative connection with Israel. In May, the National Security Council in a memo to Bush described Iraq and Saddam as '*the optimum contenders to replace the Warsaw Pact*'.[34]

Iraq invaded Kuwait on 2 August 1990. Saddam now held some 20 per cent of global oil reserves, challenging Saudi Arabia's position as the world's swing producer with 25 per cent. There was a hint of the OPEC revolt of the early 1970s, but although oil prices almost doubled after the invasion, the danger did not reside just in energy prices. As Bush Sr. later confirmed, the geopolitical rules of a post-cold war world were at stake—*the question was whether French and Russian relations with Iraq were to be allowed to hold up the establishment of a 'new world order' under American leadership.*[35] Mrs. Thatcher was prominent among those urging the Americans to use force, although she had resigned over the arms-to-Iraq scandal by the time the president declared the new world order. UK munitions deliveries to Iraq continued as late as the invasion of Kuwait, exposing British soldiers to shells just shipped in from the mother country.[36]

UN Security Council Resolution 661 meanwhile imposed, in the words of an authoritative study, 'the most comprehensive economic measures ever devised by the UN'. As late as December, many US senators still argued that fighting could be avoided given the scope of the sanctions, which brought Iraq's oil exports to a halt almost immediately; the country's GDP fell by two-thirds in 1991.[37] But the 'new world order' argument prevailed. If Iraq would have to be bribed out of Kuwait because Europe and Japan were not willing to join in a fight, this might lead to a crisis in the US world role with unforeseeable consequences.[38]

'Desert Storm' was mandated in UN Security Council Resolution 678. This mandate also tipped the balance in favour of war in the US Congress. The air attacks, eagerly awaited by the US arms industry as a means of repairing 'the damage done by the end of the cold war',[39] began in January 1991. For the first time in its history, the UN authorised a war in response to an invasion—nothing of the sort had taken place when Israel occupied parts of Syria and Lebanon and stayed there for decades in spite of one UN resolution after another. France and Britain provided troops for the invasion, but Germany and Japan remained on the sidelines. The cost of the Gulf War for the US was $61 billion, which was covered to the extent of 97 per cent by contributions from other states. Saudi Arabia paid 32 per cent of the total, Kuwait 30 per cent, Japan 19 per cent and Germany 12 per cent. By charging the allies, Britain actually made a £650 million profit on a £1.5 billion 'investment'.[40] Effectively, the war was run as a mercenary operation.

Relations with the tottering Soviet Union were more complicated. Consent for the UN resolution had been obtained by Secretary Baker, but in February the Soviet leadership suddenly sent Yuri Primakov, well-groomed in relations with Moscow's Arab allies, to Baghdad. Primakov reported that Saddam was willing to withdraw from Kuwait if his troops would not be attacked and sanctions were lifted. But Washington was in no mood to allow Moscow a role in solving the crisis. Indeed when Gorbachev negotiated a ceasefire with the Iraqi foreign minister, Tariq Aziz, the United States issued an ultimatum of its own to prevent being stopped from invading the country.[41]

The US-led coalition easily destroyed the Iraqi forces in their flight from Kuwait in what became known as a 'turkey shoot'. Between 125,000 and 150,000 Iraqi troops were killed, many of them by experimental weapons such as fuel-air explosives, the BLU 'daisy cutter', cluster bombs, and other ordnance of doubtful legal status.[42] Still uncertain about the course to follow in the post-cold war world, however, the invading armies did not push on to Baghdad. They even allowed the remnants of the Iraqi army to put down a rebellion by the Kurds in the north and the Shia Muslims in the south, which the West had encouraged them to launch.[43]

Islamists against Modernising State Classes

In the 1980s counter-revolution, the United States sought the support of all indigenous forces it could muster to combat the main challenge—the Soviet bloc and the contender state classes of the NIEO coalition. This tactic had been employed successfully in Iran in 1953, where Western agents mobilised the Shia clergy and their followers against the nationalists and communists. At the time, Washington was concerned that Iran might 'disappear behind the Iron Curtain', and this fear was still alive when Khomeini took power. As the Tower Commission reported later, in 1983 the US 'helped bring to the attention of Tehran the threat inherent in the extensive infiltration of the government by the communist Tudeh Party and Soviet or pro-Soviet cadres in the country. Using this information, the Khomeini government took measures, including mass executions, that virtually eliminated the pro-Soviet infrastructure in Iran.'[44] Otherwise, there was of course little love lost between Washington and Tehran.

There is an element of the same unease regarding the supposed alliance with the wealthiest Sunni Islamist state, Saudi Arabia. In the run-up of the Gulf War, suspicion arose that the Saudis were drifting out of control, as they are again suspected to be doing today—with China the culprit in both cases. From 1973 onwards the United States had indeed taken an active role in modernising the Saudi state and security apparatus. A joint commission set up by Kissinger and Treasury Secretary Simon (but paid for by Riyadh) worked closely with the Saudis, who were also buying US arms totalling around $100 billion through the 1980s. However, towards the end of the decade the kingdom was diversifying its weapons procurement. The purchase in 1988 of Chinese CSS2 missiles, which could reach Israel, led to a predictable storm. But then the Saudis were not necessarily grateful for having given in to Washington's pressure to bring down the oil price in 1986 in order to help undermine Gorbachev. From $227 billion in 1981, Saudi oil income fell to $60 billion a year at the beginning of the 1990s.[45]

Stationing the US-led expeditionary force on Saudi soil for landings in Kuwait thus had the additional advantage of bringing Riyadh into line. The house of Saud, however, rules with the consent of the Islamic scholars of the Wahabi sect, the most reactionary Sunni denomination in Islam. Although a US ally since the Second World War, the kingdom is therefore occasionally forced to act against Washington's interests. This was the case in the 1973 oil boycott, demanded by the ulema. The planned deployment of US troops in Saudi Arabia would always be a serious test of the monarchy's relations with the clergy, as the presence of 'infidels' on Saudi soil could be seen as desecrating Islam's holy sites. Hence the foreign policy team preparing the war first had to convince the Saudi king to override the ulema on this issue. In early August 1990, Defence Secretary Cheney travelled to Riyadh with Joint Chiefs Chairman Powell, Wolfowitz, CIA director Robert Gates and General Schwarzkopf to turn the screws on the reticent king. Their claim that Iraqi troops were amassing on the border was fiction; a Saudi reconnaissance mission failed to detect Iraqi troops, and Soviet satellite pictures confirmed that there were none. Nevertheless the king yielded. It was agreed to construct the US military presence, which increased to 540,000 on the eve of the war, as having been requested by Saudi Arabia to protect its borders. A small force would remain behind afterwards.[46]

Of course, as we know today, this was a fateful decision. Not only did it arouse the anger of the Wahabi ulema but, more importantly, it prompted Osama bin Laden, the leader of the 'Arab brigade' in Afghanistan, to claim the status of an Islamic scholar himself, in defiance of the clerics back in his homeland who were seen to have given in. The war however gave the United States new leverage on the rulers of Kuwait and Saudi Arabia, indeed 'more influence in [OPEC] than any industrial nation has ever exercised.'[47] While UN sanctions kept Iraqi oil away from the world market, the US leaned on Saudi Arabia as the swing producer to maintain prices at a sufficiently high level to keep arms sales to the OPEC countries going. Between 1990 and 1997, Saudi Arabia spent $36.2 billion on arms in the US alone, while Kuwait ordered weaponry to the tune of 4.2 billion.[48] Weapons exports to the Middle East after the end of the Gulf War saw a decline back to the level prior to the Iran–Iraq war, but the US restored its share in deliveries to around 40–45 per cent.[49]

The steady decline of Saudi oil revenue (down to $35 billion a year in 1998)[50] did not affect the country's oligarchy, whose income sources had diversified, as can be seen in Table 10.1. Yet the creeping modernisation of the country, compounded by the impoverishment of the population, is widely considered to be destabilising Saudi society. Military guarantees by the US in exchange for access to oil and Saudi purchases of US bonds are obviously not enough to ensure stability in the long run.[51] Kissinger, who had a direct hand in retooling the Saudi state through the aforementioned joint commission, makes a prophetic statement in his memoirs when he writes that in the 'artificial cities' of Saudi Arabia, a new world different from the Bedouin

Table 10.1
Wealthiest Individuals in the Middle East (2003) in US$ Billion

Name	Sector	Fortune	Country
Prince Al-Waleed Bin Talal al-Saud	Investments	17.7	Saudi Arabia
K., H., H., L. & M. Olayan	Investments	6.9	Saudi Arabia
N. al-Kharafi	Construction	5.1	Kuwait
R. al-Hariri*	Construction	3.8	Lebanon
M. Jameel	Automobile	3	Saudi Arabia
A. Bin Hamad al-Gosaibi	Finance	2.9	Saudi Arabia
K. Bin Mahfouth	Banking	2.8	Saudi Arabia
S. Sabanci*	Various	2.8	Turkey
S. Kamel	Various	2.3	Saudi Arabia
S. Bin Abdul al-Rajhi	Banking	2.1	Saudi Arabia

Source: Compiled from *Forbes* data, as in *Le Monde*, 10 November 2003 (some names include family).
Note: *meanwhile deceased.

past is developing. A Westernised cadre has come to face a 'depersonalized, detribalized proletariat', each in its own way posing serious challenges. However, 'America's relation-ship had been on the whole with the world of the princes.'[52] Under their patronage, Saudi money has woven extensive webs of charity across the Middle East, allowing the Wahabi brand of Sunni Islam to take root else-where. This takes us to two of the poorest relations of Islam, Pakistan and Afghanistan, two hotbeds of anti-Western Islamism.

Pakistan, as we saw, was part of the US-sponsored 'northern tier' against communism and Arab nationalism; towards Afghanistan, Washington preferred a low profile, leaving the country as a buffer state with the USSR.[53] Moscow however steadily gained influence through aid, and in 1973 a military coup with communist support led to a beginning of state-led development in Afghanistan. But progressive measures by the new Daud government alienated Islamic Afghan intellectuals, who had studied in Cairo and there mingled with the Muslim Brotherhood, and they turned to neighbouring Pakistan for help.[54]

State formation in Pakistan, as will be remembered, entered a crisis with the secession of Bangladesh. This event and the defeat against India in the war of 1971 deeply affected the Pakistani officer class. A new crop of military personnel, hailing from provincial and middle-class backgrounds, began to take the place of the British-trained gentlemen in uniform who had lost the war.[55] The ascendant orientation was towards radical Islamism, and when co-religionists from Afghanistan turned to Pakistan for help, they found a willing ear. The intersecting processes of state formation in ethnically heterogeneous societies form the background here. Daud hoped to build a 'Pashtunistan' around the dominant ethnic group in Afghanistan; the Pakistani military on the other hand feared that their own Pashtun minority might be seduced by this project. Hence they used Tajik minority leaders and Islamists to keep Daud 'off balance'.[56] Daud in turn moved closer to Iran (then still under the Shah) and the US. This provoked the pro-communist Afghan military to throw him out in April 1978 and embark on far-reaching land reforms and secularisation. These measures and the friendship treaty with the USSR concluded in December led rebels loyal to the landlords and Islamic traditionalists to take up arms with support from the Islamist military of Pakistan, which had meanwhile come under the rule of their own dictator, Zia ul Haq, who seized power in 1977.

This was the situation when the Soviet Union invaded Afghanistan in December 1979, partly to settle infighting between rival factions in the communist leadership in Kabul. Today we know that US policymakers saw this as a serious blunder, indeed as a trap that would bleed the Soviet contender dry if the US played its cards correctly.[57] Washington too made a cardinal mistake, however, when it let the Pakistani intelligence service (ISI), the bulwark of the new Islamist officer class, decide who among the Afghan rebels would receive US money. In addition the Americans brought in the Saudis to fund the Contra campaign, complete with an 'Arab brigade' led by Bin Laden. These forces thus became players in an Islamist project perhaps best articulated by Zia ul Haq, who remained in power during the greater part of the Soviet intervention (until his plane was blown up in 1988). Zia, Selig Harrison has argued, believed in establishing a Pakistani satellite regime in Kabul, and rolling back Indian and Soviet influence in the region. There will arise, Zia claimed shortly before his death, as part of *a strategic realignment*, an Islamic state and an Islamic confederation, part of a pan-Islamist renaissance. It would comprise—apart from an Afghan-Pakistani federation—Tajikistan and Uzbekistan, and possibly Iran and Turkey.[58]

This idea of an Islamist contender bloc taking the place of the Western-supported 'northern tier' would not materialise. It lacked the foundations of effective state power and a minimum of state-led economic development. But rebel groups financed by the ISI in Afghanistan certainly did act in the spirit of a pan-Islamist renaissance, and so would other Islamist groups with a grudge against the West. President Bush Sr. claimed at the end of the Gulf War that victory had dispelled national self-doubt and disunity,[59] but others were less optimistic. As former Japanese prime minister Nakasone remarked in a post-war magazine round-up of expert opinion, 'the victory has heightened respect for the United States in many countries, [but] it has sharpened antipathy and distrust in some Third World, Muslim and communist countries. Even in the free world there will be some uneasiness over whether the United States will tend to monopolize leadership.' Prime Minister Lee Kuan Yew of Singapore cautioned that if the US would not simultaneously push for a solution to the Israeli occupation of the West

Bank and Gaza, this would generate 'anti-American sentiments in the Arab and Muslim states of Africa, the Middle East and Asia.' More specifically, he warned against stationing Western land forces in the area.[60]

Before pursuing this in the final section of this chapter, let us look at how the contest over the newly available fossil fuel resources of the disintegrating Soviet Union affected energy and geopolitical rivalries in the wider region.

STRUGGLES OVER CASPIAN ENERGY RESOURCES AND THE 'NEW SILK ROAD'

Following the collapse of the USSR, Russian energy corporations backed by Moscow joined the competition to gain control of the energy sources in the newly independent former Soviet republics. The English-speaking states, home until then to the world's leading oil corporations, responded with a two-pronged strategy: first, prying open the Russian economy itself; and, second, trying to gain control over the Caspian states on its southern perimeter—Russia's 'near abroad'—in a further attempt to dispossess the state classes holding power. As I will argue in this section, this strategy had mixed results, but it certainly contributed to the resurrection of a strong state in Russia.

The oil reserves of the Caspian region were initially estimated at around 150 billion barrels, half those of Saudi Arabia. (Meanwhile estimates have been downgraded to half that or less.)[61] Politically, the new states in the region, shocked by the Soviet withdrawal from Afghanistan and the collapse of the USSR, were uncertain where to anchor their security. The Commonwealth of Independent States (CIS) was important to maintain the links with the Russian economy, but in January 1993 President Nazarbayev of Kazakhstan formed a regional cooperation bloc of Central Asian countries in case the CIS were not to deliver.

The first state attempting to organise the new regional constellation was Turkey. In 1992 it embarked on a programme of cultural and political rapprochement, spending more than $1.5 billion in the next six years, while covering its relations with Moscow by increasing energy imports from Russia. Certainly Ankara did not really become the regional power it had hoped to. But the barring of EU membership in 1997 and current resistance in the EU to expand further may revitalise the forces envisaging closer relations with Russia and the new Central Asia.[62]

The US government, in the words of one oilman, 'was slow to pick up on the importance of the region, [and thus the former Soviet republics] forged relations with U.S. business.'[63] The private Western entrants into the 'New Great Game' included well-placed individuals, maverick companies and large oil companies—in that order.[64] It was not until Clinton's globalisation offensive of 1994 that the US developed its own geopolitical offensive to wrest control of the region from Russia. In Azerbaijan, the historic oil centre of the Russian empire, Soviet geologists had already discovered substantial new reserves in the Caspian Sea. Ramco, an independent oil-services company from the UK, had a look in 1989 when tensions between Azerbaijan and Armenia were rising high over the Nagorno-Karabakh enclave. In January 1990, Gorbachev dispatched troops to suppress a nationalist uprising in Baku which left 200 dead, but later in the year Ramco approached BP and became a junior partner of a consortium formed by BP with Statoil of Norway. In April 1991, Amoco, the US oil company, joined in, but in the war with Armenia that followed the Azeri declaration of independence of August that year (and which would last until a ceasefire in the spring of 1994), governments came and went, and the oil companies, reinforced in the meantime by Pennzoil and Unocal, had to wait.[65]

The struggle over the Karabakh area, an Armenian enclave in Azerbaijan, led to an agitation in Turkey (the Turks are ethnically related to the Azeris), but Ankara did no want to risk its envisaged role in the wider region. In May 1992 NATO expressed concern over the war, but this occurred at a time when the organisation had not yet been active 'out of area'.[66] Neither was Washington able to play a role, given the power of the Armenian diaspora in Congress. Instead, Iran–Contra hands such as retired general R. Secord, now on the payroll of US oil companies, were reported to be active in Azerbaijan in 1993; in August, a thousand Afghan *mujahedeen*, procured through the Contra tri-continental, arrived in Baku to fight against the Armenians.[67] The CIA too was involved in the region. An American agent was killed in the summer of 1993 in Georgia, when the Russians were stoking up an uprising of the Abkhazian minority there. Clinton authorised a CIA operation in Georgia to support the Shevardnadze government, with an eye to stationing US special forces and security advisers in the strategically located republic. Today, a pro-American government installed by a 'people power' revolt is in office in Tbilisi.[68]

The initial flurry of private activity in the region fits into the picture of an unravelling of the neoliberal project into rapaciousness of its political agents. BP used the services of recently resigned prime minister Thatcher to deliver cheques totalling $30 million to the Azeris in 1992, as a downpayment for concessions.[69] Later, Mrs. Thatcher and her entourage became even bolder in the 'Great Game' opening up over Caspian energy sources, when she and former Tory party treasurer Lord McAlpine, the building tycoon, were reported to be engaged in negotiations with Chechen mafia leaders to lease the section of the pipeline running through the breakaway province (the only link available for Azeri oil to western markets) to a private consortium.[70] Indeed so many former politicians were active in private Caspian oil diplomacy (in addition to Thatcher, ex-White House chief of staff John Sununu, national security advisers Scowcroft and Brzezinski, and secretaries of state Haig, Kissinger and Baker), that questions were raised about the appropriateness of their dealings. But in July 1997 a US State Department spokesman defended the right of former officials to 'engage in normal private life—which, in the United States, is capitalism, number one'.[71]

The established oil corporations had by then taken the place of mercenaries and ex-politicians dabbling as oil traders. In Azerbaijan, former Soviet politburo member Heydar Aliyev, who took power in June 1993, concluded a deal with Amoco a year later. The Azerbaijan International Operating Co. (AIOC) consortium included Amoco, BP (which later merged with Amoco), the Azeri state oil company and also Russia's Lukoil, as well as a handful of smaller operators like Ramco, the pioneer.[72] In an earlier development, Chevron of the US negotiated a participation in Kazakhstan's Tenghiz field for four years. Discussions began when the USSR was still in existence. The agreement was concluded in the course of 1992, and doubled Chevron's worldwide reserves. This deal too was facilitated by initial contacts made by individual operators, including the former president of the US–USSR Trade & Economic Council, J.H. Giffen, and Dutch oil trader Johannes Deuss (president of Transworld Oil and Bermuda-based Oman Oil). When the USSR collapsed, Deuss' earlier assistance to Nazerbayev paved the way for the joint venture with Chevron: Tengizchevroil (TCO).[73]

The Clinton policy of viewing Caspian energy resources as a subtext of rapprochement with Moscow was led by Deputy Secretary of State Talbott (who could also be heard talking about 200 billion barrels of reserves, the reserves of Iraq and Iran combined). But Talbott was removed when the administration shifted course to NATO expansion and engagement in the Yugoslav conflict in 1994.[74] Clinton now encouraged Israel, Turkey and Pakistan to bolster Uzbekistan, Azerbaijan and Turkmenistan, while Russia consolidated its influence in Kazakhstan, Kyrgyzstan and Tajikistan.[75] The stage was obviously being set for a trial of strength, and the American intervention in the Yugoslav conflict cannot be understood in isolation from this evolving process.

With American planes flying missions against the Bosnian Serbs in Yugoslavia, Washington's aims in the Caspian region shifted to ensuring an energy transport infrastructure *beyond Russian control*, a hostile policy bound to lead to tension. The State Department endorsed the construction of a new pipeline from Baku on the Caspian to Ceyhan on Turkey's south coast, 'designed', according to *Newsweek*, 'to break Russia's grip on Central Asia's oil exports.' As the State Department energy affairs director put it, 'we will defend the commercial rights of U.S. companies. We do not recognize spheres of influence.'[76] National Security Adviser Berger convened a meeting of US oil companies operating in Azerbaijan to discuss the pipeline, which agreed not to engage in rival pipeline plans, of which several were circulating at the time. Clinton in a long personal phone call to Aliyev pushed the Baku-Ceyhan pipeline as an alternative to the pipeline crossing Russia through Chechnya.[77]

Former national security adviser Brzezinski was asked by Clinton to go to Azerbaijan and convince its leader of the wisdom of challenging Russian preferences.[78] In early 1995, William White, deputy US energy secretary, toured the region in support of a non-Russian pipeline route. This was in open defiance of Russia's attempt to encourage Azerbaijan, Kazakhstan and Turkmenistan to continue shipping oil and gas through Russia.[79] But Russia too had a number of trumps to play. The Caspian Pipeline Consortium (CPC), which it had originally set up in 1992 with Kazakhstan and Oman Oil, was to build a pipeline to Novorossiysk on the Black Sea in order to transport Tenghiz oil across Kazakh and Russian territory. In 1996, Mobil (today's ExxonMobil) joined the Tenghiz consortium and CPC; but so did Lukoil, the largest Russian oil company, and Transneft, the state-owned pipeline monopoly. Thus the aim to sideline Moscow was derailed in turn.[80]

Like BP, the UK's Conservative government under John Major was more willing to accommodate Russia than was the US. However, under American pressure, they both honed in on the projected Ceyhan route, even if in the meantime oil would have to be routed through existing pipelines under Russian control.[81] Certainly the further fall in oil prices in 1997 led BP-Amoco to question the wisdom of the Ceyhan pipeline. The estimated cost of $3 billion was not warranted at the prevailing oil price ($11 per barrel), even with Kazakh oil from across the Caspian.[82] Hence a demonstration of American willingness to back up its plans was in order. In September 1997, 600 paratroops from the US 82nd airborne division landed in Kazakhstan after a non-stop flight from North Carolina. Their commanding officer declared, with characteristic bravado, that 'there is no place on earth we cannot get to.'[83] Kazakhstan has indeed turned out to be a much greater prize than expected, with China tapping into Kazakh oil through trade and participations.[84]

Brzezinski, having done his bit for Clinton and signed up as a consultant for Amoco, also identified Ukraine and Uzbekistan as strategic interests for the United States in 1997 in his book *The Grand Chessboard*. This was not just abstract thinking, given that he was the intellectual mentor of Secretary of State Madeleine Albright, then presiding over the intervention in former Yugoslavia.[85] The strategic importance of Ukraine is closely linked with energy questions; gas and oil pipelines linking Russia with the west run for the greater part through Ukraine (e.g., accounting for 95 per cent of Europe's gas supply from Russia). The Chechnya war was helping Atlantic unity here. In the mid-1990s, the EU postponed a trade agreement with Russia because of the war in Chechnya, but signed an identical agreement with Ukraine. It was reported at the time that 'Western leaders appear to have decided that backing Kiev is a way to build up a counterweight to Moscow.'[86]

Obviously, given the size of EU trade with Russia and the country's vast energy and other mineral resources, there will always be the 'Rapallo' tendency in continental European policy, and Washington recognised early on that Ukraine offered a means for regulating this relationship.[87] But in 1995 when NATO Secretary-General Claes abandoned caution by stating that the war in Chechnya could not be considered a domestic affair, a furious reaction from Moscow followed.[88]

The subsequent period saw a back and forth process between Russian–Ukrainian rapprochement (which gave rise to Western fears that privatisations in Ukraine might be snapped up by Russian tycoons) and US interventions to steer Ukraine on a course away from Moscow.[89] Ukraine was also a key partner in GUUAM (it was one of the original members with Georgia, Azerbaijan and Moldova), the tentative regional bloc, already referred to in Chapter 8, sponsored by the US, Britain and Turkey. Uzbekistan, the strongest military power in Central Asia, and strategically located between Kazakhstan and Turkmenistan (and with Afghanistan to the south), was added in 1999 (not least because of the impending confrontation with the Taliban then in progress).[90] GUUAM aims to create mechanisms for dispute settlement and peacekeeping, and, in a sign that in this case there exists a complementarity between Anglo-American and EU objectives, it also serves as a security framework for the projected New Silk Route, an EU initiative for which the basis had been laid in May 1993. At the time, eight ex-Soviet states signed up in Brussels to the Traceca project, which aims at developing transport links across the Caspian region to provide an alternative to the traditional trade route through Russia. Marginalising other initiatives to bring the Caspian region into a single transport infrastructure—such as the 1996 'Inogate' programme of the European Commission ('Interstate oil and gas transport to Europe')—the New Silk Road was confirmed in September 1998 with the aim to link China and Mongolia to Europe, with a permanent secretariat set up in Baku, and meant to secure the participating countries' independence from Russian dominance.[91]

The EU however simultaneously cultivates Russia. While the United States and Britain have led the offensive into the former Soviet bloc, the continental EU states (notably Germany) have continued to work with Moscow in the Rapallo tradition. In mid-2001, the head of the planning staff in the German Foreign Office, Achim Schmillen, in an echo of the Lubbers plan referred to in Chapter 8, argued the case for working more closely with Russia and Russian companies to build a politically secure and economically viable, multipolar pipeline system to transport oil and gas to the world market.[92]

GUUAM, on the other hand, aimed at integration into existing Euro-Atlantic security structures, notably NATO.[93] In 1999, it worked to encourage Azerbaijan and Georgia to withdraw from the collective security treaty with the other CIS states, although Russia retains influence through a military presence in Azerbaijan and peacekeeping troops in breakaway areas within

Georgia.[94] In the meantime, 'people power', first tried out in Belgrade to remove Milosevic, has drawn a trail of Western-supported political transformations (achieved earlier in Albania) through the GUUAM countries, Georgia and Ukraine, and reaching strategically crucial Kyrgyzstan. Georgia, a key station on the Baku–Ceyhan pipeline and strategically located on the Black Sea coast, received one-third of all US aid to the Caspian basin states in 1998–2000.[95] The Aliyev dynasty in Azerbaijan and Karimov of Uzbekistan on the other hand have apparently been judged too important to be subjected to a pop concert coup. But then, a final GUUAM purpose—anti-terrorism and combating religious extremism—allows dictatorships in the region to hide under the War on Terror umbrella when things get too hot.[96]

The US-sponsored people power/'democracy' campaign and the military-strategic aspect of its advance have certainly been successful, and have now reached the Kyrgyz–Chinese border. But Russia and China have drawn nearer to each other as a result (and also because of pipeline plans related to China's growing energy needs), while Transneft was able to ward off penetration of foreign firms into the Russian pipeline grid.[97] The CPC pipeline became operational a month after the 11 September attacks in a rare moment of US–Russian agreement, but it was by all means a victory for Russia. Russia and Kazakhstan, across whose territory the pipeline passes, also have majority ownership (if Russian companies are taken into account).[98] In another clear setback to the US and the UK, in February 1999 ENI of Italy and Gazprom signed a memorandum—despite US protests that this would undermine Turkey's commitment to the 'energy corridor' from the Caspian region to Turkey—to proceed with the 'Blue Stream' project for an underwater gas pipeline across the Black Sea from the Russian coast (bypassing Ukraine) to Samsun in Turkey.[99] In 2002 Blue Stream, constructed by the original contractors jointly with Turkish and Japanese companies, became operational; the plan launched by an Anglo-American consortium to build a gas pipeline across the Caspian (to bring Turkmen gas into the Baku–Ceyhan grid and also to Turkey) has stalled as a result.[100] In May 2005, the Baku–Ceyhan oil pipeline was officially opened as well. Even this pipeline, connecting GUUAM allies Azerbaijan and Georgia with Turkey (and in which BP holds the 38 per cent majority stake), may moreover in the end benefit Turkey rather than the US. Turkey's relations with the US have weakened further because of the Iraq war; the value of its trade with the EU-12 in 2000 was already 4.5 times that with the United States.[101]

Energy Oligarchs and the Russian State

The Western role in bringing down the Soviet Union and its ruthless advance into Eastern Europe and the 'near abroad' brought home to many Russians the fact that the only way to interrupt the rampage was to build a strong state capable of defending its society against predators at home and abroad.

This has revived the ideology of 'Eurasianism'. Its two interrelated theses are that Russia is more an Asian than a European power and therefore 'should place itself at the head of Asia in the struggle against European predominance'; and that Bolshevism has activated Russia and given it new influence in world affairs. Now that the state-socialist phase of Russian resurrection has run its course, the argument goes, the country should assert its interests under a nationalist ideology developed by 'White' exiles in the 1920s. Although explicit Eurasianism in today's Russia is a minority tendency, its authoritarian, anti-parliamentarian impulses and the notion of using a modern state to further Russian power broadly characterise the development of the country since the collapse of the USSR.[102]

The 'tycoons' emerged when the state monopoly of foreign trade was dismantled. They used opportunities created by a group of westernisers led by Anatoli Chubais, who had links to the state privatisation agency and to Western financial institutions. Yeltsin was their figurehead in many respects because he had made his claim to power and obtained foreign support on the basis of their programme. The tycoons are identified in Table 10.2 (for 2003, to make comparison possible with other oligarchies).

Table 10.2
Wealthiest Individuals in Russia (2003) in US$ Billion

Name	Sector	Fortune	Age in 2003	(Age at the Time of the USSR's Collapse in 1991)
Mikhail Khodorkovsky	Oil	8	39	(27)
Roman Abramovich	Oil	5.7	36	(24)
Mikhail Fridman	Oil	4.3	38	(26)
Viktor Vekselberg	Metals/Oil	2.5	45	(33)
Vladimir Potanin	Metals	1.6	42	(30)
Mikhail Prokorov	Metals	1.6	37	(25)
Vladimir Yevtushenkov	Various	1.5	54	(42)
Oleg Deripaska	Aluminium	1.5	34	(22)
Vagit Alekperov	Oil	1.3	52	(40)
Alexei Mordachov	Metals	1.2	38	(26)

Source: Compiled from *Forbes* data, as in *Le Monde*, 10 November 2003 (age in 1991 added).

However, powerful rivals were resisting the tycoons from the start. These included a clan led by O. Soskovets, deriving its power from the metals sector and the security apparatus of Soviet times; a group around the state-owned energy sector led by V. Chernomyrdin, prime minister under Yeltsin and the head of the gas monopoly, Gazprom; and a Moscow group controlling the capital's resources, led by Yuri Luzhkov, the mayor of the city.[103] The war in Chechnya was very much a regulator of the conflicts between these groups, because, for obvious reasons, war against Chechnya's separatists in the Caucasus tended to shift resources and power to the security apparatus. Yeltsin signed a decree privatising the oil sector in 1992, but in 1994 Soskovets, who was deputy prime minister at the time, was able to mobilise a coalition including Yeltsin's bodyguard, General Korzhakov, to restore a degree of state control over the economy. They successfully appealed to the emergency created by the war in Chechnya.[104] One aim of this group was to restore the state monopoly of violence and disarm the private armies of the capitalist tycoons, such as the security guards of V. Gusinsky of Most Bank, who was speculating against the rouble and backed Luzhkov's ambition to capture government power. Yeltsin's guard however struck hard against Gusinsky, and purged state security of Luzhkov supporters in late 1994.[105]

Clinton's policy of NATO expansion, and the NATO declarations about Chechnya in 1995 referred to above, infuriated those in Russia already smarting from the loss of sovereignty and prestige after the collapse of the USSR. General Grachev, the minister of defence, identified Chechnya as 'a testing ground for the strategic enemies of Russia whose main aim is to split the country and annex part of its territory'.[106] Chernomyrdin tried to extract Russia from the war, but Grachev obtained Yeltsin's consent to step up the fighting in the early autumn of 1995.[107] The appointment of Primakov—the mediator with Baghdad and a fierce critic of NATO's eastward expansion—as foreign minister in January 1996 signalled that those willing the stand up to the Western offensive posture were gaining ground. In 1994, when still the head of the foreign intelligence service, Primakov had warned that the West was actively pursuing a further break-up of the former Soviet Union.[108] This was exactly what Brzezinski was advocating at this point. Concerned that the Russian federation remained too centralised, he claimed that 'a decentralised political system and free-market economy would be most likely to unleash the creative potential of the Russian people and Russia's vast natural resources.' A loosely confederated Russia, made up of a European Russia and what Brzezinski has already designated a 'Siberian republic and a Far Eastern republic' would therefore be welcome. This agreed with his predictions at an earlier stage that the Soviet economy should be geared to raw material exports, neutralising its military-industrial capacity.[109]

Yeltsin's close identification with the new class of tycoons and criminals made his re-election as Russia's president in 1996 highly doubtful. US polling organisations active in Russia found him trailing in third place after General Lebed, a Chechen war hero, and Yavlinski, the moderate liberal of Trilateral stripe. It was felt that the election might even result in a return of the communists, given that the notion of 'market reforms' had lost all credibility.[110] The tycoons, convening on the margin of the World Economic Forum's Davos summit of January 1996, therefore decided to join forces and entrust Chubais with the task of securing the ailing president's re-election. Boris Berezovsky (who made his fortune with the Logovaz Lada dealerships and

Aeroflot), Gusinsky, Khodorkovsky, P. Aven, M. Fridman and A. Smolensky, together controlling (according to Berezovsky) 50 per cent of the Russian economy, prevailed on Yeltsin to enlist General Lebed for the second round as his running mate and head of the security council, only to be dumped again after the election. Amidst wild-west scenes complete with illegal money transports, arrests and chases, Yeltsin's re-election was miraculously secured. When the dust had settled, Grachev, Korzhakov and Soskovets were all fired.[111] As a western banker in Moscow put it after Yeltsin's re-election, 'it was a contest of the crooks against the communists and the crooks won.'[112]

Of course the West did not fail the Yeltsin bloc at this critical juncture. In February, the IMF announced a $10.2 billion loan, the second-largest ever by the Fund, in the expectation (this was the heyday of the 'emerging markets' hype that would soon explode) that the Russian economy would grow by growth rates of 2.2–4 per cent for several years, before climbing to an 'expected' 6 per cent. In the heat of the embrace, the Kremlin in return pledged to scrap oil and gas export tariffs, thus further releasing the hold on its mineral riches, while indicating that it would stick to a tight fiscal and monetary policy. Managing Director Camdessus did not fail to add that if the communists were to win and change economic policy, the IMF would suspend the loan (which was to be disbursed in monthly instalments to keep leverage on the Russian government).[113] The re-election ignited a further inflow of foreign funds, inflating the stock market. Foreign investment bankers fell over each other predicting further growth. A Morgan Stanley strategist spoke of 'the most exciting, biggest potential play in the world'.[114] The IMF was no longer that convinced and suspended the disbursement of the last instalment of the re-election loan in October 1996, because Russia was obviously not collecting taxes from the tycoons closest to the government. Also, foreigners were excluded from the highly profitable local government debt market, where yields of more than 50 per cent were not exceptional.[115] Obviously, the capitalist class in the West is not interested in keeping an abstract capitalism in place, but wants to share in the spoils. It was only through a $1 billion Eurobond loan, the first since the Bolshevik revolution, that Russia could at this point avoid defaulting on its obligations.[116]

Yet the tide was turning. As one of Yeltsin's American campaign advisers warned after the re-election, the communists had been defeated, but the sentiment against predatory capitalism had not—only 10 per cent of Russians were positive about private ownership of industry, against 50 per cent for state ownership and one-third for workers' control. What had been achieved was merely the uncoupling of the anti-capitalist, anti-Western mood from the Communist party.[117] So even if for a short time it seemed as if the tycoons were running the country (Chubais as Kremlin chief of staff, Potanin as a first deputy prime minister, and Berezovsky as vice-chairman of the security council), the mood in the country was running against them both on economic and on geopolitical grounds. Their attack against the big state energy monopolies such as Gazprom of Prime Minister Chernomyrdin and on the surviving large industrial corporations such as Avtovaz ended in stalemate.[118] True, when Russia withdrew in humiliation from Chechnya in August 1997, the tycoons were still able to convince Yeltsin that Chernomyrdin was to blame; he was sacked in March 1998 (a year later he would emerge as a mediator in the final stages of the Kosovo war).[119]

However, the speculative nature of the financial foray into Russia and the related fragility of the tycoons' economic power were finally exposed later in the year. On 17 August, 'the most exciting, biggest potential play in the world' came to an unexpected end when the country's financial authorities defaulted on Russia's government bond obligations, paralysing its banking sector ($28.5 billion of the $183 billion foreign debt at the time was owed by Russian corporations and banks).[120] Foreign investors faced $33 billion in direct losses, and the Russian tycoons too were hard hit. Certainly most of them survived comfortably in the end (as can be seen in Table 10.2). But the crisis sufficiently weakened them to allow rival fractions to attack, sometimes under the guise of anti-fraud investigations by the state. The ubiquitous Brzezinski commented on the turn of events with the view that the financial crisis had exploded naïve ideas about Russia's privatisation and democratisation, and correctly predicted that Russia still had the capacity to restore a strong state.[121]

The crisis marks the turning point in the recent history of the formation of a new Russian state, away from the tycoon-controlled early Yeltsin period. A new type of contender posture, capitalist but with restored primacy for strategic direction by the state, and under a broadly 'Eurasian' ideology, began to take shape after 1998. Uncoupled from the global circuit of money capital, but with 70 per cent of GDP accounted for by the private sector, the long collapse of the Russian economy had bottomed out.[122] Primakov was appointed prime minister in August, only to be replaced (according to some, because his brusqueness might become dangerous in the face of Western belligerency) by another former intelligence chief, S. Stepashin, in May 1999. The next step was the promotion of another security official, Vladimir Putin, to the presidency in August. The Chechen conflict and struggles over pipelines played a part here; an attempt to re-route oil from Baku via Dagestan (on to Novorossiysk) provoked Chechen attacks in southern Dagestan, to which Moscow responded by a full-scale invasion of Chechnya.[123] In the climate of a defence of Russia's interests both against the West and against the rebels, Putin's rise as a strong man also profited from terrorist attacks in Moscow attributed to Chechens. As Mehdi Amineh writes, Putin's rise boosted the Eurasianist strand in Russian opinion that seeks a return to great power status under a broadly anti-Western aegis.[124]

With Putin, the restoration of a strong state has begun in earnest. Around a quarter of the Russian bureaucracy have a background in the security services, against 3 per cent under Gorbachev, and the merger of political and economic power is stronger than it has been for a long time. This includes regions (provincial governors have lost their parliamentary immunity and, hence, the ability to defy the central government) and municipalities.[125] The tycoons have been forced to vacate the public sphere. Significantly, the two tycoons who owned TV stations, Berezovsky and Gusinsky, are in exile today; Abramovich, the second richest among the tycoons and a former protégé of Berezovsky, has secured a measure of immunity by a high-profile purchase of Chelsea football club and residence in Britain. Khodorkovsky, the owner of Yukos and the richest man of Russia, on the other hand lost the game. When he began buying up delegates in the Duma, with an eye to influencing privatisation policy in ways challenging Putin, and negotiated privately with China about a trans-Siberian pipeline, all the while sounding out ExxonMobil and Chevron about selling participations in Yukos, he was arrested for fraud in late 2003—a charge always valid given how the tycoons obtained their fortunes. Russia wants control over its raw material wealth and a pipeline to its far eastern port, Nachodka, to diversify from its dependence on European markets to China *and* to Japan and the US, and Putin struck back against an obvious attempt to destabilise his policies. Forty per cent of Yukos shares were confiscated and in May 2005 Khodorkovsky was given a nine-year prison sentence.[126] Yukos was duly passed back, through an obvious proxy construction involving Rosneft and Gazprom, into national patrimony. Certainly the uproar in the West, especially among neoconservatives, was not long in coming. But in light of the endless broken pledges and real reversals, the Russians feel entitled to defend their interests.[127] Militarily, the country increasingly relies on its nuclear arsenal, notably the new Topol-M rocket designed to break through any US missile defence.[128]

Moscow has also organised its own economic sphere, through the formation of a customs union with Belarus, Kazakhstan, Kyrgyzstan and Tajikistan in 1995 (renamed Eurasian Economic Community, EAEC, in 2000). Significantly, the GUUAM bloc and Turkmenistan have remained outside this new bloc.[129] Moreover, in response to NATO expansion, a strategic alliance with China has taken shape. In 1996, Yeltsin and the leaders of China, Kazakhstan, Kyrgyzstan and Tajikistan signed a treaty in Shanghai, renouncing the use of force against each other in case of conflict.[130] In May 1997, the NATO–Russia Founding Act was concluded in Paris as the culminating event of a series of consolation prizes intended to compensate Russia for NATO expansion. But the solemn pledges and confessions of goodwill have begun to lose their shine. As Gilbert Achcar notes, 'at no point has the Atlantic Alliance, let alone the dominant American power, agreed to exclude from NATO expansion any former Soviet republics manifesting a wish to join. Quite the contrary.'[131]

In June 2000, the signatories to the 1996 Shanghai agreement, with the addition of Uzbekistan (still a member of GUUAM at the time), formed the Shanghai Cooperation Organisation (SCO). In 2002 it became a formal international organisation. The SCO has its secretariat in Beijing and is committed to economic cooperation and to the conservation of existing borders, an obvious concern of the states involved.[132] Whether this 'Asian Helsinki' will withstand the further forward pressure of the West remains to be seen. The US has a small military presence in Kyrgyzstan, contested by Russia; in 2003 China conducted joint military exercises with the Kyrgyz armed forces. Under existing defence agreements with Kyrgyzstan, Russia plans a large base in Kyrgyzstan, 35 miles from the US base. In March 2005, however, the president of Kyrgyzstan, A. Akayev, was toppled by an Ukrainian-style 'people power' movement and had to seek refuge in Moscow. Yet he, uniquely among Central Asian rulers, allowed an opposition and a liberal press.[133] But the strategic location of Kyrgyzstan puts a premium of direct US control.

AFGHANISTAN, 11 SEPTEMBER, AND THE INVASION OF IRAQ

The unification of global space under capitalist discipline in our age appears to be driving beyond its anchorage in the Lockean heartland. As the West loses its internal cohesion, it becomes less and less able to politically organise the space in which capital operates. The neoliberal offensive since the Reagan–Thatcher turn has certainly served capital and the oligarchic ruling classes, but it has also undermined the capacity of the West to bring anything positive and constructive to the areas it seeks to dominate. As Mark Duffield has argued, the Western approach towards the outside world is no longer inspired by a concern to aid indigenous processes of development, but to impose, if need be by force, the capitalist social model.[134] The Afghan and Iraq adventures that I will look at in this section illustrate the impotence that underlies the violent and regressive turn. In the next chapter, I will raise the question whether they have not reversed the liberal thrust of the Western advance altogether.

As we saw earlier, the neoconservative alliance between militarists in the US and a right-wing Zionist network raised the Soviet threat scare in the late 1970s; it then rode high in the Reagan and Bush I years. In the 1990s, the forces which had earlier operated through the Committee on the Present Danger and in 1992 underwritten the Defence Planning Guidance for 1994–99 regrouped again into a 'Project for the New American Century'. Their statement of principles in June 1997 reiterated the need for 'a military that is strong and ready to meet both present and future challenges; a foreign policy that boldly and purposefully promotes American principles abroad; and a national leadership that accepts the United States' global responsibilities'.[135] This approach took the trend of organising military assets in rapid deployment forces (instead of strategic zones of commitment such as Western Europe in the cold war) to its logical conclusion. With a maritime and airborne (including space) war-fighting strategy, the US should be able to take on any adversary anywhere.[136] True, the men whom Bush Jr. inherited from his father's cabinet (Cheney as vice-president, Powell as secretary of state, Rumsfeld at defence) tended to think in terms of fighting major land wars against states. Yet, soon after the Supreme Court had decided the election in his favour, Bush agreed with Rumsfeld to target the status-quo at the Pentagon and create a military strategy and appropriate forces that would secure US-centred, perpetual global supremacy—in brief, the original military programme of the Project for the New American Century.[137]

A second axis of the Bush programme was identified in a report on the US energy situation by a commission headed by Cheney. The first Gulf War entailed a return of the big Western oil companies expropriated in the 1970s nationalisation wave, because they alone would be able in the circumstances to provide the necessary investment. As oil expert Peter Odell argued in 1997, the embargoes imposed on Iraq, Iran and Libya led to a restoration of US hegemony in the international markets wrested from it by the OPEC policies in the 1970s, although others have pointed out that this has made life increasingly difficult for European oil companies unwilling to abide by the embargos.[138] In May 2001 Cheney's commission predicted that US dependence on foreign oil sources would increase from the current 52 per cent to 66 per cent in 2020. To ensure that this oil would be delivered, Washington should encourage foreign producers to produce more and then sell more to the US.[139] The problem with this strategy is that American attempts to diversify to oil producers other than the main Middle East OPEC states have largely been a failure. But as a result of US policy in the Middle East (support for Israel, war and economic warfare), the five OPEC states in the Middle East—Saudi Arabia, the United Arab Emirates, Kuwait, Iran and Iraq—have also chronically under-invested in new wells and maintenance. Although they account for 66 per cent of world oil reserves, these five accounted for only 27 per cent of world production in 1997. This should go up to at least 41 per cent in 2020 to meet global oil demand. In other words, if the projections of the Cheney commission were to be realised, a major political reshuffle would have to take place in the area.[140]

These strategic orientations (energy security and military intervention) came together when the 11 September attacks on the World Trade Centre and the Pentagon shocked the presidency into action, first in Afghanistan.[141]

Going after the Arab Brigade

Osama bin Laden, the rabble-rousing Saudi millionaire, led the volunteer 'Arab brigade' in Afghanistan on the side of the Islamist *mujahedeen* against the Soviet-backed state class. Supported by the Saudi regime (partly to get rid of him and his associates), Bin Laden used his experience in the construction business to bring ground-moving equipment into Afghanistan via Pakistan and create tunnel defences and other fortifications which the Soviet troops never succeeded in dismantling. He ran training camps for foreign fighters (notably the vast Khost camp, laid out with the help of the CIA) and set up recruiting offices in a range of countries, which would later become relays of the Islamist networks. Out of this emerged al-Qaeda in 1989.[142]

Soon after Gorbachev's accession to power in Moscow, it was decided that the Afghan war was costing the USSR too much—both in terms of loss of morale at home and in terms of exposure of the Central Asian republics to Islamist influence and actual incursions. Around 1 million Afghans had by then died in the conflict. In late 1986 Gorbachev notified the Afghan leader, Najibullah, that the Soviet commitment was finite, and in February 1988 he announced the withdrawal. Reagan however simultaneously assured Pakistan 'that the United States would stand by the rebels until they seized power', and the arrangements carefully worked out by the UN to avoid a collapse after the Soviet withdrawal were duly sabotaged by the Americans.[143] Nobody foresaw that Najibullah would hold out on his own until 1992, but then few in Washington cared. He and his fellows were eventually murdered by the Islamists and their bodies exposed on the streets of Kabul. Afghanistan now became the exclusive terrain of the Islamists in the ISI in Pakistan, concerned about the chaos into which its neighbour was descending and keen to achieve 'depth' in the strategic confrontation with India. They built up the Taliban ('seminarists') as an alternative to the unreliable Hekmatyar, whom they had earlier selected as their point man. The Taliban, unpopular inside Afghanistan itself but with a zealous following among dislocated Afghan refugees in Pakistan, assumed control in December 1996.[144]

The United States was by then, after a period of neglect, trying to revive its contacts in Afghanistan. In 1990, the US Congress even imposed sanctions on Islamabad for breaching the nuclear proliferation treaty—for if Saudi Arabia has the money, the Islamists of Pakistan have the bomb, which they brandish against their nuclear neighbour India on occasion. But with the new foray into the former Soviet republics in the Caspian area, Afghanistan became important again. 'The Clinton administration,' writes Ahmed Rashid, 'was clearly sympathetic to the Taliban, as they were in line with [its] anti-Iran policy and were important for the success of any southern pipeline from Central Asia that would avoid Iran.'[145] Turkmenistan would be the supplier of the gas: a 'second Kuwait' with its estimated 8.1 trillion cubic metres of natural gas, the world's third largest known reserve, its dictator, Niyazov, was won over by a plan for a pipeline through Afghanistan to Pakistan. This plan, originally devised by the Argentinean oil company Bridas with Prime Minister Benazir Bhutto of Pakistan, was snatched away from them in 1995 and signed into a contract with Niyazov by Unocal of the US, jointly with Delta Oil of Saudi Arabia.[146] It took another year before the Taliban too dumped Bridas for Unocal, and, when they captured Kabul, the Clinton administration threw in its lot with the Islamists to realise the pipeline. As will be remembered, this was also the juncture of support for the Bosnian Muslims and the build-up to the Kosovo campaign.[147]

Bin Laden was however becoming a problem for the Americans. The Taliban in turn were getting a bad press among feminists in the United States. In late 1997, the Clinton administration therefore came up with its plan for a Eurasian Transportation Corridor across the Caspian to Baku. In April 1998, Turkmen president Niyazov, ruling what US intelligence considers the most repressive Central Asian state (or, as his friend Haig called it, 'running a tight ship'), was feted at the White House to obtain his support for the cross-Caspian corridor.[148] By now, an anti-Taliban coalition, the 'Northern Alliance' (under the military command of Ahmad Shah Massoud and backed by Russia, Turkey and the Central Asian republics) was fighting the Taliban, who were in turn backed by Pakistan and Saudi Arabia. Bin Laden's 'Arab brigade' also fought on their side, but he and his al-Qaeda network had by then developed a wider agenda—against the Saudi monarchy over the issue of the remaining American troops; against Israel and the US itself; against the Russians in the Caucasus (Chechnya) and Central Asia (notably Tajikistan); against India in Kashmir; support for the Islamist regime in Sudan, etc. The bombing of the World Trade Centre basement in New York in 1993 was a sign of more to come, but al-Qaeda only became a major diplomatic issue for the US in its dealings with the Taliban when Bin Laden issued a *fatwa* (an authoritative scholarly interpretation of Islamic law) in early 1998 which decreed that attacks on US targets across the world were 'legal'. Washington's UN envoy, B. Richardson, visited Kabul in April to express concern; in August, two US embassies in East Africa were bombed. Only then did the US attack an al-Qaeda training camp in Afghanistan, killing 20 people but missing Bin Laden himself. In addition, the US fired Cruise missiles at a pharmaceutical factory in Sudan, claiming it was a chemical weapons facility.[149]

Putin unsuccessfully tried at the time to convince the Clinton administration to attack the Taliban by force and thus remove a source of support for the Chechen rebels. But the US had not dared to go beyond training Uzbek special forces, and they actually let Russian observers see them at work in Fort Bragg. Clinton, it would seem, to the last hoped to retain a link with the Taliban and separate them from the 'Arabs' in Afghanistan, with whom there were real tensions.[150] He actually revealed, in the wake of the 11 September attacks, that Washington had been in touch with Afghan groups supported by US special forces to kill Bin Laden, but lacked sufficient intelligence on his whereabouts.[151]

This was the situation inherited by the Bush II administration. The new government immediately shifted to a more aggressive approach. This was also motivated by its background in the energy sector (even if its key backer, Enron, was soon removed when it collapsed under the weight of its own fraudulent activities).[152] The option to attack the Taliban by using the Northern Alliance was now pursued with vigour. In January 2001 a Pentagon official visited Tajikistan; in May, General Tommy Franks, the eventual commander of the invasion of Iraq, visited the Tajik capital Dushanbe with a message from the Bush administration.[153] UN-monitored negotiations among Afghanistan's neighbours and the US and Russia (the '6 + 2' talks) had been taking place since 1997; in September 1999, a UN Security Council resolution ordered Afghanistan to expel Bin Laden to prepare the ground for reconciliation among the country's warring factions. A series of 'track-two' diplomatic meetings (in which unofficial representatives meet to sound out mutual positions without committing the governments involved), convened by the UN special representative for Afghanistan, the Spanish diplomat F. Vendrell, met to discuss implementation. In the third of these meetings, in July 2001 in Berlin, senior officials from the former Clinton state department, on Bush's behalf, conveyed a threat to the Taliban through the Pakistani representatives. Unless they surrendered Bin Laden, the US would launch military strikes against the country. Russian and Iranian delegations were present as well, as was a delegation of the Northern Alliance (according to one source, the Taliban foreign minister Mullah Mutawakil took part as well).[154] By this time, a US contingency plan to attack Afghanistan from the north was operational, and both aid from the Northern Alliance and the connivance of the Russian army had been arranged. The threat conveyed in Berlin was accompanied by sufficient operational detail to make it credible on the receiving end.[155]

On the eve of the 11 September attacks, Northern Alliance commander Massoud was assassinated by Algerians from Bin Laden's entourage. The next day, two hijacked passenger planes flew into the Twin Towers of the World Trade Centre and one into the Pentagon; a fourth crashed in a field, having been kept from flying into another target by brave passengers. Throughout the spring, the FBI had reported that Saudi jihadists were training at US aviation schools; but then, everything would have been simple in hindsight if only we had acted in light of the outcome.[156] More importantly, 10 days after the attacks, the United States organised a conference of the Northern Alliance in Rome to prepare the overthrow of the Taliban. The goodwill which existed at the time for the US was reciprocated by the Bush administration, which indicated that it was willing to involve the UN in the eventual administration of Afghanistan and give the OSCE a role too. This neutralised potential European, Russian or Chinese opposition to an American attack.[157]

Unocal meanwhile responded to the 11 September attacks by declaring it would wait for another government in Afghanistan before resuming negotiations on a pipeline again. A month later, the US launched their bombing campaign in Afghanistan, with the Northern Alliance advancing on the ground, and Russia providing facilities. Bush's special envoy, Z. Khalilzad, and Hamid Karzai, installed as head of the post-Taliban Afghan government, were both Unocal consultants. Yet in line with the outcome of several other struggles relating to energy geopolitics in Central Asia, the strength of the Northern Alliance in the actual power structure gives Russia a strong card, and their former connection with the company does not make it an American triumph even though it highlights a key aspect of the intervention.[158] For the Islamists in Pakistan, the removal of the Taliban from power weakened their strategy of achieving 'depth' for a confrontation with India. It may have reinforced the hand of those in favour of a conciliation and the development of economic ties to foster prosperity, but then the Afghan crisis has not yet been settled.[159]

Another War of Dispossession

The war to achieve regime change in Iraq is part of the same conflation of energy security and US interventionism. As early as November 2001, Bush asked his secretary of defence about the current state of war plans for Iraq; a month later a plan for a pre-emptive attack on Iraq was elaborated and made ready for execution within six months. It was 'designed for a unilateral attack by the U.S.'[160] To connect the 11 September attacks into the war plans for Iraq, the president and his speechwriters (Protestant fundamentalists like himself) came up with the theme of the 'Axis of Evil'. 'It was,' Bob Woodward writes, summing up the mood, 'almost as if Saddam was an agent of the devil.' Iran and North Korea were added to give more body to the idea of an 'axis', which evoked associations with the Second World War. 'The war on terror was going to be extended to rogue nations.' To the delight of Rumsfeld and Wolfowitz, who felt that the president 'had been listening', Bush made this the theme of his State of the Union address in January 2002.[161]

The continental European countries were however not willing to join in this crusade. In the aftermath of the first Gulf War and the collapse of the USSR, they had developed a set of policies of their own. In Eastern Europe, Germany was the main player, but southern EU states such as France, Spain and Italy wanted to develop a Mediterranean policy to offset an overly East European orientation. Indeed in light of the planned EU expansion with Austria, Finland and Sweden, it was felt that the centre of the EU might shift to the north and east. In 1991 they proposed to create a Conference for Security and Cooperation in the Mediterranean after the model of the Helsinki Agreement (and actually briefly identified in the 1975 text). A European summit in 1992 declared the Mediterranean and Middle East as 'areas of great interest to the [EU], both in terms of security and social stability.'[162] In 1994 and 1995, several steps were taken to revive the Euro-Arab Dialogue of the NIEO days, albeit this time under a neoliberal aegis. In November 1995, the project for a Euro-Mediterranean Partnership was launched at a conference in Barcelona. Its central objective is the creation of *an EU-Mediterranean free trade area for industrial goods* by 2010, backed up by a $6 billion EU aid package, complemented by an equivalent amount of soft loans and credit facilities from the European Investment Bank.[163]

As with the Euro-Arab Dialogue of the 1970s, the United States has been keen to keep oil out of this evolving relationship. US sanctions imposed in late 1995 against companies investing in Iran and Libya were obviously directed against the evolving Mediterranean partnership: the EU depends on these two countries for 20 per cent of its oil imports, and Italy for 44 per cent. EU protests that the sanctions against European companies were in breach of international trade and investment rules were in vain.[164] In the second half of the 1990s, the question arose whether Iraq was going to be included in the EU-Mediterranean free trade area. Clearly in this case oil was bound to become part of the exchanges, because Saddam had indicated that Iraq would require payment for future oil exports in Euros.[165] These issues contributed to the growing rift over the continuation of the sanctions imposed on Iraq.

In the ceasefire resolution 687 right after the Gulf War, the Security Council ordered the 'destruction, removal or rendering harmless' of Iraq's arsenal of weapons of mass destruction, i.e., its biological and chemical weapons and any facilities it might use for the manufacture of nuclear weapons.[166] In addition, the US and the UK imposed no-fly zones in the Kurdish north and Shia south. The war had however severely damaged the country. UN Under-Secretary General (and later Finnish president) Ahtisaari reported to the General Assembly that 'the conflict has wrought near-apocalyptic results and most means of modern life have been destroyed.'[167] The hardships imposed on Iraq's population by the sanctions were so drastic and obvious that the UN—after first having imposed the most comprehensive sanctions—then mounted 'the largest humanitarian relief operation in its history, the oil for food program'.[168] In late 1994, Iraq reported compliance with a number of key UN demands, including the dismantling of weapons of mass destruction, and the diplomatic recognition of Kuwait as an independent state. For the US, however, keeping the embargo in place also kept oil prices high and this reinforced its allies in the region. It was revealed in early 1992 that the director of the CIA, Robert Gates, was touring the Middle East to sound out opinion about removing Saddam and raising the military pressure.[169]

In fact, the continued embargo was beginning to reinforce the Iraqi dictator's position. The centralised food distribution system allowed the regime to reward and punish at will under the oil for food programme. In 1996, controversy erupted over US media reports that the sanctions were killing hundreds of thousands of children. The new UN secretary-general, Kofi Annan, and several senior UN special envoys unanimously reported a humanitarian catastrophe.[170] But as a result of 'the unyielding position of the United States', the Security Council failed to reciprocate Iraq's concessions, write David Cortright and George Lopez. 'For the United States the purpose of the continuing confrontation with Iraq was no longer (or perhaps was never merely) to enforce Resolution 687.'[171] Bombing raids in the no-fly zones became more intensive towards the end of the decade, especially in the southern no-fly zone, where British and US planes targeted Iraq's air defences and command structures in what National Security Adviser Berger called 'disarmament from the air'. In addition, the United States and Britain were also sabotaging Iraqi oil exports.[172] The Iraqi regime, seeing no positive result from compliance, then began its cat-and-mouse game with inspectors, hoping to wear down the UN and gain a propaganda victory restoring its image in the Arab world.

The neoconservatives by then had been raising the temperature about Iraq for several years. In 1996, Richard Perle, with Douglas Feith and his Israeli law partner Marc Zell, published a strategy document entitled *A Clean Break* for a Jerusalem institute, in which they proposed to replace the Baath regime in Iraq by a Shia leadership under a restored Hashemite monarchy (deposed in 1958, but still in power in Jordan). This would allow them to wean away the Shias in south Lebanon from the influence of the Iranians, and allow Israel to strike a direct deal with Jordan and Iraq. Its long-term problems would thus be solved without having to reach a bargain with the Palestinians. This argument had been whispered into their ear by Ahmed Chalabi, a friend of the neoconservative militarists since the late 1960s, when Albert Wohlstetter had introduced him (while he was a Ph.D. student in the US) to Wolfowitz and Perle. Chalabi's grandiose ideas were echoed in *A Clean Break*. Well-placed for the proposed reordering of the Middle East, given his family's past association with the Hashemite monarchs, Chalabi won over his Zionist friends when he promised that once in power he would conclude a peace with Israel and rebuild the pipeline from Mosul to Haifa. He also assured them that there would be no security problem after a military victory over Saddam.[173] Chalabi's Iraqi National Congress was prominent among the opposition organisations recognised by Washington under the Iraq Liberation Act signed by Clinton in October 1998, the result of strenuous lobbying by the Project for a New American Century.[174]

Meanwhile the idea began to take hold that Saddam Hussein's regime had weathered the worst. It was certainly consolidating its hold on an emaciated Iraqi society. From the spring of 1997 onwards, this led to a steady stream of contract negotiations between Iraq and non-Anglo-American oil companies, resulting in agreements for developing vast sections of the country's oilfields. The first agreement was made in 1997 with Lukoil, leading a consortium of Russian companies; followed by China National Petroleum Corporation, and then Total of France, Canada's Ranger Oil, two Indian companies, and so on.[175] Russia, France and China were already in favour of suspending the sanctions, because Iraq would then be able to pay its debts to these countries; now oil interests were added to their line of reasoning. The projected industrial free trade zone of the Euro-Mediterranean Partnership was also always looming in the background; and with European oil companies entering Iraq, it could only become more unacceptable to the United States. In early 1999 France proposed lifting the oil embargo and UN financial controls in exchange for a weapons inspections programme that was less intrusive, but the US and Britain scuttled the proposal.[176] In December 1999, the Security Council proposed that sanctions would be lifted if Iraq accepted the return of the weapons inspectors, dismissed by the Iraqis as spies, under a new scheme (UNMOVIC). Of the five permanent members, only the US and the UK voted for this, as the patience of the other permanent members was now wearing very thin.[177]

Disagreement increased further when American and British air attacks began killing civilians directly. In 2000 France called the no-fly zone patrols 'unnecessary and murderous'.[178] But then, disarming Iraq was only a pretext. As Bush told a British journalist in an obvious slip of the tongue during a Blair visit in April 2002, 'I've made up my mind that Saddam needs to go,' further confirming to the amazed interviewer, 'The policy of my government is that he goes.'[179] But attacking an undesirable regime in this way threatened to upset the accepted rules of international relations. In October 2002, Edward Kennedy, who had been on the minority resisting the mandate for war that month, qualified the doctrine of pre-emption that underlay Bush's strategy towards Iraq as 'a call for 21st century American imperialism that no other nation can or should accept.' In a newspaper comment, Dan Plesch raised the perspective of 'Iraq first, Iran and China next'.[180] To neutralise growing opposition to war, the Bush administration, with a faithful supporting cast in London, decided to play out the weapons of mass destruction theme. Neither the president nor the CIA had claimed that Saddam had weapons of mass destruction, but in August 2002 Cheney went so far as to raise the alarm over a supposed *nuclear* capability, justifying a US attack.[181] In November, the US apparently won over the other members of the Security Council to this position when Resolution 1441 was unanimously passed. It threatened Iraq with 'serious consequences' if it would not actively cooperate with the UN weapons inspectors searching for its supposed weapons of mass destruction. Votes had been garnered by making promises of all kinds, such as a pledge to Russia that its contracts with Saddam would be honoured under all circumstances.[182]

On 15 February 2003, millions marched against the prospect of war, the first truly global demonstration in world history. From early in the morning in New Zealand and Japan, marches moved westwards as the planet rolled slowly into daylight. There were rallies by more than a million people each in Rome, Madrid, and London, before demonstrations moved on to the Americas. It was an impressive call for restraint, testifying to a wisdom and concern over the future that was painfully lacking in the concerned capitals, committed as they were to making gains, if need be by force, in the global struggle over resources. The Iraqi rulers for their part went to great lengths in seeking to ward off attack after their initial grandstanding. Working through Syrian intelligence and French, German and Russian diplomatic channels, Iraq intimated that it was willing to make far-reaching concessions. In direct meetings between December 2002 and March 2003, Richard Perle and former CIA officials met representatives of the Baath regime's intelligence apparatus, who even offered to allow US troops in to assist in the search for banned weapons, and dangled oil concessions, in addition to elections. Perle's final demand was that Saddam would have to abdicate and surrender to the US military for interrogation and admit that Iraq possessed weapons of mass destruction. A meeting to discuss elections, monitored by France and the US, was still scheduled after the war had already broken out. However, two days before talks would have been held, the designated house in a town near Baghdad was precision-bombed by US warplanes.[183] The Bush II administration flatly rejected even the most amazing last-minute concessions, just as the first Bush administration had done in the case of the retreat from Kuwait.

The invasion in the spring of 2003 defeated the depleted forces of the Baathist regime in a quick campaign that left the country once more prostrate and destroyed, and that is where it remains today. James Woolsey, former CIA chief and a Project member, qualified the Iraq war as the onset of 'the Fourth World War' (the arms race against the Soviet Union being the third), with the Axis of Evil countries already identified by President Bush Jr. as targets. 'The Fourth World War,' he claimed, 'will last considerably longer' than the previous world wars, but 'for the fourth time in 100 years [the USA] and its allies are on the march.'[184] The fact that US defence expenditure for 2004 would for the first time exceed that of the rest of the world put together superficially supports the relevance of this announcement.[185]

The war served to dispossess the Sunni state class, while reclaiming Iraq's energy reserves for the English-speaking West. By disbanding the Iraqi army, against informed advice, the state itself has been destroyed.[186] As was the intention in Kosovo, the occupation of Iraq by the US and Britain is part of a privatisation strategy. In September 2003, the head of the Coalition Provisional Authority, Paul Bremer, issued Order 39, which announced that 200 Iraqi state enterprises were to be privatised, with foreign firms entitled to 100 per cent ownership and to 100 per cent repatriation of profits, an arrangement qualified by *The Economist* as a 'capitalist dream'.[187] In addition, brushing aside the foreign companies which had from 1997 struck deals with Saddam, long-term contracts for Iraqi oil were concluded with BP and Shell, with shipments starting in July 2003.[188] Ahmed Chalabi returned to Iraq immediately after the invasion. Through his nephew Ali Allawi he was in a position of influence over the posts the latter held in the US-installed interim government of his relative Iyad Allawi (trade, investment and later defence), while Chalabi nominees held posts in the central bank and the finance and oil ministries. After the celebrated elections, which allowed the Kurds in the north and the Shias to establish themselves as a governing class for the occupation powers, Chalabi rose to vice-premier under Prime Minister al-Jafaari. He also became acting oil minister, waiting for a close associate to take over. Ali Allawi is minister of finance. Chalabi has dropped all pretence about Israel and is making no secret of his close relations with Iran.[189]

Finally, in a striking riposte to the Euro-Mediterranean Partnership project of 1995, the Bush administration made public immediately after the victorious drive to Baghdad a plan to create *a comprehensive free trade area linking the United States with the Middle East by 2013* (the EU target date had been 2010).[190] The use of their military capacity by the US and Britain not only gave these countries a competitive edge over the 'civilian' EU; they could also (or at least Washington could) use its leverage over Israel. The original European declaration on the other hand had been forced to concede that 'the Euro-Mediterranean partnership, with its overall approach focused on the relationship between Europe and the Mediterranean, differs fundamentally from the peace process in the Middle East.'[191] One of the causes contributing to the problems of the EU project was in fact the Intifada provoked by Ariel Sharon's visit to the Al Aqsa mosque in September 2000.

The economic rationale of the US–Middle East Free Trade Zone, rebaptised the Greater Middle East Initiative to include the aspect of electoral democracy, is to ensure the connection between Arab oil-related purchasing power and the American economy. At the end of the accumulation cycle triggered by the Clinton globalisation offensive, the United States is experiencing the prospect of a recession—possibly a depression—complete with collapse of the dollar. Growth no longer matches productivity rises induced by both technological innovations and longer working hours. The US, as one newspaper report has it, 'compared to other countries faces a problem not unlike a driver who has switched from a family saloon to a Formula 1 car. If ... the US economy has attained a sustained higher growth rate as a result of productivity gains during the 1990s, *it needs to keep its speed higher than before for inflation not to stall.*'[192] The need therefore is to kick-start the global capitalist economy and prevent a fatal *deflation*, with the US in the driver's seat and in ways that sideline earlier projections made by the EU to do the same. This has found a focus in the incorporation of the Middle East, beginning with Iraq, into a US-dominated world market structure. Paying a pro-US government in Iraq in dollars for its oil—and seeing to it that it spends its wealth in the US—would generate a virtuous cycle benefiting both and removing the threat of an orientation towards Europe.[193]

In the end, however, the rivalries over how American military force is used to secure competitive advantages for US capital are again absorbed by a reconstituted unifying trend to capitalist globalisation, as the May UN resolution on legitimising the occupation of Iraq testifies.[194] Certainly issues of rivalry remain: Paul Wolfowitz, then deputy defence secretary and meanwhile head of the World Bank proposed in April 2003 to forgive ('some or all of') Iraq's external debt, which apart from around $55 billion to Saudi Arabia, Kuwait and other Gulf states, is owed mainly to Russia and France ($8 billion each).[195] Clearly the American proposal adds a further dimension to the motivation for the Anglo-American invasion. Yet at the same time that the plan was made public, France and Germany signalled support for a UN legitimation of the Anglo-American occupation of Iraq, leaving only Russia disgruntled.[196] In early June 2004, the UN mandate for the Anglo-American invasion was effectively granted. But instead of resistance, the Iraq issue now became a matter of apathy. At the G-8 that month on Sea Island, Georgia, the intention to reach agreement on the 'Middle East Initiative' led to nothing.[197]

The Iraq war has turned the country into a cauldron of Sunni Islamist and broader national resentment, replacing (though not entirely, given the continuing fighting there) the role of Afghanistan in this respect. It draws on rich veins of anti-Western feeling, and the Islamist message resonates powerfully among the traumatesed population. It also affects the alienated immigrant youth in Europe, from Pakistanis in Britain to Moroccans on the continent. Their parents migrated to Europe to work in a society under the corporate liberal form of capitalism, with pronounced elements of social protection; but they are growing up under neoliberalism, in a harsher environment in which the retreating state leaves people to themselves, less educated and with emaciated social support. Often lacking the skills to exploit opportunities for individual advancement, they are paradoxically more 'foreign' again than their parents or grand-parents. As prejudice returns along with unemployment and urban chaos, they acutely experience the anomie that affects migrants in general. Or are we perhaps looking at another dimension of rivalry—the US acting with impunity, while Europe (Britain included), with its large immigrant Muslim communities, pays for the consequences?[198]

Notes

1. Houweling (1999); Klare (2001: 22). On water conflicts in the Middle East, see Selby (2003).
2. Quoted in *The Washington Post*, 9 February 2004 (in a review of Coll 2004). Having risen as head of the Afghan secret police, we may assume that Najibullah knew what he was talking about.
3. Sampson (1991: 286, cf. graphs on 283).
4. Yergin (1993: 707–8). On US and Iranian funding for the Kurds, see B. Woodward (2004: 69–70).
5. In the list of shareholders of the first private bank founded in Iraq in 1991 (the first since the 1964 bank nationalisation), though, old wealth from before the revolution and newcomers having risen under the Baath state, Sunni and Shia, were all represented (al-Khafaji 2004: 291, 293; cf. 273–4).
6. The obviously well-founded mistrust of Khomeini, the need to keep Iraq's Shia population under control, claims to Iran's oil-rich Arab province (Arabistan/Khuzistan) and the Shatt-al-Arab border issue have all to be brought into the equation as well (cf. Young and Kent 2004: 548–9, 667 box).
7. Nitzan and Bichler (2002: 259, Table 5.3); Laurance (1992: 127, 183).
8. Iran suffered when its refineries at Abadan were damaged; Iraq lost when Syria, at Tehran's request, shut off the pipelines from Iraq. As a result, the greater part of the oil output lost in the early stages of the war (15 per cent of OPEC's production) was unexpectedly lost by Iraq. Saddam effectively withdrew from OPEC as the war dragged on, but when he tried to expand exports, he found himself competing with Saudi oil (which, as we saw in Chapter 7, was being marketed in great quantity to bring down the oil price in 1986 to assist US economic warfare against Gorbachev) (Yergin 1993: 711, 764; Nitzan and Bichler 2002: 258; Klare 2001: 52).
9. James (1996: 61–3, 71, 104). According to James, through the commissions gained on the successive contracts, Thatcher's son Mark rose to become the 80th richest man in the UK.
10. Ibid.: 86 and *passim*.
11. Sampson (1991: 368); James (1996: 193, 195–6).
12. Sampson (1991: 362–3).
13. *The Guardian*, 31 December 2002. Donald Rumsfeld, then in a private capacity, was sent as a personal emissary to Saddam Hussein to offer US support and the restoration of full diplomatic relations. The photo in which he shakes hands with the dictator did not fail to turn up in the press in the run-up to the Iraq war.
14. BNL Atlanta's French-Lebanese manager, probably acting on his own account and for the Bank of Credit and Commerce International (BCCI) in London, established a close relationship with Saddam's inner circle, and finances were made available under the heading 'agricultural credits'. BCCI was a money-laundering conduit for drugs and arms trafficking and a major donor to the Tory party. Among the British financiers, the Midland bank (later taken over by HSBC), enjoyed semi-official status at the centre of a web of defence suppliers (James 1996: 60–1, 67).
15. Sampson (1991: 364–5). Britain also supplied hydrogen fluoride, a component of nerve gas, to Egypt, one of Iraq's main regional defence suppliers (James 1996: 72; cf. I.F. Klich in *Le Monde Diplomatique*, August 1981, p. 5). The European nuclear fuels joint venture, Nukem, sold uranium to an Italian company, which passed it on to Iraq (Ch. De Brie and J. Brillot in *Le Monde Diplomatique*, March 1991, pp. 8–9) The Latin American source was either Brazil or Argentina.
16. Picciotto (1983: 31–2); Silk and Silk (1981: 224–5).
17. Sampson (1991: 347), quoting former Carter White House Middle East expert Gary Sick from *The New York Times*, 15 April 1991.

18. Nitzan and Bichler (2002: 259, Table 5.3); Laurance (1992: 127, 183); Sampson (1991: 346–61, 359).
19. Young and Kent (2004: 551), quoting Cockburn and Cockburn (1999: 81). In April 1988, when a US warship shot down a civilian airliner killing all aboard, Washington rushed to offer compensation.
20. B. Woodward (1991: 201); I.F. Klich in *Le Monde Diplomatique*, August 1981, p. 5; Sharon quoted in *Newsweek*, 9 February 1987. By then, the idea of striking a deal with Khomeini and restoring Iran as a regional power against the USSR was being floated in the United States too, but Iran remained on the blacklist (M. Reisman in *The Wall Street Journal*, 23 February 1987).
21. Fontaine (1995: 186).
22. Israel, as we saw in Chapter 2, had a long experience of working with Iran, including in the intelligence area. D. Kimche, the former second-in-command of Mossad, was at the centre of the covert supply operation (Cohen and Mitchell 1989: 79; B. Woodward 1987: 298–9, 305, 314).
23. Morris (1999: 603–4); Sampson (1991: 349–53).
24. *Newsweek*, 9 March 1987. In 1981 Secord and Oliver North set up lobbying activities to ensure congressional approval for the sale of AWACS radar planes to Saudi Arabia (Casey, quoted in Sampson 1991: 357); the full story is in B. Woodward (1987); cf. Chapter 6 of this book.
25. Vieille (1988: 229). On the deeper social causes of the Lebanese civil war, cf. M. Johnson (2001).
26. Names in Scott (1986: 18, 26).
27. Cover story by Roy Rowan in *Time*, 27 April 1992; a contact of Gerald James, who had spoken to two American intelligence officers the day they boarded the fatal flight, confirms this story (James 1996: 180).
28. Businessman Ross Perot, one-time independent presidential candidate, member of the President's Foreign Intelligence Advisory Board and active in a number of US prisoners of war and hostage affairs, told Vice-President Bush that on his searches for prisoners, he kept 'discovering the government has been moving drugs around the world and is involved in illegal arms deals ... I can't get at the prisoners because of the corruption among our own covert people' (quoted in Ferguson 1995: 317). In 1987, Perot in an interview added that 'if you go back and follow the trail, these guys have been working together since the Bay of Pigs' (ibid.: 318). The Lockerbie disaster also threw new light on a 1985 crash in Newfoundland that killed 248 US soldiers, including a number of special operations troops. This turned out to be a plane of a charter company working for North in the Iran–Contra operation (*Time*, 27 April 1992).
29. James (1996: 285).
30. *De Volkskrant*, 4 May 1991; Sampson (1991: 369–70, 372).
31. It also was meant to support the oil industry in the American south, then in acute financial problems (*De Volkskrant*, 22 October 1990). The original report in *The Observer* on which this piece was based also did not fail to note that both Bush and his secretary of state Baker had direct interests in the oil business in the US. Baker's Carlyle Group, in association with BDM, trains the Saudi armed forces (*Financial Times*, 19 May 1998).
32. Sampson (1991: 364, 366–7); Gerald James wrote his 1996 book on the arms-to-Iraq affair to protect himself from a similar fate. The result provides a unique insight into the British covert world associated with the City and the arms industry, including detailed accounts of the assassinations that accompanied the turnaround of the Thatcher government's policy towards Iraq.
33. Sampson (1991: 373); Hulet (1991); Glaspie quotes from B. Woodward (1991: 213).
34. NSC quote in Clark (1994: 23, emphasis added).
35. Klare (2001: 55, Table 3.1); *The New York Times*, 6 and 15 August 1990; Bush statement in *Newsweek*, 26 November 1990.

36. James (1996: 66, 94).
37. Cortright and Lopez (2000: 37, 43).
38. The case for a non-military embargo was made by K.Elliott, G. Hufbauer and J. Schott in *The Washington Post*, 9 December 1990 (reprinted in *The New York Times* on 17 December 1990); it was rejected, among others, by Paul Samuelson in *Newsweek*, 24 December 1990.
39. Sampson (1991: 380).
40. *De Volkskrant*, 16 January 1992; 3 December 1992.
41. *Newsweek*, 18 March 1991.
42. Clark (1994: 38–58).
43. B. Woodward (2004: 69).
44. Tower Commission (1987: 103–4). On the revelations on the CIA role in Iran in 1953, see M. Gasiorowski in *Le Monde Diplomatique*, October 2000, p. 11.
45. *The Washington Post*, 11 February 2002; oil revenues in $2,000.
46. B. Woodward (1991: 258–9); Clark (1994: 27–9).
47. *International Herald Tribune*, 6 March 1991. Kuwait actually asked for the US, Britain and France to take a greater role in OPEC (*De Volkskrant*, 11 March 1991).
48. Klare (2001: 66, Table 3.4); for individual weapons types, cf. ibid.: 67, Table 3.5. Oil revenue figure in $2,000, from *The Washington Post*, 11 February 2002. In spite of a stated US commitment to a less militarised Middle East, the US authorised $1.6 billion worth of F-16 jets to Egypt in the aftermath of the war. Saudi Arabia purchased F-15 jets; Kuwait actually switched an order for 250 new battle tanks from the British Challenger to the M1-A2 Abrams of the US (*International Herald Tribune*, 8 March 1991; *De Volkskrant*, 24 October 1992); for background of the Saudi deal, cf. *Business Week*, 16 March 1992. Poland too ordered fighters from the US, in a clear response to the show of force in the Middle East (Houben 2004: 26).
49. Nitzan and Bichler (2002: 259, Table 5.3). Meanwhile the mopping-up operation to erase the traces of US and UK involvement in equipping Iraq with high-grade weapons making facilities continued. In July 1991, BCCI in London was closed down by the authorities; in the same month, the Belgian politician, André Cools, was assassinated while investigating the sale by Société Générale de Belgique (Belgium's biggest finance capital group) of the munitions firm, PRB, to the UK arms industry as part of the Bull super-gun deal with Iraq. In late 1989, the key factory of PRB in Kaulille had been mysteriously blown up (James 1996: 114, 241, 248–9).
50. *The Washington Post*, 11 February 2002; oil revenues in $2,000.
51. Klare (2001: 75); *NRC-Handelsblad*, 28 December 1991.
52. Kissinger (2000: 877–8).
53. Galster (2001: 4).
54. Pohly and Durán (2001: 20–3); cf. Rashid (2002: 82–94).
55. S. Harrison in *Le Monde Diplomatique*, October 2001, p. 22.
56. Galster (2001: 7).
57. The invasion provided the United States with a chance to demonstrate, in the words of a US diplomat in Kabul, that 'our adversaries' view of the "inevitable course" of history is not necessarily accurate' (Galster 2001: 1). Even before the invasion, Carter's national security adviser Zbigniew Brzezinski famously let the president know that to draw in the Soviet Union might offer an 'opportunity of giving to the USSR its Vietnam War', while the director of the CIA at the time estimated that this would in turn 'inflame Moslem opinion against [the USSR] in many countries' (quoted in G. Kolko 2002: 47).
58. S. Harrison in *Le Monde Diplomatique*, October 2001, p. 22.
59. *International Herald Tribune*, 2/3 March 1991.
60. *Newsweek*, 11 March 1991.
61. Rashid (2002: 144). Some estimates put the reserves at the equivalent of the North Sea, or of the known reserves in the USA.
62. Ibid.: 153.

63. Quoted in Morgan and Ottaway (1998: 20); cf. D. Hirst in *De Volkskrant*, 16 March 1989.
64. According to Ahmed Rashid, the large Western corporations 'shifted their interest first to Western Siberia in 1991–92, then to Kazakhstan in 1993–94, Azerbaijan in 1995–97 and finally Turkmenistan in 1997–99' (Rashid 2002: 144).
65. Morgan and Ottaway (1998: 20); T. Dragadze in *Le Monde Diplomatique*, April 1992, p. 4.
66. Gervasi (1996: 76).
67. *Financial Times*, 26 February 1996; *Het Parool*, 5 July 1994.
68. Shevardnadze's willingness to deal with the Russians (which led to Russian interference with US military planes flying into Georgia) eventually contributed to his downfall. The responsible CIA officer in Georgia, Aldrich Ames, later turned out to have been a Soviet agent, for which he was convicted in early 1994 in the US (*De Volkskrant*, 12 August 1993 and 8 June 1994; *Financial Times*, 4 September 1995; *NRC-Handelsblad*, 11 October 1997).
69. The Azeris reportedly mistook this for British foreign policy, also because the British diplomatic mission operated from the BP offices (Morgan and Ottaway 1998: 21).
70. *Financial Times*, 16 April 1998; *De Volkskrant*, 13 March 1999. Grozny, the Chechen capital, is home to the two main pumping stations on the pipeline from Baku to the Black Sea.
71. Daily Press Briefing, US Department of State, 18 July 1997. Sununu and Scowcroft worked with Azerbaijan and oil companies investing there (*Financial Times*, 2/3 August 1997); Brzezinski was a consultant to Amoco (Morgan and Ottaway 1998: 21); Haig became the confidant of Turkmen dictator Niyazov (*Newsweek*, 17 April 1995); Baker was principal attorney of the BP-led Baku-Ceyhan pipeline consortium (Escobar 2002: 1); Kissinger became a consultant to Unocal, the company behind the projected pipeline through Afghanistan (Morgan and Ottaway 1998: 22).
72. Morgan and Ottaway (1998: 21); *De Volkskrant*, 10 October 1995.
73. Deuss, who had a dubious business reputation, had lent Kazakh leader Nazerbayev more than $100 million when the country was not yet formally independent but was already broke (*Financial Times*, 11 March 1996; *Business Week*, 21 December 1992; *Newsweek*, 17 April 1995).
74. *Financial Times*, 16 April 1998; cf. Klare (2001: 2), for the US energy department estimate of 275 billion barrels. The US State Department has recently confirmed its estimate for the Caspian of up to 200 billion barrels of oil, equivalent to eight years of world supply, and 7,000 billion cubic metres of natural gas, enough for Europe's consumption for 16 years. Russia's foreign ministry on the other hand estimates reserves (oil and gas) at 124 billion barrels of oil-equivalent (*The Guardian*, 20 October 2003; cf. Ferguson 1996: 63).
75. Russia also retained effective control in Turkmenistan through Russian officers in the Turkmen army, and troops on the borders with Iran and Afghanistan (Rashid 2002: 161–3; Klare 2001: 93).
76. Klare (2001: 83); *Newsweek*, 17 April 1995. The war in Yugoslavia, the Partnership for Peace, the association of Bulgaria and Rumania with WEU, and naval exercises in the Black Sea all testified that the West was willing to demonstrate that it did not respect a Russian sphere of influence either in Europe or in Central Asia (Achcar 1998: 109).
77. Ferguson (1996: 63); Morgan and Ottaway (1998: 21). The US also decided to throw its weight behind the claim made by Azerbaijan, Kazakhstan and Turkmenistan that the Caspian is a sea, and therefore subject to the provisions of the UN convention on the Law of the Sea; this would give them their exclusive sector, against Russia's more extensive rights under the Soviet treaties with Iran of 1921 and 1940 (Klare 2001: 99).
78. Morgan and Ottaway (1998: 21); P. Abramovici in *Le Monde Diplomatique*, January 2002, p. 10.
79. *Financial Times*, 19 April and 4 May 1995.
80. Chevron meanwhile got rid of Deuss, and Exxon-Mobil became part of the consortium as well (*OMRI Daily Digest* 213, 1 November 1995; *Financial Times*, 19 April and 25/26 November 1995; *Newsweek*, 17 April 1995; cf. Klare 2001: 87).
81. Morgan and Ottaway (1998: 21); *Financial Times*, 10 October 1995.

82. *Financial Times*, 24 November1998, 3 March and 6/7 March 1999.
83. *Financial Times*, 23 September 1997; cf. Klare (2001: 1).
84. Amineh (2003: 106).
85. Todd (2004: 22); Brzezinski (1997).
86. *Financial Times*, 2 June 1995.
87. In January 1996, a feud with Russia erupted when Ukraine raised the transit fees on the Druzhba pipeline through which Russia pumps 57 million tonnes a year to Europe (in addition to supplying Ukraine with 15 million tonnes a year) (*Financial Times*, 15 March 1996).
88. According to Georgy Arbatov, the director of the America and Canada Institute of the Russian Academy of Sciences (and since 1989 an East-West trade consultant with a Canadian partner), the war was championed by certain army circles and elements of the new elite, who apparently argued that a war would divert discontent over the collapse of the economy, which was not soon to be reversed; he also estimated that the Western attitude of recognising Russia's right to restore its sovereignty over Chechnya, while rejecting the methods used, pointed to a deal with the West (*De Volkskrant*, 7 January 1995; cf. *Financial Times*, 22 February 1996).
89. *Financial Times*, 28 February/1 March 1998. In March 1998, the US succeeded in preventing Ukraine from delivering turbines for a Russian nuclear power plant for Iran under a contract of 1995 (*De Volkskrant*, 7 March 1998).
90. In 2002, Uzbekistan left GUUAM again over trade frictions.
91. Amineh (2003: 4); *Financial Times*, 9 September and 19 December 1998.
92. A. Schmillen in *Frankfurter Allgemeine Zeitung*, 15 May 2001.
93. Amineh (2003: 75–7); *Financial Times*, 19 December 1996.
94. Klare (2001: 93); *Financial Times*, 6 May 1999; Reuters dispatch on www.russiatoday.com, 4 May 1999.
95. Klare (2001: 96, Table 4.3). Organisations like 'Kmara' (enough) in Georgia and 'Pora' (it is time) in Ukraine, sponsored by public and private money from the West, have secured the allegiance of key way-stations on the new Silk Route (cf. *Le Monde*, 26 March 2005).
96. Narcotics production and traffic in Afghanistan and the Central Asian republics do provide income, though, to independent Islamist movements, who pose a real challenge (Amineh 2003: 5, 48–9, 77); V. Cheterian in *Le Monde Diplomatique*, November 2001, pp. 16–7 (notably the maps by Ph. Rekacewicz).
97. A number of pipeline plans involving foreign operators were thwarted by the timely development of alternatives under Russian control. This, as we will see later, also played a role in the conflict with Khodorkovsky, the owner of Yukos (M.P. Amineh in *IIAS Newsletter*, July 2005, p. 6; *The Economist*, 15 March 1997).
98. Amineh (2003: 157, Figure 7.5).
99. On Blue Stream and other ventures of Italian capital in the Caspian region, see Circolo PRC (2002: 80–6).
100. Contractors for the Trans-Caspian Gas Pipeline linking Turkmenistan and Baku are Shell, Bechtel and GE Capital (Klare 2001: 100). On Blue Stream and the competition it poses for the Trans-Caspian pipeline, see Amineh (2003: 156).
101. Todd (2004: 257, Table 12); *Financial Times*, 4 February and 3 March 1999. For shareholding in AIOC and in the Baku-Ceyhan pipeline, see Amineh (2003: 147, Figure 7.1, 158, Figure 7.6).
102. Gramsci (1975, Vol. 1: 180–1); cf. Amineh (2003: 73–4).
103. *Financial Times*, 28 November 1995 and 20/21 January 1996.
104. *Financial Times*, 14/15 January 1995.
105. Ibid.; *De Volkskrant*, 8 March 1995.
106. Quoted in *Financial Times*, 22 February 1996.
107. *De Volkskrant*, 20 and 21 September 1995.

108. Amineh (2003: 79); *Financial Times*, 22 September 1994 and 10 January 1996. His predecessor Kozyrev's attempt to plead with the West for more aid and a more conciliatory approach (among others at a Trilateral Commission meeting in Copenhagen in April 1995) had failed to deliver results (*Financial Times*, 24 April 1995). In 1998, Kozyrev became a board member of ICN Pharmaceuticals in California (a firm led by Milan Panic, the Yugoslav émigré who briefly served as that country's prime minister in 1992–93) to facilitate its expansion into the former Soviet bloc (*Financial Times*, 10 February 1998).

109. Brzezinski, quoted from *Foreign Affairs*, November/December 1997, in Blackburn (1999: 113) and in Zimmerman (1981: 103).

110. *Financial Times*, 29 September 1995. A wave of capital flight, estimated at $22.3 billion for the whole of 1996 but concentrated in the first half of the year, testified to fear among capitalists that the communists would return to power (*Financial Times*, 21 March 1997).

111. Gusinsky was himself an 'institutional partner' of the WEF through his Most group (cf. www.weforum.com, 10 April 1999; *Financial Times*, 21 June and 1 November 1996).

112. *Financial Times*, 6/7 July 1996.

113. Financial Times, 23 February 1996.

114. *Financial Times*, 19 February 1997. A Swiss Banking Corp. investment brochure of August 1997 listed predictions of the Russian growth rate for that year the next as 3 and 4 per cent, respectively, pointing to immense natural resources, political solidity and restrictive monetary policy (*SBC Equity Fund Eastern Europe*, 1997, p. 4).

115. *Financial Times*, 25 October 1996.

116. *Financial Times*, 27 December 1996.

117. *De Volkskrant*, 25 July 1996.

118. *Financial Times*, 16 and 23 August 1, 28 November 1996; *De Volkskrant*, 18 October 1996; *Financial Times*, 31 January and 19 March 1997.

119. Derluguian 1999: 17; *Financial Times*, 25 March 1998.

120. Nesvetailova (2002: 259); *Financial Times*, 15 October 1998.

121. Quoted in Blackburn (1999: 114).

122. Trends and figures from Haiduk et al. (2004: 35, Diagram 1.1; 44, Table 1.9).

123. Derluguian (1999: 3 and *passim*); Klare (2001: 90).

124. Amineh (2003: 74); Eurasianism is supported by elements in the Russian security service (cf. ibid.).

125. C. Clément in *Le Monde Diplomatique*, February 2003, pp. 12–3; S. Kotkin in *FT Magazine*, 6 March 2004, p. 19.

126. S. Kotkin in *FT Magazine*, 6 March 2004, p. 19; *Financial Times*, 11/12 January 2003; *The Guardian*, 31 October 2003.

127. Proposals by Richard Perle to expel Russia again from the G-8, and other expressions of Western indignation, may be traced to Khodorkovsky's generous subsidies to neoconservative think tanks in the United States, and the presence of Henry Kissinger and Lord Rothschild on the board of his own foundation (N. Bachkatov in *Le Monde Diplomatique*, December 2003, p. 7). In September 2004, the moderate wing—M. Albright, Holbrooke, Senator McCain and others—began a campaign denouncing Putin's reversal of the earlier liberalisation (*Los Angeles Times*, 4 December 2004).

128. *Los Angeles Times*, 6 December 2004; *Neue Zürcher Zeitung*, 24 December 2003.

129. Amineh (2003: 78).

130. *Financial Times*, 27/28 April 1996.

131. Achcar (1998: 114).

132. Amineh (2003: 78).

133. *Le Monde*, 26 March 2005. Russia, in a response to 'people power' transitions in Ukraine and Kyrgyzstan, has created a new government department in charge of preventing the use by the West of Kiev-style 'Orange revolutions' as a means of 'destroying the

authority of Moscow on its periphery' by 'the enemies of Russia' (quoted in *Le Monde*, 26 March 2005; cf. *The Guardian*, 20 October 2003).

134. Duffield (2001).
135. Quoted in *The Guardian*, 11 March 2003.
136. Circolo PRC (2002: 106–8).
137. M. Klare in *Le Monde Diplomatique*, July 2001, p. 6.
138. *De Volkskrant*, 12 November 1994 and 31 October 1997. In early 2000, the US threatened Saudi Arabia with anti-trust legal action aimed to make OPEC illegal under US law if it did not increase production (*Financial Times*, 22 March 2000; N. Sarkis in *Le Monde Diplomatique*, June 2002, pp. 12–3).
139. M. Klare in *Le Monde Diplomatique*, November 2002, p. 16.
140. N. Sarkis in *Le Monde Diplomatique*, June 2002, pp. 12–3.
141. Richard Higgott (2004: 155) maintains that the original agenda was rather about avoiding foreign entanglements, although he also highlights the sources of the Bush presidency's foreign outlook in the New American Century Project.
142. Pohly and Durán (2001: 24, 36); G. Kolko (2002: 49). The jihadism that provided the recruits for the pan-Islamist renaissance had roots in Egypt, Algeria and elsewhere; it won popularity among non-Westernised intelligentsia and unemployed and uneducated masses alike, and saw a massive upsurge as a result of the Soviet invasion of Aghanistan. Sheik Abdullah 'Azzam, one of the founders of Hamas (the Palestinian Islamist movement), at this point began recruiting Muslim fighters in a range of countries, joined by Bin Laden, who funded his activities.
143. Galster (2001: 27); Nelson Mandela (quoted in *Le Monde Diplomatique*, November 2002, p. 16) considered this the most catastrophic among a series of US actions in the region.
144. Rashid (2002: 23); G. Kolko (2002: 50); Pohly and Durán (2001: 39–40).
145. Rashid (2002: 46).
146. Morgan and Ottaway (1998: 22); *Newsweek*, 17 April 1995; Rashid (2002: 159–60); *Alexander's Gas & Oil Connection*, 3 (2), 22 January 1998 (www.gasandoil.com, 24 September 2001); *The Financial Express* (Bombay), 2 June 1997. A Pakistani newspaper claims that Bhutto was removed by a coup because the Nawaz Sharif government aligned Pakistan on the US line, leaving the Taliban isolated (with Bridas relying on the Taliban); it was hoped that the Taliban could be brought in line on this issue through the ISI (*The Herald*, June 1997, www.ppp.org.pk, 24 September 2001).
147. Rashid (2002: 174); P. Abramovici in *Le Monde Diplomatique*, January 2002, p. 10; cf. *The Washington Post*, 9 February 2004 (in a review of Coll 2004).
148. Morgan and Ottaway (1998: 22); *Financial Times*, 23 April 1998; *De Volkskrant*, 2 January 1998. On Haig and Niyazov, see *Newsweek*, 17 April 1995.
149. Pohly and Durán (2001: 42); Rashid (2002: 128–42); P. Abramovici in *Le Monde Diplomatique*, January 2002, p. 10; Klare (2001: 77n.).
150. The destruction of the monumental Buddhist statues at Bamyan was done at the insistence of the Arabs (Pohly and Durán 2001: 60–1; cf. Rashid 2002: 76).
151. *The Guardian*, 26 September 2001; P. Abramovici in *Le Monde Diplomatique*, January 2002, p. 10. In all Clinton signed five orders to disrupt and destroy al Qaeda (B. Woodward 2004: 12).
152. Bush, through his two small oil companies, and Halliburton (an oil services company of which Cheney had been CEO and which had diversified into actual oil exploration itself in Turkmenistan) were partners of BP's AOIC consortium in Azerbaijan; Condoleezza Rice was a director of Chevron, the main player in Kazakhstan. Given that Cheney had been entrusted with coordinating US intelligence, these were crucial connections (Amineh 2003: 127; Circolo PRC 2002: 18). On Cheney's intelligence role in the Bush II adminnistration, see B. Woodward (2004: 29).
153. It came to light through a member of the Senate intelligence committee that the US had the information to get Bin Laden sooner rather than later (*The Guardian*, 26 September 2001). According to the same source, there were reports that Tajik and Uzbek special

forces were training in Alaska and Montana in the US (P. Abramovici in *Le Monde Diplomatique*, January 2002, p. 11).

154. The US delegation was led by the former ambassador to Pakistan; the Russian one included former foreign secretary Kozyrev, the Pakistani delegation former foreign minister N. Naik, and the Iranian delegation S.R. Khorassani, former envoy to the UN (*The Guardian*, 22 September 2001). P. Abramovici in *Le Monde Diplomatique*, January 2002, p. 11, makes the claim that Mutawakil was present.

155. *The Guardian*, 26 September 2001.

156. Ibid.

157. *The Guardian*, 21 September 2001.

158. P. Abramovici in *Le Monde Diplomatique*, January 2002, p. 11; Amineh (2003: 113).

159. Pohly and Durán (2001: 62–4).

160. B. Woodward (2004: 83, cf. 1, 54–60); L. Kleveman in *The Guardian*, 20 October 2003.

161. B. Woodward (2004: 86–7, 90, 93).

162. Colás (1997: 65). Obviously, 'security' in the European interpretation refers to migration, radicalisation and drugs trafficking rather than military issues (George and Bache 2001: 133; cf. Helsinki 1975: 91–4).

163. At the time, Turkey was the main exporter to the EU (21 per cent of all Mediterranean exports), followed by Libya and Algeria (16 each), and Israel (11 per cent); the main importers were Germany and Italy (a quarter of the total each) and France, 19 per cent (*Eurostat* data in *Financial Times*, 28 November 1995). The second pillar concerned the political and security domains: territorial sovereignty, peaceful conflict resolution; the third, an echo of the Helsinki Final Act that created the CSCE, identified human cooperation as an area of interaction (Colás 1997: 66–8).

164. The EU actually invoked the rules under the envisaged MAI (*Financial Times*, 7 August 1996; cf. 22 December 1995).

165. Th. Ferguson and R.A. Johnson in *Los Angeles Times*, 13 October 2002.

166. The eight demands of the resolution are listed in Cortright and Lopez (2000: 42).

167. Quoted in *The Guardian*, 7 July 2004; the consequences of the first years of sanctions are the main topic of Clark (1994). In March a UN mission dispatched by Secretary-General Perez de Cuéllar reported that the sanctions were producing 'near apocalyptic' destruction in Iraq, and that damage from the war had relegated the country to a 'pre-industrial age'. Cholera and typhoid fever were on the rise (Cortright and Lopez 2000: 45).

168. Cortright and Lopez (2000: 37).

169. *De Volkskrant*, 8 February 1992, quoting *The New York Times*, 7 February 1992.

170. Cortright and Lopez (2000: 47, 53). Although he was put under serious Anglo-American pressure, UN Secretary-General Annan refused to fire successive envoys to Baghdad, who all came back to report that Iraq society was disintegrating as the result of sanctions (*De Volkskrant*, 31 October 1997 and 26 February 1998; *Financial Times*, 2 November 1999).

171. Cortright and Lopez (2000: 56).

172. Berger quoted in Klare (2001: 70–1); B. Woodward (2004: 10). In the so-called 661 Committee of the Security Council set up to monitor the delivery of spare parts and equipment under the oil-for-food programme, the US and Britain insisted on denying the necessary supply of spare parts for the Iraqi section of the Kirkuk–Ceyhan pipeline. While the Turks have been upgrading their section to Ceyhan (the end-station of the Caspian pipeline from Baku), the Iraqi section was rendered incompatible as a result of sanctions, disconnecting northeast Iraq from this route (*Financial Times*, 4 February 2000).

173. Dizard (2004: 7, 2, 5–6); Fallows (2004: 2).

174. Dizard (2004: 6–7). In fact, according to the same source, Chalabi was close to Iran (his Petra Bank had been channelling Iranian funds to the Shia Amal militia in Lebanon in the 1980s), but he also was one of the key financiers of transit trade into Iraq through

Jordan. Prosecuted for fraud in Jordan, the remaking of the Middle East had meanwhile become an urgent personal need as well.

175. D. Hiro in *The Nation*, 16 December 2002.
176. Britain and the Netherlands then circulated a draft broadly following the French proposal but keeping the control over oil revenues in place (Cortright and Lopez 2000: 57–8).
177. Ibid.: 58.
178. *De Volkskrant*, 8 April 2000; *Le Monde*, 14 August 2001.
179. Quoted in B. Woodward (2004: 119).
180. Kennedy quoted in B. Woodward (2004: 203); D. Plesch in *The Guardian*, 13 September 2002.
181. B. Woodward (2004: 164).
182. D. Hiro in *The Nation*, 6 December 2002; Fallows (2004: 12).
183. *The Guardian*, 7 November 2003.
184. *The Observer*, 6 April 2003.
185. *International Herald Tribune*, 27 December 2003; cf. Golub (2004).
186. Fallows (2004: 23).
187. Naomi Klein in *The Guardian*, 7 November 2003. This step, argues Klein, is a breach of international law, which holds that an occupying power must respect 'unless absolutely prevented, the laws in force in the country' (The Hague Regulations of 1907).
188. S. Nassib in *Le Monde Diplomatique*, March 2003, pp. 12–3; *Washington Times*, 24 July 2003. Short-term contracts were concluded with ChevronTexaco, Petrobras, and Vitol of Switzerland.
189. The associate named as his successor at the oil ministry is Bahr al-Uloum. Chalabi meanwhile relies on the militias of Moqtada al-Sadr, the Shia rabble-rouser, for protection (Dizard 2004: 8; *The Independent*, 4 May 2005; *Financial Times*, 29 April 2005).
190. *Financial Times*, 10/11 May 2003. Even this newspaper adds that 'there are few regions of the world that are less prepared for the ambitious economic reforms that must accompany free trade negotiations.'
191. Quoted in Colás (1997: 66).
192. *Financial Times*, 10/11 May 2003 (emphasis added).
193. Th. Ferguson and R.A. Johnson in *Los Angeles Times*, 13 October 2002.
194. Serfati (2004).
195. *Financial Times*, 12/13 April 2003.
196. *Financial Times*, 10/11 May 2003.
197. W. Pfaff in *International Herald Tribune*, 10 June 2004. The French, through former foreign minister H. Védrine, indicated they were willing to work with Washington and contribute their experience from the Euro-Arab Dialogue and the 'Barcelona process'. But then the aspirations of the Arabs had to be respected and democratisation would have to be the work of the Arabs themselves, not of Western arrogance (H. Védrine in *Le Monde*, 26 March 2005).
198. I refer again to the report to the US government by Simon Serfaty, reported in the *Financial Times*, 3 June 2004. He argues that, as the US and Britain seem unable to disentangle themselves from their ill-fated adventure in Iraq, they risk that 'much of Europe might now view strategic separation [from the US] as a viable response to an unnecessary cultural clash with an Islamic world progressively united by the misuses of American power' (cf. Preface to this book, note 8).

11 From Human Rights to the Global State of Emergency

THE AESTHETICS OF IMPERIALIST GEOPOLITICS

The 'Global War on Terror' in many ways represents a break with prior attempts to advance the cause of the English-speaking heartland, both over current contenders and over rivals within the wider West. Yet, as I will argue in this section, it shares with these earlier forms the aspect of pretence, the projection of an image which does not conform to the substance of the policy. The *ethics* that has adorned the global aspirations of the heartland (typically represented in the US by the normative universalism espoused by Democratic presidents) is better interpreted as an imperial *aesthetics*, which reveals, on reflection, important assumptions about how the West views the people in other parts of the world.

Until the 1980s, themes in Western universalism included national self-determination and democracy (Woodrow Wilson and F.D. Roosevelt) and development plus freedom from want (Kennedy), before narrowing down to human rights. This was the theme which the Carter administration projected on the global stage in order to recapture the historic initiative from socialism after the defeat in Vietnam and setbacks in Africa and Central America. But in the context of what Jean-Claude Paye has called a 'global state of emergency',[1] the Lockean 'rights' theme has receded into the background again, further restricting even neoliberal, sanitised democracy. Under Reagan and Thatcher, the references to 'freedom' had already become so high-pitched that evoking human rights seemed soft and ineffective in dealing with the 'Evil Empire', the title bestowed on the Soviet Union at the time. By the mid-1980s, partly in response to Gorbachev's moderate line, the West again returned to a common strategy which combined propagating the Lockean set of rights (integrity of the individual, private property) against encroachment by the state, along with a campaign for the right to national self-determination (the right to statehood), applied notably to the Baltic Soviet republics. These policies and ideological themes always seemed to serve the broader strategy of undermining the contender state posture as a prelude to Lockean liberalisation, but the 'global state of emergency' under the War on Terror rather evokes the sense of a comprehensive *mutation back to a Hobbesian constellation.* The Protestant fundamentalist heritage of the heartland becomes apparent in the emphasis on the fight against 'evil' (Evil Empire, Axis of Evil, terrorists as 'absolute Evil', Iraqi insurgents as 'Satan', etc.). The democratic revolution and the historical perspective of collective emancipation have given way to an a-temporal conceptualisation of a global space in which different civilisations battle with each other, with everything that is good and noble and disinterested on the side of the West, and all that is 'evil' on the other.

Historically, the ruling classes of the English-speaking heartland (and also of France) have sought to present European expansion as the spread of civilisation per se and hence as an ethical mission. Ethics is the quest for the good by means of practical philosophy, the recurrent assessment of prevailing practices with an eye to their moral improvement. The sources of this morality can only reside in society itself, although the use of the term 'normative' in this context signals the ambition to move beyond the limits of the present.[2] Religion originally provided the framework for defining ethics. But in the imperialist age, secular mass politics, along with secularisation and science, created a need to resort to imageries other than religion to retain control of the domestic scene and justify overseas conquest and the subjugation of non-European peoples. In the English-speaking world, empire (in North America, the 'Frontier') offered the chance to redeem the authentic values of civilisation in the encounter with actual barbarians. Imperialism was an emanation of European society seeking to evade the dull compulsion of modern urban life, an outward projection of vital energy and a quest for space; a process which bankers and industrialists latched on to but which cannot be reduced to economic rationality alone. The early twentieth-century imperial frontier offered a source of revitalisation and rejuvenation, a characteristic shared with empire generally and recommended for that reason by such ancient thinkers as Confucius or Ibn Khaldun; a terrain on which strong characters are formed.[3] Late nineteenth-century contender states lacked the vast expanses of uncharted territory controlled by the heartland. Here, themes such as the decline of civilisation, the need to defend it against barbarian decay, dedication to the nation, heroism and war were propagated by philosophers such as Spengler, Nietzsche and the neo-Machiavellians. These thinkers contributed to a new language of politics inspired by an idealised reading of the Renaissance and/or Antiquity. The rejection of the corrupting influence of money, associated with Jews and the perfidious English (and set to music by Wagner) was an added ingredient. With this emotionally charged vocabulary, continental politicians hoped to arouse the passions of the masses (whom they feared would otherwise turn to socialism), while underscoring the contender posture against the English-speaking West.[4]

Today, the missionary ideology constructed around the civilisation/ barbarity dichotomy functions in roughly the same way as in the *fin de siècle* around 1900—as a powerful emotive frame of reference in which identities are constructed and then appealed to by politicians. Of course, the contemporary imagined community can only be one that takes into account the specific set of sensibilities that have developed among the populations of the West under conditions of sustained abundance. Cultural permissiveness, the exalted freedom to consume and travel, and an obsessive, mediatised fear of violence of the 'serial killer' type recycled in popular fiction, movies and daily news bulletins: these are all key determinants of the current 'social type' to which contemporary politics must cater. They add up to a particular mental substratum on which an idealised way of life can comfortably rest. Being poor is no longer just a condition that is deplorable, let alone something for which the West might bear any responsibility. It is proof of the failure of a society to organise itself like a rich society and with the rich societies—to be culturally permissive, to allow freedom of consumption and travel, etc.—in brief, to be like us.

When the collapse of the Soviet Union was followed by a systematic weakening of states (which had only been in control of their societies by virtue of the cold war)—indeed by a trail of state collapse—the cry for Western involvement mounted along with the penetration of capital in countries previously closed to it. Violence of a primitive kind, with machetes and AK-47s rather than B-52s, proved particularly offensive to people whose upper limit of sensitivity to violence has been set by the falling-over of a TV actor playing dead by a bullet. Sights of real blood on TV in Somalia or Yugoslavia only confirmed a basic prejudice that 'we' have left such barbarity behind us and should therefore should rush in to restore order. If this requires violence, it would still leave 'us' on a higher moral plane—that of civilisation. Indeed all through the history of the expanding heartland, as Calder has written, 'murdering Gaels, or foreigners, or Red Indians, ... was patriotic, heroic, and just, whereas to defend yourself and your way of life against the advancing forces of English-speaking empire showed human nature at its worst and most bestial.'[5]

The label 'ethical' for this involvement (ethical referring to the quest for the good) should therefore be read as *aesthetical* (the quest for the beautiful), because it consciously seeks to link the underlying civilisational illusion of superiority to the actual day-to-day conduct of policy. It is a construction aimed at mobilising a complex of sentiments, rather than an inherent quality born out of a prior commitment to law, equity or the survival of humanity on the planet. In a discussion of different definitions of aesthetics, Yuri Borev concludes that what we experience as beautiful is related to our *capacity to control*. We see beauty in nature only to the degree that it has been socially appropriated in the labour process; we appreciate and value certain universal qualities of natural phenomena because we are capable of objectifying/appropriating them socially. Art has this association of *ability*, for which we are ready to express admiration; what we ultimately find pleasure in when we marvel at a work of art is that we are contemplating our own collective power. Nature becomes magnificent, as it were, in the mirror of our own capacity to change it—to the point where we can enjoy without immediately exerting these powers, because an artist does it for us. The connection with an aestheticisation of politics by calling it 'ethical', I would infer, resides in the 'enjoyment' of being on the side of the good— defined as the controlling side. On the opposite side is raw nature, which we fail to control, subdue and shape to our design, and which is therefore uncivilised, 'barbarian', in one way or another. In Borev's words,

> Assessing the various phenomena aesthetically, man establishes the degree of his supremacy over the world. This degree is determined by the level and nature of the development of society and its production. The latter reveals the universal significance of the natural properties of objects and defines their aesthetic characteristics.[6]

During NATO's Kosovo war in the spring of 1999, Jamie Shea, the spokesman for the alliance, bragged that NATO, by releasing showers of tiny aluminium strips on power plants, could switch the electricity supply of Serbia on and off at will. This is an extreme example of how the might of the West was used in this conflict not just as blind destruction but, in a way that was itself awe-inspiring, by playing with the electricity switch and showing 'restraint' as a means of demonstrating a far greater power—which was yet, simultaneously, 'civilisation'. Of course, the so-called collateral damage, such as the cluster-bombing of civilian columns or the attacks on the Belgrade TV studios (to which I come back later), was not able to convey this aesthetic joy to the same degree.

The aesthetics of power, to the degree that it was effective, served to construct a mythology of authority for the NATO bloc which helped its forward march into Central and Eastern Europe. Restraint was functional and necessary here because the former socialist contender states had still generated the near-equivalent of a Western level of qualifications and attitudes—*abilities*—which make possible the element of consent and reciprocation that cannot be expected from the destructive use of power alone. Under these conditions, the promotion of neoliberal, sanitised democracy ('polyarchy', elite circulation through limited party competition) can function in a forward strategy.[7] But with the further unfolding of the neo-liberal counter-revolution, the West has in an ever-growing number of cases not been able to find populations ready to compromise and integrate. The constructive forces in societies in Africa or the Middle East are often disparate and weak, either because they still have to go through the phase of uni-fication under a single, exclusive authority, or because their confiscatory states have been undermined.[8] When such societies collapse into violence, unable to deal with the pressures to modernise dictated by the pace and power of the West, they reveal an *inability* that we experience as *un-aesthetic*, an affront to our own sensibilities. Thus there arise, in a perverse twist, calls for intervention ('we must do something'), as if the collapse itself is not already the result of conditions set by the West, by Western values, productivity levels and living conditions completely out of reach for the society in turmoil.

The New Barbarians

Reagan's 'Evil Empire' rhetoric sought to picture the USSR too as a barbarian anomaly fostering terrorism all over the globe. More fundamentally, it repre-sented a further step in shaping the Western hegemonic discourse that assumes a normative differentiation between the West itself and the world not conforming to its norms. The implication of the conviction that we represent civilisation ('the international community'), whereas the others lead an existence which is historically meaningless and ultimately illegit-imate, of course has a long pedigree. It effectively provides the moral grounds for imposing our will without reservations on any natives, whom we have first dehumanised, as Arnold Toynbee says, by considering them as part of the local 'flora and fauna'. Many contender states have added their own gruesome chapters to this dehumanisation of the 'other'—whether the victim was the 'Jew', the 'Kulak' or, under the Japanese occupation, the Chinese population. But it is important for an understanding contemporary world affairs to see that the English-speaking heartland itself was also founded on ideas of a 'chosen people' who made short shrift of any native populations they encountered—both on the British Isles and in the lands of overseas settlement.[9]

The attack on Soviet state socialism aimed to unseat and dispossess a managerial state class in the process of rejuvenating itself and switching the catch-up effort to a social democratic format. All the aims of the Gorbachev leadership—transparency, democracy, economic efficiency—were geared to that aim, without however dropping the ambition of achieving a society superior to private property and capitalism.[10] But the full fury of the English-speaking West had already been unleashed to pre-empt such a transition, with new recruits such as France under Mitterrand joining the fray. Not only was the new cold war directed against the USSR itself (we have referred to Richard Pipes' threat of war in Chapter 7), but it also aimed to destroy its Third World allies, such as Afghanistan, the former Portuguese colonies in Africa and even the Sandinista government of Nicaragua (to which Moscow no longer could afford to extend its protection). Counter-guerrilla wars and right-wing insurrections of extreme brutality were launched on all continents, mocking the ethical principles the West held up to Gorbachev. More profoundly, these interventions and proxy wars showed that a state-led modernisation strategy on principles other than those of private enterprise and subservience to the West exposes a society to the most brutal, unrestrained use of force, as the United States had already demonstrated in Southeast Asia. The local proxies employed in 'low intensity warfare' were encouraged to activate any sentiment that could bring men to fight; the example of the Western-supported Renamo guerrilla war against the progressive government of Mozambique is just one instance out of many which shows this in all its horror.[11] There was a total disconnection between presumed Western values and ethics and what happened locally. No human rights for Najibullah and the other captured pro-Soviet Afghan leaders hanging from lampposts in Kabul, their genitals stuffed in their mouths. Good morning, Afghanistan!

However, as Dick Boer has argued, the collapse of the USSR and its state-socialist allies and clients has also removed a counterweight against capitalism that was still part of 'modernity'—in the sense that it did not reject the insights and achievements of the Enlightenment but rather their perversion in late-bourgeois society. State socialism confronted capitalism with its own programme: freedom, equality and fraternity, though within the constraints of its contender status. It strove to complete the original democratic revolution, and was able to resurface *on that very programme* after having itself descended into monstrous barbarity under Stalin. Gorbachev's attempt to reach out to the West and achieve a historic compromise between capitalism and socialism, appealing to the threat to humanity's survival on the planet, was dismissed. For the West, confident of its power relative to a weakened adversary, there was no need to accept such a compromise. After the demise of the Third World's NIEO drive and after the rejection of the offers made by Gorbachev (other than their cynical use as part of a roll-back strategy), the reservoir of progressive reformism seems to have been exhausted. As a result, writes Boer, we have created 'the terrorist'.

> Since for the actual countermovement, an appeal to the ideals of the Enlightenment itself has become a totally frustrated enterprise, terrorism is the 'solution' to which the 'free world', claiming all reason for itself, compels. The opponents of the inhumanity of our 'free world' turn into the barbarians we have made out of them: the irrationality of our rationality drives them to madness. And this barbarity is then ascribed to them as their 'essence'.[12]

The withdrawal from universalism, which characterises the current stage of the revolt in the South, reflects how the 'rationality' of modern capitalism under neoliberalism wreaks havoc in pre-industrial society. By fostering privatisation in the name of universalism, notes Robert Wade, the West is driving forward liberalisation of the service sector in the WTO. This is creating 'a global market in private healthcare, welfare, pensions, education and water', creating profit opportunities for capital as part of 'a "private sector development" agenda devoted to accelerating the private (and non-governmental) provision of basic services on a commercial basis'. But the resulting 'slow economic growth and vast income disparities breed cohorts of partly educated young people who grow up in anger and despair ...[and] now the idea has spread ... that the US should be attacked directly.'[13] True, as writers like Emmanuel Todd have documented on the basis of demographic indicators, a modernisation of social relations is occurring in most countries of the Islamic world too.[14] But the desperation fed by the commodification of land rights and water, and the violent struggles over other resources which are being privatised are in evidence across the globe.[15] The mutations that occur in the belief systems of large masses of people are testimony to the degree in which they are affected by these changes and the speed at which they occur. Very often it is the slashing of education and health budgets on the recommendation of the IMF and Western governments which creates the breaches into which fundamentalists of all stripes can step in—first of all, Protestant fundamentalists operating from the US and Britain.[16] Migration to escape extreme poverty and the anomie upon arrival in a foreign environment have comparable effects, already briefly referred to at the end of the last chapter. Deadly witchcraft exorcism among African migrants in London, ascribed to 'African religions', turns out to have emerged under the guidance of Western fundamentalist preachers seeking to get hold of the levers of power over people living in destitution and fear. Indeed the mechanisms that allow us to write off the poor in/of the South as barbarians and bracket off their subjectivity from contemporary modernity can only arise in the context of the actual encounter.

Fukuyama's 'End of History' dismissed the Third World as the part of the world 'mired in history', and hence irrelevant. But the aesthetics of the 'Decline of the West' resurfaced after 1990. A new geopolitics of empire and barbarity took the place of the idea of 'development aid', and Western society appears to be reaching back to age-old notions of a realm of civilisation surrounded by savage enemies.[17] To withstand the onslaught of their less amenable brethren, semi-barbarian auxiliaries have to be recruited to defend the empire. They constitute what Jean-Christophe Rufin has labelled, in a critique of the new imperial paradigm, a new frontier, comparable to the *limes* of the Roman Empire. The violent abandonment of the South that was begun under Reagan requires a buffer zone against the barbarians; but the vassal states on this frontier are by definition barbarians themselves, unstable configurations which have to be geared to this role by Western intervention. The 'New World Order' pronounced by President Bush Sr. after the expulsion of Iraq's army from Kuwait may be interpreted as an attempt to consolidate a *limes* in this sense. Rather than destroying Iraq completely, it had to be kept in place to prevent the spread of anomie and barbarism. Mexico, Turkey, Morocco, Iran and the Western successor states of Yugoslavia can in this perspective also be seen as frontier vassals, auxiliaries of limited and temporary utility.[18] The 1991 Gulf War was perhaps the first post-cold war contest in which the stabilisation of the imperial frontier—the zone sealing off the heartland from the barbarism looming beyond it—was at issue.[19] What if we look at the Iraq war of 2003 in this light?

As argued through this study, the imperial West in the confrontations with its historic contenders, from France to the rogue states of today, has always been able to present itself as the epicentre of 'normalcy' and closeness to human nature, confronting a barbarian enemy capable of anything. In spite of the bloody interventions it undertook or commissioned from local proxies and the cruel embargoes it imposed, the heartland has always simultaneously presented itself as the enlightened champion of rationality and liberty. On the other hand, the coercive unification of real diversity to which the contenders subject their societies in the attempt to hold their own, if not to catch up with the West, have without exception produced the ugly features of overt dictatorship and repression. Who then would today be willing to speak up for Serbia in the dissolution of Yugoslavia, for Iraq under Saddam Hussein, or for North Korea or Iran? It takes a deeper understanding and courage to dissent from the moral case against repressive contender states, as E.H. Carr did by pointing out the hypocrisy of the English-speaking West concerning the Axis powers in 1939—and he was talking about the *real* Hitler.[20] But the capacity to see through the prima facie case for Western superiority and moral rectitude is not just a matter of dissenting intellectuals. Those living in those societies, often brought into the most impossible of situations by the pressures imposed on them and compelled in the end to rally to murderous causes, have critical faculties too. They may recall that before their states resorted to violent transgressions, they were often unfairly robbed, embargoed and subjected to economic blackmail and warfare by those who were victorious once overt violence erupted. This memory can be reactivated by competitive pressures even after the actual contender state posture has been abandoned—either from above, by elites seeking to reinforce their position by varying degrees of populism, as in Russia, or by populations involved in active democracy, as in Venezuela and elsewhere today.

RIVAL CONCEPTS OF HUMAN RIGHTS

Let us now look at how concepts borrowed from law, notably human rights, have evolved across the heartland/contender divide. The Global War on Terror marks a further step in the attempt to introduce the categories of penal law and prosecution into world politics: the 'barbarians' must be brought to justice.

Law is the secular expression of the ethics of a society. Unlike politics, the law is not aimed at arousing passions but meant to facilitate the reproduction of the social order by laying down enforceable rules; as a general principle, these rules will be *just* from the point of view of achieving those tasks of reproduction, and hence ethical. Certainly legal principles too have been subject to aestheticisation, most notably in the case of individual human rights. Justice and law constitute a further area in which the juxtaposition of a Lockean heartland and Hobbesian contender states is borne out.

Hobbes brought together the various strands in the legal thinking of his day (including natural law, to which I come back later) in a view of the law that reduces justice per se to the protection of life, property and the guarantee of contract; the rest is decided by the will of the Leviathan. 'Not rightness, but authority makes the law.'[21] In the nineteenth-century contender state context, the Hobbesian tradition was reproduced by thinkers like Saint-Simon and Hegel, who elaborated the idea that 'law' refers both to a legal system and to the laws of nature, the inherent rationality of things. This idea can be traced back to the rise of monotheism, which emphasises the singularity of the rational foundations of existence; but it also assumed that a state could eventually be devised in which humans would act in complete conformity with what was objectively possible.[22] Importantly, for Hobbes, individual rights, which in the society of his day were beginning to be recognised, are *alienated integrally in the social contract.*[23]

The pivotal role of the sovereign, monarch or state in domestic and international law was never easily reconcilable with the reality of what we would now call transnational relations. The relations established by commerce in the interstices between separate sovereignties fostered the emergence of rules governing private contract and forms of property, the law merchant or *lex mercatoria*. Here, in the absence of enforceable law, custom and trust play a much greater role.[24] This strand of legality emerged in the context of natural law, the implicit set of rules that applies to all human beings on the assumption of their being endowed (by God or nature) with reason. Its principles were first formulated around 300 BC by Zeno, a Phoenician (the foremost Mediterranean trading people in the era preceding the Roman empire, and the founders of Rome's early rival, Carthage).[25] Natural law henceforth became enmeshed in all political thinking in the West. But the legal universalism that it spawned would be especially prominent in eras when international commerce and, later, capital broke the confines of existing imperial or state sovereignties, and human communities were exposed to each other on an epochal scale—those giant leaps towards planetary social unification that we now denote as 'globalisation'. This applies to the age of the European discovery of the Americas and new routes to Asia (with Protestantism an added 'internal' factor) and to the final onslaught of the unified West on its contenders that began in the 1970s, which has culminated in the globalisation of capitalist discipline. The basic idea is always that the positive laws of the land, or even treaties, are of limited applicability when we encounter strangers, who may live under quite different legal arrangements; in those circumstances the idea that there exists a universal foundation of human reasonability is a powerful back-up to written laws.

Individual Rights versus the Social Contract

Hobbes interpreted natural law as the citizens' rationality, one more ingredient in the social contract underlying the strong state. On this subject, as in so many other areas, a unique and crucial mutation occurred between Hobbes and Locke, which produced the concept of individual rights *not* subsumed in the social contract. Hobbes was an admirer of modern science, but in seventeenth-century England the Church succeeded in bracketing God and the soul off from scientific enquiry. This made possible an empirical approach that was highly productive in natural science (e.g., Newton), but self-consciously agnostic about the metaphysical implications of its discoveries. As Locke put it, it is not man's concern to know everything.[26]

Locke borrowed Hobbes' idea of justice as the protection of life, property and contract, but removed the strong, all-embracing state. He introduced a novelty in terms of legal philosophy by claiming that *each man*, separately, *'has the Executive Power* of the Law of Nature.'[27] This makes the individual the equal of others, and although his right should be fused with the 'executive power' of others to achieve civil society, there is never a complete alienation of the individual right. This is also because the right is more emphatically anchored in *property*, beginning with the property of his own person. The Lockean state is therefore not the authoritative source of law but the arbiter between competitive property claims and the guardian against the breach of property in this comprehensive sense. There also emerges, in the consecration of the human individual against the state as the embodiment of the totality, a deeper strand of Judaic-Christian thought, which singles out humanity as being sacred, leaving the rest of nature for its exploitation. This in particular makes communication difficult with those societies in which the community—and hence the state—embodies the totality of humanity and nature.[28]

The spirit of Locke's legal thinking was empirical and practical. It prefigured what would later become known as the sociological approach, the third main strand in the philosophy of law, in addition to positivism and natural law.[29] In the society to which Locke's thinking is meant to apply, the law (like common law in England) is not a fixed set of rules but a *method*, which, as Gramsci writes, 'is realistic and always keeps close to concrete life in perpetual development.'[30] As a consequence of the Norman conquest and the feudal constitution, property in England was a matter of uses and rights, rather than absolute property as it developed on the continent under the influence of codified Roman law. Max Weber argues that it is precisely the medieval quality of English common law, with its highly personalised 'findings' and its guild-like professional structures, which makes it more suitable for capitalist relations than the continental, Napoleonic system of codes.[31]

In the American secession, this aspect was also made explicit in the political constitution. 'Against the tired transcendentalism of modern sovereignty, presented either in Hobbesian or in Rousseauian form,' write Michael Hardt and Toni Negri, 'the new sovereignty can arise ... only from the constitutional formation of limits and equilibria, checks and balances.'[32] This was the work of the Federalists, who rephrased and elaborated the Lockean legacy in North America. The actual sociological approach to law was influentially formulated in the 1950s by the New Haven school of Myres McDougal. McDougal argued that rules are not fixed and that definitions of what is legal are not given, but subject to deliberation in the light of changing values.[33]

Now the Lockean configuration of state and society contains, as Rosenstock-Huessy has written, a powerful conservative streak. As indicated in Chapter 1, it enshrines the rights of the existing community and its customary law against the encroaching state. 'The British tradition of 1688 made glorious revolution a return to old historical principles.'[34] These principles too date back to the time of the Norman conquest. The original 'English birthright' is the right of the community to resist the state, and resist it as a community (with a right to statehood itself); this was the central precept that inspired both the English and the American revolutions. These revolutions therefore combined conservative and emancipatory elements. Locke's innovation was to cast the property-owning *individual* endowed with freedom as the legal subject facing the state, which is itself equally under the rule of law. In the case of the American secession, however, resisting the encroaching state assumed a different form—that of self-determination. While equally a restoration of self-rule against an encroaching state (the British monarchy), *sovereign equality* (among states) in the American colonies initially overrode individual freedom or equality; this was what the Southern states would take up arms for against the North in the Civil War in the 1860s. Up to that time, the 'revolution' had not been able to interfere (although Jefferson and others did try) with slavery.

The French Revolution radicalised the ambiguities between individual equal rights as argued by Locke and the emphasis on state sovereignty in the equal rights of states, which as we saw was a product of an earlier phase of democratic revolution. In the *Déclaration des droits de l'homme*, conservatism is swept away by individual equality. Therefore the French Revolution could reach as far as Haiti, inspiring the slave revolt led by Toussaint l'Ouverture; something that Locke, who condoned slavery, would never have countenanced. But then the idea animating the French revolution—that the rest of the world had to be liberated from royal absolutism, superstition and inequality—was highly seditious from the point of view of the property-owning bourgeoisie, let alone older social forces like the land-owning aristocracy and the church. Hence it was frowned on from across the Channel, even apart from the geopolitical implications of France's revolutionary expansionism. True, the notion of equal rights itself, like so much of the European Enlightenment, was inspired by Locke. But as I noted in Chapter 1, Locke's ideas had been radicalised when they became disseminated on the continent.[35] All this led to concepts of equality which came dangerously close to communism. As Edmund Burke wrote in his *Reflections on the Revolution in France*, 'all men have equal rights; but not to equal things.'

> [Man] has not the right to an equal dividend in the product of the joint stock; and as to the share of power, authority and direction which each individual ought to have in the management of the state, that I must deny to be amongst the direct original rights of man in civil society.[36]

The French revolution, then, exposed the inherent contradiction in the Anglo-Saxon legacy between conservatism and equal rights. In E.P. Thompson's phrase, 'the ambiguities of Locke seem[ed] to fall into two halves, one Burke, the other Paine.'[37] In France itself, Napoleon would restore the country's contender state posture, with all that it entailed—but the radical democratic heritage would continue to reverberate in French society in a unique pas de deux with the directive state.

We can now understand the Lockean conception of human rights as distinct from the rights which a contender state reserves for its citizens and which are defined from the opposite vantage point originally argued by Hobbes (the state as the source of law). Three sets of 'rights' are involved here. First, *individual protection from the state*. The state should be the guarantor of life and liberty, property and contract, and the arbiter in conflicts about individual claims to these. Freedom in this sense results from the application of law, to which the state too is subject—except in an emergency, to preserve the very existence of society. In such a situation the state has the right to act 'without the prescription of the Law', under what Locke calls its prerogative.[38] But otherwise, the 'rule of law', stands in the way of enlarging state power beyond the aforementioned tasks.

Second, the positive aspect of the subject's rights: property. This begins with the *right to one's own body and mind*—the freedom to dispose of one's physical and mental abilities (e.g., to alienate them in the market). Hence, by implication of aspect one (protection from the state), this means no interference by the state either with one's physical integrity (*habeas corpus*) or with one's religious or political opinions. Since the right to one's body and mind was basically conceived to enable its free movement in the market (with the obviously positive implication of freedom of conscience), by the logic of Locke's labour theory of property we get the third component of the Lockean rights set: economic *property rights*. Everything one has gained by one's own labour, obtained by contract with free men (including of course the labour contract)—but also obtained by slave labour—is one's property. No prince can lay claim to this. This too comes under the general heading of protection from the state.

Now these rights cannot be operative in this way in the contender states. How would an activist state that seeks to mobilise its own social base in order to engage in the catch-up effort while warding off the danger of being subordinated and/or penetrated ever be able to loosen its grip on society in this way? Here the rationalism of early nineteenth-century France and Prussia paradoxically finds itself in a residual category with traditions such as the Chinese and other non-western legal civilisations. Whether argued as a totality of laws of the state and laws of nature, as in the rationalist line of thought, or as a symbiotic harmony between social life and nature in a more transcendent sense, this broad and varied set of societies is less given to privileging possessive individualism than the societies of the Lockean heartland.[39] In this group of societies, the community is therefore prior to the individual. In the contender state context, what is traditional becomes functional as well. Hegel's state-as-rationality already expresses, in the aftermath of Napoleon's sweep across Europe, the initiating role of the state in this connection. As we saw earlier, Gramsci interpreted Hegel's concept of the 'ethical state' as referring to the state's educative and moral roles, and more specifically to its obligation 'to take on the "protection" of the working classes against the excesses of capitalism.'[40]

Instead of protection *from* the state in the Lockean perspective, then, citizens in the contender state/society complex enjoy collective protection *by* the state. The contender state does not extend this privilege out of generosity or love of humanity, but because the state class considers the human community under their jurisdiction the key asset in the contest with the heartland. The social contract, as Hobbes argued, absorbs all individual rights that would claim anything else but the furtherance of the collective well-being. Certainly the protection by the state entails 'rights', for example, to health, housing, employment, etc.—but not as aspects of a right to one's own body/mind, and hence to property obtained by putting it to work one

Table 11.1
Human Rights in the Lockean and the Contender State Contexts

	Lockean Pattern	Contender State Pattern
Relation to the State	Individual Protection FROM the State	Collective Protection BY the State
Rights Concerning the Person	Freedom of Body/Conscience	Citizenship of the State
Socio-Economic Rights	Private Property	Work and Welfare

way or another, but as circumscribed *privileges* bestowed on the population by the state. The two patterns are schematically represented in Table 11.1.

The oft-heard argument that 'social and economic rights' are being left out of the 'human rights' package as propagated by the West can now be addressed as well. The Lockean package does contain social and economic rights by enshrining the right to *property*. Certainly, property is formulated from the vantage point of the sovereign individual, as a political right, if need be against the state. But as Claire Cutler demonstrates in a discussion of the work of Morris Cohen, property is much more than a political right. It entails, by its exclusionary effects and command over distribution (including taxation), 'power over the life of others'—thus effectively informing the very notion of sovereignty.[41] The state is not allowed, to put it provocatively, to interfere with the citizens' aim to provide, *for themselves*, health, housing, education and employment. That many in liberal Western society do not in the end achieve this aim is secondary here.

Now there is no need to idealise the 'ethical state' simply because the liberal, Lockean one can be demonstrated to be socially deficient.[42] In the contender state, the rights to these provisions (health, etc.) are there in principle, but this entitlement comes at a price: that of individual rights being exchanged, in the social contract, for citizenship. Simply put, all is well as long as one does not challenge the implications of citizenship in a state that requires everybody to cooperate in the state-led development effort.

The Lockean/Hobbesian dichotomy is not just a straightforward international contest between a liberal human rights approach propagating a liberal, hands-off state and private property rights approach, and a protective, confiscatory state resisting this package for reasons good or bad. It can also been seen in the pressures to dismantle welfare state arrangements in the expanding heartland itself and in former contender states restructuring towards neoliberalism. This happens when 'entitlements' under social welfare and full employment policies are replaced—in line with the neoliberal concept of control—by strategies of equal chances, participation, and employability. According to John Rawls, the modern-day Locke, the hour of freedom strikes when a certain minimum satisfaction of the needs of the 'less favoured' has been achieved, so that any restrictions on freedom (i.e., the pursuance of possessive individualism) no longer serve a pressing material need.

> Increasingly it becomes more important to secure the free internal life of the various communities of interests in which persons and groups seek to achieve, in modes of social union consistent with equal liberty, the ends and excellences to which they are drawn. In addition men come to aspire to some control over the laws and rules that regulate their association.[43]

Of course, this Aesopian language[44] only acquires its full significance when decoded as the freedom of capital in the market, and its right to actually write the laws and rules of the game. This brings us to the question of how human rights and property rights have affected international law by gradually displacing the prohibition on the original use of violence across the heartland/contender state divide.

The Lockean rights package has usually not been propagated in world politics as a programme for private property rights.[45] Likewise, the right to be protected from the state in any comprehensive sense has tended to be implied rather than claimed. What has been foregrounded are the freedoms of the body and conscience, the associated freedom of movement, right to fair trial, etc. In this resides the aesthetics of the package, because it is the part that has a truly universal import in the natural law sense. But the peculiar dynamics of developing an aesthetics of politics may equally well foreground other aspects. The human rights theme only figured prominently under Carter when the neoliberal counter-offensive against the NIEO project and the Soviet bloc began to unfold. At that juncture, notions of sovereign equality remained paramount in international law. They probably reached their zenith in that period as they began to extend to the sphere of the world economy.[46] In the neoliberal counter-revolution against the NIEO, the 'humanitarian' individualist dimension overtook the state rights' aspect behind which the contender states had entrenched themselves. But there is a profound contradiction in the furthering of human rights as a tool of Western diplomacy: the refusal, rooted in the English birthright/states' rights tradition, to be governed by an authority that is not identical to the self-governing community. Hence, the contemporary human rights ideology has been offensively deployed against other societies in ways that the United States would never countenance if it were a target of such a policy itself (the same applies, in a weaker form, to Britain, and may explain the patently demagogic resistance to a supposed European super-state). I will not further expound on the profound duplicity of its use in Western propaganda: people who were losing sleep over the fact that nuclear physicist Andrey Sakharov was banished to Gorky (a lamentable instance of injustice no doubt) happily dozed off again when the USSR broke up and its populations sank into what Princeton Russia specialist Stephen Cohen called 'an endless collapse of everything essential for a decent existence'. While silence accompanied the descent of life expectancy in Russia to levels which the world had only seen in wartime, the call to observe human rights was only heard again when, as we saw in the last chapter, oil tycoon M. Khodorkovsky, who had put together a seven-plus billion empire amidst the general collapse, was given a prison sentence for fraud.[47]

But the use of human rights as a political aesthetics is not flawed just because of media selectivity and political hypocrisy.[48] The real problem is that the West does not accept being itself subjected to that which it prescribes for the 'rest'.

FROM HUMANITARIAN 'JUST WARS' TO THE GLOBAL WAR ON TERROR

The strategic objective of the ruling classes of the heartland has all along been to dispossess the contender state classes and integrate the rival societies into the expanding West. By removing the protective state and introducing private property rights, integration clears the terrain for the sovereignty of capital—a connection first established in the history of English-speaking world, and thereafter reproduced as a Lockean package elsewhere. In this concluding section, I will analyse, by going over the three terrains identified in Table 11.1, the possible entry points of a makeover of a contender state. They would be,

- restructuring the state/society configuration through 'democracy promotion', whether or not preceded by outright 'regime change' to eliminate unwanted contestants for power; *or*
- undertaking 'humanitarian' intervention to uphold the individual human rights of those living in Hobbesian states; *or*
- achieving the privatisation of state-owned assets by turning them into private property and imposing a market regime on all property.

Note the 'ors'—the choice is really between three aspects of a single complex. Let me investigate each as an option leading to the establishment, ideally, of a liberal society. I begin with democracy promotion/regime change.

The transformation of a Hobbesian state into a Lockean state was achieved in England in the final stage of the Civil War, restoring the self-regulating society of 'English birthright'. All separate jurisdictions had been suspended under Cromwell and merged into a homogeneous social space, which then (after the dictatorship had been brought down) passed under the law. This included the state itself and hence, *civil* society, because society is now made up of citizens, each endowed with the 'executive power of the law of nature'. Elsewhere, a comparable transformation was prevented by revolutions from above by which state classes consolidated themselves to mobilise society for the contender role.

A 'global' civil society at first sight is a contradiction in terms, because there is no state or quasi-state structure at the global level; here, the heartland acts as an executor of the process. Once a contender state collapses, the West extends its helping hand to the ascendant pro-Western forces which have developed, as Gramsci terms it, 'molecularly' in the catch-up effort. If these internal forces are not strong enough, the only scene in the drama consists in knocking out the contender state and leaving the exposed society to its own internal divisions. But a change of regime by military force was unlawful in principle under the rules established in 1945.

These rules were the result of a movement against war that had been gathering strength in the course of the twentieth century. Older conceptions of *just war*, which go back to the philosophers of early Christianity, were being abandoned in the process. In the Hague Peace Conferences from 1899 onwards, and again after the First World War (in the Kellogg-Briand Pact of 1928), attempts were made to lay down an ethics that abrogated the right to go to war altogether. In 1922, the League of Nations established the Permanent Court of International Justice (the precursor of the post-1945 International Court of Justice) to settle disputes between sovereign states by arbitration, again to avoid violent conflict. But the structural conflict between the contenders, who had lost the war that preceded it, and the heartland could not be overcome by law. As E.H. Carr remarked in 1939, there is a difference between '"legal" disputes, arising out of claims which purport to be based on existing legal rights, and "political" disputes arising out of claims *to alter* existing legal rights'. Hence the Permanent Court was definitely successful in settling the dispute between Belgium and the Netherlands over the use of locks in the river Scheldt, but not the dispute between the Axis powers and the heartland states over the nature of the post-war settlement.[49]

After the Second World War, the UN Charter replaced the right to go to war (*ius ad bellum*) by a right against war (*ius contra bellum*). Article 2(4) rules that 'All members shall refrain in their international relations from the threat of use of force against the territorial integrity or political independence of any state, or in any other manner inconsistent with the Purposes of the United Nations.' The only exceptions were: a threat to the peace, breach of the peace or an act of aggression; individual or collective self-defence; and (only for the duration of the Second World War) the fight against the enemies of the United Nations.[50] In this spirit the London Charter of August 1945, building on the work of the UN War Crimes Commission set up earlier, ruled that those politicians who had launched the war would be prosecuted as war criminals. The Nuremberg and Tokyo trials (the latter of doubtful legal status given the unilateral way in which the US installed it) aimed to put the UN principles into practice. The Nuremberg Charter in Article 6 defines the crimes of war under three headings: (a) *Crimes against the peace* (the planning, preparation and initiation of a war of aggression); (b) *War crimes* (killing, maltreatment or deportation of civilians, prisoners of war and hostages, as well as wanton destruction), and (c) *Crimes against humanity* (killing, extermination, deportation and other inhuman measures against the civilian population on political, racial or religious grounds). In 1946, the United Nations unanimously sanctioned the Nuremberg Charter as an integral part of positive international law, enlarging the Hague Convention of 1907 and the Geneva Convention of 1925.[51]

The prohibition of war dovetailed with 'Realism' as it emerged at this juncture among Western international relations thinkers. Realism articulated the restraint imposed on US foreign policy by the changed balance of forces (notably, the restored power of the Left and the geopolitical gains that had accrued to the Soviet Union as a result of the collapse of Nazi Germany). Its roots in the debates of the 1920s and, more particularly, in the work of the conservative legal scholar, Carl Schmitt, tended to orient it to Hobbesian state-centrism; and certainly enough, Realism was averse to allowing Lockean liberalism and mass democracy a place in world affairs.[52] Ethical restraint, the norm of prudence, would be jeopardised if democracy and nationalist passions were to invade the realm of foreign policy making, and international morality would suffer as a result.[53]

American policy however tended to drive beyond the restraint prescribed by Realism after the war. This happened notably when Democratic administrations attempted to divert and channel democratic aspirations and industrial expansion into foreign involvement; Washington's interventions in Southeast Asia in the 1960s and early 1970s were only the most dramatic of the excesses to which this could lead. The ambition to 'make the world safe for democracy', Woodrow Wilson's old adage, thus paradoxically undermined the rules of international conduct established after the triumph of the democracies over the Axis powers. In an attempt to resurrect an ethical standard for the conduct of international affairs, Bertrand Russell, the British philosopher and peace campaigner, took the initiative for a Vietnam Tribunal. The tribunal in its two sessions—in Stockholm in May 1967 and in Roskilde, Denmark, in December of the same year—aimed to apply the principles of Nuremberg to the case of the Vietnam War, thus turning the rules established by the victors of the Second World War against one of its authors.

The Stockholm session came to the conclusion that by the norms of international law, the US government had committed aggression against Vietnam. It ruled that the United States had intentionally, systematically and on a large scale bombed civilian targets in Vietnam; repeated violations of the sovereignty, neutrality and territorial integrity of Cambodia had taken place; while the governments of Australia, New Zealand and South Korea had made themselves accomplices in the US aggression against Vietnam.[54] In the subsequent session in Roskilde, the complicity of the governments of Thailand, the Philippines and Japan was established. It was also found that the US armed forces had indiscriminately used napalm (petroleum jelly that sticks to the skin when burning), as well as fragmentation bombs, gas and defoliants, all in violation of the Geneva Protocol and other legal obligations; that prisoners had been subject to illegal killing, torture, and other forms of abuse; and that the civilian population had been systematically subjected to US army brutality, deportation, the introduction of 'free firing zones' and detention.[55] In 1971, a former prosecuting counsel at the Nuremberg trials, General Telford Taylor, confirmed that if the standards of that trial were applied to the American war in Vietnam, its architects would in all probability meet the same fate as the war criminals who were hanged or jailed for life.[56]

This list of crimes against the peace, war crimes and crimes against humanity has a familiar ring if we think of events in Afghanistan and Iraq at the time of this writing, events which are comparable, except that they have not yet come anywhere near the massive scale of the horrors of the Vietnam years. Given that the Russell tribunal was convened privately, it did not have any effect on positive international law. It did however contribute to the hardening mood against the policies pursued by the Johnson and Nixon administrations in the United States. In terms of the overall drift of the emerging global normative structure, therefore, it can be argued that the West, in the sense of a Lockean heartland, was put on the defensive in this domain too; a defensive position from which Western Europe, and as we have seen, Japan, tried to disentangle themselves by cultivating allies in the Third World and pursuing detente with the Soviet bloc. Later I will come to the response of the United States, and how the Carter administration succeeded in re-emerging from the quagmire by proclaiming itself the champion of universal human rights. This, I will argue, would eventually restore the notion of 'just war' on human rights grounds—humanitarian intervention—and in the process effectively suspend the notion of 'crimes against the peace' *for the West*. The other consequence of this change, however, was the positing of *a superior right for the West* in the process. This has given a peculiar twist to the trend, laudable in itself, towards global justice, one which reproduces the heartland/contender faultline.

At first sight, the International Criminal Tribunals for the Former Yugoslavia and Rwanda set up in 1993–94 and the International Criminal Court finally established in 1998 appear to continue the line of development that runs from the Hague Conferences to Nuremberg, and even to the Russell tribunal. But in the meantime, the neoliberal offensive has developed to the point where it is driven by the urge to 'constrain national politics and advance a human rights-oriented conception of international society'.[57] The first difference that follows from this is that the mandate of the Yugoslavia Tribunal (ICTY) includes war crimes and crimes against humanity, but *not crimes against the peace*; in addition, only individuals can be brought to trial, not states, organisations or legal persons. In other words, the criminal sphere itself has been refracted to the individual level, blotting out the sphere of structures, organisations and states. This reflects, as one observer puts it, 'the development of theory in international humanitarian law ..., in which the notion of collective responsibility had gradually yielded to that of individual responsibility.'[58] But the West, already absolved of the charge of crimes against the peace, which can no longer be made under the rules laid down for the Tribunal, could not, as it turned out, be accused of war crimes either. Thus in the case of the bombing of the RTS studio in Belgrade, in which 16 civilians were killed for the sole purpose, as Amnesty International put it, 'of disrupting Serb television broadcasts in the middle of the night for approximately three hours', the chief prosecutor, Louise Arbour, and her successor, Carla del Ponte, only conceded that 'mistakes had been made'. When pressed on the issue, an anonymous committee was established to investigate, but it concluded that there was 'insufficient evidence' of war crimes.[59]

At the time of the Tokyo trial of Japanese war criminals, the question arose whether a decision by the US commander, General Douglas MacArthur, was a sufficient basis for justice. The tribunals for Slobodan Milosevic in the Hague and Saddam Hussein in Baghdad have raised renewed questions in this domain. Milosevic has challenged the Hague tribunal from the day he was brought in to stand trial; Saddam Hussein's preliminary interrogation on the first of July 2004, led the former dictator to ask the judge

> who he was, where he studied for his law degree, whether he was properly qualified and under which law he was acting. 'I have worked since the former regime and I have been nominated by the coalition authorities,' the judge said. Saddam [Hussein] snapped back: 'This means you are applying the invaders' law to try me.'[60]

There is no question that the actions of certain leaders would therefore have to go unpunished; to move forward to a truly universal law court would be a major step towards global justice. But as Peter Gowan has written, 'we know enough about the dynamics of politics to be able to identify not only the perpetrators of atrocities, but the international actors who helped and continue to help create *the conditions in which such perpetrators arise*.'[61] Those who create the conditions—the structures and agents of transnational capital demanding 'reform', the states of the heartland backing up capitalist discipline by economic warfare or military means—know this too. Hence the International Criminal Court was not as welcome to the

West as a naïve observer would have expected. Indeed paradoxically, the more the heartland states succeed in institutionalising their policy preferences, the more their actual freedom of manoeuvre is reduced—an issue most pressing to the acting 'global policeman', the US. There is a logic to regulation, including legal regulation, which turns any set of rules, even those literally written by one interested party, against that party at some point. The rules of individual responsibility laid down by the West have a logic to them which in the end also exposes the states and social forces operating from the heartland to these very rules. Thus in the case of the WTO, the United States has already become suspicious of the rule-making powers of this body, and the same has happened with the International Criminal Court, from which Washington has sought exemptions for its military. As David Wippman points out, 'the Nuremberg, Yugoslavia, and Rwanda tribunals were all imposed on particular states by other states whose own actions would not be subject to scrutiny. But the Rome treaty [establishing the ICC] potentially subjects nationals from all states to scrutiny and possible criminal prosecution.'[62]

The US, with its conceptions of resistance to encroachment by any authority other than its own, cannot allow itself to be exposed to such jurisdiction. Militias training against the 'federal government' and repeated scares about black helicopters used by the United Nations active over US territory are only the fringe phenomena of what is essentially a foundational myth on which American society rests and which permeates the English-speaking heartland. Trapped in this contradictory position, therefore, the West and especially the United States tend to backtrack from the original radicalism of their human rights advocacy. The driving forces behind the International Criminal Court thus tend to be non-state actors such as NGOs, who are not concerned about the exposure of state sovereignty the way (powerful) states are.[63] The US attitude was well brought out when Washington called for an international tribunal to try the surviving members of the Khmer Rouge of Cambodia for war crimes, but demanded that it restrict its work to the period 1975–79, excluding, as a result, (a) the period of the US decision to widen the war to Cambodia and the carpet bombing that killed an estimated three-quarters of a million people, amounting to crimes against the peace and war crimes, and (b) the period when the US actually collaborated with the Khmer Rouge against Vietnam and thus became an accomplice of its crimes against humanity.[64] We may agree therefore with Gowan that there is

> Something deeply disturbing about a system of Western power-politics which can casually and costlessly make a contribution to plunging [countries] into turmoil and wars, can then use these wars to further their geopolitical ends and then seek to make political capital out of War Crimes Court judgements of perpetrators of atrocities, while themselves refusing all responsibility.[65]

So even if the actual shift in the relations of power has removed—for the West—the prohibition on crimes against the peace, effectively allowing regime change by force, the legal structures simultaneously put in place to administer justice on universal principles are unacceptable to the English-speaking heartland and especially to the US. The rule of law itself, in other words, must be suspended to allow its spread, which is of course a contradiction, and one that goes to the heart of the Lockean project.

Human Rights and Intervention

In 1948, in an obvious attempt to shift the normative agenda towards a Lockean interpretation centring on individual rights, the United Nations adopted the Universal Declaration of Human Rights. As colonial and neo-colonial wars waged by the West were proliferating across the emerging Third World and the Cold War was heating up in the Northern Hemisphere, the UN Charter and Nuremberg were becoming obvious anomalies from the Western perspective. The Universal Declaration aimed to restore priority to the principles of liberalism against the Hobbesian state. This Declaration is not, like the legal arrangements aimed at outlawing war, meant to consecrate sovereignty while containing the excesses that sovereign exercise of power may entail. Rather, it stands in the tradition of the French *Déclaration* and the idea of missionary dissemination of these rights. Here Locke's heritage is packaged in a militant doctrine of liberation, which had already made its appearance in US wartime pronouncements such as Roosevelt's Four Freedoms of 1941. In the Universal Declaration (the draft of which had been prepared by a committee under Roosevelt's widow Eleanor), there is an obvious implication that no state can organise its society on principles that limit individual freedom. Hence the Soviet Union and Yugoslavia abstained from the vote, not just because their states' confiscatory power over society would be implicated, but also because, as planned economies based on collective property and social organisation, they were in no position to assimilate a set of principles entirely constructed from the liberal, Lockean vantage point of the sovereign individual and private property. The English vintage is even more pronounced in the fact that the Declaration does not attribute human rights to any legislative act or treaty, but considers them innate, known to us through revelation.[66]

As indicated, the cold war was not initially conducive to a human rights policy, and it is perhaps one sign of the beginning of the erosion of the heartland's hegemony that the UN in 1966 expanded the 1948 Declaration by elaborating a separate Pact on civil and political rights, and one on economic, social and cultural rights.[67] Only after the US had withdrawn from Vietnam could Jimmy Carter raise the banner of human rights as the guiding principle of his foreign policy. This was not just propaganda, although the idea had been well prepared in the Trilateral Commission, the private planning network from which Carter recruited most of his key cabinet members.[68] Once again, the opening of a new era of global aspirations activated the natural law tradition, and this is the source from which the universalist conception of human rights emanates. The idea of humanitarian intervention now began to reassert itself, although Carter was still reticent in the use of violence.

Humanitarian intervention harks back to the idea of 'just war'. A just war is a pacifism for the future; it will bring a peace which will be eternal, if only its current enemies will have been defeated once and for all. War in this perspective is inevitable, and acquires a new quality—that of cleansing the world of evil (hence its origins, since St. Augustine, in religion).[69] Its more radical form even claims that it is 'ethical' to wage war against foreign peoples for their own good, or that, whatever the cost to the civilian population, an embargo can be imposed on a nation for political reasons. All this worked to absolve the self-styled 'international community'—in practice, the West led by the US—from the legal restraint on applying force, whereas local violence in the context of civil wars remains outlawed. To repeat the earlier quote from Angus Calder, 'to defend yourself and your way of life against the advancing forces of English-speaking empire showed human nature at its worst and most bestial'; the heartland itself, on the other hand, only acts disinterestedly, in the name of the greater good. But as Peter Malanczuk writes, the human rights doctrine which claims that 'justice' (or 'morality' or 'humanity') is a sufficient ground for action without a need for further explanation is problematic. 'This new version of *bellum justum* is based upon questionable assumptions to support the alleged universality of a moral theory drawn primarily from certain modern legal philosophers such as John Rawls and Ronald Dworkin, whose theories ... are not only controversial with regard to domestic legal systems, but seem to be confined ... to Western, or rather, Anglo-American realities.'[70] These realities, of course, were all along part of a set of universalistic aspirations against which the contender state 'reality' had to defend itself. In Wippman's words,

> International human rights law ... reject[s] the primacy of popular sovereignty rooted in national communities ... the ultimate goal is to *overcome national politics through claims of right asserted on behalf of individuals and against states and other individuals.*[71]

Here we see the role of the West as the executor of a 'global civil society', in the absence of a state at that level. In the 1960s, the US had already begun to apply its domestic legislation extraterritorially. Export prohibitions for US companies were applied to foreign subsidiaries in France and elsewhere, a policy ratcheted up under Reagan, creating tensions between transnationally applied domestic legislation and international law.[72] A critical step was taken in June 1992 when the US Supreme Court ruled 6 against 3 that the US government is allowed to abduct people from foreign countries and bring them to trial in the US, in a case concerning a Mexican doctor abducted from his office in Guadalajara (on the accusation of being involved with drug traffickers who had killed a US drugs enforcement agent operating in Mexico). Both the Mexican and Canadian governments protested against this abduction, calling it a breach of international law.[73] But this was only the beginning of an extraterritorial application of US prosecuting powers in criminal matters which would acquire its full extent in the War on Terror. Arresting a Mexican doctor on criminal prosecution grounds has at first sight nothing to do with human rights or humanitarian intervention. Its significance however is that the citizenship of another state, the counterpart to the habeas corpus of the Lockean set of rights (as in Table 11.1), can be suspended by the United States. The protests in the West over the trial against Khodorkovsky and the confiscation of assets of the Yukos oil company owned by him are significant here. The support in Western media for his appeal to the European Court of Human Rights not only underlined the extent to which human rights as habeas corpus are entwined with property rights; it also threw in doubt the sovereign jurisdiction of the Russian state, given that this confiscation affected (if only indirectly) Western business interests.[74] This takes us to the property rights issue.

Private Property for the World

It will be remembered from the discussion in Chapter 4 that the NIEO was rooted in a concern among aspirant Third World contenders over the failure to achieve control over their economies along with political independence. Building on the Bandung Conference of 1955, the 1962 UN motion proclaiming the enduring sovereignty of peoples over their natural resources identifies a strand of thinking that was to be expanded in the NIEO episode, although cracks in the reform coalition and problems with UN jurisdiction emerged at an early stage.[75] Once again, the UN had become the forum for a redefinition of global ethics, but this time the Third World seemed to be writing the rulebook. As Stephen Krasner has argued in detail, this went straight against the liberal, free-market assumptions of the Western-dominated world order.[76] Yet the very focus on the UN, with its implications for peaceful settlement of conflicts and economic equitability, carried the connotation of a worldwide, collective responsibility of/for humanity as a whole.

The challenge to the West at this juncture revealed the contrasting approaches of how the relationship of society to nature is understood in different traditions. The Judaeo-Christian lineage, which sees humanity as sacred and objectifies the rest of nature as a terrain of exploitation, differs from traditions which consider humanity as at best the *caretaker* of nature in its entirety. The boundaries are fluid here, but the idea of a society's entitlement to its own natural resources does confront the rights of private property owners; it favours the collective aspect, whether directly through the state or via the UN. The 1982 Law of the Sea Treaty signed by 117 states (basically the NIEO coalition) was duly boycotted by the US, Britain and West Germany, while Japan, France and the USSR were effectively in breach. The treaty sought to place seabed mining beyond the new 200-mile territorial limit under an international authority so as to withdraw it from control by the most powerful states and big corporations. It aimed to impose a 'Hobbesian' control regime in the face of ascendant neoliberalism, but the boycotting states and those in breach authorised seabed mining in spite of the treaty's provisions.[77] Certainly there was a manifest self-interest of the state classes and actual power elites in the states subscribing to the project. Yet the NIEO was a secular project entirely within the limits of political and economic rationality by the standards of (Western) modernity, requiring no high-pitched ideological articulation; there was no 'fundamentalism' of any kind involved which would have placed it out of bounds for the West. True, the resolution on a New International Information Order adopted in 1980 by UNESCO, intended to break the monopoly of Western media and the consumer values it propagates, was problematic in light of the credentials of most of the signatories on the issue of freedom of the press. But then the West, which indignantly rejected the idea of information outside its control in the name of freedom, has itself allowed its media to pass under the control of a handful of reactionary press barons like Murdoch, Hersant, Berlusconi, etc. US fury and actual military attacks on relatively independent media like today's Al Jazeera TV station, or the harassment of the BBC by the Blair government in the UK in the wake of the Iraq adventure, are highly revealing as to the true commitment to freedom. What was at stake in the NIEO/NIIO episodes was the priority accorded to private property.

The only property rights that are recognised in the Western tradition are those in the Lockean, individualised mould, which, like medieval law, is best suited for advanced capitalism. In the contemporary world of corporate ownership, however, property has been de-physicalised, no longer the practical ownership of land by a farmer, or a workshop and tools by an artisan. Modern property rights allow multiple overlapping claims to income and facilitate transnational restructuring of capital across different jurisdictions.[78] In most states of the South, there are millions of property owners in the classical sense; indeed as the neoliberal Peruvian and former central banker Hernando de Soto argues in *The Mystery of Capital*, people in the underdeveloped world today still make substantial savings, most of which are then used to build homes which are their property. But this is not a very interesting form of property from a capitalist point of view, because the wealth immobilised in real estate in this way is not available for circulation, transfer and profitable exploitation, but withdrawn from it. Because society in the South has not yet created a system of legally binding private contract, writes de Soto, it is 'held together by a social contract that is upheld by a community as a whole and enforced by authorities the community has selected.' A naïve observer, re-reading this line, might think that one can hardly have a more legitimate state of affairs, but that is not how de Soto sees it. Claiming that the poor of the global South in fact sit on $9.3 trillion, roughly twice the circulating US money supply, he advocates changing the law in these countries *in order to allow the mobilisation of these assets*. 'The only real choice for the governments of these nations is whether they are going to integrate those resources into an orderly and coherent legal framework or continue to live in anarchy.'[79] Anarchy by this standard is the situation in which (if there is a legal title to property at all) there is protection for ownership; and not, as in developed Anglo-Saxon law, sanctity of contract (with implications of ownership but with a much stronger emphasis on the right to dispose of property).[80] We may think here of the opposites depicted in Table 11.1, where in the 'Hobbesian' situation (ideally) there is protection *by* the state (in this case, even of individual property), whereas the Lockean pattern would imply a coercive marketisation of property, in which the protection offered by the state to those able to build a roof over their head is removed.

In fact, the changes advocated by de Soto are already being effected by the spread of capital and by Western intervention to back it up with various strategies of dispossession. The new world of capitalist property rights even moves beyond codification, because property is in the process of evacuating what Ronen Palan calls, the 'familiar world of territorial units, borders, and national production facilities, in which power is viewed as capability and is firmly anchored to a conception of "strong states",' and into an offshore 'world of flow rather than of place'.[81] Where this de-territorialisation has not yet transpired, multilateral institutions such as the World Bank offer help in the legal training of government personnel. US contract law is being replicated in the framework of the UN to 'globalise' practices developed basically in the English-speaking heartland.[82] As Christopher May observes, the rules of the contemporary world economy are being rewritten in ways in which 'it is the rights side of any balance between individual rights and public developmental benefits that are systematically privileged. And as these rights are presented as "natural" rights, their reach must be global.'[83]

This then sums up what 'disciplinary neoliberalism', as Stephen Gill calls it, is about—a global projection of the rules of contemporary capitalist property rights as they have developed in the English-speaking heartland, and their inscription into a pervasive set of legal or otherwise binding rules which the same author labels 'the new constitutionalism'.[84] The imperial aesthetics that accompanies this process was articulated, among others, by

John Rawls in his *Political Liberalism* and in an article entitled 'The Law of Peoples', both dating from 1993. In these writings, Rawls delineates an intermediary geopolitical zone in the global order, a grey area that contains political entities that approximate Rufin's 'frontier states'. They may be either 'well-ordered hierarchical regimes' and hence qualify as vassals; or be 'outlaw regimes', the 'rogue states' of the contemporary period. The criterion that Rawls uses to make these distinctions is the observance of political human rights. Crucially, this includes the respect of private property. If private property (and of course we must think here of transnational private property enforceable by Western investors in court, not the physical property that de Soto is concerned about) is not guaranteed, an authoritarian state becomes outlaw and in Rawls' view, becomes liable to 'punishment'.[85] Ultimately, it is property rights that decide the issue. Azerbaijan and Uzbekistan, which are allies of the West and work with Western companies, can torture their political dissidents; but Malaysia, which has imposed currency controls, is seen by a key US policy intellectual as drifting towards outlaw status. Milosevic is put in the dock; Pinochet can walk free. Exposure to intervention is reserved for the antiquated nation-state resisting the West, which has moved on to what Philip Bobbitt calls *market-state* concepts of sovereignty.[86]

The Demise of Liberalism?

Today, a world-wide rebellion against the degrading and exhaustive effects of globalising capitalist discipline on society and nature has been going on for at least a decade. Capitalist exploitation, expanded to global proportions, has created unprecedented inequalities of life-chances, while different peoples are directly exposed to each other to a degree never seen before. But this encounter, in which the opposing social forces often also consider each other foreigners, does not take place in the homogenised space of a capitalist 'empire' facing a disenfranchised 'multitude'.[87] It juxtaposes rival blocs, competing financial groups, transnational and national fractions of classes, and ethnic groups in ways which defy easy schematisation.

Certainly some of the poorest and most disenfranchised layers of the world's population have found a voice in the new interpretation of 'jihad' as an actual war against the West. However I agree with Emmanuel Todd that this may well have already passed its peak, and is instead mutating into a resumption of the democratic revolution; it is this that constitutes the real 'threat'.[88] The Global War on Terror is the answer to *this* threat. The neoliberal programme of the West, run aground across the globe but tenaciously pursued nevertheless, has conjured up its own nemesis, which instils fear into the ruling classes. Therefore it is depicted as a 'barbarian' uprising, so as to legitimate new forms of authoritarianism. The prison camp established at the US base in Guantánamo in Cuba, where prisoners from the Afghanistan campaign are being held without trial amidst degradation and abuse, and the crimes committed as part of interrogation practices in Abu Ghraib prison testify to the abandonment of the rule of law for 'barbarians'. In 1991 Rufin already concluded that the world was entering an era of limited universalism; the rule of law, democracy, and social justice were being restricted to the West, while the outside world had effectively been written off. He also noted that the more the ruling classes in the West would feel insecure in their own domain, the more would Serbians or Palestinians (and Arabs generally) be seen as threats.[89] But now the rule of law is also being reconsidered in the West itself. The War on Terror highlights to what extent the neoliberal globalisation project has turned in on itself, just as the medieval crusades in their closing stages became obsessed with internal heresy. The US Patriot Act of October 2001 defines terror as acts intended to influence or target the government by intimidation or coercion or to seek revenge for government actions. It specifically targets computer and internet crime. Indeed, 'hacking' that jeopardises national security will be subject to increased penalties. No wonder the act was so quickly in place after 11 September; its provisions have little or nothing to do with the suicide attacks on the Twin Towers and the Pentagon.[90]

The question of the legitimacy of war against 'barbarians' and against barbarian practices is of crucial importance for deciding whether the alternative, 'anti'-globalisation movement will be able to develop a comprehensive political programme. The paradox between the purported ethics of contemporary globalisation as the harbinger of freedom and democracy, and the reality of criminal coercion has to be exposed in order not to be caught up in a debate on economics. The pre-emptive wars waged or contemplated against the remaining non-integrated, non-Western societies, wars which try to solve by violence problems created and/or exacerbated by a century of Western involvement, are not just an aberration from what would otherwise be rational 'global governance'. They are an attempt to aestheticise globalisation as a project for which we must be willing to fight. There is perhaps even an element of mobilising the widespread resistance and disgust provoked by misery and repression per se against the victims locked in their own miserable and repressive outposts. This then turns war into 'liberation' also for us—not unlike the way German socialists in 1914 were mobilised against the autocracy of the Czar and the French socialists against the authoritarianism of the Reich. Without the ideological component of 'just war', the globalisation project will lack the energies which it can only draw from a mass base.

However, the masses to support new 'wars of liberation' are conspicuously lacking (as are, incidentally, the soldiers). What we are witnessing today is a demise of the liberal project itself, and an exacerbation of the social struggles and rivalries which that entails. In the attempt to enforce the sovereignty of capital through the primacy of the West, the people of the world are being asked to return the 'executive power of the law of nature' they are supposed to receive by entering the liberal universe, and to alienate their rights under a new, global social contract, a global state of emergency. But this call to arms to combat a largely imaginary enemy of the West's own making, in the name of a property regime that is failing the world, cannot possibly be heeded. Other emergencies, the destruction of the planet's biosphere and the descent of human society into irresponsibility and barbarity pose more urgent issues to address.

Notes

1. Paye (2004). This chapter develops arguments from van der Pijl (2002), a version of which was posted on Martin Shaw's www.theglobalsite.ac.uk.
2. Giesen (1992: 10–1).
3. On the connection between sports and British imperialism, cf. Mangan (1986).
4. Deppe (1999: 109, 112–3); Harvey (1985: 108–9). The British pre-Raphaelite school in painting (Rosetti, etc.) was also part of this movement, but without the anti-Western aspect prevalent in the contender states.
5. Calder (1981: 36). On the role of mediatised violence in mobilising the interventionist impulse, cf. Shaw (1996).
6. Borev (1985: 42).
7. Cf. William Robinson's (1996) study on the promotion of 'polyarchy' by the US, and the essays in Cox et al. (2000).
8. In this connection, cf. the analysis of the new urbanism decoupled from industrialisation in Davis (2004: 5). Vieille speaks of the chaos of the 'anti-city' after the collapse of public services (Vieille 1988: 222).
9. Toynbee (1935, Vol. 1: 211–2, 465).
10. I refer here to the collection of essays in Michael Cox (1998).
11. See, for instance, Carmen Bader in *Le Monde Diplomatique*, February 1993, pp. 20–1.
12. Boer (1991: 18). Paul Vieille (1988: 248) also highlights the connection between 'abandonment' and senseless violence.
13. Robert H. Wade in *The Guardian*, 5 January 2002.
14. If Saudi Arabia and Pakistan are the main exceptions, the radicalism they spawn may also be part of violent responses to the shifting balances from Sunni to Shia and traditionalist to rationalist interpretations of Islam (see Todd 2004: 79 and *passim*; Th. Friedman in *The New York Times*, weekly edition with *Le Monde*, 14 May 2005; Jan Selby, personal communication).
15. On the social disintegration in Nigeria's oil-producing areas, see Anna Zalik (2004).
16. Cf. Marishane (1992) and the other essays in Nederveen Pieterse (1992).
17. Fukuyama (1992) (original article, 1989); Huntington (1998) (original article, 1993); cf. critical analyses by Duffield (2001) and Senghaas (2002).
18. Rufin (1991: 193); cf. Giesen (1999).
19. Rufin (1991: 139, 159).
20. Carr (1964). See also Michael Cox's edited collection on Carr (M.E. Cox 2000).

21. Quoted in English in Battifol (1975: 13). This is the tradition of legal positivism, the idea that law is what the lawmaker has put in place as legality.
22. Supiot (2002); cf. Collins (1984: 391).
23. Battifol (1975: 58).
24. Cutler (1999: 29). The era of the seventeenth to nineteenth centuries, from Hobbes to Hegel, was the period of modern state formation in Europe and the Americas, and legally this entailed the nationalisation of the private law merchant as positive law.
25. The founder of the natural law tradition (the 'Stoa': 'hall') was Zeno, a Phoenician living in Cyprus around 300 BC. Roman 'Stoics' included Cicero, who held that 'true law is right reason in agreement with nature' (quoted in Kauppi and Viotti 1992: 102) and Seneca who developed themes such as the identity between nature and the divine, and the equality in principle between free men and slaves (Seneca 1963: 108–21, Letters 41, 47). St. Paul, the spirit behind the diffusion of Christianity in the Roman empire, shared the universalism of the Stoic tradition, which was important because Christianity would eventually provide the cocoon in which natural law was to hibernate and from which it would emerge again after the European of the Americas and the sea routes to Asia (Wagenvoort, in Seneca 1963: 7; Kauppi and Viotti 1992: 96–100).
26. Trevelyan (1961: 289–90); Locke quote in Meeus (1989: 49). Hobbes himself was keen to indicate that metaphysics should be avoided in scientific inquiry; in Engels' view, his materialism was in fact a step back from the more comprehensive approach of Francis Bacon (see Hobbes 1968: 166–7; Marx-Engels Werke, Vol. 22: 293).
27. Laslett in Locke (1965: 85, 110, 117); cf. ibid.: 312 and *passim*.
28. Dupuy (1989: 100–1).
29. Battifol (1975: 32) mentions Montesquieu, Vico and Burke as precursors, and Hume and Durkheim as articulators of this school, which wants the law to conform to the historical particularities of a society and to respond to its practical needs. Locke is not mentioned, but then history is entirely absent from Locke's argument in the *Two Treatises* (Laslett in Locke 1965: 91).
30. Gramsci (1971: 196).
31. Weber (1976: 511, cf. 394); on property, see Cutler (2002: 240), who notes that concepts of absolute property did filter into English law through the incorporation of private law merchant, the *lex mercatoria*.
32. Hardt and Negri (2000: 161).
33. Wheeler (2004: 192–3); see also Bobbitt (2003: 649–52).
34. Rosenstock-Huessy (1993: 644).
35. Jacob (1991: 111).
36. Burke (1934: 64, cf. 17).
37. E.P. Thompson (1968: 100). Tom Paine, one of the leading spirits in the American Revolution, stands for the radical democratic wing of English-speaking politics.
38. Locke (1965: 421). I was reminded of Locke's use of 'prerogative' in Locke's second treatise by Mark Neocleous of Brunel University.
39. Dupuy (1989: 101); Supiot (2002); cf. Supiot (2003), in which he works out his human rights argument.
40. Gramsci (1971: 262).
41. Cutler (2002: 237). G. Kolko (1957: 331) reminds us that Cohen was a major figure in the movement towards sociological realism in legal philosophy, the third strand identified in addition to positivism and natural law.
42. Picciotto (2000: 168) makes a useful distinction between the Hobbesian state (of authoritarian liberalism) and the ethical communitarianism based on shared values with its reactionary implications in the face of real differentiation.
43. Rawls (1973: 542). I earlier referred to Huntington's claim (in Crozier et al. 1975: 62) that Rawls' *Theory of Justice* propagates the identity between democracy and equality.

44. Aesop, a writer of fables in ancient Greece, criticised the powerful of his day in witty allegories but never mentioned them by name.
45. An exception is Hernando de Soto (2001).
46. Krasner (1985).
47. Stephen F. Cohen in *International Herald Tribune*, 13 December 1996; cf. S. Cohen (1998); Todd (2004: 210, Table 10; 22, Table 11). Cf. Table 7.1 of this book.
48. Making a mockery of rules about non-export to conflict zones, in 2003 the Blair government not only exported huge quantities of fighting equipment to Israel but also supplied the Sharon government with materials and equipment for repression and torture, such as 'leg-irons, electric shock-belts and chemical and biological agents' (*The Guardian*, 5 November 2003).
49. Carr (1964: 201, emphasis added); Eyffinger (2003: 54).
50. Malanczuk (1993: 14).
51. Regtien and van Dullemen (1968: 18–9); Eyffinger (2003: 74–5).
52. Schmitt had argued that the statesman is sovereign because he can decide who is friend and who is enemy, a decision which also included the right to go to war. 'Instead of the permanent discussion through which decisions are generated in liberal democracy, Schmitt and the other decisionists of his day (Ernst Jünger, Martin Heidegger) posited the primacy of the sovereign and solitary decision of the statesman, who, by the pathos of the state of emergency, would not be held to make his actions conform to ethical norms or to any process of communication with other political actors' (Giesen 1992: 61, emphasis deleted). See Schmitt (1963). Hitler of course fits this description and only Jünger retained certain 'aesthetic' reservations concerning the Nazi dictator.
53. Morgenthau (1964: 251), quoted in Giesen (1992: 73).
54. Regtien and van Dullemen (1968: 174).
55. Ibid.: 174–83.
56. Hitchens (2001: 24–6).
57. Wippman (2004: 156).
58. Eyffinger (2003: 78).
59. Wheeler (2004: 208–10).
60. *The Guardian*, 2 July 2004.
61. Gowan (1999b: 103).
62. Wippman (2004: 152). On the US and the WTO, see Goldstein (2000).
63. Wippman (2004: 169 and *passim*).
64. Ch. Johnson (2002: 12–3).
65. Gowan (1999b: 104).
66. H.W. von der Dunk in *NRC-Handelsblad*, 10 December 1983; Dupuy (1989: 104).
67. Dupuy (1989: 103).
68. Gill (1990).
69. Dupuy (1989: 57); Steinweg (1980).
70. Malanczuk (1993: 5). Of course, the argument of E.H. Carr's *Twenty Years' Crisis* (1964) again comes to mind here.
71. Wippman (2004: 163, emphasis added).
72. Kuyper (1984).
73. *International Herald Tribune*, 16 June 1992.
74. N. Bachkatov in *Le Monde Diplomatique*, December 2003, pp. 1, 6–7.
75. Dupuy (1989: 33); Overbeek (1982: 147).
76. Krasner (1985).
77. Dupuy (1989: 37, 44–5); *Newsweek*, 20 December 1982.
78. Cutler (2002: 242–5); see de Soto (2001: 164): 'property is not the assets themselves but a consensus between people as to how those assets should be held, used and exchanged'.
79. de Soto (2001: 23, 27).

80. Ibid.: 61–2. In his historical analysis, de Soto rightly points out that capital accumulation ensued only where politics adjusted to the requirements of new commercial practices operated outside the regulations of the guilds or the mercantilist state, as happened in England and later in the US. Of course, describing the ascendancy of a property-owning capitalist class as a process by which the law 'began adapting to the needs of common people, including their expectations about property rights', would not be everybody's choice of choice of words, but the nature of the change is identified correctly, as are the phenomena which occur if this transition is held up too long: emigration and/or revolution (ibid.: 105–7).

81. Palan (2003: 162).

82. Cutler (1999: 31–2, 42).

83. May (2004: 65); cf. May (2000) and Braithwaite and Drahos (2000).

84. Gill (1995).

85. Giesen (1999: 44).

86. Bobbitt (2003: 468, 639); the example given is the refusal by Serbia to grant minority rights to Kosovo Albanians. Pinochet, it will be remembered, was given sanctuary on British soil in 1998–98 while a request for extradition by a Spanish judge was being considered. Well taken care of by City admirers from the entourage of Mrs. Thatcher and the Pinochet Foundation, a body of businessmen who grew rich under the dictatorship, he was allowed by the then Labour home secretary, Jack Straw, to fly back to Chile (details in *Financial Times*, 11 February 1999). Craig Murray, the UK ambassador to Uzbekistan, who spoke out against the use of extreme torture in that country and against the use by the UK of Uzbek intelligence obtained in that way, was recalled from his post (*The Guardian*, 16 October 2004).

87. As argued by Hardt and Negri (2000).

88. Pohly and Durán (2001: 23, 42); Todd (2004: Chapter 2). The same point was made to me by Jan Selby.

89. Rufin (1991: 225, 237). Rufin speaks of the 'North' in the respective passages.

90. Paye (2004: 85–6).

References

Aalders, G. 1987. 'Wie vermoordde Olof Palme?', *Intermediair*, 23 (5), 29–33.

Aalders, G. and Wiebes, C. 1995. *The Art of Cloaking. The Secret Collaboration of Neutral States with Nazi-Germany.* Amsterdam: Amsterdam University Press.

Aarts, P. (ed.). 1983. *Het Midden-Oosten en Noord-Afrika. Een politiek landenboek.* Weesp, Wereldvenster & Antwerpen: Standaard.

Abdel-Malek, A. 1968. [1962]. *Egypt: Military Society. The Army Regime, the Left, and Social Change under Nasser* [transl. by C.L. Markmann]. New York: Vintage.

Abse, T. 1985. 'Judging the PCI', *New Left Review*, 153, 5–40.

Achcar, G. 1998. 'The strategic triad: The United States, Russia and China', *New Left Review*, 228, 91–127.

Adam, T.R. 1967. *Western Interests in the Pacific Realm.* New York: Random House.

Adenauer, K. 1968. *Erinnerungen 1959–1963.* Stuttgart: Deutsche Verlagsanstalt.

Adler, E. and Haas, P.M. 1992. 'Conclusion: Epistemic communities, world order, and the creation of a reflective research program', *International Organization*, 46 (1), 367–90.

Adomeit, H. 1979. 'Soviet foreign policy making: The internal mechanism of global commitment', in H. Adomeit and R. Boardman (eds.), *Foreign Policy Making in Communist Countries. A Comparative Approach.* Westmead: Saxon House.

Afanasiev, L. and Kolovnyakov, V. 1976. *Contradictions of Agrarian Integration in the Common Market.* Moscow: Progress.

Aganbegjan, A. 1989. *De Toekomst van de Perestrojka. Revolutie in de Sovjet-economie* [transl. by R. Vunderink]. Baarn: Anthos.

Agee, P. and Wolf, L. (eds.). 1987 (originally published 1978). *Dirty Work. The CIA in Western Europe.* New York: Dorset Press.

Albert, M. 1992. [1991]. *Kapitalisme contra Kapitalisme* [transl. by H. Firet]. Amsterdam: Contact.

Alff, W. 1976. *Materialien zum Kontinuitätsproblem der Deutschen Geschichte.* Frankfurt: Suhrkamp.

Ali, T. 1999. 'Springtime for NATO', *New Left Review*, 234, 62–72.

Allende, S. 1973. *Chile. Volkskampf gegen Reaktion und Imperialismus. Aus Reden des Präsidenten der Republik Chile Salvador Allende Gossens* [transl. from the Spanish]. Berlin: Staatsverlag der DDR.

Alliluyeva, S. 1967. *Twenty Letters to a Friend.* New York: Harper & Row.

Allison, G.T. 1971. *Essence of Decision. Explaining the Cuban Missile Crisis.* Boston: Little, Brown.

Allison, G.T. and Yavlinski, G. 1991. *Window of Opportunity. The Grand Bargain for Democracy in the Soviet Union.* New York: Pantheon.

Alphand, H. 1977. *L'étonnement d'être. Journal 1939–1973.* Paris: Fayard.

Amineh, M.P. 1999a. *Die Globale Kapitalistische Expansion und Iran. Eine Studie der Iranischen Politischen Ökonomie (1500–1980)* [transl. by E. Rakel]. Hamburg: Lit.

———. 1999b. *Towards the Control of Oil Resources in the Caspian Region.* Hamburg: Lit; New York: St. Martin's Press.

———. 2003. *Globalisation, Geopolitics, and Energy Security in Central Eurasia and the Caspian Region.* The Hague: Clingendael.

Anderson, P. 1979. [1974]. *Lineages of the Absolutist State.* London: Verso.

Andreff, W. 1983. 'L'organisation du travail dans les enterprises socialistes', *Reflets et Perspectives de la vie economique*, 22, 4–5.

van Apeldoorn, B. 2002. *Transnational Capitalism and the Struggle over European Integration.* London: Routledge.

van Apeldoorn, B. 2004. 'Theorizing the transnational: A historical materialist approach', *Journal of International Relations and Development*, 7 (2), 142–76.

Arendt, H. 1966. [1951]. *The Origins of Totalitarianism*. Cleveland, Ohio: World Publishing.

Armstrong, H.W. 1985. [1942]. *The United States and Britain in Prophecy*. 8th ed. Pasadena, Cal.: Worldwide Church of God.

Arrighi, G. 1978. *The Geometry of Imperialism. The Limits of Hobson's Paradigm*. London: New Left Books.

———. 1991. 'World income inequalities and the future of socialism', *New Left Review*, 189, 39–66.

———. 1994. *The Long Twentieth Century. Money, Power, and the Origins of Our Times*. London: Verso.

Arroyo, G. 1974. *Der Putsch und die Kirche in Chile*. Mainz: Stimme-Verlag.

Ashley, R.K. 1986. [1984]. 'The poverty of neorealism', in R.O. Keohane (ed.), *Neorealism and its Critics*. New York: Columbia University Press.

Augelli, E. and Murphy, C.N. 1997. 'Consciousness, myth and collective action: Gramsci, Sorel and the ethical state', in S. Gill and J.H. Mittelman (eds.), *Innovation and Transformation in International Studies*. Cambridge: Cambridge University Press.

Axt, H.J. and Deppe, F. 1979. *Europaparlament und EG-Erweiterung. Krise oder Fortschritt der Integration?* Cologne: Pahl-Rugenstein.

Baade, H.W. 1980. 'The legal effects of codes of conduct for multinational enterprises', in N. Horn (ed.), *Legal Problems of Codes of Conduct for Multi-national Enterprises*. Deventer: Kluwer.

Badeau, J.S. 1968. *The American Approach to the Arab World*. New York: Harper & Row, for the Council on Foreign Relations.

Backman, R., Giesbert, F.O. and Todd, O. 1987. [1976]. 'What the CIA is looking for in France', in P. Agee and L. Wolf (eds.), [1978], *Dirty Work. The CIA in Western Europe*. New York: Dorset Press.

Bahro, R. 1980. [1977]. *Die Alternative*. Reinbek: Rowohlt.

Barker, M. 1982. *The New Racism. Conservatives and the Ideology of the Tribe*. London: Junction Books.

Barnet, R.J. 1980. *The Lean Years. Politics in the Age of Scarcity*. London: Abacus.

Bassett, L.J. and Pelz, S.E. 1989. 'The failed search for victory: Vietnam and the politics of war', in T.G. Paterson (ed.), *Kennedy's Quest for Victory. American Foreign Policy, 1961–1963*. New York: Oxford University Press.

Battifol, H. 1975. [1960]. *La Philosophie du Droit*. 5th ed. Paris: Presses universitaires de France.

BDI (Bundesverband der Deutschen Industrie). 1984. *Jahresbericht 1983–84*. Bonn: BDI.

Beaufre, A. 1996. *NATO and Europe* [transl. by J. Green]. New York: Vintage.

Beker, M. 1996. 'The search for legitimation and liberalisation in Algeria', in A.E. Fernández Jilberto and A. Mommen (eds.), *Liberalisation in the Developing World. Institutional and Economic Changes in Latin America, Africa, and Asia*. London: Routledge.

Bell, D. 1971. 'The Cultural Contradictions of Capitalism', in D. Bell and I. Kristol (eds.), *Capitalism Today*. New York: Mentor.

Bellant, R. and Wolf, L. 1990. 'The Free Congress Foundation goes east', *Covert Action Information Bulletin*, 35, 29–32.

Beloff, M. 1963. *The United States and the Unity of Europe*. New York: Vintage.

Berend, I.T. and Ránki, G. 1982. *The European Periphery and Industrialization 1780–1914* [transl. by E. Pálmai]. Budapest: Akadémiai Kiadó.

van den Berg, M.H.J. 1995. 'Culture as ideology in the conquest of modernity: The historical roots of Japan's regional regulation strategies', *Review of International Political Economy*, 2 (3), 371–93.

Bergsten, C.F. 1973. 'The threat from the Third World', *Foreign Policy*, 11, 102–24.

Berle, A.A. 1962. *Latin America. Diplomacy and Reality*. New York: Harper & Row, for the Council on Foreign Relations.

Berlet, C. (ed.). 1995. *Eyes Right! Challenging the Right Wing Backlash.* Boston, Mass.: South End Press.

Berlinguer, E. 1976. [1973]. 'Gedanken zu Italien nach den ereignissen in Chile', in P. Valenza (ed.), *Der Historische Kompromiss.* Hamburg: VSA.

Bernard, M. and Ravenhill, J. 1995. 'Beyond product cycles and flying geese: Regionalization, hierarchy, and the industrialization of East Asia', *World Politics*, 47 (2), 171–209.

Bernstein, C. and Politi, M. 1997. *His Holiness. John Paul II and the Hidden History of Our Time.* London: Bantam.

Beschloss, M.R. and Talbott, S. 1993. *Op het hoogste niveau. Bush, Gorbatsjov en het einde van de Koude Oorlog* [transl. by J. Bertrams et al.]. Haarlem: Becht.

Bettelheim, C. 1971. *L'Inde Indépendante.* Paris: Maspero.

Beumer, T., de la Bruhèze, A., Dekker, B., Geilleit, M., Hellema, D.A. and Rodenburg, J. 1981. *The Separation of Europe. France and the Foundation of Euratom.* Amsterdam: University of Amsterdam (Mededelingen Subfaculteit Algemene Politieke en Sociale Wetenschappen, 10).

de Beus, J.G. 1977. *Morgen bij het Aanbreken van de Dag. Nederland driemaal aan de Vooravond van Oorlog.* Rotterdam: Donker.

Bichler, S. and Nitzan, J. 2004 'Differential accumulation and Middle East wars—Beyond neo-Liberalism', in K. van der Pijl, L. Assassi and D. Wigan (eds.), *Global Regulation. Managing Crises After the Imperial Turn.* Basingstoke: Palgrave Macmillan.

Biekart, K. 1999. *The Politics of Civil Society Building. European Private Aid Agencies and Democratic Transitions in Central America.* Utrecht: International Books/Amsterdam, Transnational Institute.

Black, G. 1982. 'Central America: Crisis in the backyard', *New Left Review*, 135, 5–34.

Blackburn, R. 1999. 'Kosovo: The War of NATO Expansion', *New Left Review*, 235, 107–23.

Blishchenko, I. and Zhdanov, N. 1984. *Terrorism and International Law* [transl. by L. Bobrow]. Moscow: Progress.

Bobbitt, P. 2003. *The Shield of Achilles. War, Peace and the Course of History.* Harmondsworth: Penguin.

Bode, R. 1979. 'De Nederlandse bourgeoisie tussen de twee wereldoorlogen', *Cahiers voor de Politieke en Sociale Wetenschappen*, 2 (4), 9–50.

Boer, D. 1991. 'Kerk moet steun geven aan barbaren', *Hervormd Nederland*, 10 August, 16–8.

Boni, M. and Geissler, B. 1977. 'Die italienischen Gewerkschaften, der historische Kompromiss und die Krise des Landes', *Blätter für deutsche und internationale Politik*, 22 (12), 1476–90.

Boren, D. 1990. 'Remarks by Senator David L. Boren', National Press Club, 3 April (mimeo of the transcript).

Borev, Y. 1985. [1981]. *Aesthetics—A Textbook* [trans. by N. Belskaya and Y. Philippov]. Moscow: Progress.

Bowles, P. and MacLean, B. 1996. 'Understanding trade bloc formation: The case of the ASEAN Free Trade Area', *Review of International Political Economy*, 3 (2), 319–48.

Boxer, C.R. 1965. *The Dutch Seaborne Empire 1600–1800.* London: Hutchinson.

Boyer, R. 2001. 'De la première à la seconde *pax americana*', in R. Boyer and P.-F. Souyri (eds.), *Mondialisation et regulations. Europe et Japon face à la singularité américaine.* Paris: La Découverte.

Braithwaite, J. and Drahos, P. 2000. *Global Business Regulation.* Cambridge: Cambridge University Press.

Brandt, W. 1971. *Bundeskanzler Brandt. Reden and Interviews.* Hamburg: Hoffmann & Campe.

———. 1990. [1989]. *Herinneringen* [transl. by M.W. Blok et al.]. Utrecht: Veen.

von Braunmühl, C. 1973. *Die Aussenpolitik der SPD in der Grossen Koalition.* Frankfurt: Suhrkamp.

Brennan, T. 2000. *Exhausting Modernity. Grounds for a New Economy.* London: Routledge.

Brownstein, R. and Easton, N. 1983. [1982]. *Reagan's Ruling Class.* 2nd ed. New York: Pantheon.

Brucan, S. 1978. *The Dialectic of World Politics*. New York: Free Press; London: Collier Macmillan.

————. 1998. *Social Change in Russia and Eastern Europe. From Party Hacks to Nouveaux Riches*. Westport, Conn.: Praeger.

von Brunn, R. 1973. 'Chile: Mit altem Recht zur neuen Wirtschaft?', *Vierteljahresberichte Forschungsinstitut der F. Ebertstiftung. Probleme der Entwicklungsländer*, March, 11–39.

Brus, W. 1975. *Sozialisierung und politisches System* [transl. by E. Werfel]. Frankfurt: Suhrkamp.

Brzezinski, Z. 1997. *The Grand Chessboard. American Primacy and its Geostrategic Imperatives*. New York: Basic Books.

Bufe, H. and Grumbach, J. 1979. 'Der Grif nach der Atommacht. Zur Rolle des F.J. Strauß bei der Schaffung eines atomaren Potentials der BRD', *Blätter für deutsche und internationale Politik*, 24 (12), 1439–62.

Bukharin, N. 1972. [1915]. *Imperialism and World Economy* [Foreword by Lenin]. London: Merlin.

Bukharin, N. and Preobrazhensky, E. 1969. [1918]. *The ABC of Communism* [transl. by E. & C. Paul, ed. by E.H. Carr]. Harmondsworth: Penguin.

Burchett, W. 1980. *At the Barricades*. London: Quartet.

Burke, E. 1934. *Reflections on the Revolution in France* [1790] and *Thoughts on French Affairs* [1791], Vol. IV of the *Works of Edmund Burke*. Oxford: Oxford University Press; London: Humphrey Milford.

Burn, G. 1999. 'The State, the City and the Euromarkets', *Review of International Political Economy*, 6 (2), 225–61.

Burnham, P. 1990. *The Political Economy of Postwar Reconstruction*. Basingstoke: Macmillan.

Bursk, E.C. and Bradley, G.E. (eds.). 1976. *Corporate Citizenship in the Global Community*. Washington: International Management and Development Institute.

Busch, K. 1974. *Die multinationalen Konzerne. Zur Analyse der Weltmarktbewegung des Kapitals*. Frankfurt: Suhrkamp.

Cafruny, A.W. 2003. 'The geopolitics of U.S. hegemony in Europe. From the breakup of Yugoslavia to the war in Iraq', in A.W. Cafruny and M. Ryner (eds.), *A Ruined Fortress? Neoliberal Hegemony and Transformation in Europe*. Lanham, Maryland: Rowman & Littlefield.

Calder, A. 1981. *Revolutionary Empire. The Rise of the English-Speaking Empires from the Fifteenth Century to the 1780s*. London: Jonathan Cape.

Callahan, B. 1990. 'The 1980 campaign: Agents for Bush', *Covert Action Information Bulletin*, 33, 5–7.

Calleo, D. 1976. 'The Postwar Atlantic System and its Future', in E.O. Czempiel and D.A. Rustow (eds.). *The Euro-American System*. Frankfurt: Campus; Boulder, Col.: Westview Press.

Carew, A. 1987. *Labour under the Marshall Plan. The Politics of Productivity and the Marketing of Management Science*. Manchester: Manchester University Press.

Carr, E.H. 1964. [1939]. *The Twenty Years' Crisis, 1919–1939*. 2nd ed. New York: Harper & Row.

————. 1982. *Twilight of the Comintern, 1930–1935*. New York: Pantheon.

Carrère d'Encausse, H. 1979. [1978]. *Decline of an Empire. The Soviet Socialist Republics in Revolt* [transl. by M. Sokolinski and H.A. La Farge]. New York: Harper & Row.

————. 1980. *Le pouvoir confisqué. Gouvernants et gouvernés an U.R.S.S.* Paris: Flammarion.

Carrillo, S. 1977. *"Eurokommunismus" und Staat* [transl. by H.-W. Franz]. Hamburg: VSA.

Carroll, W.K. and Carson, C. 2003. 'The network of global corporations and elite policy groups: A structure for transnational capitalist class formation?', *Global Networks*, 3 (1), 29–57.

Carroll, W.K. and Fennema, M. 2002. 'Is there a transnational business community?', *International Sociology*, 17 (3), 393–419.

Castells, M. 1998. *End of Millennium* [Vol. III of *The Information Age: Economy, Society and Culture*]. Malden, Mass.: Blackwell.

Catalán Aravena, O. 1984. 'Opkomst en neergang van het neoliberalisme van de Chicago-school', in O. Catalán Aravena and A.G. Frank (eds.), *Chili onder Pinochet. Een Latijnsamerikaans volk in gijzeling.* Amsterdam: SUA/Novib.

Caute, D. 1988. *Sixty-Eight. The Year of the Barricades.* London: Hamish Hamilton.

Cerny, P.G. 1994. 'The infrastructure of the infrastructure? Toward "embedded financial orthodoxy" in the international political economy', in R.P. Palan and B. Gills (eds.), *Transcending the State-Global Divide: A Neostructuralist Agenda in International Relations.* Boulder, Col.: Lynne Rienner.

Chahoud, T. 1987. 'Funktionswandel des internationalen Währungsfonds und der Weltbank', in E. Altvater, K. Hübner, J. Lorentzen and R. Rojas (eds.), *Die Armut der Nationen. Handbuch zur Schuldenkrise von Argentinien bis Zaire.* Berlin: Rotbuch.

Chambers' Biographical Dictionary. 1984 [rev. ed.]. [J.O. Thorne, T.C. Collocott, eds.]. Edinburgh: Chambers.

Chang, H.-J. 2002. *Kicking Away the Ladder. Development Strategy in Historical Perspective.* London: Anthem.

Chibber, V. 2003. *Locked in Place: State-Building and Late Industrialization in India.* Princeton, N.J.: Princeton University Press.

Chiesa, G. (with D. Taylor Northrop). 1993. *Transition to Democracy. Political Change in the Soviet Union, 1987–1991.* Hanover: University Press of New England.

Childs, D. 1980. 'The changing face of western communism', in D. Childs (ed.), *The Changing Face of Western Communism.* London: Croom Helm.

Chomsky, N. 1969. *American Power and the New Mandarins.* Harmondsworth: Penguin.

———. 1985. 'Interventions in Vietnam and Central America. Parallels and Differences', *Monthly Review*, 37 (4), 1–30.

Chossudovsky, M. 1996. 'Dismantling Yugoslavia, colonizing Bosnia', *Covert Action Quarterly*, 56, 31–7.

Chronologie Internationale, 1945–1977. 1979. [ed. E. Berg]. Paris: Presses universitaires de France.

Chua, A. 2003. *World on Fire. How Exporting Free-Market Democracy Breeds Ethnic Hatred and Global Instability.* London: Heinemann.

Circolo PRC Vomero-Arenella 'Che Guevara'. 2002. *Il Gioco del Capitale. Geopolitica delle risorse ed evoluzione della strategia militare.* Napoli: Lavorincorso.

Clark, R. 1994. *The Fire This Time. U.S. War Crimes in the Gulf.* New York: Thunder's Mouth Press.

Clarke, S. 1978. 'Capital, fractions of capital and the state: "Neo-Marxist" analysis of the South African state', *Capital & Class*, 5, 32–77.

Claudin, F. 1975. [1970]. *The Communist Movement. From Comintern to Cominform.* [transl. by B. Pearce and F. MacDonagh]. Harmondsworth: Penguin.

Cleveland, H. van B. 1966. *The Atlantic Idea and its European Rivals.* New York: McGraw-Hill, for the Council on Foreign Relations.

Cline, R.S. and Alexander, Y. 1986. [1984]. *Terrorism: The Soviet Connection.* New York: Crane, Russak & Co.

Club Turati. 1975. *Il Partito Americano in Italia.* Milano: Club Turati.

Cockburn, A. and Cockburn, P. 1999. *Out of the Ashes: The Resurrection of Saddam Hussein.* London: HarperCollins.

Cockett, R. 1995. [1994]. *Thinking the Unthinkable. Think-Tanks and the Economic Counter-Revolution, 1931–1983.* London: Fontana.

Cohen, B.J. 1986. *In Whose Interest? International Banking and American Foreign Policy.* New Haven: Yale University Press.

———. 1999. 'The new geography of money', in Emily Gilbert and Eric Helleiner (eds.), *Nation-States and Money. The Past, Present and Future of National Currencies.* London: Routledge.

Cohen, S.F. 1974. *Bukharin and the Bolshevik Revolution. A Political Biography 1888–1938.* London: Wildwood House.

Cohen, S.F. 1998. 'Russia: Tragedy or transition', in M.E. Cox (ed.), *Rethinking the Soviet Collapse. Sovietology, the Death of Communism and the New Russia*. London: Pinter.

Cohen, W.S. and Mitchell, G.J. 1989. *Men of Zeal. A Candid Inside Story of the Iran-Contra Hearings*. Harmondsworth: Penguin.

Cohen-Tanugi, L. 1987. [1985]. *Le Droit sans l'état* [preface by S. Hoffmann]. 3rd ed. Paris: Presses universitaires de France.

Colás, A. 1997. 'The limits of Mediterranean partnership: Civil society and the Barcelona conference of 1995', *Mediterranean Quarterly*, 8 (4), 63–80.

———. 2002. *International Civil Society. Social Movements in World Politics*. Cambridge: Polity Press.

Coll, S. 2004. *Ghost Wars. The Secret History of the CIA, Afghanistan, and Bin Laden from the Soviet Invasion to September 10, 2001*. New York: Penguin.

Collier, P. and Horowitz, D. 1976. *The Rockefellers. An American Dynasty*. New York: Holt, Rinehart & Winston.

Collins, R. 1984. *The Sociology of Philosophies. A Global Theory of Intellectual Change*. Cambridge, Mass.: Harvard University Press.

Colodny, L. and Gettlin, R. 1992. *Silent Coup. The Removal of a President*. New York: St. Martin's Press.

Conferentie van Europese communistische en arbeiderspartijen. 1976. *Voor Vrede, veiligheid, samenwerking and maatschappelijke vooruitgang in Europe*. Purmerend: Manifest.

Corson, W.R., Trento, S.B. and Trento, J.J. 1989. *Infiltraties. Sovjet-agenten in de CIA* [transl. by F. Visser]. Houten: De Haan/Unieboek.

Cortright, D. and Lopez, G.A. (with R.W. Conroy, J. Dashti-Gibson and J. Wagler). 2000. *The Sanctions Decade. Assessing UN Strategies in the 1990s*. Boulder, Col.: Rienner.

Cox, M.E. 1991. 'Requiem for a cold war critic: The rise and fall of George F. Kennan, 1946–1950', *Irish Slavonic Studies*, 11, 1–35.

——— (ed.). 1998. *Rethinking the Soviet Collapse. Sovietology, the Death of Communism and the New Russia*. London: Pinter.

——— (ed.). 2000. *E.H. Carr. A Critical Appraisal*. Basingstoke: Palgrave.

———. 2001. 'Whatever happened to American decline? International relations and the new United States hegemony', *New Political Economy*, 6 (3), 311–40.

Cox, M.E., Ikenberry, G.J. and Inoguchi, T. (eds.). 2000. *American Democracy Promotion: Impulses, Strategies, and Impacts*. Oxford: Oxford University Press.

Cox, R.W. 1979. 'Ideologies and the New International Economic Order: Reflections on some Recent Literature', *International Organization*, 33 (2), 257–300.

———. 1986. [1981]. 'States, social forces, and world orders: Beyond international relations theory', in R.O. Keohane (ed.), *Neorealism and its Critics*. New York: Columbia University Press.

———. 1987. *Production, Power, and World Order. Social Forces in the Making of History*. New York: Columbia University Press.

——— (with M.G. Schechter). 2002. *The Political Economy of a Plural World. Critical Reflections on Power, Morals and Civilization*. London: Routledge.

van Creveld, M. 1991. *The Transformation of War*. New York: The Free Press.

Crozier, M., Huntington, S.P. and Watanuki, J. 1975. *The Crisis of Democracy. Report on the Governability of Democracies to the Trilateral Commission*. New York: New York University Press.

CSE Microelectronics Group. 1980. *Microelectronics. Capitalist Technology and the Working Class*. London: Conference of Socialist Economists.

Cumings, B. 1989. 'The abortive apertura: South Korea in the light of the Latin American experience', *New Left Review*, 173, 5–32.

Cutler, A.C. 1999. 'Public meets private: The international unification and harmonisation of private international trade law', *Global Society*, 13 (1), 25–48.

Cutler, A.C. 2002. 'Historical materialism, globalisation, and law. Competing conceptions of property', in M. Rupert and H. Smith (eds.), *Historical Materialism and Globalization*. London: Routledge.

Cutler, A.C., Haufler, V. and Porter, T. (eds.). 1999. *Private Authority and International Affairs*. Albany: State University of New York Press.

Cypher, J.M. 1990. *State and Capital in Mexico. Development Policy since 1940*. Boulder, Col.: Westview Press.

Czichon, E. 1969. *Hermann Josef Abs. Porträt eindes Kreuzritters des Kapitals*. Berlin: Union Verlag.

Dallek, R. 1984. *The American Style of Foreign Policy. Cultural Politics and Foreign Affairs*. New York: Mentor Books.

Daniel, J. 1970. 'The Leader of the Free World' [*Le Nouvel Observateur*, 11 May 1970], in M. & S. Gettleman and L. & C. Kaplan (eds.), *Conflict in Indo-China. A Reader on the Widening War in Laos and Cambodia*. New York: Vintage.

Davidson, B. 1980. 'The revolution of people's power: Notes on Mozambique, 1979', *Monthly Review*, 32 (3), 75–89.

Davidson, I. and Weil, G. 1970. *The Gold War*. London: Secker & Warburg.

Davis, M. 1982. 'Nuclear Imperialism and Extended Deterrence', in *New Left Review* (ed.), *Exterminism and Cold War*. London: Verso.

———. 1986. *Prisoners of the American Dream*. London: Verso.

———. 2004. 'Planet of slums. Urban involution and the informal proletariat', *New Left Review* [new series], 26, 5–34.

Debord, G. 1967. *La société du Spectacle*. Paris: Buchet/Chastel.

Declaration Concerning the Establishment of a New International Economic Order, 3201, adopted by UN General Assembly, sixth special session, 2229th plenary meeting, 1 May 1974; reprinted in 'Appendix: Documents', in *Alternatives*, 1 (1975): 283–442.

Delaunay, J.-C. 1984. *Salariat et plus-value en France depuis la fin du XIXe siècle*. Paris: Presses de la Fondation Nationale des Sciences Politiques.

Deleuze, G. and Guattari, F. 1988. [1980]. *A Thousand Plateaus. Capitalism and Schizophrenia* [transl. by B. Massumi]. London: Athlone Press.

Deppe, F. 1992. 'The Future of the European Community. A Power Perspective', *International Journal of Political Economy*, 22 (1), 63–82.

———. 1999. *Politisches Denken im 20. Jahrhundert. Die Anfänge*. Hamburg: VSA.

Derluguian, G. 1999. 'Che Guevaras in Turbans', *New Left Review*, 237, 3–27.

Deubner, C. 1977. *Die Atompolitik der westdeutschen Industrie und die Gründung von Euratom*. Frankfurt: Campus.

———. 1984. 'Change and internationalization in industry: Toward a sectoral interpretation of West German politics', *International Organization*, 38 (3), 501–35.

Deutscher, I. 1966. [1949]. *Stalin. A Political Biography*. Rev. ed. Harmondsworth: Penguin.

Deyo, F.C. 1989. *Beneath the Miracle. Labor Subordination in the New Asian Industrialism*. Berkeley: University of California Press.

Dicken, P. 1986. *Global Shift. Industrial Change in a Turbulent World*. London: Harper & Row.

Diebold, W., Jr. 1959. *The Schuman Plan. A Study in Economic Cooperation 1950–59*. New York: Praeger.

Diligensky, G.G. 1988. 'Revolutionary theory and the contemporary world', in Lelio Basso International Foundation (eds.), *Theory and Practice of Liberation at the End of the XXth Century*. Brussels: Bruylant.

Dizard, J. 2004. 'How Ahmed Chalabi conned the neocons', http://www.salon.com, 5 May.

Djelic, M.-L.1998. *Exporting the American Model. The Postwar Transformation of European Business*. Oxford: Oxford University Press.

Doder, D. 1986. *Shadows and Whispers. Power Politics Inside the Kremlin from Brezhnev to Gorbachev*. New York: Random House.

Dorril, S. 1991. 'Willy Brandt: The "Good German"', *Lobster*, 22, 13–4.

Dorril, S. 1992. 'Heritage of Stone: JFK and *JFK*', *Lobster*, 23, 11–2.

Dorril, S. and Ramsay, R. 1992. *Smear! Wilson and the Secret State*. London: HarperCollins.

Dougherty, J.E. and Pfaltzgraff, R.L., Jr. 1971. *Contending Theories of International Relations*. Philadelphia: Lippincott.

Drainville, A.C. 1994. 'International political economy in the age of open Marxism', *Review of International Political Economy*, 1 (1), 105–32.

Duffield, M. 2001. *Global Governance and the New Wars. The Merging of Development and Security*. London: Zed Books.

Duménil, G. and Lévy, D. 2001. 'Costs and benefits of neoliberalism. A class analysis', *Review of International Political Economy*, 8 (4), 578–607.

———. 2004. 'Neo-Liberal dynamics—Towards a new phase?', in K. van der Pijl, L. Assassi and D. Wigan (eds.), *Global Regulation. Managing Crises After the Imperial Turn*. Basingstoke: Palgrave Macmillan.

Dunbar-Ortiz, R. 2003. 'The Grid of history: Cowboys and Indians', *Monthly Review*, 55 (3), 83–92.

Dupuy, R.J. 1989. *La clôture du système international. La cité terrestre*. Paris: Presses universitaires de France.

Duverger, M. 1968. [1959]. *La Ve République*. 4th ed. Paris: Presses universitaires de France.

Eakins, D.W. 1969. 'Business planners and America's postwar expansion', in D. Horowitz (ed.), *Corporations and the Cold War*. New York: Monthly Review Press.

ECE (UN Economic Commission for Europe). 1953. *The European Steel Industry and the Wide-Strip Mill*. Geneva: United Nations.

———. 1959. *Long-Term Trends and Problems of the European Steel Industry*. Geneva: United Nations.

Eden, A. 1960. *Full Circle. The Memoirs of the Rt. Hon. Sir Anthony Eden*. London: Cassell.

Elleinstein, J. 1973. *Histoire de l'URSS*. 4 vols. Paris: Ed. Sociales.

Elliott, P. and Schlesinger, P. 1980. 'Eurocommunism: Their word or ours?', in D. Childs (ed.), *The Changing Face of Western Communism*. London: Croom Helm.

Elsenhans, H. 1991. [1984]. *Development and Underdevelopment. The History, Economics and Politics of North-South Relations* [transl. by M. Reddy]. New Delhi: Sage Publications.

Elsenhans, H. and Junne, G. 1974. 'Deformation und Wirtschaftswachstum. Die Auswirkungen der wirtschaftlichen Ost-West Kooperation auf die osteuropäischen Länder', *Leviathan*, 2 (4), 534–71.

Eringer, R. 1980. *The Global Manipulators. The Bilderberg Group, The Trilateral Commission. Covert Power Groups of the West*. Bristol: Pentacle.

Escobar, P. 2002. 'The Roving Eye', *Asia Times*, 26 January [http://www.atimes.com, 1–4].

Esping-Andersen, G. 1990. *The Three Worlds of Welfare Capitalism*. Cambridge: Polity Press.

Esser, K. 1979. *Lateinamerika. Industrialisierungsstrategien und Entwicklung*. Frankfurt: Suhrkamp.

Etty, T. and Tudyka, K.P. 1974. 'Wereldconcernraden: Vakbonden en hun "kapitaalgerichte" strategie tegen multinationale ondernemingen', *Te Elfder Ure*, 21, 357–93.

Evans, J.W. 1967. *U.S. Trade Policy. New Legislation for the Next Round*. New York: Vintage.

Evans, P. 1979. *Dependent Development. The Alliance of Multinational, State, and Local Capital in Brazil*. Princeton, NJ: Princeton University Press.

Everts, P.P. 1968. *Thailand een tweede Vietnam? De Amerikaanse bestrijding van het communisme in Zuidoost-Azië*. Amsterdam: Polak & Van Gennep.

Eyffinger, A. 2003. *The Hague—International Centre of Justice and Peace*. The Hague: Jongbloed Law Booksellers.

Fall, B.B. 1967. [1965]. 'How the French Got Out of Vietnam', in M.G. Raskin and B.B. Fall (eds.), *The Viet-Nam Reader*. New York: Vintage.

Fallows, J. 2004. 'Blind Into Baghdad', *The Atlantic Monthly*, online edition, www.theatlantic.com, 9 February.

Farhi, A. 1976. 'Europe Behind the Myths', in T. Nairn (ed.), *Atlantic Europe? The Radical View*. Amsterdam: Transnational Institute.

Feldstein, M. 1998. 'Refocusing the IMF', *Foreign Affairs*. 77 (2), 20–33.

Fennema, M. 1982. *International Networks of Banks and Industry*. The Hague: Nijhoff.

Ferguson, T. 1995. *Golden Rule. The Investment Theory of Party Competition and the Logic of Money-Driven Political Systems*. Chicago: Chicago University Press.

——. 1996. 'Bill's Big Backers', *Mother Jones*, November/December, 60–6.

Ferguson, T. and Rogers, J. 1986. *Right Turn. The Decline of the Democratic Party and the Future of American Politics*. New York: Hill & Wang.

Fernandes, A.M. 1996. 'Neoliberalism and economic uncertainty in Brazil', in A.E. Fernández Jilberto and A. Mommen (eds.), *Liberalisation in the Developing World. Institutional and Economic Changes in Latin America, Africa, and Asia*. London: Routledge.

Fernández Jilberto, A.E. 1985. *Dictadura Military Oposición Política en Chile 1973–1981*. Dordrecht: Foris.

Feulner, E.J., Jr. 1976. *Congress and the New International Economic Order*. Washington, D.C.: The Heritage Foundation.

Fischer, F. 1984. *Griff nach der Weltmacht. Die Kriegszielpolitik des kaiserlichen Deutschland 1914/18* [abridged edition]. Düsseldorf: Droste.

Fischer, L. 1960. [1951]. *The Soviets in World Affairs. A History of the Relations between the Soviet Union and the Rest of the World 1917–1929* [abridged edition]. New York: Vintage.

Fisera, V. (ed.) 1978. *Writing on the Wall. France, May 1968: A Documentary Anthology* [collective transl.]. London: Allison and Busby.

Fleming, D.F. 1961. *The Cold War and its Origins 1917–1960*. 2 vols. Garden City, NY: Doubleday.

Fontaine, A. 1995. *Après eux, le Déluge. De Kaboul à Sarajevo, 1979–1995*. Paris: Fayard.

Foucault, M. 1966. *Le Mots et les Choses. Une Archéologie des Sciences Humaines*. Paris: Gallimard.

Fourth Conference of Heads of State or Government of Non-Aligned Countries. 1973. *Economic Declaration*. Algiers, 5–9 September, mimeo.

Frank, A.G. 1971. [1965]. *Capitalism and Underdevelopment in Latin America. Historical Studies of Chile and Brazil* [Rev. ed.]. Harmondsworth: Penguin.

——. 1998. *ReOrient. Global Economy in the Asian Age*. Berkeley: University of California Press.

Freyssenet, M. and Imbert, F. 1975. *La Centralisation du Capital dans la Sidérurgie 1945–1975*. Paris: CSU.

Frieden, J. 1981. 'Third World indebted industrialization: International finance and state capitalism in Mexico, Brazil, Algeria, and South Korea', *International Organization*, 35 (3), 407–31.

Friedrich, C.J. and Brzezinski, Z.K. 1963. 'Totalitarian dictatorship and autocracy', in H. Eckstein and D.E. Apter (eds.), *Comparative Politics: A Reader*. Glencoe, Ill.: The Free Press.

Füchtner, H. 1972. *Die brasilianischen Arbeitergewerkschaften, ihre Organisation und ihre politische Funktion*. Frankfurt: Suhrkamp.

Fukuyama, F. 1989. 'The End of History?', *The National Interest*, 16, 3–18.

——. 1992. *The End of History and the Last Man*. Harmondsworth: Penguin.

Fulbright, J.W. 1970. [1966]. *The Arrogance of Power*. Harmondsworth: Penguin.

Funke, R. 1978. 'Sich durchsetzender Kapitalismus. Eine Alternative zum spätkapitalistischen Paradigma', in S. Meuschel (ed.), *Sozialpolitik als soziale Kontrolle* [Starnberger Studien, Vol. 2]. Frankfurt: Suhrkamp.

Gall, N. 1976. 'Kernenergie voor Brazilië—Een wereldwijd gevaar?', *Intermediair*, 12 (42), 21–25.

Gallagher, J. and Robinson, R. 1967. [1953]. 'The Imperialism of Free Trade', in E.C. Black (ed.), *European Political History, 1815–1870. Aspects of Liberalism*. New York: Harper & Row.

Galli, G. 1995. *Il Padrone dei Padroni. Enrico Cuccia, il potere di Mediobanca e il capitalismo italiano*. Milan: Garzanti.

Galster, S. 2001. [1990]. *Afghanistan: The Making of U.S. Policy, 1973–1990* [introductory essay to the eponymous National Security Archive microfiche collection].

Garaudy, R. 1971. *Niets dan de waarheid. Krisis in de internationale communistische beweging, mei 1968–februari 1970* [transl. by H. Hom]. Amsterdam: De Bezige Bij.

Gardner, L.C. 1971. [1964]. *Economic Aspects of New Deal Diplomacy*. Boston: Beacon.

Garthoff, R. 1987. *Reflections on the Cuban Missile Crisis*. Washington, D.C.: The Brookings Institution.

———. 1994. *The Great Transition. American–Soviet Relations and the End of the Cold War*. Washington, D.C.: The Brookings Institution.

———. 1997. 'The Havana Conference on the Cuban Missile Crisis', http://www.seas.gwu.edu/nsarchive/CWIHP/BULLETINGS/b1a1.htm, 17 November.

Garton Ash, T. 1983. 'Eiserne Lady und Superman. Oder die radikale Flucht nach Hinten', *Kursbuch*, 73, 11–18.

———. 1989. 'Domestic developments in Eastern Europe: Policy implications for the West', in *Thirty-Seventh Bilderberg Meeting*, Gran Hotel La Toja, Spain (May 12–14) [original document].

———. 1993. *In Europe's Name. Germany and the Divided Continent*. New York: Random House.

de Gaulle, C. 1967. [1965]. 'News Conference, 23 July 1964', in M.G. Raskin and B.B. Fall (eds.), *The Viet-Nam Reader*. New York: Vintage.

———. 1970. *Mémoires d'espoir*. Vol. 1: *Le Renouveau 1958–1962*. Paris: Plon.

———. 1971. *Mémoires d'espoir*. Vol. 2: *L'effort, 1962–....* Paris: Plon.

Gauthier, A. [with J. Domingo, B. Elissalde and A. Reynaud]. 1993. *Le monde depuis 1945*. Paris: Bréal.

Gendzier, I.L. 1995. [1985]. *Development Against Democracy. Manipulating Political Change in the Third World*. Hampton, Conn.: The Tyrone Press.

———. 1997. *Notes From the Minefield. United States Intervention in Lebanon and the Middle East, 1945–1958*. New York: Columbia University Press.

George, S. and Bache, I. 2001. *Politics in the European Union*. Oxford: Oxford University Press.

Gerassi, J. 1965. [1963]. *The Great Fear in Latin America*. Rev. ed. New York: Collier Books.

Germain, R.D. 1997. *The International Organization of Credit. States and Global Finance in the World-Economy*. Cambridge: Cambridge University Press.

Gerretson, C. 1971. [1932]. *Geschiedenis der 'Koninklijke'*. 3 vols. Baarn: Bosch & Keuning.

Gerschenkron, A. 1962. *Economic Backwardness in Historical Perspective*. Cambridge, Mass.: Harvard University Press.

Gervasi, S. 1990. 'A full court press: The destabilization of the Soviet Union', *Covert Action Information Bulletin*, 35, 21–6.

———. 1993. 'Germany, U.S., and the Yugoslav Crisis', *Covert Action Quarterly*, 43, 41–5.

———. 1996. 'Waarom is de NAVO in Joegoslavië', in S. Flounders and S. Gervasi (eds.), *De tragedie van Bosnië. De rol van de VS en de NAVO* [transl. by W. Peters]. Amsterdam: Global Reflexion.

Geyl, P. 1969. [1939]. *Orange and Stuart, 1641–1672* [transl. by A. Pomerans]. London: Weidenfeld & Nicholson.

Giddens, A. 1985. *The Nation-State and Violence*. Vol 2. of *A Contemporary Critique of Historical Materialism*. Cambridge: Polity.

Giesen, K.-G. 1989. *L'Europe des Surrégénérateurs. Développement d'une Filière Nucléaire par Integration Politique et Économique*. Paris: Presses universitaires de France.

———. 1992. *L'Ethique des Relations Internationales. Les Theories Anglo-Américaines Contemporaines*. Brussels: Bruylant.

———. 1999. 'Charité paternaliste et guerre juste: la justice internationale selon John Rawls', *Les Temps Modernes*, 604, 40–62.

Gifford, P. 1988. *The Religious Right in Southern Africa*. Harare: Baobab Books & University of Zimbabwe Press.

Gill, S. 1990. *American Hegemony and the Trilateral Commission*. Cambridge: Cambridge University Press.

——. 1994. 'Structural change and global political economy: Globalising elites and the emerging world order', in Y. Sakamoto (ed.), *Global Transformation. Challenges to the State System*. Tokyo: United Nations University Press.

——. 1995. 'The global panopticon? The neoliberal state, economic life, and democratic surveillance', *Alternatives*, 20 (1): 1–49.

——. 1998. 'European governance and new constitutionalism. Economic and monetary union and alternatives to disciplinary neoliberalism in Europe', *New Political Economy*, 3 (1), 5–26.

——. 2003. *Power and Resistance in the New World Order*. Basingstoke: Palgrave Macmillan.

Gill, S. and Law, D. 1988. *The Global Political Economy. Perspectives, Problems, and Policies*. Brighton: Harvester; Baltimore, Md.: Johns Hopkins University Press.

Gimbel, J. 1976. *The Origins of the Marshall Plan*. Stanford, CA: Stanford University Press.

Godson, R. 1976. *American Labor and European Politics. The AFL as a Transnational Force*. New York: Crane, Russak & Co.

Goedhart, M. 1978. 'De Nederlandse landbouw als proeftuin voor Europa', unpublished MA dissertation, University of Amsterdam.

Goldmann, L. 1971. [1962]. 'Die Marxistische Erkenntnistheorie und ihre Anwendung auf die Geschichte des Marxistischen Denkens', in K. Lenk (ed.), *Ideologie. Ideologiekritik und Wissenschaftssoziologie*. 5th ed. Neuwied & Berlin: Luchterhand.

Goldstein, J. 2000. 'United States and world trade: Hegemony by proxy?', in T.C. Lawton, J.N.Rosenau and A.C. Verdun (eds.), *Strange Power. Shaping the Parameters of International Relations and International Political Economy*. Aldershot: Ashgate.

Golub, P. 2004. 'From globalisation to militarism: The American hegemonic cycle and system-wide crisis', in K. van der Pijl, L. Assassi and D. Wigan (eds.), *Global Regulation. Managing Crises After the Imperial Turn*. Basingstoke: Palgrave Macmillan.

Goralczyk, D. 1975. 'Die Marxsche Theorie der Weltmarktbewegung des Kapitals und die Rekonstruktion des Weltmarkts nach 1945', in F. Deppe (ed.), *Europäische Wirtschaftsgemeinschaft. Zur politischen Ökonomie der westeuropäischen Integration*. Reinbek: Rowohlt.

Gorbachev, M.S. 1986. *Political Report of the CPSU Central Committee to the 27th Party Congress*. Moscow: Novosti.

——. 1987. *Perestroika. New Thinking for Our Country and the World*. New York: Harper & Row.

Görg, C. and Hirsch, J. 1998. 'Is international democracy possible?', *Review of International Political Economy*, 5 (4), 585–615.

Gosovic, B. and Ruggie, J.G. 1976. 'On the creation of a new international economic order: Issue linkage and the seventh special session of the UN General Assembly', *International Organization*, 30 (2), 309–45.

Gossweiler, K. 1975. [1971]. *Grossbanken, Industriemonopole, Staat. Ökonomie und Politik des staatsmonopolistischen Kapitalismus in Deutschland, 1914–1932*. Berlin: DEB.

Gowan, P. 1999a. *The Global Gamble. Washington's Faustian Bid for World Dominance*. London: Verso.

——. 1999b. 'The NATO Powers and the Balkan Tragedy', *New Left Review*, 234, 83–105.

Gramsci, A. 1971. *Selections from the "Prison Notebooks"* [transl. and ed. by Q. Hoare and G.N. Smith]. New York: International Publishers.

——. 1975. *Quaderni del carcere* [edited by V. Gerratana for the Instituto Gramsci]. 4 vols. Turin: Einaudi.

——. 1977. *Selections from Political Writings 1910–1920* [transl. and ed. by Q. Hoare]. New York: International Publishers.

Gramsci, A. 1978. *Selections from Political Writings 1921–1926* [transl. and ed. by Q. Hoare]. New York: International Publishers.

Granou, A. 1977. *La Bourgeoisie Financière au Pouvoir et les Luttes de Classes en France*. Paris: Maspero.

Graz, J.-C. 2002. 'Diplomatie et marché de la normalisation internationale', *L'économie politique*, 13, 52–65.

———. 2003. 'How powerful are transnational elite clubs? The social myth of the World Economic Forum', *New Political Economy*, 8 (3), 321–40.

Greider, W. 1989. [1987]. *Secrets of the Temple. How the Federal Reserve Runs the Country*. New York: Simon & Schuster Touchstone.

Greiner, B. 1990 'Angst vor Rapallo. Amerikanische Reaktionen auf den Fall der Mauer', *Blätter für deutsche und internationale Politik*, 35 (2), 159–67.

Grewe, W.G. 1979. *Rückblenden. Aufzeichnungen eines Augenzeugen deutscher Außenpolitik von Adenauer bis Schmidt*. Frankfurt: Propyläen.

Grosser, A. 1978. *Les Occidentaux. Les Pays d'Europe et les Etats-Unis depuis la Guerre*. Paris: Fayard.

Guattari, F. 1976. [1965–1970]. *Psychotherapie, Politik and die Aufgaben der institutionellen Analyse* [preface by G. Deleuze, transl. by G. Osterwald]. Frankfurt: Suhrkamp

Guillou, J. and Wallis, R. 1978. 'Goodbye Bruce Hutchins', in P. Agee and L. Wolf (eds.), *Dirty Work. The CIA in Western Europe*. New York: Dorset Press.

Günsche, K.-L. and Lantermann, K. 1977. *Kleine Geschichte der Sozialistischen Internationale*. Bonn: Neue Gesellschaft.

Haas, E.B. 1968. [1958]. *The Uniting of Europe. Political, Social, and Economic Forces, 1950–1957*. 2nd ed. Stanford, Cal.: Stanford University Press.

Hager, N. 1996. *Secret Power. New Zealand's Role in the International Spy Network*. Nelson, NZ: Craig Potton.

Haggard, S. and Mo, J. 2000. 'The political economy of the Korean financial crisis', *Review of International Political Economy*, 7 (2), 197–218.

Haiduk, K., Herr, H., Lintovskaya, T., Parchevskaya, S., Priewe, J. and Tsiku, R. 2004. *The Belarussian Economy at a Crossroads*. Moscow: Actrav.

Halevi, J. and Varoufakis, Y. 2003. 'The global Minotaur', *Monthly Review*, 55 (3), 57–75.

Hall, H.D. 1971. *Commonwealth. A History of the British Commonwealth of Nations*. London: Van Nostrand Reinhold.

Halliday, F. 1979. *Iran. Dictatorship and Development*. Harmondsworth: Penguin.

———. 1986. [1983]. *The Making of the Second Cold War*. 2nd ed. London: Verso.

Halliday, J. and McCormack, G. 1973. *Japanese Imperialism Today. Co-Prosperity in Greater East Asia*. Harmondsworth: Penguin.

Halperin, S. 1997. *In the Mirror of the Third World. Capitalist Development in Modern Europe*. Ithaca, NY: Cornell University Press.

———. 2004. *War and Social Change in Modern Europe. The Great Transformation Revisited*. Cambridge: Cambridge University Press.

Hampden-Turner, C. and Trompenaars, F. 1995. [1993]. *The Seven Cultures of Capitalism. Value Systems for Creating Wealth in the United States, Britain, Japan, Germany, France, Sweden, and the Netherlands*. London: Piatkus.

Han Suyin. 1994. *Eldest Son. Zhou Enlai and the Making of Modern China 1898–1976*. London: Pimlico.

Harada, H. 1970. 'The anti-Ampo struggle', in S. Dowsey (ed.), *Zengakuren. Japan's Revolutionary Students*. Berkeley, Cal.: Ishi Press.

Hardt, M. and Negri, A. 2000. *Empire*. Cambridge, Mass.: Harvard University Press.

Hargreaves, J.D. 1988. *Decolonization in Africa*. London: Longman.

Harrison, M. 1978. 'Survey: The Soviet economy in the 1920s and 1930s', *Capital & Class*, 5, 78–94.

Hartcher, P. 1999. [1997]. *The Ministry. The Inside Story of Japan's Ministry of Finance.* London: HarperCollins.

Hart-Landsberg, M. and Burkett, P. 2004. 'China and Socialism. Market Reforms and Class Struggle', *Monthly Review*, 56 (3) [Special Book-Length Issue].

Harvey, D. 1985. *The Condition of Postmodernity. An Enquiry into the Origins of Cultural Change.* Cambridge, Mass.: Blackwell.

Haussmann, F. 1952. *Der Schuman-Plan im Europäischen Zwielicht.* München & Berlin: Beck.

Hayek, F.A. 1985. [1944]. *De weg naar slavernij* [transl. by H.L. Swart et al.]. Amsterdam: Omega.

Helleiner, E. 1999. 'Denationalising money? Economic liberalism and the "national question" in currency affairs', in Emily Gilbert and Eric Helleiner (eds.), *Nation-States and Money. The Past, Present and Future of National Currencies.* London: Routledge.

Hellema, D. 1979. 'De Duitse herbewapening 1945–1954', *Tijdschrift voor Diplomatie*, 6 (2), 112–26.

———. 1984. *Frontlijn van de koude oorlog. De Duitse herbewapening en het Atlantisch bondgenootschap.* Amsterdam: Mets.

Helsinki. 1975. *Conférence sur la Sécurité at la Coopération en Europe Acte final* [intro. by J. Denis]. Paris: Ed. Sociales.

Herde, G. 1980. 'F.J. Strauss, die Vertriebenenverbände und die Paneuropa-Union des Otto v. Habsburg', *Blätter für deutsche und internationale Politik*, 25 (1), 63–77.

Hersh, S.M. 1994. 'The Wild East', *The Atlantic Monthly*, 273 (6), 61–86.

Hess, G. 1993. 'Kennedy's Vietnam options and decisions', in D.L. Anderson (ed.), *Shadow on the White House: Presidents and the Vietnam War, 1945–75.* Lawrence: University of Kansas Press.

Hesse, R. 1984. 'AirLand Battle 2000 und deutsche Interessen', *Blätter für deutsche und internationale Politik*, 29 (1), 10–5.

Heuwinkel, L. 1978. *Autozentrierte Entwicklung und die neue Weltwirtschaftsordnung.* Saarbrücken: Breitenbach.

Hexner, E. 1943. *The International Steel Cartel.* Durham, N.C.: University of North Carolina Press.

Higgott, R. 2004. 'US Foreign Policy and the "Securitization" of Economic Globalization', *International Politics*, 41 (2), 147–75.

Hippler, J. 1986. *Krieg im Frieden. Amerikanische Strategien für die Dritte Welt: Counterinsurgency und Low-Intensity Warfare.* Cologne: Pahl-Rugenstein.

Hirszowicz, M. 1980. *The Bureaucratic Leviathan. A Study in the Sociology of Communism.* Oxford: Martin Robertson.

Hitchens, C. 2002. [2001]. *The Trial of Henry Kissinger.* London: Verso.

Hobbes, T. 1968. [1651]. *Leviathan* [intro. by C.B. Macpherson]. Harmondsworth: Penguin.

Hochraich, D. 2003. 'Les banques chinoises face à la concurrence internationale', *A Contrario. Revue internationale de sciences sociales*, 1 (2), 52–66.

Hodgson, G. 1979. 'The US Response', in P. Filo della Torre, E. Mortimer and J. Story (eds.), *Eurocommunism: Myth or Reality.* Harmondsworth: Penguin.

Hoffmann, S. 1978. *Primacy or World Order. American Foreign Policy since the Cold War.* New York: McGraw-Hill.

Holbrooke, R. 1995. 'America, a European power', *Foreign Affairs*, 74 (2), 38–51.

Holland, S. 1975. *The Socialist Challenge.* London: Quartet Books.

Holloway, D. 1984. *De Sovjet-Unie en de bewapeningswedloop* [transl. by P. Jaarsma]. Amsterdam: Mets.

Holman, O. 1986. 'Recht zonder politiek gezag of politiek zonder rechtsgrondslag', *Recht en Kritiek*, 12 (1), 6–42.

———. 1987–88. 'Semiperipheral Fordism in southern Europe. The national and international context of socialist-led governments in Spain, Portugal and Greece in historical perspective', *International Journal of Political Economy*, 17 (4), 11–55.

Holman, O. 1992. 'Transnational Class Strategy and the New Europe', *International Journal of Political Economy*, 22 (1), 3–22.

———. 1993. 'Internationalisation and democratisation: Southern Europe, Latin America and the world economic crisis', in S. Gill (ed.), *Gramsci, Historical Materialism, and International Relations*. Cambridge: Cambridge University Press.

———. 1996. *Integrating Southern Europe. EC Expansion and the Transnationalisation of Spain*. London: Routledge.

———. 1998. 'Integrating Eastern Europe. EU expansion and the double transformation in Poland, the Czech Republic, and Hungary', *International Journal of Political Economy*, 28 (2), 12–43.

———. 2004. 'Asymmetrical regulation and multidimensional governance in the European Union', *Review of International Political Economy*, 11 (4), 714–35.

Holman, O. and Fernández Jilberto, A.E. 1989. 'Clases sociales, crisis del régimen autoritario y transicion democrática: los casos de Brasil y España en una perspective comparativa', *Afers Internacionals*, 16, 5–22.

Holman, O. and van der Pijl, K. 1996. 'The capitalist class in the European Union', in G.A. Kourvetaris and A. Moschonas (eds.), *The Impact of European Integration. Political, Sociological, and Economic Changes*. Westport, Conn.: Praeger.

———. 2003. 'Structure and process in transnational European business', in A.W. Cafruny and M. Ryner (eds.), *A Ruined Fortress? Neoliberal Hegemony and Transformation in Europe*, Lanham, Md.: Rowman & Littlefield.

Houben, H. 2004. 'Het nieuwe hoofddoel van de Europese Unie: de Lissabon-strategie', *Marxistische Studies*, 65, 11–72.

Hough, J. 1986. *The Struggle for the Third World. Soviet Debates and American Debates*. Washington: Brookings.

———. 1990. *Russia and the West. Gorbachev and the Politics of Reform*. New York: Simon & Schuster.

Houweling, H.W. 1997. 'Naar een gemeenschappelijk buitenlands and veiligheidsbeleid: doelbewust ombuigen van de verandering, dat is de uitdaging', in O. Holman (ed.), *Europese dilemma's aan het einde van de 20ste eeuw*. Amsterdam: Het Spinhuis.

———. 1999. '*The Limits to Growth* na ruim 25 jaar. Een realistische terugblik op een doem-scenario', *Transaktie*, 28 (1), 71–105.

Houweling, H.W. and Siccama, J.G. 1993. 'The Neo-Functionalist Explanation of World Wars: A Critique and an Alternative', *International Interactions*, 18 (4), 387–408.

Hulet, C. 1991. 'The Secret U.S. Agenda in the Gulf War', *Open Magazine Pamphlet Series*, 5.

Hummel, H. 2000. *Der neue Westen. Der Handelskonflikt zwischen den USA und Kapan und die Integration der westlichen Gemeinschaft*. Münster: Agenda Verlag.

Huntington, S.P. 1993. 'The Clash of Civilizations?', *Foreign Affairs*, 72 (3), 22–49.

———. 1998. [1997]. *The Clash of Civilizations and the Remaking of World Order*. London: Touchstone Books.

Idenburg, P.J.A. 1961. 'Het Nederlands antwoord op het Indonesisch nationalisme', in H. Baudet and I.J. Brugmans (eds.), *Balans van Beleid. Terugblik op de laatste halve eeuw van Nederlandsch-Indië*. Assen: van Gorcum/Prakke & Prakke.

Inquilab. 1984. 'The Reagan-Botha axis threatens peace and social progress', *The African Communist*, 99, 17–30.

International Security Council. 1986. *State-Sponsored Terrorism and the Threat to International Secucrity*. New York: CAUSA International.

Jackson, R.H. 1990. *Quasi-States: Sovereignty, International Relations and the Third World*. Cambridge: Cambridge University Press.

Jacob, M.C. 1991. *Living the Enlightenment. Freemasonry and Politics in Eighteenth-Century Europe*. New York: Oxford University Press.

Jacobs, D. 1988. 'Gereguleerd staal. Nationale en internationale economische regulering in de westeuropese staalindustrie 1750–1950', Ph.D. dissertation, University of Nijmegen.

Jalée, P. 1973. *L'impérialisme en 1970*. Paris: Maspero.

James, G. 1996. [1995]. *In the Public Service. A Devastating Account of the Arms-to-Iraq Affair*. 2nd ed. London: Warner Books.

Jánossy, F. 1968. *Das Ende der Wirtschaftswunder. Erscheinung und Wesen der wirtschaftlichen Entwicklung*. Frankfurt: Neue Kritik.

Jenkins, D. 2002. *The Final Frontier. America, Science, and Terror*. London: Verso.

Jessop, B. 1983. 'Accumulation strategies, state forms, and hegemonic projects', *Kapitalistate*, 10/11, 89–111.

Johnson, C. 2002. [2000]. *Blowback. The Costs and Consequences of American Empire*. Rev. ed. London: TimeWarner.

Johnson, M. 2001. *All Honourable Men. Social Origins of the War in Lebanon*. London: I.B. Tauris.

Joint Hearings, Senate Foreign Relations Committee, Military Assistance Programme. 1949. Washington: Government Printing Office, 1976.

Jones, J.M. 1955. *The Fifteen Weeks. An Inside Account of the Genesis of the Marshall Plan*. New York: Harcourt, Brace & World.

Jung, H. 1980. 'Class Struggles in El Salvador', *New Left Review*, 122, 3–25.

Junne, G. 1985. 'Das amerikanische Rüstungsprogramm: Ein Substitut für Industriepolitik', *Leviathan*, 13 (1), 23–37.

Junne, G. and van der Pijl, K. 1986. 'Het tweeledige doel van SDI: Militaire superioriteit over the Sovjet-Unie en een technologische voorsprong op de bondgenoten', in P.P. Everts (ed.), *De Droom der Onkwetsbaarheid*. Kampen: Kok Agora.

Kahin, G. M. 1986. *Intervention. How America Became Involved in Vietnam*. New York: Knopf.

Kahn, H.W. 1979. 'Strauss und der Griff nach der Atommacht', *Blätter für deutsche und internationale Politik*, 24 (10), 1195–218.

Kaltenthaler, K. and Mora, F.O. 2002. 'Explaining Latin American economic integration: The case of Mercosur', *Review of International Political Economy*, 9 (1), 72–97.

Kannapin, K. 1984. *Imperialistische strategie gegen die Neue Internationale Wirtschaftsordnung*. Berlin: Dietz.

Kaptein, E. 1993. 'Neoliberalism and the dismantling of corporatism in Australia', in H.W. Overbeek (ed.), *Restructuring Hegemony in the Global Political Economy. The Rise of Transnational Neo-Liberalism in the 1980s*. London: Routledge.

Kauppi, M.V. and Viotti, P.R. 1992. *The Global Philosophers. World Politics in Western Thought*. New York: Lexington Books.

Kautsky, K. 1914. 'Der Imperialismus', *Die Neue Zeit*, 1913–1914, 2. Band, 908–22.

de Kemp, A. 1985 *Internationale Regulering van Multinationale Ondernemingen*, Nijmeegse Studies, 6. Nijmegen: University of Nijmegen.

Kennan, G.F. 1951. *American Diplomacy 1900–1950* [includes two articles originally published in *Foreign Affairs* in July 1947 and April 1951]. New York: Mentor.

Kennedy, P. 1987. *The Rise and Fall of the Great Powers. Economic Change and Military Conflict From 1500 to 2000*. New York: Random House.

Kenwood, A.G. and Lougheed, A.L. 1971. *The Growth of the International Economy 1820–1960*. London: Allen & Unwin; Sydney: Australasian.

Keohane, R.O. and Nye, J.S., Jr. (eds.). 1973. [1971]. *Transnational Relations and World Politics*. Cambridge, Mass.: Harvard University Press.

al-Khafaji, I. 2004. *Tormented Births. Passages to Modernity in Europe and the Middle East*. London: I.B. Tauris.

Kim, Y.-H. 2004. 'Foreign direct investment in China: Recent trends and impacts on the international division of labor in Asia', *The Journal of East Asian Affairs*, 18 (1), 157–75.

King, P. 1974. *The Ideology of Order. A Comparative Analysis of Jean Bodin and Thomas Hobbes.* London: Allen & Unwin.

Kirchheimer, O. and Menges, C. 1965. 'A free press in a democratic state? The *Spiegel* case', in G.M. Carter and A.F. Westin (eds.), *Politics in Europe. 5 Cases in European Government.* New York: Harcourt, Brace, & World.

Kissinger, H.A. 1965. *The Troubled Partnership. A Re-Appraisal of the Atlantic Alliance.* New York: McGraw-Hill.

——. 2000. [1982]. *Years of Upheaval.* London: Phoenix Press.

Klare, M.T. 2001. *Resource Wars. The New Landscape of Global Conflict.* New York: Henry Holt Metropolitan Books.

Klinkenberg, W. 1971. *De ultracentrifuge 1937–1970. Hitlers bom voor Strauss?* Amsterdam: van Gennep/In den Toren.

Kloss, H. 1969. *Grundfragen der Ethnopolitik im 20. Jahrhundert.* Wien: Braumüller; Bad Godesberg: Verlag Wissenschaftliches Archiv.

Kniazhinsky, V. 1984. *West European Integration: Its Policies and International Relations* [transl. by P.F. Medow]. Moscow: Progress.

Knieper, R. 1976. *Weltmarkt, Wirtschaftsrecht und Nationalstaat.* Frankfurt: Suhrkamp.

Knight, S. 1985. [1983]. *The Brotherhood. The Secret World of the Freemasons.* London: Grafton.

Kolk, A. 1996. *Forests in International Environmental Politics. International Organisations, NGOs and the Brazilian Amazon.* Utrecht: International Books.

Kolko, G. 1957. 'Morris R. Cohen: The scholar and/or society', *American Quarterly*, 9 (3) 325–36.

——. 1968. *The Politics of War. The World and United States Foreign Policy 1943–1945.* New York: Vintage.

——. 1985. *Anatomy of a War. Vietnam, the United States, and the Modern Historical Experience.* New York: Pantheon.

——. 1988. *Confronting the Third World. United States Foreign Policy 1945–1980.* New York: Pantheon.

——. 1989. 'Varieties of Third World elites: A framework for analysis', in P. Limqueco (ed.), *Partisan Scholarship: Essays in Honour of Renato Constantino.* Manila: Journal of Contemporary Asia Publishers.

——. 1997. *Vietnam: Anatomy of a Peace.* London: Routledge.

——. 2002. *Another Century of War?* New York: The New Press.

Kolko, G. and Kolko, J. 1972. *The Limits of Power. The World and United States Foreign Policy, 1945–1954.* New York: Harper & Row.

Kolko, J. 1974. *America and the Crisis of World Capitalism.* Boston: Beacon.

——. 1988. *Restructuring the World Economy.* New York: Pantheon.

Konrád, G. and Szelényi, I. 1981. [1978]. *Die Intelligenz auf dem Weg zur Klassenmacht* [transl. by H.-H. Paetzke]. Frankfurt: Suhrkamp.

Koopmans, R.W. 1977. *Jazz. Improvisatie en organisatie van een groeiende minderheid.* Amsterdam: SUA.

——. 1978. 'Turkey, The Limits of Modernisation', Ph.D. dissertation, University of Amsterdam.

Kornbluth, J. 1992. *Highly Confident: The Crime and Punishment of Michael Milken.* New York: Morrow.

Korzeniewicz, R.P. and Moran, T.P. 1997. 'World economic trends in the distribution of income, 1965–1992', *American Journal of Sociology*, 102 (4), 1000–39.

Kosovo Agreement. 1999. *Interim Agreement for Peace and Self-Government in Kosovo* (23 February 1999), www.monde-diplomatique.fr/dossiers.

Kosta, J. 1978. *Abriss der sozialökonomischen Entwicklung der Tschechoslowakei 1945–1977.* Frankfurt: Suhrkamp.

Kotz, D.M. [with F. Weir]. 1997. *Revolution from Above. The Demise of the Soviet System.* London: Routledge.

Kowalewski, D. 1997. *Global Establishment. The Political Economy of North/Asian Networks.* Basingstoke: Macmillan.

Kowaljow, E. and Malyschew, W. 1986. *Terror. Drahtzieher und Attentäter. Das Netz der CIA in Westeuropa* [transl. by W. Hanke]. Berlin: Militärverlag der DDR.

Krägenau, H. 1975. *Internationale Direktinvestitionen 1950–1973. Vergleichende Untersuchung und statistische Materialien.* Hamburg: HWWA.

Krasner, S.D. 1985. *Structural Conflict. The Third World Against Global Liberalism.* Berkeley: University of California Press.

Kriegel, A. 1977. *Un autre Communisme?* Paris: Hachette.

Kreitzman, L. 1999. *The 24 Hour Society.* London: Profile Books.

Kristol, I. 1971. '"When virtue loses all her loveliness"—Some reflections on capitalism and "The Free Society"', in D. Bell and I. Kristol (eds.), *Capitalism Today.* New York: Mentor.

Kubálkova, V. and Cruickshank, J.J. 1980. *Marxism-Leninism and Theory of International Relations.* London: Routledge.

Kuyper, P.J. 1984. 'European community law and extraterritoriality: Some trends and new developments', *The International and Comparative Law Quarterly*, 33, 1013–1021.

Kwon, Y. 2004. 'East Asian tegionalism focusing on ASEAN plus three', *The Journal of East Asian Affairs*, 18 (1), 98–130.

Lacouture, J. 1966. *Vietnam: Between Two Truces* [intro. by J. Kraft, transl. by K. Kellen and J. Carmichael]. New York: Vintage.

Laffey, M. and Dean, K. 2002. 'A flexible Marxism for flexible times', in M. Rupert and H. Smith (eds.), *Historical Materialism and Globalization.* London: Routledge.

Lafontaine, O. 1999. *Das Herz schlägt links.* München: Econ.

Laird, R.D. and Laird, B.A. 1970. *Soviet Communism and Agrarian Revolution.* Harmondsworth: Penguin.

Lake, D.A. 1987. 'Power and the Third World: Towards a realist political economy of North-South relations', *International Studies Quarterly*, 31 (2), 217–34.

Lamounier, B. 1989. 'Brazil: Inequality Against Democracy', in L. Diamond, J.J. Linz and S.M. Lipset (eds.), *Democracy in Developing Countries—Latin America.* Boulder, Col.: Rienner; London: Adamantine Press.

Landau, S. 1983. *Nieuw Rechts in Amerika* [transl. by C. van Splunteren]. Amsterdam: Van Gennep.

Landgraeber, W., Sieker, E., Wagener, M. and Wisnewski, G. 1992. 'Im Brennpunkt: Die Zerstörung der RAF-Legende. Ein Kronzeuge packt aus ...' (printed text of a TV documentary produced by HR and WDR networks and broadcast on 1 July 1992, by ARD).

Lane, J.-E. 2000. *New Public Management.* London: Routledge.

Langley, P. 2002. *World Financial Orders. An Historical International Political Economy.* London: Routledge.

Larson, H.M., Knowlton, E.H. and Popple, C.S. 1971. *New Horizons. History of Standard Oil Company (New Jersey) 1927–1950.* New York: Harper & Row.

von Laue, T.H. 1967. [1961]. 'Russian peasants in the factory', in V.R. Lorwin (ed.), *Labor and Working Conditions in Modern Europe.* New York: Macmillan.

Laurance, E.J. 1992. *The International Arms Trade.* New York: Lexington Books.

Lefebvre, H. 1976. *De l'Etat,* 4 vols. Paris: Ed. Générales, 10/18.

Leggewie, C. 1989. 'CDU—Integrationsmodell auf Widerruf? Die zwei Modernisierungen der deutschen Rechten nach 1945', *Blätter für deutsche und internationale Politik*, 34 (3), 294–308.

Leigh, D. 1989. *The Wilson Plot. The Intelligence Services and the Discrediting of a Prime Minister.* London: Heinemann-Mandarin.

Lenin, V.I. (published from 1964). *Collected Works* [transl. from the Russian]. Moscow: Progress.

Leontief, W., Carter, A.P. and Petri, P.A. 1977. *The Future of the World Economy.* New York: United Nations.

Lerner, D. and Gorden, M. 1969. *Euratlantica. Changing Perspectives of the European Elites.* Cambridge, Mass.: MIT Press.

Lerouge, H. 2004. 'Een te verwerpen grondwet', *Marxistische Studies*, 65, 73–84.

Levathes, L. 1994. *When China Ruled the Seas. The Treasure Fleet of the Dragon Throne, 1405–1433.* Oxford: Oxford University Press.

Levi, A. 1979. 'Eurocommunism: Myth or reality?', in P. Filo della Torre, E. Mortimer and J. Story (eds.), *Eurocommunism: Myth or Reality*. Harmondsworth: Penguin.

Levinson, C. 1978. [1977]. *Wodka-Cola. Die gefährliche Kehrseite der wirtschaftlichen Zusammenarbeit zwischen Ost und West* [transl. by H. Gaethe and K.A. Klewer]. Reinbek: Rowohlt.

Lewin, M. 1985. *The Making of the Soviet System. Essays in the Social History of Interwar Russia.* London: Methuen.

Lindberg, L.N. 1983. 'Wirtschaftswissenschaftler als Politikberater. Der Rückzug aus Keynesianismus und Staatsinterventionismus in den USA nach 1970 (Teil II)', *Journal für Sozialforschung*, 23 (2), 185–204.

van der Linde, C. 1991. 'Dynamic International Oil Markets. Oil Market Developments and Structure 1860–1988', Ph.D. dissertation, University of Amsterdam.

Lipietz, A. 1982. 'Towards Global Fordism', *New Left Review*, 132, 32–47.

———. 1984. 'How monetarism has choked Third World industrialization', *New Left Review*, 145, 71–87.

Lipp, E.-M. 1997. 'Auf dem Weg zur transatlantischen Wirtschaftsgemeinschaft', in W. Weidenfeld (ed.), *Partnerschaft gestalten. Die Zukunft der transatlantischen Beziehungen* [Bellevue-Gespräche II]. Gütersloh: Bertelsmann Stiftung.

Locke, J. 1965. [1690]. *Two Treatises of Government* [intro. by P. Laslett]. New York: Mentor.

Lockwood, L. 1974. 'Two Comments on the Energy Crisis (II)', *Monthly Review*, 25 (11), 55–60.

Lombard, D. 1981. *Pantjasila, trente années de débats politiques en Indonésie* [Etudes insulindiennes, vol. II]. Paris: Editions de la Maison des sciences de l'homme.

London, A. 1970. [1968]. *The Confession* [transl. from the French]. New York: Morrow.

Löwy, M. 1981. *The Politics of Combined and Uneven Development. The Theory of Permanent Revolution.* London: Verso.

Lundberg, F. 1969. [1968]. *The Rich and the Super-Rich. A Study in the Power of Money Today.* New York: Bantam.

Mabey, N. 1999. 'Defending the legacy of Rio: The civil society campaign against the MAI', in S. Picciotto and R. Mayne (eds.), *Regulating International Business. Beyond Liberalization.* Basingstoke: Macmillan.

MacEwan, A. 1986. 'Latin America: Why not default?', *Monthly Review*, 38 (4), 1–13.

———. 1991. 'Banishing the Mexican revolution', *Monthly Review*, 43 (6), 16–27.

Macintyre, D. 2000. *Mandelson and the Making of New Labour*. London: HarperCollins.

Mackinder, H. 1962. [1919]. *Democratic Ideals and Reality.* New York: W.W. Norton & Co.

Maddison, A. 1971. [1969]. *Twee modellen van economische groei* [transl. by P.J.J. Seebregts]. Utrecht and Antwerpen: Spectrum.

Magdoff, H. 1969. *The Age of Imperialism. The Economics of U.S. Foreign Policy.* New York: Monthly Review Press.

Malanczuk, P. 1993. *Humanitarian Intervention and the Legitimacy of the Use of Force* [inaugural lecture, University of Amsterdam]. Amsterdam: Het Spinhuis.

Mandel, E. 1974. *Der Spätkapitalismus.* Frankfurt: Suhrkamp.

Mangan, J.A. 1986. *The Games Ethic and Imperialism.* New York: Viking Penguin.

Mankoff, M. 1974. 'Watergate and Sociological Theory', *Theory and Society*, 1 (1), 103–10.

Maraveyas, N. 1996. 'The agricultural strata in the European Union and the Common Agricultural Policy', in G.A. Kourvetaris and A. Moschonas (eds.), *The Impact of European Integration. Political, Sociological and Economic Changes.* Westport, Conn.: Praeger.

Marcou, L. 1979. *L'internationale après Staline.* Paris: Grasset.

Marcuse, H. 1971. [1958]. *Soviet Marxism*. Harmondsworth: Penguin.

Marijnissen, J. and Glastra van Loon, K. 2000. *De laatste oorlog. Gesprekken over de nieuwe wereldorde* [interviews with G. Arbatov, C. Beal, H. van den Broek, Lord Carrington, N. Chomsky, R. Detrez, J. Kobaladze, V. Lukin, K. van der Pijl, Sir Michael Rose, H.C. Ströbele, P. de Waart, R. de Wijk]. Amsterdam: Veen.

Marishane, J. 1992. 'The religious Right and low-intensity conflict in southern Africa', in J. Nederveen Pieterse (ed.), *Christianity and Hegemony. Religion and Politics on the Frontiers of Social Change*. New York: Berg Publishers.

Marjolin, R. 1989. *Architect of European Unity. Memoirs 1911–1986* [foreword by Eric Roll]. London: Weidenfeld & Nicholson.

Marx, A. 1974. 'Two Comments on the Energy Crisis (I)', *Monthly Review*, 25 (11), 52–5.

Marx, K. 1973. *Grundrisse. Introduction to the Critique of Political Economy* [transl. and intro. by M. Nicolaus]. Harmondsworth: Penguin/New Left Review.

Marx-Engels Werke. 1965. *Collected Works edition*. Berlin: Dietz.

Mattera, P. 1992. *World Class Business. A Guide to the 100 Most Powerful Global Corporations*. New York: Henry Holt & Co.

May, C. 2000. *A Global Political Economy of Intellectual Property Rights. The New Enclosures?* London: Routledge.

———. 2004. '(Re)producing intellectual property norms: Capacity building programmes in developing countries', in K. van der Pijl, L. Assassi and D. Wigan (eds.), *Global Regulation. Managing Crises After the Imperial Turn*. Basingstoke: Palgrave Macmillan.

Mayer, H. 1979. 'Neokolonialistische Lösungsversuche in Rhodesien/Zimbabwe', *Blätter für deutsche und internationale Politik*, 24 (9), 1117–31.

Mayer, U. 1979. 'Die Verfassungsentwicklung der Bundesrepublik', in U. Albrecht, F. Deppe, J. Huffschmid et al. (eds.), *Beiträge zu einer Geschichte der Bundesrepublik*. Cologne: Pahl-Rugenstein.

McAuley, M. 1977. *Politics and the Soviet Union*. Harmondsworth: Penguin.

McCoy, A. 1991. *The Politics of Heroin. CIA Complicity in the Global Drug Trade* [rev. ed. of *The Politics of Heroin in Southeast Asia*, 1972]. New York: Lawrence Hill.

McGeehan, R. 1971. *The German Rearmament Question. American Diplomacy and European Defense After World War II*. Urbana, Ill.: University of Illinois Press.

Medvedev, R.A. 1976. [1971]. *Let History Judge. The Origins and Consequences of Stalinism* [transl. by C. Taylor and ed. by D. Joravsky]. London: Spokesman.

Meeus, M. 1989. *Wat betekent arbeid? Over het ontstaan van de westerse arbeidsmoraal*. Assen: Van Gorcum.

Melman, S. 1970. *Pentagon Capitalism. The Political Economy of War*. New York: McGraw-Hill.

Menshikov, S. 1973. [1969]. *Millionaires and Managers. Structure of U.S. Financial Oligarchy*. Moscow: Progress.

Merk, J. 2004. 'Regulating the global athletic footwear industry: The collective worker in the product chain', in K. van der Pijl, L. Assassi and D. Wigan (eds.), *Global Regulation. Managing Crises After the Imperial Turn*. Basingstoke: Palgrave Macmillan.

Merkx, G.W. 1976. 'Argentina: Peronism and Power', *Monthly Review*, 27 (8), 38–51.

Meskill, J.T. (ed. with J.M. Gentzler). 1973. *An Introduction to Chinese Civilization*. Lexington: Mass. Heath.

Mickolus, E.F. 1980. *Transnational Terrorism: A Chronology of Events, 1968–1979*. London: Aldwych Press.

Middendorf, J.W., II. 1986. *A Free Market Prescription for Third World Debt* [The Heritage Lectures, no. 46]. Washington, D.C.: The Heritage Foundation.

Middlemas, K. 1995. *Orchestrating Europe. The Informal Politics of European Union 1973–1995* [with introductory chapters by R.T. Griffiths]. London: Fontana.

Migdal, J.S. 1988. *Strong Societies and Weak States. State-Society Relations and State Capabilities in the Third World*. Princeton, NJ: Princeton University Press.

Miller, R.E. 1971. *Innovation, Organization and Environment. A Study of sixteen American and West-European Steel Firms* (nouvelle série no. 6). Louvain: Université Catholique de Louvain.

Milward, A.S. 1984. *The Reconstruction of Western Europe 1945–51*. London: Methuen.

———. 2000. [1992]. *The European Rescue of the Nation-State*. 2nd ed. London: Routledge.

Mitrany, D. 1975. *The Functional Theory of Politics*. London: Robertson.

Mittelman, J. 1977. 'Some reflections on Portugal's counterrevolution', *Monthly Review*, 28 (10), 58–64.

———. 1997. 'Restructuring the global division of labour: Old theories and new realities', in S. Gill (ed.), *Globalization, Democratization and Multilateralism*. Tokyo: UNU Press; Basingstoke: Macmillan; New York: St. Martin's Press.

Monnet, J. 1976. *Mémoires*. Paris: Fayard.

Moore, B. 1981. [1966]. *Social Origins of Dictatorship and Democracy*. Harmondsworth: Penguin.

Morgan, D. and Ottaway, D.B. 1998. 'Central Asian riches alter the chessboard' [original series from the *Washington Post* edited by E. Haider], *The Friday Times*, 23–29 October, 20–3.

Morgenthau, H.J. 1964. [1948]. *Politics Among Nations. The Struggle for Power and Peace*. 3rd ed. New York: Knopf.

Morin, F. 1974. *La structure financière du capitalisme français*. Paris: Calmann-Lévy.

Morris, E. 1999. *Dutch. A Memoir of Ronald Reagan*. New York: Random House.

Morris, J. 1982. 'The revenge of the rentier or the interest rate crisis in the United States', *Monthly Review*, 33 (8), 28–34.

Morton, A.D. 2003. 'Structural change and neoliberalism in Mexico: "Passive revolution" in the global political economy', *Third World Quarterly*, 24 (4), 631–53.

Muhal-Leon, E. 1980. 'The PCE in Spanish Politics', in D. Childs (ed.), *The Changing Face of Western Communism*. London: Croom Helm.

Müller, L.A. 1991. *Gladio—das Erbe des Kalten Krieges*. Reinbek: Rowohlt.

Müller-Plantenberg, U. 1981. 'Die mögliche historisch-politische Bedeutung der dritten Großen Depression', *Probleme des Klassenkampfs*, 11 (3), 24–39.

Murphy, C.N. 1994. *International Organization and Industrial Change. Global Governance since 1850*. Cambridge: Polity.

Nair, K. and Opperskalski, M. 1988. *De CIA-moorden in de Derde Wereld* [transl. by B. & I. Voskuil]. Weesp: Centerboek.

Nairn, T. 1973. [1971]. *The Left Against Europe*. Harmondsworth: Penguin.

Nederveen Pieterse, J. 1985. 'Israel's role in the Third World: Exporting West Bank expertise', *Race & Class*, 26 (3), 9–30.

———. 1990. *Empire and Emancipation*. London: Pluto.

——— (ed.). 1992. *Christianity and Hegemony. Religion and Politics on the Frontiers of Social Change*. New York: Berg Publishers.

Nesvetailova, A. 2002. 'Asian tigers, Russian bear and international vets? An excursion in the 1997–98 financial crises', *Competition & Change*, 6 (3), 251–67.

Newhouse, J. 1967. *Collision in Brussels: The Common Market Crisis of 30 June 1965*. New York: W.W. Norton & Co.

Nitzan, J. and Bichler, S. 1995. 'Bringing capital accumulation back in: The Weapondollar-Petrodollar coalition—Military contractors, oil companies and Middle East "energy conflicts"', *Review of International Political Economy*, 2 (3), 446–515.

———. 2000. 'Capital accumulation: Breaking the dualism of "economics" and "politics"', in R. Palan (ed.), *Global Political Economy. Contemporary Theories*. London: Routledge.

———. 2002. *The Global Political Economy of Israel*. London: Pluto Press.

Norman, E.H. 1940. *Japan's Emergence as a Modern State. Political and economic Problems of the Meiji Period*. New York: Institute of Pacific Relations.

Nove, A. 1978. [1969]. *An Economic History of the USSR*. Harmondsworth: Penguin.

Ognev, A.P. 1984. 'International trade and peace', in V.S. Shaposhnikov (ed.), *Problems of Common Security*. Moscow: Progress.

Ognev, A.P. 1985. *Economic Co-operation, An Instrument of Peace*. Moscow: Nauka.

Ohmae, K. 1985. *Macht der Triade. Die neue Form des weltweiten Wettbewerbs* [transl. from the English]. Wiesbade: Gabler.

O'Leary, G. 1980. *The Shaping of Chinese Foreign Policy*. London: Croom Helm.

Önder, N. 1998. 'Integrating with the global market. The state and the crisis of political representation. Turkey in the 1980s and 1990s', *International Journal of Political Economy*, 28 (2), 44–84.

Ortiz, C. 2004. 'Regulating private military companies: States and the expanding business of commercial security provision', in K. van der Pijl, L. Assassi and D. Wigan (eds.), *Global Regulation. Managing Crises After the Imperial Turn*. Basingstoke: Palgrave Macmillan.

Overbeek, H. 1979. 'Twintig jaar Europese ontwikkelingshulp. Het Europees ontwikkelingsfonds 1957–1977', *Cahiers voor de Politieke en Sociale Wetenschappen*, 2 (2), 55–81.

———. 1982. 'Internationale ontwikkelingshulp and de nieuwe internationale economische orde', *Tijdschrift voor Diplomatie*, 9 (3), 144–64.

———. 1986. 'The Westland Affair: Collision over the future of British Capitalism', *Capital and Class*, 29, 12–26.

———. 1990. *Global Capitalism and National Decline. The Thatcher Decade in Perspective*. London: Unwin Hyman.

———. (ed.). 1993. *Restructuring Hegemony in the Global Political Economy. The Rise of Transnational Neo-Liberalism in the 1980s*. London: Routledge.

———. 2000. 'Transnational Historical Materialism', in R. Palan (ed.), *Contemporary Theories in Global Political Economy*. London: Routledge.

Overbeek, H. and van der Pijl, K. 1993. 'Restructuring capital and restructuring hegemony: neo-liberalism and the unmaking of the post-war order', in H. Overbeek (ed.), *Restructuring Hegemony in the Global Political Economy. The Rise of Transnational Neo-Liberalism in the 1980s*. London: Routledge.

Packenham, R.A. 1973. *Liberal America and the Third World. Political Development Ideas in Foreign Aid and Political Science*. Princeton: Princeton University Press.

Padfield, P. 2000. *Maritime Supremacy and the Opening of the Western Mind. Naval Campaigns that Shaped the Modern World, 1588–1782*. London: Pimlico.

Palan, R. (ed.). 2000. *Global Political Economy. Contemporary Theories*. London: Routledge.

———. 2003. *The Offshore World. Sovereign Markets, Virtual Places, and Nomad Millionaires*. Ithaca, NY: Cornell University Press.

Palan, R. and Abbott, J. [with P. Deans]. 1996. *State Strategies in the Global Political Economy*. London: Pinter.

Panah, M.H. 2002. 'Social revolution: The elusive emergence of an agenda in international relations', *Review of International Studies*, 28, 271–91.

Parboni, R. 1981. [1980]. *The Dollar and Its Rivals. Recession, Inflation and International Finance* [transl. by J. Rotschild]. London: Verso.

Park, H.J. 2004. 'Ideas, interests, and construction of a Northeast Asian community', *The Journal of East Asian Affairs*, 18 (1), 78–97.

Parteitag der KPdSU, XXIV (30 March/9 April 1971). Moscow: APN.

Pasche, C. and Peters, S. 1997. 'Les premiers pas de la Société du Mont-Pèlerin ou les dessous chics du néoliberalisme', in H.U. Jost (ed.). *L'Avènement des Sciences Socials commes Disciplines Académiques (Les Annuelles*, no. 8). Lausanne: Antipodes.

Paterson, T.C. 1989. *Meeting the Communist Threat. Truman to Reagan*. New York: Oxford University Press.

Patomäki, H. and Teivainen, T. 2002. 'Critical responses to neoliberal globalization in the Mercosur region: Roads towards cosmopolitan democracy?', *Review of International Political Economy*, 9 (1), 37–71.

Paul, J.A. 2001. 'Der Weg zum Global Compact. Zur Annäherung von UNO und multinationalen Unternehmen', in T. Brühl, T. Debiel, B. Hamm, H. Hummel, J. Martens (eds.), *Die Privatisierung der Weltpolitik*. Bonn: Dietz.

Pavlovski, G. 1992. 'Drie dagen', in Progress Publishers (eds.), *Staatsgreep in Moskou* [transl. by P. Brouwer et al.]. Weert: M & P.

Paye, J.-C. 2004. 'De strijd tegen het terrorisme en de algemene uitzonderingsstaat', *Marxistische Studies*, 65, 85–104.

Pelissier, R. 1965. [1963]. *La Chine—Le troisième géant*. 4 vols. Illustrated ed. Paris: Les Presses de France.

Pellegrin, J. 2000. 'European competitiveness and enlargement: Is there anyone in charge?', in T.C. Lawton, J.N.Rosenau and A.C. Verdun (eds.), *Strange Power. Shaping the Parameters of International Relations and International Political Economy*. Aldershot: Ashgate.

Petras, J.F. 1970. *Politics and Social Structure in Latin America*. New York: Monthly Review Press.

Pfeiffer, H. 1993. *Die Macht der Banken. Die personellen Verflechtungen der Commerzbank, der Deutschen Bank und der Dresdner Bank mit Unternehmen*. Frankfurt: Campus.

Phillips, C. 2000. *The Atlantic Sound*. London: Faber & Faber.

Pianta, M. 1987. *Economia in decline, technologie di guerra. Il potere Americano negli anni 80 e l'Europa*. Rome: Archivio Disarmo.

Picciotto, S. 1983. 'Jurisdictional Conflicts, International Law and the State System', *International Journal of the Sociology of Law*, 11, 11–40.

———. 2000. 'Liberalization and democratization: The forum and the hearth in the era of cosmopolitan post-industrial capitalism', *Law and Contemporary Problems*, 63 (4), 157–78.

van der Pijl, K. 1978. *Een Amerikaans Plan voor Europa. Achtergronden van het ontstaan van de EEG*. Amsterdam: SUA.

———. 1984. *The Making of an Atlantic Ruling Class*. London: Verso. Integral text posted at www.theglobalsite.co.uk.

———. 1987. 'Neoliberalism against a New International Economic Order', *The Marxist Review*, 20 (1) (January), 13–32, 97–104.

———. 1989. 'Ruling classes, hegemony, and the state system. Theoretical and historical considerations', *International Journal of Political Economy*, 19 (3), 7–35.

———. 1992. *Wereldorde en Machtspolitiek. Visies op de internationale betrekkingen van Dante to Fukuyama*. Amsterdam: Het Spinhuis.

———. 1993a. 'Soviet socialism and passive revolution', in S. Gill (ed.), *Gramsci, Historical Materialism, and International Relations*. Cambridge: Cambridge University Press.

———. 1993b. 'The sovereignty of capital impaired: Social forces and codes of conduct for multinational corporations', in H. Overbeek (ed.), *Restructuring Hegemony in the Global Political Economy. The Rise of Transnational Neo-Liberalism in the 1980s*. London: Routledge.

———. 1994. 'The Reich resurrected? Continuity and change in German expansion', in R.P. Palan and B. Gills (eds.), *Transcending the State-Global Divide. A Neostructuralist Agenda in International Relations*. Boulder, Col.: Lynne Rienner.

———. 1995. 'The Second Glorious Revolution: Globalizing Elites and Historical Change', in B. Hettne (ed.), *International Political Economy. Understanding Global Disorder*. London: Zed Books.

———. 1996a. 'A theory of transnational revolution: Universal history according to Eugen Rosenstock-Huessy and its implications', *Review of International Political Economy*, 3 (2), 287–318.

———. 1996b. *Vordenker der Weltpolitik Einführung in die internationale Politik aus ideengeschichtlicher Perspektive* [transl. by W. Linsewksi]. Opladen: Leske+Budrich.

van der Pijl, K. 1997. 'Atlantic rivalies and the collapse of the USSR', in S. Gill (ed.), *Globalization, Democratization, and Multilateralism*. Basingstoke: Macmillan; Tokyo: United Nations University Press.

———. 1998. *Transnational Classes and International Relations*. London: Routledge.

———. 2001a. 'From Gorbachev to Kosovo. Atlantic rivalries and the re-incorporation of Eastern Europe', *Review of International Political Economy*, 8 (2), 275–310.

———. 2001b. 'International relations and capitalist discipline', in R. Albritton, M. Itoh, R. Westra and A. Zuege (eds.), *Phases of Capitalist Development. Booms, Crises and Globalizations*. Basingstoke: Palgrave Macmillan.

———. 2002. 'Imperiale Ethik und Ästhetisierung der Weltpolitik', *Das Argument. Zeitschrift für Philosophie und Sozialwissenschaften*, 248 [44(5/6)], 802–817.

———. 2004. 'Two faces of the transnational cadre under neo-liberalism', *Journal of International Relations and Development*, 7 (2), 177–207.

van der Pijl, Kees and van Zon, Hans. 1989. 'The new Soviet concept of international relations and the transition to socialism', *Amsterdam International Studies*, Working Paper no. 6.

Piore, M. and Sabel, C.F. 1984. *The Second Industrial Divide. Possibilities for Prosperity*. New York: Basic Books.

Pistorius, R. and van Wijk, J. 1999. 'The Exploitation of Plant Genetic Information. Political Strategies in Crop Development', Dissertation, University of Amsterdam.

Pluvier, J. 1999. *Zuidoost-Azië. Een eeuw van onvervulde verwachtingen*. Breda: de Geus.

Pohly, M. and Durán, K. 2001. *Osama bin Laden und der internationale Terrorismus*. Frankfurt: Ullstein.

Polanyi, K. 1957. [1944]. *The Great Transformation. The Political and Economic Origins of Our Time*. Boston: Beacon.

Pollin, R. and Zepeda, E. 1987. 'Latin American debt: The choices ahead', *Monthly Review*, 38 (9), 1–16.

Ponting, C. 1989. *Breach of Promise. Labour in Power 1964–1970*. London: Hamish Hamilton.

Posner, A.R. 1977. 'Italy: Dependence and political fragmentation', *International Organization*, 31 (4), 804–25.

Poulantzas, N. 1971. *Pouvoir politique et classes sociales*. 2 vols. Paris: Maspero.

Presidential Transcripts, The. 1974. [with commentary by the staff of the *Washington Post*]. New York: Dell.

Pringle, P. and Spigelman, J. 1983. [1981]. *The Nuclear Barons*. London: Sphere.

Pursey, S.K. 1980. 'The trade union view on the implementation of codes of conduct', in N. Horn (ed.), *Legal Problems of Codes of Conduct for Multinational Enterprises*. Deventer: Kluwer.

Rakovsky, M. 1978. *Towards an East European Marxism*. London: Allison & Busby.

Ramsay, R. 2002. *The Rise of New Labour*. Harpenden: Pocket Essentials.

Rashid, A. 2002. [2000]. *Taliban. Islam, Oil and the New Great Game in Central Asia*. 2nd ed. London: I.B. Tauris.

Rawls, J. 1973. [1971]. *A Theory of Justice*. Oxford: Oxford University Press.

Regan, D.T. 1988. *For the Record. From Wall Street to Washington*. San Diego: Harcourt Brace Jovanovich.

Regtien, T. and van Dullemen, M. 1968. *Het Vietnam-tribunaal Stockholm-Roskilde 1967* [preface by J.-P. Sartre]. Amsterdam: Polak & Van Gennep.

Reiding, J. 1975. *Ontwikkelingshulp, neo-kolonialisme en nationale vrijheidsstrijd*. Amsterdam: IPSO.

Reischauer, E.O. 1965. [1950]. *The United States and Japan*. 3rd ed. New York: Viking.

Richardson, K. 2000. 'Big business and the European agenda', *Working Papers in Contemporary European Studies*. Falmer, Brighton: Sussex European Institute.

Richelson, J.T. and Ball, D. 1990. [1985]. *The Ties That Bind. Intelligence Cooperation Between the UKUSA Countries—The United Kingdom, the United States of America, Canada, Australia and New Zealand*. 2nd ed. Boston: Unwin Hyman.

Rijkens, P. 1965. *Handel en Wandel. Nagelaten gedenkschriften 1888–1965*. Rotterdam: Donker.

Risse-Kappen, T. 1994. 'Ideas do not float freely: Transnational coalitions, domestic structures, and the end of the cold war', *International Organization*, 48 (2), 185–214.

Ritsert, J. 1973. *Probleme politisch-ökonomischer Theoriebildung*. Frankfurt: Athenäum.

Roberts, K. 1985. 'Democracy and the dependent capitalist state', *Monthly Review*, 37 (5), 12–26.

Robinson, W.I. 1996. *Promoting Polyarchy*. Cambridge: Cambridge University Press.

———. 2004. *A Theory of Global Capitalism. Production, Class, and State in a Transnational World*. Baltimore: Johns Hopkins University Press.

Robison, R. and Hadiz, V.R. 2004. *Reorganising Power in Indonesia. The Politics of Oligarchy in an Age of Markets*. London: RoutledgeCurzon.

Rodinson, M. 1977. [1966]. *Islam and Capitalism* [transl. by B. Pearce]. Harmondsworth: Penguin.

Roosevelt-Churchill. 1975. *Their Secret Wartime Correspondence* [F.L. Loewenheim, H.D. Langley, and M. Jonas, eds.]. London: Barrie & Jenkins.

Rosecrance, R.N. 1968. *Defense of the Realm. British Strategy in the Nuclear Epoch*. New York: Columbia University Press.

Rosenberg, J. 1998. 'Isaac Deutscher and the lost history of international relations', *New Left Review*, 227, 3–15.

———. 2000. *The Follies of Globalisation Theory*. London: Verso.

Rosenstock-Huessy, E. 1961. [1931]. *Die europäischen Revolutionen und der Character der Nationen*. 3rd ed. Stuttgart: Kohlhammer.

———. 1993. [1937]. *Out of Revolution. Autobiography of Western Man*. Providence, R.I.: Berg.

Ross, G. 1995. *Jacques Delors and European Integration*. New York: Oxford University Press.

Roth, J. and Ender, B. 1984. *Dunkelmänner der Macht. Politische Geheimzirkel und organisiertes Verbechen*. Bornheim-Merten: Lamuv Verlag.

Rother, B. 1987–88. 'Socialist economic policy in the crisis. The case of Portugal', *International Journal of Political Economy*, 17 (4), 88–105.

Roy, A. 1978. *'Euro-Communism'—An Analytical Study*. Calcutta: Pearl.

———. 1986. *Contemporary India—A Perspective*. Bombay: Build.

———. 1994. 'New interrelations between Indian big bourgeoisie and imperialism', *The Marxist Review Occasional Letters*, 16.

Rufin, J.-C. 1991. *L'empire et les nouveaux barbares*. Paris: Lattès.

Ruggie, J.G. 1982. 'International regimes, transactions and change: Embedded liberalism in the post-war order', *International Organization*, 36 (2), 379–415.

Ruhwedel, K. 1976. 'Der Europäische Gewerkschaftsbund und die westeuropäische Integration', in F. Deppe (ed.), *Arbeiterbewegung und westeuropäische Integration*. Köln: Pahl-Rugenstein.

Ruigrok, W. and van Tulder, R. 1995. *The Logic of International Restructuring*. London: Routledge.

Rupert, M. 1995a. *Producing Hegemony. The Politics of Mass Production and American Global Power*. Cambridge: Cambridge University Press.

———. 1995b. '(Re)Politicizing the global economy: Liberal common sense and ideological struggle in the US NAFTA debate', *Review of International Political Economy*, 2 (4), 658–92.

———. 2000. *Ideologies of Globalization. Contending visions of a New World Order*. London: Routledge.

Russo, G. 1979. 'Il compromesso storico: The Italian Communist Party from 1968 to 1978', in P. Filo della Torre, E. Mortimer and J. Story (eds.), *Eurocommunism: Myth or Reality*. Harmondsworth: Penguin.

Rustow, D.A. 1965. 'Turkey: The modernity of tradition', in L.W. Pye and S. Verba (eds.), *Political Culture and Political Development*. Princeton: Princeton University Press.

Ryner, J.M. 1998. 'Maastricht convergence in the Social and Christian Democratic heartland', *International Journal of Political Economy*, 28 (2), 85–123.

Ryner, J.M. 2002. *Capitalist Restructuring, Globalisation and the Third Way. Lessons from the Swedish model*. London: Routledge.

Sabri Abdallah, I. 1979. 'La place du Dialogue euro-arabe dans les relations internationals contemporaines', in J. Bourrinet (ed.), *Le Dialogue Euro-Arabe*. Paris: Economica.

Samary, C. 1995. *Yugoslavia Dismembered* [transl. by P. Drucker]. New York: Monthly Review Press.

Sampson, A. 1968. *Anatomy of Europe*. New York: Harper & Row.

———. 1974. *The Sovereign State of ITT*. Greeenwich: Fawcett-Crest.

———. 1982. *The Money Lenders. Bankers in a Dangerous World*. London: Coronet.

———. 1987. *Black and Gold. Tycoons, Revolutionaries and Apartheid*. London: Coronet.

———. 1991. [rev. ed. of *The Arms Bazaar*, 1977]. *The Arms Bazaar in the Nineties. From Krupp to Saddam*. London: Coronet.

Sanguinetti, G. 1982. [1979]. *Over het terrorisme en de staat* [transl. from the French]. Bussum: Wereldvenster.

Sansom, G.B. 1950. *The Western World and Japan. A Study in the Interaction of European and Asiatic Cultures*. New York: Alfred A. Knopf.

Scheer, R. 1982. *With Enough Shovels. Reagan, Bush, and Nuclear War*. New York: Random House.

Schmitt, B.E. and Vedeler, H.C. 1984. *The World in the Crucible, 1914–1919*. New York: Harper & Row.

Schmitt, C. 1963. [1932]. *Der Begriff des Politischen*. Berlin: Duncker & Humblot.

Schneer, C.J. 1969. *Mind and Matter. Man's Changing Concepts of the Material World*. New York: Grove Press.

Scholten, Y. (ed.). 1975. *De sociale strijd in Italië. Teksten uit Il Manifesto en Lotta Continua*. Amsterdam: van Gennep.

Schwartz, H.M. 1994. *States versus Markets. History, Geography, and the Development of the International Political Economy*. New York: St. Martin's Press.

Schweizer, P. 1993. *Friendly Spies. How America's Allies are Using Economic Espionage to Steal our Secrets*. New York: Atlantic Monthly Press.

———. 1994. *Victory. The Reagan Administration's Secret Strategy That Hastened the Collapse of the Soviet Union*. New York: Atlantic Monthly Press.

Sciascia, L. 1978. *De zaak Moro* [transl. by J. Tuin]. Antwerpen: Lotus.

Scott, P.D. 1986. 'Transnationalised repression: Parafascism and the U.S.', *Lobster*, 12, 1–30.

Scott, P.D. and Marshall, J. 1991. *Cocaine Politics. Drugs, Armies, and the CIA in Central America*. Berkeley: University of California Press.

Scott-Smith, G. 2002. *The politics of apolitical culture. The Congress for Cultural Freedom, the CIA and post-war American hegemony*. London: Routledge.

Seagrave, S. 1996. [1985]. *The Soong Dynasty*. London: Corgi.

Seidman, A. and Makgetla, N. 1980. *Outposts of Monopoly Capitalism: Southern Africa in the Changing Global Economy*. Westport, Conn.: Lawrence Hill; London: Zed Books.

Selby, J. 2003. *Water, Power and Politics in the Middle East. The Other Israeli-Palestinian Conflict*. London: I.B. Tauris.

de Senarclens, P. 1990., 'La transnationalisation des clercs. Essai sur les experts internationaux', *Revue européenne des sciences sociales*, 28 (87), 231–50.

Senate Foreign Relations Committee. Executive Sessions of the Senate Foreign Relations Committee (Historical Series) plus year of session (Washington, D.C.).

Seneca, L.A. 1963. [1917]. *Brieven aan Lucilius* [ed. and intro. by H. Wagenvoort]. Utrecht: den Boer.

Senghaas, D. 1982. *Von Europa Lernen. Entwicklungsgeschichtliche Betrachtungen*. Frankfurt: Suhrkamp.

———. 2002. *The Clash within Civilizations. Coming to Terms with Cultural Conflicts*. London and New York: Routledge.

Senin, M. 1973. *Socialist Integration* [transl. from the Russian]. Moscow: Progress.

Serfati, C. 2004. 'American military power—Global public good or competitive advantage?', in K. van der Pijl, L. Assassi and D. Wigan (eds.), *Global Regulation. Managing Crises After the Imperial Turn*. Basingstoke: Palgrave Macmillan.

Servan-Schreiber, J.-J. 1969. [1967]. *Le défi américain*. Paris: Denoël.

Shaw, M. 1996. *Civil Society and Media in Global Crises. Representing Distant Violence*. London: Pinter.

———. 2000. *Theory of the Global State*. Cambridge: Cambridge University Press.

Shevchenko, A.N. 1985. *Breaking with Moscow*. New York: Ballantine.

Shoup, L.H. and Minter, W. 1977. *Imperial Brain Trust. The Council on Foreign Relations and United States Foreign Policy*. New York: Monthly Review Press.

Silk, L. and Silk, M. 1981. *The American Establishment*. New York: Avon.

Simon, W. 1976. *Macht und Herrschaft der Unternehmerverbände BDI, BDA und DIHT im ökonomischen und politischen System der BRD*. Cologne: Pahl-Rugenstein.

Singer, D. 1988. 'Twenty years on: May 68 Revisited', *Monthly Review*, 40 (2), 18–37.

Singh, T. 1984. 'Why world capital backs South Africa. The role of transnational corporations and foreign investment in South Africa', *The African Communist*, 99, 82–93.

Singham, A.W. and Hune, S. 1986. *Non-Alignment in an Age of Alignments*. London: Zed Books.

SI Report on Multinationals. 1978. In *Socialist Affairs* (November/December), 168.

Sklar, H. (ed.). 1980. *Trilateralism*. Boston: South End Press.

Sklair, L. 2001. *The Transnational Capitalist Class*. Oxford: Blackwell.

Skolnik, R. 1969. *1803: Jefferson's Decision. The United States Purchases Louisiana*. New York: Chelsea House.

Smith, D. 1979. 'The alternative: Portuguese communism', in P. Filo della Torre, E. Mortimer and J. Story (eds.), *Eurocommunism: Myth or Reality*. Harmondsworth: Penguin.

Sohn-Rethel, A. 1975. [1973]. *Grootkapitaal en fascisme. De Duitse industrie achter Hitler* [transl. by E. Vonk]. Amsterdam: Van Gennep.

Sonntag, R.H. 1973. 'Der Staat des unterentwickelten Kapitalismus', *Kursbuch*, 31, 157–83.

Sörgel, A. 1985. 'Ermittlungen gegen die Deutsche Bank', *Blätter für deutsche und internationale Politik*, 30 (10), 1225–37.

de Soto, H. 2001. *The Mystery of Capital. Why Capitalism Triumphs in the West and Fails Everywhere Else*. London: Black Swan Books.

Spaak, P.H. 1971. *The Continuing Battle. Memoirs of a European 1936–66* [transl. by H. Fox]. London: Weidenfeld and Nicholson.

Späth, L. 1985. *Wende in die Zukunft. Die Bundesrepublik auf dem Weg in die Informationsgesellschaft*. Reinbek: Rowohlt; Hamburg: Der Spiegel.

Spohn, W. 1975. 'Die technologische Abhängigkeit der Sowjetunion vom Weltmarkt', *ProKla*, 5 (19/20/21).

van Splunter, J. 1993. *Kernsplijting en diplomatie. De Nederlandse politiek ten aanzien van de vreedzame toepassing van kernenergie, 1939–1957*. Amsterdam: Het Spinhuis.

Stalin, J.V. 1972. [1952]. *Economic Problems of Socialism in the U.S.S.R.* Peking: Foreign Languages Press.

Statz, A. 1975. 'Zur Geschichte der westeuropäischen Integration bis zur Gründung der EWG', in F. Deppe (ed.), *Europäische Wirtschaftsgemeinschaft. Zur politischen Ökonomie der westeuropäischen Integration*. Reinbek: Rowohlt.

Stegmann, D. 1976. 'Kapitalismus und Faschismus in Deutschland 1929–1934: Thesen und Materialien zur Restitutierung des Primats der Großindustrie zwischen Weltwirtschaftskrise und beginnender Rüstungskonjunktur', in G. Dill, E. Hennig, J. Hirsch, M. Küchler and H. Reichelt (eds.), *Gesellschaft: Beiträge Zur Marxschen Theorie* Frankfurt: Suhrkamp.

Steiner, H. 1964. *Grossenordnung und horizontale Verflechtung in der Eisen- und Stahlindustrie*. Kiel: Institut für Weltwirtschaft.

Steinweg, R. (ed.). 1980. *Der gerechte Krieg: Christentum, Islam, Marxismus*. Frankfurt: Suhrkamp.

Stikker, D.U. 1966. *Bausteine für eine neue Welt. Gedanken und Erinnerungen an schicksalhafte Nachkriegsjahre* [transl. by W. Petwaidic]. Vienna/Düsseldorf: Econ.

Stockwell, J. 1978. *In Search of Enemies. A CIA Story*. New York: W.W. Norton.

Stone, D. 1996. *Capturing the Political Imagination. Think Tanks and the Policy Process*. London: Frank Cass.

Strauss, E. 1962. *European Reckoning. The Six and Britain's Future*. London: Allen & Unwin.

Struik, A. (ed.). 1938. *Waakzaamheid tegen het fascisme. Het proces tegen het 'blok der rechtsen en trotzkisten' Boecharin—Rykow—Jagoda* [transl. from the Russian]. Amsterdam: Pegasus.

Studiegroep (Studiegroep voor Reconstructie Problemen). 1942. 'Een blijvende economische voorlichtingsinstantie', *Rapporten 9de Reeks* (publications of the Dutch government in exile) (December).

———. 1944. 'Bevordering der Buitenlandsche Handelsbetrekkingen', *Rapporten 9de Reeks* (publications of the Dutch government in exile) (November).

Sulzberger, C.L. 1972. [1970]. *The Last of the Giants*. London: Weidenfeld and Nicolson.

Supiot, A. 2002. 'Ontologies of law', *New Left Review* [2nd Series], 13, 107–24.

———. 2003. 'The labyrinth of human rights. Credo or common resource?', *New Left Review* [2nd Series], 21, 118–136.

de Swaan, A. 2001. *Words of the World. The Global Language System*. Cambridge: Polity.

Swann, D. 1992. [1970]. *The Economics of the Common Market*. 7th ed. Harmondsworth: Penguin.

Talbot, K. 1999. 'Backing up globalization with military might', *Covert Action Quarterly*, 68, 30–36.

Tanzer, M. 1980. *The Race for Resources. Continuing Struggles over Minerals and Fuels*. New York: Monthly Review Press.

Tawney, R.H. 1952. [1926]. *Religion and the Rise of Capitalism*. New York: Mentor Books.

Teacher, D. 1993. 'The Pinay Circle Complex 1969–1989', *Lobster. Journal of Parapolitics*, 26, 9–16.

Teschke, B. 2003. *The Myth of 1648. Class, Geopolitics and the Making of Modern International Relations*. London: Verso.

Teubal, M. 1996. 'Structural adjustments, democracy and the state in Argentina', in Alex E. Fernández Jilberto and André Mommen (eds.), *Liberalisation in the Developing World. Institutional and Economic Changes in Latin America, Africa, and Asia*. London: Routledge.

Therborn, G. 1979. 'The travail of Latin American democracy', *New Left Review*, 113/114, 71–109.

Thompson, E.P. 1968. [1963]. *The Making of the English Working Class*. Harmondsworth: Penguin.

Thompson, P. 1980. 'Bilderberg and the West', in Holly Sklar (ed.), *Trilateralism*. Boston: South End Press.

Thorsson, I. 1984. *In Pursuit of Disarmament. Conversion from Military to Civil Production in Sweden, Volume 1B. Summary, Appraisals and Recommendations*. Stockholm: Report to the Ministry of Foreign Affairs.

Tiedtke, J. and Tiedtke, S. 1978. [1976]. 'The Soviet Union's internal problems and the development of the Warsaw Treaty Organisation', in E. Jahn (ed.), *Soviet Foreign Policy. Its social and economic conditions* [transl.]. London: Allison & Busby.

Tinbergen, J. (coordinator). 1977. *Naar een Rechtvaardiger Internationale Orde*. Amsterdam: Elsevier.

Todd, E. 2004. [2002]. *Après l'empire. Essay sur la décomposition du système américain*. 2nd ed. Paris: Gallimard.

Tolchin, M. and Tolchin, S. 1989. *Buying Into America. How Foreign Money is Changing the Face of Our Nation*. New York: Berkley Books.

Tosi Rodrigues, A. 2000. *Brasil de Fernando a Fernando. Neoliberalismo, corrupção e protesto na política brasileira de 1989 a 1994*. Ijuí, Rio Grande do Sul: UnIjuí.

Tower Commission Report [by J. Tower, E. Muskie and B. Scowcroft]. 1987. New York: Times Books.

Toynbee, A.J. 1935. *A Study of History*. 3 vols. 2nd ed. Oxford: Oxford University Press; London: Humphrey Milford, for the RIIA.

Trevelyan, G.M. 1961. [1944]. *Sociale geschiedenis van Engeland* [transl. by D.J. Blok]. Utrecht: Aula.

Trotsky, L. 1978. [1936]. *Geschiedenis der Russische Revolutie* [transl. by J. Valkhoff]. 3 vols. Amsterdam: van Gennep.

Tuccille, J. 1989. *Rupert Murdoch*. New York: Donald Fine.

van Tulder, R. and Junne, G. 1988. *European Multinationals in Core Technologies*. Chichester: Wiley.

UNCTC (UN Centre for Transnational Corporations). 1980. *Progress made towards the establishment of the new international economic order. The role of transnational corporations. Report of the Secretariat*. New York: United Nations.

———. 1986. *The United Nations Code of Conduct on Transnational Corporations*. New York: United Nations.

———. 1989. *The Process of Transnationalization and Transnational Mergers*. New York: United Nations.

Van Ness, P. 1970. *Revolution and Chinese Foreign Policy. Peking's Support for Wars of National Liberation*. Berkeley: University of California Press.

Vergopoulos, K. 1987–88. 'Economic Crisis and Modernization in Greece', *International Journal of Political Economy*, 17 (4), 106–41.

Vernon, R. 1973. [1971]. *Sovereignty at Bay. The Multinational Spread of US Enterprises*. Harmondsworth: Penguin.

Vieille, P. 1988. 'The World's Chaos and the New Paradigms of the Social Movement', in Lelio Basso Foundation (eds.), *Theory and Practice of Liberation at the End of the Twentieth Century*. Brussels: Bruylant.

Virilio, P. and Lotringer, S. 1997. [1983]. *Pure War* [transl. by M. Polizzotti]. New York: Semiotexte.

Voslensky, M. 1984. [1980]. *Nomenklatura. Anatomy of the Soviet Ruling Class* [transl. by E. Mosbacher]. London: Bodley Head.

Wade, R. 1990. *Governing the Market: Economic Theory and the Role of Government in East Asian Industrialization*. Princeton: Princeton University Press.

Wade, R. and Veneroso, F. 1998. 'The Asian crisis: The high debt model versus the Wall Street-Treasury-IMF Complex', *New Left Review*, 228, 3–24.

Wahl, J. 1962. *Tableau de la Philosophie Française*. Paris: Gallimard.

Wallerstein, I. 1974. *The Modern World System. Capitalist Agriculture and the Origins of the European World Economy in the Sixteenth Century*. New York: Academic Press.

Walpen, B. 2004. *Die offenen Feinde und ihre Gesellschaft. Eine hegemonietheoretische Studie zur Mont Pèlerin Society*. Hamburg: VSA.

Weber, M. 1976. [1921]. *Wirtschaft und Gesellschaft. Grundriss der verstehenden Soziologie*. 5th rev. ed. Tübingen: J.C.B. Mohr.

Weber, N. 1973. *Privilegien durch Bildung. über die Ungleichheit der Bildungschancen in der Bundesrepublik Deutschland*. Frankfurt: Suhrkamp.

Wehler, H.-U. 1985. [1973]. *The German Empire, 1871–1918* [transl. by K. Traynor]. Leamington Spa: Berg.

Werner, J. 1985. 'A short history of the war in Vietnam', *Monthly Review*, 37 (2), 14–21.

Werth, A. 1967. *De Gaulle. A Political Biography*. Harmondsworth: Penguin.

Wertheim, W.F. 1992. [1978]. *Indonesië van vorstenrijk tot neo-kolonie*. Meppel: Boom.

van Wesel, A. 1992. 'Catholics and Politics in Western Europe', in J. Nederveen Pieterse (ed.), *Christianity and Hegemony. Religion and Politics on the Frontiers of Social Change*. New York: Berg Publishers.

Weston, B.H. 1987. 'The Reagan administration versus international law', *Case Western Reserve Journal of International Law*, 19 (3), 295–302.

Wheeler, N.J. 2004. 'The Kosovo bombing campaign', in C. Reus-Smit (ed.), *The Politics of International Law*. Cambridge: Cambridge University Press.

Wiebes, C. 1988. 'A spy in the sky?', *Intermediair*, 24 (28), 5–9.

———. 2002. *Intelligence en de oorlog in Bosnië 1992–1995. De rol van de inlichtingen- en veiligheidsdiensten* [one of a 5-volume report on Srebenica]. Amsterdam: Boom.

Wiebes, C. and Zeeman, B. 1983. 'The Pentagon negotiations March 1948: The launching of the North Atlantic treaty', *International Affairs*, 59 (3), 351–63.

Wildenberg, I.W. 1990. *De revolte van de kapitaalmarkt. Over fusies, overnames en de terugkeer van de eigenaar-ondernemer*. Schoonhoven: Academic Service.

Willan, P. 1991. *Puppet Masters. The Political Use of Terrorism in Italy*. London: Constable.

Williams, W.A. 1962. [1959]. *The Tragedy of American Diplomacy*. Rev. ed. New York: Delta Books.

Williamson, J.G. 1968. [1962]. 'The long swing: Comparison and interactions between British and American balance of payments, 1820–1913', in A.R. Hall (ed.), *The Export of Capital from Britain 1870–1914*. London: Methuen.

Wilson, C. 1968. *Unilever in de Tweede Industriële Revolutie 1945–1965* [transl. and ed. by H. Baudet]. Gravenhage: Nijhoff.

Wilson, T.A. 1970. *The First Summit. Roosevelt and Churchill at Placentia Bay 1941*. London: Macdonald.

Wilson, W.A. 1919. *Die Reden Woodrow Wilsons* [bilingual edition published by the Committee on Public Information of the USA]. Bern: Freie Verlag.

Wippman, D. 2004. 'The International Criminal Court', in C. Reus-Smit (ed.), *The Politics of International Law*. Cambridge: Cambridge University Press.

Wisnewski, G., Landgraeber, W. and Sieker, E. 1993. [1992]. *Das RAF-Phantom. Wozu Politik und Wirtschaft Terroristen brauchen*. 2nd ed. Munich: Knaur.

Wolf, E.J. 1973. *Peasant Wars of the Twentieth Century*. Berkeley: University of California Press.

Wolf, M. [with A. McElvoy]. 1997. *Man zonder gezicht. Memoires* [transl. by J. van der Wijk]. Amsterdam: Balans.

Wolfe, A. 1979. *The Rise and Fall of the "Soviet Threat". Domestic Sources of the Cold War Consensus*. Washington: IPS.

Woodward, B. 1987. *Dekmantel. De geheime oorlogen van de CIA* [transl. by J. Koesen]. Houten: de Haan.

———. 1991. *The Commanders*. New York: Simon & Schuster.

———. 2004. *Plan of Attack*. New York: Simon & Schuster.

Woodward, S.L. 1995. *Balkan Tragedy. Chaos and Dissolution After the Cold War*. Washington, D.C.: The Brookings Institution.

Wright, G. 1997. *The Destruction of a Nation. United States' Policy Towards Angola since 1945*. London: Pluto.

Wright, P. [with P. Greengrass]. 1987. *Spycatcher. The Candid Autobiography of a Senior Intelligence Officer*. New York: Viking Penguin.

Wright, S. 1998. 'An appraisal of technologies of political control' [working document, consultation version]. Luxemburg: European Parliament.

van der Wurff, R. 1993. 'Neo-Liberalism in Germany? The "Wende" in perspective', in H. Overbeek (ed.), *Restructuring Hegemony in the Global Political Economy. The Rise of Transnational Neo-Liberalism in the 1980s*. London and New York: Routledge.

Yallop, D. 1984. *In God's Name*. London: Jonathan Cape.

Yergin, D. 1977. *Shattered Peace. The Origins of the Cold War and the National Security State*. Harmondsworth: Penguin.

Yergin, D. 1993. *The Prize. The Epic Quest for Oil, Money, and Power*. London: Simon & Schuster.

Young, H. 1999. *This Blessed Plot. Britain and Europe from Churchill to Blair*. London: Papermac.

Young, J.W. and Kent, J. 2004. *International Relations Since 1945. A Global History*. Oxford: Oxford University Press.

Zalik, A. 2004. 'The peace of the graveyard: The voluntary principles on security and human rights in the Niger delta', in K. van der Pijl, L. Assassi and D. Wigan (eds.), *Global Regulation. Managing Crises After the Imperial Turn*. Basingstoke: Palgrave Macmillan.

Zamoshkin, Y.A. and Melvil, A.Y. 1982. 'Between Neo-Liberalism and Neo-Conservatism', in E. D'Angelo, D.H. DeGrood, P.N. Russo and W. W. Stein (eds.), *Contemporary East European Marxism*, Vol. II. Amsterdam: Grüner.

Zhou, Y. and Lall, S. 2005. 'The impact of China's FDI surge on FDI in South-East Asia: Panel data analysis for 1986–2001', *Transnational Corporations*, 14 (1), 41–66.

Ziegler, R., Reissner, G. and Bender, D. 1985. 'Industry and banking in the German corporate network', in F.N. Stokman, R. Ziegler and J. Scott (eds.), *Networks of Corporate Power*. Cambridge: Polity.

Zimmerman, W. 1981. 'Soviet-East European relations in the 1980s and the changing international system', in M. Bornstein, Z. Gitelman and W. Zimmerman (eds.), *East-West Relations and the Future of Eastern Europe. Politics and Economics*. London: Allen & Unwin.

Index

About the Author

Kees van der Pijl teaches international relations at the University of Sussex and is director of the Centre for Global Political Economy at the same university. He previously worked at the University of Amsterdam and has also taught courses as a visiting professor at the University of Auvergne at Clermont-Ferrand, France.

His work deals with transnational classes and global political economy, and his writings include *The Making of an Atlantic Ruling Class* (1984) and *Transnational Classes and International Relations* (1998). He has also published on the history of international theory, including *Vordenker der Weltpolitik* (1996, in German), a revised version of an earlier Dutch study of 1992. Recently he (co-)edited works in the area of global norms and regulation. Between 1989 and 1994, he also published three novels in Dutch, his mother tongue. He is married with two children.

The author lives in Hove, East Sussex, and is currently working on a project entitled 'Tribal and Imperial Antecedents of Contemporary Foreign Relations', for which he has been awarded a Leverhulme Major Research Fellowship for 2006–2009.

14395474R00269

Printed in Great Britain
by Amazon.co.uk, Ltd.,
Marston Gate.